Institutions, Goals, Policies and Analytics in Economic Development

Institutions, Goals, Policies and Analytics in Economic Development

Solomon I Cohen
Erasmus University Rotterdam, The Netherlands

World Scientific

NEW JERSEY • LONDON • SINGAPORE • BEIJING • SHANGHAI • HONG KONG • TAIPEI • CHENNAI • TOKYO

Published by

World Scientific Publishing Co. Pte. Ltd.
5 Toh Tuck Link, Singapore 596224
USA office: 27 Warren Street, Suite 401-402, Hackensack, NJ 07601
UK office: 57 Shelton Street, Covent Garden, London WC2H 9HE

Library of Congress Cataloging-in-Publication Data
Names: Cohen, S. I., 1942– author.
Title: Institutions, goals, policies and analytics in economic development /
Solomon I Cohen, Erasmus University Rotterdam, The Netherlands.
Description: New Jersey : World Scientific, [2024] |
Includes bibliographical references and index.
Identifiers: LCCN 2023022691 | ISBN 9789811277078 (hardcover) |
ISBN 9789811278518 (paperback) | ISBN 9789811277085 (ebook for institutions) |
ISBN 9789811277092 (ebook for individuals)
Subjects: LCSH: Economic development--Developing countries. |
Development economics--Developing countries. | Developing countries--Economic policy. |
Developing countries--Economic conditions.
Classification: LCC HC59.7 .C5884 2024 | DDC 338.9009172/4--dc23/eng/20230518
LC record available at https://lccn.loc.gov/2023022691

British Library Cataloguing-in-Publication Data
A catalogue record for this book is available from the British Library.

For any available supplementary material, please visit
https://www.worldscientific.com/worldscibooks/10.1142/13431#t=suppl

Desk Editors: Balasubramanian Shanmugam/Claire Lum/Geysilla Jean

Typeset by Stallion Press
Email: enquiries@stallionpress.com

This book is dedicated to the memory of Jan Tinbergen. His thoughts, ideals, conduct and methods for resolving urgent world development problems are present throughout the collected works in the book.

Preface

This collection of works in development economics by the author has been carefully curated and updated to reflect important messages and insightful contributions accumulated over the years. For the seasoned reader of development economics or for the newcomer, this updated collection is sure to provide new insights and fresh perspectives. Each piece has been carefully selected for its relevance and timelessness and has been updated to reflect the current state of knowledge in the area and the author's latest thoughts and findings thereupon.

While the book treats major topics that are commonly included in development economics textbooks such as those of Thirlwall and Lopez (2017), Todaro and Smith (2020), Taylor and Lybbert (2020) and Janvry and Sadoulet (2021), the current book does not pretend to be categorized as a comprehensive textbook of development economics. The coverage of topics in this book is targeted and limited when compared to the above quoted textbooks. The book aims at presenting an appealing approach towards economic development that emphasizes the crucial importance of several sets of institutions that are prerequisite for development, and it aims at focusing on the primary twin goals of growth with progressive redistribution of endowments (GWR). The development policies studied and the analytical methods pursued deal mostly with the goals of growth and redistribution.

So, while some readers may view this book as another book on development economics, there are also reasons for considering it as a different book on development economics. The book carries several messages which are laid down below.

The first message that many will not dispute is that the starting phase of development economics in the 1950s to about 1980s was its golden times, with Nobel awards to some 10 economists with renowned works in development economics. Since then, other fields in economics took the lead. In the last decade, there is some revival of interest in development economics as more developing countries have become leading economies and as it is increasingly realized that their economic systems and their development paths are different than those of the mainstream advanced market economies. One and the other require reshaping the agenda of development economics to meet the new challenges. This book is meant to contribute to the reshaping or to what can be named the compartmentalization of development economics in ways that can lift and recover its status and push its future perspectives to levels that meet future challenges.

The second message is that institutions matter. The economic behavior of agents is circumscribed by more or less binding formal and informal institutions. Institutions are foundational roots, and they determine growth and development. As the twig is bent, so grows the tree. The message that institutions matter is commonly accepted and is not new. What this book conveys with respect to institutions is the important distinction between the politico-economic system institutions and the socio-cultural circumventing institutions. The system institutions are created and enforced by the politico-economic regime and are changeable, adjustable, and controllable. They are to a large extent quantifiable and analyzable and would belong to mainstream development economics, and this book deals with them as such. The socio-cultural outer institutions are intergenerationally transmitted, stubborn, and sticky and can take a generation or so before they change. They are qualitative, and they overlap, which makes them difficult to integrate in DE. Nevertheless, the breakup of the socio-cultural outer institutions in a few categories in terms of their significance for development is an important step forward. The following four behavioral patterns representing outer institutions are singled out and reviewed: corruption, stratification, distrust, and violence.

The third message is that when the twin goals of economic growth with endowments redistribution (for short growth with redistribution, GWR) are posed as the primary goals in the development of a nation, it can be shown (in the respective chapters on development goals) that the combination of growth with redistribution is necessary for any society with groups of people and with individuals who entertain high and low productivities and have significantly different earning capabilities. Since this is the reality in all nations, and the twin goals of growth with redistribution are universal and would apply to both developing and advanced countries. It will be noted that the relationship between growth and redistribution is mutual in both directions (growth allows redistribution and redistribution secures growth), though the relationship is complex and is long termed. Success in this endeavor requires taking collective and repetitive actions to shore up human capabilities and to rebalance them over time. The twin goals of growth with redistribution are necessary but are not insufficient for addressing all other development problems and issues. The category of secondary goals and related policies comes into the picture to tackle the other development problems and issues, but these are logically of a lower order. The compartmentalization of decision-making along these ways simplifies the stage, promotes transparency, allows the policy makers to be more effective, and allows the development economists (whether as academics or advisors) to be more focused in their analysis and advice.

The fourth message relates to applied studies of development policies. The truth of the message is that over a span of 40 or 50 years, the devoted scientist gets involved in many kinds of auxiliary topics on the borders of one's own core topics of interest. It is important to concentrate and be selective. Accordingly, the book contains a selection of fourteen chapters on development policies that are broadly linked to the core interest of economic growth with endowments redistribution. Eight of these chapters relate to sector developments economy-wide. The other six chapters focus on human resource development and utilization. The work done on human resources is consistent with my view that the upgrading of the capabilities of human resources is the shortest and most effective development strategy for reaching sustainable growth with redistribution. All the policy chapters are country applications. Most of them make use of economy-wide models for the analysis of the policy problem and in reaching conclusions on the development impacts of alternative policies.

The fifth message is directed to readers who are technically practicing development economists, academic staff, and students in development economics. The content of most chapters of this book is a mixture of (a) descriptions, studies, and analysis on the one hand and (b) quantitative applications of economy-wide models, partial equations, and indicator analysis on the other hand. By combining and presenting (a) and (b) together, it becomes easy for this concerned technical category of readers to have all in one. Admittedly, the general reader may not like to be interrupted by equations and formulas. We have put most formulas and equations in boxes which the general reader can skip if desired.

The sixth message is that development economics and global governance are becoming close cousins. Increasingly, more development economists are studying and contributing to the multi-disciplinary field of global governance, and correspondingly, global governance specialists are increasingly engaged in the study of development externalities and the developing regions. In the last three to four decades, quite a number of developing countries have become leading countries in the world at large, and projections of the GDP and population show that this trend is strengthening and will continue. The close link between development economics and global governance raises challenging questions and has consequences which we shall touch upon.

Currently, the highest echelon of global governance is entrusted to the G20 (these are the presidents and PM of countries with the largest GDP). Our messages on development economics stated above could similarly apply to global governance. Regarding institutions, is the G20 institution representative of the development regions? Should regions precede countries in representation? Regarding global goals, to what extent can the thesis of growth with redistribution at the national level be transplanted at the global level (having in mind that the twin goals of growth with redistribution are much more than reductions in inequality and poverty)? These are some of the questions that our studies of global governance raise.

As to acknowledgments, this book would not have been possible without the contributions of many professionals, officials, and students from many countries. Several persons mentioned in the following have since then unfortunately passed away. I would like to take this opportunity to honor and to acknowledge their contributions to the formation of this book. First is Jan Tinbergen whose methods and style are noted throughout most chapters. The impact of shared discussions with Hollis B. Chenery is found in our chapters on growth with redistribution as the primary development goal. Shared insights with Irma Adelman impacted the chapters on computable general equilibrium models. Various co-authored works with Hector Correa impacted the chapters on human resources. The interactions with the four persons and many more, their insights, and guidance have been invaluable and are not forgotten. I am deeply grateful for the cooperation with them and the positive impact they have had on published outcomes.

On reflection, belonging to and affiliation with the developing world and development economics are obvious. It started with birth and childhood in the desert oases of El Fayoum, Egypt, and continued with manhood at the University of Khartoum, Sudan. Two books that were compulsory for the bachelor's degree in development economics in Khartoum 1962 became career determining: One was by W.A. Lewis: *The Principles of Economic Planning*, Allen & Unwin, London, 1949. The other was by J. Tinbergen: *On the Theory of Economic Policy*, NHPC, Amsterdam, 1952. The follow-up was amazing. I was fortunate to obtain via World University Service a study scholarship in 1963 for the master's degree at the Netherlands School of Economics in 1962, with Jan Tinbergen as supervisor, and later on as his assistant, doctoral candidate, and staff member of his research team. To the three countries in which I lived most, I am deeply indebted for their generous hospitality, proud to be and/or have been a citizen of each, and always willing to pay back.

The fieldwork and advisory investigations started in Colombia in the late 1970s. In the framework of a technical assistance project financed by the Netherlands, we had the opportunity of forming an international team at Servicio Nacional de Aprendizaje (SENA) which worked on developing a plan for human resource development and utilization. One of the outcomes of the cooperation is the edited book *Sistema de Planeacion de Recursos Humanos*, Sena Press, Bogotá, 1982. Among the contributors to that book are A. Sarmiento, B. Kugler, and D. Otero. One of the chapters in this book makes use of these contributions. To all three Colombians, many thanks and appreciation for the learning experiences and wonderful times spent together.

The next country was Pakistan, as will be apparent from the country applications in this book. Several investigations on labor markets and manpower planning took place at the Manpower Division, Ministry of Labor, Pakistan, in the context of technical assistance projects sponsored by the ILO and the Netherlands for the preparation of the Five-year Development Plans. Special thanks go to N. Hussein and M. Javaid, Chief and Deputy Chief Manpower Division, and to B. Herman, H. de Kruijk, K. Van Elk, and T. van Galen who coordinated different parts of the project. The fieldwork was extended to a very fruitful collaborative research with the Pakistan Institute of Development Economics (PIDE), Islamabad, in the 1980s and 1990s, which resulted in a large number of published papers. I am grateful for the facilities provided by PIDE, especially for the close friendship with Prof. Syed Nawab Haider Naqvi, who was the director of PTDE at that time. Mention should be made of valuable contributions by I. Havinga and F. Mohammed in Islamabad and supplementary computations by H.J. Boehlé and J.B.W. Waterman in Rotterdam.

Opportunities for advisory and research work arose along similar lines and in diversified areas of development economics in Indonesia, Malaysia, India, Korea, Ghana, Zimbabwe, Kenya, Egypt, Ethiopia, and the Netherlands Antilles. Here again, there were many officials and colleagues in these countries who contributed in one way or another to the studies included in this book, via discussions and elaborations of the analysis and/or data provision and computations. To all of them, many thanks. Various chapters in this book drawback on the fieldwork in these countries.

In the 1990s and for one or two decades later, technical assistance, fieldwork, and advisory research shifted from the field of development economics to transition economics. What was expected had to happen. The fieldwork, research activities, and related publication program shifted at that time from topics in development economics to those in transition economics, microeconomics, and economic systems. Fortunately, the supervision of various doctorate dissertations with focus on and application to developing countries opened many avenues for continuing doing research in many areas of development economics. These opportunities were made possible by the supervised PhD graduates, some of whom have become colleagues and close friends. I wish to thank them all and especially mention B. Rettab, E. Abdelgalil, S. Acharya, A. Anwar, A. Khan, F. Shaheen, F. Ssennoga, S. Shahab, S. Safdar, M.A.A. Sargana, and M. Nosheen. Chapters 11 and 12 relate to Phd studies.

The comeback to development economics and extensive travel to developing countries in the last six years focused on the United Arab Emirates and Suriname; chapters 14 and 13 relate to the works done in the two countries, respectively. The work done in UAE was as Senior Advisor to the Ministry of Labor and to the Dubai Chamber of Commerce and as Visiting Professor at Dubai University. In this context, I like to thank all three instances for their invitations to participate in their regular activities and deliver some contributions. My work in Suriname was partly as Expatriate Advisor to the National Planning Department Suriname (NPD Suriname) and partly as Visiting Professor at the University of Suriname.

The first task was sponsored and supported by the ILO mission in the Caribbean, and the second task was sponsored and supported by the Faculty of Economics, Erasmus University Rotterdam, to which I belong. I like to acknowledge my deep thanks for the hospitality and cooperation provided by the director and staff of the NPD Suriname, D. Lachman, L. Menke-Tangali, S. Wallerlei, and T. Elstak, staff at the General Bureau of Statistics Suriname, especially G. Koornaar, D. Sjahkit, S. Bisshop, and S. Presierie-Nijon, and to D. Rei and M. La Marca from the ILO. The same thanks and appreciation go to R. Woodly-Sobhi and S. Debipersad of the University of Suriname.

In reading this collection, the reader will have the opportunity to delve deeper into the six messages mentioned in this preface. Whether you are searching for inspiration, guidance, methods, or just a new way of looking at things, this updated collection can be helpful in your search. So, dive in and share the experience and vision.

Contents

Part I
Background

Chapter 1

Introduction

1. The Rise, Decline, and Shallow Comeback of Development Economics

Wikipedia states: Development Economics (DE) is the branch of economics which deals with economic aspects of the development process in (low-income) developing countries. Further on, DE covers developing country studies for promoting economic growth and structural changes that eventually improve the well-being of massive populations in terms of income, employment, health, education, environment, etc. The studies can be theoretical or applied, analytical or documentary, technical or general, and originate in academic, advisory, commissioned, or official contexts.

Informative websites state that common topics in DE include (a) economic growth, (b) agriculture and land reforms, (c) industrialization and foreign trade, (d) distribution and poverty, (e) dual sector economy, (f) rural–urban divides, (g) human resources, employment, and education, (h) institutions and development, among others. Other statements: DE involves the creation of theories and methods that aid in the determination of policies and practices spheres. Unlike in many other fields of economics, for DE approaches to be successful, they may need to incorporate social, political, and cultural aspects to supplement the economic aspects.

The above statements rightly suggest that DE is an elastic and flexible branch of economics, which carries advantages as well as disadvantages. There are varied opinions on the performance of the branch of development economics. Since the institution of Nobel Prizes in economics in 1969, there are some 8 Nobel Prize winners with outstanding works in DE out of a total of about 85 awards in economics. Taken over all awarded years, the performance of DE is highly respectable when compared to other branches of economics as reflected in their share of Nobel Prize awards. However, when these numbers are placed in the context of the history of DE, it cannot be avoided to state that the esteem of the discipline was much higher in the past than it is currently.

The performance of DE had its ups and downs as can be gathered from this section's heading "The Rise, Decline, and Shallow Comeback of Development Economics". Development economics had its highest times in the fifties, sixties, seventies, and early eighties (some five decades ago), when it started as a forum for theorizing on economic development, analyzing development problems, appraising development policies, and setting up suitable methods for planning and monitoring. The best early years of DE were associated with awards to economists who, next to their awarded specialization, have contributed major works in DE (bracketed areas): Tinbergen (development planning), Myrdal (development institutions), Lewis, Kuznets, and Schultz (development theory), Sen (development goals), and Stiglitz (development policy). The decline period from the 1990s to 2018 went unawarded. The comeback has been signaled by the 2019 award to Duflo (development experiments).

The decline in the esteem of DE started in the later eighties and has continued since then. The decline is due to two main causes which can be sketched as follows: (1) Disappointing economic growth and social progress in developing countries and failure of state and development planning were perceived by some economists as a failure of DE. These economists argued that the same market economics for developed countries would apply to developing countries. And hence DE is redundant. (2) There has been an undisciplined outgrowth of research works assigned to DE that can be described as beyond the original intentions of DE. The outgrowth added little substance and brought confusion on the depth and boundaries of DE.

First, with the independence of most developing countries in the fifties, development economists generally agreed with the proposition that given traditional institutions in developing countries which discourage entrepreneurship and markets, it is the task of the government and state planning to transform the lagging economies into growing economies that can feed and prosper their people. Two to three decades later, many developing economies failed to take off with only four countries/city-states that were able to transform. These are the Republic of Korea, Taiwan, Hong Kong, and Singapore, which have presumably relied on free markets rather than state plans. Their successful performance was interpreted by some economists to mean that market forces are more able than state development plans in realizing development. More economists saw the failed performance of development planning as a failure of DE and challenged the rationale for the existence of DE. These thoughts were accentuated with the breakup of the Soviet Union and the transition of the ex-Soviet countries from state planning to market economies. The truth is that in the four Asian countries mentioned above, the governments worked closely with market leaders under a common consensus and devised interventionist policies that were mutually coordinated. This was also the case with the spectacular growth of China a decade later. Opportunities for state-market coordination in other developing countries are less ample. Besides, disappointing development performances due to political failures cannot be simply interpreted as failures of DE. Irrespective of counterarguments, the late eighties brought significant damage to the image of DE.

Second, there has been a tremendous outgrowth of case studies that use data on one or the other developing countries on diverse topics, many of which are hardly related to DE, and yet such publications are assigned to DE. This applies also to cross-country studies applying regressions on economic growth, and indicators of institutions, trade, government, education, health, and tens of other indicators, which pool together data of USA and European countries side by side with data of individual developing countries, without taking into account regional differentiation or country sizes. Many of these studies are incorrectly assigned to DE. Most of these studies have their origin in academics and are awarded PhD degrees. It is as if DE is being used as a collective basket for whatever economic studies that refer to a developing country. The result is a randomly constructed configuration of DE with highly fragmented and remarkably fluid content, and far away from the original reference framework of guiding the developing countries in their transformation to an industrialized and welfare economy. DE loses its seriousness when it becomes an open destination for all kinds of economic papers that deal with one or the other developing country.

The confusion was further accelerated by overloading DE with tens of development goals that were added to supplement the primary goal of economic growth and that DE is supposed to consider in its deliberations on development policy. To mention an example, the Millennium Development Goals (MDGs) state eight development goals: to eradicate poverty and hunger, achieve universal primary education, gender equality, and empower women, reduce child mortality, improve maternal health, combat HIV/AIDS, malaria, and other diseases, ensure environmental sustainability, and develop a global partnership for development. While all these goals are legitimate and should be addressed, the technical art of development planning and policymaking is in how to bring order and consistency in the coordination of these overlapping goals and to link specific goals to specific policies so as to make available quantitative parameters of goal/policy that policy makers can use in deciding policies. During its rise in the past century, DE used to give more attention to the technical art of development planning, than currently.

In summary, the undisciplined outgrowth of DE brought confusion and chaos. It is not strange to read on informative websites that "Unlike other branches of economics, in DE there is no consensus on what students should know."[6] The conclusion is that in spite of the transformation successes of many developing countries, there are still many more in the process, and to meet their expectations, DE needs to keep its random outgrowth within boundaries and to dig in rather than to grow out. Toward that end, Section 2 of this introductory chapter tabulates several steps that pertain to the compartmentalization and consolidation of the field of DE and discusses them in some detail. Section 3 is a brief review of the various chapters.

2. The Compartmentalization of Development Economics

Compartmentalization is the brain's way of processing complex and extensive information. Applied to DE, one can say that there is a rush of development studies/information coming in daily from various sources and sometimes without a clear direction. To combat this wild growth in information, one can compartmentalize the information field by organizing it into different parts and asserting the links between them. Within the compartments, one can simplify further by distinguishing between primary and secondary preoccupations, or one can make use of hierarchical orders in dealing with multiple topics. Doing so will help the development economist to focus on the task at hand and avoid feeling overwhelmed.

Compartmentalization is the process of organizing information and activities into separate, distinct areas. By doing this, one can minimize the amount of confusion that comes from having to deal with too many things at once. This helps to focus on one thing at a time and not get distracted. This helps in improving productivity, control, and communication.

The compartmentalization and redirections in DE that we desire and wish to emphasize can be grouped under five headings: regions, institutions, goals, policies, and analytics. Our suggestions on the handling of regions, institutions, goals, policies, and analytics in DE are summarized in Table 1.

Classification and treatment of the developing countries into *development regions* is a crucial first compartment in DE. The count gives more than hundred developing countries and territories spread in the southern hemisphere. There exist tens to hundreds of DE works in each of these countries. The number of DE works on individual countries is overwhelming, making it quite difficult for the engaged economist to see light through in a forest of packed and diverging trees. While the need for a tailored approach to development policy for each individual country or territory is appreciable, there is also something called the economics of doing effective research in the field of DE. This would call for the application of aggregative approaches and regional consolidations. One of the aims of this book is to advance DE analysis in terms of development regions.

Although each developing country has different cultural backgrounds and has gone through different histories, many countries, with proximity in terms of geographical location, have similar cultural and historical backgrounds as well as comparable economy/polity systems and related institutions, as well as shared development policies. A regionalization approach in DE is long due. There are

Table 1. Compartmentalization of development economics.

Compartment	Consolidation principles	Book Plan
Development regions	Large diversity among developing countries and accelerated research and information lead to fragmented oversight, which can be controlled by applying regionalisation. There are also country and regional interests at the global level that require applying regionalisation. These are arguments for grouping countries in development regions (DR) and treating DR as analytical units, next to the country level.	Ch. 2
Development institutions	Socio/economy/polity systems have gone through significant and different structural changes in the different development regions. It is important to highlight the systemic changes, as well as the transmitted and created institutions per development region as these determine the pace and shape of the development process. Some specific institutions retard development. Other institutions promote development. Case studies of underlying institutions and their upgrading are an essential part of DE.	Ch. 3
	Examples of case studies: modelling of bygone institutional barriers. Feudal regime in India. Political impasse in Chile.	Ch. 4
Development goals	DE is overloaded with a significant surge in proposed development goals which are meant to supplement or replace GDP growth. There is a need to bring simplification and order in the controversy on goals. The dualistic character of the development process with a persistent high productivity high earnings segment, and a persistent low productivity low earnings segment requires formulation of the primary development goal as growth with redistribution, in short, GWR. Other goals are supplementary to GWR.	Ch. 5
	For each goal there are goal relevant theories. For the growth goal there are the growth theories: Macro growth (Harrod-Domar), Neoclassical growth (Solow), Human capital (Becker), Endogenous growth (Romer), segmented growth (Baumol), Dual sectors (Lewis), Multi sectors (Chenery), Social accounting matrix (Stone), Computable general equilibrium models (Adelman). For the distribution goal there are distribution theories: Positive, Normative. For the growth with redistribution goal: (Tinbergen, Cohen, Chenery, Kuznets, Lewis, Stiglitz).	
	GWR performances at country and region level.	Ch. 6
Development policies at national level	Multi sector development and policies	Chs. 7–14
	Human resource development and policies	Chs. 15–20
DP at regional, world levels	Development policies at regional level.	Ch. 21
	Development policies at world level.	Ch. 22
Analytics, models	Analytics and development indicators	a
	Economy-wide policy modeling	b

Notes: a = Chs. 2, 3, 5–8, 13–22
b = Chs. 4, 7–13, 16–19

other considerations such as regional externalities and global policies which support the regrouping of developing countries in development regions. World development agencies such as the World Bank, UNDP, ILO, WHO, and OECD often present their results and recommendations in regionalized forms. Accordingly, the following chapter will distinguish between six regional development groups and will review briefly their backgrounds and recent economic history.

Development institutions is another compelling compartment in DE. A significant portion of DE works deals with the impact of institutions on development. Institutions can play significant roles in obstructing/promoting development goals. Some countries experience institutional barriers and regime characteristics that often stand in the way of rapid development and adoption of fruitful development policies. The remedies are removing institutional obstacles to development and encouraging institutions that advance development. While development economics can direct attention to the positive and negative impacts of specific institutions on the development process, and where feasible recommend and elaborate on institutional reforms related to the economy and polity system, there are many institutions that are culturally entrenched in society and that go beyond the frontiers of development economics.

Institutions refer to the formal and informal rules, norms, and practices that shape economic behavior and decision-making in a society. The role of formal and informal institutions in shaping and determining the pace of economic development has been a central topic in past and recent economic literature. There are earlier and important contributions to institutions in development by Myrdal, North, and Williamson, among others. More recent contributions have examined how different institutions, such as property rights, political systems, and the rule of law, shape economic outcomes and the impact of institutional quality on economic growth and development. The contributions offer insights into the challenges and opportunities for upgrading institutions to the levels required for promoting economic growth and development. For example, North (2003) examines the role of institutions in economic growth from a historical perspective. Amendola *et al.* (2013) examine the impact of institutions on income distribution in an empirical analysis. Acemoglu and Robinson (2010) and Bardhan (2005) emphasize the political economy of institutions. There are subtle differences when the above contributions are compared to our approach as will be displayed in Chapter 3. We distinguish between inner institutions that are created by and are attached to the economic political system present in a country (such institutions are controllable and adjustable) and the outer institutions which relate more to socio and cultural traits in the country; these are primarily informal, intergenerationally acquired, and are less controllable and less adjustable for policymaking. We shall elaborate on the subtle differences as we proceed in the forthcoming chapters.

It is worth mentioning that next to the above-quoted works, there are some works on institutions that are allocated to DE because the country studied is a developing country. Some of these publications are messy and are too eager to enter into a discussion of political solutions to institutional reforms and their details. A correct approach would pursue strict separation between economic analysis and political judgment.

Development goals is the next compartment in DF. Welfare economics teaches that the appraisal of economic growth is not independent of the appraisal of the income distribution underlying it. Growth paths are preceded by distribution patterns. Hence, policymaking is always confronted with the twin development goals of growth and distribution. Due to the complexity of the relationship between growth and distribution, the general practice is to act on and apply policies relating to the goal of economic growth in the first round and to act and apply policies relating to the goal of distribution in the second round. We shall accordingly treat the economic growth goal first and the income distribution goal later.

The economic growth goal (represented by annual growth rates of the Gross Domestic Product (GDP) and/or GDP per capita) is the prominent development goal in DE. GDP is rightly challenged regarding its representation of national well-being. For supplementing the GDP per capita by a measure of fair distribution of the income on the population, DE resorts to the Gini index of income distribution or similar indicators. The Gini index gives the gap between the actual distribution and full equality. The lower the Gini index, the more equal the income distribution.

Each goal is backed by several theories on how the goal is impacted and how the goal impacts. The economic growth goal is backed up by several growth theories. For income distribution, there is distribution theory and welfare theory. In this section, we shall review briefly various theories of growth and distribution.

Next to the growth of the GDP and its distribution, which we shall call primary goals, there are many other development goals that are as important, but because they are partially derivable from the primary goals, the other goals can be called secondary goals. These cover fulfillment of basic needs for all (which implies eradication of poverty), development and utilization of human resources, and the satisfaction of collective needs that involve externalities, such as civil security, environmental sustainability, fair justice, and democratic representation. Generally speaking, if the development effort is successful and there are significant advances in the two primary goals of growth and distribution, there may be then sufficient trickle-down effects that contribute to the fulfillment of the secondary goals. If in turn it is found *ex post* that there are still shortcomings in the fulfillment of the secondary goals, then additional and more specific policies can be tapped to tackle the shortcomings. The staged approach as described here brings a much needed simplification and principled ordering and coordination in the vast number of development goals put forward.

Regarding economic growth theories, a very much needed simplification of the extensive writings on growth theories is the distinction between the not relevant and the more relevant. Growth theories that are not relevant or non-operational in applied development economics include Mercantilist thoughts. Some economists mistakenly link growth theory in DE to Mercantilist thoughts that emerged in the 17th century with the rise of the nation-state, which emphasized restricted imports and mobilization of national *resources* to foster national economic growth. Mercantilist thoughts of the 17th century Europe are off point for understanding or theorizing on the underdevelopment situation of developing countries in the fifties, which stayed underdeveloped for centuries in colonial rule. One first simplification in the theory curriculum of DE is to drop Mercantilists and start from 1950. Add to this, that on its own, Mercantilist thought was not worked out in any precise form that can be scientifically tested or applied in development policy.

The classical growth theory postulates that a country's economic growth will decrease with an increasing population and limited resources. The idea is that a temporary increase in real GDP per person inevitably leads to a population explosion, consumes the nation's resources, and lowers real GDP. The theory is handicapped by assuming subsistence wages and ignoring technology in determining growth.

Big push, balanced growth, and stages growth theories are from works by Paul Rosenstein-Rodan, Ragnar Nurkse, and W. W. Rostow, respectively. Rostow presented the growth stages by which all countries were supposed to go through traditional society, pre-conditions for take-off, take-off, drive to maturity, and the age of high mass consumption. He focused on utilization of both domestic and international savings for spurring investment and moving toward the take-off. The theories are too general to be of use for development policy.

Dependency theories (Singer and Prebisch) viewed underdevelopment and low economic growth as being caused by the past foreign occupation and current foreign interests. The theory has no operational use in planning or implementing development.

Geo-economic theories (Sachs) emphasize the geographical location and topography of the developing country as key determinants and predictors of its economic prosperity. In contrast, resource-rich countries can sit back and extract rent, which reduces the pace of economic growth. The theories are valid but their relevance for operationalization and use development policy is limited.

Unity theories show that uniformity in ethnicity, belief, and language tends to facilitate communication, trust, and exchanges and thus contribute positively to growth and higher levels of development, as contemplated in important contributions on Indexes for ethnic heterogeneity and fractionalization by Easterly and Levine, and Alesina and La Ferrara. The unity theories are valid but their relevance for operationalization and use development policy is limited.

Turning to the more relevant growth theories, many of these were developed in the context of developed economies and they are equally relevant for developing economies. There are five of them. The first is the macro growth theory (Harrod–Domar model, 1950's), which provided an algebraic illustration of savings put into capital investment leading to greater economic growth.

The second is the neoclassical growth theory (Solow), which brought together the functioning of capital, labor, and technology in determining growth. Technology increases labor productivity (and labor earnings). Technology increases total output. The long-term growth rate of an economy is determined by technological progress.

The third is human capital theory (Gary Becker). Human capital stands for knowledge, skills, know-how, good health, and education of the workforce. More human capital raises productivity and individual earnings. Households, firms, and the state can invest in human capital, for example, through education and training, enabling higher earnings, productivity, and growth.

The fourth is endogenous growth theory (Paul Roemer), which states that economic growth is generated internally in the economy, i.e. through endogenous forces and not through exogenous ones. The theory contrasts with the neoclassical growth model, which claims that external factors such as technological progress are the main sources of economic growth. Governmental policies can raise an economy's growth rate if the policies are directed toward enforcing more market competition and helping stimulate innovation in products and processes. There are increasing returns to scale from capital investment in the "knowledge industries" of education, health, and telecommunications. Private sector investment in R&D is a vital source of technological progress for the economy.

The fifth is the segmented growth model of Baumol (1967) applied to developed countries and is very relevant for developing countries as well. In his analysis, he distinguishes two types of sectors: progressive (private) and non-progressive (public) sectors. The progressive sector is characterized by economies of scale and technological change, which lead to increases in productivity per unit of labor. In the non-progressive sector, labor productivity grows at a much lower rate. This difference in productivity is caused by differences in the nature of the product that is produced, whereby the public sector is in fact a service sector with little possibilities of substituting capital for labor. The scope for improving technology is very limited. What happens over time with labor costs crucially depends on the productivity differential. In the progressive sector, increases in labor productivity are followed by equal increases in wage rates. As a result, unit costs remain constant over time. In the non-progressive sector, the growth in productivity stays behind relatively to the progressive sector (this gives rise to the productivity differential). But, in order to prevent labor moving from the non-progressive to the progressive sector, wages in the non-progressive sector have to match those in the progressive sector, which the public sector does. The public sector becomes exhaustive with negative effects on economic growth. Baumol's model is highly relevant for developing countries where the public sector accounts for a big portion of employment.

The first and foremost growth theory with focus on developing economies is the dual growth theory of Lewis. Lewis was the first to emphasize the dualistic character of the developing economy. He introduced labor next to capital in a two-sector dualistic economy, and viewed agrarian societies as consisting of large amounts of surplus labor which can be utilized to spur the development of an urbanized industrial sector. Equivalent thoughts on the dual economy were developed by Todaro and de Soto among others focusing on the dualistic economy with low-productivity low-income underemployed labor in the informal/traditional sector versus a high-productivity high-income labor in the formal/modern sector.

A major refinement of the dual economy model is Chenery's extensions of the development model to multi-sectors and to input–output relations, and thus contributing to economy-wide models. Chenery shows that developing countries can follow different specializations and trajectories in their transformation within general patterns of industrial development.

An important and significant extension of the input–output analysis is in the construction and analysis of the social accounting matrix (SAM) first initiated by Stone. With the SAM, it became possible to link statistically the multi-sector input–output relations with the other dimensions of the circular flow of the economy, such as consumption, savings, and investments of households, businesses, and government, as well as foreign trade, savings, and investments.

The SAM provided a framework for applying computable general equilibrium (CGE) models to many developing countries, led by Adelman, among others. CGE models are applied in the chapters on sector development policies, which focus on growth and distribution in the framework of economy-wide models. This book contains several chapters with applications of SAM and CGE models to various countries.

The income distribution goal: We turn now to the distribution goal which is backed up by various distribution and welfare theories. There are positive and normative theories of income distribution. For an elaborate discussion and analysis of distribution theories, see Cohen (2001). *Positive* theories that explain income distribution in countries at large are empirically verified. A summary of 10 factors causing differences in acquired incomes is listed in the following:

1. working in low-productivity low-earnings activities versus high-productivity high-earnings activities,
2. differences in personal talents, capabilities, and health,
3. differences in personal choices regarding specific jobs and work intensity,
4. schooling achieved,
5. work experience and age profile,
6. good luck and risk-taking,
7. bad fortune and corner solutions,
8. distortive starting positions regarding ethnicity, gender, location (rural/urban), and parents (rich/poor),
9. biased assortative mating where people tend to marry within their own socio-economic class,
10. disadvantage/advantage in case of absence/presence of inherited wealth.

Five of the ten factors presume an economic valuation of the work at hand (i.e. paid-out earnings) based on market-priced productivity considerations. To remain a competitive economy, the total system may need to accept the general rule of compensation differences in accordance with productivity differences, with due consideration of externalities that are not accounted for by the market. The other five factors stand for predominantly non-market forces that determine realized distributional differences. These factors are non-economic in origin and are eventually controllable by non-economic institutional reforms. Recent empirical studies for developing countries relating to one or more of the 10 causal factors of income inequalities are covered in Ravallion (2014).

The normative theories of income distribution come into the picture along the following lines. Welfare economics postulates that for a given income distribution, the market mechanism will result in an economically efficient outcome, where cost is minimized and satisfaction is maximized. However, the market mechanism can provide as many technically efficient outcomes as there are possible distributions of income and wealth. An implicit assumption is required that the existing or some other distribution of income and wealth is "fair" or "equitable". Normative theories of what constitutes a "fair" distribution rest upon what is meant by "fairness" and whether fairness can be objectively specified.

In normative theories of distributive justice, cross-distinctions are made between outcome theories (what matters is the outcome at the finishing line) and process theories (what matters is an equal opportunity during the whole running race) and between exogenous and endogenous; each of the four alternatives ends up with a different view of what constitutes a fair distribution. Exogenous justice theories define concepts of justice by relying on principles formulated without taking into account the individual ethical preferences of the population under discussion. These theories impose those principles from above upon the population. Exogenous concepts of justice developed in one society would not be accepted by a society with a significantly different culture because the people here would reject the right of an external authority to impose its view of justice on their society. Endogenous justice theories focus on the economy's internal causation of inequality. See Box 1 for leading contributors.

Box 1. Normative theories of income distribution and distributive justice.

	Process theories	Outcome theories
Exogenous theories	Nozick, Sen	Utilitarianism, egalitarianism, Rawls
Endogenous theories	Blame freeness Schotter	Envy freeness Varian

Combined goals of growth with redistribution (GWR): While there is general agreement among economists and policy makers that there is no escape from treating the goals of growth and distribution separately and in the order of growth first and distribution second, there are some refinements to this position dating back to the mid-seventies. Several development economists collaborated to consolidate the wide range of development goals into a unified goal that was dubbed growth with redistribution as well as redistribution with growth. Foremost among them were Chenery and related World Bank economic advisors: Chenery (1974) and Cohen (1975). The idea is that in a dualistic developing economy, which may remain dualistic for a very long time, there will be always high productivity modern sectors paying high earnings and low productivity informal sectors paying low earnings with the latter overcrowded by underemployed labor. Hence, there is a persistent income inequality in the earnings market. A win-win development strategy would strive to elevate the modern sectors to even higher growth and higher incomes by extra taxing this income and using these taxes to upgrade over time the productivity levels of the lagging low productivity sectors and the working population attached to them in years to come. The modern sectors can then count on more upgraded skills. The extra tax which the modern sectors would pay can be seen as their investment in enlarging and upgrading human resource inputs that the modern sectors require. Investment in human resource development covers income maintenance, education, health, shelter, etc. The optimal or satisficing income distribution in the context of GWR can be named a functional income distribution that allows for positive, mutual, and cumulative feedback between growth and redistribution.

Theoretical and empirical contributions to the relationship between growth and distribution started with Kuznets in the 1950s, famously propounding the view that there is an inverted U curve relating levels of per capita income to income distribution, with income distribution first becoming more unequal, and at a later state, more equal, as per capita incomes rise. Kuznets derived this from cross-country evidence, which was later supported by others using time series on the changing income distribution in industrialized countries. It should be noted that the Kuznets work relates to levels of income per capita, not to the growth rate. How is the U curve caused? Take the first part of the curve. The case is that of a dualistic economy as modeled by Lewis, with a low productivity agrarian sector and a high productivity industrial sector. Development causes a sectoral shift to occur. Consequently, inequality rises, both because of the differences in average incomes between the sectors and because some labor is shifting from a less to a more productive sector. The first part of the U curve is thus derivable from the Lewis growth model, i.e. productivity and incomes' growth are confined to the modern sector, where the profit share rises, while in the stagnant traditional sector, incomes remain low (and may even fall as population growth occurs) so that between-sector inequality rises. As for the process underlying the second part of the curve, one explanation is that when the whole economy becomes part of the modern industrial sector, the inequality arising from the between-sector differences disappears, which signals the disappearance of dualism in an advanced economy. Besides, when full employment is reached, income inequality diminishes as well.

These explanations assume that the U-turn is caused by imperfect markets in a dualistic economy and that in the advanced economy, the dualistic characteristic disappears and markets become more perfect and contribute to a more progressive income distribution. These explanations are incomplete because empirical analysis for advanced countries, which is presented in Chapter 5 and earlier in Cohen (2002), show that if left to the market forces, the primary distribution of income is either stable or regressive, and it is the state which causes the U to turn via tax levies of the modern industrial sector that are redistributed to low and no income earners, thus resulting into a more equal distribution. Making use of SAM analysis for advanced economies, we show later in Chapter 5 that tax transfers are determinants of the U-turn. Besides, dualistic and segmentation features are amply present in the advanced market economies (in the sense of differential productivities between old and knowledge-based new economy activities). In summary, the downward phase of the U-curve is typical of the dualistic developing economy, while the upward phase is typical of a welfare-advanced economy.

We join many other economists in defining and focusing on growth with redistribution, GWR, as the core goals of socio-economic development. Development goals and policies for developing countries aiming at promoting both economic growth and redistribution of endowments among the population at large have been the focus of many governments and scholars. Our focus on the twin goals of growth with redistribution and on policies that promote growth with redistribution is shared by many other development economists as manifested in Stiglitz agenda for inclusive development in Stiglitz (2016). Other thoughts in the same direction were started by Tinbergen and Chenery in the 1970's and are recently recalled in Berg *et al.* (2018) and Basu and Stiglitz (2017). However, there are subtle differences when the above-quoted references are compared to our approach. Due to possible trade-offs between growth and redistribution in the early stages of development, we tend to view (a) progressive redistribution as subsequent to growth in time perspective and (b) progressive redistribution of endowments rather than incomes as necessary and inevitable for assuring sustainable growth in the context of both developing and developed countries. In the long run, progressive redistribution of endowments and raising up well-balanced capability levels of all human resources is necessary for sustainable growth. We shall elaborate on the subtle differences as we proceed in the following in forthcoming chapters.

The next compartment in DE is that of development policies. Development policy studies count in the thousands per year. The choices of development policies that are treated in this book are directly related to the development goals of growth and redistribution. This does not diminish the importance of other policies dealing with other issues than growth and distribution.

The development policies for growth with redistribution (GWR) that are treated in this book can be grouped under two headings: (i) multi-sector development and policies and (ii) human resource development and policies. The two distinguished policy areas of multi-sector development and human resource development are viewed to be two pillars for a successful and sustainable achievement of the combined goals of growth with redistribution.

There are alternative strategies for the achievement of (higher) growth with (efficient) redistribution. All strategies require increased taxation of more productive activities and higher incomes. The strategies differ regarding the redistributive use of the collected revenue. Economically speaking, the search is for the most efficient redistribution avenues in year t to assure the highest growth for the future in year $t + 1$, that allows again for more redistributions and higher growth in $t + n$. A short-term GWR strategy would be a simple transfer of the collected revenue to the less productive activities and their low-income earners, which may achieve little in terms of sustained development. Other more compelling GWR strategies have medium and long-term horizons and would invest the collected revenue in physical, and human, educational, and /informational infrastructures that would raise the productivity and remuneration levels of the less productive sectors with poorly paid agents, and in the education of their children and raising their skills with the perspective of joining the more productive sectors and contributing to a higher growth of the economy and to more redistribution in a cobweb fashion. To be successful, GWR must rely on sustained feedback cycles between growth and redistribution.

This book contains (i) eight chapters relating to multi-sector developments and policies and (ii) six chapters relating to human resource development and policies. Most of the chapters demonstrate the developments and policies making use of case studies for developing countries.

Development policies at the regional and world levels: This area of DE has become increasingly demanding and active as the presence of regional and world externalities in epidemics spread, climatic change, resource use, and national security is being increasingly recognized. We introduce the subject matter in this book in Chapters 21 and 22, and this we do by reflecting on the growing relative power of the development regions (and countries) in the world at large.

We shall make use of two indicators of the relative power of a country or a region. The two indicators are derived from economy/polity system theory in Chapters 2 and 3, and these are the GDP which measures the volume of activity, and population which measures the scale of agents engaged in producing and consuming these activities. The indicators show the rising power of the development regions and their constituent countries (as measured by GDP and population). These changes need to be reflected in the structure and operation of world governance.

Analytics and modeling methods: One of the major contributions of DE to social sciences concerns the elaboration of analytical methods in the collection, organization, analysis, and use of data, and the development of monitoring and evaluatory indicators. The planning and policy side of DE made possible the formulation and application of a wide range of economy-wide models and analyses which did not exist before. Each chapter of this book gives ample space for explaining the applied methods which can be adapted and applied to more countries and more years. The applied methods can be grouped into two categories: indicator analysis and economy-wide models. As indicated in Table 1, some chapters work exclusively with indicator analysis, while other chapters make use of economy-wide models or both.

Indicator analysis for developing economies is an immense area of research. Our focus is on institutional indicators, goal indicators, and the overlapping area of analytical and policy indicators, which are reviewed briefly here. We make use of institutional indicators that are developed by others, such as the corruption perception indicator (CPI) and Destratification Mobility Index (DMI). But we also develop and apply our own institutional indicators. The Dominance Index (DI), which combines relative shares of GDP and population, grades the influential power of a member entity among the set of all member entities. Other institutional indicators that we develop are based on respondent replies in opinion surveys. Examples are respondent attitudes to free markets and government interventions in Chapter 3. Regarding goal indicators, we develop in Chapter 5 a quasi-elasticity that gives the percentage change in the Gini distribution associated with a percentage change in the growth of the GDP, a similar elasticity for poverty reduction, and a basic needs index, among others. Next to structural indicators that measure long-term changes in sectoral development at the country and regional levels, a large number of analytical and policy indicators are developed and applied in the chapters on development policies. Following are a few examples: key sector indicators based on the extent of backward and forward linkages in input–output table analysis, gainer–loser index that identifies sectors with built-in relative growth and decline, outcome–input index for the knowledge economy, various labor market indicators, alternative benefit–cost ratios in human resource development, and intra and intergenerational mobility indicators.

Economy-wide models for developing countries can be grouped into models that assume constant prices, CP models, and those which work with endogenous prices, such as computable general equilibrium CGE models. The Social Accounting Matrix (SAM) puts the national accounts in a matrix form and is a prerequisite basis for CGE models. The SAM itself can be handled as a static model of the economy that assumes constant prices. In many ways, the SAM is a bridge between the CP models and the CGE models. This book contains various chapters that apply CP, CGE, and SAM models in the analysis of multi-sector development policies. Furthermore, the book makes use of partial models of the economy in the analysis of human resource development policies.

3. Summary Contents of the Chapters

This book brings some collected works in DE over the past years, next to recent works undertaken as recently as 2022. All the works are re-edited and often redone, shortened, and updated. There is special focus in all chapters on analytics methods and policy modeling. These are durable methods which can be adapted and applied to more countries and at more times. While the topic of analysis may become less relevant over the years, the methods of analysis remain intact and usable in more contexts. In this section, we review briefly the abstracts of each chapter.

Chapter 1 is the current introduction.

Chapter 2. The development regions: The chapter aims at grouping developing countries in development regions (DR) based on geographic proximity, historical background, and other shared cultural, socio, economic, and political features. Important determining factors are data availability, and the World Bank practices in separating regional groups. The classification results in six DR which are utilized throughout this book where relevant. The chapter goes further to reflect on the historical backgrounds of the DR and examines the main structural changes relating to population, state, and economic activities in each DR.

Chapter 3. System dominance and institutions conduct in developing countries: Theory and application: The chapter starts by positioning the six development regions in terms of prototypes of the socio-economy-polity systems, i.e. total system. The system prototypes describe the concentration of agents and activities in the traditional familial households subsystem, the modern firm, business, and market-led subsystem, and the polity, government, and state-led subsystem. The positioning of DR is helpful in highlighting major system and institutional changes and differences between the DR, especially regarding their institutional inclinations regarding market coordination versus state coordination. The chapter recalls as well empirical research that emphasizes the impact of institutions on development. Specific behaviors of the interacting agents may retard a speedy socio-economic development process. Following are examples: (1) corruptive practices in business and state contexts distort fair competition, (2) social distrust between transacting agents (due to differential attitudes) discourages exchange, (3) societal stratification (feudal system) has a rent-extracting character that discourages agent mobility and efficient allocation of resources, (4) polarization (due to non-compromising ideologies, beliefs, ethnicity, and nationalism) excludes co-operation and in the extreme can lead to violent conflicts.

Chapter 4. Modeling of bygone institutions that obstructed development: Case studies of India and Chile: The chapter dares to innovate and model the impact of two institutional areas on development prospects. Chapter 4 is an economy-wide model and a case study of the bygone societal stratification and the feudal system in India of the 1950s and 1960s. The same economy-wide model was adapted to represent the polarization due to opposite and non-compromising ideologies with supportive powers during the Allende regime in Chile in the 1970s that ended with military violence.

Chapter 5. Growth with redistribution in the development process: The chapter elaborates on the twin development goals of growth with redistribution, GWR. It treats the processes behind the U-shape of the Kuznets curve and finds the dualistic economy model of Lewis as best suited in describing the downward part while the social accounting matrix analysis by Cohen as best suited in describing the upward part of the curve. The chapter develops and demonstrates for a few countries the application of a GWR performance indicator that divides the relative change in the Gini index by the growth rate of the GDP. The sign of the elasticity tends to reverse as the turning point in the U-curve is passed.

Chapter 6. Growth with redistribution performances at region and country levels: The chapter is a continuation of the previous chapter. The GWR performance indicator is quantified for the six development regions and the major countries in each region. Results are analyzed and country performances are distributed along a ranking index of the GWR performance indicator.

Chapter 7. The social accounting matrix as analytical framework for growth with redistribution: Applications to ten developing countries: The chapter introduces the social accounting matrix, SAM, and treats the conversion of the SAM into an economy-wide model that employs fixed relative prices and clears market imbalances via flexible quantities. The chapter reviews multiplier results relating to the trade-off between economic growth and income distribution for 10 developing countries. It then continues with decomposing these multipliers in various effects, identifying sector and agent gainers and losers, and highlighting the significance of dual structures in production (formal and informal sectors) and earnings (poor and rich household groups) in generating interdependent patterns of growth and distribution.

Chapter 8. Macro-sector and micro-economics of dualistic sector development: Case studies of Indonesia and Pakistan: The chapter models the dualistic structure of the developing economy in two sectors and two population groups using the SAM framework for Indonesia and Pakistan. The results show the growth bias in the two sectors and the corresponding distribution bias for the two population groups. The chapter shifts to a micro analysis of capital returns of small enterprises in the formal and informal segments in the two countries. The analysis is based on survey data from a few locations in the two countries. The results show bias in favor of the modern segment, and elaborate on explaining the co-existence of both segments in spite of lower profitability of one on the other. The bias favoring the modern segment is in correspondence with the earlier obtained results at the macro level using the SAM.

Chapter 9. Social sectors introduced in economic models: An application to past Korea: The chapter explores quantified ways of incorporating social development goals and basic needs indicators in economy-wide models. We evaluate the welfare and productivity effects of higher satisfaction against the costs involved and examine the optimal ordering of various social and economic development goals in the policymaking process. The model is applied to the Republic of Korea during its period of take-off. The modeling application demonstrates high degrees of positive complementarities between social development and economic growth in the Korean context that can be replicable elsewhere.

Chapter 10. Simplified statics and dynamics in a Computable General Equilibrium, CGE, model: Indonesia: This chapter demonstrates how a simple static computable general equilibrium model of the Indonesian economy can be constructed and parameterized using the social accounting matrix as a database. It will also convert the constant labor supply and capital stock in the static model to dynamic specifications allowing formulation and solution of a dynamic version of the CGE model.

Chapter 11. Growth with redistribution through liberalization with restructuring in a CGE policy model: Nepal: The CGE model is modified to include prospective restructuring of the economy and its distribution mechanisms and apply it to Nepal. The restructured CGE model showed that the combination of import and export liberalizations generates higher growth but the distribution pattern does not become pro-poor. Liberalization under a flexible exchange rate regime, when compared to the fixed regime, can work negatively since the currency may appreciate much and eliminate the comparative advantages. We also find that a piece-by-piece external reform gives better economic results than implementing all external reforms together.

Chapter 12. Sustained development of agricultural resources in a CGE policy model: Sudan: The chapter develops a model that shares common features with the computable general equilibrium (CGE) models. It is used to address two questions. First, what are the future prospects of a green gross domestic product (GDP), should we be concerned about resource degradation or not, and to what extent and under which conditions? Second, which policies are more effective than the others? Different model closures are simulated relating to different specifications of exogenous variables. Furthermore, alternative policies are treated: human capital, price incentives, property rights, and poverty reduction. In the African context, we show that while the prospects of environment-friendly economic development, i.e. a rising green GDP, are weak in the medium run, yet under certain structural conditions, there is a range of effective policies that resolve the conflict between economic growth and resource degradation, and contribute positively to a rising green GDP.

Chapter 13. Development analysis and policy modeling with minimal data: IOT and SAM of Suriname: The chapter reports on the construction of the input–output table and the social accounting matrix of Suriname making use of minimal data. Multiplier analysis in various forms is done for the IOT and SAM and compared. Growth and distribution issues are examined showing which sectors score most in achieving growth and progressive distribution effects. Negative savings by poor household groups are generated by the SAM as a measure of poverty. The SAM framework is extended into a medium-term planning model that was used, among other sources, in projecting the GDP targets for the Suriname development plan 2023–2027.

Chapter 14. Oil-rich labor short development with focus on growth only: Comparative performance of UAE and GCC: Oil-rich labor-shortage economies such as the GCC countries are guided by the goal of economic growth only. The income distribution goal is considered not applicable. While this simplifies socio-economic development issues, the achievement of economic growth in the GCC is significantly dependent on migrant workers, which raises complex issues regarding the optimal net inflow of migrant workers over the years. This is complicated further in the context of the introduction of the knowledge economy which saves on migrant labor but which also favors the luxury of being serviced by cheap migrant labor. Individual GCC countries face conflicting pressures such as increasing national power via enlarging the migrant labor force and the total resident population versus minimizing security risks of dependence on foreign resident citizens. The chapter examines the comparative performance of UAE and the other GCC countries in handling the above-mentioned issues.

Chapter 15. Labor market information and matching assessments: The objectives of this chapter are to upgrade the use of labor force information to meet more demanding analysis and policy preparations in the areas of the longer-term development and utilization of human resources, and the short-term balancing of the labor market and unemployment reduction. The objectives are reached by developing and applying suitable analytics and methods that broaden the use of these data. The chapter falls into two parts. One part develops labor force survey data into a labor force information system that takes the form of a labor force matrix. The other part organizes labor market matching statistics in ways that allow simple regressions which highlight short-term tendencies and imbalances in the labor market and policy remedies to relieve these imbalances. Both applications were done in the context of technical assistance to the Ministry of Labour Affairs, Pakistan.

Chapter 16. National and regional manpower modeling and projections for development plan: Indonesia: The chapter reports on a simulative model that confronts projections of the demand for manpower types by sectors, occupation, education, and status with projections of the supply of manpower classified in the same categories. The model analyses alternative ways to resolve the imbalances between demand and supply. The model and its results served as a primary input among others in the preparation of the development plan of Indonesia (1986–1990) in the areas of manpower and education. The model gives for the period of 1980–1990 projections of human resources in the labor force and the educational system at the national level and their distributions at the regional level.

Chapter 17. Labor market imbalances and adjustments: Korea, Pakistan, and Colombia: The chapter makes use of conventional manpower and educational planning methods by formulating and applying a forecasting model of labor imbalances in terms of demand and supply for occupational types and educational levels. The aim of public policy is to close the gaps in the absence of labor market interactions between demanders and suppliers. In a mixed economy, *a priori* market expectations on the occupational demand side would not match with the market expectations on the educational supply side. In the real world, both types of expectations adjust to each other in processes that clear imbalances. The chapter goes beyond the planning methods and simulates labor market adjustments by applying an iterative fitting model (using the RAS algorithm) to simulate the clearance of the imbalances in the labor market. The RAS method allows the demands and supplies for labor quantities of various types to meet, adjust to each other, and end up in the matched mix of occupational types against educational levels. The model is applied and validated to Colombia, Korea, and Pakistan making use of plans and labor market data for the periods 1970–1990.

Chapter 18. Imbalances in earnings expectations and educational returns: Supply and demand imbalances in the labor market in terms of labor quantities have their counterpart in expectations imbalances regarding earnings. This is demonstrated in Chapter 18 by formulating and applying earnings expectations based on two contrasting expectations as viewed by suppliers (school leavers) and by demanders (job employers). One is based on human capital (HC) theory which tends to overestimate educational returns and underestimate occupational returns. The other is based on job competition (JC) theory which puts more emphasis on returns by occupations than by education. The cost–benefit analysis along with the two contrasting theories on returns expectations is applied to Indonesia and Pakistan. The results from the two contrasting theories are found to be consistent with the forecasted scarcities and surpluses. The results show also that returns to education based on HC (supply-side educational returns expectations) tend to be biased upwards when compared to returns based on JC (demand-side occupational returns expectations).

Chapter 19. Normed planning of human resource development: Ethiopia: The chapter develops a normed planning model with regressed parameters from the data sets of the selected best performing countries. The model is then applied to Ethiopia with outcomes on the targeted education mix regarding enrolments, teachers, expenditure, etc. at the various educational level, shortfall gaps between the targeted education mix and the existing education mix, crucial features that account for the shortfall gaps, implications for the public and private financing of the educational 'plans, etc.

Chapter 20. A survey analysis of generational mobility: Pakistan: The chapter reports on a specially designed questionnaire applied to Pakistan with the purpose of describing the changing socio-economic positions of the workforce in the modern segment over different generations and their association with their endowments of social, human, and physical capital and other socio-economic characteristics. The assessment of the incidence and nature of mobility trends would make it possible to identify the processes through which different socio-economic groups attempt to improve their positions in a changing society. The chapter describes the data set of the field inquiry, gives the socio-economic profiles for two generations of "sons" and "fathers", and applies a framework which studies the results of inter and intragenerational mobility.

Chapter 21. The shifting economic power of countries and regions: Studies and discussions of global dominance focus on the relative size of the GDP of individual countries. This focus suffers from two biases: the one criterion GDP bias and the isolated individual country bias. The chapter aims at proposing and applying solutions to these two bias problems. First, we present basic premises for measuring global dominance via a dominance index that avoids the GDP bias by combining population size with GDP size. This dominance index is quantified to give the list of leading countries. Second, the world cannot be seen as a loose collection of individual countries. Any individual country is allied to other countries in a regional formation and is as such a member of a regional interest group that has common interests. The remedy to the isolated individual country bias is to move to interregional and intraregional dominance, which is shown to add analytical insights.

Chapter 22. World governance and the G-20: An alternative design: An expanding globalization causes global failures, similar to economy failures encountered in the national economic system. Global failures are likely to be more severe in the coming years as new leading countries from the development world join leading incumbents of the developed world, whereby the newcomers (for instance, China and India) and the incumbents (US and EU) have distinctly different economic systems. It is crucial in such circumstances to have a design of world governance that can respond adequately to global failures. The G-20 is one such design, but this is handicapped by its narrow scope (composition based on GDP size) and undemocratic composition (selection of individual countries is not based on regional representation, next to being inconsistent and outdated). The chapter formulates and applies an index of influence potential that combines population and GDP, which is measurable at the region and country levels. The chapter produces an alternative design for the G-Top that has more representative participation by regions/countries than the G-20.

Chapter 2

The Development Regions

1. Introduction

Consistent and meaningful regional grouping of developing countries is necessary and useful for various purposes. The economic development of a specific country is better understood when it is supplemented by knowledge of the development of the region in which the country is situated. There are always minor and major externalities which involve countries within the same region, and the resolution of these externalities requires pursuing regional approaches. At the global level, different regions in the world are confronted with different problems that require regional approaches to examine and solve the regional problems. Finally, a democratically based world governance would need to include the representation of regional interests by regional entities. This chapter aims at grouping developing countries in development regions (DR) based on geographic proximity, historical background, and other shared cultural, socio, economic, and political features. This chapter goes further to reflect on the historical backgrounds of the DR and examines the main structural changes relating to population, state, and economic activities in each DR.

This chapter sets up in section 2 the classification of development regions (DR) making primary use of the World Bank classification which will be followed in this book, where relevant. Section 3 adds brief historical backgrounds on the various DR. Section 4 examines major developments and structural changes in the DR. We distinguish between three major transitions with transformational impacts on the socio-polity-economy system, in short, the total system. The three transitions occurred in and centered around the three broad subsystems of (a) the households/population, (b) the state/polity, and (c) the firms/markets/economy. Section 5 brings together several structural indicators resulting from the above transitions. The structural indicators are tabulated for the development regions and main constituent countries.

2. Classification of Development Regions

There are tens of international agencies that have set up their own databanks resulting in a multitude of overlapping country groupings. We shall focus on and make

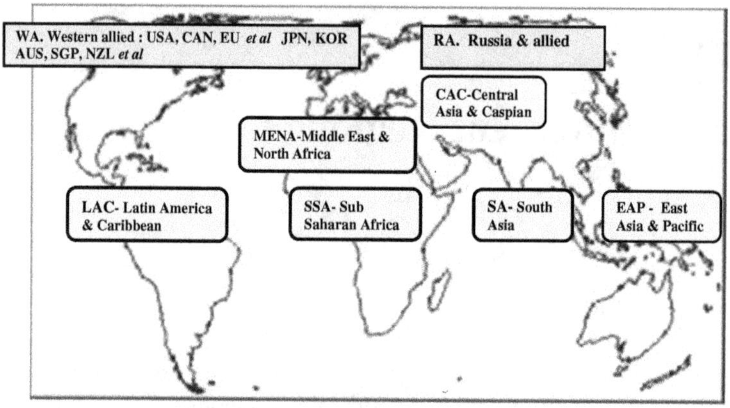

Figure 1. World regions containing two developed regions and six development regions.

Table 1. Country groupings and subsequent modifications applied to the World Bank databank.

Distinguished country groups	Specification of countries included
Two Developed Regions	
WA Western allied developed countries	USA, Canada, and EU *et al.* extended to include next to the EU, all other European countries not included elsewhere. Total 46 countries. Japan, Korea, Australia, New Zealand, Brunei Darussalam, French Polynesia, New Caledonia, and Singapore.Total 8 countries.
Six Development Regions	
EAP East Asia and Pacific	All income levels excluding EAP-high income: China, Cambodia, Indonesia, Korea DR, Lao PDR, Malaysia, Micronesia, Myanmar, Mongolia, Papua NG, the Philippines, Thailand, Timor-Leste, Vietnam, and other Oceania small territories and islands. Total 26 countries.
SA South Asia	All income levels: India, Afghanistan, Bangladesh, Bhutan, Maldives, Nepal, Pakistan, and Sri Lanka. Total 8 countries.
CAC Central Asia and Caspian	Turkiye, Iran, Azerbaijan, Kazakhstan, Kyrgyz R, Tajikistan, Turkmenistan, and Uzbekistan. Total 8 countries.
MENA Middle East and North Africa	All income levels: Egypt, Algeria, Bahrain, Djibouti, Iraq, Israel, Jordan, Kuwait, Lebanon, Libya, Morocco, Oman, Palestine, Qatar, Saudi Arabia, Syria, Tunisia, the UAE, and Yemen. Total 19 countries.
SSA Sub-Saharan Africa	All of Africa except Algeria, Egypt, Libya, Morocco, and Tunisia, which are included in MENA. Total 48 countries.
LAC Latin America and Caribbean	All income levels in Latin America and the Caribbean: Brazil, Mexico, etc. Total 41 countries.

use of the databank of the World Bank (WB) as our main source, as it is the one most used.

It is acknowledged that country groupings using databanks, once done, become sticky. The classified groupings may have been meaningful and useful when they were initiated in the past, but some may have become less meaningful over time. A reset would damage the continuity of the data series, so things are kept as they were, resulting in a less effective use of the databank. This holds for the WB classification as well. This is why we shall update the WB classification with two adjustments.

First, the WB databank lumps together all ex-Soviet Union and allied countries, all European countries, and some Asian countries in the so-called Europe and Central Asia. This country grouping is less useful today. Our approach would split these countries into three country groupings: EU *et al.*, together with the USA and others belonging to the Western alliance (WA), Russia and Russian allied countries (RA), and the separate development region of Central Asia and Caspian (CAC). The CAC is a development region consisting of the ex-Soviet Islamic Republics, supplemented by the border countries of Turkiye and Iran. This development region has strong dynamics and has shown a high degree of integration and increased influences of Turkiye and Iran powered by common belief, ethnicity, rich resources, and border proximity.

Second, the WB databank includes Iran and Malta in the predominantly Arab group of the Middle East and North Africa (MENA). The Arab-inclined configuration of the region is diluted by the inclusion of a major Persian county as Iran. Another unfitting detail is the inclusion of Malta in MENA, which is already a member of the EU since 2004. Our adjustment of MENA deletes Iran and Malta from the group and assigns them to CAC and EU, respectively.

We have adjusted the WB databank to the above-mentioned modifications. The adjusted groupings and databank are sketched in Figure 1 and Table 1. All regional data for all indicators employed in this book have been re-aggregated in line with these modifications.

3. Historical Backgrounds

The objective of this section is to summarize briefly the historical epochs of enduring influence on the polities and economies of the development regions. We treat two historical epochs: colonial rule and nation-building.

Colonial epoch: While the European colonization was driven by unified political, economic, religious, and discovery motives, the impact of the colonization on the host development regions was highly diversified. Climatic conditions, resource endowments, and geographical location of the host country, as well as the colonial resistance, cultural remoteness, and cheer numbers of the host population in relation to the colonial power, have all played central roles in determining differentiated colonial configurations. The colonial rule evolved into four configurational forms: (a) from a fully absorbed commonwealth country, to (b) settled colonies, (c) occupied colonies, and (d) loosely linked strategic relationships with autonomous regions.

The first form is that of the fully absorbed commonwealth countries, such as the US, Canada, and Australia. Very large European migrations took place to these countries, allowing them to form, in a relatively short time, the over majority of the total population. Soon afterward, they went for nationhood and independence in the 17th and 18th centuries and remained closely affiliated with their European ancestors and institutions. Ultimately, most of Europe and the newer countries of the US, Canada, and Australia have come to share a common heritage with many similarities in their social, political, and economic systems.

The second form is that of regions settled by migrants, and supported by armies, but nevertheless with substantial native populations working in mining and plantations, and residing in rural areas, such as in Latin America. The colonial epoch in these countries manifested regular conflicts between settlers and their descendants and the native population, leading to militant actions. Realization of nationhood and independence in these countries took more time to mature, i.e. in the 19th century.

The third form took the shape of army-occupied and annexed colonies and applied to many countries in Asia and Africa. There was no permanent role for colonial settlers, instead there were relatively limited numbers of foreign soldiers and related officials who maintained the colonial rule. Colonization took place later in time in this category, and consequently, national leadership and demands for independence took more years to develop. The colonial epoch endured longer in this category than in the other categories, and the accomplishment of political independence was mostly accompanied by resistance and wars of liberation. Especially, where pockets of colonial settlers existed, the armed struggle was heavier. In general, the transfer of European institutions has been much more limited in this category than in the other above categories.

The fourth form was based on relationships of a more calculative nature that emerged between the colonial powers and autonomously run countries that have remained politically independent. One can include here bigger countries, such as Japan and China, and also much smaller and distanced Islamic countries, such as Iran and the Arab peninsula. The colonial powers and these countries stood culturally, ethnically, and religiously very remote from each other to sustain a relationship other than that of strategic interest. Besides, the sizes, densities, histories, and cultures of the populations in these countries would exclude the introduction of colonial rule. Hence, the systemic impact of the colonial epoch is the least in this category of countries.

In summary, the impact of the colonial epoch on the total systems of the host countries was highly diversified in content and size. There were commonly shared impacts as well. The colonial epoch carried a bias against the traditional modes of work and living and for the modern modes. The traditional surroundings, undergoing little or no change, continued to center in household settings in rural areas as they used to be for centuries. At the same time, some young people left the traditional (rural/formal segments) and joined the modern (urban/formal segments). In the modern surroundings, the significance of household settings in establishing and maintaining behavioral rules deteriorated as interactions in state and firm settings grew more. The small elite groups managed to exit the traditional settings, enter schools, occupy leading positions in their communities, and communicate and interact with the modern world. The select elites were able to transform themselves, partly through skill mobilizations set into motion by the colonial regimes and partly through making use of their own inborn capabilities and kinship support. The select elites became the dominating actors in the next phases of nationhood, economic development, and global integration.

Nation building: With the advent of national independence, in one country after another, political authority was transferred from colonial powers to national governments guarded by elite leaders. In contrast to the colonial period that stretched over centuries, the nationhood phase was a matter of a few decades only and with significant impacts on the total systems in most development regions. Already in the colonial period political authority was gradually transferred to national elite leaders. Independence opened more opportunities for the national elite leaders and state settings, as defenders of national independence, identity, and integration. State settings increased their roles as focal points of interaction and overriding authorities in shaping the total system.

Running a government requires appointing officials that can be trusted. In the development context, these were often recruited from the networks of ethnic groups, regions, and kinships to which the political leaders belonged.[1] Not only the distribution of political positions but also the funding of development schemes and the allocation of rich licenses reflected the ethnic and regional divides. Sooner or later, this was bound to lead to an intensification of ethnic divides. It is natural, therefore, that in some countries, the first rounds of national governments were challenged by political leaders from excluded networks of ethnic groups, kinships, sects, or regions. In the EAP region, Cambodia is the foremost example. In the South Asia region, the split up of Pakistan was the foremost example. Ethnic exclusion has been a major cause of civil violence in the Middle East with foremost examples being Iraq and Syria. In some African countries, i.e. Nigeria, Burundi, Congo, Rwanda, and Sudan, this type of conflict led to civil violence and in some cases to civil war with winning and losing groups. It can be postulated that state institutions must have increased their influence among the winning networks and reduced their influence among the losing networks.

Indifferently, in most of the developing world, the nation-building period led to the institution of strong military defense forces and to the strengthening of supportive interest groups along lines of vast land ownership, business, industry, and religion. Military regimes are not permanent, however. The military leadership can be peacefully transformed into a civil leadership[2] and legitimized by electoral vote. The alternative is mostly an unstable cycle of military successions that can develop into civil unrest or ethnic wars. In some countries, successions of military leaders faced regular clashes with popular calls for stepping down, i.e. Myanmar in EAP, Pakistan in SA, and Congo, Ghana, Ivory Coast, and Nigeria in SSA. In other countries, the military disintegrated and collided with affiliated ethnic groups in self-defense or in search of dominance over others, i.e. Afghanistan in SA, Syria and Iraq in MENA, and Angola, Congo DR, Liberia, Mali, Mozambique, Sudan, and Somalia in SSA. These countries experienced substantial violence and mistrust in state institutions. This is likely to lead to a reduction in the institutional influence of the state in the longer run in some of these countries; while in others, the situation has evolved to that of a failed nation-state and has become riper for split-ups.

Finally, ideological confrontations between conformists and reformers disrupted the stability of national governments in many countries of the developing world and tended to have mixed effects on the focalizing of the state in the system. The confrontations between a "capitalist" and a "socialist" ideology were often reinforced by foreign military support in the context of the cold war, and this led to greater casualties, such as in North Korea and Vietnam. Countries handicapped by violent rightist-leftist confrontations included Laos, Nepal, Philippines, Yemen, Angola, and Mozambique, among others. The other major ideological confrontation is that between a fundamentalist and a modernist interpretation of religious belief. This has been a major challenge to nation-building in the MENA and SSA regions and in some Asian countries with highly non-integrated ethnic and religious minorities.[3]

The degree of political instability in the nationhood phase varied significantly in the various development regions. Taking civil war casualties as a proxy measure of political instability,[4] records show for the period 1945–2003 that in absolute terms, regions and countries with the largest populations such as in the Asian regions have had high casualties, but when casualties are expressed in relative terms, per thousand inhabitants of the year 2000, a different picture is obtained. Table 2 shows SA to have the lowest relative casualties of about 1 person per 1000. EAP is higher at about 4.7 per thousand. MENA occupies an intermediate position with about 1.9 casualties per 1000, with Iraq as the leader in civil war casualties, with 7.1

Table 2. War casualties in the development regions (millions of casualties per thousand people).

Development region	War casualties in whole region	Country with highest war casualties	War casualties in whole region	Country with highest casualties
	Civil wars 1945–2003		Foreign wars 1945–2003	
EAP	8.45(4.7)	China 3.19 (2.5)[a]	5.94(3.3)	Korea, 3.00[f]
SA	1.24(0.9)	India 1.10 (1.1)[b]	2.04(1.8)	Afghanistan, 1.01[g]
CAC	0.53(1.9)	Iraq .18; (7.1)[c]	1.79(6.5)	Algeria, 1.00[h]
SSA	8.77(13.2)	Nigeria 2.02 (17.1)[d]	1.07(1.6)	Ethiopia, 0 .85[i]
LAC	0.67(1.3)	Colombia 0.30 (7.1)[e]	0.01(0.02)	Honduras, 0.006[j]
Total number of countries	68		36	

Notes: a = followed by Cambodia, b = followed by Sri Lanka, c = followed by Iran, d = followed by Congo, e = followed by Guatemala, f = followed by Vietnam, g = followed by Bangladesh, h = followed by Iraq-Iran war, i = followed by Angola, j = followed by Argentina-UK war.

Source: Raw country data on war casualties are found in the database of the Centre for Systemic Peace, University of Maryland, at *http://members.aol.com/cspmgm/warlist.htm*. We aggregated war casualty figures into the regional groups. To obtain casualties per thousand people of the average population, we use the population figures by region for 2000, shown in Table 4.

casualties per 1000. Sub-Saharan Africa appears to be the most unstable region with casualties of about 9 million over five decades related to a total population in 2000 of about 660 million, giving casualties of about 13 people per thousand of the population. In the SSA region, figures show Nigeria as the highest, with 2.2 million casualties and a relative figure of 17 casualties per 1000. Table 2 gives also casualty figures as a result of foreign wars. The origins of these wars are diverse. Some were liberation wars that occurred toward the end of the colonial rule, such as in Ethiopia and Algeria. Some were inflamed by the cold war, such as in Korea and Vietnam. Some were between bordering countries, such as the Iraq–Iran war.

Although national governments were installed in Latin America about a century earlier than for other regions, similar periods of nation-building and civil divides followed each other and were caused by ideological confrontations based on uneven endowments between the haves and have-nots, empowered at a later stage by powerful interest groups in drug production and trafficking.[5] It is generally observed that the ideological camps of capitalists versus socialists, and rightists versus leftists, tend to coincide with the "haves" versus the "have-nots", respectively. In this respect, the distribution of endowments in the social system is crucial for understanding the stability and unity of the system. In the LAC region, Colombia had the highest casualties, which coincided with high inequalities as well. Nevertheless,

Table 3. Political regimes in the development regions: percent of applicable countries in region.

	Authoritarian rule		Restricted parliament		Multi-party democracy		Total	
Development region	1982	2000	1982	2000	1982	2000	1982	2000
East Asia, Pacific (EAP)	67	38	14	10	19	52	100	100
South Asia (SA)	72	58	14	28	14	14	100	100
Central Asia, Caspian (CAC)	88	78	12	4	0	18	100	100
Middle East, Nr Africa (MENA)	88	65	12	24	0	11	100	100
Sub-Saharan Africa (SSA)	84	30	7	23	9	46	100	100
Latin America, Caribbean (LAC)	88	5	6	5	6	91	100	100
Total number of countries	73	31	13	17	15	53	100	100

Source: Regional distributions of political regimes are aggregated and calculated in accordance with our regional classification from country data in Kidron and Smith (1983), for 1982, and from Heritage Foundation (2000), for 2000.

the LAC as a whole shows low relative casualties of 1.3 per thousand people. War casualties due to foreign wars were also the least significant in LAC. Honduras was leading.

More recently, more countries have adopted parliamentary elections and majority rules, these being political solutions that are the most logical if violence is to be avoided in reaching political compromises between different factions. As Table 3 shows, the share of authoritarian regimes has declined from 73 to 31%, while the share of multi-party democracies increased from 15 to 53%. By the turn of the 20th to the 21st century, the shift toward democratic institutions is seen to be the highest in the Latin American region, followed by the Asian, African, and Arab regions.

What are the implications of the democratization tendencies for the total system and its components of households, firms, and state settings? A more democratic rule can shift power from the state to individual agents in household and firm settings, but this is conditional on the presence of many other social institutions which limit the interference of the state in the domains of individuals, households, and firms. The following chapter will deal with institutional aspects of the development process.

4. Major Transitions

We shall make use of the analytical framework of system theory in elaborating on major transitions in the development regions. System theory treats the socio-polity-economy system, as a total system, and models the interplay of its broad subsystems of (a) the households/population, (b) the state/polity, and (c) the firms/markets/economy. Each of the three subsystems has undergone major shakes and reshaping causing significant structural changes not only in its own subsystem but also more importantly in the other subsystems and thus the total system. We distinguish between three major transitions with transformational impacts. The three transitions occurred in and centered around the three broad subsystems, namely (a) household-led demographic transition, (b) state-led economic development, and (c) firm-led integration with the world economy.

Household-led demographic transition: The demographic factor had far-reaching systemic impacts in the developing world. Demographic transition refers to the transition from high birth rates and death rates to low birth and death rates in the process of economic development. Works on the Demographic Transition Model (DTM), due in 1929 to Warren Thompson, and elaborated by many others,[6] explained population growth and its changing composition relatively well in developed countries over the last two centuries.

Demographic transition theory applies also generally to the development regions of the present world. The initially high death rates decline significantly due to better hygiene and nutrition and improvements in well-being that accompany economic development. With birth rates remaining high, causing relatively younger populations and hence raising fertility further, and with death rates declining, the rate of population growth accelerates and reaches a peak. In due course, as households move from rural to urban areas and become subjected to modernization, education, emancipation, rising incomes, and considerations of opportunity cost, the reproduction behavior of households changes toward smaller size families, thus causing birth rates to decline. The growth rate of the population retreats then gradually from its peak and tends in the long run toward a replacement rate.

Although the DTM applied generally to the past demographic transition of the developed countries, the demographic transition in the developing countries differs due to different encountered circumstances. Economic development of the developed countries, which happen to possess a firm intensive economic system, was spread over two to three centuries, the initial populations were relatively small, and the urbanization was gradual and became evenly spread and standard for practically all households. In the economic analysis of developed countries, it is commonplace to speak of the representative household as an urban/modern household, as the extent of rural/traditional households is very tiny. This stands in contrast with developing countries where there are distinctively rural/traditional households in significant numbers, separate from urban/modern households. The rural/traditional households are in an early phase of reproductive behavior and demographic transition, and the urban/modern households are in a later phase. The composition of the population between the dual household types changes in the economic development process.[7] Hence, the average death, birth, and population growth rates are

Table 4. Population and urbanization trends in development regions.

Region	Population annual growth rate, % 1950–1955	Peak rate (a)	2000–2005	2025–2030 (b)	Population millions 1950	2012	Population % 1950	2012	Rural: Urban rates, % 1950	2012
EAP	1.98	2.47	1.28	0.62	609	1992	23.8	28.3	86:14	50:50
SA	2.05	2.35	1.63	0.92	366	1649	14.3	23.4	83:17	69:31
CAC	..	..	1.60	0.90	..	225	..	3.2	..	39:61
MENA	2.50	2.87	1.91	1.17	104	318	4.1	4.5	73:27	43:57
SSA	2.18	2.93	2.28	1.82	134	912	5.2	13.0	89:11	63:37
LAC	2.65	2.75	1.42	0.73	164	609	6.4	8.6	58:42	21:79
Subtotal					1377	5705	53.9	81.0		
Rest World					1179	1339	46.1	19.0		
World total					2556	7044	100.0	100.0		

Sources: Columns s1–4 are from UN Population Division. The 2005 Revision is at http://www.un.org/esa/population/unpop.htm. Other columns are from World Bank at http://data.worldbank.org. (a) Highest periods were 1965–1970 for SA and EAP, 1980–1985 for SSA and MENA, and 1960–1965 for LAC. (b) projections.

better seen as the result of a changing mix between opposite types of reproductive behavior than that of the representative household. Urbanization rates, next to rates of population growth and their peaks in the development regions, are displayed in Table 4. This shows that the demographic transition in developing countries is squeezed into a handful of decades implying historically more significant and abrupt declines in reproductive household behavior. The trend toward a smaller family size has been accelerated by government interventions in favor of birth control in countries like China and India, among others, which contribute to explaining an early peak in 1965–1970 at a low population growth rate in EAP and SA, 2.47–2.35% per year, as compared to MENA and SSA where birth control was discouraged because of cultural and religious objections, leading to a delayed peak, 1980–1985, and at a higher population growth rate of 2.87–2.93. The case of LAC is different. Table 4 shows that although the peak was reached in LAC in 1960–1965, and the region is characterized by the highest urbanization rate, the population growth rate remained at higher levels than would have been expected, mainly due to religious belief that discourage birth control. The demographic trends have resulted in a declining share of EAP in world population, though with its 36% of the world population, EAP remains the largest. SA and SSA show increasing shares. SA and MENA show stable shares. FIS and SIS-related countries, that is the rest of the world, experience declining population shares.

State-led economic development: Economic development required structural transformation from an agricultural into an industrializing economy and from a closed to an open economy, raising and upgrading the factors of production of capital and labor to assure a greater production on the supply side and an expansion of purchasing power to assure an equal balance on the demand side. The structural transformation required active intervention by the newly installed states in the development regions. Because the business sector in the 1950s was still relatively undeveloped, the state had to assume the responsibility of formulating development plans, financing and implementing them, next to implementing regulatory measures. As the capability of the private sector would increase during the economic development process, the engagement of the public sector could then be phased out. Where the public sector did not withdraw in time and/or public mismanagement of economic development occurs, this has led to inflation and recession. The correction of such crisis situations required implementing strict stabilization and structural adjustment programs which required again the full involvement of the state.

As economic development is commensurate with the reallocation of resources from the low productivity agriculture to the high productivity industry, state strategies for applying this structural transformation in developing countries were elaborated and followed.[8] The governing elite in the newly independent nations led the drive for economic development with the support of development planners, policy advisors, economists, and statisticians who played an important role in defining and formulating 5 year economic development plans, strategies, policies, and spending programs.

With respect to agriculture, it was evident that given the low yield per acre, agriculture was unable to feed the unexpected rapid surge in the population in many developing countries. Surplus labor could be only generated if agriculture would become more productive and remunerative. State policies were directed to productivity and remuneration enhancing measures such as land reform and the green revolution, which were supposed to especially benefit such target groups as poorer peasants and small farmers and relieve more workers for work elsewhere. Such benefits would materialize if the governments in charge are popular and committed to such policies and if the institutional arrangements that exist are not biased against the target groups. As it has turned out in the SA region, particularly in India, land reform and the introduction of new varieties of seeds and cultivation evolved in unexpected ways and had unintended consequences. Although plans and schemes of land reform targeted a significant redistribution of land from large landowners to landless farmers and small landowners, the actual implementation was very marginal in a country where large landowners were politically strong and in a position to overpower the “soft state”.[9] At the same time, the green revolution brought higher productivity to large landowners, elevated the price of cultivated land, and led to more landless farmers and urban migration. In the EAP region, particularly in China, the opposite took place. A strong state was able to break down the concentration of land ownership, even though it took the state many years of experimentation with the status and organization of land ownership before settling at a mixture between private and community ownership. The benefits of the introduction of new varieties of seeds and cultivation were also more equally shared.

With respect to industry, it was accepted by policy advisors that a take-off required next to skill formation and capital deepening, an investment program across all industrial sectors that makes use of industrial linkages and economies of scale. There are many positive externalities that could be simultaneously exploited, design and implement a big push, and achieve an early take-off.[10] Such investment programs have to be well timed and coordinated by well-informed economic agents. It was generally recognized that the developing world did not possess sufficient business resources or initiatives to engage in the risky and intricate investment programs of economic development. These arguments justified an extended interpretation of the role of the state, beyond policy incentives, that allowed the state to own, build, and run significant portions of the industrial sector. Many of these actions could be justified at the time as rational state responses to market failures, on the expectation that once established and well operating such state enterprises can be shifted in time and sold to the private sector. Furthermore, it was recognized that an export orientation of the industrial output is necessary given the advantages of economies of scale, the large size of the world market, and the small size of the domestic market. The protection of infant industries by restricting imports was seen as an intermediate step in a strategy of export promotion. The striking of a balance between incentives for export promotion and import substitution, which generates high levels of net foreign exchange, is a major challenge for the state's management of economic development. In principle, import protection and foreign trade regulations are supposed to be temporary and are to be phased away as the concerned industry realizes its comparative export advantage. In some countries of EAP, SA, and LAC, the phasing out of state control occurred as was rationally scheduled: the state started retreating from public entrepreneurship, liberalized domestic prices, and deregulated foreign trade just in time to allow private firms to compete globally in open economies.[11] Other countries, especially in MENA and SSA, were slower in reforming their economies. Economic growth did much better in the more reforming countries. Under increased national and international pressure to introduce more reforms in all developing economies, further privatization and liberalization took place.[12] Liberalization measures required freeing prices in the product and factor markets, both domestically (abolition of subsidized prices) and in foreign trade (abolition of import quotas, tariffs, and licenses), eliminating the monopoly of pricing boards in agriculture, and eliminating bailing out of unprofitable firms and projects in industry. As stabilization may lead to economic recession, the IMF opened the possibility of conditional funding of encountered financial gaps.

Some SSA countries, with overextended public sectors and regulations, encountered in the eighties increasing problems in reducing inflation, avoiding recession, and balancing their state budgets and foreign payments. Furthermore, faced with increased oil prices, the SSA experienced a fall in its GNP by about a quarter between 1980 and 1990.[13] To fix matters for a troubled economy, the International Monetary Fund (IMF) prepared in the 1980s a structural adjustment package (SAP) consisting of two components: stabilization and market liberalization with public sector reforms. SAP can be seen as the forerunner of the stabilization and liberalization measures that were proposed and implemented a decade later in the transition countries. To reduce inflation, stabilization measures included controlling wages and raising the interest rate. To balance the state budget, the measures included raising taxes, cutting expenditures, and real financing of budget deficits. To stabilize the foreign payments balance the measures included devaluation of overvalued exchange rates, so as to raise exports and reduce imports, and restructuring foreign debts. About half of the SAPs were in support of the SSA region, and the other half in other development regions. The economic performance of countries that implemented the SAP improved, but in some cases, the packages increased poverty. This was a reason for the IMF and WB to require assisted countries to develop poverty reduction strategies and incorporate corrective measures in their assistance programs.

Political leaders in the DR expanded the influence sphere of the state subsystem. An important question to deal with is as follows: How do the internal dynamics, and the functioning levels, of the state subsystem fare in the development regions? An empirical assessment would throw light on the ability, strength, sustainability, and contribution of the state subsystem in the various development regions. Table 5 gives the results of the Country Policy and Institutional Assessment (CPIA) database of the World Bank, which is a rating system that WB officials use in their lending operations.

The database provides interesting material that illustrates the effectiveness and dynamics of the state subsystem. Aggregation is done for four of the six development regions from 2009 to 2012. The data for CAC are missing while data for the SSA region are too diverse to allow for a meaningful aggregation. Table 5 shows four indicators that reflect on the institutional strength of the state subsystem; these are the efficiency of revenue mobilization and the qualities of macroeconomic management, fiscal management, and public administration. The ratings put the state subsystem of LAC ahead of other regions. There is little change over the reported years.

Firm-led integration with the world economy: Economic development requires the economy to become more open and outward-oriented. Business firms deliver the central role in this outward orientation. Foreign exchange is required to import

Table 5. CPIA indicators on viability of the state subsystem in the development regions: 2009, 2012.

Region year	Efficiency of revenue mobilization	Macroeconomic management	Budgetary and financial management	Public administration	Average (Change)
EAP2009	3.4	3.7	3.4	3.0	3.38
2012	3.4	3.6	3.2	2.9	3.28 (−0.10)
SA2009	3.5	3.6	3.4	3.2	3.43
2012	3.5	3.3	3.3	3.3	3.35 (−0.08)
MENA2009	3.3	3.5	3.3	2.8	3.23
2012	3.3	3.5	2.8	2.8	3.10 (−0.13)
LAC2009	3.8	3.8	3.6	3.1	3.58
2012	3.8	3.8	3.5	3.1	3.56 (−0.02)

Source: World Bank Group, CPIA database (http://www.worldbank.org/ida). CPIA Rating is 1 = low to 6 = high.

modern capital equipment and other inputs in the industrialization process, and selling outside enlarges the extent of the market and exploits economies of scale. Exporting is the primary mean for obtaining foreign exchange and the key actors here are profit-maximizing exporting firms. Given the enormous size of the global economy relative to that of any individual economy, the firm-led outward development was able to link and integrate with the global economy and supplement and/or replace the state in realizing sustained development.

While exports are the primary source of foreign exchange, other sources are official development assistance (ODA), net foreign loan transfers (FLT), and net foreign direct investment (FDI). Table 6 sums up the trends in these sources for the development regions as a whole. The table shows that export proceeds to the developing world grew remarkably in the last three decades. The share of exports from developing countries in total world exports increased from 16% in 1990 to 20% in 2000 and to 34% in 2012. With respect to foreign financial flows, the prominence of official development assistance (ODA) in the early development decades gave way to foreign loans and foreign investment in the latter decades. While practically all regions experienced declines in their shares in world ODA over the years, SSA increased its share and has become in recent years the major recipient of ODA with about a quarter of the total ODA in 2012. Nevertheless, given its pattern, its use, and its limited and diminishing size, the contribution of ODA to the restructuring of the SSA economies was marginal. The flow of net FLT, which was previously positive, reversed direction into net transfers of foreign debt repayments from the late 1980s onwards, mostly due to debt repayments that were higher than fresh loans and investment booms creating financial crises; this applied particularly for the LAC and EAP regions. In contrast, net FDI has become

Table 6. Development regions. The changing pattern of foreign exchange sources, US$ million 1970–2012.

	Export proceeds by recipient			Financial flows by recipient				
Year	Developing countries	Developed countries	World total of exports (a)	ODA to developing countries	net FLT to developing countries	Net FDI to developing countries	Net FDI to developed countries	World total of net FDI (b)
1980	567595	1739703	2307298	34513	15136	8807	42694	51500
1990	688009	3666478	4354487	58479	−8258	42560	147440	190000
2000	1732669	6257695	7990364	49673	−1540	275930	1044070	1320000
2012	7814992	14954070	22769062	133039	..	874001	635999	1510000

Sources: World Bank at http://data.worldbank.org/, except for column 3 on FLT which is from World Bank (2003): Global Development. (a) = columns 1 + 2, (b) = columns 6 + 7.

by the turn of the century the dominant force in the financial global integration of development regions, with the EAP and LAC regions as the main beneficiaries.

Given the past and recent trends of foreign exchange resources, it is sufficient to focus on exports and FDI (both are led and managed by firms) as the main driving forces in the global integration of the development regions. Table 7 illustrates how the different development regions reacted to export and FDI opportunities. Column 1 shows the share of EAP in world exports rising to 14.3% in 2012 (mainly due to Chinese exports), MENA is next with 7.3% (mainly due to oil exports), followed by LAC at 6.1% (partly due to Brazilian exports). The realized gain in the share of all development regions in world exports between 1990 and 2012 amounted to 18%; this is also by definition the decline that occurred in the share of developed countries. In the process, the developing economies have become significantly more dependent on exports. Column 2, giving exports/GDP, shows MENA in 2012 as the most dependent with a proportion of 54%, with other regions between 23% and 35%. The share of the total exports of the six development regions in their total GDP amounted to 27.0% and 31.5% in 2000 and 2001, respectively. These shares are remarkably close to the figures for the developed countries where the share of their exports in their GDP amounted to 23.7% and 31.2% in 2000 and 2012, respectively. In 2012, developing and developed countries share the same level of export dependence.

Regarding FDI, in Table 7, columns 3 and 4 show how the development regions have responded to the FDI opportunities. Column 3 gives regional shares of FD in the world total of FDI, showing a progressive gain for EAP from 0% in 1970 to 35% in 2012; these gains are mainly at the cost of a decreased share for developed countries, falling from 71% in 1970 to 45% in 2012. In spite of the significant flow of FDI to the development regions, the dependence of these economies on FDI, expressed by FDI/GDP in column 4, has been limited to an average of 2.4% in 2012. Dependence on exports is about 14 times dependence on FDI.

Table 7. Indicators of global influence: Shares of exports and net foreign direct investment of development regions in world totals and in GDP, 1980–2012.

	Exports of goods and services		Net foreign direct investment (FDI)			Exports of goods and services		Net foreign direct investment (FDI)	
Region/ year	Exports/ world ttl	Exports/ GDP	Net FDI/ world ttl	FDI/ GDP	Region/ year	Exports/ world ttl	Exports/ GDP	Net FDI/ world ttl	FDI/ GDP
EAP					SSA				
1980	3.5	16.2	9.5	0.3	1980	3.6	31.7	0.5	0.1
1990	3.8	21.3	15.7	0.6	1990	1.8	26.2	0.6	0.4
2000	7.6	33.2	12.4	2.0	2000	1.4	34.5	0.5	2.0
2012	14.3	33.5	34.5	2.6	2012	2.2	35.1	2.6	3.0
SA					LAC				
1980	0.7	7.5	0.4	0.1	1980	5.5	15.6	12.5	0.9
1990	0.8	8.5	0.3	0.1	1990	4.9	19.6	4.4	0.7
2000	1.1	13.7	0.3	0.7	2000	6.1	21.6	6.6	3.7
2012	2.3	22.5	1.8	1.2	2012	6.1	24.7	12.7	3.3
CAC					Total development regions				
1980	..	..	..	..	1980	24.6		17.1	
1990	..	..	..	..	1990	15.8		22.4	
2000	1.2	22.9	0.2	07	2000	21.7	27.0	20.9	4.3
2012	2.2	29.2	2.7	2.4	2012	34.3	31.5	57.9	3.5
MENA					Total developed countries				
1980	11.3	44.3	−6.0	−0.4	1980	75.4		82.9	
1990	4.5	32.6	1.4	0.5	1990	84.2		77.6	
2000	4.2	38.7	0.8	1.2	2000	78.3	23.7	79.1	3.9
2012	7.3	54.4	3.6	1.8	2012	65.7	31.2	42.1	1.3

Source: World Bank at http://databank.worldbank.org.

In rounding up, it is important to draw attention to short-term tribulations which associate with global integration and an increased dependence on foreign finance. The greater openness of an economy to the international financial markets makes it usually vulnerable at times to serious financial crises. In LAC, this occurred in 1982 when Mexico was unable to meet its obligations to pay foreign debts after an over-borrowing spree in preceding years. Fearful of risk of default payment, international lending banks reduced their financial flows to defaulting and other countries in LAC and beyond. This combined with a surge in oil prices led to a slow economic growth in most development regions for a couple of years. The vulnerability of the integrating developing economies in unstable world financial markets reappeared again in EAP in 1998, when the devaluation of the Thailand currency was followed by other devaluations in the EAP, downfalls in stock markets, and withdrawals of foreign financial resources from the region.[14] The confidence crisis was fueled by the lack of transparency in corporate governance and state dealings and a future economic outlook that was seen to be bleak against the background of over-expanded investment in construction and other production capacities. The greater openness of an economy to the international financial markets makes it usually vulnerable at times to serious financial crises. In LAC, this occurred in 1982 when Mexico was unable to meet its obligations to pay foreign debts after an over-borrowing spree in preceding years. Fearful of risk of default payment, international lending banks reduced their financial flows to defaulting and other countries in LAC and beyond. This combined with a surge in oil prices, led to a slow economic growth in most development regions for a couple of years.

The vulnerability of the integrating developing economies in unstable world financial markets reappeared again in EAP in 1998, when the devaluation of the Thailand currency was followed by other devaluations in the EAP, downfalls in stock markets, and withdrawals of foreign financial resources from the region.[15] The confidence crisis was fueled by the lack of transparency in corporate governance and state dealings, and a future economic outlook that was seen to be bleak against the background of over-expanded investment in construction and other production capacities.

Although analysts would agree that the globalization epoch has been functional in strengthening both the firm and the state subsystems in all development regions, opinion differs as to which of the two gained more and in which development region. These issues can be more fruitfully treated in an analytic model of the total system complemented by available empirical data to reach conclusions on how the relative dominance of the firms and state subsystems are affected. The following chapter employs an analytical framework for the study of systemic and institutional changes and will be able to reflect on these issues.

5. Structural Indicators of Economic Activities

The developments reviewed in the above sections have repercussions on the structural patterns of economic activities. Of special significance and interest for this and the following chapter are the system changes that occurred regarding (a) the relative distribution of the GDP on the sector activities of agriculture, industry, and services, (b) the relative distribution of employment and the associated dependent population on these sectors, (c) the shares of GDP and employment in the public sector as a proxy for state influence, and (d) the share of exports and foreign direct investment (FDI) in GDP as proxies' for the changing dependence and integration of countries and regions in the world economy.

Measurement of these structural indicators by region on the basis of totals for nominator and denominator is not feasible. What is available are the values of these structural indicators by country. In this context, what we do is the conventional practice of computing the simple average values of member countries to give the regional value for the indicator concerned. Furthermore, we shall represent the region by taking the mean of the constituent six leading countries in the region. The selection of the six leading countries in a region is based on the relative sizes of the population and of the GDP, equally weighted. (The two dimensions of population and GDP are the constituents of the dominance index, which is treated at more length in the following chapter.) The selection is sufficiently wide to give a representative picture of regional diversity. Table 8 sums up the coverage degree by region. For regions like EAP, SA, and CAC, the six leading countries account for practically 100% of the region's total population and total GDP, respectively. For LAC, the average is 80%, which is very satisfactory. This is less so for MENA at 67% and for SSA at 57%. We have experimented with adding more countries to MENA and SSA, but the mean and standard deviation for most indicators treated remained the same with the additions; besides for every three countries added, two had no or incomplete data on the studied indicators. Our review will elaborate also on the regional mean, x, the standard deviation, s, and the variation coefficient (that is, $v = s/x$) for the various indicators we analyze so as to form an opinion on tendencies over time and across space on regional diversity. In calculating the values of s and v, we propose to correct for the coverage gap by specifying the so-called Bessel's correction as the number of observations, $n = 6$, *less* the coverage shortfall, outlined in Table 8. Growths of GDP and GDP per capita are in constant prices of 2000.

In the rest of this section, we bring together the average indicator values of development regions based on country averages for various structural indicators of special interest for the research done in this book. A couple of forthcoming chapters will make use of the structural indicators displayed here.

Table 9 gives GDP shares and Table 10 gives employment shares of main economic activities over two periods. A global comparison between the six regions would place the two regions of LAC and EAP ahead of the other regions regarding industrial development as indicated by the high shares of the GDP that is due to industry and low shares in agriculture. The two regions with the lowest industrial shares and highest agricultural shares are SA and SSA. The two regions which lie in between are MENA and CAC. The GDP shares of industry in 2012 have regional means that vary between 28% and 46%. Turning to Table 10, the regional means

Table 8. Cumulative share of the six leading countries in the population and GDP of their regions: Coverage degree and coverage shortfall, 2012.

Region	Population	GDP	Coverage	Shortfall	Region	Populationon	GDP	Coverage	Shortfall
EAP	0.94	0.98	0.96	0.04	MENA	0.70	0.63	0.66	0.34
SA	1.00	1.00	1.00	0.00	SSA	0.48	0.66	0.57	0.44
CAC	0.96	0.98	0.99	0.01	LAC	0.77	0.83	0.80	0.20

Table 9. GDP shares by sector, 2000, 2012 (in percent).

	2000			2012				2000			2012		
Region	agr	ind	srv	agr	ind	srv	Region	agr	ind	srv	agr	ind	srv
EAP							MENA						
CHN	15.1	45.9	39.0	10.1	45.3	44.6	EGY	16.7	33.1	50.1	14.5	39.2	46.3
IDN	15.6	45.9	38.5	14.4	46.9	38.6	SAU	4.9	53.9	41.1	2.2	62.6	35.2
PHL	14.0	34.5	51.6	11.8	31.1	57.1	DZA	8.9	58.6	32.5	9.3	48.5	42.2
THA	9.0	42.0	49.0	12.3	43.6	44.2	IRQ						
MYS	8.6	48.3	43.1	10.1	40.8	49.1	ARE	2.3	48.5	49.2	1.0	51.8	47.2
VNM	22.7	34.2	43.1	19.7	38.6	41.7	MAR	14.9	29.1	56.0	14.6	29.6	55.8
Mean	14.2	41.8	44.0	13.1	41.1	45.9	Mean	9.6	44.6	45.8	8.3	46.3	45.3
SA							SSA						
IND	23.0	26.0	51.0	17.5	26.2	56.3	ZAF	3.3	31.8	64.9	2.6	28.4	69.0
PAK	25.9	23.3	50.7	24.4	22.0	53.6	NGA	26.0	52.2	21.8	33.1	40.6	26.3
BGD	25.5	25.3	49.2	17.7	28.5	53.9	ETH	48.7	12.3	39.0	48.8	10.1	41.1
LKA	19.9	27.3	52.8	11.1	31.5	57.5	ZAR						
NPL	40.8	22.1	37.0	37.0	15.4	47.6	AGO	5.7	72.1	22.2	10.0	59.7	30.3
BTN	27.4	36.0	36.6	15.9	43.9	40.2	SDN	42.2	20.8	37.0	27.7	31.2	41.1
Mean	27.1	26.7	46.2	20.6	27.9	51.5	Mean	25.2	37.9	37.0	24.4	34.0	41.6
CAC							LAC						
TUR	11.3	31.5	57.2	9.1	27.0	63.9	BRA	5.6	27.7	66.7	5.2	26.3	68.5
IRN	13.7	36.7	49.5	10.2	44.7	45.1	MEX	3.5	35.7	60.8	3.6	35.7	60.7
KAZ	11.0	35.0	55.0	5.0	40.0	56.0	ARG	5.1	28.1	66.9	9.1	30.5	60.4
UZB	34.0	23.0	43.0	19.0	32.0	49.0	COL	8.9	29.4	61.6	6.5	37.5	56.0
AZE	17.0	45.0	38.0	6.0	63.0	31.0	VEN	4.2	49.7	46.1	5.8	52.2	42.1
TJK	27.0	39.0	34.0	27.0	26.0	48.0	PER	8.5	29.9	61.6	7.0	34.6	58.4
Mean	19.0	35.0	46.1	12.7	38.8	48.8	Mean	6.0	33.4	60.6	6.2	36.1	57.7

Source: http://databank.worldbank.org.

of the employment shares of industry in 2012 vary less within a range between 19.1% and 35.1%. Tables 9 and 10 combined throw light on significant differences in labor productivity among the six regions. Division of the GDP shares in Table 9 by the employment shares of Table 10 shows the EAP to be highest in industrial labor productivity in 2012, i.e. $41.1/22.7 = 1.81$. At the other extreme is SSA with the lowest agricultural productivity in 2012, i.e. $24.4/2.1 = 0.579$.

Table 11 gives the shares of the public sector employment and public revenue in the GDP. The CAC region heads all regions in terms of the share of public employment which amounted in 2012 to 13.2% and the share of public revenue at 26.8%. Most of the countries in the CAC region were ex-Soviet Republics with large public sectors. Other countries in CAC such as Turkiye and Iran have also large public sectors. Less expected is to note that the LAC region entertains also a large public sector with shares of public employment at 13.5% and 25.3%.

Table 10. Employment shares by sector, 2000, 2012 (in percent).

	2000			2012				2000			2012		
Region	agr	ind	srv	agr	ind	srv	Region	agr	ind	srv	agr	ind	srv
EAP							MENA						
CHN	50.0	22.5	27.5	36.7	28.7	34.6	EGY	29.6	21.3	49.1	28.2	25.3	46.5
IDN	45.3	17.4	37.3	35.1	21.7	43.2	SAU	6.1	19.9	74.0	4.7	24.7	70.6
PHL	37.1	16.2	46.7	32.2	15.4	52.4	DZA	21.1	24.3	54.6	10.8	30.9	58.3
THA	48.8	19.0	32.2	39.6	20.9	39.5	IRQ						
MYS	18.4	32.2	49.4	12.6	28.4	59.0	ARE	7.9	33.4	58.7	3.8	23.1	73.1
VNM	65.3	12.4	22.3	47.4	21.1	31.5	MAR	44.4	20.1	35.5	39.2	21.4	39.4
Mean	44.1	20.0	35.9	33.9	22.7	43.4	Mean	21.8	23.8	54.4	17.3	25.1	57.6
SA							SSA						
IND	59.9	16.0	24.1	47.2	24.7	28.1	ZAF	15.6	24.2	60.2	4.9	24.5	70.6
PAK	48.4	18.0	33.6	47.1	20.7	32.2	NGA	68.7	10.3	21.0	56.3	18.8	25.0
BGD	62.1	10.3	27.6	48.1	14.5	37.4	ETH	86.6	4.6	8.8	79.3	6.6	14.1
LKA	30.7	25.6	43.7	24.2	32.9	42.9	ZAR						
NPL	70.9	11.6	17.5	65.2	13.3	21.5	AGO	21.9	20.3	57.8	15.0	21.6	63.4
BTN	79.8	2.7	17.5	62.2	8.6	29.2	SDN	56.9	25.5	17.6	55.2	28.4	16.4
Mean	58.6	14.0	27.3	49.0	19.1	31.9	Mean	50.0	17.0	33.1	42.1	20.0	37.9
CAC							LAC						
TUR	36.0	24.0	40.0	23.6	26.0	50.4	BRA	20.5	21.4	58.1	20.5	21.4	58.1
IRN	23.0	31.0	46.0	23.0	32.0	45.0	MEX	18.0	26.8	55.2	13.1	25.5	61.4
KAZ	27.0	20.0	53.0	26.0	19.0	55.0	ARG	0.7	22.7	76.6	0.6	23.4	76.0
UZB	39.0	19.0	42.0	32.0	25.0	43.0	COL	22.0	18.0	60.0	16.9	20.9	62.2
AZE	41.0	11.0	48.0	38.0	14.0	48.0	VEN	10.6	22.8	66.6	7.7	21.2	71.1
TJK	52.0	18.0	30.0	40.0	30.0	31.0	PER	33.3	14.7	52.9	25.8	17.4	56.8
Mean	36.3	20.5	43.2	30.4	24.3	45.4	Mean	17.5	21.1	61.6	14.1	21.6	64.3

Source: http://databank.worldbank.org.

The two Asian regions of EAP and SA show the lowest shares for public employment and public revenue which suggest a greater influence of private market forces in these regions. The other regions are positioned in between.

Table 11 contains indicators reflecting on regional integration in the world economy. The indicators of exports/GDP and FDI/GDP are highest for EAP at 54% and 3%, respectively, in 2012. MENA is very high in export/GDP at 53% due to oil exports but low in FDI/GDP at 1%.

The variation coefficient, υ, is important for assessing regional homogeneity and convergence tendencies. Low values of υ represent homogeneity, and decreasing values of υ over time indicate integration and convergence. Focusing on the four indicators in Table 11, it is shown that with the exception of SSA which shows rising υ, the other five regions show decreasing values of υ between 2000 and 2012.

Table 11. Indicators of the shares of public sector in employment and GDP. Shares of exports and foreign direct investment in GDP. Six Development Regions. 2000 and 2012.

EAP 2000	Public emp/ total	Public rvn/ GDP	Exports/ GDP	FDI/ GDP	EAP 2012	Public emp/ total	Public rvn/ GDP	Exports/ GDP	FDI/ GDP
China	2.0	7.1	23.3	3.2	China	4.0	11.6	27.3	3.1
Indonesia	6.2	16.7	41.0	−2.8	Indonesia	8.3	19.3	24.3	2.2
Philippines	7.1	15.2	51.4	2.8	Philippines	7.6	14.5	30.8	1.1
Thailand	6.3	19.5	66.8	2.7	Thailand	8.1	20.5	75.0	2.9
Malaysia	8.7	17.5	119.8	4.0	Malaysia	13.0	22.1	87.1	3.2
Vietnam	..	..	50.0	3.9	Vietnam	..	..	80.0	5.4
Mean x	6.0	15.2	58.7	2.3	Mean x	8.2	17.6	54.1	3.0
Stdv s	2.2	4.3	30.4	2.3	Stdv s	2.9	3.9	27.0	1.3
Vrcf υ	0.37	0.28	0.52	1.02	Vrcf υ	0.35	0.22	0.50	0.44

SA 2000	Public emp/ total	Public rvn/ GDP	Exports/ GDP	FDI/ GDP	SA 2012	Public emp/ total	Public rvn/ GDP	Exports/ GDP	FDI/ GDP
India	2.9	12.0	12.8	0.8	India	3.5	12.4	24.0	1.3
Pakistan	4.7	14.0	13.4	0.4	Pakistan	4.0	12.6	12.3	0.4
Bangladesh	2.7	9.8	14.0	0.6	Bangladesh	4.5	12.0	23.2	1.0
Sri Lanka	7.3	16.8	39.0	1.1	Sri Lanka	6.0	13.9	22.8	1.5
Nepal	1.9	10.6	23.3	0.0	Nepal	3.4	15.9	10.0	0.5
Bhutan	4.0	22.9	29.0	0.3	Bhutan	6.7	22.9	34.6	0.5
Mean	3.9	11.7	11.5	0.4	Mean	4.7	17.9	21.2	0.9
Stdv s	1.8	4.5	9.7	0.4	Stdv s	1.2	3.8	8.2	0.4
Vrcf υ	0.46	0.38	0.84	1.01	Vrcf υ	0.26	0.21	0.39	0.49

CAC 2000	Public emp/ total	Public rvn/ GDP	Exports/ GDP	FDI/ GDP	CAC 2012	Public emp/ total	Public rvn/ GDP	Exports/ GDP	FDI/ GDP
Turkiye	12.5	31.2	20.1	0.4	Turkiye	17.4	34.6	26.4	1.6
Iran	10.8	23.4	22.7	0	Iran	15.7	22.2	23.0	0.9
Kazakhstan	4.6	8.6	56.6	7.01	Kazakhstan	8.3	15.1	47.6	7.43
Uzbekistan	4.5	12.8	24.6	0.54	Uzbekistan	11.0	25.5	27.9	2.14
Azerbaijan	8.5	17.6	39.0	2.46	Azerbaijan	20.1	41.8	53.7	7.95
Tajikistan	3.2	10.6	98.8	2.74	Tajikistan	6.6	21.3	18.2	2.60
Mean	7.3	17.4	43.6	2.2	Mean	13.17	26.74	32.80	3.77
Stdv s	3.50	7.87	27.6	2.39	Stdv s	4.89	8.91	13.10	2.82
Vrcf υ	0.48	0.45	0.63	1.09	Vrcf υ	0.37	0.33	0.40	0.75

(*Continued*)

Table 11. (*Continued*)

MENA 2000	Public emp/ total	Public rvn/ GDP	Exports/ GDP	FDI/ GDP	MENA 2012	Public emp/ total	Public rvn/ GDP	Exports/ GDP	FDI/ GDP
Egypt	9.6	21.3	16.2	1.2	Egypt	9.7	21.5	17.4	1.1
Sd Arabia	10.9	22.2	43.7	−1.0	Sd Arabia	9.8	21.0	56.2	1.7
Algeria	20.8	38.0	41.2	0.5	Algeria	23.7	40.6	37.2	0.8
Iraq		..	75.7	0.8	Iraq		..	44.5	1.6
UnArabEm	28	2.5	49.2	..	UnArabEm	38	3.2	95.2	..
Morocco	10	33.3	28.0	0.5	Morocco	12	35.6	36.2	0.4
Mean x	26.7	29.1	42.3	0.4	Mean x	18.5	24.4	53.0	1.1
Stdv s	18.8	7.0	19.0	0.8	Stdv s	11.3	13.5	26.9	0.5
Vrcf v	0.70	0.24	0.45	1.89	Vrcf v	0.61	0.55	0.51	0.46

SSA 2000	Public emp/ total	Public rvn/ GDP	Exports/ GDP	FDI/ GDP	SSA 2012	Public emp/ total	Public rvn/ GDP	Exports/ GDP	FDI/ GDP
Nigeria	3.0	14.1	51.7	2.5	Nigeria	2.2	8.8	55.4	2.7
S Africa	16.5	27.4	27.9	0.7	S. Africa	20.6	29.2	28.3	1.2
Ethiopia	1.1	12.0	12.1	1.7	Ethiopia	1.6	11.1	14.0	0.7
Congo DR			22.4	1.7	Congo DR			55.5	16.8
Angola	21.8	42.0	89.6	9.6	Angola	30.4	47.9	60.1	−1.6
Sudan	15.9	2.8	16.0	3.2	Sudan	16.2	2.7	6.3	4.2
Mean x	9.0	22.3	36.6	3.9	Mean x	11.5	22.6	36.6	4.0
Stdv s	8.8	11.6	27.9	3.1	Stdv s	12.3	15.0	22.3	6.2
Vrcf v	0.97	0.52	0.76	0.79	Vrcf v	1.07	0.66	0.61	1.56

LAC 2000	Public emp/ total	Public rvn/ GDP	Exports/ GDP	FDI/ GDP	LAC 2012	Public emp/ total	Public rvn/ GDP	Exports/ GDP	FDI/ GDP
Brazil	14.1	24.2	10.0	5.1	Brazil	15.1	26.0	12.6	3.4
Mexico	6.8	12.4	26.0	2.6	Mexico	8.5	13.8	32.9	1.3
Argentina	10.7	14.1	11.0	3.7	Argentina	13.8	18.2	19.7	2.6
Colombia	14.9	25.2	15.9	2.4	Colombia	16.4	26.4	18.3	4.2
Venezuela	14.1	21.2	29.7	4.0	Venezuela	15.6	22.1	26.2	0.6
Peru	8.5	16.4	21.5	2.3	Peru	11.2	19.8	28.6	4.5
Mean	11.5	18.9	19.0	3.4	Mean	13.5	25.3	23.1	2.8
Stdv s	3.1	5.0	7.5	1.0	Stdv s	2.8	4.5	7.0	1.5
Vrcf v	0.27	0.26	0.39	0.31	Vrcf v	0.21	0.18	0.30	0.53

Source: http://databank.worldbank.org.

6. Concluding Remarks

The end results of structural changes in economic activities take shape in the GDP per capita (GDP pc), and its growth rate. This section will deal exclusively with values of the GDP pc and answer the following questions. In terms of the GDP pc expressed in USD on the basis of regional totals, what is the extent of convergence between the regions on the GDP pc? In terms of the GDP pc expressed in purchasing power parity dollars, ppp$, what is the extent of convergence between the regions? What kind of significance should be attached to the difference between USD and ppp$? Moving to a disaggregated level, what are the patterns of variance in GDP pc expressed in USD for the individual countries within the regions, and is the variance in GDP pc increasing or diminishing over the reported decades, and what are the implications for regional development?

Table 12 gives the GDP per capita in current USD for 2000 and 2012. Between 2000 and 2012, MENA, CAC, and EAP have come closer to catching up with LAC, while SA and SSA, although reversing positions, are still far away from the other four regions in terms of GDP pc. South Asia and Sub-Saharan Africa having the lowest well-being are conventionally described in development circles as the two lowest-income regions.

Table 12. GDP per capita in the development regions: Valuations, variation, and convergence.

	GDP pc based on regional totals			GDP pc based on mean of countries in the region				
Region	USD	Valued in ppp $	Conversion factor ppp$/USD	USD	Highest/ Lowest country	Standard deviation s	Variance coefficient υ	Convergence elasticity
EAP 2000	1060			1298	13.39	903	0.70	
2012	5349	7836	1.46	3437	11.05	2148	0.62	−0.06
SA 2000	453			497	3.61	226	0.46	
2012	1396	3506	2.51	1515	4.27	899	0.59	0.15
CAC 2000	2134			1158	8.83	1236	1.07	
2012	7607	12780(a)	1.68 (a)	5976	12.72	4032	0.67	−0.09
MENA 2000	3544			7294	36.40	8967	1.23	
2012	9341	17800	1.90	14821	37.45	15263	1.03	−0.16
SSA 2000	519			703	46.19	978	1.39	
2012	1456	2356	1.62	1832	42.46	2426	1.32	−0.03
LAC 2000	4292			6738	48.99	6341	0.94	
2012	9560	12673	1.33	12529	61.74	11008	0.88	−0.08

Source: World Bank at http://databank.worldbank.org. (a) Because of unavailable data, the conversion factor applied to CAC is assumed to be the average of EAP and MENA. Conversion factor col. 8 = col 7/ col. 1. Variance coefficient υ col. 7 = standard deviation col. 6/mean col. 4. Convergence elasticity col. 8 = change in υ] / [% change in GDP pc]. For example, −0.06 = [(0.62 − 0.70)/0.70] / [(3437 − 1298)/1298].

Table 12 gives also GDP pc in purchasing power parity dollars, ppp$. A purchasing power parity exchange rate equalizes the purchasing power of different currencies in their home countries for a given basket of goods. It is a better measure of standards of living between countries, more so than GDP per capita in US dollars. Because the share of non-traded goods and services, and their prices, is lower in countries with lower income levels, the standard of living of poorer countries is raised and that of richer countries lowered when ppp$ is used instead of USD.[15] As a result, the gap in the income per capita between richer and poorer regions is reduced remarkably when ppp$ is applied. Notwithstanding, LAC, MENA, CAC, and EAP continue to rank in the same order. SA and SSA reverse their order under ppp$. The last column gives the conversion factor ppp$/USD for the development regions. The conversion factor is highest for SA. The conversion factor has a significant meaning since in the long run foreign exchange rates tend to converge from their current market rates toward their values in ppp$, via a combination of higher domestic inflation and appreciation of nominal exchange rates. The convergence factor is thus an important determinant of the GDP gap between developed and developing countries, next to the other determinant, i.e. growth rates of the GDP.

It is noted that these GDP pc figures are based on consolidated regional totals for each region. Within each region, there can be considerable differences among countries in GDP per capita, as will be elaborated here. Descending to data at the country level allows observing variance and treating questions on convergence tendencies within the regions, and the implications thereof for regional integrations and economic systems. Column 4 calculates the GDP pc per region as the mean of all countries within the specific region, excluding outliers (these are a few islands and territories with GDP pc levels that can exceed those in rich countries).Column 5 reports significant variations within the regions. For example, in 2012, within EAP, the GDP pc of Malaysia is 11 times that of Korea D.R, in SA, the GDP pc of Sri Lanka is 10 times that of Nepal, in CAC, the ratio for Kazakhstan to Tajikistan is 13 times, in MENA, the ratio for Kuwait to Yemen is 37, in SSA, the ratio for Gabon to Congo is 43, and in LAC, the ratio for Curacao to Haiti is 62. The variance within the regions is formalized via the standard deviation s and the variance coefficient υ in columns 6 and 7. The regions ranked with the highest to lowest variance coefficient show SSA as the most heterogeneous region, followed by MENA, LAC, CAC, EAP, and SA. There is a general tendency for the variance coefficients to diminish in all regions for the reported decades. This tendency can be formalized in the form of convergence elasticity (column 8), that divides the percentage change in the variance coefficient in column 7, by the percentage change in GDP pc in column 4. The value of the convergence elasticity is highest for MENA, which can indicate the presence of spillover effects from the oil-rich to the non-oil countries in the region. In all regions, except SA, there is a negative elasticity and falling variance among member countries with the rise of their regional GDP pc, which is indicative of catching up processes and regional integration toward what may become regional economic systems. The exception is South Asia, which in the last two decades was the playground for an extra-large and a rapidly growing India, and relatively speaking, politically unstable neighboring countries with lower performances (Pakistan, Nepal, Bangladesh, and Afghanistan). Our explanation of the divergence in SA is that it is incidental in character and should turn into a convergence like in other regions.

Endnotes

1. This is a case where the kinship setting has its bearing on the state setting.
2. Military leadership in some countries succeeded in transforming their military into civil regimes that were subsequently nationally endorsed, i.e. Egypt, Libya, and Indonesia, among others.
3. Religious identity combined with regional ethnicity form the backbone of separatist movements in India (Kashmir) and Indonesia (Banda Aceh) and less pronounced confrontations in China, Malaysia, Thailand, and the Philippines.
4. See also Szirmai (2005), pp. 448–449, and 452, for a similar analysis.
5. Civil casualties are high in Colombia and some Central American countries.
6. Caldwell *et al.* (2006).
7. Section 4 of this chapter will elaborate further on the dualistic nature of the economic system.
8. See related works of Chenery, Kuznets, and Lewis. among others. For an updated review, see Ranis (2003).
9. See Myrdal (1968) on agrarian reform, Griffin (1972) on the green revolution, and Cohen (1978) on related aspects between agrarian reform and the green revolution.
10. See Rosenstein-Rodan (1943) on the “Big Push" and Krugman (1981) on economies of scale and scope.
11. Among the successful examples of achieving an early outward balance are Korea, Hong Kong, Taiwan, and Singapore, which served as leading examples that countries of the EAP and SA would follow later on. Although China and India are relatively latecomers in the outward orientation, the large size of their economies and diversification allows them to capture accelerated gains in world exports. Brazil, Mexico, Chile, and Argentina took the lead in the outward orientation in LAC.
12. See World Bank (1997) on privatization in LDC.
13. Mohan *et al.* (2000) elaborate on differences between SSA and other development regions regarding the functioning of the state and its bias toward liberalization.
14. The leading Asean countries were those most affected by the financial crises that started in Thailand. China was financially less globally integrated at the time and was less affected.
15. It is generally conceived that exchange rates based on ppp are realizable equilibrium rates in the long run.

Part II

Systems and Institutions Shaping Development Prospects

Chapter 3

Systems and Institutions in Developing Countries: Theory and Application

1. Introduction

Institutions refer to the formal and informal rules, norms, and practices that shape economic behavior and decision-making in a society. The role of formal and informal institutions in shaping and determining the pace of economic development has been a central topic in past and recent economic literature. Various contributions have examined how different institutions, such as property rights, political systems, and the rule of law, shape economic outcomes and the impact of institutional quality on economic growth and development. The contributions offer insights into the challenges and opportunities for upgrading institutions to the levels required for promoting economic growth and development. North (2003) examined the role of institutions in economic development from a historical perspective. Amendola *et al.* (2013) examined the impact of institutions on income distribution from an empirical perspective. Acemoglu and Robinson (2013) and Bardhan (2005) emphasized the political economy of institutions.

There are subtle differences when the above contributions are compared to our approach. We distinguish between inner institutions that are created by and are attached to the economic political system present in a country (such institutions are controllable and adjustable) and the outer institutions which relate more to socio and cultural traits in the country; these are primarily informal, intergenerationally acquired, and are less controllable and less adjustable for policymaking. We shall elaborate on the subtle differences as we proceed in the following in this chapter.

(Social) institutions are broadly defined as endorsed norms of conduct in agent interactions. Some countries (developing or developed) are more fortunate to have institutions that promote the development process, but there are some countries that are stuck with institutions that hinder speedy development. It follows that for these less fortunate countries, the positive impacts of development policies are significantly reduced, irrespective of how well intended, well designed, and well implemented these development policies are. The questions posed are as follows: Which types of institutions are there? What are their origins? What are their conducts and displays? How to design them so that they advance development? This chapter attempts to answer these questions.

Institutions can be categorized into two types based on their origin and maintenance: *system institutions* and *outer institutions*. System institutions are created in the socio-economy-polity system or simply system. Outer institutions are created and maintained in the context of socio-cultural communal discourses in the nation as a whole. The outer institutions circumscribe and are outside the system. This chapter is concerned with both, though we focus more on the system institutions than on the outer institutions.

The socio-economy-polity system creates system institutions to coordinate interactions between its constituent subsystems and their interacting agents (members). System institutions take the forms of (a) legalized rules that are written and administered, and sanctioned, or (b) conventions which are unwritten and generally agreed upon rules of conduct that are manifested in attitudinal values and common practices and that agents generally adhere to. Conventions are created and maintained in the interactions of agents within and between firms and markets (the economy) and interactions of agents with the state regarding political representation and governmental matters (the polity). While there is a general agreement on the broad definition of institutions as endorsed rules of conduct in agent interactions, there are overlapping views on how institutions come into being and develop. Different views see institutions as the result of evolution, contract, convention, game theory, political power, or legal necessity. For example, there is the evolutionary view of Hayek (1960), which sees norms to emerge spontaneously in a bottom-up manner as individuals interact and to evolve subsequently allowing the more fitting norms to become the regular norms. The contract view of Williamson (1985) sees social institutions as efficient solutions to problems of asymmetric and incomplete information. The convention view of Lewis (1969) sees the individual agent in optional situations, standing to gain from coordinated behavior in the form of conventions bolstered by common experience and focal points. The game theory view of Schotter (1981) considers agents to be goal oriented and to act strategically to create institutions that serve such goals. The political power view of Knight (1992) sees social institutions as the by-products of distributional struggles between powerful and weak agents. Last but not least, a major portion of legalized institutions are backed by the legal necessity view of Sened (1997). This perceives the state's enacting of statuary rules and state sanctions as essential conditions for establishing a conscious top-down institutionalization process. The literature on the functioning of institutions adds more complexity. Once created, and functioning, institutions succeed when they constrain agent behavior within intended boundaries, but institutions can live their own life beyond the once-intended boundaries. Once created, institutions can live their own life and gain influence on the whole economy/society in respect beyond their intrinsic origins.

The wide range of views on the issue of the origin and functioning of institutions gives the sense that, in addressing the issue, piecemeal approaches were pursued. In these views, little or no attention is given to the system or to its differentiated subsystems wherein the institutions actually originate and function. Treating issues of institutional formation and development in the framework of system theory and analysis will be shown to simplify the picture appreciably and bring more insight. System theory views the more powerful and more dominant subsystems as being able to enforce their institutions on less dominant subsystems and their institutions, resulting in hierarchies of institutions with some overruling the others. System theory aligns with Knight and Sened quoted above in highlighting the association between specific institutions and the power and dominance of interest groups (subsystems), as well as the hierarchical character of the institutions that is supported by the distribution of power among groups subsystems). Identification for a specific country of the dominant subsystem (say firms/markets or the state/government) is often sufficient for comprehending the kind of institutions which hold for the specific country and the development prospects that associate with these institutions.

The outer institutions are less identifiable than the system institutions. In general terms, communities are guided by religious and cultural rules and norms that they inherit, create, and maintain via parental transmission and non-parental interactions. Members of the community adopt these communal institutions in guiding expectations and coordination of their mutual behavior. Some of the outer institutions may be expressed in written forms (tales, traditions, proverbs, or religious text) but mostly are unwritten conventions that take the forms of beliefs, values, attitudes, practices, and customs. Conventions can be conceptualized as behavioral norms and traits that are historically transmitted and learned over time partly from parents to children and partly as the result of many other interactions beyond the years and settings of the household childhood: in school, with a married partner, in the residing neighborhoods, in and with circles of friends, clubs, etc. A country with several ethnic and cultural groups is bound to have several sets of outer institutions that are group-attached and hence a variety of diverging conventions.

Convention-based behaviors can thus have their origin in the context of the socio-economy-polity system or in the outer context. Given the qualitative nature of conventions, their origin can be mixed, and they can overlap. Conventions are difficult to define in quantitative terms. Though many conventions are indirectly observable in terms of their manifested belief, practices, attitudes, and values, many of these can be categorized and scaled and their impact on development can be studied in a quantitative manner. Indirectly, because a specific subsystem has its own set of institutional manifestations in the forms of rules, conventions, attitudes, etc., observation of the one implies the identification of the other. The same reasoning applies to outer institutions.

All types and forms of institutions (system-based or outer-based, and whether they take the form of legally sanctioned or conventions backed) play crucial roles in shaping the development process and promoting and/or retarding achievement of the development goals of growth with redistribution.

The larger part of this chapter is devoted to system theory and system institutions. Section 2 gives a brief introduction on system theory (subsystems, influence, dominance, and prototypes of dominance). Section 3 formulates an index of system dominance. Section 4 applies the index to quantify the institutional inclinations of the system in terms of more alignment with the firm–market subsystem versus the state–government subsystem in a given country. This is done for the six development regions. Section 5 does some verifications by reflecting on surveyed agent attitudes toward free markets versus state interventions in the six development regions. Section 6 elaborates on the required system institutions.

Section 7 is devoted to outer institutions and highlights behavioral traits that retard development. These are (1) corruptive practices that distort fair competition, (2) social distrust between transacting agents (due to differential attitudes) that discourages exchange and transactions, (3) societal stratification (feudal system) with a rent-extracting character that discourages agent mobility and efficient allocation of resources, and (4) polarization (due to non-compromising ideologies, belief, ethnicity, or nationalism) that excludes cooperation and in the extreme can lead to warlike conflicts. The four types of institutions can be briefly labeled as corruption, distrust, stratification, and polarization. Section 8 includes concluding remarks.

2. System Theory: Subsystems, Influences, Dominance, and Prototypes

General: (Social) system theory is an offshoot of general systems theory which is a cross-disciplinary collection of scientific thought that developed during the 20th-century offering potential for systemic description and integration of separated theories into a single framework. The main proponents of (social) system theory research program were Parsons (1956) and Luhmann (1995). Their transdisciplinary framework saw the economic system as one functional subsystem, next to other functional subsystems pertaining to sociology (families and social groups), politics, law, education, science, theocracy, etc. These subsystems act and interact in forming together the socio-economy-polity system, i.e. total system. Agents inhabit each subsystem and engage in pursuing a specific goal that is characteristic to each subsystem. In its pursuit of fulfilling its specific goal, each subsystem functions by itself, sets up its organization, withholds its institutions, and interacts with and adapts itself to other subsystems and the changing external environment.

The system theory of Parsons and Luhmann failed to mobilize economists and other social scientists to rethink and integrate their fields of specialization along the proposed lines. The main reason is that the mono-disciplinary approaches are strongly established in each field and have produced intelligible outcomes that serve their purposes. Besides, moving toward a trans-disciplinary approach requires the presence of conceptual frameworks with common principles that describe how the various subsystems operate and interact with each other to produce the whole system. The development of such conceptual frameworks requires, in turn, substantive organized cooperation and pooling of joint resources. Since these conditions were not present, it was more rewarding to keep to one's own discipline. Additionally, while Parsons and Luhmann are to be accredited for proposing system theory, they did not go in depth in formulating general principles, entities, and variables that relate to the evolution of the subsystems and their interactions with each other. In Cohen (2009), and with further elaborations in Cohen (2014, 2015), we laid out a system theory that connects the social with the polity and the economy in ways that can be quantified and verified. We give in the following a brief review of the system theory.

The system and its subsystems: The socio-economy-polity system consists of interacting subsystems. In turn, a specific subsystem, call it B, consists of a vast number of behavioral settings b of the same specific type. Behavioral settings relevant for economic analysis are those that generate for their participants added value from the economic transformation of some production and/or exchange activity. Settings of significance and interest for economic analysis are those of *household*, *firm*, and *state* settings, that is, *government*.[1] These three types of settings will be denoted by h, f, and s. There are other settings like those of schools, worship, military, etc. Agent behavior and transformation processes are driven by intrinsically distinct goal functions and reinforced by regulating institutions. For example, affinity sharing is the underlying intrinsic motive in household settings. Agents in household settings are united by kinship, ethnic, locality, or religious ties and adopt initially institutions of reciprocal exchanges and the collective sharing of benefits and costs. In contrast, profit maximization is the intrinsic motive in firm and market settings, while the acquisition of a polity rent and political advantages attached to the political intermediation are the intrinsic motives in state settings, in short, rent politicization.

Proceeding from the level of settings to the level of subsystems involves objectifying and depersonalizing the settings, turning them into entities, and supplementing these entities with supportive institutions that safeguard the sustainability and expansion of the subsystem.[2] Accordingly, each subsystem B has its own institutional rules and information schemes for guiding the actions of the agents present in that subsystem. Corresponding with household, firm, and state settings, their subsystems are denoted by capital letters H, F, and S, respectively.

The goal functions are distinct and intrinsic for the three subsystems. The intrinsic goal in the household subsystem is described as affinity sharing, and coordination mechanisms have a sociologic character. The goal in the firm subsystem is profit maximization and coordination mechanisms are economic in character. The goal in the state subsystem is rent politicization, and coordination mechanisms are political in character. The distinct behavioral motives of the three subsystems can be expressed formally in equational forms.[3]

Expanding on the above, in the household subsystem, the motto of the *homo sociologicus* is most applicable: from whom according to his/her ability and to whom according to his/her needs, resulting in social sharing and committed reciprocity. The firm market subsystem functions along the *homo economicus* where choices in production and exchanges are made to assure that material benefits less costs are maximized. From whom according to his/her abilities and effort and to whom in accordance with his/her relative abilities and efforts is the rule of the game. In contrast, the state government subsystem is represented by the *homo politicus;* this is a state authority that brokers a settlement among insecure and/or differing parties in ways that guarantee security and resolve conflict peacefully, with simultaneously strengthening institutions that bolster power and protective rent for the state authority. The rule of the game in the state subsystem is close to what can be described as from whom according to his/her maximum negotiable ability and to whom according to his/her minimum negotiable needs. The difference between the two volumes is the polity rent that the state agent acquires.

While each subsystem B is in some sense a sum of its own constituent behavioral settings b, there is more to that than being a simple sum. The subsystems are functional wholes by themselves. Any of the subsystems engage in (a) establishing and applying internal rules of conduct aiming at eliminating free riding among members and securing the sustainability of the subsystem, thus leading to a deepening of the goal function of the subsystem; and (b) acting to improve and expand the scope of the transformations in the face of emerging challenges.

Pioneering leaders within the subsystem level play major roles in initiating the above actions. Followers sustain these actions. Pioneers in the F subsystem are innovative, entrepreneurial, and risk-takers, while pioneers in the S subsystem are state reformers and are highly devoted to public service. Finally, changes in the external environment open external opportunities that encourage pioneering as well as freeriding to take place. Events in the external environment impact significantly the expansion and exhaustion of the comparative advantage of a subsystem in activities that the subsystem is most suited to transform.

Influences: Subsystems influence each other, with usually one overgrowing and the others declining or growing but lagging behind. Focus is on two dimensions of influence: *interactive influence* and *regulative influence.*

Interactive influence relates to the intensity of participation and activity of the agents in one subsystem relative to other subsystems. The same agents can be members of more than one subsystem simultaneously. Agents communicate with other agents within their own subsystem and with other subsystems. The exchange of information and communication on the performances of subsystems activates the realignment of agents toward the more promising (overgrowing) subsystem. This leads over lengthy periods of time to relatively greater concentrations of agents in the overgrowing subsystem, say subsystem B gains on subsystems B', opening the way for the spread and dominance of the institutions of B over B' and of the behavioral traits of subsystem B over those of B'. Once a threshold is reached regarding accepting a specific behavioral type, say that of B, this can be expected to gain momentum in view of network externalities and spread further to all other $B's$.

There is vast literature on the adoption and spread of a particular behavioral type among more agents. Some six mechanisms of agent interactions can be singled out as determining the formation of the common behavioral pattern, its spread, and its dominance: (1) Sharing of the same external environment and history fosters convergence toward a common behavioral type. (2) Agents observe the transformation outcomes in alternative settings and *move* to the advantaged setting or *copy* its behavior thus resulting in the prospect that the typical behavior of the advantaged subsystem becomes prevalent. (3) Intensive and extensive interactions and communications of agents participating in several subsystems are prone to extend the prevalence of the advantaged behavioral type that associates with the most growing and dominant subsystem. (4) Network externalities enforce convergence toward the advantaged behavioral type. (5) The deep-rooted social-psychological inclination of individuals toward consistency in their relationships and cognition ends up in adopting a positive attitude toward the preferential behavior of the dominant counterpart. (6) Other related mechanisms include imitation, convention, focal points, information cascades, reciprocal behavior, group learning, Markov chain inversions, melting pot, and power of dominant shares, among others.[4]

Next to all the interactive mechanisms, external events and environments play major roles in strengthening or weakening the relative dominance of the competing subsystems, and thereby contribute significantly to speeding up or obstructing the convergence tendencies toward one integral system that associates with the dominant subsystem.

Regulative influence refers to a situation in which a behavioral setting b happens to stand higher in relation to b' in the hierarchy of settings, allowing b to set behavioral rules typical of b that other settings b' should abide with. In this way, the behavioral type of b overrides b', allowing the further spread of behavioral norms of b at the cost of those of b'. The origin of the regulative influence lies in the ability of the higher settings to impose binding rules of conduct on the lower settings. It is not feasible to devise measures of regulative influence along the lines of interactive influence. Besides, comparative analysis of the degree of public regulation between countries is limited due to difficulties in standardizing diversified measures of regulation. It is likely that there is a positive association between the two notions, in the sense that a subsystem powerful in interactive influence is also powerful in regulative influence.[5]

The nature of the horizontal channels makes its effect more endurable as it is generated via experiencing, learning, and adoption. In the case of vertically accommodated behavioral attitudes, the regulative influence can terminate abruptly if the regulative mechanisms become too demanding due to technological loopholes or the rationale for the binding restrictions disappears.

System Dominance: Summing up, the better performing subsystem attracts more agents from the less performing subsystems, gains in interactive influence, and gains system dominance. Supported by the above interactive mechanisms, the lead is strengthened, and the behavioral motive of the dominant subsystem is likely to become the norm for the whole system in the long run. Thus, one subsystem is very likely to evolve into dominance, and the whole system tends to become identifiable with the dominant subsystem.

As an illustrative example, it can be reasoned that in the US, the high concentration of agent interactions in firms has allowed over time the goal of profit maximization (which is intrinsic to the firm subsystem) to overshadow the intrinsic goals typical of the household and state subsystems. Similarly, it can be reasoned that comparable assimilation processes tended to oblige agents in household and firm settings in Soviet Russia to follow a politicized behavioral motive typical of the state subsystem. As a result, all three subsystems in the US behave in ways typical of firm settings, while in Soviet Russia, they manifested behavior typical of state settings.[6] The above implies that agent behavior, institutional conduct, and outcome performance of the whole system will tend to be relatively homogeneous and reasonably predictable. It is logical to expect high degrees of consistency and correlation between the sociological, economic, and polity aspects of a specific social system.

System prototypes: In summary, agent mobility and communications between subsystems in the direction of the better performing subsystem together with regulatory influence in the same direction end up in one dominant behavioral type typical of subsystem B over other B'. As such, the result is a homogeneous social system that can be approximately described in terms of the dominant subsystem, that is, *H, S, or F.* The following three schemes in Figure 1 show the configurations of the system when the system is dominated by the H, S, and F, subsystems, respectively. The dominant subsystem is in bold print, and its interactions with and impact on other subsystems carry more weight, hence their lines of communication are also drawn in bold.

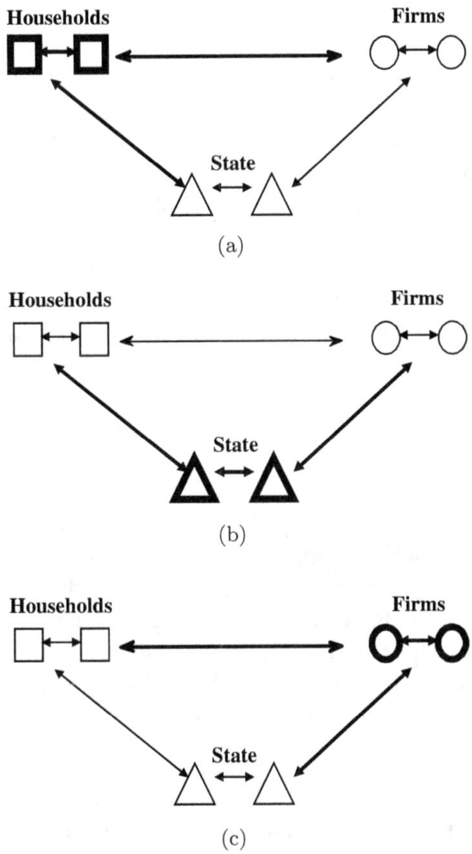

Figure 1. (a, b, c). Configurations of three social systems: H-dominated, S-dominated, and F-dominated.

3. Measurement of Dominance Index

The interactive influence of subsystem B on other subsystems B' can be quantified using a *Dominance Index (DI)* denoted by DI_B. The index has two arguments: the relative share of agents of B in the whole system and the relative share of transacted transformations of B in the whole system.

$$DI_B = (\omega_1 A_B + \omega_2 C_B) \tag{1}$$

In this equation, there are two share parameters that affect prevalence. A_B is the share of agents in subsystem B, with respect to all agents in the system. C_B is the share of commodities demanded that are most suitably transformed in subsystem B, with respect to all demanded commodities in the system. *Personal* commodities are most suitably transformed in firm settings. *Collective* needs are most suitably transformed in state settings. Eq. (1) proposes that the greater the shares of those agents and commodities associated with a particular setting, the greater the probability that the behavioral type underlying this setting prevails over other behavioral types. In this equation, $\omega 1$ and $\omega 2$ are weights applying to these two shares, whereby $\omega_1 + \omega_2 = 1$.[7]

The dominance index, DI_B, is indicative of the interactive power of subsystem B over all the other subsystems B'. Quantification of this index can be done at lower levels (for specific firms within an industry, for specific industries within the whole economy, and for specific agencies within the state subsystem). It can be applied also at higher levels, i.e. for individual countries within a world region or the world economy as an indicator of the relative influence of individual countries, as will be shown in later chapters.

The dominance index focuses on a limited and system-led interpretation of the power of subsystems. For example, a discourse on the degree of state power in a given country should consider many aspects falling under the control of the state, such as state budget, defense spending, foreign exchange financial reserves, property ownership, appointment rights, and mass media. These considerations are outside the scope of the dominance index. To the extent that there is a positive correlation between state influences in adjacent spheres, the dominance index may do the trick of conveying a wider and general coverage.

4. Application of Dominance Index to Developing Countries: Firms versus State

To quantify the dominance index for the firm and state subsystems, we need data on participating agents and transformed produce in the two contexts. These data are not readily available on comparable basis for the developing countries. What is available are data on the three sectors of agriculture, industry, and services, giving the sectoral shares of employment (i.e. participating agents) and the sectoral shares of generated value added (i.e. transformed produce), next to the share of public revenue in the GDP, see appendix. Working with what is available in the appendix required reorganizing and reinterpreting these available data in ways that can coincide with the notions in the dominance indexes for the firms and state subsystems. The main presumptions are to look at the agriculture workplace as representative of the household self-employed and to perceive the industry workplace as representative of the modern firm, next to supplementary assumptions that are worked out in Tables A.1 and A.2.

The outcomes from the appendix are brought together and summarized in the following table, which shows the two components of the dominance indexes for the firms and state subsystems by development region over a number of years. The two components are the shares of participating agents (i.e. employment) and the share of transformed produce (i.e. GDP). The dominance index gives equal weights to the two shares. Overall, the DI shows greater dominance of firms over the state for all regions and years, but the degrees of dominance and their tendencies over time differ by region.

The last column in Table 1 gives the ratio of DI(F)/DI(S) over the years. A rising ratio means a gain in the dominance of firms over the state. A falling ratio means the state gaining dominance over firms. The results show that in the period 1990–2000, the firm subsystem, *F*, booked more influence in all development regions to more or less the same degree (with the exception of CAC which favored the state subsystem *S*). In the years 2000–2012, the state gained influence (with the exception of SA where firms continued gaining influence). The years 2000–2012 coincided with the financial crises of 2007–2009, which enlarged the regulative influence of the state and in which the recession in the developed world reduced economic activity causing a retreat in the growth of the private sector in the development regions.

Table 1. Extent of the influence of firm and state subsystems, *F* and *S*, 1990, 2000, 2012 (in percentage).

	Dominance of firms DI(F)			Dominance of state DI(S)			Ratio
Region year	Employment shares	GDP shares	Dominance index firms	Employment share state	GDP share state	Dominance index state	DI(F)/ DI(S)
EAP 1990	22	67	*45*	5.2	16.7	10.9	4.13
2000	33	75	*54*	6.0	15.2	10.6	5.09
2012	42	73	*59*	8.2	17.6	12.9	4.57
SA 1990	18	46	*32*	3.2	13.2	8.2	3.90
2000	21	50	*35*	3.9	11.7	7.0	5.00
2012	29	58	*43*	4.7	17.9	7.7	5.58
CAC 1990	33	58	*45*	5.9	14.5	10.2	4.41
2000	37	65	*51*	7.3	17.4	12.3	4.15
2012	44	75	*60*	13.2	26.7	20.0	3.00
MENA	36	67	*52*	11.5	24.4	17.9	2.91
2000	57	81	*69*	26.7	29.1	19.7	3.50
2012	65	84	*74*	18.5	24.4	21.5	3.44
SSA	11	43	*27*	4.6	16.5	10.6	2.55
2000	32	61	*46*	9.0	22.3	15.6	2.95
2012	42	61	*52*	11.5	22.6	17.1	3.04
LAC 1990	47	75	*61*	10.0	18.8	14.4	4.24
2000	51	84	*71*	11.5	18.9	13.9	5.11
2012	67	85	*75*	13.5	25.3	15.7	4.78

Source: Appendix.

Note that the sum of the two dominance indexes is below one. DI(F) + DI(S) < 1.0. The remaining portion would represent an approximation of the dominance of the household subsystem.

The "tug of war" between *F* and *S* is illuminated in Figure 2, where the values of the dominance index of *F*, column 3, are plotted along the horizontal axis, meaning that moving along this axis represents more influence of the firm subsystem over the state subsystem. The dominance index of the state, column 6, is plotted along the vertical axis, meaning that moving upward implies greater influence of the public sector versus the private sector. The outcomes are interesting in that they show a tendency in all six regions for the *F* orientation to increase in the two periods but also to bend more toward the *S* orientation in the second period.

Furthermore, the diagram shows MENA to be the first highest in state influence *S*, which is a prolongation of a centuries-long tendency for the authoritarian state in MENA. CAC is second highest on *S*, and SSA is third highest. The hike in state influence in the two regions of CAC and SSA is much more rapid than the movements of other regions along either axis. The CAC consists of ex-Soviet Islamic Republics with built-in state influences, as well as Iran and Turkiye with likewise tendencies. In LAC, influential changes moved within small ranges, the range for F being larger than for *S*, but here too, the state appears to have increased its influence in the past decade.

In contrast, the cases of EAP and SA show influences of the firm and state subsystems to vary within a smaller range than the other regions, suggesting a greater degree of continuity in power sharing in both regions. In reference to the previous chapter on regional performances, the higher economic performance of

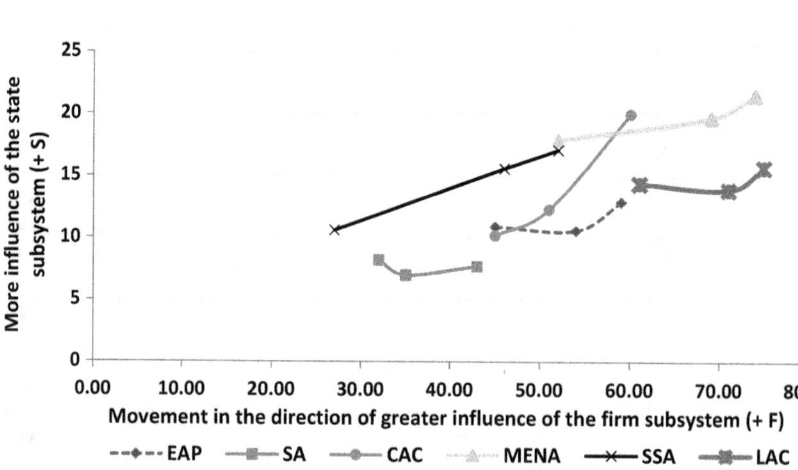

Figure 2. Directions of changing dominance of firms and state in the development region.

EAP and SA as compared to MENA, CAC, SSA, and LAC can be reasoned to be partly due to the greater institutional continuity in EAP and SA when compared to the other four development regions of MENA, CAC, SSA, and LAC.

As was expected, the end result is that LAC is highest regarding the relative dominance of firms. MENA is also approaching the same level as LAC regarding the strength of the F subsystem, but while the F was anchored in LAC for a long period, the surge of F in MENA is more recent and more rapid. Next on the F axis are EAP and CAC with equal influences. They are followed by SSA and SA, which can be described to have the lowest business-like orientations.

5. Institutional Attitudes Reflecting System Dominance

System dominance shows up in institutional displays as exemplified by people's attitudes toward firm growth manship and state coordination. An important data source on agent attitudes is the World Value Survey (WVS). The survey is a compilation of national surveys on values and norms on a wide variety of topics. It started in 1981 and was carried out in 1981–1984, 1990–1993, 1995–1997, and 1999–2004.[8] We use this last survey, and where necessary, compliment it with the previous survey for missing country data. The WVS contains relevant information relating to the perceived importance of the household family in an agent's life, as well as information on perceived preferences for business firms contra preferences for state bodies in managing the economy.

In focus, here are the perceived preferences for firms versus the state. The World Value Survey gives national results around 2000 on a relevant question in this context. The question was the following:

{*'How would you place your views regarding the following statements on the scale of 1 to 10?'*
1 = Private ownership of business should be increased; 2= . . . etc. . ..; 9= . . ..;
10 = Government ownership of business should be increased.}

The respondent is requested to mark the statements with which he/she completely agrees. There are ten statements numbered 1–10 that range from one extreme to the other.

Figure 3 shows that in countries that are generally classified as being oriented toward the firm subsystem and where firms are dominant, the WVS opinion response was found to favor private ownership of business significantly. The score for the US is 83%, with Western Europe and Japan at 76% and 70%, respectively. In Russia, ex-Soviet Union countries, and previous East European allies, the response was found to be less favorable to private ownership. Preference toward private ownership dwindles to a range between 64% and 50%. The majority of responses in Russia is seen to reverse and favor government ownership, i.e. 55%.

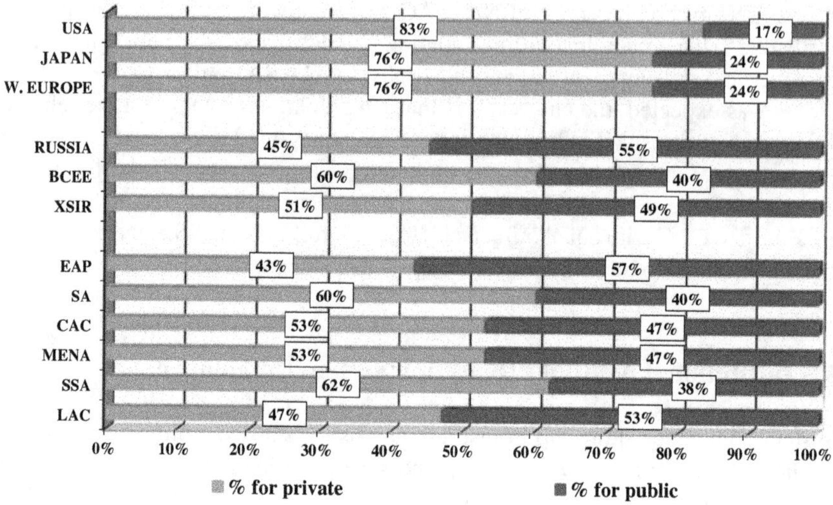

Figure 3. Pro-firm and pro-state attitudes.
Source: Compiled from World Value Survey 1999–2000, at http://www.worldvaluessurvey.org. The results of the responses from 1 to 5 are summed and are denoted as favoring private ownership, and responses from 6 to 10 are summed and denoted as favoring government ownership. BCEE stands for Balkan, Central, and East European countries formerly allies of the Soviet Union. XSIR stands for Ex-Soviet Union Islamic Republics. These countries are included again in the CAC development region, in addition to bordering Turkiye and Iran.

Figure 3 shows and summarizes a pattern of diminished preference for firm settings and a rising preference for management of the economy by state settings as one moves from the US to Russia, which is consistent with the theory. The developing regions show a mixed picture with SSA as the region that favors private ownership of business most, followed closely by SA, MENA, and GCC. On the other hand, the majority of responses in EAP and LAC favor state ownership over private ownership. These outcomes are for a part interpretable along the lines of theory whereby the private versus public attitude in a specific region is consistent with the respectively dominant F or S regime in the specific region. In case of countries in the developing regions where the attitude response does not comply with this line in the theory, the non-compliance can be interpreted as a logical reaction to disappointments with the outcome performances of the standing regimes. For example, in Sub-Saharan Africa, South Asia, and the Arab countries, a pro-private attitude can be seen as a logical reaction to dissatisfaction with the increased role of the state and the ensuing development performance of the country. In contrast, in EAP and LAC, i.e. China and Brazil among others, the pro-state attitude can be seen as a logical reaction to dissatisfaction with displacement outcomes and high-income differentials in rapidly changing economies led by firms and markets.

In Cohen (2015), other results from the WVS are reported. It is interesting to recall here some striking results. Country groups that tend to have pro-business attitudes were found to assign very high importance to familial institutions and household settings, while country groups that favor pro-state attitudes tend to assign low priority to familial institutions. This is generally true for the industrial and transition country groups and applies also to the six development regions. The association at the country group level suggests the presence of a synergy between pro-family and pro-business attitudes and an affinity between indifference to familial sentiments and support of pro-state attitudes.

In summary, the quantified system dominance and the World Value Survey show consistent features of system dominance and institutional attitudes in the six development regions whereby (a) systems which contain more state influence associate with institutional attitudes that are more positive toward state intervention and state influence and whereby (b) in countries where the firms/market system is overwhelming, institutional attitudes are more welcoming to free enterprise and market competition.

6. Required versus Available System Institutions

For the whole system to survive and expand, each subsystem has to create and maintain its own subsystem institutions which members of the subsystem need to abide with and the subsystems need to support each other and cooperate in supplementing each other. This holds for the firm subsystem and for the state subsystem. This section will list the required basic system institutions.

In order to work as they should, to maximize their profits, firms would take action to create and maintain formal and informal institutions that define the rules of the game to which all firms need to adhere. A flourishing firm subsystem sees to it that market-supporting institutions exist and are sanctioned to ensure four conditions:

(1) Free competition, entry, and exit are to be fostered and non-competitive practices are to be sanctioned.
(2) Exchange uncertainties associated with the exchangers and the exchanged goods and services need to be reduced to the minimum. This requires that property rights are legally respected, that agents can be trusted to live up to their contracted promises, fair settling of disputes when they arise, and that near to perfect information exists and flows smoothly between buyers and sellers.
(3) Externalities caused by one firm are held in check and are internalized back to the causing firm.
(4) Factor remuneration: While supply and demand considerations will always influence rewards to the factors of production in the short run, factor rewards

should reflect their factor productivities within the firm and across firms in the longer run.

Since it is impossible for the firm subsystem to fulfill these four conditions on its own, the state subsystem is called upon to correct for the market failures. For interventions by the state subsystem to be optimal, these are equally required to be governed by serving institutions and regulations that are transparent, unbiased, and non-exploitive. While there is ample empirical literature on the presence and functioning of the firm and state institutions in the developed countries, there is as yet very scarce investigation for developing countries.

A central question which is often addressed in development economics is whether the pro-firm (market) system associates with high economic growth, while the pro-state (government) system associates with low economic growth. Quantitative and verifiable answers to these questions require in-depth research and can fill a separate volume, which may not be meaningful after all. The posed question assumes that there is a system that can be labeled as optimal. Because the sample of countries regressed empirically have many specific differences to which their systems are adjusted and tailored, there is no one optimal order that can be labeled as such. Each country-specific situation produces its own optimal systemic mix.

Notwithstanding, some hints and tentative answers can be posed based on the findings of this chapter and the previous chapter. The general findings of the two chapters would suggest that countries with relatively more firm than state dominance had better economic performance, but there are many intervening factors behind the association. China defies the suggested association with its system of firms subordinated to state policy directions, and nevertheless, the country's ability to achieve the highest ever realized economic performance in three decades. The point is that China was successful in creating and maintaining the market institutions and state institutions required for the China system to work. Decades earlier, South Korea, Singapore, Taiwan, and Hong Kong had their own combinations of well-implemented market and state institutions that allowed them to achieve swifter development than their contemporaries. The central question is whether the required market institutions and state institutions are present and are well functioning in the investigated developing country.

7. Outer Institutions

Outer institutions are understood as practiced behavioral traits and conventions that circumscribe and are exterior to the system. It is now established that there are several outer institutions that retard a speedy socio-economic development process. We limit the listing to four instances: (1) corruptive practices in business and state contexts distort fair competition, misallocate resources, and encourage exploitation, (2) social stratification (feudal system *et al.*) has a rent-extracting character that discourages agent mobility and efficient allocation of resources, (3) social distrust between transacting agents (due to their opposite backgrounds) reduces exchange, and (4) polarization (due to non-compromising ideologies, belief, ethnicity, and nationalism) excludes cooperation and in the extreme can lead to violent conflicts. The four types of outer institutions can be briefly labeled as corruption, distrust, stratification, and polarization.

The first area of corruptive practices relates to violations of legalized institutions. Although we see corruption as an outer institution, there is acknowledged evidence that corruption is associates with the state-led system. But since corruption exists in all systems, it is rightly labeled as an outer institution. The three other areas relate to behavioral manifestations of transmitted and acquired conventions. Their origin and persistence are due to transmitted socio-cultural behavioral patterns at highly differentiated community levels. They are as such outer institutions and not system institutions. Nevertheless, there can be situations in which the outer institutions and the system institutions collide and strengthen each other. An ethnically exclusive, self-enriching, or non-cooperative polarized state system can embolden outer institution conducts of distrust, stratification, and violent conflicts, which retard development.

The objective of this section is not to demonstrate once again the significant impact of these outer institutions on economic development. This is already done by many and is proven. More of the same is wasteful. Development economists can better monitor and document the lags and successes accomplished in the four areas by country and region, and where feasible contributes indirectly to identifying and transferring the conditions of success in the successful country to the lagging country. Progress in the four areas involves long-term socio-cultural changes. Accordingly, the section humbly reviews some data available on the outer institutions in the development regions in Table 2.

Corruption perception: The Corruption Perceptions Index (CPI) by Transparency International (2022) ranks 180 countries and territories around the world by their perceived levels of public sector corruption as determined by expert assessments and opinion surveys, see www.transparency.org › en › cp. The index does not treat corruption in the private sector which can be as extensive as in the public sector.

The results for 2020 are given on a scale of 100 (very clean)–0 (highly corrupt). Results in Table 2 reveal that corruption levels are at a worldwide standstill. The global average remains unchanged for the tenth year in a row, at just 43 out of a possible 100 points. Two-thirds of countries score below 50, indicating that they have serious corruption problems. The results for the six development regions range between 52 and 26 points and rank as follows from cleanest to corrupt: MENA, LAC, EAP, SSA, CAC, and SA.

Table 2. Four indexes referring to outer institutions.

	CPI 2020		DMI 2020		STI 2016		CVI 2013	Reversed	Average
Region	Index	Rank	Index	Rank	Index	Rank	Index	Rank	Rank
Western allied	66.3		74.8		47.5		na		
Russian allied	39.4		60.1		20.0		19		
EAP	37.4	3	54.8	2	42.0	1	15.8[a]	2	2.0
SA	26.0	6	43.0	5	42.0	2	33.2[b]	6	4.5
CAC	28.1	5	58.6	1	25.0	3	22.2[c]	4	3.3
MENA	51.6	1	49.3	4	24.5	4	25.5[d]	5	3.8
SSA	32.3	4	39.4	6	13.0	6	15.8[e]	3	4.8
LAC	40.5	2	52.0	3	14.0	5	14.6[f]	1	2.8

Notes: CPI = Corruption Perception Index, From Transparency International CPI 2020.
DMI = Destratification Mobility Index. From World Economic Forum 2020.
STI = Social Trust Index From World Value Survey 2016, as reported in Mattes and Moreno (2017).
CVI = Civil Violence Index 2017. From Feindouno *et al.* (2016). Countries with highest scores by region. [a]Thailand 38. [b]Afghanistan 57, Pakistan 64. [c]Index for ex-Soviet Islamic republics approximated at value of Russia, Turkiye. [d]Iraq 68, Syria 56, Yemen 58. [e]Nigeria 55, Somalia 53, DR Congo 39, Zambia 50. [f]Colombia 51.

Social stratification hindering mobility: Social stratification ranks the relative position of a group or persons belonging to a group in the whole population. For example, caste is viewed among the lowest ranks with members of the cast immobile and unable to move upward. In caste systems, all aspects of social status are ascribed such that one's social position at birth persists throughout one's lifetime. Development opportunities are missed in this institutional setup. Social mobility is the movement of individuals and social groups between the layers. Mobility can be intragenerational or intergenerational. Countries/societies with high upward intragenerational mobility make use of progressive institutions that promote development. Little mobility retards development.

The Global Social Mobility Report produced by the World Economic Forum (2020) includes a Destratification Mobility Index (DMI) that ranks countries in 2020 according to their performance across five key pillars: healthcare, education, technology access, working conditions, and social protection. Western-allied countries score high at 75 points out of 100 points. Within the West, the Scandinavian countries have the top index scores of 83–85 points. If a person is born into a low-income family in Denmark, the WEF estimates it would take two generations to reach a median income. In contrast, for someone in India, Egypt, South Africa, or Guatemala (with scores of 40–44 points), it would take nine generations to reach the median at the current pace of growth. The development regions are ranked in

Table 2 from high to low as follows: CAC, EAP, LAC, MENA, SA, and SSA. The low score on mobility in the South Asia region at 43 points reflects the high occurrence of caste and related stratifications in India and neighboring countries. The following chapter includes a case study for India that reflects on related aspects of feudal systems, stratification, and mobility.

Social trust: Levels of social trust in a nation predict national economic growth as powerfully as financial and physical capital. Low trust implies a society where one has to keep an eye over one's shoulder, which ultimately limits exchange and misses economic opportunities to grow. To assess the relative level of interpersonal trust, the World Values Survey (WVS) asks the following: "Would you say that most people can be trusted?" The percentage of respondents giving a yes answer forms the Social Trust Index (STI), as reported in Mattes and Moreno (2017).

Table 2 shows the Western-aligned countries scoring on average 47% (with Scandinavian countries scoring 66%), compared to Russia at 20%. The development regions vary between values of 42 and 13 ranked in the following order: EAP, SA, CAC, MENA, LAC (14), and SSA (13). It is important to note the low level of social trust in LAC at 14% for a region that is more economically developed than others. The following chapter includes a case study for Chile that reflects on related aspects.

Polarized violence: Polarization is tearing at the seams of democracies around the world. Some ask why has polarization come to a boil in so many places in recent years. The truth is that in many development regions, polarization was present since the 1950s when the principal question of "Where to?" was addressed. Polarized thoughts in some LAC countries led to opposed views on which ways to follow: capitalist, socialist, and cut dependency links. In some MENA countries, the extreme choices were between the secular order and Islamic laws. The polarization developed often in violent conflicts. Severe polarization and recurring violence chatters cooperation and damages basic conditions for economic development. The following chapter includes a case study of Chile that reflects on polarized violence.

A Civil Violence Index (CVI) was developed and applied by Feindouno *et al.* (2016). The index focuses on polarized violence. It is a composite indicator of four clusters: internal armed conflict, criminality, terrorism, and political violence in the forms of political assassinations and riots. They applied the index to Russia and 130 developing countries. We aggregate their results for the six development regions on the basis of simple averages for each region. There is a high country variation by region as can be read from the footnote to Table 2, sitting countries with the highest index of violence.[9]

The results in Table 2 show South Asia (SA), MENA, and SSA having the highest levels of violence which are easily recognized in view of the high figures observed for Afghanistan and Pakistan in SA, and Iraq, Syria, and Yemen in MENA, and Nigeria, DR Congo, Somalia, and Zambia in SSA. Except for Nigeria which is fortunate to have rich natural resources, all the above-mentioned countries are progressing very slowly in terms of economic development.

8. Concluding Remarks

This chapter distinguished between system institutions that are tied to the economic polity system particular to a specific country, and the outer socio-cultural and historically formed institutions which tend to exist overall irrespective of the economic polity system.

With the help of system theory, it was possible to demonstrate system manifestations in the six development regions. The six regions show different combinations of the economically oriented firm-based system and the politically oriented state-based system. The two Asian regions of EAP and SA were found to show greater occurrence of firm-based than state-based system characteristics. This applies less to the other four development regions. In contrast, and in general terms, the other four regions of SSA, CAC, MENA, and to a lesser extent LAC show an increased influence of the state since the turn of the century.

As regards outer institutions, four dimensions were treated: corruption, stratification, trust, and polarized violence. If their stands are averaged as done in the last column of Table 2, the EAP region comes out as best equipped with outer institutions, followed by LAC, CAC, MENA, SA, and SSA. The development prospects of the six regions may very well follow this ranking, indeed with exceptions for specific countries within each region. In general, some minimum commonality of shared endowments, attributes, values, and custom in the population of a nation puts the nation on safer tracks of fair competition, more trust, more mobility, and a cooperation path with less polarized violence that promote the development process. Countries with more commonalities of shared endowments enjoy easier paths of economic development.

The following chapter dares to innovate and model the impact of two areas of outer institutions on development prospects. Chapter 4 is an economy-wide model and a case study of the bygone societal stratification and the feudal system in India of the 1950s and 1960s. The same economy-wide model is adapted to represent the polarization due to opposite and non-compromising ideologies with supportive powers during the Allende regime in Chile in the 1970s that ended with military violence.

Appendix. Calculation of the Dominance Index (DI)

The available data that can be used for DI are limited to the distribution shares of employment and GDP by sector of activity for a large number of countries (Table A.1).

These data are reset to fit with the calculation of the dominance indexes DI for firms and the state. It is generally agreed that the traditional household mode of production is prevalent in agriculture, while the modern firm settings are prevalent in industry. So, there are justifications for approximating the H subsystem with agriculture and the F subsystem with industry. The shift of agents and value added from agriculture to industry constitute a configuration of behavioral types in favor of that of F at the cost of that of H.

Regarding the employment figures, the share of households H is calculated as agriculture/(agriculture + industry). The share of firms F is calculated as industry/(agriculture + industry). The two shares add to 1.0. They are expressed as ratios $H{:}F$ in Table A.2. The same procedure is applied to the GDP figures. The footnote at the bottom of Table A.2 gives an example.

Table A.1. Changing concentrations of agents and the GDP.

Region: Year	Distribution of employment, %			Distribution of GDP, %			Public revenue/GDP
	Agriculture	Industry	Services	Agriculture	Industry	Services	
EAP1990	53	15	32	20	41	39	16.7
2000	44	20	36	14	42	44	15.2
2012	34	23	43	13	41	46	17.6
SA 1990	60	13	27	28	24	48	13.2
2000	59	14	27	27	27	46	11.7
2012	49	19	32	21	28	51	17.9
CAC 1990	40	19	41	23	31	46	14.5
2000	36	21	43	19	35	46	17.4
2012	30	24	45	13	39	49	26.7
MENA 1990	36	20	44	19	39	42	24.4
2000	22	24	54	10	45	46	29.1
2012	17	25	58	8	46	45	24.4
SSA1990	67	10	23	32	24	44	16.5
2000	50	17	33	29	35	36	22.3
2012	42	20	38	28	32	40	22.6
LAC 1990	27	23	50	10	30	60	18.8
2000	18	21	62	6	33	61	18.9
2012	14	22	64	6	36	58	25.3

Source: The raw country data on employment and on GDP per sector are from World Bank at http://databank.worldbank.org. The regional distributions are averages for the six leading countries in each region, which are fairly representative and complete.[10]

Table A.2. Dominance of firm and state subsystems, F and S, 1990, 2000, 2012 (in percentage).

	Dominance of Households (agriculture) versus dominance of Firms (Industry)			Dominance of State			Ratio
Region year	Employment shares Hhlds: Firms	GDP shares Hhlds: Firms	Dominance index *Firms*	Employment share State	GDP share State	Dominance Index State	DI(F)/DI(S)
EAP 1990	78:22	33:67	*45*	5.2	16.7	*10.9*	4.13
2000	67:33	25:75	*54*	6.0	15.2	*10.6*	5.09
2012	58:42	24:73	*59*	8.2	17.6	*12.9*	4.57
SA 1990	82:18	54:46	*32*	3.2	13.2	*8.2*	3.90
2000	79:21	50:50	*35*	3.9	11.7	*7.0*	5.00
2012	71:29	42:58	*43*	4.7	17.9	*7.7*	5.58
CAC 1990	67:33	42:58	*45*	5.9	14.5	*10.2*	4.41
2000	63:37	35:65	*51*	7.3	17.4	*12.3*	4.15
2012	56:44	25:75	*60*	13.2	26.7	*20.0*	3.00
MENA 1990	64:36	33:67	*52*	11.5	24.4	*17.9*	2.91
2000	43:57	19:81	*69*	26.7	29.1	*19.7*	3.50
2012	35:65	16:84	*74*	18.5	24.4	*21.5*	3.44
SSA 1990	89:11	57:43	*27*	4.6	16.5	*10.6*	2.55
2000	68:32	39:61	*46*	9.0	22.3	*15.6*	2.95
2012	58:42	39:61	*52*	11.5	22.6	*17.1*	3.04
LAC 1990	53:47	25:75	*61*	10.0	18.8	*14.4*	4.24
2000	41:51	16:84	*71*	11.5	18.9	*13.9*	5.11
2012	36:67	15:85	*75*	13.5	25.3	*15.7*	4.78

Source: World Bank at http://databank.worldbank.org. The regional figures are averages for the six leading countries in each region, which are fairly representative and complete.

Example: Column 1 refers to relative agent density in households and firms and is calculated from the employment shares in AT1. For EAP, in 1990, the ratio 78%:22% gives the relative shares of agent employment in agriculture and industry; i.e. $53/(53+15) = 78$ and $15/(53+15) = 22$. Column 2 refers to GDP density and is calculated similarly to give 33%:67%. Focusing on firms and taking the average of columns 1 and 2 gives the Dominance Index of F in column 3, that is $(22+67)/2 = 45$. In the above, the firm domain is proxied by industry.

Columns 4, 5, and 6 refer to state influence and are done similarly.

How do agents engage in producing services fare in this approximation? They form a mixture of (a) informally operating households that rely mostly on self-employed and family workers and thus associate with the household subsystem, (b) formally operating firms that maximize profit and where the mode of employment is that of employer-employee, (c) a fluent combination of the informal and formal modes, and (d) employment in the public sector. Rough estimates for the developing world[11] suggest that over half or more of agents delivering services are found in the informal household settings relating to (a) and the other half is spread on (b), (c), and (d), whereby public sector employees are often higher than the formally engaged service workers in the private sector. Due to productivity differentials, the generated GDP in the informal services is lower than in the formal services. The above gives ground for splitting agent activity in services proportionately between subsystems H and F, approximated here by agriculture and industry. This simplification allows us to distribute agent presence and transformed GDP in services in proportion to agriculture and industry.[12] The simplification can also be seen as neutralizing the impact of services on the spread of agent activity between H and F. The result is equalizing the relative distribution of agents between H and F, denoted as $H \quad F$, to the ratio of employment of agriculture to industry. We obtain the ratio of $H \quad F$ in columns 1 and 2, respectively, in Table A.2.

State dominance: Available data on public employment are scanty and their coverage is highly incomplete. Due to lack of usable data, we propose to construct and apply an equivalent indicator for the share of public employees in total employment defined as (employment in services/total employment) $*$ (public revenue/GDP). This indicator should not be read as the absolute share of public employment in total employment in the country concerned. The values of the indicator should be viewed as indicative of where and when the state is more or less influential in comparisons between countries and over time. This indicator is inserted in column 4. The state share in the GDP is in column 5. This share ranged between 11% and 31% for the development regions in 2012, being lowest in the Asian regions and highest in MENA, reflecting a greater influence of the state in the Arab countries than in other regions. The share has been rising in all regions between 2000 and 2012, by some 4% on average. The dominance index of the state is in column 6 and is the equally weighted average of columns 4 and 5.

Note that the sum of the two dominance indexes is below one. $\text{DI(F)} + \text{DI(S)} < 1.0$. The remaining portion would represent an approximation of the dominance of the household subsystem.

Endnotes

1. By state settings, we mean the legislative and executive branches, i.e. government. The state subsystem does not include the judiciary, which is a separate functional subsystem, though it becomes a part if the government is fully controlling the judiciary in the context of the country concerned.
2. Our modelling of the formation of subsystems draws on thoughts on interaction within social groups in Simon (1952) and on institutional growth in Zysman (1994).
3. In the household setting, h, agents lump together their benefits and costs in an effort to make total benefits exceed total costs. In eq. (1), V_h stands for the value added in the household setting, while rewards R and efforts E of agents i and i' are lumped together and somehow shared among all i.

$$V_h = R_i + R_{i'} - E_i - E_{i'} = 0. \tag{1}$$

In the firm setting, f, each agent aims at the highest economic returns to oneself, as shown in eq. 2, which implies aiming at realizing the highest return to the firm as a whole, above an opportunity cost margin ρ.

$$V_f = \Sigma(R_i - E_i)/\Sigma E_i = \rho. \tag{2}$$

To model the state setting, introduce the subscript *ps* to denote the pre-state situation (before engagement of the state), subscript s to denote the situation after engagement of the state, and *k* to represent state. Eq. (3) shows lower value added in pre-state situation compared to situation with state engagement.

$$V_{ps} = \Sigma R_{psi} - \Sigma E_{psi} = 0, \quad V_s = \Sigma R_i - \Sigma E_i - \Sigma E_{ik} = 0. \tag{3}$$

Institutional rules in state settings give the governing agent, *k*, the exclusive authority to acquire a polity rent from all agents for the polity services rendered, denoted by $E_{ik,}$. Furthermore, institutional rules in state settings tend to be molded in manners that require prolonged dependency of agents, *i*, on agents with state authority, *k*, and collection of polity rent in the future if transformation is to be realized and maintained in future transactions.

4. See Banerjee (1992), Bikhchandani, Hirshleifer, and Welch (1998), Frank (1988), Goodin (1993), Schelling (1978), Brueckner and Smirnov (2004), and Simon (1993).
5. There is some evidence for OECD countries of a positive correlation between the degrees of public regulation and public spending correlate. See Borcherding *et al.* (2002) on the correlation between public regulation and public spending.
6. The examples can be elaborated further. For instance, in the US, the polity can be described to have adapted itself to the economy. Next to constitutional checks and balances, and an independent judiciary system, that keep state discourse in control, profit maximizing firms and utility maximizing agents have installed more institutions for controlling state conduct and bent, the polity toward behaving along the same norm of maximizing economic returns. In contrast, in Russia, the polity can be seen as exogenous to the economy.
7. The two shares are not independent of each other. For instance, C_f affects A_f positively in the long run, while when relatively more agents go in *f*, thus increasing A_f, the potential for demanding and producing the *f* type of commodities is enhance, and thus C_f is influenced positively. Despite the interdependence, the two shares stand for different aspects that feature the identification of the economic system. It can be expected that the two shares correlate, which is an argument for giving them equal weights in the simple aggregation equation.
8. The questionnaire collects information on different types of attitudes, preferences, and beliefs, as well as information on demographic and socio-economic attributes of respondents. The responding national samples vary from several hundred to several thousands. See for more details http://www.worldvaluessurvey.org.
9. The selected variables are initially expressed in different units and must be standardized to make them comparable. While different standardization or normalization methods can be used, the authors use the max-min method: Index = 100 ∗ (variable value – min) /(max – min) with min and max being the observed minimum and maximum values for each variable's distribution. Every indicator then lies between 0 and 100.
10. For obtaining the dominance index DI from the distributions of employment and the GDP, there are two ways open: (a) find DI at country level and then take average at regional level for the concerned countries. (b) it is feasible to compute DI at the regional level straightaway by pooling country data and computing regional. The results would be fairly the same if either way is followed if the variation among the countries in the specific region is mild, but the gap widens with more variation; this is especially so for SSA where countries are highly varied not only in their distribution of employment but in most respects as well. In computing DI, we applied processing along (a). Besides, processing along (b) is objectionable in terms of substance for it assumes employment and GDP of one country to be continuously additive and substitutable with those of other countries in the specific region.
11. See Cohen (2009), pp. 257–258.
12. Results are marginally different whether agent interaction in the services sector is distributed proportionately or evenly. For the sake of simplicity, we choose a proportionate distribution.

Chapter 4

Modeling of Bygone Institutions That Obstructed Development: India and Chile

1. Introduction

The background of this chapter is of special interest. In the sixties and early seventies, the UN/Committee for Development Planning, chaired by Tinbergen, held an optimistic view about governments playing prominent roles in promoting development. The view was criticized by Myrdal in *Asian Drama*. Myrdal saw government in the development context as "soft state" with powerful landowners obstructing land reform and economic development.[1] Tinbergen was awarded the Nobel Prize in 1969. Soon after, Tinbergen acknowledged the limits of development planning and the critique of Myrdal, and he devoted the Nobel Prize award to fund research on land reform in India. The funded research culminated in a book on the modeling of agrarian structures and agrarian reform, Cohen (1978), and several published articles.[2] Reflecting in retrospect, the book is best described as a modeling exploration representing a cross-fertilization between socio-political structures and economic interactions in which Myrdal excelled and the unique mix of strict modeling approaches with positivist policymaking that is typical of Tinbergen.

This chapter reworks parts of the above-mentioned book. It formulates an economy-wide model in the tradition of the combined econometric multi-sector models, even though econometric estimation is restricted to regressing saving and consumption functions, while estimates of other coefficients were obtained from various statistical sources. The model incorporates socio-political structures and is used to draw boundaries for feasible land reform and related development policies in the given socio-political settings of India and Chile. This chapter is organized as follows. Section 2 describes the main features of the model. Section 3 specifies the basic model and explains its adaptation to different socio-political systems, and displays the leftover feasible areas for conventional economic policymaking. Section 4 adapts and applies the model to feudal India or what we have called "landlord-leader" socio-political structure of India. Section 5 adapts the model to suit Chile in the period 1966–1972 under president Allende, a highly politically polarized country at the time with a leftist government pleading for land reform in an otherwise highly conservative and rightist-oriented coalition of landowners, business proprietors, and military interests. It will be seen that the Chile impasse obstructs economic development policy and prospects. Section 6 concludes. In both countries at those times, the socio-economy polity systems and their institutions formed obstacles to economic development. The fading out of the conflicting regimes in the two countries was the pre-condition for further economic development.

2. Main Features of the Model

In spite of many analytical and policy studies done on agrarian reform, there is little work on addressing the problem within an economy-wide development model. One reason lies in the argument that the implementation of agrarian reform is not so much a matter of policy modeling as it is of political decision. The argument is not valid, however, since all government actions require political decisions, and many of them are commonly modeled. Starting from scratch, the model distinguishes between four actors: landlords, peasants, the non-agricultural sector, and the government. The main features of the actors and their interrelationships are summarized in the following.

Peasants and landlords are assumed to behave differently according to their own separate institutional attitudes, production functions, savings and consumption patterns, tax and interest rates, and so forth. Several links are modeled between peasants and landlords: (i) transfer of land assets between the two groups, (ii) financial lending by landlords to peasants, (iii) crop sharing between the two groups in case of tenancy, and (iv) a functioning of the landlord as an employer and the peasant as a hired worker with paid farm employment. When a transfer of land occurs from one group to another, it is assumed that transferred land acquires the characteristic production function and value of the new owner group and ceases to function with the parameters of the previous owner group.

Several links are modeled between agriculture and non-agriculture: (i) net financial assets of agriculture are invested in non-agriculture and (ii) since the model is formulated within an input–output framework, we note that intermediate goods are delivered to all sectors while capital formation goods are delivered solely by the non-agricultural sector, and final consumption goods demand for each sectors' goods depends on the income created in the concerned sector and the other sectors.

The new element in the research venture is to start first with a basic model that is not fully specified and, second, adapt the model to represent different socio-political situations and thereby make the model specific and solvable. Therefore, in the first step, we formulate a basic model that is under determinate (in this case, the model contains 24 unknowns and 22 equations). In the second step, values of two variables regarded as crucial in defining a particular political structure are pre-set, yielding thus a determinate model. Exactly which two variables to specify exogenously will depend on the particular leading actor who moves the economy and his preferences. The remaining actors and their variables are followers.

The *government* functions explicitly as a collector of a lump-sum land tax which can be redirected to investment and can within limits adjust credit and wage policy. There are other parameters that the government can influence, but the variation of any of the controllable instruments happens within the prescribed socio-political closure of the model. The closure can be dominated by the interests of (a) the landlords' group, (b) the peasants' group, (c) the non-agricultural population, or coalitions of them.

3. The Modeling Framework

3.1. *Specification of the model*

The model makes use of the notations in Table 1. All variables refer to the end of the year, and variables in monetary units are expressed in constant prices. The model is summarized in four blocks: Boxes 1–4. Eqs. (1)–(7) refer to the peasant group, eqs. (8)–(14) refer to the landlord group, eqs. (15) and (16) concern the agricultural sector as a whole, eqs. (17)–(19) deal with the non-agricultural sector, and eqs. (20)–(22) specify national accounting balances, typical of economy-wide models.

Box 1 contains equations for the peasants and landlords' groups. Eq. (1) formulates gross production, X_1, as a function of the number of acres that peasants possess, NQ_1, initial productivity per acre, π_{1o}, and an exponential growth of productivity per acre, π_1.

Eq. (2) relates investment requirements I_1 to production growth from actually possessed land. This reflects a Harrod–Domar production function, where investment in capital is directly related to the growth of production, i.e. π_{1o} and π_1.

Eq. (3) determines the price of land, NP_1, in several steps. First, the owner's valuation of an acre of owned land is defined as the future return to that acre, that is (land rental × future productivity levels), i.e. $\rho_1\pi_{10}(1+\pi_1)^t$; discounted by the peasant group's own discount rate $\imath_1$ and obtained as the sum of a geometric series to give present value, thus $\rho_1\pi_{10}(1+\pi_1)^t(1+\imath_1)/(\imath_1-\pi_1)$. Second, the owner's valuation differs from the market price for the same acre due to different discount rates that sellers and buyers may have, cultural attachment of farmers to own land, liquidity needs, indivisibility of offered land, non-transparent market information, and the like. To obtain the market value, the above expression is multiplied by a discrepancy ratio of market to own valuation, denoted by δ_1. Third, when a

Table 1. Notations.

Indices: h = Household groups and associated sectors of production, wherein 1 = peasants' group 2 = landlords' group, and 3 = non-agriculture. All agriculture is denoted by subscript $(1+2)$.

Endogenous variables	
$E_{(1+2)}, E_3$	Exports less imports of the agricultural sectors (1+2) and non-agriculture (3)
F_h	Value of financial assets possessed by group h = I, 2
I_{31}, I_{32}, I_{33}	Gross investment purchased by group/sector h and delivered by non-agriculture, $h = 3$
N_h	Value of land assets by group, $h = 1,2$
NP_h	Price per acre of land possessed by group h, $h = 1, 2$
NQ_h,	Land acreage possessed by group h, h = I, 2
S_h	Savings by group, h = I, 2, 3
W_h	Value of total wealth by group, $h = 1, 2$
X_h	Gross production by group (sector), $h = 1, 2, 3$
Y_h	Disposable income by group, $h = 1, 2, 3$
Exogenous variables	
BNY_1	Minimum of basic needs income per person for the poor farmers' population group 1
FCF	Foreign capital flow expressed in national currency
$NQ_{(1+2)}$	Total agricultural land acreage
P	Total population
Coefficients	
$\alpha_{hh'}$	Input–output coefficients of intermediate deliveries from sector h to sector h', h =1, 2, 3
δ_h	Discrepancy proportion between owner's valuation and market value of land, $h = 1, 2$
φ_{23}	Proportion of financial assets of landlords group (2) invested in non-agriculture (3)
φ_{21}	Proportion of financial assets of landlord group (2) lent to peasants' group (1)
$\gamma_{hao}, \gamma_{ha}$	Intercept and propensity to consume agricultural goods in total consumption of group h, $h = 1, 2, 3$. The corresponding coefficients for non-agricultural goods are $(1-\gamma_{hao})$ and $(1-\gamma_{ha})$
ι_h	Rate of discount used by a group for discounting its future income, h = I, 2
ι_{12}, ι_{32}	Rate of interest applied to loans lent by rich farmers (2) to poor farmers (1), and to financial assets held by rich farmers (2) in the non-agricultural sector (3), respectively.
κ_{31}, κ_{32}	Investment per unit of land in farmland 1 and 2 that is required to sustain productivity; investment is delivered by the non-agriculture sector 3
κ_{gh}	Publicly financed investment per acre in land belonging to farmer group h, h =1, 2
κ_3	Incremental capital–output ratio in the non-agricultural sector, 3
ν_1	Proportion of the peasant population in the total population
π_{ho}, π_h	Initial production per acre, and its growth rate, $h = 1, 2$
ρ_h	Proportion of land rental (includes capital rental) in gross output, $h = 1, 2$

(Continued)

Table 1. (*Continued*)

$\rho_{hh'}$	Proportion of land rent of sector $h$which is transferred to sector h, $h = 1, 2$
$\sigma_{ho}, \sigma_h, \sigma'_h$	Intercept, propensity to save from income, and propensity to save from wealth, $h = 1, 3$. The savings equation for peasant households follows other arguments
τ_h	Land tax per acre, $h =$ I, 2
ω_h	Labor earnings share in gross production, $h = 1, 2$
ω_{21}	Wage payments received by peasants $h = 1$ as proportion of labor earnings of landlords, $h = 2$

constant land tax per acre is levied, τ_1, the price of the taxed land is reduced; following geometric series, the present value of the reduction is $-\tau_1(1 + \imath_1)/\imath_1$. The three steps combined give the price of a unit of land.

Eq. (4) specifies the value of land possessed, N_1, which is simply quantity multiplied by price.

Eq. (5) defines wealth, W_1, to consist of two assets, namely value of land and all that goes with it, such as capital and inventory, N_1, and financial assets, F_1. In the case of the peasants' group, the financial assets consist of held cash and negative borrowings from the landlords' group which usually surpass the cash held so that financial assets can be expected to be negative.[3]

Eq. (6) defines income to consist of value added on own land, wages earned from hiring out labor to group 2, crop-sharing returns earned from tenancy arrangements with group 2, less interest paid on borrowed loans from the landlords' group, and less land taxes. There can also be some income from non-agricultural activities, but this is assumed to be absent for simplification.

Eq. (7) formulates savings as a residual of income after meeting basic needs of the population group, expressed as a basic needs income per capita BNY_1 multiplied by the peasant population, $\nu_1 P$. It is usual that savings are negative, which pushes peasant households to borrow from the landlords' group.

Eqs. (8)–(14) refer to the landlords' group, indexed as 2. This is a set of equations similar to those of the peasants' group, indexed as 1, except for the following differences. Landlords do not hire out their own labor to peasants and do not function as tenants in land possessed by peasants. The contrary is the case so that part of group 2's value added is transferred to group 1. In contrast, the landlords' group lends loans to the peasants' group and gets rent in return. They also have property in non-agriculture and receive rent in return. The financial assets of landlords consist of cash held, loans lent to peasant farmers, and property in non-agriculture. The loans and the property are specified as proportions of their total financial assets. The cash held is not explicitly specified but can be derived as residual.[4] The savings behavior of the landlord group is formulated otherwise in eq. (14). Next to the positive dependence of savings on income, the

Box 1. Equations applying to the peasants' group and landlords' group.

Peasants' group: output, investment, land price, land assets, financial assets, income, and savings

$$X_1 = \pi_{1o}(1+\pi_1)^t NQ_1 \tag{1}$$

$$I_{31} = \kappa_1\, \pi_{1o}\, \pi_1\, NQ_1 \tag{2}$$

$$NP_1 = \{\delta_1\, \rho_1\, \pi_{10}(1+\pi_1)^t(1+\imath_1)\}/(\imath_1-\pi_1) - \tau_1(1+\imath_1)/\imath_1 \tag{3}$$

$$N_1 = NP_1 \cdot NQ_1 \tag{4}$$

$$W_1 = N_1 + F_1 \tag{5}$$

$$Y_1 = (\omega_1+\rho_1)X_1 + (\omega_{21}\omega_2+\rho_{21}\rho_2)X_2 - \imath_{12}\varphi_{21}F_2 - \tau_1 NQ_1 \tag{6}$$

$$S_1 = Y_1 - BNY_1\, \nu_1\, P \tag{7}$$

Landlords group: output, investment, land price, land assets, financial assets, income, and savings

$$X_2 = \pi_{20}(1+\pi_2)^t\, NQ_2 \tag{8}$$

$$I_{32} = \kappa_2\, \pi_{2o}\, \pi_2 NQ_2 \tag{9}$$

$$NP_2 = \{\chi_2\, \beta_2\, \pi_{2o}(1+\pi_2)^t(1+\imath_2)\}/(\imath_2-\pi_2) - \tau_2(1+\imath_2)/\imath_2 \tag{10}$$

$$N_2 = NP_2 \cdot NQ_2 \tag{11}$$

$$W_2 = N_2 + F_2 \tag{12}$$

$$Y_2 = (1-\omega_{21})\omega_2 + (1-\rho_{21})\rho_2 X_2 + \imath_{12}\varphi_{21}F_2 + \imath_{32}\varphi_{23}F_2 - \tau_2\, NQ_2 \tag{13}$$

$$S_2 = \sigma_{2o} + \sigma_2 Y_2 - \sigma_2' W_2 \tag{14}$$

landlord is assumed to target a desired level of wealth. The closer the realized to the desired wealth, the less there is an incentive to save, thus giving a negative relationship.

Box 2 specifies equations applicable to the whole agricultural sector. Eq. (15) sums land quantities owned by peasants and landlords to give total agricultural land, $NQ_{(1+2)}$, which is fixed in acreage.

Eq. (16) defines financial assets in agriculture as a whole, done in several steps: (i) Financial assets of peasants in year t are those in year $t-1$, plus savings, less capital investment on land, plus (less) the amount collected (spent) in the sale (purchase) of transferred land. These transactions can be displayed as $F_1 = F_{1,t-1} + S_1 - I_1 +$ *land sales and/or purchases.* (ii) A similar equation holds for landlords: $F_2 = F_{2,t-1} + S_2 - I_2 +$ *land sales and/or purchases.* (iii) Since the sum of transferred acreage is zero and land is transferred at a common price, the two expressions can be equalized to give the outcome for eq. (16).

Box 2. Agriculture: Land distribution, financial assets, and value added.

$$NQ_I + NQ_2 = NQ_{(1+2)} \tag{15}$$

$$F_1 - F_{1,t-1} + F_2 - F_{2,t-1} = S_1 + S_2 - I_1 - I_2 \tag{16}$$

Box 3 contains equations relating to non-agriculture. Eq. (17) is a Harrod–Domar production function[5] where investment determines the change in gross production, via incremental capital–output ratio, k_3.

Eq. (18) specifies Leontief input–output technology to derive the value added from the gross output. Eqs. (17) and (18), together with eqs. (20) and (2), specify production for non-agriculture. The same has also been followed for agriculture.[6] To obtain in eq. (18) the income of the rest of the economy (i.e. non-agriculture), adjust the gross value added to two items: deduct interest payments on financial assets owned in non-agriculture by the landlords' group and add land tax revenue collected by the government (the latter being part of the rest of the economy).

Eq. (19) is the savings function for the rest of the economy.

Box 3. Non-agriculture.

$$(X_3 - X_{3,t-1}) = k_3(I_{33,t-1}) \tag{17}$$

$$Y_3 = (1 - \Sigma_h \alpha_{h3})X_3 - \imath_{32}\phi_{23}\, F_2 + \tau_1\, NQ_1 + \tau_2\, NQ_2 \tag{18}$$

$$S_3 = \sigma_{30} + \sigma_3\, Y_3 \tag{19}$$

Box 4 contains national accounting balances. Eqs. (20) and (21) specify the product balances for agriculture and non-agriculture. In eq. (20), agricultural production for peasants and landlords is aggregated to give the total supply, which is equal to the total demand for agricultural goods consisting of intermediate deliveries, final consumption specified via consumption functions for spending agent groups, and net exports, noting that agriculture does not deliver investment goods. Eq. (21) is the equilibrium balance of supply and demand for the non-agricultural products. The difference between the two balances lies in the fact that non-agriculture delivers all investment goods in the economy. These consist of investment made by the two farming groups in agriculture and by non-agriculture.

Government, indicated by subscript g, is additionally engaged in public investment in the farming lands via the terms $\kappa_{g1}NQ_1 + \kappa_{g2}NQ_2$.

Eq. (22) is the savings–investment balance showing the supply of domestic savings plus foreign savings (taking the form of foreign capital flow FCF) equal to the investment demand.[7]

Eq. (A.1) is the foreign payments balance that equalizes net exports (exports less imports) to FCF. This balance is automatically realized when the other national accounting balances in eqs. (20–22) are realized and is not counted as an independent equation of the model; hence its numbering as eq. (A.1).[8]

Box 4. National accounting balances.

$$X_1 + X_2 = \Sigma_{h'} \Sigma_h \alpha_{h'h} X_h + \{\Sigma_h \gamma_{\mathrm{ha},o} + \gamma_{\mathrm{ha}}(Y_h - S_h)\} + E_{(1+2)} \quad (20)$$

$$X_3 = \Sigma_h \alpha_{3'h} X_h + \{\Sigma_h(-\gamma_{\mathrm{ha},o} + (1 - \gamma_{\mathrm{ha}})(Y_h - S_h)) + I_{31} + I_{32} + I_{33}\} + \kappa_{g1}NQ_1 + \kappa_{g2}NQ_2 + E_3 \quad (21)$$

$$S_1 + S_2 + S_3 + FCF = I_{31} + I_{32} + I_{33} + \kappa_{g1}NQ_1 + \kappa_{g2}NQ_2 \quad (22)$$

$$E_{(1+2)} + E_3 = FCF \quad (\mathrm{A}.1)$$

The basic model contains 24 endogenous variables, specified in Table 1, in 22 equations. The exogenous variables are total farmland $NQ_{(1+2)}$, population P, basic needs income BNY_1, and foreign capital flow FCF. The model is underdetermined and possesses two degrees of freedom. The following section will examine how the socio-polity determines these two degrees of freedom and the closure of the model.

3.2. *Adaptation of the basic model to different socio-political contexts*

The solutions of the model are directed toward the fulfillment of predetermined targets of one of the main actors. This represents the case where one actor has absolute control of the socio-political structure and is the sole decision-maker in the country while the other actors are passive. For example, in a feudal society, the landlords are assumed to determine the future course of their welfare variables while other actors are followers. The model is *adaptable* to represent different socio-political structures, i.e. cases in which the respective dominant actors are peasants, non-agriculturalists, and the state.

In terms of adapting the model to different socio-political situations, the procedure followed was, first, to formulate a basic model that is under determinate with 24 unknown variables and 22 equations and, second, to assume that the two variables regarded as crucial in defining a particular political structure can be exogenously set, yielding a determinate model. Exactly what two variables to specify exogenously will depend on the particular actor who moves the economy, the "leader," and his or her preferences, the "leader's welfare variables." The remaining actors are "followers".

The approach is to hypothesize *different exogenous variables for different socio-political systems.* In a political system characterized by a feudal agrarian structure, what is called here a landlord-leader model, it can be realistically assumed that the sole movers and decision-makers in the economy are the landlords' group; their two target variables may be described by landlord's wealth, W_2, and landlord's income, Y_2. When both variables are fixed, a determinate model is obtained.

To take a different example, in a socio-political system in which peasants are powerful enough to be the leaders, the predetermined variables can be such representative target variables as possession of more land, NQ_1, and reduction or acquittal of financial liabilities $(-F_1)$. This is a different determinate model than the previous.

Another example is that in which the mover of the economy is the non-agricultural sector and its managers. As a country becomes more modernized and urbanized, the emergence of a strong urban-oriented leadership can be expected. This leadership usually consists of the intelligentsia, the industrialists, labor unions, and the military. If the urban sector acts as the leader, then one of these subgroups, or a combination of them, via the government or in spite of the government, will dominate political developments. Predetermined variables that would represent the welfare of the urban sector should differ in accordance with the distribution of power within the urban sector. One applicable target variable is the income of the non-agricultural sector Y_3. Another target variable is non-agricultural wealth, which, although not explicitly specified in the model, can be represented by setting the agricultural financial assets $(F_1 + F_2)$ at lower values, thereby increasing the financial assets of the non-agricultural sector.

In the above examples, the socio-political system assigns the model closure: the combination of exogenous and endogenous variables. It is a matter of further research and judgment to identify the type of socio-political system of particular countries. Once identified, each socio-political system produces a different causal structure. The system structure of a model can be displayed in terms of causal ordering as done in Figures 1 and 2, following Simon (1953).[9] The causal orderings of the landlord-leader and of the peasant-leader regimes are displayed in Figures 1 and 2.

In Figure 1, the predetermined target variables Y_2 and W_2 are shaded. They are fed in eqs. 8, 11, 12, and 13, shown bracketed, which are simultaneously solved to give values of F_2, Y_2, X_2, and the important variable of landlord land, NQ_2. Once known, its counterpart variable, peasant land, NQ_2, becomes known and the solution of the model proceeds further by simple substitutions from lower to higher orders along a diagonal pattern. The peasant-leader model, Figure 2, has a simpler structure. The predetermined target variables are shaded: NQ_1 and

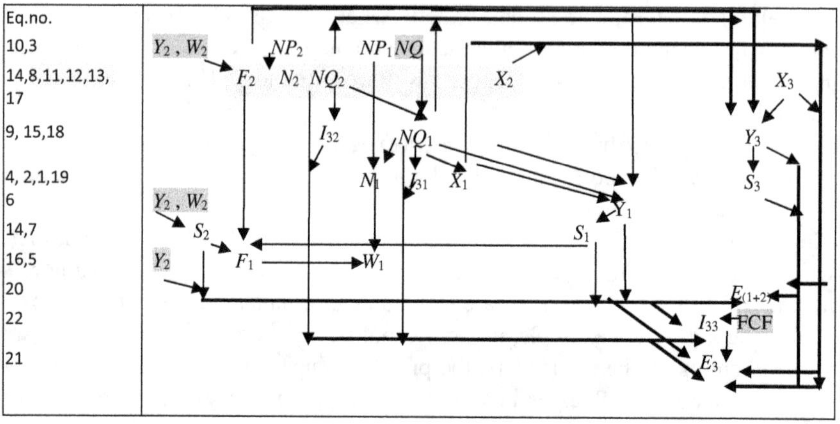

Figure 1. Causal ordering in the landlord-leader model.

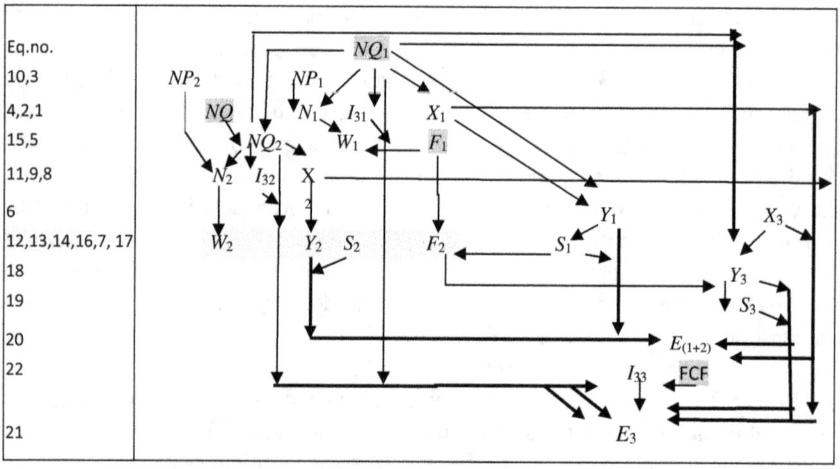

Figure 2. Causal ordering in the peasant-leader model.

F_1. These allow for quick solutions for the peasant variables. Again, once NQ_2 becomes known, the landlord variables are solved in a simultaneous system of four equations, marked in bracket. In both cases, the sector product balances of agriculture and non-agriculture and foreign payments balance active at the higher orders and take decisive roles in determining the trade balances by sector, $E_{(1+2)}$ and E_3, and capital formation, I_{33}.

We consider now the role of *government.* Depending on the particular socio-political power structure, the model considers various agrarian policies as being under different degrees of government control. These policies can be (radical) direct reforms as in the case of land confiscation and redistribution and debt cancelation, or can take the form of various indirect policy measures.

Direct reforms cannot be realistically simulated in a landlord-leader setting where landlords have targeted variables that defy direct reform. But confiscating and redistributing land and debt acquittal are plausible in a peasant-friendly socio-political setting and can be simulated by fixing N_h and F_h.

Indirect policy measures apply in principle to all settings irrespective of the socio-political power distribution. The model is able to consider and run the following policies:

1. Yield rates, $\pi_{h,o}$ and π_h, can be raised by productivity-promoting measures.
2. Credit policy can be pursued toward adjusting discount and interest rates: $\imath_h$, $\imath_{12}$, and $\imath_{32}$.
3. Land tax policy can be entered via changes in tax rates: τ_1 and τ_2.
4. Tenure and wage regulation policies can be entered via changes in crop sharing arrangements and remuneration levels: $\rho_{hh'}$, $\omega_{hh'}$. Furthermore, the framework allows for additional policies, such as new land settlements that can be introduced through certain extensions in the model.

The degree of intervention and the choice of means would depend on the socio-political power setting and the political color of the government. This can be illustrated by a few examples. If in a landlord-leader society the government is also dominated by landlords, there is little chance that any agrarian reform favoring peasants would take place. However, when the composition of the government is not biased in favor of landlords, the government is usually able to pursue indirect policy measures. In substantive terms, in a landlord-leader setting, the government tacitly accepts the setting and works within that realm. When the socio-political power structure is more favorable to peasants, and the government has also the same inclination, the scope for policymaking is wider and can include direct reform as well as indirect policy measures.

4. Selected Results from Application to India

Our classification of the Indian socio-polity in the early 1960s as a landlord-leader type is essentially in agreement with Bardhan (1974). Application of the landlord-leader soft-state model to India is consistent with thorough analysis made by authorities on India, for example, Thorner (1956), Myrdal (1968), and Joshi (1975). For the substantive discussion and justification of the characterization of India as a landlord-leader society, see Cohen (1978).[10]

The initial year chosen for applying the model is 1961. Estimation of the model is derived from data from the seventies. Table 2 gives values of a few parameters on which we focus. Among these are the predetermined growth targets for wealth

Table 2. Basic run projection parameters and changes therein under different policy simulations.

Parameters	Values in basic run projections	1. Higher Productivity	2. Credit Advances	3. Higher taxes	4. Tenure reform
Leader targets					
$Y_2 = Y_{2,0}(1+y_2)^t$	$y_2 = 0.0259$				
$W_2 = W_{2,0}(1+w_2)^t$	$w_2 = 0.0259$				
Parameters					
$\langle \pi_{1o} \rangle$ $\langle \pi_{2o} \rangle$	$\langle 355 \rangle$ $\langle 230 \rangle$			$\langle 357 \rangle$ $\langle 234 \rangle$	
$\langle \pi_1 \rangle$ $\langle \pi_2 \rangle$	$\langle 0.028 \rangle$ $\langle 0.026 \rangle$	$\langle 0.031 \rangle$ $\langle 0.027 \rangle$			
$\langle \kappa_{g1} \rangle$ $\langle \kappa_{g2} \rangle$	$\langle 0.6 \rangle$ $\langle 0.6 \rangle$	$\langle 0.77 \rangle$ $\langle 0.74 \rangle$			
$\langle \iota_1 \rangle$ $\langle \iota_2 \rangle$	$\langle 0.3 \rangle$ $\langle 0.15 \rangle$		$\langle 0.27 \rangle$ $\langle 0.14 \rangle$		
$\langle \iota_{12} \rangle$ $\langle \iota_{32} \rangle$	$\langle 0.3 \rangle$ $\langle 0.22 \rangle$		$\langle 0.27 \rangle$ $\langle 0.22 \rangle$		
$\langle \tau_1 \rangle$ $\langle \tau_2 \rangle$	$\langle 4 \rangle$ $\langle 4 \rangle$			$\langle 6 \rangle$ $\langle 8 \rangle$	
$\langle \rho_{12} \rangle$ $\langle \omega_{hh} \rangle$	$\langle 0.045 \rangle$ $\langle 0.4 \rangle$				$\langle 0.052 \rangle$ $\langle 0.46 \rangle$
FCF	$-5.1(1. - 0.1)^t$		$-5.0(1. - 0.1)^t$		

and income of the landlord group, w_2 and y_2, which are assumed to continue their past trends of a growth rate of $w_2 = y_2 = \pi_2 = 2.6\%$ *per annum*, reflecting the conservatism of *traditional* landlords to maintain wealth and income growth in line with the growth of land productivity. The model is solved consecutively to give the initial values for 1961 ($t = 0$) and 20 following years. Results for the main variables are found in Table 3. The results reflect the path of the Indian economy fairly well, giving an annual projected growth rate of GDP of about 3.5% over the whole 20 years against an observed rate of about 3.3%.

One important result of these basic run projections is the almost unchanged distribution of possessed land between landlords and peasants. In the projected 20 years, only 3 million acres (ma) shift hands from landlords to peasants of a total land of 330 million acres. A second important result relates to the distribution of financial assets, which becomes increasingly concentrated in the hands of landlords at the cost of increasing debts of peasants. As a result of the above shifts in land and financial assets, the distribution of wealth among landlords and peasants, that formed a ratio of 3:1 in the initial year, kept to about the same rate of 3:1 in year 20. The ratio for income shifted from 2.2:1 to 2.4:1, respectively. The non-agricultural production and income are realistically projected to grow at higher rates than those for agriculture.

The outcome regarding land distribution, NQ_2 and NQ_1, is very significant in determining other results. Substituting eqs. (10)–(13) into each other gives NQ_2 in terms of the future targeted growth rates of w_2 and y_2 and a large host of parameters that include ω_{21}, ω_2, ρ_{21}, ρ_2, ι_{12}, φ_{21}, ι_{32}, φ_{23}, τ_2, χ_2, β_2, π_{2o}, π_2, and ι_2. Substituting values of these except π_2 gives the solution for NQ_2 as in eq. (A.2).

Deducting this from total land as in eq. (15) gives NQ_1.

$$NQ_2 = 54900(1 + y_2)^t - 80204(1 + w_2)^t/2.75 - 98.51(1 + \pi_2)^t \quad \text{(A.2)}$$

Eq. (A.2) indicates that under a common growth rate of targeted wealth and income that is equal to π_2, and if the term 2.75 would have been zero, then NQ_2 would remain constant at its initial year value of 264 million acres. Due to the term 2.75, there is a slight annual reduction but at a diminishing rate so that NQ_2 stabilizes after 20 years at 261 million acres.

Next to basic run projections, it is conceivable to simulate an alternative future in which a *modern* landlord leadership predominates, whose wealth and income aspirations are more ambitious than the traditional, less bounded to agriculture and who would aim at $y_2 > w_2 > \pi_2$. It can be seen from eq. (A.2) that this would lead to decreasing values of NQ_2, as modern landlords are better off substituting financial assets for land assets. Under $y_2 = w_2 > \pi_2$ or $w_2 > y_2 > \pi_2$, representing a commercialization wave, the opposite would occur making it more attractive for modern landlords to increase their land possession. We shall maintain here the basic run projections where traditional landlords predominate.

Within the boundaries of the basic run projections, the question is as follows: How big is the scope for policymaking that can raise the welfare of the subordinate group without touching the predetermined targets of the dominant group? Notwithstanding the softness of the state, can it still pick successful policies in the margin? A few policy simulations applied to the Indian model will treat these questions. We have stated before that direct reform measures of de-owning and redistributing land are excluded in the landlord-leader model. But there are ample possibilities for indirect policy measures that can be simulated: (1) promotion of levels of land productivity with special emphasis on land of peasants, (2) provision of more credit facilities at lower interest rates in particular to peasants, (3) fixation of higher taxes, and (4) tenure reform in the form of increases in the agricultural wage rate and in the peasants' share in crop sharing. The model contains parameters on each of these that can be adjusted, the model is rerun, and effects of each adjustment are studied. Table 2 shows relevant parameters and how they were adjusted. Table 3 gives the results of each of the four policy simulations, and these can be compared with the basic run projections in the first and second columns, all for year $t = 20$.

One remark is still to be made before looking at the results. First, to permit an unbiased appraisal of the effectiveness of alternative policies, we aimed at stimulating relative changes in the policy measures that are equivalent in terms of the public effort needed in implementing them. A common adjustment in the policy parameters of 15% was followed. When one policy involves adjustment in more parameters, the sum of the adjustments should also amount to 15%.

The first policy raises farm productivity. A policy can be formulated in a "discriminate" form (for example, public investment in lands possessed by landlords,

Table 3. Selected results of basic run projections and policy simulations: India, year 20.

Variables		$t = 0$ Initial year	$t = 20$ Basic run projections	Policy simulations to $t = 20$: 1. Higher productivity	2. Credit advances	3. Higher taxes	4. Tenure reform	Combined policies (b)
Peasants								
Land ownership acres	NQ_1	65	68	82	105	69	84	156
Price per acre	NP_1	1911	3346	3571	3675	3357	3346	3940
Financial assets	F_1	−3	−26	−43	−82	−25	−56	−74
Wealth	W_1	122	203	251	303	205	225	541
Output	X_1	23	42	54	65	43	52	129
Income	Y_1	25	38	43	42	39	38	54
Landlords								
Land ownership acres	NQ_2	264	261	247	225	261	246	174
Price per acre	NP_2	1222	2058	2135	2177	2064	2080	2775
Financial assets	F_2	42	70	80	118	69	97	125
Wealth	W_2	365	608	608	608	608	608	608
Output	X_2	61	100	97	86	102	94	54
Income	Y_2	55	92	92	92	92	92	92
Other variables								
Total agri output	$X_1 + X_2$	84	143	151	151	145	146	182
Tot agri fin. assets	$F_1 + F_2$	39	45	37	37	44	41	51
Output non-agri	X_3	126	281	281	282	283	283	723
Income non-agri	Y_3	126	166	169	170	168	170	455
Net exports agri	$E_{(1+2)}$	12	4	9	9	5	6	−83
Net exports non-agri	E_3	−17	−5	−10	−10	−6	−7	82
National income	ΣY	150	296	303	303	299	300	601
Income distribution	$Y_1/\Sigma Y$	0.1648	0.1292	0.1409	0.1380	0.1295	0.1270	0.0906
Rank by effectiveness				III	II	V	IV	I

Notes: (a) Land in million acres, value variables in billion rupees. Shaded rows are predetermined.
(b) The policy simulations have an immediate impact on NQ_1 instantly in the initial year, which is not realistic and results in exaggerating the long-run result. While NQ_1 in the initial year $t = 0$ amounted to 65 million acres, the immediate average impact of the four policy simulations was to raise it to 82 million acres. To neutralize this bias, the terminal value of NQ_1 is adjusted downwards by the factor 65/82, and the outcome is carried forward throughout other variables where applicable.

κ_{g2}, can be cut down and thus reduce their productivity growth π_2) or in a "neutral" form (both κ_{g1} and κ_{g2} are raised, and thus the productivity growth of both farmlands are raised: π_1 and π_2, with the rises higher for group 1 than 2). We ran both policies. Results of the discriminate policy are inferior to the neutral one. For example, wealth and income of the landlords are unaffected by counterproductive measures to their land productivity; instead, they will shift the incidence of the discriminate policy to peasants and will buy more land to meet their targets, leaving less land for peasants. Besides, income earnings by peasants from work they perform on farms of landlords would fall with falling land productivity. In contrast, under the neutral policy, rich farmers have higher produce yields on possessed land and need less land to maintain their targets and sell some land to peasants who will now benefit twice from having higher yields and more land. We ran for each of the four policy measures both the discriminate and neutral forms. All results show that the discriminate policy is detrimental to all parties concerned and is always deficient to the neutral one. As discriminate policies are self-defeating, the results in Table 3 will focus on the neutral policies.

The credit policy employs part of the available foreign capital inflow, FCF, to finance credit advances to all farmers, giving relatively more to poor than rich farmers. This easing of credit reduces the discount rates of peasants and landlords by 10% and 5%, respectively (sum $=$ 15%, see preceding remark). The lower discount rates stimulate landlords to sell land to peasants, thus increasing the latter's output and income. Besides, under lower interest rates, peasants pay less for their borrowings. As land moves from landlords to peasants, where land productivity is higher, agricultural output is raised. Output of non-agriculture is unaffected but income increases as liabilities fall.

The third policy simulated is raising the land tax by 15%; to maintain the same income net of the land tax, the farmer is assumed to raise productivity per acre by the same amount of the tax. Being only a small change in productivity, it is assumed that this is made possible by raising labor input. Results of the tax policy do not differ much from the basic projections. In many policy discussions that took place in the development context, some great expectations were built around land taxes, but the simulations here show poor results in this direction.

The fourth policy simulates changes in the tenancy regime by which the shares of peasant income in the wage bill and land rental of farmland possessed by landlords are increased by 15%. The results are confined to some redistribution of land, with the feedback effects to the rest of the economy limited, when compared with the basic run projections.

When results of the four policies are assessed against such criteria as reaching the highest levels of land redistribution, rural welfare, agricultural production, agricultural income, and non-agricultural income and reaching the lowest financial liabilities for the non-agricultural sector (as the net financial assets of farming groups, $F_1 + F_2$, are held in non-agriculture, these assets are also the latter's liability), the conclusion is that policies of *credit advances* perform best, and then in a descending order followed by *productivity measures*, then *tenancy measures* and *higher taxation*, all of them compared with the basic projection, which ends as last. The positive effects of the credit policy are somewhat exaggerated since the policy leads to an immediate redistribution of land in the initial year 0, due to the newly stipulated discount and interest rates, which are not realistic. In practice, it will take a number of years before realization. We will correct this bias in the following paragraph.

One interesting question that can be raised concerns the relative performance of a combination of indirect reform measures. Would such a combined run give a better or a worse performance than the best of the individual runs? Why? A combined simulation was carried out. This starts from the input of the basic run projections and incorporates into it the combined adaptations of the four policies shown in Table 2. The results obtained for the combined policies, shown in Table 3, last column, *outrank* in a remarkable way all other results found earlier. For example, the combined simulation predicts (above the base run) an additional transfer of land from rich to poor amounting to 88 million acres, when the sum of the additional transfers achieved by each indirect measure separately counts only 68 million acres. This better performance is due to multiplicative effects of combining independent measures that are nonlinearly related. Rates of taxes, discount, interest, yield, and yield growth are nonlinearly related. These rates determine also the prices per acre, which reach their highest levels under the combined simulation. These effects enhance the prospects for increasing the wealth and income of rich farmers. To keep to their wealth and income targets, the rich farmers require less land than they possess. Land is sold to the poor farmer, therefore, which explains the simulated rise in F_2 as against a fall in F_I. The higher agricultural production and income, via inter-industrial deliveries and consumption demand, increase non-agricultural production and income, which are further pushed up by rising net exports and investment. Under the combined simulation, the national income would grow at a yearly average rate of 7.2%; all other runs gave a figure of about 3.5%. GDP growth rates achieved by India in the seventies and eighties were somewhere between the two rates. This is not meant to suggest that if the proposed policy simulations were followed a higher growth rate toward 7.2% would have been achievable. Even though the model applied is an economy-wide model, its focus is specific and abstains from treating savings, investment, consumption, and trade in any good detail, which are the main determinants of GDP growth.

It is interesting also to point out that the share of the income of the peasants' group in the GDP, which is a measure of income distribution, is highest under the combined policy at 9%.

5. Application to Chile

The Chilean socio-polity has been for a long time a sensitive mixture of the landlord-leader, peasant-leader, and industrialist-leader types discussed earlier; the balance of power has shifted from the first to the second and the third over a period of three decades and is still under pressures. Chilean governments (Allessandri 1957–1964, Frei 1964–1970, Allende 1970–1973, and Pinochet 1973–1990) played important roles in either actively promoting these shifts in power or in simply giving legality and shape to them.

Although there is a long history of sporadic conflict between landlords and peasants on farms all over Chile, it has never yielded a sustained organized movement among peasants. However, during Frei's regime, rural workers organized when the state offered them patronage and protection. During Allende's period, the peasant movement was able to multiply its power. Rural union's membership increased from 53,000 in 1967 to 140,000 in 1970 and 218,000 in 1972. This period also saw an upsurge in rural strikes, farm seizures and land expropriation by peasants, the convening of the first Peasant Assembly in 1971, and the drawing of official demand declarations by peasant leaders. By 1973, the peasantry have become too independent to be orderly managed, but that year was also its climax year of power. The military overthrew the Allende government and installed the Pinochet regime.

The agrarian problem has drawn vast attention from politicians and laymen and greatly influenced Chilean events. Yet, Chile is highly urbanized (urbanization rate = 90%) and has a non-agricultural sector accounting for more than 90% of the GDP. *A priori*, it can be reasoned that agrarian solutions that are unacceptable to the industrial population have little chance of realization in a society with this socio-political balance. There is substantial evidence that the movement of the peasantry was looked upon with distrust by the industrial population (and industrial leaders). The political obsession with the agrarian problem derives as much from catching the political support of the peasantry votes as it does from attempts to reform the economically lagging tenure system and its low agricultural productivity.

The socio-political structure of Chile in the 1960s and early 1970s can be conceived in our analytical framework as a mixture between the peasant-leader model and the industry-leader model. The peasant-leader model, it is recalled, is the one in which peasant's welfare variables are considered predetermined, especially land property, NQ_1,and financial debt, F_1. To allow for the fact that the industrial leadership is not a follower at any cost, we incorporate boundary conditions on certain variables; these represent minimum solutions that are acceptable to the industrial leadership. The socio-political sphere in Chile at the time was also overloaded with political polarization between rightist and leftist sentiments to the extent that the polarized conflicts culminated in counterviolence and military-backed regime change that replaced Allende with Pinochet.

Data organization and parameter estimates of the model were calculated from various sources and made consistent for the initial year 1965. The distinction between small (peasant) and large farmers (rich) was made along the lines of CIDA (1966). This resulted in a population distribution in the ratio of 92% to 8%, as against a land distribution ratio of 4% to 96%, which is extremely skewed worldwide. Distribution of agricultural output is less skew due to higher productivity of peasant farms: $\pi_{1,0} > \pi_{1,0}$.

A determinate solution of the model requires fixation of target variables NQ_1 and F_1. Although problematic, we took as representative of NQ_1 the actual transfer of land to peasants that occurred in Chile between 1965 and 1972, being an indication of the will of the peasantry. This is a period in which peasants had recourse to farm seizure and thereby *expedited,* and perhaps *determined,* the confiscation of land at a tempo that was quicker than that anticipated by the state. The land transfer from rich to poor is targeted at 0.09 million hectares per year, which forms only a meager 0.003 of land held by landlords. For the approximate fixation of the future values of the peasantry financial debt F_1, we have assumed that the peasantry would feel satisfied with the elimination of the debt within half a generation. This is a period that present peasant leaders would outlive. This assumption would reduce debts by 25 million escudos per year noting that total debts amounted to 365 million Escudos in 1966.

The model was solved for 1966 and 20 consecutive years to give basic run projections (BRP). The projected annual growth of the GDP over 20 years, 4.5%, is higher than the actual growth rate reached in Chile: 4.1% for 1965–1970 and 2.0% for 1970–1975. Although the model overestimates growth prospects, the projections do reproduce structural relationships that determined Chilean development.

The projections show that in spite of the targeted transfer of land and reduction of the liabilities, the income share of peasants deteriorates during the 20 years. There is an improvement in the income share of rich farmers and a very substantial increase in the rich farmer's wealth due to an increasing price for their land and increased financial assets due to the sale of some land and accumulated savings from higher income. The projections indicate a development impasse.

It is important to analyze the implications of these projections for the industrial leadership, who may have the last word. The assumed target for land transfer leads to a high accumulation of financial assets by landlords F_2. Peasants too are targeted to cut their financial liabilities, i.e. increase their financial assets F_1. As a result, the non-agricultural sector, including the public sector, becomes increasingly in debt to rich farmers. This financial debt is projected to reach 40% of the non-agricultural income after 20 years. These are outstanding debts that the non-agricultural sector has to pay back. In other words, the incidence of the targeted NQ_1 and F_1 would fall on the non-agricultural earners. In addition, interest payments on this debt cut into the income of non-agricultural earners. The targeted NQ_1 and F_1 can be shown to affect the interests of the industrial sector unfavorably in other ways too. Prosperity in the industrial sector requires a strongly growing agricultural output with an export surplus that can be used, among other things, to import investment goods for industrial growth. The projections indicate that, in spite of the higher agricultural output, the demand for agricultural consumption goods overexceeds its output with the result that net food imports (exports less imports) would rise from a value of $E_{(1+2)} = -2{,}541$ in the initial year to $-3{,}912$ in year 10 and $-7{,}918$ in year 20, thereby using up both the net industrial trade balance, E_3, and the foreign capital inflow, *FCF*.

The conclusion that can be drawn at this stage is that although in the BRP the welfare of peasants rises, this is small when compared to the gain of rich farmers, and more importantly, they have an unfavorable effect on the relative position of the otherwise politically very strong industrial sector as shown above. This would seem to be a sufficient reason why industrial leadership would not allow these specific projections to materialize. If the industrial leadership can be assumed to set up boundary conditions on such variables of interest to them as $(F_1 + F_2)$, Y_3, and $E_{(1+2)}$, the obtained projections would have most likely violated these boundaries. Results signal an accentuating *impasse.*

No doubt the significant changes in socio-political power which occurred in Chile in 1973 and thereafter are just too complex to be clarified or predicted by means of an exploratory model simulating the Frei and Allende regimes, but this much is evident: the simulations suggest that the stipulated land reforms would have implications that are politically unacceptable by the industrial leadership and would sooner than later be cut short, obstructed, or modified.

Given the above *impasse,* the object of the subsequent alternative policy simulations that we ran was to propose,adapt, and study in several steps more moderate strategies of agrarian reform that have a greater chance of achieving a future redistribution of wealth and income from rich to peasant farmers without undermining industrial interests. With the complexity of Chilean politics at the time, finding ways and means of securing this delicate balance appeared to be the central development issue. We report here on five policy simulations that were run, among others. Policy A is a less ambitious land redistribution and debt acquittal along the 1967 Agrarian Reform Law (ARL). Comparing: Targeted NQ_1 in year 20 in (ARL) = 0.6 (BRP). Targeted annual fall in F_1 in (ARL) = 0.3 (BRP).

Policy B adds to policy A credit advances, thus reducing $\iota_1, \iota_{12}. \iota_2, \iota_{32}$.

Policy C adds to policy B public investment to increase farm productivity, thus raising $\pi_1, \pi_2, \kappa_1, \kappa_1$.

Policy D adds to policy C a harmonized tax at a higher level: $\tau_1. = \tau_2$. The actual situation was discrimination against poor farmers and in favor of rich farmers $\tau_1 > \tau_2$.

Policy E adds to policy D higher agricultural wages, via raising ω_{21}.

Results in Table 4 show a persisting stalemate under policy simulations A (moderate land reform) and B (credit advances): a failing output and rising inequality in agriculture and a high financial liability of non-agriculture to agriculture. This indicates a helpless role for national policy in producing a coherent development pattern that satisfies the expectations of all actors. Among all policy runs, the combination of C (public investment to raise agricultural productivity) with E (higher agricultural wage rates) is the most promising policy package. Policy D (tax policy) does not improve on C or D. The combination of higher productivity and higher wages reinforces each other. The proposed package gives the highest levels obtained for the income of poor peasants as their share in the GDP doubles compared to BRP. Agricultural output, which is a very strategic variable in the Chilean context, is also highest under this simulated package. Results show that non-agricultural income appears not to be very sensitive to alternative strategies. On the other hand, the

Table 4. Initial year $t = 0$, basic run projections (BRP), and policy simulations for year $t = 20$.

		$t = 0$	BRP $t = 20$	Policy A	Policy B	Policy C	Policy D	Policy E
Income poor farmers	Y_1	783	2,231	1,537	1,647	3,378	3,367	5,234
Income rich farmers	Y_2	915	2,716	2,801	2,850	3,774	3,287	1,028
Income non-agriculture	Y_3	16,301	38,187	38,352	37,715	36,633	36,391	36,848
Gross Domestic Product GDP	$\Sigma_h Y_h$	17,999	43,134	42,690	42,212	43,785	43,585	43,110
Share poor in GDP	$Y_1/\Sigma_h Y_h$	0.044	0.052	0.036	0.039	0.077	0.077	0.121
Output agriculture	$X_{(1+2)}$	2,416	4,637	4,190	4,515	8,247	8,165	8,145
Output non-agriculture	X_3	30,981	75,784	75,363	74,185	71,496	71,203	70,444
Net exports agriculture	$E_{(1+2)}$	−2,541	−7198	−7,416	−7,283	−3,947	−3,934	−4,258
Net exports non-agriculture	E_3	2,707	4,564	4,782	4,649	1,313	1,300	1,625
Financial liability	$F_1 + F_2$	235	8,177	7,676	8,328	6,165	4,638	2,547

findings show that financial liabilities of the non-agricultural sector — another strategic variable in the Chilean context — reach their lowest levels under this simulated package. The combination of higher agricultural productivity and higher wages for poor farmers appears to be the most favorable scenario for solving the Chilean agrarian development impasse. Besides, this scenario may need the least effort to achieve in view of long-term free labor market forces which tend to raise wage rates with rises in labor productivity.

6. Concluding Remarks

Incorporation of the socio-political structure in economic models introduces more realism in evaluating policymaking. The approach followed here to incorporate and specify the socio-polity is realistic, simple, and flexible. Six remarks can be added as ways of elaborating on the approach:

First, the division of the total population into groups with common interests and incorporating their relative strength brings more realism to policymaking. The relative strengths of interest groups determine who leads and who follows and, subsequently, the socio-political profile of the nation. Different socio-political profiles of power distribution represent different model closures, yield different model structures, and show different solution sets over time. When predicted performances are compared with observed ones in a particular economy, it is possible to reveal the socio-political structure of that particular economy. In this respect, it is interesting to quote a supporting statement made later in Taylor (1990), ch. 2: "...Setting (model) closure is impossible unless class structures and economic power relationships have already been defined."

Second, the procedure of constructing first an under-determinate model consisting of economic relations with an n number of degrees of freedom and second, making the model determinate by fixing n unknowns belonging to the leader is a handy simplification of a complex problem.

Third, the translation of the objectives and desires of a leader group into numerical targets is problematic. Lacking substantive quantitative studies of this kind, we were inclined to use some approximate procedures for India and Chile. The setting of precise targets is nowhere required, however. In fact, it can even be useful to inflate the targets of the leader group and study the effectiveness of measures under extreme conditions. There is perhaps another reason why the targets of the leader groups can better be overrated: for the actual implementation of most government measures, the cooperation of the leader group is necessary, i.e. in the Indian context, and to assure this cooperation, a premium on the targets of the leader group may prove to be necessary.

Fourth, the impact of one and the same government measure may vary under different socio-political leaderships. However, if the impact of certain measures is found to be constant (or ranks consistently high in terms of effectiveness), irrespective of the socio-political system in which the measures function, this would indicate that such measures may form a policy core in all situations. The approach can then be employed as a simulation method to find the more basic policy measures, in which case, difficulties that may be encountered in identifying the real leaders or in fixing the predetermined values for their welfare variables become secondary.

Fifth, the approach permits testing the feasibility of reformist policies in controversial regimes. If, in spite of functioning within the boundaries set by the leader group(s), reformist policies are still not feasible, this can be considered as an indication that there is something wrong with the foundation, in which case a deeper change in the foundation is necessary, as was shown for Chile.

Sixth, the particular model closure demonstrated here can be called a fixed closure as it represents a situation where the dominant actor group fixes its target(s). It is possible to adapt the model to flexible closures. For instance, each actor group can be modeled to maximize its preferred targets within a bounded range, with greater weights for more dominant actors. The government can be modeled as the arbiter in reaching a bargained solution. The government may then maximize a common aim whose benefits go to all groups, i.e. national product, subject to technical and behavioral constraints of the model and the bargaining constraints.

In closing, it can be stated that few governments (and political parties) are likely to sponsor models that explicitly incorporate power structures. The utility of the type of models presented here lies more in their exploratory signaling of reform deadlocks and exploratory search for feasible policies.

Endnotes

1. Myrdal (1968) presented in "Asian Drama" a pessimistic and a rebuffing perspective in which development planning, plans, and targets did not matter and in which the benefits of economic development went primarily to the wealthy and the feudal landlords.

2. Cohen (1978): Agrarian Structures and Agrarian Reform, Kluwer, Boston. See also Cohen (1981) and Cohen (1977). I am greatly indebted to Jan Tinbergen for giving me the opportunity to undertake the study. Thanks go also to ex-colleagues for their useful comments, among whom are F. Bishay, H. Bos, P. Cornelisse, L. Mennes, J. Sandee, A. Waarts, as well as S. Chakravarty, who was visiting professor in Rotterdam in 1975–1976.
3. The model does not specify explicitly the cash held, but it can be derived as a residual from the following identity: $F1 = (\text{cash held}) + \phi_{21}F_2$.
4. See previous endnote.
5. In the Harrod–Domar production function, the minimal of labor and capital supply determines production. If labor is assumed in abundance, (incremental) capital becomes the constraining factor that determined (the growth of) the output. This setup was a standard use in early models for developing countries and in UN modeling of the first, second, and third development decade's policy programs.
6. In eqs. (2) and (9), the maintenance of agricultural gross production at the stipulated levels X_1 and X_2 would require investments I_1 and I_2 along the lines of a simple Harrod–Domar production function. This combines with the input–output technology that enters in eqs. (18), (20), and (21) to give a two-level production technology, as is common in economy-wide models.
7. It was empirically handy to make use of given projected values for the foreign capital flow FCF; this led to investment I_{33} being determined in the savings−investment balance, eq. (24). When I_{33} is then fed into the product market balance (non-agriculture), eq. (23), solution for net exports (non-agriculture), E_3 is obtained. The same outcomes could be secured if instead the ordering is reversed: Take E_3 as given, which is then fed into eq. (23) to give I_{33}; that is then entered in the savings−investment balance, eq. (24), thus solving for an endogenous FCF. Most of the models in this book follow the latter, where FCF is made endogenous. In this respect, the difference between this model and the others is only formal.
8. In a circumscribed and interdependent accounting system of n rows, knowledge of $n - 1$ rows is sufficient to solve the system. The nth row is not required and is left out. Correspondingly, Walras law states that in general equilibrium, specification of market clearance for $n - 1$ markets is sufficient, and the nth market clearance can be dropped, this being automatically guaranteed.
9. The causal ordering of a system can be decomposed along the lines of Simon (1953). Endogenous variables of the first order are those which are influenced by parameters (and pre-determined variables) and/or by each other mutually. Endogenous variables of the second order are those which are influenced only by parameters (and predetermined variables) and/or endogenous variables of the first and second orders, etc.
10. Of course, it is an oversimplification to maintain that the peasantry do not resist rich farmers in India. There are regions where growing awareness has slowly and steadily eroded dominance of landlords. Agrarian studies in a vast country like India require a multi-regional analysis as suggested by Joshi (1975, p. 96).

Part III

Goals: Growth with Redistribution

Chapter 5

Growth with Redistribution in the Long Run

1. Introduction

It was argued in Chapter 1 that if there has to be a choice for an overall primary goal in development, this choice should be formulated as growth with redistribution, GWR. Development goals and policies for developing countries aiming at promoting both economic growth and redistribution of endowments among the population at large have been the focus of many governments and scholars. Our focus on the twin goals of growth with redistribution and on policies that promote growth with redistribution is shared by many pioneer economists writing on development including Tinbergen and Sen, and contemporary economists as manifested in Stiglitz agenda for inclusive development, in Stiglitz (2016). Other thoughts in the same direction are found in Berg *et al.* (2018) and Basu and Stiglitz (2016), and Piketty (2017).

There are nevertheless some subtle differences between our approach and those of the above-mentioned contributions. Because of possible trade-offs between growth and redistribution in the early stages of development, we tend to view (a) progressive redistribution as subsequent to growth in time perspective and (b) progressive redistribution of endowments rather than incomes as necessary and inevitable for assuring sustainable growth in the context of both developing and developed countries. In the long run, progressive redistribution of endowments and raising up well-balanced capability levels of all human resources are necessary for sustainable growth. We shall elaborate on these aspects as we proceed in this chapter.

Achievement of the twin goals is not as simple as it looks since growth and redistributions have a complex interrelationship of trade-offs which change over time. This is evident in the empirically verified Kuznets curve which depicts that in the early stages of economic development, economic growth (context A) is usually accompanied by some regressive income redistribution and only at later stages of economic development (context B) the picture reverses, thus allowing economic growth and positive redistribution to take place.

This chapter digs deeper into the relationship between twin goals of growth with redistribution. Section 2 reviews the rationale for GWR. Section 3 discusses the shift in the trade-offs between growth and redistribution in the early and later stages of development, i.e. stage A and stage B. Section 4 introduces a measurable performance indicator of GWR, i.e. the inequality to growth (ITG) ratio. Section 5 quantifies the ITG ratio in the development context (stage A), making use of country data of China and India. Section 6 formulates and analyzes the growth with redistribution trade-off in the context of the welfare state (stage B), making use of the SAM as an economy-wide model. The European countries treated, for which comparative SAMs were readily available, are Germany, Hungary, Italy, and the Netherlands. Section 7 discusses policy options for achieving sustained GWR over the long run. Section 8 ends with concluding remarks.

This chapter aims to develop, model, and explain the trade-offs for the distinct contexts of A and B; and subsequently quantify and analyze results for both contexts, as will be simulated for Asian and European countries, respectively. The modeling of the trade-offs and their quantification should serve to identify countries that are more able than others in minimizing the conflict between income equality and economic growth, and where possible how this is done. Results will be useful in achieving less costly and speedier development paths.

2. Rationales for the Goal of Growth with Redistribution (GWR)

What are the rationales for formulating the primary goal of economic development as growth with redistribution? There are at least six reasoning approaches that draw on economics which lead to the same conclusion and reenforce its significance. The six approaches can be titled as: (1) theorems of welfare theory, (2) the law of diminishing marginal utility, (3) theories and empirics of economic growth accounting in terms of inputs and productivity, (4) theories and empirics of human capital implying GWR, (5) interdependence dynamics in social systems implying GWR and (6) theories and empirics on growth and distribution in the long run as reflected by the Kuznets curve.

The first rationale proceeds from welfare economics that states that any Pareto-optimal state is an equilibrium for some initial distribution of endowments. The competitive market equilibrium is by no means optimal in the absolute sense because the outcome depends entirely on the agreed upon original satisfising distribution of endowments. While it is very complex to reach agreement on the satisficing distribution, it is logical to presume that in cases where there is maldistribution of endowments, more people would rationally agree to a more progressive redistribution of endowments.

The second rationale relates to the well-known phenomenon in economics that the marginal utility of an additional dollar decreases with more accumulated wealth. This concept is known as the law of diminishing marginal utility; and it implies that a progressive redistribution of endowments culminating in a redistribution of dollars would increase the total utility of all the generated dollars.

The third rationale is based on economic growth accounting which emphasizes the significant contribution of the growth in factor productivity as compared to the growth in factor inputs. Rise in factor productivity is primarily the extensive and intensive upgrading of skills and technology which in essence is the enrichment of labor, and the population at large, with greater human capital endowments. This is equivalent to a progressive redistribution of skill endowments among the population; and a demonstration of how progressive redistribution of skill endowments enhances economic growth. The next chapter will examine empirics of growth accounting by development region.

The fourth rationale views the mechanisms for the contribution of human capital to economic growth as basically the extension and progressive redistribution of educational and skill endowments to a lesser endowed population, that becomes more productive, and allows more economic growth that can be partly invested again in expanding human capital. The mechanism corresponds with goal of growth with redistribution. Human resource development and policies are extensively treated in later chapters.

The fifth rationale relates to the dual economy, and can be explained using two propositions. First proposition: A person does not choose to be born or not. Any born person has basic living entitlements. These entitlements are relative to the norms in the concerned community. It is the obligation of the community to meet the community's norms of basic living entitlements. Second proposition: Due to normal distributions of abilities at the personal level and normal distributions of efficiencies at the activity level (firm, sector, and location), there are always(H) high-earnings persons with high abilities working and earning in activity segments with high productivity, in contrast to (L) low-earnings persons with lower abilities working in activity segments with low productivity, minimal productivity, and sometimes zero productivity or not working/earning at all. It follows from the first and second propositions that continuous growth of H is necessary to permit redistribution of part of the growth outcome to (L) so as to catch up with the relative norms of basic living entitlements. In similar ways, the upgrading of L to higher levels would feed H and assure its continuous growth.

The sixth rationale relates to the Kuznets curve which postures that while in the early stages of economic development higher economic growth is likely to associate with regressive income, wealth and endowment distributions, this reverses at later stages into a scenario of growth with progressive redistribution. This rationale will be treated at more length in the next section.

Next to these six approaches that draw on economic research, there are fundamental contributions from other social sciences that that support the rationale of

GWR, and that can easily surpass the economic contributions in terms of significance, and which go as far back as K. Marx, J.J. Rousseau, R. Owen, and J. S. Mill. It is sufficient to mention here the sociological alienation of societal factions which rises with increasing income and wealth disparities and which may end up in breaking up society. Similarly, political unrest and violence are characteristic features of regressive distributions of income and wealth.

The development goal of GWR is especially relevant for the developing economy given its dualist character where higher productivity activities (modern sectors) and their high-income earning agents prosper significantly, while the low-productivity activities (mostly informal sectors) and their low-income dependent agents move very slowly, are stable or some may fall down in terms of well-being. The duality is apparent in many forms: absentee landowners (with rural and urban residences) versus rural peasant workers, high-productivity urban sectors in industry and services versus low-productivity self-employed informal enterprises, and high-productivity and well-salaried professionals in private and public services versus low-income (less productive) manual workers. Furthermore, there are poverty households with no income earnings.

It is important to underline that the goal of GWR is not only logical and necessary for the (dualistic) developing economy, but GWR is also applicable for the developed economy which equally contains segments that can be denoted by H and L, for the simple reasons that the normal distribution of personal abilities and activity productivities which generates H and L are general laws that are applied and are common to all peoples and activities. The very quick advance of hi-tech and digitalized activities in developed economies is not evenly spread over all segments, resulting in an increased gap between the H and L segments in developed economies.

The rationale for GWR as the primary goal does not exclude the relevance of secondary goals such as employment, the satisfaction of basic needs, and various aspects of well-being. But there is an essential difference between primary and secondary goals. An improvement in the primary goal leads automatically to improvements in the secondary goals. We refer here to Chapter 10 which displays an economy-wide model for Korea that contains a large number of secondary goals. Structuring the model along the causal ordering premises of Simon (1953) showed that the goal of earned income (and its summation to give the GDP) precedes other goals and determines them directly or indirectly. It is logical that development policy proceeds from primary to secondary phases, which makes the evaluation of growth and distribution goals ahead of secondary goals. If the outcomes of implementing the primary goal of GWR are considered as insufficient in meeting the secondary goals, additional measures can be implemented in a supplementary round to satisfy the secondary goals. See Chapter 10 with the application to Korea.

3. Empirics of Growth and Distribution in the Long Run

Turning to development histories and empirics, the twin development goals of growth and redistribution have a complex empirical relationship over time that is named after its discoverer, the Kuznets curve. Kuznets (1955) showed what seems to be an unescapable trade-off in the early phases of economic development whereby growth take-off is accompanied by regressive distribution. Only after a certain threshold in economic development is passed, then other processes enter the picture and allow for accomplishing growth with progressive distribution.

The inverted U form of the Kuznets curve is a suitable starting point for elaborations on the upside and downside of the curve. The left-hand upward slope applies for development settings, where increasing income inequality coincides with high economic growth. Call it stage A; the right-hand downward slope applies for the advanced stages of economic development, where greater income equality is accompanied by income transfers, greater public shares, and lower economic growth. Call it stage B.

What are the economic processes which determine the upward slope of the Kuznets curve in the early development stage (developing country) and the processes that determine the downward slope for the later development stage (developed country)? The generally noted association of rapid economic growth and an increase in income inequality during the development phase (stage A) can be explained predominantly in terms of purely *market mechanisms of demand and supply* of production activities with high H and low L productivity levels (think of agriculture and traditional sectors versus industry and modern sectors along the dualistic model of Lewis) and subsequently the factor suppliers to these activities. Working in differentiated activities with H and L productivities, the workers have also differentiated productivities and earnings termed H and L. With economic development, there is greater demand for H activities and H workers, which raises the share of income earned by H. In contrast, with economic development, there is a lesser rise in the demand for L activities and L workers, which diminishes the share of income earned by L. Hence, the distribution of earnings in stage A shows regressive tendencies. The above is the standard economic theory that states that economic growth over more years sets into motion demand shifts and resource reallocations from low-productivity activities (L) to high-productivity activities (H). The result is that earnings of factors of production (labor and capital) engaged in L lose, while those entering H gain, in relative terms. With inelastic magnitudes of factor inputs in L, more economic growth for H is bound to create more inequality in the primary income distribution. As usual, there are mitigating factors that can intervene and affect supply and demand. Demographic surge increases labor supply in L, depresses their earnings, and accentuates income inequality. While if the scope of economic growth is manifold and diversified in terms of high and medium productivity activities, then these can absorb L labor, raise the overall earnings of L labor, and decrease income inequality.

How empirically valid is the phenomenon of the upward slope? Many empirical tests of the left-hand portion of the Kuznets curve were applied to developing economies, using various indicators of income inequality and of the pace of economic development. While empirics tend to support the upward slope for many developing countries, they do not have full unanimity; see among others for various appraisals and tests Anand and Kanbur (1993), Kanbur (2000), Sala-i-Martin (2002), and Garth (2006).

This book contains data on economic growth and income distribution for 36 developing countries (6 countries by 6 regions) over three periods of 10 years each, giving a total of about 140 observations (data are not available for all countries for earlier years). The data are displayed in the following chapter. We find that the growth and distribution data for earlier years, that is, before 2000, aligned more with the upward part of the Kuznets curve implying regressive income redistribution with economic growth. But for later years, the exceptions increased, thus defying the upward part of the Kuznets curve and confirming reductions in the Gini index as the countries developed. The reversed change in some developing countries of the trade-off as development progresses can still be held as consistent with the Kuznets curve as the concerned countries advance in their economic development and move from the upward part toward the downward part of the curve.

The mixed empirical evidence on the upward slope of the Kuznets curve does not invalidate the theory that resource reallocation from low- to high-productivity activities in economic development shifts the income distribution from low- to high-productivity earners. At best, development empirics that contradict the hypothesis are explainable in terms of mitigating factors that redirect the outcome between inequality and development, which would apply to some countries but not all. Moreover, some developing countries were able to shorten the time path appreciably toward the turning point. Besides, as the developing economy advances along the upward slope, the trade-offs are bound to reduce allowing for the accompaniment of economic growth with progressive redistribution, as was just mentioned above and as will be shown in Chapter 6.

Proceeding further to the downward slope of the Kuznets curve, this is stage B where the country can be classified as developed and typical of the welfare state. In principle, the above same economic mechanisms, albeit in other forms, work in the same direction of bringing about economic growth with an increase in inequality in the primary distribution of income. But motivated by social and political considerations, state collective actions intervene in the form of publicly administered substantial income transfers to non-earners and low-income earners, to reverse the rise in income inequality that accompanies economic growth in the primary markets that remunerate H and L factors of production. Redistribution policies in the welfare state are usually formulated in terms of the income transfers

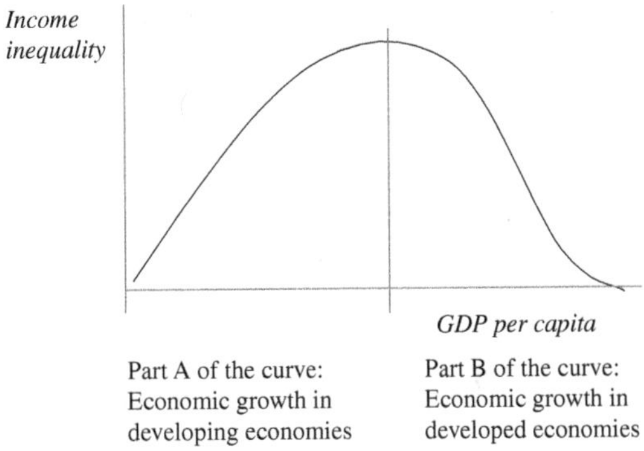

Figure 1. Split-up of the *U*-turned Kuznets curve in parts A and B.

required to erase the rise in earning inequalities and the *foregone potential* economic growth due to the income transfer.

Although there is empirical evidence that in stage B redistribution is accompanied by slower economic growth (which implies a trade-off and a zero-sum game), the trade-off and the zero-sum game are not imminent. The redistribution in stage *B* can be designed in ways that raise endowments in the *L* low-productivity segment that trickle up to the H high-productivity segment and enhance mutual and sustained overall growth. That is why we speak of *foregone potential* economic growth because what matters is the design of the redistribution, and this can be done in ways that bring about a potential oncoming sustainable and higher economic growth. There is a famous statement by Tinbergen that fits with the above thoughts and can be quoted here: "(Re)distribution brings growth".

The use of the term trade-offs in our context can be confusing as it was first used by Okun (1975) to express an indicator which evaluates the gain in equality against the loss in the GDP, following a tax levy on the rich that is paid to the poor. The instrument and the time perspectives of our GWR strategies go beyond tax transfers in one or the other year. The standpoint of the GWR perspective is that there are development strategies which secure mutual gains in win-win strategies rather than trade-offs that assume zero-sum games. Besides, our focus is on growth and not the GDP level. To avoid confusion and complement language use, we shall equally speak of trade-offs and win-win as applicable.

4. Measurement of the Inequality to Growth (ITG) Ratio

This section formulates the inequality to growth (ITG) ratio which is a performance indicator of the increase in income inequality that is created by economic growth in the early phases of economic development (this corresponds with the upward part of the inverted Kuznets curve in Figure 1). The ITG ratio is defined as the absolute change in the Gini index between t and $t - 1$ divided by the average growth rate of the GDP per capita in t and $t - 1$. As an alternative, if we use the relative change in the Gini index in t over $t - 1$ in the nominator instead of the absolute change in the Gini index, the ratio becomes an elasticity measure of the impact of growth on inequality. We shall focus on absolute form since the alternative form is less comprehendible, and anyhow the change in the Gini index and the growth rate of GDP per capita are both expressed in percentage points.

$$\text{ITG ratio} = (\text{change in average Gini index between periods } t \text{ and } t-1)/ \\ (\text{average growth of GDP per capita per annum in periods } t \text{ and } t-1) \quad (1)$$

The ITG ratio computed for a specific developing country and for several periods is meant to assess how far the country has to go before reaching or bypassing the turning point in the inverted Kuznets curve. For the developing country in the development phase, the value of the ratio is expected to be much above 1 in early periods as significant inequalities are caused by takeoff growth. Normally speaking, the ratio diminishes gradually hereafter to reach ITG ratio $= 1$. This would mean that the country, in the periods concerned, experiences equal increases in inequality and growth and would thus lie exactly along the turning point in Figure 1. Values of ITG ratio < 1 would position the country in the downward part of the curve. This is the part that characterizes developed economies where economic growth is likely to be accompanied by diminished income inequality.

Assessment of the journey trajectory and the remaining distance toward reaching the turning point is crucial in monitoring the pace and prospects of economic development. If the ITG ratio keeps increasing over time or becomes sticky at high values, this can be a sign that the country is in trouble of being caught in a spiral trap of more inequality and less growth, or a stagnant standstill in both. Such situations often lead to socio-political instabilities and civil disorder that can eliminate economic growth for years and postpone the economic development process until the system and its institutions are overhauled. By the same token, an assessment of the ITG ratio for the country concerned that shows a falling ratio is a sign that the country in question is proceeding successfully along the upward slope and that the country is likely to pass some time in the future through the turning point and make the transformation from developing to developed.

5. Application of the ITG Ratio in the Development Context: China and India

What are the prospects of a specific developing country traveling across the upward slope and passing through the turning point? The upward slope does not tell how long it takes for a developing country before the plateau and turning points are reached. The technical and educational upgrading of the labor force toward higher levels of productivity and availability of opportunities for their remunerative employment is generally believed to be prerequisites for making the turn in the inequality–growth relationship. While some developing countries have crossed the turning point, others are on the way to do that, and still others may take a very long time to do that, to the extent that lying across the upward slope becomes a stationary state. This is the case where income inequality becomes institutionally strengthened under the influence of special interests, leading to a stagnation of economic development. Why is it important to ask the above question and try to answer it? Ultimately, realization of the transition would require a swift economic development process within stable and sustainable social and political settings. While these issues are highly complex and least predictable, it can be logically proposed that in situations where the trade-offs between growth and equality are within tolerably experienced fair values, the risk of social and political instability is the least. When the inequality costs of growth benefits are excessive and unfair, the risks of instability tend to mount. Achieving incremental reductions in the inequality growth ratio over time is essential for the sustained development of the social system. Convergence in the economic welfare of agents belonging to the same national economic system is a necessary condition, since agents, rightly or wrongly and justified or not justified, do compare their lots with the lots of others. And if the gaps in living go beyond some reference range, agents will be inclined to object, voice, or exit. The result is that the sustained development of the social system is challenged and is at risk.

The economic history of developing countries included cases of countries and periods when ITG was excessively high and rising, leading to fragile socio-political environments and weak economic development performances. South Africa and Brazil have gone through lengthy periods of this kind. Recently, they are joined by Mexico and Venezeula experiencing high ITG, as will be seen in Chapter 6. Here, the focus will be on the two leading countries of China and India, showing their performance regarding ITG. Table 1 gives values of the Gini index g, GDP growth per capita y, and calculation of the ITG ratio for the two countries over several periods.

Probably, China has had the highest decades-long economic growth ever recorded. Table 1 shows an annual growth rate of GDP per capita in real terms of about 9% for three decades. At the same time, moving from a state ownership system with a relatively equitable income distribution in 1980 to a mixed market and open economy with significant reallocations of resources and rewards led to significant shifts of income distribution in favor of earners in high-productivity activities at the cost of the rest. Concentration of income in the richer portions of the population as indicated by the Gini index, g, has increased in the period between 1980 and 2000 by 21 points, compared to other countries in EAP, i.e.

Table 1. The ITG ratio in China and India.

	y = Average annual growth in GDP per capita, percent in constant prices			*g = Gini index, percent*			*ITG* = $(g_t - g_{t-1})/0.5$ $(y_t + y_{t-1})$	
	Col. 1	Col. 2	Col. 3	Col. 4	Col. 5	Col. 6	Col. 7	Col. 8
	1981–1990	1991–2000	2001–2012	1981–1990	1991–2000	2001–2012	1981–2000	1991–2012
China	7.8	8.7	9.4	25.7	40.3	42.4	1.77	0.23
India	3.6	3.8	5.4	32.1	35.0	33.6	0.78	−0.30

Source: Col.1 to 6 from http://devdata.worldbank.org/query. Col. 7= (Col. 5 – Col. 4)/(Col. 1+ Col. 2)/2. Col 8= (Col. 6 – Col. 5)/(Col. 2+ Col. 3)/2.

5 points. Computation of the ITG ratio over three decades permits making a balanced judgment on the transition of China. China had a very high ITG ratio over the two decades of the eighties and nineties, reaching 1.77, a scenario which fits fully with the upward slope of the Kuznets curve. The ITG ratio falls down in the next decade of 2000–2012 to 0.23. This significant downfall of the ITG ratio strongly suggests that the critical threshold of an inequality–growth trade-off for avoiding disruptive crises has been already passed with success.

In the case of India, the range and the pace of the increase in growth and inequality were much smaller. The annual growth of the GDP per capita in India over the 20 years of 1981–2000 was about 3.6–3.8%. The Gini index increased from 32.1 to 35.0 points, a rise of 2.9 points, in the same period of 1981–2000. Together, these result in an ITG ratio of 0.78 for 1981–2000. The positive ITG fits with the upward slope. In the next decade of 2001–2012, GDP per capita annual growth rises to 5.4% while the Gini index is reduced in 1991–2000 to 33.6 points, giving together a reduced ITG ratio of −0.3. This means that the previously observed trade-off of the past periods has turned into a win-win, indicating that India is proceeding along the inequality growth curve smoothly and in the right direction.

In summary, a comparison between China and India with respect to the trade-off measure would support the statement that China's pattern of growth was realized with a more negative redistribution than the case of India's growth pattern that so far has been realized with less negative redistribution. The calculated ITG ratios for China for the two periods are very high at 1.77 and 0.77, compared to India at the lower rates of 0.78 and −0.30. The much higher ratios in China are in part due to the transition from the state ownership system to a mixed state–market system. Most importantly, in both cases, the ITG fell over time and is nearing <1 in China and is already negative for India. Both countries seem to have passed the critical test of balancing growth with inequality in sustainable and stable societies and polities and are on their way to reach and/or go beyond the turning point in the direction of stage B and along the downward slope.

6. The GWR Analysis for Developed Countries

This section deals with the downward slope in the Kuznets curve, which presumably applies more to the developed country context. The downward slope is characterized by a slower growth of the GDP with a fall in income inequality. What are the mechanisms behind these tendencies?

First, the market-driven economic mechanisms that were described above for the development context are fully active in the developed context as well. Techno-economic growth and change push higher-productivity activities and their earners at the cost of the lower-productivity activities and their earners, thus leading to an increase in income inequality in the primary distribution of earned incomes.

In this respect, the economic process in developing and developed economies is the same and shares in common that, ceteris paribus, and conditioned by the extent to which demand and supply for activities and factors of production are elastic, economic growth has as a side effect a skewer primary income distribution.

Second, and more specifically for the developed country that has become richer and in some sense a welfare economy, the skew primary income distributive results of the market-driven economic forces are not left unattended. The state takes actions to reduce inequality in a secondary redistribution via taxes and transfers. More inequality is considered a demerit good in the sense that it reduces social cohesion and increases social unrest, thereby weakening society. Alesina *et al.* (2001) find that inequality negatively affects happiness in Europe, though less so in the United States. Because a more inequitable income distribution is considered a demerit good in the welfare state, parliaments and governments implement measures of minimum earnings and employment protection to affect the primary income distribution positively and apply substantive income transfers to avoid fallbacks of disadvantaged groups in the secondary income distribution. There are two possible interpretations for the shift in public policy toward income inequality at later stages of development. It can be interpreted as a conscious change in collective preferences that has become necessary over time or that the developed economy has become rich enough to afford undertaking the income transfers to reduce income inequality. There are similar shifts in public policy in other areas at later stages of development. There is evidence supporting the claim that the relation between environmental health pollutants and economic development shows the same inverted U-shaped curve, the so-called environmental Kuznets curve, cf. Dasgupta *et al.* This phenomenon may apply to other aspects of social welfare that gain priority at the cost of economic growth in the context of the welfare state.

There is a trade-off as reflected in the negative relationship between a bigger public share (necessitated by income transfers to avoid worsening income inequalities) and higher-economic growth. This has been empirically tested in developed economies, and the negative relationship is not in doubt, cf. Cohen (2009). But this need not mean that specific developed countries are unable to escape this trade-off.

It is obvious that analysis of the equality growth relation in the welfare state involves economy-wide interactions with an explicit role in government policy. Short of a dynamic model of the economy, the social accounting matrix (SAM) is convertible into a static economy-wide model that implies dynamics and that can serve the purpose. Chapter 7 will describe the model in detail. The SAM displays in matrix form for a particular year the actually carried national accounts transactions between the main actors in the economy: sectors of activity, factors of production, receiving and spending agents such as households of various types, firms, government, and the rest of the world. Transactions cover production, income, consumption, investment, and savings, among others. SAM includes entries for government taxes and other receipts, as well as sectoral injections and income transfers to households. SAM includes also entries of imports, exports, and transfers to and from the rest of the world.

Assuming proportional relationships for the cells in terms of their column totals, an SAM coefficient matrix, S, is obtained which links the endogenous part of the economy denoted by y (that is, growth and distribution) to the exogenous part denoted by x (this is spending by government and rest of the world). The system can thus be described in matrix form as $y - Sy = x$. By inversion of the S matrix, the model generates SAM multipliers, denoted by M, giving the impact of a simulated change in an x variable on the y variables, as in eq. (2).

$$y = (I - S)^{-1}x = Mx \tag{2}$$

The SAM multipliers give the final result of a simulated change in x traveling through the circular flow of the whole economy and thus impacting the y variables. The model generates many multipliers, expressed as Mij, whereby j stands for the exogenous stimulus and i for the endogenously impacted. We focus here on those in Table 2. For instance, Maa tells the effect of a unit injection in economic activities on the output growth of economic activities. Mpa and Mra give the impact on the primary incomes of poorer and richer households, respectively. In contrast, Mpa, Mpp, and Mrp show the corresponding impacts if the injection takes the form of an income transfer to poorer households. These six parameters are sufficient to construct the trade-off between the first-column policies of economic growth versus the second-column policies of income redistribution.

The construction of an SAM for a specific country can be a very lengthy exercise, and there are not many available for countries for more years. Besides, for a comparative analysis of the trade-offs as is intended in this chapter, the SAMs employed for the countries concerned should be basically comparable. The choice of countries and periods for the current analysis is thus restricted by the availabilities of comparative SAMs for Hungary (1990), Italy (1984), the Netherlands (1987), and Germany (1984). These four SAMs are reported upon in Cohen (2002), where more details on each are included. We have applied further compression of these SAMs and their results in the context of this chapter. All four SAMs divided

Table 2. Relevant SAM multipliers for studying growth and distribution in the welfare state.

Endogenous \ Exogenous	1. Injected spending in sectoral activities *a*	2. Income transfers to poorer households *p*
Effect on output growth of sectoral activities *a*	*Maa*	*Mpa*
Effect on primary incomes of household groups, of which		
Poorer *p*	*Mpa*	*Mpp*
Richer *r*	*Mra*	*Mpr*

household groups into 10 income deciles groups. We have summed deciles 1–5 to give the poorer income earning group, denoted by p, and deciles 6–10 are summed to give the richer earning group denoted by r.

The results summarized in Table 3 show that a one-unit stimulus in economic activities is predicted to result in output growth effects that are highest in Italy 3.89, followed by Germany 3.45, Hungary 3.01, and the Netherlands 2.29. In general, the size of the multipliers of an inverted matrix is relatively small if the exogenously assumed part of the economy is relatively high. It is noted that government and ROW are stipulated as exogenous in the SAM model. For instance, in the Netherlands, the combined shares of government and ROW in the economy are among the highest in Europe, which explains the low size of the output multiplier.

Besides the output growth effects, of special interest here are the predicted earned income effects and their distribution on poor and rich households, *Mpa* and *Mra*. In particular, how does the predicted distribution compare to the actually *observed* distribution of income on poor and rich households *Dp* and *Dr*? These parameters are displayed in the second and third parts of Table 3. In the fourth part, a simple division of *Mpa* by *Dp* and of *Mra* by *Dr* gives a measure of the multiplier distributive bias, MDB, of activity injections. For values of $MDB < 1$, > 1, and $= 1$, there are positive, negative, and neutral redistributive effects. For example, taking the poorer half in Germany, a predicted multiplier share of 19% and an actual share of 26.5% gives an *MDB* of 0.717, which is an indication of a regressive income bias. In contrast, the rich can get richer as indicated by *MDB* of 1.1035. All four countries show the same predicted association of economic growth with a regressive primary income distribution.

That, nevertheless, the actual income distribution in all four countries shows more equality than the SAM predicted multiplier distribution is due to the positive effect of annually repeated secondary income transfers to the poorer half of the population, usually concentrated in the first and second deciles. The SAM

Table 3. SAM multipliers and their implications for growth-related increases in income inequality.

	Formula	Hungary	Italy	Netherlands	Germany
Multiplier gains from injection in activities *a*					
Output growth of activities *a*	Maa	3.01	3.89	2.29	3.45
Earned income of all households *h*	Mah	0.77	1.50	0.85	1.32
Earned income of poorer group *p*	Mpa	0.22	0.37	0.16	0.25
Earned income of richer group *r*	Mra	0.55	1.13	0.69	1.07
Share in multiplier gains %					
Poorer group	Mpa%	29	25	19	19
Richer group	Mra%	71	75	81	81
Poorer/richer	Mpa%/Mra%	0.41	0.33	0.23	0.23
Share in observed income distribution					
Poorer group	Dp%	34.1	30.2	28.3	26.5
Richer group	Dr%	66.0	69.9	71.7	73.4
Poorer/richer	Dp%/Dr%	0.5167	0.4329	0.3947	0.3610
Simulated fall in poorer/richer income shares: SAM multipliers — observed income distribution shares					
Equality gap to be recovered by income transfers, proportion	EGR= (Dp%/Dr%) − (Mpa%/Mra%)	0.1096	0.1014	0.1617	0.1265
Measure of distribution bias, MDB					
Poorer group index	Mpa%/D p%	0.8475	0.8245	0.6678	0.7170
Richer group index	Mra%/D r%	1.0758	1.0773	1.1311	1.1035

framework allows computing the equality gap that occurs in the primary phase of income distribution, which is normally recovered by income transfers during the secondary phase of income redistribution. The equality gap recovered, denoted by EGR, is defined in eq. (3).

$$\text{EGR} = (Dp\%/Dr\%) - (Mpa\%/Mra\%) \tag{3}$$

While EGR indicates the predicted higher inequality in the primary income distribution, it represents the improvement in the secondary income distribution due to implementation of income transfers and is thus the appropriate nominator for measuring equality gains in the measurement of the trade-off in the developed economy, i.e. welfare state. Table 3 shows EGR to vary between 10% and 16% for the four countries examined, in the following order: Hungary, Italy, Germany, and the Netherlands being highest at 16%. It is logical and interesting to note that in the real world, the countries with the higher EGR are those that redistribute more and have also higher public shares so as to execute greater income transfers. For example, *EGR* is higher, transfers are relatively higher, and government share in national income in the Netherlands is higher than in Hungary, Italy, and Germany.

To close the emerging inequality governments, initiate and sustain income transfers to the poorer portion of the population, and thus allow the countries to move swiftly along the second portion of the Kuznets curve, i.e. the downward slope, manifesting thus a recovery in equality as the country grows, though that growth may be bound to be lower in the case of the transfer than without transfer. As was stated earlier, when the reallocative, disincentive, and administrative aspects of the redistributive income transfers are taken into account, the economic growth potential after the redistribution could be less than the potential without the redistribution. There is, thus, a trade-off between income transfers to sustain equality and economic growth that characterizes secondary transfers in the welfare state.

The SAM multiplier analysis can be extended to calculate the required z units to recover the equality gap as formulated in eq. (4.1). The equation requires that the ratio of the sum of the multiplier effect of the one unit injection in economic activities on the poor group in the first round and of the z units of income transfers to the poor group in the second round, represented by $(Mpa + z^* Mpp)$, to the sum of the above effects for the rich group, represented by $(Mra + z^* Mrp)$, should be equal to the ratio of the actual incomes of poor to rich. By shifting terms, the value of z is determined in eq. (4.2).

$$(Mpa + z^* Mpp)/(Mra + z^* Mrp) = (Dp\%/Dr\%) \tag{4.1}$$

$$z = ((Dp\%/Dr\%)^* Mra - Map)/\ (Mpp - (Dp\%/Dr\%)^* Mpr)) \tag{4.2}$$

Table 4 shows for the four countries the value of the required units of income transfer z. Hungary requires the least. To remove the equality gap brought about by a 1.0 unit of activity injection, Hungary needs no more than an income transfer of 0.07. For the Netherlands, Germany, and Italy, the required z are 0.12, 0.15, and 0.29, respectively.

Now that z is known, it can be employed to predict the increases in the incomes of poor and rich groups and in the output. The income of the poor will increase by more than the transfer z because the transfer travels through the circular flow of the economy and generates additional income for the poor. Similarly, the rich will gain some income from the transfer, and the total output of sectoral activities will increase. The three effects are represented by the multipliers *Mpp*, *Mrp*, and *Map*, respectively.

Of special interest for the trade-off are multipliers that give the output growth effects of activity injections versus income transfers, i.e. *Maa* and *Map*, respectively. We need to compare (i) the output resulting from the one-unit injection in

Table 4. SAM calculations of trade-off between equality and growth in developed economies.

	Formula	Hungary	Italy	Netherlands	Germany
Multiplier gains from a unit income transfer to poorer group *p*					
Gain in output of activities *a*	*Map*	2.16	2.95	1.55	2.26
Gain in income of all households *h*	*Mhp*	1.53	2.08	1.42	1.86
Gain in income of poorer group *p*	*Mpp*	1.1520	1.2689	1.0798	1.1626
Gain in income of richer group *r*	*Mrp*	0.3740	0.81	0.34	0.69
Calculation of trade-off					
Required income transfer z to poorer group to recover simulated equality gap	*z as in eq. (4.2)*	0.0669	0.287	0.1189	0.1494
Two rounds output in case of income transfers, *OIT*	$OIT = Maa + z\,Map$	3.1547	4.2692	2.4743	3.7877
Two rounds output in case of activity injections, *OAI*	$OAI = (1+z)Maa$	3.2114	4.3906	2.5623	3.9655
Foregone output, *FO*	*FO = OAI-OIT*	0.0567	0.1214	0.0880	0.1778
Foregone output proportion, *FOP*	*FOP = FO/OIT*	0.0177	0.0276	0.0343	0.0448
Equality gap recovered, proportion	*EGR, Table 3*	0.1096	0.1014	0.1617	0.1265
Trade-off expressed as equality gain to foregone output	*EGR/FOP*	6.1921	3.6739	4.7143	2.8237
Trade-off expressed as foregone output to equality gain	*FOP/EGR*	0.1615	0.2722	0.2121	0.3542

economic activities in the first round, plus the output from the income transfers of z units required and applied to close the equality gap recovery in the second round, i.e. $Maa + z\,Map$, denoted by *OIT*, and (ii) output resulting from the one unit injection in economic activities in the first round, and in case z units are injected also in economic activities in the second round, i.e. $Maa + z\,Maa$, denoted by *OAI*. The difference between *OAI* and *OIT* constitutes the foregone output, *FO*, when z is employed as an income transfer instead of an activity injection. Table 3 gives the four countries *OIT*, *OAI*, and the foregone output, *FO*, as well as the foregone output as a proportion of the maximal output, *FOP*. For comparative purposes, the foregone output expressed as a proportion, *FOP*, is a better measurement than units of foregone output, *FO*. This is so because the specific details of the SAMs for the individual countries, which can influence the results, are neutralized; besides, the trade-off is better measured between proportional equality improvement in equality and proportional output foregone.

The table shows the foregone output proportion, *FOP*, to be lowest for Hungary and increases gradually for Italy, the Netherlands, and Germany. Italy's loss in the proportion of foregone output is less than the Netherlands and Germany due to the higher output effects of income transfers in Italy, as expressed by *Map*.

As was stated earlier, a measure of the trade-off between equality and growth should be able to show which countries are more effective in achieving, in proportionate terms, greater income equality with the least foregone growth. This is done by a simple division of *EGR* by *FOP*. As an alternative, dividing *FOP* by *EGR* tells how much of the GDP is foregone for a one-point improvement in equality.

Results shown in Table 4 suggest that Hungary is more effective than the other examined countries in achieving more equality at lesser forgone growth in output, with a score of *EGR/FOP* of around 6.2, compared to 4.7, 3.7, and 2.8 for the Netherlands Italy, and Germany, respectively. As an alternative, *FOP/EGR* gives the same trade-off but is intuitively more directly comprehendible, showing Hungary to lose 0.16 of a percent in foregone GDP for a 1% improvement in income equality. The loss is somewhat greater in the Netherlands at 0.21, higher in Italy at 0.27, and highest in Germany at 0.35.

The low level of conflict between equality and growth in Hungary, as indicated by a trade-off of 0.16, is not a surprise given its socialist historical background. The Netherlands shows a higher conflict level between growth and equality in the primary income distribution, but the removal of the emerging inequality from the primary income distribution via income transfers involves relatively low foregone growth so that the total result of a loss of 0.21% output for a 1% improvement in equality suggests a moderate level of conflict. The trade-off in Italy at 0.27% loss in output for a 1% improvement in equality is higher, suggesting a greater conflict between the two goals. The conflict between equality and growth is highest in Germany, with a loss in GDP of 0.35% for a 1% improvement in equality.

The SAM–multiplier analysis applied above comes closest to a simplified economy-wide model including government that allows the measurement and analysis of the equality growth trade-off. There are two major limitations of the SAM–multiplier approach that need to be mentioned. (1) Cell entries of the SAM are amounts, i.e. products of prices × quantities. However, quantities and prices are not explicitly disentangled. In the fixed price multiplier model, supplied amounts are supposed to adjust to demanded amounts. They will, but if there is restricted capacity, the result is inflation. This may require a revision downward in the real sizes of multipliers. (2) Many linear relationships are assumed: constant shares of factor remunerations in total output, of household incomes in the various factor payments, of commodities in household expenditure, and of sectors in commodity production. Following the uniform proportional assumption in cross-country comparisons is an advantage in contrast with incomparable specifications for individual countries. For a detailed account of limitations, see Chapter 7.

7. Policy Options for Achieving Sustained GWR

Regarding alternative policies to achieve GWR, the optimal redistribution policies are those that maximize the continuous growth of H and L along relative norms that are held in the community context concerned. Annual taxations of H and transfers to L are one policy. This short-term policy is likely to be much less efficient than longer-term policies that aim at sustained investments in and enriching the human resource endowments of both H and L, and the physical and informational infrastructures associated with their production activities. On policies to achieve growth with redistribution, GWR, are there policies other than taxation and transfers for achieving higher growth and more equity in the longer run, thus avoiding Okun's trade-off? If the time horizon is expanded to consider intergenerational mobility and endowment strategies to enrich the productive levels of those child segments of future generations which are currently denoted as poor, the outcome can be the creation of new long-run mechanisms of growth with equity which escape the trade-off.

The above applies to both developing and developed countries with one very important qualification that has been referred to above in reference to the Kuznets curve. Empirics show that it is almost unavoidable in the early phase of economic development that economic growth is accompanied by some regressive redistribution of income but that GWR is easier to achieve at more advanced levels of economic development. The more developed the economy, the more it is in a position to apply GWR fruitfully.

8. Concluding Remarks

The Kuznets curve highlights the conflict and complementarities between the twin goals of growth and redistribution. Most studies of the Kuznets curve look at the developing and developed countries as a continuum of observations. Major differences require splitting the Kuznets curve and analyzing the trade-off between growth and inequality in separate and distinct portions for developing and developed countries. In developing countries, the disposable income is basically determined during the primary distribution of factor earnings. The inequality to growth ratio, ITG ratio, falls gradually over time as differential productivities and their attached earnings diminish as the dualistic economy integrates and develops. In the welfare economies of developed countries, governments engage in income transfers in a round of secondary income redistribution to mend income inequalities arising during the round of primary distribution. Measurement and analysis of the relation between growth and distribution in the welfare state require working with an economy-wide model with a central role for government. The social accounting matrix, SAM, proves to be insightful in reflecting on growth and distribution in this context.

Whether it is a developing or a developed economy, or it is a rapidly growing or a slowly growing economy, by nature, all countries experience *some* degree of income inequality. Besides, the optimal distribution of income should always involve *some* inequality because the total amount of income in society is not independent of how it is distributed. Given these facts on the inevitability of income inequality, some raise questions on the paradox and consistency of a discussion on the feasibility of equal opportunities with inevitable income inequalities. The discussion becomes sensible and relevant if the intrageneration analytical context is supplemented by an intergeneration analytical context where a neutral mobility of earners across generations could guarantee that all earners have equivalent probabilities of becoming rich or poor. Mobility introduces degrees of freedom that can resolve the paradox. If the intragenerational income distribution with its inevitable inequalities remained the same but substantial fractions of the population changed position each year from rich to poor and poor to rich, then there would be nevertheless more equality occurring over time, defined in the *superior* terms of the equality of probabilities of moving upward and downward.

Chapter 6

Development Performances at Region and Country Levels

1. Introduction

The complementarity of the twin goals of sustained economic growth and progressive endowment redistribution (GWR) is a main theme in this book. The combined goal has been the focus of some prominent scholars such as Tinbergen and Sen. The GWR perspective is shared by contemporary economists in the contexts of developing and developed countries, i.e. Piketty (2014), Stiglitz (2016), respectively. There are at least six theories and related empirics that support *why* the GWR perspective needs to be pursued as the primary goal of socio-economic development. Next to addressing the *why* question, we shall briefly comment on alternative policy strategies on *how* and *when* to go for GWR. The thrust of the chapter discusses problems in the measurement of country performances in terms of GWTR and applies approximative performance indicators of GWR to some thirty leading countries in the world development regions, and shows *where* the GWR perspective has been more successful and most lagging.

The six theories and related empirics that support this perspective and reenforce its significance. can be titled as: (1) theorems of welfare theory, (2) the law of diminishing marginal utility, (3) economic growth accounting, (4) human capital, (5) dual economy, and (6) structural transformation as implied by the Kuznets curve.

The first rationale proceeds from welfare economics that states that any Pareto-optimal state is an equilibrium for some initial distribution of endowments. The competitive market equilibrium is by no means optimal in the absolute sense because the outcome depends entirely on the agreed upon original satisfising distribution of endowments. While it is very complex to reach agreement on the satisficing distribution, it is logical to presume that in cases where more people feel that there is a skew distribution of endowments, more people would rationally agree to a more progressive redistribution of endowments.

The second rationale relates to the well-known phenomenon that the marginal utility of an additional dollar decreases with more accumulated wealth. The law of diminishing marginal utility it implies that a progressive redistribution of endowments leading in the longer run to a progressive redistribution of dollars would increase the total utility of all the generated dollars.

The third rationale is based on economic growth accounting which emphasizes the significant contribution of the growth in factor productivity as compared to the growth in factor inputs. Rise in factor productivity is primarily the extensive and intensive upgrading of skills and technology which in essence is the enrichment of labor, and the population at large, with greater human capital endowments, OECD (2021). Productivity growth is equivalent to a progressive redistribution of skill and technological endowments among the population that sets into motion higher economic growth.

The fourth rationale which dates back to Becker (1964), views the contribution of human capital to economic growth as basically of the extension and progressive redistribution of educational and skill endowments to children and youngsters who happen to belong to a lesser endowed population, enhancing upward labor mobility, and resulting into a more productive labor force that allows for more economic growth and more resources that can be partly reinvested again in expanding human capital.

The fifth rationale relates to the dual economy and Lewis (1955), and can be paraphrased in terms of two propositions. First proposition: A person does not choose to be born or not. Any born person has basic living entitlements. These entitlements are relative to the norms in the concerned community. It is then an obligation of the community to meet the community's norms of basic living entitlements. Second proposition: Due to normal distributions of abilities at the personal level and normal distributions of efficiencies at the activity level (firm, sector, and location), there are always (H) high-earnings persons with high abilities working and earning in activity segments with high productivity, in contrast to (L) low-earnings persons with lower abilities working in activity segments with low productivity, minimal productivity, and sometimes zero productivity or not working/earning at all. It follows from the first and second propositions that continuous growth of H is necessary to permit redistribution of part of the growth outcome to L, so as to catch up with the relative norms of basic living entitlements. In similar ways, the upgrading of L to higher levels would feed H and assure its continuous growth.

The sixth rationale relates to the Kuznets curve, Kuznets (1964), which postures that while in the early stages of economic development higher economic growth is likely to associate with regressive income, wealth and endowment distributions; this reverses at later stages into a scenario of growth with progressive redistribution. By implication, growth and redistribution complement each other in the longer run.

Next to these six rationales, there are fundamental contributions from other social sciences that equally support the perspective of GWR, and which go as far back as K. Marx, J. J. Rousseau, R. Owen, and J. S. Mill. It is sufficient to mention here the sociological alienation of societal factions which rises with increasing income and wealth disparities and which may end up in breaking up society. Similarly, political unrest and violence are characteristic features of regressive distributions of income and wealth.

In commenting on how to realize GWR, a broad distinction can be made between direct intra-generational and indirect inter-generational strategies towards realizing GWR. The first strategy would tax the rich and transfers income and wealth to the poor. The second strategy perceives a longer horizon whereby part of the accumulated taxes are invested in upgrading human capital endowments of the younger generation whose majority would by definition belong to the less privileged. In time this would lead to a progressive redistribution of endowments, income and wealth. The first strategy may not lead to a sustainable GWR if the redistributed income is consumed and not reinvested. The second strategy would be more effective in realizing GWR.

In principle, enriching human capital endowments happens also in the process of regular investments in physical infrastructure as when skill training, better housing and health services are provided and are part of the investment projects. Notwithstanding, since returns to physical investments do not consider the positive endowments involved, the designs of most investment projects may not be geared towards exploiting the positive human capital endowment effects. A plausible rule of the thumb would be to suggest devoting some 20% of an investment budget to upgrading human endowments and the 80% to the physical component. The ratio of 20:80 is motivated by the commonly observed practices at the macro level, where the shares of public expenditure allocations to human capital development departments versus physical infrastructural departments are also in the range of 20% to 80%, as documented in Cohen (2015). Theoretical modelling of the optimal resource allocation on physical and human capital by Yi–Chia Wang (2024) suggest a recommended equivalent allocation of approximately 25% and 26% of real GDP towards developing human capital and accumulating physical capital, respectively, to attain long-term economic optimality in the United States.

In commenting on the when timing of GWR, the following can be stated. A possible trade-off between growth and distribution in the early stages of development as suggested by the Kuznets curve, would imply that a higher economic growth may have to proceed the progressive redistribution of endowments. This does not deny that there are some fortunate countries in East Asia which have been able to combine GWR fairly quickly. In contrast, if the progress towards GWR is low or does not occur, it becomes more difficult to make the transition as the less privileged group become more demanding and challenging, and the benefiting interest groups become more powerful and distrustful. This appears to be the case in some Latin American countries where progress towards GWR is much slower than elsewhere, as will be shown in a later section.

2. Measurement Problems of Growth with Redistribution

While growth and redistribution considerations can be commonly integrated in many development policies and actions, a simple joint measurement of GWR performance at for a county for a specific year faces many complexities due to intricate relationships between growth and distribution over time and space, and may not be feasible. There are four complexities which we shall list in this section. These complexities lead us to approach the measurement of GWR performance in a grossly fashion in this chapter, making use of the regional context of individual countries and doing that over longer periods.

The first complexity lies in the schism between the postulates of welfare theory and their implementation in the real world The First Theorem of Welfare Economics states that, the market prices are equilibrium prices whereby it is impossible to make a change without making someone worse off, making the resulting competitive market equilibrium as most efficient and Pareto-optimal. Under these conditions and other things remaining the same, higher economic growth is guaranteed to be efficiently done.

The Second Theorem of Welfare Economics emphasizes that any such competitive equilibrium is defined in terms of given initial endowments; and thus states that any Pareto-optimal state is an equilibrium for some initial distribution of endowments. The significance of the theorem is that if the postulated assumptions are fulfilled in a real market economy, then economic efficiency will be guaranteed by market forces. Accordingly, the competitive market equilibrium is by no means optimal in the absolute sense because the outcome depends entirely on the original distribution of endowments. The second theorem suggests that the initial distribution of endowments can be reset beforehand at the socially desired pattern, after which market forces will take care of efficient allocation. The role of the state would then be restricted to applying a priori lump-sum transfer payments which are consistent with the desired initial distribution of endowments.

The reset beforehand does not work in this way in the real world. The process is reversed in the real world. What happens is that governments go for economic growth and tend to review the income distribution situation at the end of the year and reset this ex-post, giving due consideration to the perception of a desirable initial distribution and unintended differential outcomes during the year. Transfers are then affected in consistency with the resetting. If the resetting is well-done and duly implemented, then the model of the perfect market economy can be described to stand firm with regard to the equity dimension, even though this happens with a lag in time. And should the government be non-responsive, it can be argued that it will be replaced in time by a responsive government which could correct the distribution ex-post. And this involves again more time lags. The political complications and the time lags make the measurement of the simultaneous performance of growth with redistribution for a particular year less meaningful. The evaluation of GWR over a period of time of a decade or so seems to be more meaningful and useful.

The second complexity relates to the resetting of the desirable distribution. It is not easy to reach consensus on the desired distribution norms in relation to growth which is specific for the country/region and year/periods concerned; and there can be wide differences on the distribution norms within one and the same country and over time. Recognition of these limitations requires giving more consideration to the regional context in which the specific countries find themselves; and our classification of the world development regions in eight regions can be helpful in this respect.

As for complexities surrounding divergent norms, these are partly mitigated by considering extended years of observation when measuring and evaluating the GWR performance for the specific countries and regions.

The third complexity relates to the empirical relationship between economic growth and income distribution in the course of economic development, whereby in the early stages of economic development growth tends to associate with regressive income distribution while as countries develop and become richer they tend to have progressive income distribution. The relationship is known as the Kuznets curve, and is due to Kuznets (1955). Performance evaluation of GWR for a specific country needs to give due consideration to the development stage and the regional context of the country concerned; which renders a simple comparison across countries for a certain year less meaningful.

The fourth complexity is in some sense the opposite of the Kuznets curve. Some economists perceive long term economic development in terms of strategies that redistribute endowments so as to elevate higher economic growth and progressive income distributions. This can be rightly named the Tinbergen-strategy, given the pronounced role that this cause effect relationship play in Tinbergen's writings, see Dekker (2021). Economic growth accounting (to be discussed in the next section) does show that growth in factor productivity may contribute more than growth in factor inputs to the growth the GDP. When it is recognized that growth in factor productivity is basically the extension of human skills endowments and technology, it follows that Tinbergen-strategies can have significant positive effects on economic growth. Since these GWR strategies have long gestation lags, it follows that GWR performance evaluation for countries which apply such strategies become meaningful when the evaluation period is long enough; and this need not hold for other countries. The complication makes simple comparisons between divergent countries less conclusive.

The four complexities discussed above impose limitations on GWR performance measurement and the drawing of conclusive results. The task is made easier when the GWR performances are evaluated in the context of regional comparisons and over a longer period of time. This chapter does that and will be able to reach some considerate conclusions on GWR performances in developing countries.

The contents of the chapter fall in the following sections. Section 2 is an overview of development performances at the regional level. The performance analysis of economic growth is extended to examine the decomposition of growth into factor inputs and factor productivities, while performance analysis of income distribution is extended to poverty reduction. Section 3 will elaborate on development performance at the country level along the GWR perspective. Section 4 will make an attempt at ranking country performances along the GWR perspective. Section 5 concludes.

3. Overview of Development Performances by Region

This section gives an overview of regional performance in terms of economic growth and income distribution. To start with growth of the GDP and GDP per capita, Table 1 gives these values over various periods. The data show that the two Asian regions of EAP and SA perform better than other regions in terms of GDP growth and GDP growth per capita. At the other end are the GCC, MENA, SSA, and LAC regions with lower economic growth performances, the lower performance being due to different forces specific to the regions. The structural transformation of the MENA economy from agriculture to industry is noted to be stagnant. The region was also handicapped by political instability. The SSA region shows depressing

Table 1. Annual growth rates of GDP and GDP per capita over five decades 1960–2012.

Region, years	GDP	GDP per capita	Region, years	GDP	GDP per capita
EAP			MENA		
1961–1970	4.7	2.5	1961–1970	8.5	5.7
1971–1980	6.6	4.5	1971–1980	5.1	2.3
1981–1990	7.6	5.8	1981–1990	3.0	0.0
1991–2000	8.4	7.1	1991–2000	4.0	1.8
2001–2012	6.0	4.7	2001–2012	4.8	1.6
SA			SSA		
1961–1970	4.4	2.0	1961–1970	4.9	2.3
1971–1980	3.0	0.7	1971–1980	3.7	0.8
1981–1990	5.6	3.4	1981–1990	1.9	−1.0
1991–2000	5.2	3.2	1991–2000	2.3	−0.3
2001–2012	5.9	4.3	2001–2012	6.6	4.2
GCC			LAC		
1961–1970	..	..	1961–1970	4.9	2.6
1971–1980	9.3	3.7	1971–1980	3.7	3.2
1981–1990	0.1	−4.9	1981–1990	1.9	−0.9
1991–2000	3.1	0.4	1991–2000	2.3	1.7
2001–2012	7.51	6.01	2001–2012	4.0	2.7

Source: World Bank at http://devdata.worldbank.org/query. The GDP and GDP per capita columns give average annual growth rates of GDP and GDP per capita, respectively, in constant prices of US dollars of 2000 for four 10-year periods. The fifth period of 2000–2012 is the mean of the largest six countries in the region.

performances: economic growth in SSA is the lowest and has declined over time, partly due to increases in oil prices but also political unrest, civil wars, and state interventions aggravated the situation. There is a reversal in SSA as indicated by a moderate recovery in the years 2000–2005.

The better performances in economic growth in EAP and SA are partially accounted for by more significant structural transformations from agriculture to industry in EAP and SA, as well as early and stronger shifts from import protection to export promotion in EAP and SA.

Table 2 displays results of GDP growth accounting analysis. Economic determinants of the better performance of the two Asian regions, EAP and SA, as compared to other regions are highlighted by an analysis of growth accounting factors covering the period 1960–1994. For EAP, annual GDP growth of 7.0% over the years 1960–1994 is accounted for by annual growth in the labor and capital factors of production of 2.3% and 3.4% and annual growth in total factor productivity for the remaining 1.3%. The SA region enjoyed annual growth in total factor productivity of 0.8%. In the other three regions of SSA, MENA, and LAC, productivity growth was negative or slightly positive: −0.6, −0.3, and 0.2, respectively.[1] It is interesting to note that in economic growth accounting the contribution of the rise in factor productivity is substantive. Rise in factor productivity is primarily the extensive and intensive upgrading of skills and technology which in essence is the enrichment of labor, and the population at large, with greater human capital endowments. This is equivalent to a progressive redistribution of skill endowments among the population; and evidence to how progressive redistribution of skill endowments enhances economic growth. The regional results in the table suggest that there was more attention and effort given to the progressive redistribution of skill endowments in enhancing economic growth in EAP and SA regions than is the case for the other development regions; allowing the two Asian regions to achieve higher economic growth.

Table 2. GDP growth accounting, all values are in growth rates.

Region	GDP	Labor	Capital	Factor productivity
East Asia & Pacific (EAP)	7.0	2.3	3.4	1.3
South Asia (SA)	4.2	1.6	1.8	0.8
Arab Gulf (GCC)	..	..	..	..
Middle East, Nr Africa (MENA)	4.5	2.3	2.5	−0.3
Sub-Saharan Africa (SSA)	2.9	1.8	1.7	−0.6
Latin America, Caribbean (LAC)	4.2	2.2	1,8	0.2

Source: Adapted from *Brookings Papers and Proceedings* 2:135–91. The GDP growth accounting equation is the growth rate of GDP = growth rate of labor + growth rate of capital + growth rate of total factor productivity. The equation is applied to the six development regions.

How did the development regions combine higher well-being (that is, growth in GDP pc) with performance on the dimensions of income distribution and poverty reduction? Table 3 gives the answers, but there is a statistical problem that has to be clarified before studying the table. Table 3 presents the mean of these indicators for the leading six countries in each region in the past four decades. Note that for the GDP pc, there is a difference between the consolidated regional total (column 2) and the regional mean (column 3). For the indicators on income distribution and poverty reduction, it is not feasible to estimate consolidated regional totals; the calculations are regional means of the six leading countries per region.

To start with, compare the mean annual growth of GDP pc with the mean Gini index, columns 3 and 4. In the two Asian regions, while EAP did better than SA in GDP pc growth, the SA did better than EAP in restraining tendencies toward more income inequalities. MENA had a moderate to low GDP pc growth combined with a reduction in income inequalities. SSA also had a moderate to low GDP pc growth but the increases in income inequality in SSA were among the highest in the developing world. LAC entered the 1950s with a higher GDP pc and a more unequal income distribution than other regions. Between 2000 and 2012, LAC had a GDP pc growth of 2.1% that went together with an unchanged Gini index at 53.2%, which is still the highest among the development regions.

Another relevant indicator of income inequality is the ratio of income shares of the richer top 20% of the population (T20%) to the poorer bottom 20% of the population (B20%), column 5. This indicator, denoted as T/B (20%), has increased most in SSA and LAC. This indicator modified to apply to 10% of the population (that is, T/B 10% in column 6) shows even greater tendencies toward income inequality, again led by SSA and LAC. Situations where low-income growth combines with significant and increasing concentrations of income go together with persistent dualism in the economy and weak integration in the system.

Next, column 7 in the table refers to the inequality to growth (ITG) ratio that was treated earlier in Chapter 5. This ratio divides the change in the Gini index by the growth in the GDP pc and comes close to representing a quasi-form of an inequality growth elasticity. It is defined as follows:

ITG = Inequality to growth ratio = Change in average Gini index between periods t and $t - 1$/average growth rate GDP per capita in period t.

Generally speaking, the elasticity is positive but less than one, meaning that distribution worsens with higher well-being but at a diminished rate. The elasticity fell from 0.78 to 0.09 in EAP and increased from 0.47 to 0.80 in SA in the last two decades. Other regions show contrasting results but the data are incomplete to draw hard conclusions. CAC shows no change. MENA shows negative elasticities in the early period turned into no change in the later period. SSA has insufficient data, and LAC shows a positive elasticity in the early period turned into no change in the later period.

Another dimension of the distribution problem is the poverty ratio, column 8. This is the share of poverty headcounts at 1.25 dollars a day in purchasing power

Table 3. Growth of the GDP per capita and indicators of income distribution, 1980–2012 (in percent).

Periods	GDP per capita Annual growth: Region totals	GDP per capita Annual growth: Mean	Gini index	(T/B) 20%	(T/B) 10%	Inequality change to growth, ITG (a)	Poverty ratio	Poverty change to growth, PTG (b)
EAP: 1981–1990	5.8	3.8	36.3	6.3	9.7		44.6	
1991–2000	7.0	4.5	39.8	7.6	12.2	0.78	31.2	−0.25
2000–2012	8.0	4.7	40.2	7.8	12.5	0.09	14.8	−0.29
SA: 1981–1990	3.1	3.3	31.1	4.6	6.8		50.5	
1991–2000	3.3	3.1	32.6	4.8	7.3	0.47	48.7	−0.05
2000–2012	5.2	4.3	36.0	5.8	8.9	0.80	24.0	−0.48
CAC: 1981–1990	..	..	..	..	..		..	
1991–2000	3.9	−2.4	38.1	7.8	14.3	..	3.6	
2000–2012	6.0	6.0	35.9	6.2	10.0	0.05	3.4	−0.00
MENA:1981–1990	−1.5	−1.1	40.5	9.4	16.5		2.7	
1991–2000	1.8	1.0	38.0	7.0	11.5	−5.3	4.0	0.11
2000–2012	2.8	1.6	35.4	6.2	9.9	−0.6	2.2	−0.09
SSA: 1981–1990	−1.3	−1.1	42.0	6.2	9.4		..	
1991–2000	−0.6	−1.4	46.2	12.1	21.0	n.a.	49.1	..
2000–2012	2.1	4.2	44.2	11.2	19.1	−0.5	40.8	−0.16
LAC:1981–1990	−0.5	−1.1	50.7	15.0	31.4		10.7	
1991–2000	1.5	1.4	53.5	17.1	41.5	2.0	9.6	−0.07
2000–2012	2.0	2.7	52.0	17.8	45.7	−0.5	8.7	−0.03

Source: World Bank at http://databank.worldbank.org/. With the exception of column 1 that gives GDP pc growth figures based on consolidated regional totals, all other columns are regional averages of each region's six leading countries, which are practically fully representative for all regions, though less so for MENA and SSA. Periodical figures are averages of available yearly observations for the specified period in the leading countries. While the World Bank provides total poverty ratios for EAP and SA based on regional totals, there are only simple averages available for other regions. To maintain the same basis for regional comparisons for this indicator, and for the other income distribution indicators, we kept to simple averages.[2]

Note: (a) The ITG ratio is the change in the average Gini index between periods t and $t-1$/average growth of GDP per capita per annum in period t. For example, for EAP 2012, this is (40.2 – 39.8)/(4.7) = −0.09. (b) The poverty change to growth PTG ratio is the reduction in poverty ratio over period t normalized per 1 year, divided by the average growth of GDP per capita per annum in period t. For example, for EAP 2012, this is [(15.4 – 32.0)/12 years] / [4.7] = −0.29.

parity in the population. In EAP in 2000–2012, the poverty ratio is reduced by −1.37% per annum (that is, (31.2 – 14.8%)/12 years).

It is reasonable to expect that the poverty ratio falls more when the GDP per capita grows more. In Table 4, we add a last column 9 defining the poverty change to growth ratio PTG, which is a poverty reduction elasticity defined as:

PTG = (annual reduction in poverty ratio in period t)/(annual growth rate of GDP pc in period t).

For the EAP in the period 2000–2012, the results show a PTG elasticity of −0.29 (that is, −1.37% / 4.7%). The poverty reduction elasticity for SA in 2000–2012 was higher at −0.48, which can be expected given the greater poverty base. EAP and SA appear to be more effective than other regions in reducing the poverty ratio as their income levels grow higher. On the other end, SSA and LAC are least effective in combining reduced poverty with higher well-being. This is in one sense more severe in the case of SSA where the poverty ratio is remarkably high but also as severe in the other sense that the elasticity is remarkably low in LAC given its much high level of GDP pc. The two regions of CAC and MENA have the lowest poverty ratios at their lowest unavoidable level. This makes the poverty reduction elasticity irrelevant in this contest.

4. Growth with Redistribution Performances by Region and Country

Excessive conflicts between the twin goals of growth and redistribution are generally perceived to be undesirable. Countries that combine maximum reductions in income inequality with maximum rates of economic growth are envied by others. This section will assess the performance of the six leading countries in each region. The analysis for China and India in the previous chapter is expanded to include the 36 leading countries in the six development regions. This is done in Table 4 which is compacted to include GDP growth pc, Gini index, poverty ratio, and the two analytical indicators of inequality change to growth ratio ITG and poverty to growth (PTG) ratio. These two analytical indicators take the form of elasticities.

Table 4. EAP: Performance indicators of growth and distribution, averages of period (%).

	1991–2000			2001–2012				
Country periods	GDP pc, growth	Gini index	Poverty ratio %	GDP pc, growth	Gini index	Poverty ratio %	ITG ratio	PTG ratio
China	8.7	36.8	49.9	9.4	42.4	17.4	0.60	−0.6
Indonesia	3.3	29.9	48.5	3.9	34.3	22.6	1.13	−1.1
Philippines	0.6	44.7	25.7	2.9	43.8	21.0	−0.31	−0.5
Thailand	4.0	43.6	3.9	3.6	40.8	0.8	−0.78	−1.6
Malaysia	4.6	48.4	1.4	2.8	43.4	0.2	−1.79	−2.8
Vietnam	5.9	35.6	56.7	5.3	36.4	26.6	−0.64	—
Mean	4.5	39.8	31.0	4.7	40.2	14.8	−0.30	
Stdv s	2.5	6.3	22.3	2.3	3.6	10.5		
Vrcf v	0.55	0.16	0.72	0.49	0.09	0.71		

Source: http://databank.worldbank.org/. Annual growth rates of GDP and GDP pc are in constant prices of 2000.

East Asia Pacific (EAP) performance is summarized in Table 4. China's GDP and GDP pc growth rates per annum were remarkably higher than the other countries, and the difference between the two rates was the lowest, which is due to success in restraining population growth. The higher economic growth in China has been associated with a higher rise in income concentration in China when compared to other EAP countries. The Gini index in the period 2000–2012 shows a higher concentration of income distribution in China, at 42.4, compared to an average for EAP of 40.2. The association of unequal income redistribution with higher growth is a common phenomenon in the early phases of economic development. The results show ITG ratios of 0.6 and 1.1 for China and Indonesia, implying about a half to 1% increase in the Gini index (increase in income inequality) for an additional growth of 1% in GDP pc. The other EAP countries show falls in Gini (progressive distribution effects) accompanying economic growth and higher levels of well-being.

The poverty ratio is highest in Vietnam, Indonesia, and the Philippines, lowest in Thailand and Malaysia, and is about average in China, which can be seen as reflecting differences in general levels of well-being. The poverty change to growth elasticity (PTG ratio), column 9, highlights the significance of trickle-down effects in individual countries. PTG has higher trickle-down effects in rates in Malaysia and Thailand and lower rates in China and the Philippines.

Table 5 is on South Asia (SA)\ performance. In 2000–2012, the GDP growth per capita of 4.3% was accompanied by an increase in the Gini index of 2.4 percentage points (pp). The ITG is calculated at 0.58, meaning that for a 1% income growth, there is a rise in inequality of half a percent. India is close to this figure at 0.52. Sri Lanka and Nepal show regressive effects at 1.0 and 1.2 and Bangladesh and Pakistan

Table 5. SA: Performance indicators of growth and distribution, averages of period (%).

	1991–2000			2001–2012				
Country periods	GDP pc, growth	Gini index	Poverty ratio %	GDP pc, growth	Gini index	Poverty ratio %	ITG ratio	PTG ratio
India	3.8	30.8	49.4	5.4	33.6	37.2	0.52	−0.4
Pakistan	1.4	31.6	47.3	2.2	31.1	25.5	−0.23	−1.7
Bangladesh	2.5	31.3	63.1	4.5	32.7	23.4	0.31	−1.2
Sri Lanka	4.0	33.9	15.7	5.1	39.2	6.3	1.04	−1
Nepal	2.4	35.2	68.0	2.5	38.3	39.0	1.24	−1.4
Bhutan	4.4	38.0	..	6.3	41.2	12.7		
Mean	3.1	32.6	48.7	4.3	36.0	24.0	0.58	−1.1
Stdv *s*	1.1	1.7	18.3	1.5	3.7	11.9		
Vrcf *υ*	0.34	0.05	0.38	0.35	0.10	0.49		

Source: http://databank.worldbank.org/. Annual growth rates of GDP and GDP pc are in constant prices of 2000.

Table 6. CAC: Performance indicators of growth and distribution, averages of period (%).

	1991–2000			2001–2012				
Country periods	GDP pc, growth	Gini index	Poverty ratio %	GDP pc, growth	Gini index	Poverty ratio %	ITG ratio	PTG ratio
Turkiye	2.3	41.5	5	3.1	41	4.4	−0.16	−0.3
Iran	2.9	43.6	1.3	3.2	38.3	0.7	−1.66	−1.2
Kazakhstan	−2.4	34.0	4.6	6.9	32.8	2.0	−0.17	
Uzbekistan	−1.9	45.3		5.5	35.6	..	−1.76	
Azerbaijan	−5.3	35.0		11.6	35.1	3.4	0.01	
Tajikistan	−9.8	29.0		5.8	32.4	6.56	0.59	
Mean	−2.37	38.1	3.63	6.01	35.9	3.42	−0.53	
Stdv *s*	4.35	5.81	1.66	2.85	3.01	2.01		
Vrcf *υ*	−1.84	0.15	0.46	0.47	0.08	0.59		

Source: http://databank.worldbank.org/. Annual growth rates of GDP and GDP pc are in constant prices of 2000.

show progressive effects at 0.3 and −0.2. The differences can be rationalized in terms of systemic features. The average poverty reduction elasticity, PTG, in the SA region is around 1, with an average poverty ratio of 24%. It can be calculated that if GDP pc growth can be sustained at 4% pa, the poverty ratio of 24% (on the defined basis of 1.25$ per person) can be reduced to zero in some 5–6 years.

Table 6 is on the CAC region. For most of the Central Asia and Caspian (CAC) region, the period 1990–2000 was a period of transition from a Communist/Russian regime to a development/national regime in the XSIR countries. GDP and GDP pc declined in these countries by annual rates that reached −10.0%. Recovery came in 2000–2012 allowing some of these countries to reach growth rates of 12%, i.e. Azerbaijan. GDP growth pa and GDP pc growth pa for the whole region in 2000–2012 amounted to 7.5% and 6.0%. In spite of this high-income growth, the Gini index has fallen on average from 38.1 to 35.9 as most of the ex-Soviet countries in the region moved on and left the transition period behind. The ITG ratio is negative at −0.53. The underlying tendency of more equality with higher growth after a distribution regressive transition period is a systemic property. The poverty ratio is not relevant in the CAC region, i.e. the poverty ratio in the richer countries of Kazakhstan and Azerbaijan stood at 0.1 and 0.4 in 2011.

Table 7 is on the Middle East and North Africa (MENA). Performance in terms of growth of the GDP is fairly similar among MENA countries and the variation tends to fall. While the topic of income distribution would apply to most countries of MENA, it is not applicable in the context of the six countries of the Gulf Cooperation Council (GCC). In the oil-rich labor shortage GCC, there are ample income resources for the nationals to the extent that the income distribution issues are acknowledged to be statistically irrelevant, and such notions as the Gini index are non-applicable to the nationals. The migrant population forms

Table 7. MENA: Performance indicators of growth and distribution, averages of period (%).

	1991–2000			2001–2012				
Country periods	GDP pc, growth	Gini index	Poverty ratio %	GDP pc, growth	Gini index	Poverty ratio %	ITG ratio	PTG ratio
Egypt	2.6	31.6	2.9	2.7	31.5	0.9	−0.037	−2.1
Sd Arabia	0.8	..	..	2.7	..	..		
Algeria	−0.2	35.3	6.8	2.2	36.6	..		
Iraq	..	..	..	3.2	30.9	2.8		
UAE	0.6	..	..	−5.0	..	..		
Morocco	1.0	39.3	4.6	3.8	40.8	4.4	0.395	
Mean	1.0	35.4	4.8	1.6	34.4	2.7		
Stdv s	0.9	3.2	1.6	3.1	4.6	1.5		
Vrcf v	0.97	0.09	0.34	1.94	0.13	0.54		

Source: http://databank.worldbank.org/. Annual growth rates of GDP and GDP pc are in constant prices of 2000.

Table 8. SSA: Performance indicators of growth and distribution, averages of period (%).

	1991–2000			2001–2012				
SSA	GDP pc, growth	Gini index	Poverty ratio %	GDP pc, growth	Gini index	Poverty ratio %	ITG ratio	PTG ratio
Nigeria	0.4	45.7	65.2	5.5	45.9	43.7	0.036	−0.5
S. Africa	−0.8	57.9	24.0	2.0	65.3	15.6	3.700	−1.5
Ethiopia	−0.6	35.0	58.1	5.8	31.7	34.8	−0.569	−0.6
Congo DR	−8.3			1.5	44.4	87.7		
Angola	−1.6			6.9	42.7	43.4		
Sudan	2.6	..		3.4	35.3	19.8		
Mean	−1.4	46.2	49.1	4.2	44.2	40.8	1.056	−0.8
Stdv s	3.5	9.7	18.7	2.1	11.1	24.5		
Vrcf v	−2.53	0.21	0.38	0.50	0.25	0.60		

Source: http://databank.worldbank.org/. Annual growth rates of GDP and GDP pc are in constant prices of 2000.

the majority of the population in most GCC. Chapter 14 of this book is on the GCC countries. As far as the non-GCC are concerned, Gini indexes available for Egypt and Morocco show stable income distributions. The limited availability of data restricts further analysis of inequality trade-offs and poverty reduction in MENA.

Table 8 is on Sub-Saharan Africa (SSA). Economic growth of the Sub-Saharan African region up to the year 2000 was least among the developing world. The association between frequent political instabilities and slow economic growth in

SSA has been noted, tested empirically, and found significant in various studies.[3] There is tension between insiders (those identified with the political establishment) and various groups of outsiders. The distinction between insiders and outsiders is often based on kin groups, ethnic origin, and regional and religious affiliation. As violence erupts, economic infrastructure is hit the most. Besides, in an unstable political environment, the allocation of economic resources is distorted. Some governments, and their running heads, are known to have diverted national resources to non-developmental ends and/or personal gains. Under these circumstances, the investment climate is weak, and openness to foreign direct finance and trade is discouraged. Add to this a high population growth. The result was an average annual growth of the GDP per capita that was negative in the years before 2000, Table 8. The period 2000–20012 brought a turnaround in economic growth making it possible to achieve GDP growth rates pa of 8.3% in Nigeria and 3.5% in South Africa.

Income inequality as represented by the Gini index increased in Nigeria between 1980 and 2000 by some 7% but appears to have stabilized at the level of 46% in 2012, which is generally in line with the average for the whole SSA region. However, performances in the SSA region are full of diversity. For example, the Gini index continued rising in South Africa to make its income distribution become one of the most unequal in the world, at 65% in 2012. The South African path does not conform to the normal path consistent with economic theory and can be best explained in terms of socio-economic systemic features typical for South Africa. At the opposite end, Ethiopia shows diminished income concentration around a Gini index which has a value of only 32% in 2012; this is one with the least income concentration in the world, coinciding with a growth in the GDP per capita of 5.8% in the period 2000–2012, giving an ITG ratio of −0.57, which is accountable solely in terms of systemic properties.

Table 9 is on Latin America and Caribbean (LAC). The table shows for all six leading countries similar growth rates of GDP per capita. Distribution tendencies differ. Three countries (Brazil, Mexico, and Peru) reverse their positive ITG of 1990–2000 (i.e. regressive distribution tendencies) into negative ITG in 2001–2012 (i.e. progressive distribution tendencies). The other three countries (Argentina, Colombia, and Venezuela) show an opposite switch. In all three countries, the ITG ratio is positive implying a shift toward more inequality and is consistently associated with a positive PTG ratio rise, meaning that the poverty ratio has increased with economic growth.

Tables 4–9 above made evaluations of changes in performance indicators for the six development regions, based on mean values, and produced results on country variations within ear region. Table 10 focuses on the indicators of growth and distribution and summarizes results for the variation coefficient, υ, which is an important source of information for assessing regional homogeneity and convergence tendencies. Low values of υ represent homogeneity, and decreasing values

Table 9. LAC: Performance indicators of growth and distribution, averages of period (%).

	1991–2000			2001–2012				
LAC	GDP pc, growth	Gini index	Poverty ratio %	GDP pc, growth	Gini index	Poverty ratio %	ITG ratio	PTG ratio
Brazil	0.3	59.5	13.3	2.3	57.3	8.8	−0.957	−1.2
Mexico	1.7	50.5	6.1	1.1	48.4	2.2	−1.909	−4.8
Argentina	3.2	48.2	3.2	3.5	49.3	5.3	0.314	1.6
Colombia	1.0	55.4	12.3	2.8	57.8	14.0	0.857	0.4
Venezuela	0.0	46.3	8.8	1.9	47.7	13.4	0.737	2.3
Peru	2.2	60.8	14.1	4.6	51.5	8.4	−2.022	−0.7
Mean	1.4	53.5	9.6	2.7	52.0	8.7	−0.497	+0.4
Stdv s	1.1	5.6	4.0	1.1	4.2	4.2		
Vrcf v	0.80	0.10	0.42	0.42	0.08	0.49		

Source: http://databank.worldbank.org/. Annual growth rates of GDP and GDP pc are in constant prices of 2000.

Table 10. Variation coefficients for growth and distribution in the development regions, two periods.

	1991–2000		2001–2012	
Region: year	Annual growth of GDP per capita	Gini index	Annual growth of GDP per capita	Gini index
EAP	1.15	0.47	0.49	0.40
SA	0.34	0.15	0.35	0.26
CAC	−1.84	0.38	0.47	0.28
MENA	0.97	0.21	1.94	0.31
SSA	−2.53	0.40	0.50	0.57
LAC	0.80	0.37	0.42	0.33

Sources: Tables 4–9.

of v over time indicate integration and convergence. With slight exceptions, each of the six regions shows that its member countries are converging to the regional modes over the two decades. However, the degree and speed of integration vary between the regions. The three regions that show the highest uniformity among their member countries and integrative tendencies are LAC and CAC followed by EAP. In all three regions, the values of v for the two indicators of growth and distribution fall down over the last 2–3 decades. It is not surprising to observe high uniformity and integrative tendencies in the LAC countries given their long and shared history together. But it is surprising to note the high uniformity and integration in the Central Asia and Caspian (CAC) region which was never treated as a regional group. It is also interesting to find that among the widely spread and highly populous group of countries in Asia that the South Asia region shows less variance in performance than the EAP. The MENA region shows high diversity in the growth of GDP per capita which is due to the presence oil-rich small population with high growth, though the region is more uniform regarding distribution, again excluding the GCC countries where the distribution goal is not relevant and is not data accessible. Finally, the Sub-Saharan region appears to be the most diversified scoring the highest variation coefficients and these show that they increase over time. One and the other support the idea of viewing the Sub-Saharan Africa region as consisting of an upper belt (led by Nigeria) and a lower belt (led by South Africa). This would bring more sense to the analysis. Notwithstanding there are significant differences between individual countries within the two belts.

5. Performance Ranking of Developing Countries in terms of Growth with Redistribution

This chapter made an assessment of country performances regarding the twin goals of growth with redistribution (GWR). The inequality to growth ratio, ITG ratio, was a helpful tool in this assessment. The comparative performance of a specific country was limited to a comparison of the ITG ratio with neighboring countries in the applicable development region. Ideally, one would like to view an assessment for all developing countries ending up with a ranking of countries over several periods with respect to their achievement of GWR. Such a ranking faces problems mentioned in the introduction, which can be somehow mended:

(a) One problem is the arbitrariness of any one-year ranking. This is solvable by defining the period to cover several years and applying ranking over more periods.
(b) A second problem is the presence of observations with abrupt or outlier values that may distort representation. The problem is solvable by ignoring outliers but this distorts the coverage. A better solution is by abiding to ordinal ranking instead of cardinal numerals.
(c) A third problem lies in the scale normalization of the two goals of growth and redistribution. This is complex given the trade-offs in early and later phases of economic development which differ by country. The problem is solvable by tracing ranking over more periods to catch the trade-off transformation and by applying ordinal instead of cardinal ranking.
(d) Last but not least is the problem of fixing preferential weights for the growth and redistribution objectives so as to obtain a unified general performance index. The problem is solvable by working initially with equal weights and supplemented by simulated weights.

The performance ranking that is applied in Table 11 takes the above specifications into consideration. The ranking is done for two periods, each period

Table 11. Performance rankings of growth with redistribution index for 30 countries, two periods.

	Country score 1991–2000			Country score 2001–2012		
Country	GDP per capita annual growth	Gini index inversed	GWR index	GDP per capita annual growth	Gini index inversed	GWR index
China	30	17	**23.5**	29	11	**20.0**
Indonesia	23	29	**26.0**	17	23	**20.0**
Philippines	11	11	11.0	11	9	10.0
Thailand	26	12	19.0	15	15	15.0
Malaysia	28	6	17.0	10	10	10.0
Vietnam	29	18	**23.5**	21	20	**20.5**
India	25	28	**26.5**	22	24	**23.0**
Pakistan	14	26	20.0	5	30	17.5
Bangladesh	19	27	23.0	18	26	22.0
Sri Lanka	24	24	24.0	20	16	18.0
Nepal	18	20	19.0	7	18	12.5
Bhutan	27	16	21.5	27	12	19.5
Turkiye	17	14	15.5	12	14	13.0
Iran	21	13	17.0	13	17	15.0
Kazakhstan	3	23	13.0	28	25	**26.5**
Uzbekistan	4	10	7.0	24	21	**23.0**
Azerbaijan	2	22	12.0	30	22	**26.0**
Tajikistan	1	30	15.5	26	27	**26.5**
Egypt	20	25	22.5	8	29	18.5
Algeria	7	19	13.0	4	19	11.5
Morocco	13	15	13.0	16	13	14.5
Nigeria	10	9	9.5	23	8	15.5
S. Africa	5	3	**4.0**	3	1	**2.0**
Ethiopia	6	21	13.5	25	28	**26.5**
Brazil	9	2	5.5	6	3	**4.5**
Mexico	15	5	10.0	1	6	**3.5**
Argentina	22	7	14,5	14	5	9.5
Colombia	12	4	8.0	9	2	5.5
Venezuela	8	8	8.0	2	7	**3.5**
Peru	16	1	8.5	19	4	11.5

consisting of about 10 years: thus 1991–2000 and 2001–2012. Some of the 36 developing countries considered do not have full data coverage for all these years on the two objectives of economic growth and progressive redistribution (i.e. lower Gini index). The number of countries with the required data is 30. The performance ranking of countries is done along ordinal numbers separately for the economic growth objective and for the progressive redistribution objective. The country with the highest economic growth scores 30 on the growth objective. Similarly, the country with the lowest Gini index scores 30 on the redistribution objective. Finally, equal weights are applied for the ordinal rankings of the growth and redistribution objectives by simply calculating the average of the two scores to obtain a unified performance index of growth with redistribution.

In the period 1990–2000, out of a maximum score for the GWR index of 30, the highest scores are found for India, Indonesia, China, and Vietnam, ranging between 26.5 and 23.5. The lowest score is for South Africa and Brazil at 4.0 and 5.5.

In the next period 2001–2012, the four countries of India, Indonesia, China, and Vietnam continue to score high between 23.0 and 20.0 but are now joined with higher scoring countries of the CAC region, namely Kazakhstan, Uzbekistan, Azerbaijan, and Tajikistan, next to Ethiopia, with scores of around 26.0. The lowest scores continued to be found among South Africa and Brazil with even lower levels at 2.0 and 4.5. They are joined at the lower end by Mexico and Venezuela with scores of 3.5 and 3.5.

The results over the two periods show an increasing gap between high- and low-performing countries in the combined area of growth with redistribution. Especially in the cases of South Africa, Brazil, Venezuela, and Mexico, their rank performances in terms of growth and redistribution have been falling relative to other countries. Most of the other 26 countries show rank improvements in growth and/or redistribution.

6. Concluding Remarks

Welfare economics teaches that the appraisal of economic growth is not independent from the appraisal of the income distribution underlying it. The joint development goals of growth with redistribution (GWR) can be fully derived from welfare theory. As such, growth with redistribution form the cornerstone of development policy, actions and performance.

While growth and redistribution considerations can be commonly integrated in many development policies and actions, a joint measurement of GWR performance at the country level faces many complexities due to intricate relationships between growth and distribution, and may not be feasible. There are four complexities. First, nations (via their current and future governments) tend to go first for growth, and subsequently evaluate the impact of growth on distribution, and when needed governments may take posterior actions in time to rebalance the distribution. This renders a joint measurement of growth with redistribution performances at one and the same year an incomplete exercise. Second, consensus on the distribution norm in relation to growth (which would function as the evaluation base) is specific for the country/region and year/periods concerned. Third, economic growth and income distribution tend to move along the Kuznets curve during the process of economic development, which makes performance evaluation dependent on the stage of economic development, and that complicates simple comparisons. Fourth, as redistribution of endowments enhances economic growth along the lines of

Tinbergen strategy, which require long gestation periods; yearly comparisons of GWR performance among divergent countries are less meaningful.

This chapter accommodated for the above complexities and limitations by applying what can be called considerate comparisons of GWR in the context of regional development and over longer periods than commonly done. The results show that the LAC countries Brazil, Mexico, Venezuela and South Africa are caught in the trap of a moderate to low economic growth with most regressive income distribution among the studied thirty leading developing countries. Having in mind that the four countries belong to the upper income per capita compared to other developing countries, the results suggest that the four countries have difficulties and fare failing in switching sides along the Kuznets curve.

At the other end, China, Indonesia, Vietnam and India (the EAP and SA regions), and some ex-Soviet countries in Asia appear to be the best performers regarding GWR over three decades of economic development. Their positive performances on GWR suggest that they have made good use of the Tinbergen strategy (redistribute endowments to facilitate growth) in their development plans.

Endnotes

1. See calculations in Bosworth and Collins (1996) and reviews in Crafts (2001).
2. The total poverty rates are higher than the averages in EAP and SA, reflecting the weights of China and India in the two regions. For example, for EAP in 2012, the total poverty rate is 17.9 while the average is 15.4; the difference for SA in 2012 is greater: 37 and 23, respectively. The difference between the total and the average tends to disappear in the other regions where divergence in country sizes is much less.
3. Nkurunziza and Bates (2003).

Part IV

Multi Sector Development and Policies

Chapter 7

The Social Accounting Matrix as Analytical Framework for Growth with Redistribution: Applications to Ten Developing Countries

1. Introduction

The social accounting matrix (SAM) is a unified statistical framework that is capable of collapsing the economy-wide circular flow in a compact whole. SAM includes the national accounting balances required for modeling equilibrium and allows for an appraisal of growth and distribution, next to other development issues. The SAM was first conceptually developed as an integrated system of national accounts by Stone and brought to life again via a large number of applications and refinements carried by many contributors, including Pyatt, Thorbecke, Adelman, Robinson, and Cohen, among others.

The idea of a social accounting matrix, SAM, is traceable to Quesnay's Tableau Economique in 1758. The idea was revived some 200 years later. Hicks coined the term social accounting in 1942; the realization of a SAM was the work of Stone (1947), and it was associates of Stone, working in the context of developing countries, who presented 30 years later the first comprehensive publication of a SAM for a developing country, cf. Pyatt and Roe (1977). In the two to three decades following the introduction of the SAM, there has been a remarkable shift of interest from the input–output matrix and multi-sector models to the social accounting matrix as a basic framework for economic modeling. Most developing countries have now some reference available on a constructed SAM and many have used the SAM as a benchmark for calibrating a related computable general equilibrium (CGE) model.

In this chapter, we select and study the results of a few SAM applications from the many SAM multiplier analysis we applied to developing countries. The objective is to highlight the impact of sector development policies on the twin goals of growth and distribution. Section 2 introduces the basics of the SAM. Section 3 converts the SAM into a circular flow model. Section 4 reviews multiplier results. Section 5 decomposes the SAM multipliers in separate effects. Section 6 uses the SAM multipliers to identify gainers and losers. Section 7 ends with closing remarks on the scope and limitations.

2. Tabulation and Construction of the Social Accounting Matrix

By way of introduction, it can be stated that the social accounting matrix, SAM, is compiled according to the same accounting principles as input–output tables, each transaction being recorded twice so that any ingoing in one account must be balanced by an outgoing of another account. However, the SAM contains a complete list of transactions describing income, expenditure, and production flows among sectors, factors of production, and groups of households. These transactions are usually grouped into several sets of accounts belonging to various economic agents, as will be elaborated on later. The SAM itself is nothing more or less than the transformation of the circular flow among agents in the national economy, as depicted in Figure 1, into a matrix of transactions between the various agents as displayed in Table 1.

In the first line of the figure, production activities produce goods. Second production activities employ factors of production and pay them. Third, institutions (including households, firms, and governments) earn their incomes from supplying

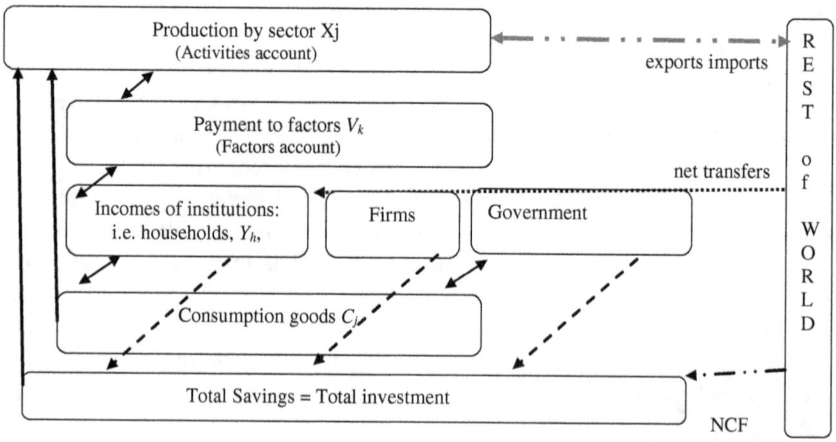

Figure 1. Circular flow.

factors of production. Fourth, institutions spend their incomes on the consumption of commodities that feedback as demand for consumption goods in the production activities, and fifth, institutions spend the rest of their incomes on savings that are turned into demand for capital goods in the production activities. Separated on the right-hand side are transactions with the rest of the world (ROW). At the upper bound, the production activities export and import goods and services to and from the ROW. At the lower bound, ROW supplements savings and investment by the foreign capital flow. In between ROW is engaged in transfer transactions with the institutions.

In correspondence with the circular flow, the SAM contains the following account categories: (1) Activities accounts consist of payment received and paid for in and out deliveries among the sectors. (2) Factors of production accounts receiving earnings and paying them to factor owners, i.e. the institutions of households, firms, and government. (3), (4), and (5): These are current institutions accounts of households firms, and governments describing their receipts and spending. (6) Capital account consists of total savings transactions aggregated over all institutions and supplemented by ROW whereby total savings are equal to total investments that are distributed on the production activities. (7) Rest of the world account. It is worthwhile to mention that the SAM accounts can be alternatively ordered, though the above ordering is the most commonly used.

The circular flow transactions are presented in a simplified social accounting matrix form in Table 1.

The construction of the SAM is usually done in two steps: In the first step, the published estimates of the national accounts are sufficient to construct an aggregate matrix of incomings and outgoings for the accounts. In the second step, the accounts undergo disaggregation. The required data for disaggregating the SAM include (a) the input–output table for disaggregating the production activities by producing sectors and converting data for transforming the product classification into the sector classification. It can happen that for a couple of cells in the disaggregated SAM, the data are not available or are less reliable; in these cases, sound judgments on the initial values are required. (b) Household budget surveys for breaking up the household account into specific household groups and specifying their incomes by source and expenditures by type of consumption commodity, (c) conversion of commodities to the sector classification and (d) government revenues and expenditures. The definitive values are obtained by applying the RAS method to the whole matrix, which simultaneously assures consistency of the grand totals of the rows and columns.

The quantified SAM matrix giving values of national accounts transactions can be converted into a coefficient matrix which divides each cell by its vertical total cell, as is done in deriving input–output coefficients. The assumption of a stable proportional relationship between the parts and their whole is basic and defendable in a static modeling analysis.

Table 1. A simplified version of the social accounting matrix.

	1. Activities j	2. Factors	3. Households	4. Firms	5. Government	6. Capital (investment)	7. Rest of World (ROW)	Totals
1. Activities j (Production sectors)	Domestic intermediate goods j to j'		Private consumption spending on j		Public consumption spending on j	Domestic investment j	Exports j	Gross output j = gross input j
2. Factors	Factor earnings							Factors payments
3. Households		Incomes earned			Government Transfers		ROW Transfers	Private incomes = spending
4. Firms		Corporate profits					ROW Transfers	Firms incomes = spending
5. Government	Indirect taxes received		Income taxes	Corporate taxes			ROW Transfers	Government income = spending
6. Capital (savings)			Private savings	Corporate savings	Government savings		Foreign capital flow (FCF)	Total savings = total investment
7. Rest of world	Imported intermediate goods		Imported consumption		Imported consumption	Imported investment		ROW receipts = ROW payments
Totals	gross input j	Factors payments	Private spending	Firms spending	Government spending	Total investment	Payments by ROW	Grand total

3. The SAM as an Economy-Wide Model

In converting the obtained coefficient matrix of the SAM into a SAM model, it is necessary to distinguish between endogenous and exogenous variables so that an analysis can be made of how the endogenous variables are impacted by the exogenous variables. We assume the government account, the capital account, and the ROW account to be exogenous (that is, government consumption, all investment, and all transfers). This allows all other variables in the SAM to be endogenous.

More generally formulated, let the endogenous variables on the left-hand side be denoted by vector υ (consisting of production by sector, earnings by factor, income, consumption, and savings by households, among others), the exogenous variables on the right-hand side by vector e (consisting of governments, investments, and ROW variables), and the SAM coefficient matrix for the endogenous variables by A_s, then the system can be described generally by $\upsilon - A_s\upsilon = e$. Inverting the SAM matrix of coefficients and solving gives eq. (1), where M_s stands for the SAM matrix of multipliers:

$$\upsilon = (I - A_s)^{-1}e = M_s e, \tag{1}$$

Depending on the disaggregation of the SAM, M_s can be a very large matrix. For most analytical purposes, a small selection of specific multipliers is sufficient. This chapter will focus on the multiplier impacts of exogenous spending injections in sectors j (these can be via government consumption, investment, or exports) and of exogenous income transfers to household groups h (these can be via transfers from government or ROW). One can trace these multiplier impacts on such endogenous variables as the output by sector X_j and the income by household group Y_h. As such, the analysis can be restricted to four types of multipliers. These are the multipliers showing impacts by two types of exogenous impulses that are spending and transfers, on two endogenous variables: sector output and household incomes, Table 2.

There are several uses for these multipliers. For a couple of years directly before and after the year of computation, the SAM multipliers can be employed to show applicable economic effects of exogenous stimulus caused by governments, investments, or exports, directed to a particular sector. The two economic effects

Table 2. Selected output and income multipliers.

Impact of exogenous impulse on endogenous variables	Spending injection in sector j'	Income transfer to household group h'
Output of sector j, X_j	$M_{s,jj'}$	$M_{s,jh'}$
Income of household group h, Y_h	$M_{s,hj'}$	$M_{s,hh'}$

to be examined are the output effects (i.e. the growth of output and its distribution on sectors) and the income effects (i.e. generation and distribution of income on household groups). In a similar way, one can assess output and income effects of income transfers from government and ROW which are directed to specific household groups.

4. Output and Income SAM Multipliers: Results for Ten Countries

The comparative analysis of this section considers SAMs for Colombia, Korea, Pakistan, and Suriname, constructed by the same team of investigators, and for six other countries: Egypt, Kenya, India, Indonesia, Iran, and Sri Lanka, from various published sources.[1] The SAMs of these countries are very diversified in content. However, appropriate aggregation and modifications brought the various SAMs to a common base. In the process, we necessarily exclude some valuable information on some countries but enhance drawing more general conclusions on the relationships between growth and distribution. Foremost are the specific disaggregations of the activity and household accounts. The classification of activities had to be limited to four large groups of sectors: agriculture, mining, industry, and services. Distinguishing more sectors would reduce the uniformity and comparability of the 10 SAMs reported here. The classification of households emphasizes dualities in the location of the population in urban and rural areas and the differentiation within urban and rural groups by level of income earned. This differentiation is done by distinguishing urban households into three groups: employers, employees, and self-employed, and breaking down rural households into three groups: large landowners, medium landowners, and small/landless households. For a couple of countries, a seventh residual group was incorporated so as to accommodate classifications which did not fit the standardized six categories. The SAMs of Egypt and India form exceptions to the above as they follow personal income distributions in distinguishing between household groups with different income levels.

The focus in the applications reported here obviously lies with the contributions of the SAM framework to deliberations on development policies. Accordingly, the analysis will start with (a) a review of results for output and income multipliers linked to sectoral injections and household transfers, (b) decomposition of these multipliers in transfer, open-loop, and closed-loop effects, (c) analysis of the growth and distributionary built-in bias in the structure of the economy as reflected by the SAM, which will allow identifying gainers and losers, and (d) the compact use of SAM simulations to highlight strategic choices for growth with redistribution.

Table 3 shows output multipliers for spending injections in sectoral activities. The multiplier reported here is $M_{Sjj'}$. Most of the countries fall in the middle

Table 3. Output multipliers $M_{s,jj'}$ and income multiplier $M_{s,hj'}$ following an exogenous spending injection of one unit in activity sectors.

Country	Multiplier	Agriculture	Mining	Industry	Services	Average
Colombia 1970						
output	$M_{s,jj'}$	4.447	4.952	4.287	4.678	4.591
income	$M_{s,hj'}$	2.146	2.512	1.651	2.230	2.135
Suriname 1979						
output	$M_{s,jj'}$	1.967	1.871	1.849	1.911	1.900
income	$M_{s,hj'}$	1.153	0.777	0.816	1.220	0.992
Egypt 1976						
output	$M_{s,jj'}$	2.897	1.721	2.537	2.997	2.538
income	$M_{s,hj'}$	1.570	0.854	0.893	1.473	1.073
Kenya 1976						
output	$M_{s,jj'}$	2.872	3.099	2.541	2.934	2.861
income	$M_{s,hj'}$	1.867	1.127	0.910	1.501	1.351
India 1968/69						
output	$M_{s,jj'}$	6.910	5.185	5.977	5.711	5.946
income	$M_{s,hj'}$	4.427	3.384	3.328	3.599	3.684
Indonesia 1975						
output	$M_{s,jj'}$	4.176	na	2.414	3.579	3.390
income	$M_{s,hj'}$	2.567	na	1.395	2.395	2.119
Iran 1970						
output	$M_{s,jj'}$	4.358	3.025	3.576	3.595	3.639
income	$M_{s,hj'}$	2.584	1.470	1.752	2.085	1.973
Korea 1973						
output	$M_{s,jj'}$	3.514	3.994	3.198	3.766	3.618
income	$M_{s,hj'}$	1.883	2.080	1.144	1.809	1.729
Pakistan 1978/9						
Output	$M_{s,jj'}$	9.457	8.911	8.227	8.483	8.770
Income	$M_{s,hj'}$	4.430	4.116	3.534	4.033	4.028
Sri Lanka 1970						
output	$M_{s,jj'}$	3.334	na	2.929	3.007	3.090
income	$M_{s,hj'}$	2.289	na	1.714	2.163	2.055

Note: na: not available

range: Colombia, Korea, Iran, Indonesia, Sri Lanka, and Kenya, scoring 4.6, 3.6, 3.6, 3.4, 3.1, and 2.9, respectively.[2] In general, output multipliers are highest for impulses in the agricultural sector, followed by the services sector, which is second in 7 out of the 10 countries. Industry ranks between third and fourth. Mining does not show a common ranking among the 10 countries. The five Asian countries of

Iran, Pakistan, India, Sri Lanka, and Indonesia show a particularly homogeneous pattern of sectoral ranking regarding their output multipliers.

Turning to income multipliers, $M_{S,hj'}$, it is observed from Table 3 that for all countries together, the size of the income multipliers is about half the output multipliers, 0.53 on average. For individual countries, it is noted that Egypt, Pakistan, Colombia, Kenya, and Korea extract a lower income proportion from the output, around 0.45, while Sri Lanka, Indonesia, and India extract a higher proportion, around 0.64. In the latter countries, it takes less of an output effort to produce a unit of household income.

Table 4 summarizes results regarding multiplier effects of income transfers to household groups. The impacts of income transfers on output and income are denoted by $M_{s,jh'}$ and $M_{s,hh'}$, respectively. Compared with the previous table, in all cases, average output multipliers of income transfers are lower than output multipliers of sectoral injections, but income effects from income transfers are higher than income effects from sectoral injections.

For most of the 10 countries, it is found that income transfers to the poorer household groups — mostly in rural areas — generate the highest output and income multipliers. Injections into richer households — mostly urban — have lower output and income multipliers. These results suggest that a redistribution of incomes from urban to rural household groups may increase growth and equality.

5. Decomposition of SAM Multipliers into Transfer, Open, and Closed-Loop Effects

The decomposition of the aggregate multipliers into meaningful effects will be the focus of this section. Recalling eq. (1), the aggregate multiplier matrix M_S in this equation can be decomposed into three multiplier matrices M_1, M_2, and M_3, as in eq. (2). See Appendix for the derivation of the decomposition.

$$v = A_S v + e = (I - A_S)^{-1} e = M_S e = M_3 M_2 M_3 e \tag{2}$$

M_1, which is known as the transfer multiplier, captures intra-effects resulting from transfers that happen between one variable and other variables belonging to the same endogenous account (i.e. effects of an impulse in a production activity on other production activities or in other words, the Leontief multipliers).

M_2, known as the open-loop effects, captures the effects of one endogenous account on other endogenous accounts (i.e. from production to factor income to household income).

M_3, standing for the closed-loop effects, ensures that an effect from a specific account is subjected to circular flows through all endogenous accounts (i.e. from household income to product consumption to production activities to factor income

Table 4. Output multiplier $M_{s,jh'}$ and income multiplier $M_{a,hh'}$ following an exogenous income transfer of unit to household groups.

Country: variable	multiplier	Urban			Rural			Other groups	Average all
		Poor	Middle	Rich	Poor	Middle	Rich		
Colombia									
output	$M_{s,jh'}$	4.117	4.417	4.014	4.809	4.356	3.108	3.958	4.083
income	$M_{a,hh'}$	2.795	2.913	2.756	2.965	2.863	2.341	2.728	2.766
Surinamee									
output	$M_{s,jh'}$	1.539		1.147	1.45		1.261		1.349
income	$M_{a,hh'}$	1.869		1.669	1.839		1.735		1.785
Egypt									
output	$M_{s,jh'}$	2.593	2.464	1.662	2.108	1.582	1.482		1.982
income	$M_{a,hh'}$	2.124	2.083	1.759	1.901	1.692	1.651		1.87
Kenya									
output	$M_{s,jh'}$	2.463	2.088	1.309	2.507	2.31	2.4	2.088	2.195
income	$M_{a,hh'}$	2.353	2.224	1.743	2.339	2.36	2.299	2.071	2.198
India									
output	$M_{s,jh'}$		6.288			4.433			5.361
income	$M_{a,hh'}$		4.932			3.752			4.342
Indonesia									
output	$M_{s,jh'}$	3.146		2.727	3.916		3.366	3.413	3.314
income	$M_{a,hh'}$	3.011		2.761	3.44		3.104	3.142	3.092
Iran									
output	$M_{s,jh'}$		2.568			3.459			3.014
income	$M_{a,hh'}$		2.414			2.916			2.665
Korea									
output	$M_{s,jh'}$	3.206	3.388	3.146	3.041	2.798	2.515		3.016
income	$M_{a,hh'}$	2.475	2.557	2.445	2.387	2.773	2.143		2.38
Pakistan									
output	$M_{s,jh'}$	7.525	7.698	7.536	8.561	8.123	7.378	7.579	7.774
income	$M_{a,hh'}$	4.421	4.496	4.435	4.875	4.579	4.359	4.433	4.52
Sri Lanka									
output	$M_{s,jh'}$		1.962			2.33		2.305	2.265
income	$M_{a,hh'}$		2.323			2.378		2.689	2.53

and then to household income, and so on again and again through all four types of endogenous accounts). The understanding of the terms direct and indirect effects in the traditional output–input context may cause confusion in the SAM context. The following can be stated on terminology: the transfer effects are the Leontief effects and they include both the direct and indirect effects in the limited sense and scope of the activities accounts. Similarly, the open-loop effects can be interpreted to include direct and indirect effects. However, the closed-loop effects are exclusively indirect effects but then in the broader sense of the whole SAM framework.

We shall limit the presentation here to the decomposed impacts of exogenous demand injections in activities on activities, $M_{s,jj'}$, and comment briefly on the decomposition of other impacts. The decomposition of $M_{s,jj'}$ in terms of the three effects is shown in eq. (3):

$$\begin{aligned} &M_{s,jj'} = M_{3,jj} * M_{2,jj} * M_{1,jj'} \\ &\text{aggregate} = \text{closed} * \text{open} * \text{transfer} \end{aligned} \tag{3}$$

Since $M_{2,jj}$ does not engage other accounts than its own account of activities j, the open-loop effects are not applicable here, $M_{2,jj}$ being an identity matrix. The aggregate multiplier falls thus into the transfer effects (which are the Leontief multipliers), $M_{1,jj'}$, and the closed-loop effects, $M_{3,jj}$. Table 5 displays the aggregate effects of $M_{s,jj'}$ next to the transfer effects, $M_{1,jj'}$, the latter representing the Leontief multipliers. The difference between the two effects is the closed-loop effect. With the exception of Suriname, in all other countries, the closed-loop effects overshadow the transfer effects by large margins. For the 10 sampled countries as a whole, the transfer or Leontief effects form only about one-third while the closed-loop effects form two-thirds of the SAM multipliers. While the transfer effects, i.e. the Leontief multipliers, point to manufacturing as the key sector with the highest multiplier effects and the foremost contributor to the growth of production activity from an additionally allocated unit of spending, these conclusions are turned upside down when the closed-loop effects are incorporated, resulting in SAM multipliers that are higher for agriculture, mining, and services than for manufacturing. Many development policy recommendations on key sectors for economic growth and employment creation that were based on inter-industry analysis, typical of the fifties and sixties, lost their validity within the SAM framework.

The results should not be interpreted to mean that if the 10 countries would have expanded in the past relatively more in agriculture than in manufacturing, they would have necessarily achieved a higher overall growth, since realization of the multiplier potentials requires significant exogenous expansion of spending both domestically and in the rest of the world in agriculture versus manufacturing, which is the point for discussion. Besides, both the SAM and the input–output emphasize the demand side of the economy and do not consider limits on the supply side.

It is now easy to consider and comprehend the decomposition of the multiplier effects of sectoral demand injections on household incomes, eq. (4):

$$M_{s,hj'} = M_{3,hh}{}^{*}M_{2,hj}{}^{*}M_{1,jj'} \tag{4}$$

In eq. (4), a production injection creates $M_{1,jj'}$ transfer effects (i.e. Leontief multiplier) and carries these through $M_{2,hj}$ open-loop effects, thereby creating household incomes, after which these household incomes are engaged in a circular flow

Table 5. Breakdown of SAM multipliers, M_S, into transfer effects (Leontief multiplier), M_1, and closed-loop effects, M_3, 10 countries.

	Agriculture	Mining	Industry	Services
Colombia SAM multiplier	4.447	4.953	4.287	4.679
Transfer effect (Leontief multiplier)	1.478	1.499	1.985	1.558
Suriname SAM multiplier	1.968	1.871	1.849	1.912
Transfer effect (Leontief multiplier)	1.218	1.385	1.316	1.121
Egypt SAM multiplier	2.898	1.722	2.537	2.997
Transfer effect (Leontief multiplier)	1.321	1.348	1.575	1.353
Kenya SAM multiplier	2.871	3.099	2.540	2.934
Transfer effect (Leontief multiplier)	1.160	2.118	1.755	1.615
India SAM multiplier	6.910	5.184	5.977	5.711
Transfer effect (Leontief multiplier)	1.350	1.240	1.936	1.411
Indonesia SAM multiplier	4.176	na	2.414	3.579
Transfer effect (Leontief multiplier)	1.584	na	1.345	1.240
Iran SAM multiplier	4.357	3.025	3.576	3.594
Transfer effect (Leontief multiplier)	1.396	1.454	1.668	1.344
Korea SAM multiplier	3.515	3.995	3.198	3.767
Transfer effect (Leontief multiplier)	1.388	1.451	1.847	1.619
Pakistan SAM multiplier	9.463	8.924	8.110	8.610
Transfer effect (Leontief multiplier)	1.865	1.888	2.187	1.671
Sri Lanka SAM multiplier	3.335	na	2.929	3.007
Transfer effect (Leontief multiplier)	1.378	na	1.524	1.193
Average all countries SAM multiplier	4.39	3.28	4.68	4.08
Transfer effect (Leontief multiplier)	1.41	1.55	1.71	1.41
Closed-loop effect	2.98	1.73	2.96	2.67
Ratio closed/transfer	2.11	1.12	1.73	1.89

Note: na = not available

through the whole system and back to incomes, i.e. the closed-loop effect of $M_{3,hh}$. The latter are behind the phenomenon that income redistribution injections, after rotating through the circular flow of the SAM, have a tendency to vanish and reproduce the initial situation. The expenditure patterns of the different household groups tend to benefit sectors, earnings, and their households' incomes in the same ways.

Turning to multipliers of exogenous income transfers to household groups their decomposition can be decomposed along the lines of eq. (5):

$$M_{s,hh'} = M_{3,hh}{}^{*}M_{2,hh}{}^{*}M_{1,hh'} \tag{5}$$

The decomposition is simple. Because of lack of data on transfers among household groups, the transfer effect may not be fully traced. Also because the open-loop effect is not relevant in this context, the implication is that the closed-loop effect is about equal to the aggregate multiplier.

Finally, the decomposition of the multiplier effects of household income transfer injections on sectoral production is displayed in eq. (6):

$$M_{s,jh'} = M_{3,jj}{}^{*}M_{2,jh}{}^{*}M_{1,hh'} \tag{6}$$

Given that $M_{1,hh'}$ is not applicable, the transfer injections will be passed directly to sectoral activities through $M_{2,jh}$ and from thereon subjected to a circular flow through $M_{3,jj}$.

6. Identification of Gainers and Losers in SAM Multipliers

Besides studying the level of a multiplier and the decomposable mechanisms that determine them, it is important to uncover the built-in distributive inclinations of the multiplier effects with respect to sectoral growth. Which sectors can be described as gainers and which as losers in terms of their comparative multipliers relative to their comparative shares in total output (production)? The structural pattern of the SAM determines the built-in growth pace of the individual sectors in the near future. To identify the built-in growth pace, a gainers and losers index for the sector-to-sector effects, $GLI_{jj'}$, is defined as follows[3]

$$GLI_{jj'} = [(M_{s,jj'} - 1)/(\Sigma_j M_{s,jj'} - 1)]/[\text{Output}_{j,o}/\,\Sigma_j \text{Output}_{j,o}] \tag{7}$$

where j and j' denote receiving and injecting sectors and J is the total number of sectors. In the *nominator*, the multiplier effect of the concerned sector is measured after deducting the unit injection of 1 and stated in ratio to the sum of multipliers of all sectors after deducting the unit injections of $1 * J$. The *denominator* is the share of sector j in the total output of all sectors in the actual year 0, i.e. the year to which the SAM refers. Division of nominator by denominator gives GLI. For values of $GLI_{jj'}>1$, <1, and $=1$, there are positive, negative, and neutral redistributive effects. For instance, values of $GLI_{jj'} = 1$ mean that sectoral injections would exactly reproduce the sectoral dispersion pattern of the base year.

Similarly, we can calculate a gainer and loser index, $GLI_{hj'}$, for the multiplier effects of sectoral injections j' on the income of household group h, as done in eq. (8), which gives in the *nominator* the share of the multiplier income that goes to one h in all h's, and in the *denominator*, the share of the actual income received to one h in all h's. Division of nominator by denominator gives GLI. Values of $GLI_{hj'} = 1$ mean that sectoral injection would reproduce exactly the share group

i had in the base year in total income. A higher value would mean an increase in its income share; a negative value would mean a decrease.

$$GLI_{hj'} = [(M_{s,hj'})/(\Sigma_h M_{s,hj'})]/[\text{Income}_{h,o}/\,\Sigma_h \text{Income}_{h,o}] \quad (8)$$

The two indices in eqs. (7) and (8), that is, $GLI_{jj'}$ and $GLI_{hj'}$, are calculated for the 10 countries in Table 6. First take the $GLI_{jj'}$. In general, agriculture scores a positive $GLI_{jj'}$ for most countries except for India. Mining shows also a positive and high $GLI_{jj'}$ in all countries, but the data on mining for the studied past periods were incomplete and distorted as some parts of the mining sector seem to have been included in the industry sector. For a couple of countries, data were not separately available for mining. The sectors of industry and services show negative $GLI_{jj'}$ for most countries except Kenya, Indonesia, and Sri Lanka. It is observed that these results relate to the early development phases of development in the 10 countries. Their SAMs for recent years are likely to show the opposite results as the sectors quoted to be gainers (agriculture and mining) have grown less than the sectors quoted to be losers (industry and services) in most of the 10 studied countries.

Turning to the impact of injections on the incomes of household groups in urban and rural areas, all countries show $GLI_{hj'}$, that is, positive for rural households and negative for urban households except for Colombia and Kenya which show the SAM multipliers to favor urban over rural.

The same analysis of *GLI* is applicable for the case where the injections are in the form of income transfers to household groups. In correspondence with the case for sectoral injections, two types of *GLIs* for household transfers can be formulated, giving the impact of the transfers on the incomes of household groups: $GLI_{hh'}$ and on the output of the sectors $GLI_{jh'}$.

$$GLI_{hh'} = [(M_{s,hh'} - 1/(\Sigma_h M_{s,hh'} - 1)]/[\text{Income}_{h,o}\,\Sigma_h \text{Income}_{h,o}] \quad (9)$$

$$GLI_{jh'} = [(M_{s,jh'})/(\Sigma_j M_{s,jh'})]/[\text{Output}_{j,o}/\,\Sigma_j \text{Output}_{j,o}] \quad (10)$$

Both equations can be applied to simulate equal unit transfers to each household group, summed and averaged over all household groups to give average results of gainers and losing among household groups and sectors.

The pattern of results for household transfers corresponds with the earlier results for sector injections displayed in the table and need not be shown again. The results confirm the general tendency of obtaining a high GLI for the poorer household groups, especially the rural ones, which is an indication of the existence of progressive inclinations in the mechanisms of income distribution. The fact that the actual distribution of income in the 10 countries is worse than what the income multipliers indicate can be explained by the actualized presence of regressive patterns of exogenous impulses.

Table 6. Gaining and losing sectors and households following equal units of injections in all sectors.

	Gainers and losers indexes GLI following equal injections in all sectors					
	GLI among sectors				GLI among households	
Countries	Agriculture	Mining	Industry	Services	Urban	Rural
Colombia						
nominator	0.24	0.28	0.23	0.26	0.6289	0.3731
denominator	0.21	0.01	0.41	0.37	0.62	0.38
GLI	1.17	19.38	0.56	0.69	1.01	0.98
Suriname						
nominator	0.27	0.24	0.24	0.25	0.58	0.42
denominator	0.0748	0.2923	0.1808	0.4522	0.57	0.43
GLI	3.59	0.83	1.31	0.56	1.00	1.00
Egypt						
nominator	0.31	0.12	0.25	0.32	0.56	0.44
denominator	0.21	0.05	0.39	0.34	0.66	0.34
GLI	1.44	2.17	0.64	0.96	0.85	1.30
Kenya						
nominator	0.25	0.28	0.21	0.26	0.41	0.59
denominator	0.24	0.22	0.18	0.34	0.38	0.62
GLI	1.07	1.28	1.15	0.76	1.08	0.95
India						
nominator	0.30	0.21	0.25	0.24	0.56	0.44
denominator	0.37	0.02	0.36	0.25	0.60	0.40
GLI	0.81	9.62	0.70	0.95	0.93	1.10
Indonesia						
nominator	0.51	na	0.23	0.42	0.29	0.70
denominator	0.36	na	0.34	0.30	0.34	0.66
GLI	1.42	na	0.68	1.40	0.84	1.07
Iran						
nominator	0.32	0.19	0.24	0.25	0.69	0.31
denominator	0.22	0.08	0.34	0.36	0.75	0.25
GLI	1.42	2.48	0.72	0.69	0.92	1.23
Korea						
nominator	0.24	0.29	0.21	0.26	0.67	0.33
denominator	0.11	0.14	0.38	0.37	0.67	0.33
GLI	2.18	2.04	0.56	0.71	0.99	1.01
Pakistan						
nominator	0.27	0.25	0.23	0.24	0.3134	0.6866
denominator	0.25	0.01	0.44	0.30	0.34	0.66
GLI	1.08	26.80	0.53	0.80	0.93	1.04
Sri Lanka						
nominator	0.44	na	0.37	0.38	0.2663	0.7337
denominator	0.33	na	0.32	0.35	0.28	0.72
GLI	1.36	na	1.14	1.08	0.95	1.02

Note: *GLI= nominator / denominator*

7. Discussion of Scope and Limitations

In some sense, any consistent economy-wide model must be congruent with some accounting matrix that frames the model. The advantage of the SAM is that by specifying a compact SAM, the underlying model of the economy is kept compact and can nevertheless reflect on a wide range of issues in development policy. The SAM framework has other useful contributions. First, the SAM serves as a helpful tool in setting up an integrated statistical system of accounts for differentiated agents in the economy. The advantage of forcing national statistics into a social accounting framework is that the statistician can discover inconsistencies and gaps, which went unnoticed before. Second, SAM facilitates the initialization of corresponding economy-wide models, in particular CGE models. Third, once a SAM is available, it can be used to give a quantitative diagnosis of the structure of the whole economy. Fourth, the availability of SAMs for different countries and for more years allows for the investigation of economic mechanisms behind superior and inferior performances.

Any analytical framework has its limitations next to its contributions. Several limitations of the SAM, and counterpart arguments, are in place. First, cell entries of the SAM are amounts, i.e. products of prices × quantities. However, quantities and prices are not explicitly disentangled. In the fixed price multiplier model, supplied amounts are supposed to adjust to demanded amounts. They will, but if there is restricted capacity, the result is inflation. This may require a revision downward in the real sizes of multipliers. Of course, if the size of the injection is relatively small, which is usually the case, the fixed price multiplier results can still be seen to represent realizable quantity effects. It is also feasible to check in a single way within the SAM framework whether the capacity limits will be violated or not. The supply side can simply be modeled as a relationship between the investment rate and economic growth via an incremental capital–output ratio, κ, as in $K/X = \kappa(\Delta X/X)$. From the SAM, we obtain multiplier effects for K and X. If division of the multiplier effects of K by those of X gives values equal to or above K/X for the base period, this implies that the SAM solves for sufficient investment to meet the projected capacity increase.

Second, it is commonly perceived that a SAM-inverted model belongs to the prototype of demand-oriented models. However, under general equilibrium conditions, the SAM can be seen as a representation of both the demand and the supply side as well, which is why in computable general equilibrium (CGE) models, the SAM is directly used to initiate CGE models.

Third, the SAM model describes an endogenous economy with fixed relative prices and complementarities-based production and consumption functions. Producers and consumers are assumed to face fixed prices, and in their pursuit of profit and utility maximization, respectively, adjustment takes the form of changes in quantities supplied and demanded. As regards the assumption of producers and consumers facing given relative prices, this is common practice in short-run models. Moreover, even in the longer run, having in mind the broad categories of sectors and products in the SAM, analysts can draw on empirical evidence over long periods which supports indefinite shifts in relative prices between such broad categories, cf. Bleaney and Greenaway (1993).

Fourth, there is the shortcoming that the SAM is a static model and its reflections are valid only for the year for which it is observed. Since more SAMs can be quantified for more years, the statics shortcoming may need to be assessed in relative terms.

Fifth, it is noted that the coefficient matrix in the SAM model, A_S, is a matrix of fixed average proportions. Linear relationships are assumed throughout: constant shares of factor remunerations in total output, of household incomes in the various factor payments, of commodities in household expenditure, and of sectors in commodity production. Compared to averages, observed marginal coefficients are better since they incorporate income and scale effects, but they can be disputable as their estimated values may carry other than income effects, which is inconsistent with the SAM framework. While consumption propensities can be calculated sensibly as marginal instead of average values, the problem is severe for input–output coefficients, factor earnings coefficients, and other coefficients in the model, which do not usually depict stable marginal propensities. Taking a portion of the coefficients as marginal and the other as average propensities introduces an estimation bias. Under the circumstances, many analysts of cross-country data would prefer assuming and using uniform fixed coefficient systems over incomparable specifications for individual countries.

Sixth, the size of the multiplier depends to some degree on the level of aggregation. This argument is less relevant in the context of a uniform aggregation for the compared countries. The differences in multipliers due to alternative aggregations were tested for the 10 countries studied. The differences do not go beyond 8% for individual countries, which is a moderate margin of uncertainty.

Last, but not least, evaluation of the multipliers of the SAM model cannot be done in isolation from the closure rules applied. The size of the multipliers depends on the choice of the exogenous and endogenous variables, which, in turn, depends on the problem studied. However, for the short-term horizon, there is a tacitly accepted rationale among most economic modelers to consider various types of government spending and variables of the rest of the world as exogenous. This rationale was postulated in Koopmans and Montias (1971) and is particularly relevant in the early phases of economic development where decisions on investment are dominated by the government.

Appendix: Decomposition of SAM Multipliers

The aggregate multiplier matrix can be decomposed into three multiplier matrices M_1, M_2, and M_3 as in the following equation. M_l gives transfer effects, M_2 captures the open-loop effect which is the interaction among and between the endogenous accounts, and M_3 is the closed-loop effect that ensures that the circular flow of income is completed among endogenous accounts

$$v = Av + e = (I - A)^1 e = M_S e = M_3 M_2 M_1 e \tag{i}$$

The formal derivation of the decomposed multipliers proceeds by separating matrix $\tilde{A}$ from A, provided that $\tilde{A}$ is of the same size as A and that $(I - \tilde{A})^{-1}$ exists.

$$v = Av + e = (A - \tilde{A})v + \tilde{A}v + e = (I - \tilde{A})^{-1}(A - \tilde{A})v + (I - \tilde{A})^{-1}e = A^* v + (I - \tilde{A})^{-1}e \tag{ii}$$

Here, $(I - \tilde{A})^{-1}$ refers to the transfer multiplier M_1. Derivation of M_2 and M_3 proceeds further as in eqs. (iii)–(v).

Both sides of eq. (ii) can be multiplied by A^*, substituting for $A^* v$ from eq. (ii) and rearranging terms to give

$$v = A^{*2} v + (I + A^*)(I + \tilde{A})^{-1}e \tag{iii}$$

The same manipulation can be repeated with A^{*2} up to A^{*k} so that in general

$$v = A^{*k} v + (I + A^* + A^{*2} + \cdots + A^{*(k-1)})(I - \tilde{A})^{-1}e \tag{iv}$$

For any positive value for k, it is true then that

$$v = (I - A^{*k})^{-1}(I + A^* + A^{*2} + \cdots + A^{*(k-1)})(I - \tilde{A})^{-1}e \tag{v}$$

Here then, $(I - A^{*k})^{-1}$ is identified with M_3. $(I + A^* + A^{*2} + \cdots + A^{*(k-1)})$ is identified with M_2 and, as was just mentioned, $(I - \tilde{A})^{-1}$ refers to M_1. The multipliers can also be rearranged in an additive form. The multiplicative decomposition can be rearranged, as done by Stone (1978), into four additive components, namely the initial injection I and the net contributions of the transfer effect T, open loop effect 0, and closed-loop effect C, as follows:

$$M_a = I + (M_1 - I) + (M_2 - I)M_1 + (M_3 - I)M_2 M_1 = I + T + O + C \tag{vi}$$

Endnotes

1. For the sources of the ten SAMs, see Cohen (2002).
2. India and Pakistan are shown to have the highest average output multipliers, 5.9 and 8.8, respectively, which is partly due to a treatment of imports in their SAMs that does not fully consider leakage due to imports. At the other extreme, Suriname and Egypt show the lowest output multipliers, 1.9 and 2.5, respectively, reflecting low degrees of interdependence.
3. *GLI* was first discussed and applied in Cohen (1988, 1989). In these publications, the index was named relative distributive measure (RDM). Reflecting on the indicator *ex post*, it is sounder to call it a gainers and losers index (*GLI*).

Chapter 8

Macro, Sector, and Microeconomics of Dualistic Development: Case Studies of Indonesia and Pakistan

1. Introduction

The previous chapter demonstrated the use of the social accounting matrix (SAM) in the assessment of the relationship between economic growth and income equality under different combinations of policy instruments. In this chapter, the assessment gains more transparency when the SAM is grossly simplified to represent a macro dualistic economy along the lines of W.A. Lewis, with two activities only: a modern sector with high productivity and high growth prospects, and a traditional sector with low productivity and is less prosperous. The analysis goes beyond Lewis as we introduce a corresponding classification of household groups into high-income and low-income earners. The macro dualist approach focuses on two contrasting sectors through which growth is caused, and on two contrasting household groups which compose the shape of income distribution.

The striking contrasts between the modern and traditional sectors are not only present and apparent in the macro and sector analysis but are also present and gain more substance when these contrasts are studied and highlighted in the microeconomic context. Micro survey analysis of small enterprises in the modern and traditional sectors shows contrasting conditions of factor productivity and growth prospects. The market appears to be conditioned to accept and promote the co-existence of its dualistic character.

Section 2 will apply the SAM analysis in the macro context of the dualistic economy. Section 3 will apply enterprise survey data to highlight market imperfections in the dualistic economy. Both sections will use comparable data for two large developing countries: Indonesia and Pakistan. Although the empirics refer to large developing countries of the eighties and nineties, the validity of the results and the analytical methods used for the developing countries as a whole and for current years are not in doubt, as witnessed by more recent studies.[1] Section 4 includes concluding remarks.

2. Macro Sector Dualistic Developments and Policies

In the process of economic development, there are the high-productivity sectors that lead the economy into higher economic growth, and there are the low-productivity sectors that lag behind. The first tends to correspond with the formal or modern sectors; the second contains what is generally known as traditional and informal sectors. Households whose earnings are coupled to the more productive sectors become better off, while households whose incomes come from the work they do in the low-productivity sectors will get relatively less income. This relative independence of the two segments is the essence of the growth–equality relationship in the Kuznets curve in the early processes of economic development. But there are also dependence relationships between the two segments that are dubbed as "trickle-down" and "evaporation upwards", which mitigate the growth–equality relationship.

Economic prosperity in the informal sector, in the sense of a higher income per head and consequently a reduction in overall poverty, is dependent not only on the economic growth of the informal sector itself but also on that of the formal sector. The informal–formal sector relationship can be viewed within a macroeconomic framework. There are two main relationships that require emphasis. One is a direct relationship in the production sphere. The tiny and small establishments in the informal sector are deliverers of intermediate goods and other partially processed goods to the formal sector where they are processed further into final goods. Households associated with the informal sector deliver also labor services, mostly less skilled, to the formal sector. In both cases, the formal sector is a major source of income for the informal sector and associated households. Correspondingly, the formal sector is able to produce cheaply by drawing on the goods and services of the cheaply priced informal sector. Even though the production dependence of the two sectors is mutual, the formal sector commands much more economic resources and has greater access to national and foreign financial and non-financial markets. Thus, the mutual dependence is not one of equals.

The other relationship is an indirect one and relates to the income–consumption spheres. For labor and capital services used in the production sphere, households get income earnings that they spend on consumption, thus funding back the production process. Households associated with the formal and informal sectors do not exclusively spend on the consumption of goods produced in their respective sectors. Generally speaking, the informal sector and associated households would secure a net gain from this mutual spending on consumption. Given the wide income differentials between the formal and informal households, it can be expected that there will be a relatively higher portion of spending by the formal households to the benefit of the informal households, than the other way round. A positive result of the consumption link is a rise in the incomes of the households associated with the informal sector and a reduction in overall poverty; the result is commonly known as the "trickle-down" effect. Again, the mutual consumption pattern implies also that the portion of the income of informal households that is spent on the consumption of modern or formal goods (goods produced in the formal sector) can be considered as a partial "evaporation upward". It is not a complete evaporation because the informal sector and informal households would be once again engaged in the production process of these formal goods, and they will benefit from this participation.

The simplest way to highlight this mix of independence and dependence is by reclassifying the SAM so as to distinguish between (better-off) households working in the modern and formal sectors (the more productive sectors, M) and (less-off) households working in the traditional and informal sectors (the less productive sectors, L). An assessment of the growth and distribution problem along these lines of classification would illuminate the basic linkages that characterize the problem. To increase focus, we regrouped activities into a formal/modern sector that depicts the more productive segment (M) and an informal/traditional sector that depicts the less productive segment (L). Household groups were regrouped into the richer household group and the poorer household group. Other accounts in the SAM are left untouched.

The following can be repeated as a reminder. The SAM is a transformation of the circular flow of economic activity into a matrix of transactions between the various agents. In the rows of such a matrix are the factors, the institutions consisting of households, firms, and government, the activities, and the rest of the world. The columns are ordered similarly. Transactions between these actors take place at the intersecting cells. The absolute values of transactions can be converted into proportional coefficients in terms of the column totals, giving a square coefficient matrix. This can be partitioned into an exogenous and an endogenous part.[2] Inversion of the endogenous part results in output and income multipliers.[3] These multipliers show the effects of changes in the exogenous variables on endogenous variables. SAM multipliers tell (a) what the final effects of an exogenous injection in the formal or informal sector (due to government spending or foreign exports) on the growth of output in both sectors and on the distribution of income between the poorer and richer household groups are and (b) what the final effects of exogenous transfers to poor or rich household groups on their respective incomes and the output growth of the formal and informal sectors are.

The multipliers in Tables 1 and 2 give for Indonesia[4] and Pakistan[5] the final effects of exogenous sector injections on output and income. For Indonesia, in

Table 1, an injection of a unit, of say a million rupiahs, in the informal sector gives a potential increase in total output of 4.9, two-thirds of which benefits the informal sector itself and one-third benefits the formal sector. The injection generates a total income of 2.3 units but only a minor share of this income, about 23%, goes to poorer households and 77% to richer households. This multiplier distribution reproduces the actual distribution in the country of the income between the two household groups. If the injection is done in the formal sector, the output and income effects would be less, 3.6 and 1.6, respectively, the informal sector will benefit relatively more than the formal sector, and the relative distribution of benefits on the household groups will not be affected. Although the results show that the relative distribution of incomes between poor and rich households is neutral with respect to the expansion of either the informal or formal sectors, the absolute levels of the income multipliers are higher in case of informal sector injections and expansion than the formal sector, and this would imply that more households are likely to cross the poverty line upwards. The policy growth and income implications are clear. First, whatever growth source is stipulated, the output of the informal sector tends to grow more than that of the formal sector. So, the informal sector is there and its production activities can only grow further. Second, while the growth of the formal sector reduces poverty, the growth of the informal sector reduces poverty even more, but the relative income distribution is unaffected in both cases.

Table 1 gives also the output and income effects of another type of instrument: income transfers to households. Government or the rest of the world can make the transfers. It is noted that a transfer to the poorest group creates more output and income than a transfer to the richest group of urban upper income. The reasons lie in the intensity of the circular flows. Poorer households consume and spend most incomes they receive, and given their numbers, the incomes re-enter the circular flow more extensively and intensively than in the case of the richer households. There is a greater leakage in the latter case. The results show also that, in contrast to the policy of sector injections, the actual income distribution between the two household groups will be significantly affected by the direction of the income transfer. The poor households in Indonesia of the eighties appear to end up with holding back in their own group about 50% of the income transfer, which represents a higher share than their actual income distribution of about 24%. Therefore, the "evaporation upward" effect appears to be relatively weak. In similar ways, the results show also that the "trickle-down" effect is also very low, with only 15% of a simulated transfer to rich households trickling down to poor households, a substantial portion of 85% remaining with rich households. Of course, while it is possible that these magnitudes may be approaching each other over time, the gap is too wide to be reversed in two decades.

Finally, a comparison of the results of injections in the production sphere with transfers in the income–consumption spheres allows for the following conclusion.

Table 1. The impact of formal and informal sector injections and of transfers on output and the incomes of poorer and richer household groups. Demonstration of results for Indonesia 1975.

		Impact of a unit injection in approximated sectors (a)		Impact of a unit transfer to household groups (b)	
	Actual percentage distribution (1975)	Informal sector	Formal sector	Poorer households	Richer households
Output Multiplier		**4.9**	**3.6**	**4.2**	**3.9**
Percentage distribution of the output (multipliers) on sectors:					
Informal sector	36.1%	65.8%	53.6%	62.0%	39.3%
Formal sector	63.9%	34.2%	46.4%	38.0%	60.7%
All sectors	100.0%	100.0%	100.0%	100.0%	100.0%
Income Multiplier		**2.3**	**1.6**	**3.0**	**2.8**
Percentage distribution of the income (multipliers) on household groups:					
Poorer households	23.5%	22.6%	23.7%	49.5%	15.3%
Richer households	76.5%	77.4%	76.3%	41.5%	84.7%
All households	100.0%	100.0%	100.0%	100.0%	100.0%

Note: (a) The informal/formal sectoral distinction is approximated by combining the analytical results of traditional agriculture and small-scale manufacturing to represent the informal sector and taking the rest of the economy to represent the formal sector (including among others commercial agriculture and large-scale manufacturing). (b) Poorer household groups include rural landless farm workers and urban lower-income earners; richer household groups include land owners and upper-income earners in rural and urban areas.
Source: Biro Pusat Statistik Indonesia (1982).

In achieving economic growth, with poverty reduction and a more equitable income distribution, policies pursuing transfers to poor households in the income–consumption spheres are shown to be more effective than those of injections in the production sphere.

Similar results as the above apply to Pakistan, as shown in Table 2. First, injections in the informal sector bring more overall growth in output and income than injections in the formal sector, but each sector injection tends to benefit its own sector more. Second, while growth of the formal sector reduces poverty, growth of the informal sector reduces poverty even more, but the relative income distribution is unaffected in both cases. Third public transfers to poor groups benefit the informal sector the most and are very effective in reducing poverty. Fourth, in contrast, the benefits of public transfers to rich groups go mostly to the formal sector and the rich groups linked to the formal sector; the informal sector and the poor groups encounter relative deteriorations in their positions from such transfers.

Table 2. The impact of formal and informal sector injections and of transfers on output and the incomes of poorer and richer household groups. Demonstration of results for Pakistan 1978/1979.

		Impact of a unit injection in approximated sectors (a)		Impact of a unit transfer to household groups (b)	
	Actual percentage distribution (1975)	Informal sector	Formal sector	Poorer households	Richer households
Output Multiplier		**4.79**	**4.56**	**3.82**	**3.51**
Percentage distribution of the output on sectors:					
Informal sector	42.2%	53.0%	31.6%	49.7%	34.7%
Formal sector	57.8%	47.0%	68.4%	51.3%	65.3%
All sectors	100.0%	100.0%	100.0%	100.0%	100.0%
Income Multiplier		**3.17**	**2.62**	**2.21**	**2.04**
Percentage distribution of the income on household groups:					
Poorer household groups	31.1%	30.9%	31.7%	36.6%	22.1%
Richer household groups	68.9%	69.1%	68.3%	63.4%	77.9%
All households	100.0%	100.0%	100.0 %	100.0%	100.0%

Note: (a) The informal/formal sectoral distinction is approximated by combining the analytical results of agriculture, mining, small-scale manufacturing, and diversified services to represent the informal sector and taking the rest of the economy to represent the formal sector (including among others large-scale manufacturing, utilities, construction, transport, banking, and public services). (b) Poorer household groups include landless and off-farm workers in rural areas and manual labor and self-employed in urban areas. Richer household groups include large, medium, and small land owners in rural areas and employers and non-manual labor in urban areas.
Source: PIDE (1985).

3. Micro Economics of Dualistic Development

Economists and politicians dealing with development problems of the third world are anxious to know about the extent, nature, and consequences of displacement of traditional enterprises by the more competitive firms and to gain insight into alternative collective mechanisms for handling the consequences. International development agencies are equally facing new challenges in designing development programs that combine economic efficiency with social protection.

In competitive markets, the more competitive and market-driven firms which produce better quality and sell their goods at relatively lower prices will increase their share of the market at the cost of traditional enterprises, which operate in the informal sector. Traditional firms that produce and sell goods that buyers consider as less competitive will eventually close down. Firms that close down lay off factors of production, capital, and labor, which can be used elsewhere or not at all if they happen to be very specific to the closing firms. In such cases, capital is scrapped and labor remains unemployed. Without incomes, most of these unemployed and their households fall under the poverty line. If this scenario is realized, then it would be the start of a pessimistic and a very problematic perspective. Normally speaking, equilibrating mechanisms and collective actions would then come into being to assure that the chronically unemployed will be in a position to cover their living expenses if negative externalities and the consecutive disruptions of the whole economic process and development failure are to be avoided and a stable society is to be maintained. Do such equilibrating mechanisms and collective actions exist? And what are their forms, roles, and effects?

In this section, we assess the prospects of traditional enterprises in the context of the enhanced competitive market forces of the past decade both nationally and globally and discuss the rationale for the mutual coexistence of traditional with modern market-driven enterprises at the micro level.

Lewis and Kuznets were among the earlier economists who saw economic development to be a competitive market process that reallocates physical and human resources from low-productivity sectors to high-productivity sectors, whereby the redundant physical and human resources, read labor, will become unutilized and impoverished. In particular, traditional agriculture and cottage industry — belonging mostly to the informal sector — would include enterprises with low factor productivity, while commercial agriculture, modern industry, and related services constitute the more productive segment of the economy, where new enterprises are initiated, grow, and flourish further, i.e. the modern or formal sector. While the informal sector is intensive in the least skilled labor, the modern or formal sector is intensive in capital and employs more skilled labor. The replacement of informal firms by formal firms would thus ultimately lead to a rise in unemployment of less skilled labor and some increase in poverty seems unavoidable, other things remaining the same.

The above pieces of development theory and evidence would suggest a bleak projection for the informal sector and poverty reduction. The basic assumption behind these expectations is that the conditions of one joint market in which traditional and modern enterprises compete for the same consumer demand exists and are continued. However, there is contrasting evidence that emphasizes the significant roles of structural barriers and collective actions in bypassing the competitive drive. These factors can be seen as equilibrating mechanisms that convert the competitive dichotomy between the formal and informal sectors into a complementary relationship or, in the least case, into a relationship of mutual co-existence in multi-equilibriums.

A case can thus be made for a different reality in which modern and traditional enterprises, *Em* and *Et*, respectively, are serving two different population groups which can be described as modern and traditional, thus *Pm* and *Pt*. In this segmented market, *Pm* and *Pt* are institutionally, and often spatially, detached from each other. The average income level of *Pm* is far above that of *Pt* and the personal valuation of the marginal dollar that *Pm* receives is lower than in the case of *Pt*. The spending habits of the two population groups differ substantially. The design and pricing of goods supplied by *Em* and the margins placed on them by the retail sectors are usually quite high and are directed for the use and purchase by *Pm*. Such goods, at the offered high prices, are too expensive for *Pt* to buy. Moreover, the retail trade for such goods is usually located in modern urban centers from which most of *Pt*, especially in rural areas, is practically spatially remote. In contrast, the traditional enterprises, *Et*, produce and sell mainly less sophisticated goods at low prices, primarily to *Pt*.

Large countries with large rural populations have started the development process with a relatively large *Pt* and a small *Pm*, and the above configuration fits particularly such countries as China, India, Indonesia, Pakistan, Bangladesh, Egypt, and Nigeria, to mention a few. In smaller countries, the size of *Pt*, and the supporting *Et*, may be relatively too small to stand firm against the purchasing power from *Pm* and the supporting *Em*, resulting in the inability of the traditional segment and tiny enterprises to survive as a distinct low-income purchasing population with its own market providers.[6]

The rationale for the mutual coexistence of both an *Et* and *Em* in countries with large populations is, in fact, of a more basic nature. About three-quarters of the labor force in the countries quoted are engaged in self-employment, and only about a quarter are working as paid employers in the modern segment which includes both public and private market activities. While the informal activities in *Et* are able to absorb self-employed populations of hundreds of millions, the modern segment faces stable or diminishing employment output elasticities, inhibiting any substantial increases in labor absorption. In such a situation, the existence and continuation of self-employment activities in traditional enterprises is a godsend. A very gloomy and politically unstable scenario can be sketched if employment opportunities for masses of the labor force would be solely restricted to the modern segment. It is evident that modern employment cannot be forthcoming in the neighborhood of the required members.

The mutual coexistence of the segmented market was demonstrated in field investigations of small enterprises in large to very large countries, including Bangladesh, Indonesia, India, and Pakistan. These investigations were carried out in the mid-eighties. Their contemporary relevance in terms of content has validity three decades later. For the sake of brevity and consistency with previous sections, we explore here the results for Indonesia and Pakistan.

The Indonesian data belong to a survey of small-scale industrial (SSI) enterprises carried out in Banda Aceh, Indonesia, in late 1985, and revalidated a decade later. The sample covered 181 units, which constituted 5% of the units existing in the area. The sample covered 996 workers making the average size of the enterprise equal to 5.5 workers. The sample is distributed over three modes of enterprises that can be described as cottage, tiny, and larger firms.[7] Household production units that share the same roof as the household run the traditional cottage workshops. This would fit fully into the concept of the informal sector. The larger firms would belong to the modern sector, while the tiny firms would lie in between.

The employed questionnaire allowed estimation of the total assets of the firm, among other aspects. It collected data on fixed capital and working capital and the value of owned premises. The average cottage firm was found to have an asset value of 1.3 million rupees as compared to 3.3 million rupees in tiny firms and 13.0 million rupees in small firms. We deducted from the owner's income an equivalent labor income based on the average wage of hired workers for the whole sample to give the average imputed value of profits in the three modes, 0.73, 0.95, and 1.6 million rupees, respectively. We then calculated three profit rates for the three modes of enterprise: 54, 29, and 12%. The above results are displayed in Table 3. The material is plotted in Figure 1 to show profit values and profit rates that coincide with total assets of the three firm types.

The mutual coexistence of three significantly different profit rates among establishments competing in the same locality is remarkable. The phenomenon indicates a high degree of segmentation between different modes of enterprise. For some reason, small industry entrepreneurs with a profit rate of 12% cannot or are not willing to move to tiny and cottage businesses where the profit rates are 29 and 54%. First, one reason lies in the limited extent of the traditional market. Even though the profit rate in the traditional sector is very high, the turnover is too small to be attractive for modern businesses. Such limitations on turnover would not permit a modern business owner to earn profits beyond 730,000 or 946,000 rupees, while with a lower profit rate of 12% but a bigger market and turnover, it is able to make a profit of 1,601,000 rupees. Second, modern entrepreneurs may realize also that overcrowding the cottage and tiny industry market can reduce both the absolute profit per owner and profit rates significantly, hence the preference to operate in modern markets with a higher level of purchasing power but a lower profit rate. Third, the traditional firm may not like that the modern firms intrude in their traditional market and may act collectively to obstruct third-party entry. Fourth, consumers are segmented into traditional and modern goods consumers given their income differentials and their distinguishable reference consumption patterns: one segment consists mostly of households with income and consumption patterns below the poverty line, and the other segment is better off and has a larger purchasing power. The coupling of spending of traditional and poor households to the informal production of these and related households gives this segment an autonomy that allows it to survive and co-exist with modern business.

The above four reasons represent a combination of segregating and equilibrating mechanisms at the micro level that holds a dualistic economy in a stable balance and prevents the societal configuration from breaking up and shifting to opposite extremes and corner solutions. The above account does not mean that households and enterprises do not have an opportunity to move from the traditional to the

Table 3. Average values of assets and profits in thousand rupees and profit rates, Indonesia.

	Cottage industry	Tiny industry	Larger industry
Average value of assets per firm	1347	3291	12977
Average profit amount earned per firm	730	956	1601
Average profit rate achieved per firm (a)	54%	29%	12%

Source: Sample surveys carried out by the author in the context of development assistance projects financed by the Directorate of International Cooperation, the Netherlands. (a) = Second row/first row.

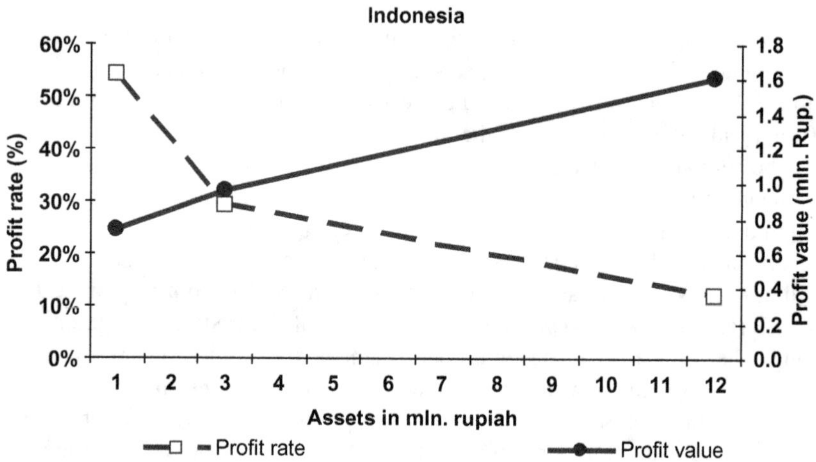

Figure 1. Profit rates, profit values, and asset values of SSI in million rupiahs, Indonesia.

modern sector. The Indonesian material shows the presence of an intermediate category of firms that can be placed between the two sectors. But there is no evidence found that a modern enterprise "now" has evolved over time from a traditional enterprise "then". Generally speaking, when upward mobility occurs for a particular household production unit from the informal to the formal sector, this would be mostly applicable for second-generation youngsters.[8]

Table 3 and Figure 1 display evidence that supports the rational co-existence of dualistic economic systems within the same country. Three modes of entrepreneurs that were investigated appear to be equally satisfied with their profitability position in spite of significant differences in their profit rates. This again substantiates the conclusion that these types are sufficiently detached and shielded from each other to avoid being competitive with each other. They produce differentiated products and serve different markets even though they may share similar problems and prospects in different degrees, as will be clear from additional results to be discussed further in this section.

Table 4. Average values of assets and profits in thousand rupees and profit rates, Pakistan.

	Informal segment	Formal segment
Average value of assets per firm	142	350
Average profit amount earned per firm	12	20
Average profit rate achieved per firm (a)	8.5%	5.7%

Note: (a) = Second row/first row.
Source: Sample surveys carried out by the author in the context of development assistance projects financed by the Directorate of International Cooperation, the Netherlands.

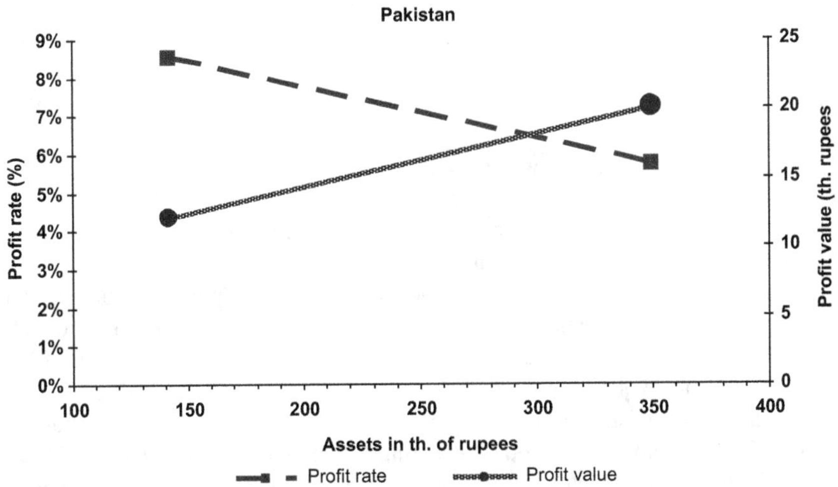

Figure 2. Profit rates, profit values, and asset values of SSI, in thousand rupees, Pakistan.

The second set of similar results we present refers to a survey of small enterprises conducted in 1980 and 1981 in four cities of Pakistan: Lahore, Karachi, Peshawar, and Rawalpindi. The interviews, which covered enterprises active in manufacturing and not exceeding five workers per enterprise, produced 806 valid responses at the establishment level; see Table 4 and Figure 2.

The heterogeneity of the enterprises, and their positioning between formal and informal types, called for the subdivision of the sample into two sub-samples. The traditional segment contained family-based firms with forward and backward linkages usually to the local consumer market. In contrast, the modern segment employed non-family labor and maintained backward and forward linkages with the rest of the economy.[9]

The survey data for the four cities in Pakistan allow the construction of Figure 2, which is similar to that of Figure 1, for the Indonesian case. Traditional enterprises are on the left-hand side, with lower average assets per enterprise, and the modern on the right-hand side. It is noted that traditional enterprises report an average profit rate of 9.2% while modern enterprises report 5.9%. In terms of profit value, an opposite picture is obtained. While a traditional enterprise generates on average 12.4 thousand rupees, the modern goes beyond that to achieve 20.22 thousand rupees. There seems to be a rationale for the mutual coexistence of both types based on the combination of different performance criteria that are conditioned to two different entrepreneurial environments.

Public policy that aims at enhancing pro-poor economic growth has a heavy agenda in the context of the formal–informal dichotomy. The evidence examined showed that the informal sector is bound to grow in production and income. Next to its own autonomous economic growth mechanisms, there is also complementary growth due to the growth of the formal sector. Thus, economic growth of the informal sector is secured for the future and is not a problematic issue. The real problem is that the informal sector may be absorbing more people at a rate that overgrows the rate of its economic growth, resulting in a prolongation of poverty.

Eventually, the issue is how to raise the average labor productivity in the informal sector to a level above that coinciding with the poverty line. Moreover, given the relative notion involved in the poverty line, the ultimate aim is to narrow the gap between factor productivities in the informal and formal sectors.

The previous section examined some macroeconomic policy measures that could raise productivity in the informal sector and promote thereby pro-poor development strategies. It was suggested that income (and asset) transfers to household groups associated with the informal sector are likely to be very effective. This implies a partial redistribution of the growth in national income from the formal to the informal sector. In development settings where the poor spend most of their income in the informal sector, this will advance the growth of the sector furthermore and contribute to a further reduction in poverty. Although belonging to a different realm of policymaking, any human resource development policy that leads directly or indirectly to reducing the family size of households associated with the informal sector, and restraints in population growth, will help raise productivity levels and reduce poverty.

Policies aiming at raising the output level of informal enterprises are the other major areas of state intervention. Microeconomic surveys of the informal sector in developing countries have highlighted several obstacles facing these enterprises. Policy directed toward removing these obstacles is a high priority.

We give the following selected results from the sample surveys of the targeted establishments undertaken in Indonesia and Pakistan. Establishments were asked to report on five types of difficulties that they faced at the time of the inquiry and which they felt were obstructing future growth, noting that the number of reported difficulties may exceed the number of surveyed establishments.

A rough picture is obtained by ranking the problems encountered in the last column of the table, even though the picture hides important country differences.

For instance, the difference in problems faced in the two segments appears to be more pronounced in Pakistan than in the Indonesian context, which draws attention to the requirement of elaborating distinct public policies and approaches in different countries.

Giving due consideration to the above country differences, the overall picture that emerges is one in which limited financial resources and weak demand conditions are the two major obstacles in both sectors. Financial problems appeared to come up more frequently than demand problems in the informal sector; the opposite was observed for the formal sector. Lack of qualified skills is another important obstacle to the growth of the informal sector, reflecting its comparative disadvantage as a producer of technologically less developed products.

Although there is a consistent continuum in faced problems by enterprises in informal and formal sectors, Table 5 shows the magnitude of specific problems to differ appreciably by country. Therefore, local diagnosis is necessary for coming up with effective local policies.

Informal enterprises in the context of Pakistan perceived the lack of skills, finance, and demand as the major problems, in a declining order. The interviewed informal enterprises in Indonesia saw lack of finance and demand as more problematic than skill shortages. On the whole, the lack of finance, skilled labor, and raw materials next to a sluggish demand appeared to be on average the more significant problem. Modern enterprises, having more outward orientations, have a different perception of problems encountered, which draw attention to the requirement of elaborating distinct public policies and approaches toward the two segments. Finally, differences in problems faced by the two segments appear to be more pronounced in Pakistan than in the Indonesian context.

Some of the obvious conclusions from the above are that more credit facilities and upgrading of technical skills would relieve the often encountered shortages of finance and skills on the supply side. But to resolve the problems of low demand

Table 5. Percentage share of difficulties reported by surveyed establishments, grouped by informal and formal market segments. Selected countries.

Country	Pakistan		Indonesia		Average rank (a)	
Reported difficulties	Informal	Modern	Informal	Modern	Informal	Modern
Weak demand, purchasing power	11.4	17.6	37.2	20.7	1.5	3.0
Location too small, unsuitable	15.5	16.5	4.2	1.1	1.5	2.0
Lack of financial resources	16.5	15.2	39.5	27.4	3.5	2.5
Lack of qualified skills, machines	23.7	12.7	12.6	29.7	3.0	2.5
Others	33.4	38.0	6.5	21.1		

Note: (a) This column is found by ranking the four specified difficulties in terms of their frequency (highest 4, lowest 1) and by taking a simple average over the two countries.
Source: Sample surveys carried out by the author in the context of development assistance projects financed by the Directorate of International Cooperation, the Netherlands.

and a weak purchasing power that enterprises face in the informal sector would require increased earnings, and expenditures, of households allied to the informal sector as well as greater trickle-down effects from the formal sector, and households attached to it, toward the informal sector.

In a discussion of public policies toward the informal sector, it cannot be avoided mentioning that public policies, already since the independence of most developing nations in the 1950s and 1960s, were heavily oriented toward favoring the formal sector. The term "urban bias", coined by Lipton several decades ago, is still generally valid.[10] In spite of the greater attention given in state policies to the urban/formal sector as compared to the rural/informal sector, past and recent developments show that the rural/informal sector and the populations associated with this sector survive and are self-sustainable. There are significant potentials in the informal sector that can be realized with only moderate shifts from past and current biased policies.

4. Concluding Remarks

The most prominent feature of the development economy is its dualistic structure and performance. What are then the characteristics, magnitudes, and impacts of this dualism on the low-productivity activities? Would they disappear? New classical market competition reasoning would predict a bleak future for the traditional enterprise sector under conditions of one joint market in which traditional and modern enterprises compete for the same consumer demand.

In contrast, this chapter demonstrated a different reality in which modern and traditional sectors at the macro–sector levels and their counterparts at the micro level, that is, modern enterprises (*Ern*) and traditional enterprises (*Et*), are serving two different population groups which can be described as traditional and modern. The two population groups can be denoted by *Pm* and *Pt*, respectively. In this segmented macro economy and micro market, the earning populations attached to the modern and the traditional *Prn* and *Pt* are institutionally detached from each other. The income levels of *Prn* are far above those of *Pt* and the marginal valuation of the additional rupee which *Prn* receives is lower than in the case of *Pt*. The spending habits of the two groups differ substantially. The design and pricing of goods supplied by *Ern* and the margins placed on them by the retail sectors are usually quite high and are directed for the use and purchase of *Prn*. Such goods at the offered high prices cannot be afforded by *Pt*. Besides, the retail trade for such goods is usually located in modern urban areas from which *Pt* are practically spatially isolated. In contrast, *Et* produce and sell mainly less sophisticated goods at low prices to *Pt*. There is an element of personal servicing which *Et* provide and

Pt expect. The characteristic needs of one segment cannot be provided by the other segment, which is a sufficient rationale for both segments to co-exist. The market is segmented and there are different returns for the same activity. This confirms the thesis on imperfect markets as postulated by Banerjee and Duflo (2005).

Endnotes

1. See Cohen, S.I. (2002).
2. We assume for a typical developing country receipt and payment transactions of government and rest of world as exogenous so that the remaining variables can be treated as endogenous variables.
3. The output multipliers are higher than the income multipliers due to leakages into intermediate inputs and imports, and undistributed earnings of institutions.
4. SAMs of Indonesia were assembled by Biro Pusat Statistik (1982) for the calendar years of 1975 and 1980, respectively. The assembled version we shall adhere to is one that falls into a matrix of 28 rows and 28 columns. For the purpose at hand, we aggregate the results of the multiplier analysis for Indonesia to represent in some approximate ways the division between a predominantly informal sector and a predominantly formal sector, and the division between households with a high incidence of poverty and the better off households, see footnote to Table 1.
5. The source of the SAM of Pakistan is PIDE (1885). The multiplier results are aggregated to approximate the distinctions of formal and informal sectors and of rich and poor groups; see footnote to Table 2.
6. This phenomenon supports the contention reached earlier that there can be relatively more incidence of poverty in smaller than bigger countries.
7. Cottage industries, tiny industries = 1–4 workers. Small industries = 5–20 workers. The difference between cottage and tiny enterprises relates to the nature of the product: traditional versus non-traditional, respectively. Small industry is the outgrowth of tiny industries. The 181 enterprise units are distributed on industrial activities as follows: food 46, textiles 19, wood 36, printing, chemical and non-metal 29, metal 23, miscellaneous, and workshops 28.
8. Moving to the modern sector often requires received modern education that is more present in the second than the first generation.
9. The subdivision was accomplished as follows: A sliding scale of five indicators was designed and applied. The five indicators were the share of hired workers, the share of local sources of raw material, the share of local outlets of product scales, the size of fixed capital investment, and whether the enterprises is legally registered. For each of these five indicators, threshold values were specified for qualifying in the modern segment. If an establishment is assigned twice or more times to the modern segment, then it was counted as definitely belonging to the modern segment. The other establishments were then counted as belonging to the traditional segment. The subdivision resulted into the grouping of 153 firms (19%) in the modern segment and 653 firms (81%) in the traditional segment. The empirical results on averages and standard deviations for 30 other indicators on enterprises characteristics showed that the resulting division of the sample in the two segments is significant and analytically consistent with economic theory.
10. Cf. Lipton, M. (1977), and a contemporary overview of the urban bias in Eastwood R. and Lipton, M. (2004).

Chapter 9

Social Sectors in Economy-Wide Models: An Application to Past Korea

1. Introduction

In the early decades of development economics, mainly in the 1950s and 1960s, economic development was analyzed and planned in terms of economic growth. The central development objective was the growth of the GDP and sometimes the GDP per capita. Empirical data on the actual performances in most developing countries gave a different picture, showing increasing income inequalities, more population groups falling behind poverty lines, increasing underemployment and unemployment, and deteriorating food and other living conditions. The new picture brought a revision in interests and insights by economists and planners dealing with development problems. One of the reactions that emerged was the social economic development perspective, which saw the misplaced focus on GDP as the fault in the planning framework and went for reformulating development models and plans in terms of broader social economic development aims.

Despite the accelerated interest in social economic development perspective, there were no attempts made to put up an operational framework that would unify new goals in the development planning models that were commonly used at the time. There was a flood of definitions and concepts on basic needs, social indicators, social aims, etc., but most of them were dispersed and not accessible in economic models. Our contribution in this area was to broaden the scope of policy modeling and planning practices toward the social economic development perspective. This chapter reports on work which formulated and applied a social economic development model that extended aim variables to include next to GDP growth, income and employment aim variables belonging to social groups, and indicators on the attainment of well-being. The scope of policy instruments and other relationships was extended accordingly. Primarily for reasons of data availability at the time, the Republic of Korea was selected as a test case. The model was estimated on the basis of data for the sixties and employed to simulate development up to the early eighties. Interestingly, the empirical applications around 1970 showed positive and coherent future performances for Korea on the GDP, distribution, employment, and basic needs attainment for the 1970s and early 1980s; these outcomes were also confirmed by the realized development performance of Korea years later.

This chapter is organized as follows: Section 2 is devoted to laying out an operational framework for specifying an integrated system of social economic development goals. Section 3 specifies the model. Section 4 displays some detail on the estimation of the model and the projected results and examines multiplier properties of the model. Section 5 shifts the model from its analytical form to a planning form. The analytical form of the model treats aim variables as unknown and instruments as given. The complete planning form is usually described as the reverse, with aim variables taking the form of fixed targets and instrument variables becoming unknown. The shift from analysis to planning raises questions on the decomposition of the model for planning purposes and the structural properties of the outcome. The section deals with these questions and demonstrates its application via a few simulations and adds some elaborations. Section 6 ends with concluding remarks.

2. A Unifying Approach toward Social Economic Development Goals

In identifying and selecting aim variables in the context of social economic development policy, it is essential to distinguish between social groups of common interest, followed by listing the goal variables for each group separately, which can be of a monetary nature (i.e. income) or of a non-monetary nature (i.e. well-being). The literature on well-being indicators is long and overlapping. United Nations Research Institute for Social Development (UNRISD) was one of the starters.[1] It implemented during 1966–1968 a research program on identifying and quantifying indicators of basic needs relevant to developing countries. Soon after, various agencies of the UN came up with their own basic needs indicators. As is well known, the interest in quantifying well-being indicators has a long history. One of the first articles to quantify basic needs indicators at the international level was by Bennet (1948). The concepts and measurements of well-being have undergone substantive refinements since then in terms of depth and width, with the most comprehensive system in Sen (1982). In the past years, tens of foundations worldwide have developed various quality-of-life and well-being indicators.

The integration of any set of these social indicators in applied economic models is a different story. We shall review the various steps required and comment on how we approached them. The first step is to incorporate some division of the total population into social groups with more or less homogeneous interests, whose well-being levels can be traced in the available statistics. The outcome is subordinate to available data on consumption, expenditure, employment, and labor supply on such social groups. Data at the time did not go beyond a disaggregation into household groups headed by (1) wage earners, (2) salary earners, and (3) the large group of employers, self-employed and family workers,[2] with possible subdivisions into rural and urban areas. The data for Korea allowed for the distinction between these three social groups; the terms household groups are also used interchangeably; they will be denoted by index h, $h = 1, 2, 3$, respectively.

The next step is to specify/select the aim variables thought to be of relevance. To distinguish aim variables from other variables, we attach the letter Á to the aim variables. The selection of aim variables was guided by two survey reports at the time, United Nations (1966) and United Nations (1971), which were particularly helpful in justifying in quasi-objective ways the selection, which would have been otherwise a subjective choice. The surveys that were conducted among planning bureaus of 48 developing countries listed income, employment, and four basic needs: food, housing, health, and education, next to macroeconomic monitoring indicators. To start with, the aim variable with the highest score in the surveys was *GDP* growth, which we shall denote by *AG*. Income was next. This is represented by the disposable income per capita received by each household group, denoted by AY_h, $h = 1, 2, 3$. It is obvious, as *AG* can be derived from the weighted sum of the growth AY_h and population growth, any predetermined double fixation of *AG* and AY_h has growth and distributive implications. If planning is done in terms of the AY_hs, then the aggregate *AG* follows. The aim variable with the next highest score in the survey of planning bureaus was a minimal unemployment rate, which can be expressed in the form of employment rates that relate employment to labor supply, which is to be denoted by AM_h, where $h = 1, 2$. Since the unemployed are those who are seeking work for pay, that is, potentially hired employees, this aim variable would by definition apply to the hired workforce only, which are the groups of wage earners and salary earners only, and exclude an unemployment status for the group of employers and the self-employed. This group may suffer from underemployment, but that should show up in a low income, which is taken care of AY_h. The income and employment goals in the UN surveys were directly followed by the satisfaction of basic needs with respect to nutrition, shelter, health, and education. As the focus is on the attainment of such basic needs, it can be justifiably assumed that for all households with higher incomes, the satisfaction of these basic needs is not a problem. Basic needs attainment variables are thus especially relevant for population groups with the lowest incomes, in this case, wage earners. As such, the model specifies an aim variable of average daily intake of calories per capita for wage earners group $h = 1$, denoted by AC_1, and not for

Table 1. List of aim variables by household group (h.g.).

Wage earners h.g.:1	Salary earners h.g.:2	Employers, etc. h.g.:3	Whole nation
Disposable income per capita AY_1	Disp. Inc. p.c. AY_2	Disp. Inc. p.c AY_3	Economic growth AG
Employment rate AM_1	Employment rate AM_2		
Calorie intake p.c. AC_1			
Dwelling space p.c. AD_1			
Health level for households group 1, approximated by survival rate AH			
Educational level for households group 1, approximated by primary school enrolment rate AN			
Composite index of basic needs attainment, ABN_1, consisting of AC_1, AD_1, AH, and AN, specified in eq. (30).			

other groups. Similarly, dwelling levels, expressed as the average number of rooms per capita, are relevant as an aim variable for group 1, e.g. AD_1. For education, we take the primary enrolment ratio. Any increase in this ratio, although referring to the eligible school-going population for the country as a whole, thus *AN*, would tend to benefit primarily the children of the lowest income group. With respect to health needs, we shall work with the national survival rate as an aim variable, *AH*, partly because available data do not make possible the division of health benefits by social groups but mainly because the characteristic external effects which accompany health levels in the whole nation make it more desirable to formulate this aim for the whole nation.[3] We shall also make use of a composite index of basic needs attainment consisting of the four indicators to be denoted by ABN_1, which would apply to the lowest income group. Table 1 is a summary.

The introduction of these aim variables requires the incorporation of suitable instrument variables that could enhance their values. The model contains many policy instruments controllable by the government. The analysis will concentrate on budget items such as various taxes and government spending related to the distinguished aim variables, as well as income transfers to social groups and public investment by sector of activity j, as indicated in Table 2.

Next steps are to address such questions as how the values of these aim variables are generated, and how to incorporate and measure their productivity effects in an economy-wide model. In the formation of aim variables, the levels of income among the social groups determine how much is consumed privately of each good or service. This private consumption, together with public allocations, determines final demand by sector and in turn production by sector and demand for and supply of labor by skill type and social group. As a result, labor productivity rates and employment rates are obtained. These two rates play dominant roles in the formation of the factor earnings accruing to each social group. This completes the circular flow.

Table 2. List of instrument variables.

Wage earners h.g.:1	Salary earners h.g.:2	Employers, etc. h.g.:3	Whole nation
Direct tax rate	Direct tax rate	Direct tax rate	Indirect tax rates by sector Foreign trade taxes
Income transfers food subsidies rent subsidies	Income transfers	Income transfers	Public expenditure on health education other social services Public investment by sector

Regarding productivity effects of better living conditions, the model attempts to integrate what various studies have already established, namely higher levels of $AC_1 \cdot AD_1$, AH, and AN, up to a certain degree, increase the capacity of labor. The productivity effect of higher well-being is long established in economic thinking.[4] There are many empirical studies for different countries that have tested and confirmed the productivity effect. Studies on the effects of higher nutrition show that the higher energy produced allows labor to work near his full capacity. The housing effect is supported by empirical evidence of positive influence on labor productivity from rehousing projects. Higher health levels save work time lost due to morbidity, while the quality of work improves and life and economic activity increase. Furthermore, the productivity effects of more education are very well established. The combined effects of the above factors are usually considered to be more crucial at low-income levels but may not hold at higher incomes.

How to incorporate the productivity effect of higher well-being in an economy-wide policy model? This is done in several rounds. (a) In a Cobb–Douglas production function at the sector level with factors of production capital and labor, the productivity effect will be more applicable to low skill and not high skill. (b) Assume for the benchmark year that employed labor of low skill, indexed as 1, in activity j, thus LD_{1j}, is functioning below its full working capability due to shortfalls in well-being attainment from some desired level; denote well-being attainment for this labor type by the general index introduced earlier ABN_1, the highest attainment level is at $ABN_1^* = 1.0$, and thus $ABN_1 < ABN_1^*$. Define full capability labor in year t as labor multiplied by the welfare attainment index $(ABN_1 \cdot LD_{1j})$. Because for the benchmark the term $(ABN_1 \cdot LD_{1j})$ is less than LD_{1j}, the calibration coefficient for the benchmark will be raised. (c) As the well-being attainment rises in coming years to its maximum level, the impacted labor recovers its full capacity and contributes to a larger production level. (d) Note that the productivity effect of higher well-being is conditional on which labor is impacted and on what is included in the well-being indicators. Of course, once $ABN_1^* = 1.0$ is reached, new concepts of what constitutes the next stage of well-being can be formulated and incorporated for the next round of enhancing functioning capabilities.

3. Specification of the Model

3.1. *General*

The model that we use belongs to the so-called category of combined econometric multi-sector (CEM) models.[5] The limiting feature of the model is that most of the adjustments in the balancing of factor and market balances take place via quantity changes, under unchanging relative prices.

The original model contained many sectors. To increase focus, we report here on four combined sectors: agriculture, industry, commercial sectors, and social sectors, which include housing, health, education, and other social services.

As was mentioned above, the model generates the 10 aim variables in Table 1, which are specified to be partly influenced by the instrument variables in Table 2. Regarding the productivity effects of higher well-being, the model integrates what various studies have established, namely that basic needs attainment, ABN_1, increases labor quality and labor productivity and, in turn, can contribute to enhancing economic growth. The model does not consider ABN_1 effects on demographic transitions and economic growth, which are known to be substantial.

One central question in development planning at the time was how to proceed with policymaking when there are so many aim variables to be targeted and instrument variables to be solved. The model reverts to the ordering structures of Simon (1953) to answer the question. Practically speaking, the analytical model is a simultaneous system which has to be solved in one shot. Conversion of the analytical model into a planning model simplifies the system substantially. It turns out that the prefixing of income variables by social groups is the most logical first move in the policymaking process, and when accompanied by basic needs and employment targets, the planning model would presume a significantly simplified diagonal structure that can readily be split into stages of policymaking.

3.2. *Notations*

In the notations in Table 3, unless otherwise stated, all variables are measured at the end of a period of 6 years. The model solves for three six-year periods: 1968, 1974, and 1980. Monetary variables are expressed in constant prices of 1965, in billion won (thousand million). Demographic variables are in 1000 persons.[6]

Table 3. Notations.

Endogenous variables	
C_j	Total private and government consumption expenditure on activity j
C_{hc}	Consumption expenditure by household group h on commodity c, $h = 1,2,3;\ c = 1,.,6$
E_j	Exports of sector j
FCF	Foreign capital flow expressed in foreign currency
GBD	Government budget deficit
I	Total installed investment
I_p	Private demand for installed investment
ICH_j	Inventory change in sector j, $j = 1,2$, agriculture and industry, etc., respectively
KDj	Capital utilized in sector j, $j = 1,2$, agriculture and industry, etc., respectively
KSj	Capital supply in sector j, $j = 1,2$, agriculture and industry, etc., respectively
LD_{qj}	Labor demand for skill q in sector j; $q = 1,2$; $j = 1 \ldots, 4$
LD_h	Employed number of workers belonging to social group h, $h = 1,2$
M_j	Imports of sector j
NT_e	Enrolment total in educational level e
NE_e	Enrolment of new school entrants in first year in educational level e
LR_h	Remuneration rate of wage earners and salary earners, $h = 1,2$
LS_q, LS_h	Labor supply by skill q and by household group h, $h = 1,2$
V_j	Gross product of activity j, i.e. value added of activity j
X_j	Gross output of activity j
Y_h	Disposable income of household group h, $h = 1,2,3$
Z_h	Factor and other income receipts of social group h, $h = 1,2$
Z_3	Factor and other income receipts of social group 3
Z_g	Government revenue
The following endogenous variables are aim variables	
AG	GDP growth rate
AY_h	Income per capita specified by social group, $h = 1,2,3$
AM_h,	Employment rates of wage and salary earners, $h = 1,2$
AC_1	Food and nutrition aim variable is daily calorie intake per capita for the lowest income group, i.e. wage earners and related dependents
AD_1	Housing aim variable is dwelling space (rooms) per capita for the lowest-income population group, i.e. wage earners and related dependents
AH	Health aim variable, i.e. survival rate applying for the whole population
AN	Education aim variable is enrolment ratio for primary education
ABN_1	Basic needs attainment index for (low skilled) wage earners, maximum=1.0
Exogenous variables	
C_{gc}	Gvernment consumption expenditure on good c
FXR	Foreign exchange rate
I_{gj},	Government investment expenditure in sector j
P	Total population

(*Continued*)

Table 3. (*Continued*)

T_{gh}	Transfers from government to institutions
T_{rh}, T_{rg}	Transfers from rest of world to household group h and to government g
Coefficients	
$\alpha_{jj'}$	Input–output delivery coefficients from sector j to sector j'
α_{jo}	Calibration coefficient in Cobb–Douglas production functions for the sectors j, $j = 1$ (agriculture), $j = 2$ (industry, construction and transport)
α_{rj}	Non-competitive imports share in the output of sector j
β_{qj}	Labor elasticities of production by skill and sector. Capital elasticity $= 1 - \Sigma_j \beta_{qj}$
χ_{eo}, χ_e	Intercept and slope coefficient in a regressed costing function that relates enrolments to spending by educational level: $e =$ primary, secondary, higher
χ_{te}	Expenditure share of educational level e in the total gross spending on education
δ_j	Depreciation rate of capital in sector j, $j = 1, 2$
ε_j	Export growth rate for sector j, $j = 1, 2, 3, 4$
$\phi_{1,1,o}, \phi_{1,1}$	Intercept and slope coefficient in a regressed costing function of total expenditure on food per capita per unit of nutritional intake made dependent on income per capita. Equation applies for wage earners, 1st subscript 1, and for expenditure on food, 2nd subscript 1
$\phi_{1,2,o}, \phi_{1,2}$	Intercept and slope coefficient in a regressed costing function of expenditure on housing per capita per unit of housing space. made dependent on income per capita. Equation applies for wage earners, 1st subscript 1, and for expenditure on housing, 2nd subscript 2
$\phi_{3,o}, \phi_3$	Intercept and slope coefficient in a regressed costing function of health expenditure per capita per unit of survival rate, taken as dependent on income per capita. Equation applies for the whole nation and for expenditure on health, denoted by subscript 3
$\gamma_{\text{hco}}, \gamma_{\text{hc}}$	Intercept and slope coefficient in regressed household consumption functions relating consumption on commodity c to disposable income of social group h; $c =, 1 \ldots, 6$; $h = 1, 2, 3$
$\eta_{\text{qho}}, \eta_{\text{qh}}$	Intercept and slope coefficient in a regressed labor supply function of wage earners and salary earners relating to skill q; $h = 1, 2$; $q = 1, 2$
$\iota_o, \iota, \iota\prime\, \iota\prime\prime$	Intercept and slope coefficients in a regressed private investment function relating private investment demand to GDP, profit rate, public investment, and other exogenous variables
ι_j,	Investment delivery share by activity j in the total delivery of installed investment Sector of industry, etc. ($j = 2$) delivers all investment, thus $\iota_2 = 1$. All other $\iota_j = 0$
φ_{jc}, ϕ_{gjc}	Distribution coefficients of private consumption expenditure by good c to sector j and same for government consumption expenditure. $c = 1, \ldots, 6$; $j = 1, \ldots, 4$
κ_{pj}	Installed investment destined for use in sector j as a proportion of total installed investment. $\Sigma_j = \kappa_{oj}$
κ_j	Incremental capital output ratio for sector j. See endnote 10, on relation of κ_{pj} to κ_j

Table 3. (*Continued*)

$\lambda_{eo}, \lambda_e, \lambda'_e$	Survival rate of enrolled students from previous period and two flow operators for the newly entering students within the educational system approximated in terms of current period t and previous period 6 years earlier, $t-6$
$\lambda_{qo}, \lambda_{eq}, \lambda'_{eq}$	Survival rate of labor force from previous period and two flow operators for students passing through and exiting from the educational system and eventually joining the labor force, approximated in terms of current period t and previous period 6 years earlier, $t-6$
μ_{jc}, μ_{ji}	Competitive imports shares in consumption and in investment by sector j. Because sector 2 is the only one delivering investment goods, it follows that μ_{ji} is zero for sectors 1, 3, 4
ν_{qjo}, ν_{qj}	Intercept and slope coefficient in an economically defined labor requirement function giving number of workers of skill q required for producing gross value added by sector j
π_1, π_e	Population belonging to wage earners in the total population and proportion of the age group eligible for primary education in the total population
$\rho_{ho}, \rho_h, \rho'_h$	Intercept and slope coefficients in a regressed remuneration rate function that relates average labor earnings to productivity and unemployment rate; $h = 1, 2$
ρ_g	Factor income share in the GDP due to government
σ_h	Savings rate of household group h
τ_{hg}, τ_{jg}	Rates of direct taxes on income of household group h and indirect taxes on gross output of sector j
$\tau_{jg,imp,}; \tau_{jg,\exp}$	Rates of import tariff and export duty collected by government
ϖ_j	Utilization rate of capital in sector j, $j = 1, 2$

Notes: j = sectors of activity (whereby 1 = agriculture, 2 = industry, construction, and transport combined, 3 = commercial services, 4 = social services). c = categories of consumption (1 = food, 2 = housing, 3 = health, 4 = education, 5 = other commodities, 6 = other services). e = educational levels (i = primary, ii = secondary, iii = higher). q = labor skills (1 = low, 2 = high). h = social groups defined by head of household (1 = wage earners, 2 = salary earners, 3 = employers and self-employed). Subscript g to identify government and r for rest of the world.

3.3. *Equations*

The first block, in Box 1, of the model relates to factors of production and the factor market. Eq. (1) specifies Cobb–Douglas production functions by sector j (for agriculture and for industry) with three factors of production: capital KD_j, high skilled labor LD_{2j} and low-skilled labor measured in fully productive labor units, where LD_{1j} is the number of demanded (employed) low-skilled workers and BNA_1 is the basic needs attainment level of low-skilled workers. When ABN_1 is at 100%, the worker performs at his full productivity level. The term $(LD_{1j} \cdot ABN_1)$

attempts to measure the workforce in fully productive units. A workforce LD_1 of 5 million with ABN_1 at a level of 90% is equivalent to 4.5 million workers with a 100% productive capability. Higher levels of nutrition, housing, health, and general education lead to a higher ABN_1 and a higher labor quality, as will be formulated in eq. (30), and has the same effect on production as increased labor inputs. Consequently, substitution possibilities can occur between labor quantity and quality.[7] In this equation, β_{qj} are labor elasticities of production, $1 - \Sigma\beta_{qj}$ is the capital elasticity, and α_{jo} is the calibration coefficient.

Eq. (2) incorporates the second level of production technology typical of economy-wide models, i.e. Leontief input–output system. The gross value added by sector, V_j, is derived as a proportion of the gross output by sector, K_j, after deduction of domestic and imported intermediate deliveries and indirect taxes. The equation holds for all sectors.

Eq. (3) states that the utilized capital in non-service sector j is equal to the installed supply of capital. The utilization rate ϖ_j is a given data.

Eq. (4) specifies the supply of capital in non-services sector j as that of the previous year less depreciation at rate δ_j, plus the share of the destination sector in newly installed private investment, plus government investment destined to the sector. The destination shares of private investment, κ_{pj}, when summed over all sectors add to 1. The values of these shares take account of the relative requirements for investment goods among the destination sectors; hence, they may be periodically updated.[8]

Eq. (5) gives the demand for manpower skills q by sector j. The quantity demanded would depend on technical rates of manpower inputs per unit produced and the sector product X. The closest approximations available to estimate these functions are the input rates implicit in development plans (the Korean Second Five-Year Plan). We assumed the technical requirements to be a linear function of the plan requirements with values of ν_{qjo} and ν_{qj} to be found from regressions on plan data. To account for the fact that the potential effects of higher labor quality have still to be realized, the potential is multiplied by realization coefficients which are calibrated by regressions on observed data.

Eq. (6) specifies the supply of manpower skills, as depending partly on survival and retirement from the previous stock and partly on various flows of students that leave the school system and enter the labor force. These flows are the result of combined rates of student transitions, graduation, and labor participation applied to new enrolment of students to various educational levels in the past. These yearly flows are summed and approximated in terms of two periods: t and $t-6$. The final form of this equation falls into three terms.[9]

Eq. (7) specifies the number of new enrolments as the number of total enrolments less the outflow of students leaving the educational system. This outflow is the result of past new enrolment less mortality, dropping out, and graduation. The same approximations in the previous equation are followed here so that the specification of the equation is done in terms of periods t and $t-6$ and falls also in three terms. (See the previous endnote.)

Eq. (8) makes total enrolments by educational level dependent on total spending on education, that is, consumption category 4, by households and by government, $\Sigma_h C_{h4} + C_{g4}$. The spending is distributed on the three educational levels via proportions χ_{te}. The obtained financial resources available to a specific educational level undergo a regressed costing function of costs per student to determine total enrolment at each level. Eqs. (6)–(8) are very closely linked. In eq. (8), spending determines total enrolment places at each educational level, NT_e. Deducting from these the present stock of enrolled students and school leavers gives the new enrolments NE_e in eq. (7). When these go through the educational system and after several years graduate, many of them will participate in the labor force, hence eq. (6).

Eq. (9) converts the demand for and supply of manpower by skill types into demand and supply by social groups, LD_h and LS_h, respectively. The following conventions facilitate the conversion. Commonly, unemployment data are collected from compulsory insurance schemes, trade unions, or employment offices. In this context, people in unemployment are defined as workers whose employment contracts have been terminated, have been suspended, or have to be started for the first time and who are seeking paid work at the prevailing market wage rates. As such, the state of involuntary unemployment, often defined as simply unemployment, occurs exclusively among employees and potential employees. Because of lack of appropriate data at the time, it was assumed that unemployment among wage earners would correspond to unemployment among the lower skills and similarly for the case of salary earners and the higher skills. Given our previously mentioned classification of occupations into low and high skills, these correspond very closely with the wage and salary modes of payment.

Eq. (10) counts on the above considerations and follows consistently the assumption that the bulk of the supply of manpower with lower skills can be classified as wage earners while that of higher skills is mainly salary earners. The conversions allow for regressed estimates.

Eq. (11) gives a regressed explanation for the remuneration rates for wage and salary earners. After testing alternative formulations, two main factors appeared to be the most relevant for explaining the variances in labor earnings, LR_h. These are the labor productivity rate and the gap between supply and demand forces of the labor market. The unemployment rate (i.e. 1− employment rate WM_h) reflects these labor market forces.

Box 1. Production functions and factor market equations.

Cobb–Douglas production functions for the sectors of agriculture and industry

$$X_j = \alpha_{jo}(ABN_1 \cdot LD_{1j})^{\beta 1j} \cdot LD_{2j}^{\beta 2j} \cdot KD_j^{(1-\beta 1j-\beta 2j)} \qquad j = 1,2 \quad (1)$$

Leontief technology-based value added by sector

$$V_j = (1 - \Sigma_{j'}\alpha_{j'j} - \alpha_{rj} - \tau_{jg})X_j \qquad j = 1,..,4 \quad (2)$$

Capital supply

$$KD_j = \varpi_j KS_j \qquad j = 1,2 \quad (3)$$

$$KS_j = (1 - \delta_j)KS_j, t - 1 + \kappa_{pj} I_p + I_{gj} \qquad j = 1,2 \quad (4)$$

Labor demand by skill type

$$LD_{qj} = \nu_{qjo} + \nu_{qj} V_j \qquad q = 1,2, \ j = 1,..,4 \quad (5)$$

Labor supply by skill type

$$LS_q = \lambda_{qo} LS_{q,t-6} + \Sigma_e \lambda_{eq} NE_e + \Sigma_e \lambda'_{eq} NE_{e,t-6} \qquad q = 1,2 \quad (6)$$

Enrolments at educational levels

$$NT_e = \lambda_{e0} NT_{e,t-6} + \lambda_e NE_e + \lambda'_e NE_{e,t=6} \qquad e = i,ii,iii \quad (7)$$

Financing and costing of total enrolments

$$NT_e = \chi_{eo} + \chi_e[\chi_{te}(\Sigma_h C_{h4} + C_{g4})] \qquad e = i,ii,iii \quad (8)$$

Employment, unemployment, and remuneration by earning group

$$LS_h - LD_h = LS_q - \Sigma_j LD_{qj} \qquad q = 1,2 \quad (9)$$

Labor supply of wage employees and salary employees

$$LS_h = \eta_{qho} + \eta_{qh} LS_q \qquad q = 1,2 \quad (10)$$

Remuneration rates of wage employees and salary employees

$$LR_h = \rho_{oh} + \rho_h(\Sigma_j V_j / LD_h) - \rho'_h(1 - AM_h) \qquad h = 1,2 \quad (11)$$

The next block of equations in Box 2 reviews private and government income and their demand for consumption goods, investment goods, exports, and imports. Eq. (12) specifies income received by household groups, Z_h, headed by wage earners and salary earners, $h = 1, 2$. Additional sources of income are transfers from the government and rest of the world.

Eq. (13) specifies income received by the group of self-employed and employers, $h = 3$, as the total *GDP* less factor incomes received by wage earners, salary earners, and government. Private profit is thus defined as the residual: the value added less other factor payments. An additional source of income for the group is foreign transfers.

Eq. (14) specifies disposable incomes by social group, Y_h, as incomes received less taxes paid.

Eq. (15) specifies consumption of commodity c by social group h, C_{hc}, within consumption functions that are dependent on disposable income.

Eq. (16) specifies government revenue Z_{g} as consisting of factor incomes, direct and indirect taxes, and import and export duties.

Eq. (17) equalizes government current expenditure on consumption and transfers plus government investment expenditure (on the right-hand side) to government revenue and government budget deficit, *GBD* (on the left-hand side).

Eq. (18) gives the private and government demand for consumption goods converted to the sector level. Commodities are distributed in sectors via converter coefficients.

Eq. (19) formulates the private demand for installed investment goods. There are very few examples known of multi-sector models which include a function for private investment demand, the exception being Japan (1965) and Byung-Nak Song (1972). In general, more reality is built into the model when a behavioral equation for investment demand is incorporated. In short-term econometric models, it is common practice. Empirically, private investment is found to be explained by expectations of economic growth, profit rates, and interest rates. Additional explaining variables can be enumerated, such as complementary versus competitive effects of government investment, liquid reserves, and foreign commitments to invest domestically. The scope of the model allows for incorporating a few effects but not all. To account for economic growth, lagged variables of the *GDP* were tested, giving the current *GDP* as the best fit. One candidate explaining variable is profit income divided by employed capital, meant to approximate the profit rate. Another variable is public investment, $\Sigma_j I_{gj}$, which can be expected to show a positive complementary effect in the development context.[10]

Eq. (20) adds private investment demand to government investment to give total installed investment.

Eq. (21) specifies, in a simple way, exports by sectors.

Eq. (22) specifies competitive imports as proportions of consumption and investment.

Box 2. Household income, consumption, investment, and government accounts.

Receipts of household groups of wage and salary earners

$$Z_h = LR_h \cdot LD_h + T_{gh} + T_{rh} \qquad h = 1,2 \quad (12)$$

Income of the group of employers and self-employed

$$Z_3 = \Sigma_j V_j - Z_1 - Z_2 - \rho_g \Sigma_j V_j + T_{r3} \qquad (13)$$

Disposable incomes by social group

$$Y_h = (1 - \tau_{hg}) Z_h \qquad h = 1,2,3 \quad (14)$$

Private consumption by social group h of commodity c

$$C_{hc} = \gamma_{\text{hco}} + \gamma_{\text{hc}}(1 - \sigma_h) Y_h \quad h = 1,2,3 \qquad c = 1,..,6 \quad (15)$$

Current Revenue of government

$$Z_g = \rho_g \Sigma_j V_j + \Sigma_h \tau_{hg} Z_h + \Sigma \tau_{jg} X_j + \Sigma_j \tau_{jg,\text{imp},} M_j + \Sigma \tau_{jg,\text{exp}} E_j + T_{rg} \quad (16)$$

Government expenditure and budget deficit

$$\Sigma_c C_{gc} + \Sigma_h T_{gh} + \Sigma_j I_{gj} = Z_g + GBD \qquad (17)$$

Consumption demand converted to sector level j

$$C_j = \Sigma_c \varphi_{jc} \Sigma_h C_{hc} + \varphi_{gjc} C_{gc} \qquad j = 1,..,4 \quad (18)$$

Private investment demand

$$I_p = [\iota_o + \iota_i \Sigma_j V_{j,t} + \iota [Z3/(KD_1 + KD_2)] + \iota' \Sigma_j I_{gj} \qquad (19)$$

Total investment demand

$$I = \Sigma_j I_{pj} + \Sigma_j I_{gj} \qquad (20)$$

Exports demand

$$E_j = E_{j,t-1}(1 + \varepsilon_j) \qquad j = 1,..,4 \quad (21)$$

Competitive imports

$$M_j = \mu_{jc} \Sigma_j C_j + \mu_{ji} I \qquad j = 1,..,4 \quad (22)$$

The third block, in Box 3, lays down conventional aim variables and what has become known as basic needs aim variables and their formation. Together, they are eight sets of aim variables: the *GDP* growth rate, denoted by *AG*, in eq. (23). Next is the per capita disposable income by social group h, denoted by AY_h in eq. (24). Next are the employment rates for wage earners, and for salary earners, they are denoted by AM_h in eq. (25). Then, there are the basic needs aim variables for the lowest income group that relate to satisfaction with food and nutritional calorie intake, AC_1, dwelling needs, AD_1, health needs, *AH*, and education needs, *AN*. There is also the basic needs attainment index, ABN_1, which combines the above.

As was stated earlier, the basic needs indicators are relevant in the case of population groups who are not able to satisfy these needs considering the level of income they receive. In terms of the population groups considered in the model, this would apply most to the group of wage earners. Hence, subscript 1 is attached to the nutrition and housing aim variables: AC_1 and AD_1. In the case of health and education, it is difficult to identify these indicators at the group level. The average level reached for the whole population is taken to be representative of what is reached at the wage earner level.

Eq. (26) specifies the formation of nutritional levels. The derivation of calories from a certain amount of food expenditure would require knowledge of the average cost per calorie. For example, realized calories per capita = (consumption expenditure on food per capita)/(average cost per calorie) or written otherwise, average cost per calorie = consumption expenditure on food per capita/realized calories per capita. The model is concerned with the nutritional conditions of the lowest income group, $h = 1$. Their consumption expenditure on food, which consists of a private component, $C_{1,1}$, plus public allocations of food directed to this group, $C_{g,1}$. Consumption expenditure of food per capita per annum is, therefore, $(C_{1,\cdot 1} + C_{g\cdot 1})/\pi_1 P$. The realized calorie intake per capita for the group is denoted by WC_1. Dividing the first by the second term gives the average annual cost per calorie per day, which can be assumed to be a linear function of the general level of living of the group, represented by the income per capita of the group, thus $(Y_1/\pi_1 P)$. Usually, the unit cost tends to increase rapidly as the general level of living approaches higher levels, owing to the gradual shift in the pattern of food composition from cheap food articles to more expensive food articles with the same calorie content. As a result, the equation can be written for estimation purposes in the form of eq. (26), in which $\phi_{1,\,1.o}$ and $\phi_{1,\,1}$ are the parameters which require estimation by regression.

Eq. (27) specifies the formation of housing levels in similarity with the above formulation. A specification for the supply of rooms per capita for the lowest income group can be written wherein the numerator is the rent expenditure per capita and the denominator stands for the average rent per room (assumed a function of income per capita).

Eq. (28) follows the preceding formulations to define the survival rate (which is 1-mortality rate) for the whole nation in terms of a numerator (the health expenditure per person) and a denominator (the average health costs of avoiding one death). Although the equation fitted with regressed data, its predictions of the mortality rate were at variance with those from established demographic projections; besides, the link of the equation with the model turned out to be empirically weak. Hence, it was decided to reformulate eq. (28) into eq. (28.1), i.e. $AH = \lambda$, as eq. (28.1), where λ is the exogenously given survival rate for the whole nation and use given projections of the mortality rate, which is $1 - \lambda$. This proved to be also more functional since the model required values of mortality rates for manpower with different skill types and pupils of different ages and these were simply set at levels proportional to the mortality rate for the whole population.

Eq. (29) is the enrolment rate defined as enrolment in primary education in percent of the eligible child population. Derivation of enrolment levels was specified in eq. (8).

Eq. (30) is a basic needs attainment index for the wage-earning/ low-skilled group, ABN_1. The index is close to the human development index, developed by the UNDP and often used in assessing country ranks. The attained values of the four basic needs indicators are divided by their requirement levels, and the outcome is averaged. The specification of the index chooses to exclude substitution possibilities between the four indicators but otherwise is also justified. The first equation of the model assigns a role for ABN_1 in influencing the labor input equivalent of low-skill workers. Labor works at its full capacity when ABN_1 attains the value of 100%, i.e. basic needs are fully satisfied. To repeat, in demonstration of the argument, a workforce of 5 million with ABN_1 at a level of 90% is equivalent to a workforce of 4.5 million with a 100% productive capability. In eq. (30), the following is observed: $AC_1/ac > 1$ to be reduced to 1, similarly for AD_1/ad, AH/as, and AN/an.

Box 3. Well-being variables (aim variables).

GDP growth

$$AG = (\Sigma_j V_{j,t}/\Sigma_j V_{j,t-1}) - 1 \quad (23)$$

Disposable income per capita

$$AY_h = Y_h/\pi_h P. \qquad h = 1,2,3 \quad (24)$$

Employment rates

$$AM_h = LD_h/LS_h \qquad h = 1,2 \quad (25)$$

Food: Calorie intake

$$(C_{1,1} + C_{g\,1})/(\pi_1 P.AC_1) = \phi_{1,1,o} + \phi_{1,\,1}(Y_1/\upsilon_1 P) \quad (26)$$

(*Continued*)

Housing: Dwelling level	
$(C_{1,2} + C_{g,2})/(\pi_1 P.AD_1) = \phi_{1,2,o} + \phi_{1,2}(Y_1/\upsilon_1 P)$	(27)
Health: Survival rate(= 1 − mortality rate)	
$(\Sigma_h C_{h.3} + C_{g3})/(P.\ AH) = \phi_{3,0} + \phi_{,3}(V/P)$	(28)
Education: Enrolment rate in primary education	
$AN = NT_e/\pi_e P$ $e = i$ *(primary education)*	(29)
Basic needs index	
$ABN_1 = (^1/_4)(AC_1/ac + AD_1/ad + AH/as + AN/an)$	(30)

The fourth block, in Box 4, consists of national accounts balances referring to product market balance, savings–investment balance, and foreign payments balance. Eq. (31) equalizes the supply of goods to their demand. Supply consists of gross output by sector, X_j, and imports, M_j. Demand consists of intermediate deliveries, consumption, investment, inventory change, and exports. Two notes need to be added. The only sector that delivers investment goods is the industry sector ($j = 2$). Thus, $\iota_{2\text{industry}}) = 1$, and $\iota_j = 0$ for other sectors. Inventory changes, ICH_j, applies to the non-service sectors. The product market balances for the services sectors have $ICH_j = 0$.

Eq. (32) equalizes total savings to total gross capital formation in what can be called the financial market balance. Total savings consist of private savings, government savings, and foreign savings, i.e. foreign capital flow converted into national currency, *FXR.FCF.* Total savings are equal to installed investment and inventory change.

Box 4. Product market balances.

Sector product balances	
$X_j + \mathrm{M}_j = \Sigma\alpha_{jj'}X_{j'} + C_j + \iota_j I + ICH_j + E_j\, j = 1,\ldots,4$	(31)
Financial market balance (Savings investment balance)	
$(\Sigma_h \Sigma_h Y_h) + (Z_g - \Sigma_c C_{gc} - \Sigma_h T_{gh}) + FXR \cdot FCF = \mathrm{I} + \Sigma_j ICH_j$	(32)
Foreign payments balance	
$\Sigma_j \alpha_{rj} X_j + M_j + \Sigma_h T_{rh} + T_{rg} = \Sigma_j E_j + FXR \cdot FCF$	(A1)

With its 32 sets of equations, the model contains the equivalent number of 32 sets of endogenous variables. It is a determinate model. There is the additional equation of the foreign payments balance, but this is automatically obtained when the model of 32 equations is solved and as such stands outside the model. Hence, it is numbered as eq. (A1). The equation is useful in checking the consistency of solutions of the model. When one of the three balances is left out, and the remaining balances are substituted in each other and solved, they will automatically reproduce the balance which was left out. This is also the rule that guides the construction of a social accounting matrix and is common use in guaranteeing the consistency of the interdependent accounts. So, to maintain the model as a square matrix, we choose to leave out the foreign payments balance, but the same results are obtained if instead of skipping the foreign payments balance the modeler skips the investment savings balance. Deleting one of the balances is interpretable in terms of Walras law that states that in general equilibrium, the modeler may impose market clearing for $n-1$ markets and drop the nth market, this being automatically guaranteed, and thus redundant to specify. In principle, the same rule applies to a state of general equilibrium, irrespective of whether the general equilibrium has come through price adjusters, quantity adjusters, or a combination of both. The structure and closure of the model will be reviewed in Figures 2 and 3.

4. Application

4.1. *Estimates and projections*

The model contains coefficients whose estimation falls into two categories: technical or institutional coefficients that are directly available from published material and behavioral coefficients estimated via regressions. The basic data for the estimation of the first category are Korean single-year data, especially the input–output tables of 1963 and 1966, estimates of Korean capital, and inventory in 1968. Production function parameters for agriculture and industry, eq. (1), are from various publications of Korea Development Institute.[11] Initial labor input rates by skill and sector, eq. (5), are derived from the Korean Second Five-Year Plan. We applied these rates to the observed value added by sector for the observation period to give the "plan requirements". These were regressed against observed employment to generate calibration coefficients that were used to adjust the initial planning input rates to their actual values.[12] Data on the progress of cohorts of pupils at various educational levels, participation in the labor force, and mortality are from various Korean ministerial sources. Estimates of all transition rates λs in eqs. (6) and (7) assure consistency for the observation period.[13]

Estimation of behavioral parameters was done by applying OLS to observations for 1960–1971. The data used are Korean time series of household surveys, labor surveys, and national accounts. All estimates selected are econometrically viable and are in conformity with expectations based on economic theory. Few remarks follow on the obtained estimates. Eq. (8), which specifies costing coefficients, fitted better for primary and secondary education than for higher education. In terms of relative current costs per student, the three levels are related in the ratio 1.0:3.0:14.2, respectively. Eq. (10), which specifies conversion coefficients of manpower supply by skill types into social groups, fitted very well with the data.[14] Several regressions of eq. (11), which explains separately wage and salary rates for low- and high-skilled labor, were tested and the best fits selected. The estimates allow calculating the elasticity of the remuneration rate by earner type h, LR_h, with respect to average productivity, $\Sigma_j V_j / LD_h$, calculated at mean values. The elasticities are above unity and are found to be higher for wage earners than that for salary earners, which may indicate that economic growth in Korea favored wage earners relatively more than salary earners. Calculated elasticities of remuneration to unemployment are -0.933 and -0.177 for wage earners and salary earners, respectively. These results emphasize the greater dependence of the wage rate on the employment situation; salary formation is more autonomous.[15]

Next are well-fitted 18 consumption functions covering 3 household groups and 6 consumption categories, eq. (15). The equations fitted slightly better for wage and salary earning groups than for the employers and related group, which is expected given the latter's heterogeneity and the fact that their consumption and income data were obtained as residual after deducting figures for other groups (obtained from surveys of households and labor) from national aggregates (available from national accounts). The estimates are in general conformity with well-known changing patterns of consumption with rising incomes. Calculated consumption elasticities at mean values show for the three groups: elasticities lower than one for food and housing, higher than one for health and education, and about one for commercial and other social services. In contrast, eq. (19), specifying the private investment function, performed the least of all equations and had to be slightly modified to produce reasonable estimates.[16]

Finally, there are the regressed coefficients relating to the formation of nutrition, housing, and health. Eq. (26) explains the variance in unit cost of daily calories by the annual disposable income per capita. The regressed data fitted well, allowing calculating an elasticity of calorie cost with respect to income per capita, evaluated at mean values, at the value of 0.606. This implies that a 1% increase in income per capita adds 0.6% to calorie cost, thus leaving less for more calorie consumption.[17] Eq. (27), which relates to housing levels, gave a well-performing regression as well. The calculated elasticity of the cost of a room per capita with respect to income per capita, evaluated at mean values, amounts to 0.5891.[18] The elasticities are practically equal for both nutrition and housing. Eq. (28), which relates to health, performed well too. But the calculated elasticity of survival cost with respect to income per capita came out to 1.0393, implying that growth in income per capita accelerates the growth in the costs of avoiding death. This reflects the general tendency for costs of medical care to rise more than incomes. As was stated earlier, because the equation is not able to connect functionally with the rest of the model, we chose to replace eq. (28) with eq. (28.1), which takes over given mortality rates from demographic projections instead of predicting them endogenously.

Estimated on the basis of data for 1960–1972, the model is solved for three six-year periods: 1966, 1974, and 1980. Comparisons between projected solutions and observed values for the sixties show that the employed model represented the Korean economy fairly well. With respect to the post-observation periods, the predictions for the *GDP* and its composition for 1974 and 1980 were in a close range of values actually observed. More insight into the validation of the outcomes can be gained from an evaluation of structural ratios between the solved variables. The investment share in the *GDP* increases remarkably from 0.24 to 0.34 and to 0.39 over three periods which is consistent with the high growth of *GDP* at 9.0%. Regarding financing of investment, the ratio of domestic savings to foreign capital inflow increases from 0.57 to 0.74 to 0.94, indicating increasing self-sufficiency. The general labor coefficient that divides total employment by total product undergoes remarkable reductions in each period, i.e. from 8.4 to 5.1 and to 2.7 in 1968, 1974, and 1980, reflecting the remarkable growth in labor productivity. Concurrently, labor input shifts substantially to the high skilled and away from the employer and self-employed category. Employment rates AM_h develop gradually toward fuller employment indicating that by 1980 unemployment is reduced to 5% for wage earners and to 2% for salary earners. The combined employment rate for both groups reached 0.96 in 1980; see Figure 1.[19]

The remarkable growth in labor productivity, together with a favorable labor market, raised earnings appreciably. Results show that with respect to the disposable income per capita WY_h, while in 1962 the group of employers, etc. had the highest value, from 1968 onward, salary earners were the best off. Wage earners were the least off. The income gap between the two earner groups appears to widen, but that between groups 2 and 3 is shown to shrink. For 1968 and 1980, the Gini index of income concentration derived from the income forecasts of the model and population projections indicates a general progress toward more equality, as shown in Figure 1. The Korean combination of high economic growth ($AG = 9.6\%$) with fair distribution tendencies (Gini index falling from 0.48 to 0.46) is often quoted as exemplary in the development context.

Regarding the progress of general living conditions for the (lowest income) wage earners group, the aim variable of calorie consumption per day per person, AC_1, is the first to reach its minimum requirements level, i.e. 2,290, followed by the enrolment rate AN and the survival rate AH. The housing indicator, AD_1, is the most remote from its "satisfaction point".[20] The progress of the composite index of the general living conditions, ABN_1, with special reference to wage earners, is shown in Figure 1. This index is found to progress gradually from its observed

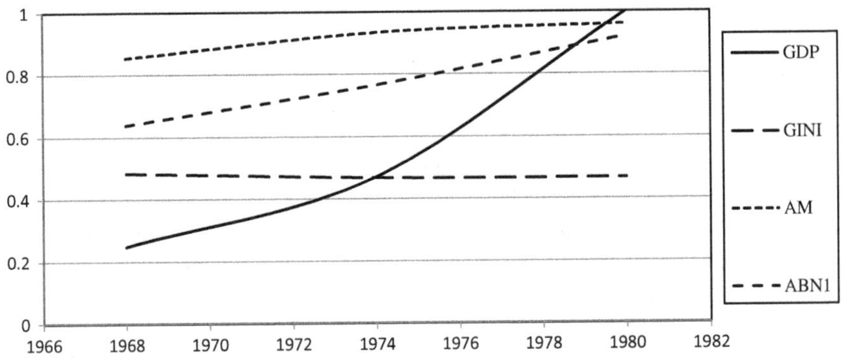

Figure 1. Model solutions: Indices of selected aim variables. GDP index takes 1982 = 100.

level of 64% in 1968 to a predicted level of 92% in 1980, and at this rate to reach its maximum of 100% in a couple of more years. The improvement amounts to 28 percentage points over a period of 12 years. It can be inquired what the relative contribution of the productivity effect to the economic growth in the 12 years is. Raising the 28% to the low-skill labor supply elasticities in the agriculture and industry production functions (0.24 and 0.34), and weighing the outcomes by the GDP shares of agriculture and industry (0.32 and 0.48 in 1971) gives a contribution of 6.44% over the 28 years or an average annual contribution of 0.54%, whereas the solved average growth rate of the GDP amounted to about 9.0%. The share of the contribution of the productivity effect in GDP growth can thus be roughly estimated at about 6%, i.e. 0.54% / 9.0%. The contribution is a once and for all effect that ceases as ABN_1 reaches its satiation level at the beginning of the 1980s.

4.2. *Multiplier properties*

To bring more policy practices into the analytical framework, the conventional multiplier analysis was extended in two respects. First, while the model generates impact multipliers that measure the immediate effect of a unit increase in an exogenous variable on endogenous variables and generates interim multipliers that give the effect of a sustained change in the exogenous variable in period t on endogenous variables in later periods; there is another notion of the multiplier that is applicable in this model. When a government makes plans in period t for a specific addition to public expenditure, i.e. food and housing subsidies, health and educational allocations, or income transfers or a revision in tax rates, these measures are not only sustained in later periods t' but often tend to recur in later periods t', especially when there is a commitment to maintain the extended services. Assuming that the magnitude of the manipulated addition in a particular exogenous variable in each period is the same, one obtains what can be called recurring multipliers, which were simulated.

Second, in the real world, government allocations to consumption and investment are closely tied. Often, an increase in public consumption C_{gc} implies a certain proportionate increase in public investment I_{gj}. This complementarity relationship makes it essential to evaluate the combined multipliers of C_{gc} and I_{gj}. For example, the ratios of I_{gj} to C_{gc} in Korea in the observation years were stable and amounted to zero for food and housing subsidies, 1.0, 1.4, 2.0, and 3.4 for spending on health, primary, secondary, and higher education, and 3.0 and 3.3 for spending on other goods and other services.

To save space, we report briefly the findings on the recurring multiplier effects of current and associated capital spending bundles on the distinguished budget spending categories: food, housing, health, education, and other goods and services. We focus on two recurring multiplier effects: one is on the gross domestic product, *GDP*, i.e. $\Sigma_j V_j$, is plotted along the x-axis in Figure 2, and the other is on the income of the poorest population group Y_1, which is plotted along the y-axis in Figure 2. When the two variables are considered together, they would reflect on both growth and distribution. The upper right quarter of the figure is where positive growth is combined with positive redistribution. The joints indicate transition of the multiplier effect from one six-year period to a later period. As can be directly seen, there are trade-offs between immediate and later returns, whereby the immediate returns in the first period are not rewarding in terms of both growth and distribution, but accumulated returns over a couple of periods are positive in both terms and tend to accelerate. The sluggish effect on the *GDP* in the first period tends to diminish somewhat the income accruing to wage earners Y_1. Both effects change sign as the *GDP* increases in later periods.

The results show that the multiplier as defined here is insignificant for food and housing subsidies and barely shows in the figure. Health spending contributes to

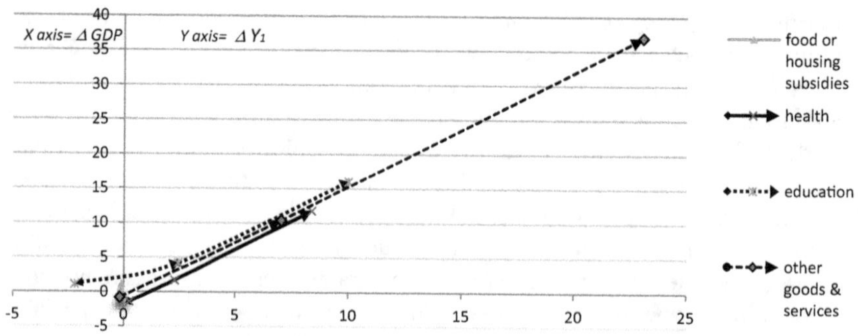

Figure 2. Recurring multiplier effect of public current plus associated capital expenditure.

both aim variables. Education spending contributes somewhat more. Allocations to other goods and other services perform better. The main mechanism behind these effects is that capital appears to be more scarce than labor in determining economic growth, while skill upgrading counts too. In this context, public current allocations that are associated with higher capital expenditures would over time increase the availability of investment goods and upgrade leading to higher economic growth. If food and housing subsidies were accompanied by agricultural and housing investment projects, their multipliers would have been positive and significant. The results can explain to some extent why impatient governments often show little readiness to wait for longer periods before reaping the rewards of public spending. Another mechanism already mentioned is the productivity effect of higher levels of ABN_1; this is less active in the Korean context as the relevant satiation level of ABN_1 was practically reached.

5. Analytical versus Policy Uses: Breakdown of Policymaking

5.1. *Structure and functioning of the analytical model*

In conformity with accepted uses, the analytical form of the model treats aim variables as unknown and instruments as given. The complete policy form is usually described as the reverse, with all aim variables taking the form of fixed targets and instrument variables becoming unknown. In this section, we assess both forms. Figure 3 gives the causal ordering of the analytical form, showing the equation number and the equation endogenous variables, and controllable policy instruments that can be employed to influence solutions. Simon (1953) defines the general rule for establishing causal ordering: endogenous variables of the first order are those which are influenced by parameters (and pre-determined variables) and/or by each other mutually. Endogenous variables of the second order are those which are influenced only by parameters (and predetermined variables) and/or endogenous variables of the first and second orders, etc. A model containing one order is a complete simultaneous system in which, in principle, any controllable policy instrument or data can influence all unknowns.

All the 32 equations and variables are solved within one order, except those at the very end of the figure: eqs. (16), (17), and (32) that relate to Z_g, *GBD*, and *FCF*.[21] The very high simultaneity in the model is due to various interdependences that exist between the sectors that produce goods, i.e. agriculture and extended industry, marked by G, and the sectors that produce services, marked by S. Although production technology is modeled differently in the two categories, whereby production in the G sectors combines the two levels of production function and input–output technologies, the S sectors produce their services along input–output technologies. The types of sectors interact at the input–output level

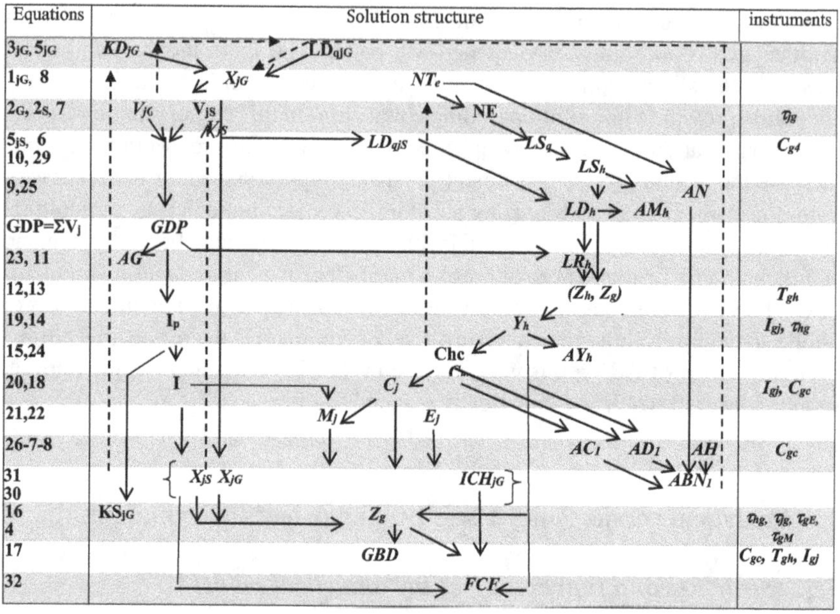

Figure 3. Causal ordering of the analytical model.

and compete for labor and investment inputs. While the formation of labor supply is dependent on educational spending (mostly placed on the right-hand side in the figure), this spending is only known if incomes are determined. Capital formation is delivered and primarily purchased by the goods sectors (on the left-hand side), but this can only be known if outputs and incomes are determined. If the two sector categories would fall in lower and higher causal orders, the structure of the model would have been diagonal and simpler, but this is otherwise. Furthermore, the productivity effect of basic needs attainment brings more simultaneity in the model since they enter the production function in the very first equation, but the solution of BNA_1 can only be obtained at the end of the circular flow and after realization of consumption. The dashed arrows in the figure showing an upward direction highlight the high degree of interdependence and simultaneity.

5.2. *The planning form: a decomposed structure*

In redesigning the model toward its planning (which comes to fixing aim variables and solving for suitably selected policy instruments), the question presents itself whether there exist meaningful causal orderings that can tell which specific aim variables should be fixed first and which others should follow later. Granted for the moment that there are no political preferences that dictate the form in which the planning model should be shaped, the planning advisor may search, on purely technical grounds, for the logically simplest structure. By comparing the matrix structures of a number of conceivable alternative policy forms that with the simplest structure can serve as a starting point. It logically follows also that after starting with the simplest structure, one should extend it later to more complex structures. In this way, the analytical form of the model is adapted in a step-wise manner to the fixation of targets for more aim variables of a more complex nature until the complete policy form is approached. For our particular purpose, we shall consider that as we move to forms whose mathematical structures fall into a larger number of orders, we approach a simpler structure. By shuffling rows and columns, we can triangulate the particular structures of alternative forms and observe which structure is simpler.

Application of this procedure shows that *first*, the planning form which fixes targets for disposable incomes per capita AY_h and uses direct tax rates and/or income transfers as unknowns has a simpler structure than the analytical form. Figure 4 displays the case where income transfers are the adjusters, but the same can be done via direct taxes or a combination of them. As was mentioned earlier, fixing Y_h for all groups is equivalent to fixing *GDP* and choosing for a targeted distribution of income. In the formulation of distribution policy, various alternatives are supposed to be evaluated in the light of their effects not only on the welfare of the immediate beneficiaries but also on the whole economy. In the following section, we shall examine some applications of alternative distributions.

After this *first* policy form, the most logical step is that in a *second* round, such supplementary aims as higher nutrition, housing, education, etc. for the lowest income social group can be fixed, in particular, AC_1,AD_1, (AH is already predetermined), and AN. Public allocations toward these ends are the instruments to be solved: these are C_{g1}, C_{g2}, C_{g3}, and C_{g4}, respectively. This simplifies the structure of the model appreciably since the labor productivity effect of the targeted higher quality of life can be immediately fed into the production functions in eq. (1); see upper left hand, Figure 4, while the allocations to education C_{g4} allow determining straightforward NT_e, NE_e, and LS_q, which are further converted into LS_h; see upper right hand, Figure 4.

In a *third* round, with the labor supply known, fixation of employment targets implies that the distribution of production on the sectors of activity has to adjust itself so as to absorb the labor supply consistent with employment targets; this occurs in equations in the upper shaded order in Figure 4. Once production levels of all sectors and labor inputs are solved, the main adjustors in the final analysis become (a) distribution of install investment in the goods-producing sectors become, leading to solve for the unknown policy instruments of public investment I_{gj} in sectors $j = 1, 2$, see lower left hand, Figure 4, and (b) distribution of inventory changes ICH_j as adjusters of product balances in the goods-producing sectors, $j = 1,2$, shown in the lower shaded order. This third round can be described as the

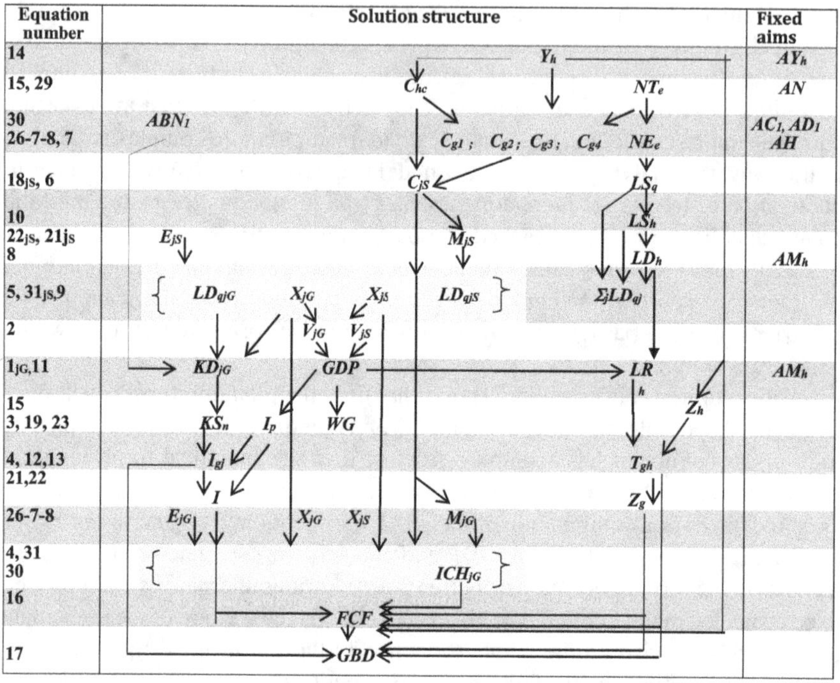

Figure 4. Causal ordering of the planning model.

complete planning form since it incorporates fixed targets for all target variables (GDP and ABN_1 follow indirectly).

Contrasting Figures 3 and 4 shows the planning model to be fully decomposable in clearly defined diagonal orders, which increases insight and control of the model and its outcomes. The crux of the analytical model fell in one order that had to be simultaneously solved. The planning model falls into some 13 subsequent orders that are solved one after another. There are two more orders common to both models; these are at the bottom where *FCF* and *GBD* are determined. The planning model is not only more helpful than the analytical model in increasing analytical insight and management control, but policy makers would prefer it too. As policy makers are equally interested in aim variables and in the achievement of a balanced government budget, they like to see how the budget is shaped by targeted variables. The planning model does not set all policy instruments as unknowns. It contains additional degrees of freedom (instruments that are *a priori* fixed and can be modified to suit a balanced budget). These are tax rates τ_{hg}, τ_{jg}, τ_{gE}, and τ_{gM}, current expenditures C_{g5} and C_{g6}, and capital expenditure in the services sectors, I_{gj}, $j = 3, 4$.

How do the above forms treat clearance of the product and financial market balances? This comes to the specification of closure rules. In both forms, clearance of the product market balances happens via inventory changes in the goods-producing sectors. With respect to the savings–investment balance, as domestic savings and investments are determined in preceded equations and as the foreign exchange rate, FXR, is fixed, it is foreign capital flow, FCF, which is the primary adjuster. Because all the equations in the analytical model are involved in a simultaneous solution of the unknowns, specific adjusters cannot be assigned per equation. However, under the planning form of the model, the solution structure of the model is more diagonal, which allows for the above assignment of adjuster status to particular variables.

5.3. *Some illustrations*

The first policy form where incomes of social groups are fixed and taxes are made unknown can be planned via alternative strategies of income redistribution. The results of three alternative strategies are shown in Table 4. The first strategy I stipulated increases in the disposable income of wage earners by 10 billion won in 1968, 1974, and 1980 without affecting other incomes. This led to lower *GDP* at the end of the third period, in 1980, involving a reduction of −15.68 billion won (bw), higher requirement of foreign capital inflow +16.94 bw, and higher budgetary deficit +25.68 bw. In addition, this strategy raises unemployment for both manpower types. A second strategy II applied income transfers from salary earners to wage earners, at the same rates and periods. This strategy reduces the above strains on *GDP*, *FCF*, *GBD*, and unemployment rates. A third strategy III applied the income transfers from employers, etc. to wage earners, at the same rates and periods. This strategy brought about the best performance with respect to the four macro variables. Historically, too, in the process of development, a trend is often observed toward a larger income share for wage and salary earners at the cost of employers and related.

When the development objective is to raise basic needs attainment, there is the choice between indirectly raising income (via reduced taxes or via transfer payments) versus provisions in kind. Eqs. (26) and (27) allow reflecting on the

Table 4. Alternative strategies of fixing income targets by social groups: Deviations from analytical solutions for 1980 (in billion won and thousand persons).

	Fixed income strategies				Fixed income strategies		
	I	II	III		I	II	III
GDP	−15.68	−6.57	−1.48	BGD	25.68	6.57	1.48
FCF	16.94	4.44	0.83	$LD_l + LD_2$	−83	−35	−7

Table 5. Predictive performance of the analytical and policy forms

Analytical	(1) Observed	(2) Solution	(1)/(2)	Policy	(3) Observed	(4) Solution	(3)/(4)
$Y11$	0.33	0.2973	0.9009	Z11	0.0082	−0.0454	wrong sign
$Y12$	0.1288	0.1287	0.9992	Z12	0.0070	0.0058	1.21
$Y13$	0.4941	0.5187	1.0502	Z13	0.0443	0.0884	0.5

affectivity of cash transfers versus provisions in kind. Besides the obvious fact that not all the cash transfers would be spent on the targeted food or targeted housing, there is the second and more important aspect that cost is a function of income, and increases in income are bound to increase the unit cost of the basic needs and diminish the amounts purchasable. As a result, direct cash transfers can be shown to be less effective than provisions in kind in raising levels of living.

5.4. *Other elaborations*

The empirical investigation of the model in both its analytical and policy forms allows for making a few observations of a general nature. In a comparison between the multiplier effects of (the common) exogenous variables in both the analytical and policy forms, it is found that for most unknowns, the effects can be substantially different between the two forms. This testifies to the high sensitivity of the reduced form to the particular specification of the model structure.

It is also worthwhile to investigate and compare the predictive performances of the analytical and policy forms in other respects. Tinbergen (1970) mentions that highly ordered model structures would give solutions which are more reliable than the outcome of model structures with fewer orders. This is not always supported, as the comparisons in Table 5 show a prediction advantage for the analytical over the policy form. The results are consistent with the nature of the aim variables and instrument variables. In the analytical model, the unknown aim variables of disposable income have a bigger base so that an absolute error in the unknown becomes a relatively small one. But in the policy model, where income taxes are the instrument variables, and which have a smaller base, an absolute error in their prediction can become relatively speaking a very high one. In general, in most economic models, aim variables carry higher values than instrument variables.

6. Concluding Remarks

The advance made in defining, measuring, applying, and comparing well-being indicators stands in contrast with little work achieved in incorporating such well-being indicators in economy-wide policy models. This is to some extent understandable in view of the difficulties encountered in formulating and verifying relationships that link well-being indicators with conventional variables in an economic model. In this chapter, we attempted to close the gap and incorporate basic needs indicators, next to other development goals, in an economy-wide model, and with some success.

Several lessons can be summed up. First, because the number of indicators that can be integrated is by nature quite limited, a systematic and consensus-oriented approach had to be followed in choosing/minimizing the selection of indicators. Our approach was to stick to the income per capita goals of household groups and supplement these with well-being indicators in case income is around or below the poverty line.

Second, handy shortcuts worked well in areas of food, housing, and education, but there is less success with concise specifications for health indicators. It is also interesting to note the empirical verification of an increasing cost per well-being unit with higher income per capita.

Third, incorporation of the productivity effect of higher well-being is best and simplest done via defining the affected (number of) worker units in terms of capability worker units, whereby full capability is reached when basic needs are attained. It was possible to estimate the contribution of this productivity effect to GDP growth at about 6% of the whole GDP growth. The contribution is a once and for all effect that ceases as the well-being indicators reach their satiation level, i.e. in Korea in the early 1980s.

Fourth, when there are so many aim variables to be targeted and instrument variables to be solved, there is the central question in policymaking on how to proceed with policymaking, i.e. which aim variables should be planned first (or treated first) and which other should logically follow. Causal ordering of the modeled system due to Simon (1953) is very useful in decomposing the analytical model in its planning forms. It turns out that the prefixing of disposable incomes by social groups is the most logical first move in the policymaking process, followed by basic needs and employment targets. The GDP variable appears down the list following causal ordering. It is understood, of course, that the conversion of the analytical model into its planning forms (where goal variables are fixed) does not imply that a central planning machinery is assumed. Working with planning forms is a device in policymaking that increases insight into and control over the mechanisms of the model.

Endnotes

1. The UNRISD list of basic needs indicators was applied to developing countries in Drewnowski and Scott (1967). The application was extended in Cohen (1968). This application was later updated to cover the period 1920–1975 and published in Cohen (1986).

2. It can be rightly argued that the group of employers, self-employed workers, and family workers is a very heterogeneous group and cannot have common interests. The group usually contains the richest and some of the poorer parts of the population. Its distribution between rural and urban areas is even more subtle. Disaggregated data on the constituents of this group are very scarce, however.
3. The national survival rate is 1 minus the national mortality rate.
4. Quoting from Adam Smith, more than two centuries ago, he stated the following: "......... The liberal reward of labor, as it encourages the propagation, so it increases the industry of the common people. The wages of labor are an encouragement of industry, which, like every other human quality, improves in proportion to the encouragement it receives. A plentiful subsistence increases the bodily strength of the laborer, and the comfortable hope of bettering his condition, and ending his days perhaps in ease and plenty, animates him to exert that strength to the utmost. ....." Ed. E. Cannan, ... in A. Smith (1961), Vol. 1, p. 91.
5. See Cohen (2013).
6. As a result, Y_h becomes in million won per person, WC_1 is in thousand calories p.p., and WD_1 is rooms pp.
7. As it is assumed that high-skilled labor has already reached $BNA > 1$, specification of a basic needs attainment productivity effect in the case of high skill labor is not applicable. The specification is limited to low-skill workers only.
8. Although the distribution of destination proportions is assumed fixed for a period t, the coefficients need to be updated for distributional changes between periods. The basis for the specification of the coefficient is the relative investment requirement of a sector in relation to all sectors: $\kappa_{pj} = (1/\kappa_j)(X_j - X_{j,t-1})/\Sigma_{j'}\left((1/\kappa_{j'})(X_{j'} - X_{j',t-1}\right)$ where κ_j stands for the incremental capital output ratio. The destination proportions should be consistent with the weights of relative growth among the sectors.
9. These equations contain transition rates on demographic survival, promotion of students from one class to another, repetition, graduation, certification by educational level, and participation in the labor force. When the three variables over more t years are approximated linearly to give their values at the end of 6-year periods, we obtain eqs. (6) and (7) as they are expressed in the current model. For more details, see Cohen (1975).
10. See, for instance, Grier and Tullock (1989) and Easterly and Rebelo (1993).
11. The supply elasticities of production for low skill and high skill amount to 0.24 and 0.006 and for capital to 0.754, in the Cobb–Douglas production function of the agriculture sector. The three elasticities are 0.34, 0.08, and 0.58 for the extended industry sector.
12. The calibration of plan requirements to observed employment performed econometrically very well with $R^2 = 0.98$ and high t-value. The results show that a 1% increase in planned requirements of manpower skills has been implemented with 1.1–1.2% increase in actual employment. For the past period, the derivation of manpower input rates from planned requirements can be described to underestimate the actual manpower absorption, the discrepancy between planned and realized being higher in the case of the high skill than in that of the low skill.
13. For derivation of the transition rates, see endnote 10.
14. $R^2 = 0.97$ and 0.99 for regressed labor supply equations for $h = 1,2$, respectively.
15. The equation explains the remuneration rate for wage earners performed better than that for salary earners, with $R^2 = 0.83$ and 0.67, respectively. In the case of wage earners, the variance is explained for 80% by labor productivity and for 20% by the unemployment rate.
16. Compared with other regressed equations, the proposed private investment equation performed least. It had to be modified to a simple dependence on the GDP, which did very well with $R^2 = 0.96$, t-value high, and serial correlation low. Transformation of the slope coefficient into an elasticity at mean values gave an elasticity of private investment to GDP of 2.75, which is characteristic of

the accelerating effect of economic growth on investment and likewise a high feedback effect of investment on future economic growth, both typical for Korea.

17. As Korean data on the daily calorie consumption available were insufficient for testing the equation, we have relied on mixed data from cross-sections (from countries of the ECAFE) and time series (between 1957 and 1967). In total, 20 observations were employed. The following regression results were obtained: $(C_{h1} + C_{g1})/(\pi_1 P.\ WC_1) = 0.0051 + 0.0498(Y1/\pi\, 1P)$. Estimates are highly significant with $R^2 = 0.97$.
18. Estimation of the equation for housing gave intercept at 0.0032 and a highly significant slope coefficient at 0.0427, with $R^2 = 0.91$.
19. The more general employment ratio meant to include all earners, employers, self-employed, and family workers divided by the labor force is, by definition, lower than *WM* as used here.
20. These conclusions are in agreement with results of the Bari Loche world model for Latin America obtained in a different context; see Herrera (1974).
21. GBD and FCF are positioned in the highest orders in the CEM prototype model. They do not influence other variables.

Chapter 10

Statics and Dynamics in a Basic Computable General Equilibrium CGE Model: Indonesia

1. Introduction

In general, there are two types of applied economy-wide models focussing on economic development: (1) combined econometric models (CEM) based on macro data and often combined with input–output multi-sector specifications. The Korean model in Chapter 9 is an example of the CEM type. (2) The computable general equilibrium model (CGE) is the second type, and this takes various forms, static and dynamic, and may focus on different topics ranging from growth and distribution to trade, liberalization, finance, energy, environment, etc. Chapters 10, 11, and 12 are examples of CGE models. This chapter demonstrates how a simple static computable general equilibrium model of the Indonesian economy can be constructed and parameterized using the social accounting matrix as a database, which is instructive for the reader who engages in modeling and calibration. This chapter will also elaborate on converting the constant labor supply and capital stock in the static model to dynamic specifications allowing formulation and solution of a dynamic version of the CGE model.

As background to CGE models, it can be mentioned that the discovery of the CGE as an operational model that can be readily calibrated for the economy-wide circular flow can be traced back to Johansen (1960), where he presented a multi-sector general equilibrium model for the Norwegian economy. But Johansen's work was not immediately picked up. It was only later, in the mid-seventies and eighties, when the launching phase of the CGE model took place. A limited number of pioneers, mostly advising in the context of developing countries, together with the active support of the World Bank, set the scene for the first generation of

CGE models. There is a recurring controversy on who was first, second, or third in leading the launching phase. The launching can be also perceived as a collective effort at mapping a barely discovered territory at the time. Each contribution added something that was missing from the map. The following list of contributors is illustrative of the collective effort. Adelman and Robinson (1978) provided the first CGE model for a developing country: Korea. A somewhat different direction introduced structural constraints. The structuralist approach is apparent in Lysy and Taylor (1977), who developed and applied the CGE model for an analysis of income distribution in Brazil. At about the same time, the World Bank initiated country studies on structural adjustment, trade, and distribution that made use of CGE models with elements from both neoclassical and structural thought. The work by Dervis, De Melo, and Robinson (1982) is in part an outcome of the World Bank initiative. In the next few years, tens of CGE models for developing countries followed. For a related survey, see Decaluwe and Martens (1988). The launching phase of the CGE model was a success story. Other factors that helped elevate the CGE model to the mainstream were the preceding experience gathered in constructing social accounting matrices, which is essential for calibrating the CGE models, the advances made in quick computations, the recognition that endogenous prices are essential in economy-wide models, and the flexibility of the CGE modeling framework in incorporating modifications and extensions. The contributions mentioned above are incomplete without due mention of works by Scarf (1969) and Scarf and Shoven (1984) which aimed at developing the links between the theoretical framework of general equilibrium, applied general equilibrium models, and the empirical CGE models as we know them today.

The extensive application phase that started around 1990 and continued expanding ever since is overwhelming. CGE models proved to be very useful tools for the analysis of many policy areas including tax reforms, international trade, economic integration, environment policy, resource allocation, income distribution, regional development, and financial policy. A compact review of the applied extensions of CGE models is impossible due to the rapid and extensive expansion of CGE modeling and applications. Though, as the following chapters will treat CGE models that focus on some of the just mentioned policy areas, it is natural that we shall review related works.

In recent years, but not exclusively, there were retrospective evaluations of the CGE models' research program as well as efforts to link them with other modeling directions; see, for instance, Robinson *et al.* (1999) and Taylor (1990). In the meantime, the CGE modeling activity has become a world industry with its teaching curricula, software, data banks, graduate dissertations, and advisory teams. The CGE model paradigm has finally become part of the academic establishment. This advance has not gone unnoticed by rebels on the sidelines. Some critical views are justifiable; others are not sufficiently founded. McKitrick (1998) and Mitra-Khan (2008) are two such examples.

The CGE model in this chapter dates to the year 1980 and belongs to the launching phase of CGE models. The other CGE models in this book are more recent and would belong to the extension phase. Does it make sense to pay attention to a demonstration model that was developed three decades ago in view of the many advances made in CGE modeling since then? Probably not for some, and likely it is useful for others. In particular, there are some presentation features of the CGE model that were already there and others that we have added and revised, which highlight alternative formulations of the model and specifications of its working mechanisms. There are elaborations on the links between the SAM and CGE models, not only with regard to empirical calibrations but also regarding shared structures and mechanisms. The CGE model is also reformulated at first in a more elaborate form in correspondence with contemporary specifications, and in a process of deduction, we arrive at the simplified form which was applied then. The static CGE model is also extended to incorporate dynamic paths for labor skill formation and capital accumulation. The policy simulations that we apply relate to raising efficiency in alternative production activities, which are important ingredients of economic development but are often neglected in policy discussions.

The choice made to apply the model to Indonesia goes back to circumstances associated with the launching phase of SAMs and CGE models. Various Dutch institutions collaborated with Biro Pusat Statistik Indonesia in constructing the first social accounting matrix for Indonesia dated 1975, made available in 1979 and published officially in BPS Indonesia (1982). The availability of the SAM for Indonesia was followed by a rush among several economists working on Indonesia to fit CGE models to the SAM.[1]

This chapter is organized as follows: In Section 2, we specify the static CGE model and examine its structure. In Section 3, we estimate the CGE parameters from the available SAM for Indonesia at the time. In Section 4, the model is used to run policy simulations that investigate the effects of policy measures to enhance productivity in alternative economic activities. The analysis is done with the object of highlighting the mechanisms of the CGE model. In Section 5, several dynamic aspects will be introduced in the model. In Section 6, the policy simulations are repeated in the context of the dynamic model. Finally, in Section 7, concluding remarks will be made.

2. The Static CGE Model

In this section, the core of the general equilibrium model is presented. It is a general-purpose model, which contains only a minimal number of equations necessary to describe the economic process. It has the advantage that all parameters needed are derived from the SAM. For more specialized applications, the model needs to be elaborated, in which case supplementary data are required to estimate additional parameters. Because we are primarily interested in domestic transactions, we keep the relations with the rest of the world as simple as possible. Foreign prices are assumed to be equal to domestic prices to keep the model homogeneous in all prices. The foreign exchange rate is fixed. Table 1 lists the notations used.

The 18 equation sets of the model can be grouped into four blocks. The first block, Box 1, comprises eqs. (1)–(6) forming together the factor market. In eq. (1), sector output is determined from a two-level production structure and is derived in several steps of subequations, ending up in eq. (1). To start with, at the lower level, value added in volume terms, or quantity terms, VQ_j, is expressed as the product of a Cobb–Douglas production function with (demanded) employed factors of labor $LD_{q\,j}$ and capital KD_j with β_{qj} standing for production elasticities relating to labor type q and activity j and $(1 - \Sigma_q \beta_{qj})$ denoting production elasticities relating to capital in activity j. Thus, smooth substitution possibilities are assumed in the Cobb–Douglas production function, expressed by $VQ_j = \alpha_{jo} LD_j^{\beta qj} KD_j^{(1-\Sigma q\, \beta qj)}$.

At the higher level sector, value added in quantity terms, VQ_j, is a fixed proportion of the sector output in quantity terms, XQ_j, after deduction of domestic and imported intermediate inputs coefficients and indirect tax rates, following Leontief, thus $VQ_j = (1 - \Sigma_j(\alpha_{j'j} - \alpha_{rj} - \tau_{jg})XQ_j$. By definition, nominal gross output, X_j, equals output quantity, XQ_j, times the output price, XP_j, thus $X_j = XP_j \cdot XQ_j$. Substitution of the three subequations in each other gives the final form of eq. (1), displaying the generation of sector gross output, in terms of the sector price and parameters of the two-level production structures. The further elaboration and solution of the model make no more use of the two specific variables of XQ_j and VQ_j. For the sake of simplification, these two variables are left out from the list of notations, which is done on purpose. The outcome of the above handlings is eq. (1).

In eq. (2), making further use of Leontief coefficients, the value added by sector, V_j, is found by subtracting the cost of domestic intermediate deliveries, imported intermediate deliveries, and indirect taxes from the gross output by sector, appropriately priced.

In eq. (3), producers are assumed to maximize profits under perfect competition in product and labor markets; as a result, in the short run, they will hire employees until wages equal the value of their marginal product.

Eq. (4) shows that the remuneration of capital as the remainder of nominal value added after labor is paid its share. Because the volume of capital is fixed in the short run, the remuneration rates of capital may differ among sectors.

Eq. (5) states that the demand for (employment of) labor by skill level is equal to the supply of labor by the corresponding skill type. The latter is exogenously fixed in the short run. At full employment, wages carry the burden of adjustment.

Eq. (6) states that the demand for (employed) capital is equal to its supply for each activity level j. The latter is given in the short run. Here, too, the remuneration

Table 1. Notations.

Endogenous variables	
C_{hj}	Value of consumption expenditure of institution h on commodities od activity j
C_j	Value of total consumption expenditure by activity j
E_j	Value of exports of activity j
FCF	Foreign capital flow expressed in foreign currency
LD_{qj}	Demand for labor of skill qualifications q in activity j
KD_j	Demand for capital in activity j
GBD	Value of government budget deficit
I	Value of installed investment
ICH	Value of inventory change
M_j	Value of total competitive imports
KR_j	Remuneration rate of capital in activity j
LR_q	Remuneration rate of labor of qualification type q
V_j	Value of the gross product of activity j (i.e. gross value added)
X_j	Value of the gross output of activity j
XP_j	Price index of the gross output of activity j, whereby XP $_{1(\text{agriculture})}$ is taken as numeraire
Y_h	Disposable income of households h. Index h is extendable to include the category of firms
Z_h	Value of total incomings of households h. Index h is extendable to include the category of firms
Z_g	Value of total revenue of government
Exogenous variables:	
C_{gj}	Government consumption expenditure on activity j
FXR	Foreign exchange rate
I_g	Government expenditure on installed investment
I_{psi}	Private sector demand for installed investment
KS_j	Value of capital stock in activity j
LS_q	Labor supply of qualification type q
T_{gh}	Government transfer payments to household group g, extendable to firms
Coefficients and data:	
a_{jo}	Calibration constant in the production function of activity j
$\alpha_{jj'}$	Input/output delivery coefficients between activities j
α_{pj}	Non-competitive imports share in the output of activity j in benchmark year
β_{qj}	Labor elasticities of production relating to labor type q and activity j
ε_{jo}	Quantity of exports as proportion of the quantity of output of activity j in benchmark year
ε_j	Price elasticity of demand for exports of activity j
γ_{hj}	Consumption budget shares of spending institution h on products of activity j
ι_j	Delivery share of installed investment by activity j in the total installed investment
μ_{rj}	Competitive imports proportion in domestic supply of products of activity j
μ_j	Price elasticity of imports of products of activity j
$\pi_{jh}, \pi_{jg}, \pi_{jr}$	Profit distribution shares of activity j to households h; to government g and rest of world r
$\rho_{hh;}$	Transfer rates of households to households h. The h index is extendable to include firms
τ_{hg}	Rate of direct tax paid by households h to government g; the h index is extendable to include firms
τ_{jg}	Rate of indirect taxes on output of activity j collected by government g
υ_j	Inventory change of activity j as proportion in total inventory change
ω_{qh}	Earnings distribution shares from labor type q to households h

Notes: The index j represents sectors, h stands for institutions which can be a specific household group, firms, or government, q stands for types of labor, and r is used to denote actors abroad, that is, rest of the world.

of capital in each activity adjusts to the particular demand and supply of capital in the sector.

Box 1. Production function and factor market balances.

$X_j = XP_j\{1/\left(1 - \Sigma_j(\alpha_{j'j} - \alpha_{rj-}\tau_{jg})\right\}\left[\alpha_{jo}\Pi_{LD_{qj}^{\beta qj}}KD_j^{(1-\Sigma q\,\beta\, qj)}\right]$	j	(1)
$V_j = (1 - \Sigma_j\alpha_{j'j}XP_{j'}/XP_j)X_j - \alpha_{rj}X_j - \tau_{jg}X_j$	j	(2)
$LR_q \cdot LD_{qj} = \beta_{qj}V_j$	$q \cdot j$	(3)
$KR_j \cdot KS_j = (1 - \Sigma_q\beta_{qj})V_j$	j	(4)
$\Sigma_j LD_{qj} = LS_q$	q	(5)
$KD_j = KS_j$	j	(6)

The next block, in Box 2, presents the formation of the institutional accounts of household groups (and firms)[2] denoted by index h, and government, indicated by g. In eq. (7), the total income of recipient household groups (and firms) is specified. Factor remunerations are distributed over household groups h via wage and profit shares ω_{hq} and π_h. Income transfers paid to and received from other household groups are fixed proportions, $\rho_{hh'}$, of the income of the paying party. The equation incorporates the net results of these transfers. Furthermore, there are net income transfers received from the government, T_{gh}. [There are also net transfers received from the rest of the world, but these are not reported in the current SAM of Indonesia; they are left out.]

In eq. (8), direct taxes are subtracted from the incomings of households and firms to arrive at disposable income.

Eqs. (9) and (10) specify consumption expenditure by private institutions and government. This can be done in detail, but under some assumptions, it can be compressed in an abridged form. Suppose that the household group h spends their consumption expenditure on consumer commodities denoted by c, which is the usual case. In eq. (i), this consumption by h of c, denoted by C_{hc}, is dependent on the relatives' prices of commodities c, denoted by SP_c, and on the disposable income of household group h, Y_h, and on the applicable own and cross-price elasticities and income elasticities. The sum of the elasticities adds up to unity, in conformity with the Cobb–Douglas functional relationship that is also used above in the production sphere. Hence, the specification of the income elasticity is $(1 - \Sigma_c\gamma_{hc})$. The relative prices are taken relative to one of the commodities or a package of commodities c. In this equation, γ'_{hc} are the start budget proportions spent on c, γ_{hc} are the price elasticities, and γ_{hco} is a calibration coefficient. In eq. (ii), the realized consumptions classified by c are converted into consumption by activity j, making use of converter coefficients θ_{jc} and dividing by SP_c to obtain quantities that are again converted into value in terms of activity prices XP_j. Government consumption by sector j is added to give consumption demand by sector.

$$C_{hc} = \left[\gamma_{hco}\,\Pi_{hc}\,SP_c^{\gamma\,hc}\{\gamma'_{hc}Y_h\}^{1-\Sigma c\gamma\,hc}\right] \qquad h.c \quad \text{(i)}$$

$$C_j = XP_j\,\Sigma_c\theta_{jc}(\Sigma_h C_{hc}/SP_c) + C_{gj} \qquad \text{(ii)}$$

The first equation can be cut down in size if it can be assumed for the sake of demonstration that the price elasticities equal zero, so that the income elasticity would equal 1.0, and the distribution of spending on commodity c will be consistent with the initial budget shares γ_{hc}. The price effect disappears and C_{hc} becomes proportionately dependent on Y_h. Furthermore, both equations are greatly simplified if it is assumed that the classification of commodities c corresponds exactly with activities j, which is common in many SAMs that lack data to do it, otherwise the SAM of Indonesia is one such case. When θ_{jc} takes the value of 1 in the diagonal and zero otherwise, SP_c and XP_j disappear from the equation. Substitution of these assumptions in the two equations results in the simplified form of eqs. (9) and (10) which will be kept in this model.

Eq. (11) specifies the demand for installed investment[3] by the private sector and government. As the possibility of specifying an investment function for private investors was not feasible, the formulation had to choose for fixing the whole investment level autonomously at its known value for the benchmark year. This is sufficient for solving the static model for the base year. A forecast of I is required for future years when the model is run in its dynamic version. The forecast will be based on semi-autonomous grounds.

In eq. (12), government revenue consists of factor income from the ownership of public enterprises, plus direct taxes from households and firms, plus indirect taxes. [There are also net transfers from abroad but the current SAM of Indonesia does not show them; we leave them out.]

In eq. (13), the government's current expenditure consisting of consumption and transfers plus government fixed expenditure, i.e. investment, I_g, are put in balance with government revenue, Z_g, and a government budget deficit, GBD_g.

Box 2. Income and spending of private sector and government.

$$Z_h = \Sigma_q\omega_{qh}LR_q \cdot LS_q + \Sigma_j\pi_{jh}KR_{j.} \cdot KS_j + \Sigma_{h'}\rho_{hh'}Z_{h'} + T_{gh} \qquad \{h = 6 \text{ groups, firms}\} \quad (7)$$

$$Y_h = (1-\tau_{hg})Z_h \qquad \{h = 6 \text{ groups, firms}\} \quad (8)$$

$$C_{hj} = \gamma_{hj}Y_h \qquad h \cdot j \quad (9)$$

$$C_j = \Sigma_h C_{hj} + C_{gj} \qquad j \quad (10)$$

(*Continued*)

(*Continued*)

$I_j = \iota_j(I_{psi} + I_g)$	(11)
$Z_g = \Sigma_j \pi_{jg} KR_j \cdot KS_j + \Sigma_h \tau_{hg} Y_h + \Sigma_j \tau_{jg} X_j$	(12)
$\Sigma_j C_{gj} + \Sigma_h T_{gh} + I_g = Z_g + GBD$	(13)

The third block, in Box 3, relates to demand, supply, and price formation in the product markets. Preliminary equations are specified in Roman numbers, after which simplifications are applied to the preliminary equations with the object of highlighting the role of price formation in the CGE model and reducing the model to a minimum of equations. The model still remains a CGE model but with less reliance on prices in clearing the product markets. In eq. (iii), the quantity of exports of activity j is initially specified as the quantity of exports for the benchmark year $\varepsilon_{jo}(X_j/XP_j)$ and further made dependent on relative prices of domestic production XP_j, a fixed foreign exchange rate and foreign exports prices, $FXR.ep_j$, and a price elasticity ε_j.

$$E_j/XP_j = \varepsilon_{jo}(X_j/XP_j)(FXR.ep_j/XP_j)^{\varepsilon j} \qquad j \quad \text{(iii)}$$

In eq. (iv), the quantity of competitive imports is initially specified as a proportion μ_{rj} of the quantity of consumption and investment and further made dependent on relative domestic and foreign prices, fixed FXR, and a price elasticity μ_j.

$$M_j/XP_j = (\mu_{rj}(C_j + I_j)/SP_j)(XP_j/FXR.mpj)/)^{\mu\, j} \qquad j \quad \text{(iv)}$$

In eq. (v), the composite price of sector j is a weighted average of domestic and import prices.

$$SP_j = \mu_{rj}(FXR.mp_j) + (1 - \mu_{rj})XP_j \qquad j \quad \text{(v)}$$

The first basic simplification in this block is to assume that FXR is fixed and prices of export j, import j, and activity j are equal, which is feasible and realized in various situations, i.e. eq. (vi).

$$ep_j = mp_j = XP_j \qquad \text{(vi)}$$

When this assumption of equal prices is substituted in the above equations, the simplification would eliminate the effects of relative prices and the foreign trade elasticities in influencing foreign trade streams and clearance of the product markets. The supply composite price will be equalized to the sector product price, making the supply composite price a redundant variable in this simplified model.

Although the model keeps all features of the CGE model, the effect of the simplification is to reduce the role of prices and increase the role of quantities in balancing the supply and demand of the product market. The equations are reduced to take the form of eqs. (14) and (15), in Box 3.

It is noted that the foreign trade equations do not explicit a specification for the foreign exchange rate. Assuming a fixed foreign exchange rate is done on purpose. This is a second basic simplification that is representative and consistent with situations of fixed foreign exchange regimes. If the model focused on foreign trade in an open economy with free operations with the rest of the world, the specification of an endogenous foreign exchange rate would be the obvious choice.

Finally, because the model can only determine relative prices, a price normalization rule is required. It would have been possible to make use of a consumer price index as a numeraire, but the required data on commodities were not separable from those on activities. This being the case at the time, we chose the agricultural price as numeraire, as specified in eq. (16). The agricultural price level can be considered a good approximation for consumer prices in situations where food commodities take up the largest share in consumption expenditure. All price and nominal variables are thus defined relative to the price in agriculture. [Despite choosing the agricultural price as numeraire, we compute later on, when we analyze results of policy simulations, a consumer price index for an approximate evaluation of changes in real welfare.]

Box 3. Foreign trade and product markets.

$E_j = \varepsilon_{jo} X_j / XP_j$	j	(14)
$M_j = \mu_{rj}(C_j + I_j)$	j	(15)
$XP_1 = 1.0$		(16)

The fourth block, in Box 4, consists of national accounting balances. Eq. (17) gives product market balances that assure equilibrium in the product markets. For each activity j, the supply side consisting of the produced output, X_j, supplemented by competitive imports, M_j, is equal to the demand side, consisting of the delivery of intermediate goods appropriately converted to the applicable price index of the delivering activity, XP_j, final consumption goods delivered by j, the part of investment goods delivered by j, inventory change occurring in j, and exports of j. Which variables are the adjusters of the product balances? These must be j in number. Domestic prices of the activities, XP_j, in total $(j - 1)$ in number, carry the burden of adjustment between the supply and demand by sector, together with the variable of inventory change for the economy as a whole, ICH. In the equalization of supply and demand in the product markets, XP_j represent the adjustments at the specific product level, while inventory change, *ICH*, represents adjustment at the macro level of the whole economy.

Eq. (18) specifies the savings–investment balance, which can also be called the financial market balance. It states that total savings (the sum of private savings, government savings, and foreign savings) are equal to total investment (i.e. "fixed" installed investment plus inventory change). While private savings are positive, government savings are usually negative reflecting a budget deficit. Net foreign savings are net foreign capital flows converted to national currency, *FXR.FCF*. The gap between total investment and domestic savings is filled by foreign capital flow, *FCF*, which takes the role of adjuster.

Eq. (A1) is the foreign payments balance. It equalizes outgoing foreign payments (these are competitive imports and imported intermediate inputs) to incoming foreign payment (these are exports and foreign capital inflow). The model, consisting of equation sets 1–18, is a determinate model that solves for all endogenous variables as enumerated in the list of notations, also counting 18 sets of unknowns. The solutions so obtained will reproduce the consistency of the foreign payments balance automatically, hence denoting this accounting balance as an additional equation that is laid outside the model.

Box 4. National accounting balances.

Sector product balances

$$X_j + M_j = \Sigma_j(\alpha_{jj'}XP_j/XP_{j'})X_{j'} + C_j + I_j + \upsilon_j ICH + E_j \qquad j \quad (17)$$

Investment savings balance

$$\Sigma_h(Y_h - \Sigma_j C_{hj}) + (Z_g - \Sigma_j C_{gj} - \Sigma_h T_{gh}) + FXR.FCF = I + ICH \qquad (18)$$

Foreign payments balance

$$\Sigma_j M_j + \Sigma_j a_{rj} X_j + \Sigma_j \pi_{jr} KR_j.KS_j = \Sigma_j E_j + FXR.FCF \qquad (A1)$$

3. Parameterization of the CGE Model

A Social Accounting Matrix (SAM) is a prerequisite for the calibration of the CGE model. The SAM is a statistical presentation of the circular flow and transactions between agents, which the CGE model specifies in equation form. A supporting description of the ways in which a CGE model and the SAM are linked to each other is in Robinson *et al.* (1999). The objective of this section is to demonstrate the basic links between the primary form of CGE models and the SAM and the use of the SAM for calibrating the CGE model. To facilitate the objective, and as an illustration, Table 2 displays the 1975 SAM of Indonesia. This SAM has the activities account of four sectors of activities/commodities, namely agriculture,

Table 2. SAM Indonesia 1975.

	Activities				Factors earnings			Institutions										ROWS	
	1	2	3	4	5	6	7	8	9	10	11	12	13	14	15	16	17	18	
	Agriculture	Industry	Trade	Services	Low skill	High skill	Profit	Rural farm owner	Rural farm worker	Rural nonfrm high	Rural nonfrm low	Urban high	Urban low	Firms	Government	Indirect taxes	Capital accou	Rest of worldd	Total
Activities																			
1 1.Agriculture	2571	292	310	21				2422	467	346	882	534	698		2			423	8968
2 2.Industry	204	1348	306	121				351	68	105	196	351	301		218		3410	907	7886
3 3.Trade	1353	758	77	31				268	61	61	160	221	298		194			772	4254
4 4.Services	56	98	195	37			711	268	53	60	131	233	222	62	769			−26	2096
Factors																			
5 low skill	1945	694	1248	276															4163
6 high skill	20	81	168	794															1063
7 profits	2503	3218	1637	739															8097
Institutions																			
8 Rrl frm ownrs					1627	61	1970								73				3731
9 Rrl frm wrkrs					440	32	131								12				615
10 Rrl nfrm high					205	251	84							88	14				642
11 Rrl nfrm low					824	90	354	46	2	14	13	3	2	33	31				1412
12 Urban high					322	545	326							467	24				1684
13 Urban low					745	84	652	5	1	2	2	73	47	43	28				1682
14 Firms							3810												3810
15 Government							59	39	2	5	6	40	26	1448		277			1902
16 Indirect taxes	87	141	42	7															277
17 Captial Acc								332	−39	49	22	229	88	1669	567			493	3810
Rest of world																			
18 ROW	229	1256	271	70											−30				2569
Total	8968	7886	4254	2096	4163	1063	8097	3731	615	642	1412	1684	1682	3810	1902	277	3410	2569	

industry, trade, and services, whereby commodities and sectors are directly aligned. The SAM distinguishes between three factors of production, six household groups, firms, and government, capital account, and the rest of the world account.

The parameters of the CGE model are derived from benchmark values of nominal variables in the SAM under the assumption that the benchmark SAM represents the *ex post* equilibrium situation. Furthermore, because price variables in the CGE model are expressed as indices, and they take the value of 1 for the benchmark, the values of variables and their relationships in the SAM are interpretable in quantity (real) terms. The estimates of the parameters should be such that calibration of the CGE model reproduces the same SAM.

The first block of the model contains input–output coefficients and factor elasticities of production. The coefficients of input–output deliveries, non-competitive imports, and indirect taxes, α_{jj}, a_{rj}, and τ_{jg}, respectively, are calculated simply by dividing the appropriate cells in the SAM by their column totals, giving their estimates in Table 3. The labor elasticity β_{qj} is calculated by dividing the factor payments,[4] LR_1,LD_{1j}, by the value added, V_j. Furthermore, by defining sectoral prices as indices, as described above, V_j/XP_j becomes equal to V_j, which is readily obtainable from the SAM, and is thus inserted in eq. (1). From the assumption that capital supply, *KS*, is equal to capital in use, *KD*, the benchmark values of SK_j are estimated at 10,541 for agriculture, 13,552 for mining, industry, and construction, 6,894 for trade and transport, and 3,112 for services. When all these data are inserted in eq. (1), the calibration coefficients α_j, for the four sectors are obtained as shown in Table 3. The resulting calibration constants are close to unity for agriculture and trade and transport, nearly three for services, and slightly above one-half for industry.

Turning to the second block of the model, the coefficients that distribute factor income over households, ω_{hq} and π_h, in eq. (7), are calculated by dividing the

Table 3. Coefficients relating to sectoral production functions, eqs. (1) and (2).

Coefficients	SAM columns rows	18. agriculture	19. industry	20. trade	21. services
τ_j	12. Gov. indirect taxes	0.0097	0.0179	0.0099	0.0033
α_{1j}	14. Agriculture	0.2867	0.0370	0.0729	0.0100
α_{2j}	15. Industry	0.0227	0.1709	0.0719	0.0577
α_{3j}	16. Trade	0.1509	0.0961	0.0181	0.0148
α_{4j}	17. Services	0.0062	0.0124	0.0458	0.0177
μ_j	18. Rest of the world	0.0255	0.1593	0.0637	0.0334
Production function coefficients					
β_{1j}	1. low-skill earnings	0.4353	0.1738	0.4088	0.1526
β_{2j}	2. high-skill earnings	0.0045	0.0203	0.0550	0.4389
$1 - \beta_{1j} - \beta_{2j}$	3. profits	0.5602	0.8059	0.5362	0.4085
αj	Calibrated off SAM	0.9154	0.5635	1.1791	2.8154

Table 4. Coefficients of factor income distribution to institutions, ω_{qh}, π_h, eq. (4).

SAM columns rows	Low skill earnings ω_{ih}	High skills earnings ω_{2h}	Profits π_h
4. *R* farm owners	0.3908	0.0574	0.2433
5. *R* farm workers	0.1057	0.0301	0.0162
6. *R* non-farm upper	0.0492	0.2361	0.0104
7. *R* non-farm lower	0.1979	0.0847	0.0437
8. *U* upper income	0.0773	0.5127	0.0403
9. *U* lower income	0.1790	0.0790	0.0805
10. Firms	0.0000	0.0000	0.4705
11. Gov. general	0.0000	0.0000	0.0073

Table 5. Coefficients of income transfers between institutions, $\rho_{hh'}$, eq. (7).

SAM columns rows	*R* farm owners	*R* farm workers	*R* non-farm upper	*R* non-farm lower	Urban upper	Urban lower	Firms
4. *R* farm owners	0	0	0	0	0	0	0
5. *R* farm workers	0	0	0	0	0	0	0
6. *R* non-farm upper	0	0	0	0	0	0	0.023
7. *R* non-farm lower	0.012	0.003	0.022	0.009	0.002	0.001	0.009
8. *U* upper income	0	0	0	0	0	0	0.122
9. *U* lower income	0.001	0.002	0.003	0.001	0.043	0.028	0.011
10. Firms	0	0	0	0	0	0	0.008
11. Gov. general	0.011	0.003	0.008	0.004	0.024	0.016	0.377

applicable cells into the factor account columns of the SAM, by the column totals. As can be expected, the estimates in Table 4 show lowskilled labor income accrue mainly to low-income households. High-skilled labor income goes mainly to urban upper-income groups. Recipients of capital income are mainly landowners and firms.

Transfer coefficients between institutions, τ_{hh}, defined as the ratio of outgoing transfers to income of the transferring institution, are calculated by dividing the respective income transfers by their respective column totals. Transfers are dominated by flows of funds from firms to households and government, for which transfer rates are 0.122 and 0.377, respectively, Table 5.

Coefficients of institution's expenditure on consumption by activity, γ_{hj}, generally known as budget shares, are calculated by dividing consumption expenditures for the various commodities in the institutions' columns by disposable income $(1 - \tau_{hg})Z_h$. For households, the largest share of income is spent on agricultural products. The government spends nearly half of its income on services, Table 6.

The Indonesian data at the time did not classify commodities differently from sectors. As can be noted in the SAM in the appendix, the sectors and commodities correspond to each other. The product market can thus be formulated throughout

Table 6. Coefficients of institution's expenditure on commodity consumption γ_{hj}, eq. (9).

SAM columns rows	*R* farm owners	*R* farm workers	*R* non-farm upper	*R* non-farm lower	Urban upper	Urban lower	Firms
13. Agricultural	0.665	0.766	0.557	0.634	0.341	0.434	0.000
14. Industrial	0.096	0.112	0.169	0.141	0.224	0.187	0.000
15. Trade	0.074	0.100	0.098	0.115	0.141	0.185	0.000
16. Services	0.074	0.087	0.097	0.094	0.149	0.138	0.000

in terms of the produce of activities j. It was stated earlier in the description of eqs. (9) and (10) that the model is substantially simplified by working with one set of prices for the activities that hold also for commodities instead of having two separate sets of prices for commodities and sectors, which is more usual in CGE models.

Among the government parameters in eq. (12), direct taxes are computable from the intersection of rows 4–10 with column 11 in the SAM. Indirect taxes are computable from the intersection of rows 13–16 with column 12 in the SAM. Other data on exogenous government consumption, C_{gj}, and transfers, T_{gh}, are directly obtainable from column 11 in the SAM.

Foreign trade parameters specified in eqs. (14) and (15), export data ε_{jo} and import coefficient μ_{rj}, are derived from the "Rest of the World" column and row the.

The coefficients allocating investment goods to sectors of origin, ι_j, which show up in eq. (17), are also simplified since the sector of industry ($j = 4$) is the sole deliverer of investment goods, meaning that $\iota_4 = 1$ and $\iota_1 = \iota_2 = \iota_3 = 0$.

Finally, the SAM for the benchmark year does not specify the inventory changes *ICH*; these are summed up together with the installed investment I. Since the model is calibrated for the benchmark year with the given value of I, the solution of the model for the base year for *IHC* is also zero. However, this need not be so for years beyond the base year as when the model will be solved in its dynamic version. As an aggregate adjuster of supply with demand in the future, *IHC* can take positive or negative values. To allow for the distribution of the *IHC* on the sectors, we defined υ_j as the shares of the output of sector j in the total output of all sectors and fixed their estimates from the benchmark data.

4. Static Policy Simulations

In this section, we demonstrate the functioning of the 18 equations model by simulating two supply impulses to economic growth. The results will be reviewed with the object of highlighting the mechanisms of the model and need to be cautiously interpreted as being demonstrative and specific to the simplified database employed for Indonesia. Besides, it is important to take into account the generality of the assumptions and the absence of qualitative structural characteristics of the Indonesian economy in the CGE model. The two simulations are as follows: (1) 10% productivity increase in industry and construction and (2) 10% productivity increase in services.

Simulation 1: 10% productivity increase in industry and construction: The efficiency parameter in the production function in industry is increased by 10%. The result is an 8.78% increase in the volume of output. However, because demand is inelastic,[5] the favorable volume effect is reversed by a −10.01% price decrease, resulting in a reduction of value added in industry in relation to other sectors. So all factors employed in the sector with the increased productivity undergo a decline in their income. The increased productivity makes more than 5% of the labor employed in industry redundant, while the owners of capital see their remuneration reduced by 5.35% because of the declined value of the marginal product of capital. Because a relatively large share of the national capital stock is installed in industry, total remuneration of capital falls with the reduced value added in industry. The wage rate of high-skilled labor increases slightly, relative to the low-skilled wage rate, 0.42% versus 0.21%, because very little high-skilled labor is employed in industry.

The change in factor incomes is not large enough to cause a change in income distribution: there is a small fall in income for all groups varying from −0.65% for landowners to −0.14% for farm workers.

The fall in nominal income does not mean that welfare has decreased, however. We have computed a consumer price index, *CPI*, which is a weighted average of sector price levels, making use of sector shares in the total *GDP*. This consumer price index has decreased by more than the fall in nominal income so that it can be concluded that purchasing power has increased for all household groups. The welfare increase of the different groups is confirmed by the +2.5% increase in real *GDP* (average increase in the volume of value added).

Simulation 2: 10% productivity increase in services: As in the previous experiment, the efficiency parameter of the production function is increased by 10%. The resulting production increase in the service sector is +9.17%, which is only slightly higher than the increase in industry production in the previous simulation. However, in this simulation, there are hardly any spillover effects to other sectors, in which the increase in production does not exceed 0.2%. This is due partly to the fact that in Indonesia the service sector is rather small and partly to the lack of backward linkages. The resulting increase in real *GDP* is less than one-half of the increase in the industry experiment: +1.19%.

Again, as a result of inelastic demand, the value added of the sector with the productivity increase falls relative to the sectors without productivity increase (−2.52%), although the fall is less than in the previous simulation. Because the majority of high-skilled workers are employed in the service sector, the decrease in value added is detrimental to their relative wage rate; this decreases by −0.21%. The decrease in the remuneration for the highly skilled leads to a worsening of the income position for non-farm upper-income groups (both rural and urban: −0.58% and −0.45%, respectively). These groups consist of a large part of high-skilled workers. But as the consumer price index, *CPI*, has decreased by even more, this would allow an increase in real *GDP* to reach all households.

5. The Dynamic Model

Incorporation of dynamics in the CGE models proceeded already in the 1980s, once the static CGE model was established as a useful tool for economic analysis and policymaking. Economists worked first extending the static model to a sequence of static equilibria with the object of tracing price changes and quantity reallocations following exogenous shocks and/or parameter modifications in each sequence. In a later stage, the modeling of dynamics was improved by considering intertemporal optimization and forward-looking behavior, resulting in two different approaches: the recursive equilibrium approach and the full dynamic approach. A classification of dynamic CGE models along these lines is in Dixon and Parmenter (1996). The recursive equilibrium approach assumes that the model is solved for a sequence of static equilibrium. The equilibria are connected through accumulation in the factors of production. The approach does not incorporate intertemporal aspects of decision-making. One of the early attempts to introduce dynamic elements into a CGE model for the US economy, in Ballard *et al.* (1985), assumed that consumers have myopic expectations regarding future prices, especially regarding the future rate of return to capital. An example of recursive dynamics with adaptive expectations for the Australian economy is in Dixon and Rimmer (2002). The full dynamic approach derives consumers' behavior and producers' behavior, as in Knudsen *et al.* (1998) and Babenberg (1985), respectively, from both intra- and intertemporal optimization. These models are based upon the perfect foresight hypothesis and describe the transition path to the new equilibrium point. The models are exploratory and generally require a great computational effort because all the equations defined over the whole time horizon are solved at once. Their scope is usually short of economy-wide policy models.

The dynamic features that we apply in this chapter would fall under the recursive sequence equilibrium approach. They make use of both myopic and adaptive expectations. The basic steps to make the model dynamic lie in updating the variables of labor and capital availabilities that so far were kept fixed. The updating can be based on behavioral relationships or on extrapolated growth. This will be done mostly based on behavioral relationships and for a part on extrapolated growth. For the extensions, additional notations are required as shown in Table 7.

Table 7. Additional notations.

Newly introduced endogenous variables	
AKR	Average profitability of investment aggregated over all sectors, i.e. weighted average
$I_{\mathrm{dst}\,j}$	Nominal investment in destination sector j
IDS_j	Investment in destination sector j expressed as proportion in total investment, whereby the following condition is observed: $\Sigma_j = IDS_j = 1$
KS_j	Capital stock of sector j
RHL_{t+n}	Ratio of high-skilled labor ($q = 2$) to low-skilled labor ($q = 1$) in a future prospective year $t + n$
SL_1	Supply of low-skilled labor ($q = 1$)
SL_2	Supply of high-skilled labor ($q = 2$)
Newly introduced coefficients	
δ	Depreciation rate of capital goods
η_q	Educational cost incurred and earnings forgone in acquiring skill
κ	Elasticity of intersector investment shifts to profitability differentials
λ'	Growth rate of the total labor force
λ_o	Calibration coefficient in the equation of the skill ratio
λ	Elasticity of skill upgrading in response to wage differentials
φ	Distributed lag adjustment for realizing long-term change in the labor ratio between low and high skills

The extension of the static to the dynamic model involves adding 7 sets of equations to the static model of 18 sets, thus resulting in a total of 25 equation sets. In correspondence with these, there are seven newly introduced sets of endogenous variables, as listed in the notations above. These extensions bring back the model in its determinate form, and allow its solution via simple substitutions, and matrix inversion. The extensions are summarized in Box 5.

Eq. (19) states that the total labor force, consisting of low and high skills, grows annually. [The growth rate that applied to Indonesia was $\lambda' = 0.025$.]

Eq. (20) distributes labor over the two skill types for the long term along endogenous lines. The skills ratio of high to low skills, *RHL*, grows over time influenced by what is generally acknowledged as social demand (or sometimes called non-economically motivated behavior) and economically motivated behavior. Given the close association between the two factors, especially with regard to occupational education, it is functional to focus on the economically motivated behavior, which can give a reasonable approximation of the effects of the combined behavior. The workers' choice between offering himself (or herself) to high-skilled versus low-skilled employment depends on the relative benefit–cost ratios associated with the two skill types. Benefits are the remuneration of labor, LR_2 and RL_1, respectively. Costs are indicated by η_2 and η_1, respectively, and they include the education costs incurred in acquiring skill q and foregone earnings during the formal acquisition of the higher skill.[6] The incurred costs of η_2 and η_1 are interesting policy parameters; they can be varied and their long-term effects on the structure of the labor force can be evaluated. To keep things simple, the application assumes that the cost of higher education in Indonesia is four times the cost of lower education, that is, $\eta_2 = 4\eta_1$.

Once earners make their choice as to what skill level they will pursue, it takes several years, say (n) years, before the effects of the choices are realized in a changed structure of the labor supplies. The (n) years may vary from about 4–10 years depending on the educational system and the classification range of high and low skills. The ratio of higher to lower labor skills, RHL_{t+n}, can be written for the long-term period $t+n$ as in the following equation, which starts with the benchmark for the ratio at $(SL_2/SL_1)_o$, allows for some growth due to social demand expressed by λ', and goes further to specify its dynamics in terms of net relative returns to both skills, with λ as the elasticity of skill upgrading due to differentials in skill returns, thus $RHL_{t+n} = (1+\lambda')(lS_2/lS_1)_0\{(lR_{2,t}/\eta_2)/(lR_{1,t}/\eta_1)\}^{\lambda}$.

For estimation purposes, the equation can be edited as in eq. (20), in Box 5, where the calibration coefficient λ_o can have a value equal to or higher than the benchmark for the skill ratio. There is an estimation problem here in that the period (n) cannot be specified *a priori* since behind it are many lags and overlapping variables of the educational and demographic systems that do not permit a short cut. The value of (n) can only be specified along empiricist lines. It is clear also that when the period (n) is longer, then RHL_{t+n} will tend to be higher and thus leading to a higher value of the skill upgrading elasticity. In principle, the equation can be regressed for various fixations of the (n) years, and the best fitting regression for λ_o and λ can be selected, in this way determining how long the number of years (n) should be. This may require many data that are usually not available. An alternative approach is to postulate that the elasticity λ assumes the value of unity and iterate from available data series the gestation years (n) that correspond with the postulate of $\lambda = 1$. [The application for Indonesia produced a value of (n) close to 6 years.]

Finally, in eq. (21), the change in the skill ratio for the current year t, as from past year $t-1$, is assumed to follow a distributed lag pattern in terms of its value in the future year of $t+n$ and in the past year $t-1$. This is done via a distributed lag adjustment coefficient, ϕ. In this equation, the proportion φ is definable as $t-(t-1)/(t+n)-(t-1)$, giving a value of $(1/n+1)$. [With $n = 6$ years in Indonesia, the value of φ is fixed at 0.14.]

Turning now to the capital stocks, in the static model, these were fixed for each sector and were not allowed to reallocate between the sectors. The dynamic model allows these stocks to grow and to reallocate in search of the highest profitability. For updating the capital stock and for making its distribution on the sectors endogenous, use is made of four equations, eqs. (22)–(25). Eq. (22) distributes newly made investment expenditure over using sectors in proportions which are a function of the ratio of sectoral profitability to average profitability Ki_{rja}/AKR. Sectors which show high profitability in period $t-1$ will increase their share in total investment in period t, in line with an intersector investment adjustment elasticity denoted by κ that is set equal to 1. Sectors with higher profitability would thus experience relatively greater increases in their capital stock and in their production than other sectors. The share of investment destined to sector j in total investment, IDS_j, is defined in eq. (21), holding $\Sigma_j IDS_j = 1$. The benchmark investment shares, $IDS_{j,t-1}$, are approximated by taking the sectoral shares in the total operating surplus: $Ki_{rja} \cdot Sc/\Sigma_j KR_j \cdot Sc$. [The approximation resulted in the following investment shares 0.3091 for agriculture, 0.3974 for industry and construction, 0.2022 for trade, and 0.0913 for services.]

Eq. (22) defines the average profitability for all sectors.

Eq. (10.23) distributes total investment expenditure over sectors of destination to give the nominal investment in destination sector j, denoted by $D_{\text{ist}}., j$. This is obtained by multiplying the newly introduced share variable by total investment.

Eq. (24) subtracts depreciation from the capital stock and adds new investment to it. Note that the investment outlays have to be divided by the price of investment goods, Ex_{pr}, to determine the investment in physical units.

Box 5. Newly introduced equations.

$$LS_{1,t} + LS_{2,t} = [LS_{1,t-1} + LS_{2,t-1}](1 + \lambda') \tag{19}$$

$$Rhe_{tt+n} = (LS_2/LS_1)t_{-1}\left[\{(LR_{2,t}/\eta_2)/\left(LR_{1,t}/\eta_1\right\}/\right.$$
$$\{(LR_{2,t-1}/\eta_2)/(LR_{1,t-1}/\eta_1)\} \tag{20}$$

$$(LS_2/LS_1)_t = (LS_{2,}/LS_1)_{t-1+}\varphi[RHL_{t+n} - (LS_{2,}/LS_1)_{t-1}] \tag{21}$$

$$IDS_{j,t} = IDS_{j,t-1}\{(KR_{j,t}/AKR_t)/(KR_{j,t-1}/AKR_{t-1})\}^{\kappa} \quad j \tag{22}$$

$$AKR = \Sigma_j(KR_j \cdot KS_j)/\Sigma_j KS_j \tag{23}$$

$$I_{\text{dst},j} = IDS_j \cdot I \quad j \tag{24}$$

$$KS_j = KS_{j,t-1}(1 - \delta_j) + I_{\text{dst},j,t-1}/XP_{j'} \tag{25}$$

6. Dynamic Policy Simulations

To set the dynamic model into motion, the path of the following exogenous variables needs to be specified, C_{gj}, $T_{gh}T_{rh}$, T_{rg}, I_g, I_{psi}. See Table 1 for notations. Government consumption expenditure and transfers were projected based on past trends. In the case of I_g and I_{psi}, which together add up to installed investment I, we considered initially an annual growth rate of the GDP at 5% and making use of an average incremental capital-output ratio, at 2.2, predetermined the required value of I for each year between 1975 and 1980. The preliminary runs of the model showed a lower growth of the *GDP* than was initially considered by about 0.5%. This justified resetting the predetermined required values of ($I = I_{psi} + I_g$) at a lower level.

The dynamic model was applied to simulate the time path from 1975 to 1980. The time path is the sequence of temporary equilibrium under unchanged policies. To get an idea of changes that would take place over time in the base time path, we will first discuss the predicted rates of growth between 1979 and 1980. The growth of *GDP* would amount to 4.40% per annum. The largest contribution to this growth would come from the industry sector scoring a real value-added growth of 5.37%. The better performance of industry is mainly the result of the increased demand for investment goods (+6.73%) of which industry is the only supplier. This would lead to higher profit rates for industry and a faster accumulation of capital in this sector (+5.89%). As a result of increased supply, the price level of industry would tend to decline, reaching a reduction of −0.27% in 1980.

The distribution of income would change, although only slightly, in favor of the higher income groups, which can be traced back to the deteriorating position of low-skilled labor in the factor market. The sectors that employ mainly low-skilled workers, such as agriculture and trade, would grow at a lower rate than other sectors: 4.12% and 3.78%, respectively.

We also applied simulations of the static model to the dynamic model, starting with the year 1975. A few reflections can be made on the results with the object of highlighting the working mechanisms of the model. In the first policy simulation, a 10% *productivity increase in industry and construction* was applied. Substantial differences are found between the results of the dynamic and static simulations. The effect on *GDP* is more than twice as large in the dynamic simulation: 6.1% as compared to 2.5% in the static simulation. This can be explained by the decline in the price index of the industrial sector by 9.14%, which makes it possible to buy more capital goods at a given level of savings. Therefore, capital is accumulated faster than in the base time path. This effect has been reinforced by the fact that an increased inflow of foreign savings pushes up total investment expenditure by 5.59%.

The performance of the industry sector would improve in the dynamic as compared to the static simulation. This can be attributed to both demand and supply factors. Demand for the sector's output would increase resulting from the increase in total investment. On the other hand, the supply of the sector would be reduced because the low profit rate would lead to a decrease in investment in this sector. Thus, capital accumulation would be lower than in other sectors and so is the growth of output. Combined with the inelasticity of demand, the reduced supply would have a favorable effect on value added. However, although the decrease in value added would be reduced in comparison with the static simulation, value added generated in industry and construction would still be lower than in other sectors.

So, also in the dynamic simulation, the effect of an increase in industrial productivity would lead to a reduced importance of industry and construction in the domestic economy.

The second policy simulation stipulated a 10% *productivity increase in services*. The results of the static simulation, which can take into account the effects for 1975 only, are similar to those of the dynamic simulation. The largest difference appears in the predicted decline of the wage rate of the highly skilled. Because potential suppliers of high-skilled labor would be discouraged by the lower wage, they would tend to quit the education system and would prefer to offer themselves low-skilled labor. As a result, the supply of highskilled labor would drop by −0.83%. This together with an expected diminished demand would result in a reduction in the remuneration rate by −0.74%.

7. Concluding Remarks

This chapter demonstrated how a static CGE model is harmonized with and parametrized from the SAM.

The static CGE model is expandable to a dynamic version that allows factors of production to grow over time and reallocate among alternative activities moved by incentives of relative returns in these activities. The dynamic model developed shortcuts for approximating time lags between responding to incentives and realization of factor reallocations.

Policy simulations were run and their results analyzed with the objective of tracing the work mechanisms of the models. The first policy simulation envisaged a 10% productivity increase in the sectors of industry and construction. The second policy simulation applied a 10% productivity increase in the sector of services. Although the results of the static and dynamic simulations differ in magnitude, both predict that a productivity increase makes the innovating sector worse off in comparison with non-innovating sectors. This outcome occurs in cases of (a) low-demand elasticities, i.e. constant budget shares in eq. (9), and (b) non-sensitive quantities of exports and imports to relative price changes as specified in eqs. (14) and (15). While the simplifications introduced in the model are functional in highlighting and comprehending the structure of the model and its mechanisms, these same simplifications may reduce empirically the utility of the model in policy simulations.

Notwithstanding the advantages and shortcomings of the simplifications introduced, policies directed solely to rising productivities in the various sectors (and thus saving on labor use) may fail in sustaining demand if they are not accompanied by measures to stimulate the employment of the laid-off labor. The US experience serves as a good example. [Productivity for all of 2009 rose 3.5%, the best showing in six years and a reflection of companies' ability to produce more with fewer workers. Still, many economists contend that the big productivity gains are actually harming the economy's prospects for a sustainable rebound. Companies may need to stop slashing their workforces and rehire laid-off workers. That will boost incomes and give households the support they need to increase consumer spending, which accounts for 70% of economic activity.]

The results suggest that policymaking which relies solely on the supply side (i.e. enhancing productivity as was simulated here is an example) may fail to accomplish sustained development if they are not accompanied by policies that handle the demand side as well. By analogy, it is also logical to expect that policies focusing solely on the demand side would not accomplish sustained development if policies for tackling the supply side are left out. The following two chapters will show greater policy gains when instruments from the demand and supply sides are appropriately phased and combined.

Endnotes

1. See Thorbecke (1990) for a broad discussion of Indonesian CGE models.
2. Different household groups are denoted by index $h = 1.2$, etc. We also use a subset of h to represent firms. There is no need to introduce a separate index for firms. Household groups and firms have in common that they both receive a profit income, pay taxes, and engage in transfer payments. Otherwise, they differ: households earn wage income, firms do not; households consume, while firms do not have consumption expenditures.
3. Installed investment is fixed investment. However, the word "fixed" may bring misunderstandings as we use the same word in the sense of fixing an exogenous value of the variable. To avoid such overlapping, we shall refer to fixed investment as installed investment or simply investment.
4. By defining low-skilled wage rate as index, factor payments to the low-skilled wage becomes equal to $RL_1 DL_{1j}$, which is a readily available figure in the SAM. For high-skilled labor and capital, the same approach can be followed. However, for reasons of converting the static model into a dynamic model later on, a different approach was followed regarding these production factors. In the dynamic model, low skilled labor and high skilled labor have to add up to total labor supply. Thus, high skilled labor has to be expressed in the *same productive units* as low skilled labor. To obtain this result, it is assumed that differential productivity is reflected by differential earnings and that a unit of high skilled labor earns four times the wage of a low-skilled worker in the benchmark period, which is empirically supported in the Indonesian context. This implies that in the benchmark DL_{2j} is equal to $RL_2/4DL_{2j}$. Similarly, in the dynamic model, new investment has to be added to the existing capital stock, so capital has to be expressed in the *same physical units* as investment. The way in which this is done is elaborated in Section 5.
5. Aggregate demand consists of demand categories with a (negative) unitary (consumption and investment) and with a zero elasticity of demand (intermediate deliveries, exports, and competitive imports). As a consequence, the aggregate demand elasticity lies between 1 and 0.
6. Taking ε'_q for the unit cost of educating labor of skill type q, ε''_q for the part of educational costs charged to the user, and ε'''_2 for foregone earnings during n years of educational upgrade from low to high skill, the total cost for skill type 2 can be abridged into $\varepsilon_2 = \varepsilon'_2 + \varepsilon''_2 + \varepsilon'''_2$. Similarly, the total cost for skill type 1 is $\varepsilon_1 = \varepsilon'_1 + \varepsilon''_1$. The equation makes use of the aggregated costs ε_2 and ε_1.

Chapter 11

Growth with Redistribution through Liberalization and Restructuring in a CGE Policy Model: Nepal

1. Introduction

Many developing economies have undergone trade liberalization in the context of the structural adjustment program of the IMF and the World Bank during the last couple of decades. The motivation is straightforward: If a regulated economy is to benefit from growth opportunities offered by the increasingly globalizing world, then the economy should open up and implement trade liberalization and structural adjustments. There are various empirical studies on whether the predicted gains from trade liberalization were materialized in countries that applied them. Most of the studies find that trade reform is accompanied by productivity growth, technological advancement, falling mark-ups, and a reshuffling of resources toward more efficient firms, among others. In contrast, there are detrimental effects that have drawn equal attention such as higher unemployment among workers displaced from less competitive industries and substantial rises in wages for the more competitive industries, resulting in a widening of income inequalities. Moreover, there is also some evidence that the impact on employment growth is small and adjustment costs are high. An elaborate list of references to these studies is found in Acharya (2011).

The focus of this chapter is modeling the growth and distribution effects of trade liberalization and structural adjustment. A few of the many models that dealt with this issue can be mentioned as a means for positioning our model. For example, in case of South America, Ianchovichina *et al.* (2001) modeled the effects of price changes on poverty and income distribution following the tariff reform of Mexico as a salient feature of its membership to the North American Free Trade Agreement (NAFTA). The impact on household welfare was found positive. Moreover, when non-homothetic individual preferences were modeled, import liberalization had a good prospect of benefiting the poor more than the rich. Models for South Asian countries, Bandara and Yu (2003), reveal that small economies benefit more from unilateral liberalization than multi-lateral preferential trading agreements. But these benefits are not sustained in the long run. In the African context, Chitiga *et al.* (2005) applied a CGE model for Zimbabwe showing that trade liberalization benefits unskilled labor employed intensively in agriculture, mining, and services, while most of the manufacturing sectors shrink leading to a fall in demand for skilled labor and capital. Poverty is reduced more in urban than in rural areas, but the income distribution pattern remains stable. In the Arab context, reference can be made to Lofgren *et al.* (1999), which is another dichotomy CGE model applied to Morocco that studies the effect of liberalization on rural and urban incomes. The review of models for individual countries that are related to our model is more extensive in Acharya (2011). It suffices here to state the shared conclusion that the review does not lead to a robust conclusion regarding the distributional impact of unilateral import liberalization. Even if the liberalization could generate pro-poor growth, the sustainability of this impact is questionable. Moreover, the combinations of modeling details, model structures, choice of variables, and data overlapping make the whole significantly incomparable. Furthermore, the sustainability of the pro-poor growth following unilateral trade openness must have the fulfillment of some initial conditions, which are not laid down and are rarely explored in the reviewed models.

The present modeling effort responds to the above-mentioned gaps and attempts to contribute some approaches toward resolving them. There are two objectives of the modeling effort. The first objective is to measure the impacts of various unilateral trade liberalization measures on a small open economy of Nepal in a general equilibrium framework. Second, as the impact of liberalization is found to be ineffective in promoting pro-poor growth, further modeling focuses on reformulations, tests, and redesigns of the economy structure in ways that could generate economic growth that is higher and pro-poor.

The outline of this chapter is as follows: Section 2 formulates a general equilibrium model that is highly representative of the Nepalese economy. Section 3 reports on the calibration of the model and simulation results of various unilateral trade liberalization policies. Section 4 presents specific modes of economic restructuring that are hypothesized to be conducive to pro-poor growth. The formulation of the modes is based on a thorough understanding of how this representative model of the economy works in generating its results. Section 5 again repeats the simulated liberalization policies analysis but under the restructured economy. Section 6 concludes.

2. Key Features

The CGE model of this chapter shares some associations with two other specific CGE models, and it is functional to signal them, mention the similarities, and emphasize the differences. One model is built by the International Food Policy Research Institute (IFPRI) and described in Lofgren *et al.* (2001). The common feature that we share with this model is the detailed specification of the supply and demand for commodities in the product markets versus activities in the production sphere, whereby foreign prices of imported and exported commodities are comprehensively incorporated in determining composite commodity prices. Another relevant model in the present context is by Cockburn (2001) who conducted a CGE analysis on trade liberalization and poverty in Nepal, though his study relates to regional poverty, while ours define poverty in terms of socio-economic groups at the national level.

There are minor and major differences between our model and the models of Lofgren and Cockburn. Besides differences in the specification of model closures, government budget balances, product market balances, and numeraire, the major difference is that we evaluate a wider combination of trade liberalization and structural adjustment measures than present in the above models. Furthermore, and more importantly, while the quoted models are static, we supplement the static version with a dynamic version that is particularly designed to meet the policy modeling tasks that are derived from the analysis of shortfalls in the policy simulation results of the static version. Because poverty reduction requires more time to achieve, the extension of the static CGE model to a dynamic CGE model is the logical step to undertake.

Before entering into the specification of notations and equations, some main features of the model can be summarized. The model contains the four characteristic accounting balances in economy-wide models, which link the various parts of the model in a systemic whole and characterize its equilibrium conditions. These are the factor market balances, product market balances, investment–savings balances, and foreign payments balances. As the model specifies the government explicitly, there is the additional government budget balance that equalizes its outgoing spending to its incomings, though the inclusion of this budget balance is not a prerequisite condition in economy-wide models. A few comments will be made on each of these accounting balances.

The factor market balances consider three factors of production: manpower with lower skills, manpower with higher skills, and capital, employed in various activities. The remuneration rates of these factors and their allocation among the sector activities are fully the results of interactions between demands for them and their supplies. All three factors are movable from one activity to another.

The model contains four activities denoted by j (agriculture, industry, commercial services, and other services). The product market balances are similarly broken down into four commodities denoted by c. Although there is a high correspondence between j and c, the correspondence is not diagonal. The model uses different types of prices for commodities. There are the price levels of exports and imports by commodity c (i.e. EP_c and MP_c, these are based on given world market prices quoted in foreign currency, converted to national currency via the foreign exchange rate, and adjusted to levies collected by the government). Then there are price variables at the domestic production levels, XP_c, composite prices of commodities appropriately weighted by the shares of domestic productions and imports, SP_c, and domestic supply prices of domestic productions inclusive of indirect taxes, DP_c. In a general equilibrium model, only relative prices can be established. In specifying these relative prices, the model uses as numeraire one of the DP_c commodities, namely that of industrial goods, which is an important normed base in Nepal; this is denoted by $DP_{c=2(\text{industrial})}$. Next to $c - 1$ commodity prices, which are adjusters in clearing the product market, there is the aggregate inventory change, IHC, which acts also as an adjuster in balancing the product markets.

The closure specification for the savings–investment balance is formulated along the lines displayed in Cohen (2014). The model determines domestic savings ahead of installed investment which is autonomously determined by the private and government investors. The adjustment mechanism for balancing the financial market of savings and investment is one of two alternatives: It is either the foreign savings (this is foreign capital flow, denoted by FCF) which takes the role of the adjuster, keeping the foreign exchange rate fixed, or the adjuster is the FXR, which is the unknown, while FCF is prefixed. For a deductive study of the effects of alternative policy simulations, the model considers initially foreign capital flow, FCF, as endogenous and the foreign exchange rate, FXR, as exogenous, and we end up with the policy simulation where FXR is unknown and FCF is prefixed.

Finally, in correspondence with the underlying SAM, the CGE model distinguishes between three institution accounts: households, firms, and the government. To keep it simple, households and firms are denoted by the same index h, so there is no need for separate equations for firms. It will be taken for granted for the model as a whole, therefore, that when reference is made to h, this would cover various household groups and firms, with the understanding that contrary to the household groups whose factor income consists of wages and profits, the firm's income consists of profits only, and contrary to household groups who spend on consumption, the firm's income is fully saved and invested. Otherwise, both households and firms pay taxes on incomes and may be involved in transfers.

Among the households, four groups are distinguished. This subdivision of households is based on various socio-economic and locational characteristics applicable to Nepal. The first two groups, Urban Residing Households (URH) and

Rural Upper households (RUH), are rich households, whereas Rural Small Households (RSH) and Rural Landless Households (RLH) are poor with the latter being the poorest. Government enters the model with equations and variables for revenue, consumption expenditure, transfer payments, investment spending, and a budget deficit.

The model applies detailed distribution of factor incomes by household, factor, and activity types. These three crosslinks allow linking changes in the production of activities to changes in factor remunerations and household incomes and highlight the impact of activity and factor reallocations on household incomes and the consequences thereof for the poverty situation. This is one of the aspects often overlooked in many CGE models.

3. Model Specification

The model contains 28 equation sets in 28 sets of unknown variables that can be described to fall into 4 blocks. Table 1 summarizes all indices used and defines variables and coefficients.

The first block, Box 1, comprises the factor market equations. Eq. (1) combines the Cobb–Douglas production function and Leontief input–output coefficients in determining the volume of gross output per sector, $X_j \cdot XP_j$, as a function of the employed labor skills and capital, and technical coefficients of input–output deliveries.

Eq. (2), making further use of Leontief input–output coefficients, the value added by sector, V_j, is found by deducting from the gross output the appropriately re-priced value of the composite commodities c used in the production of activity j and the value of intermediate imports per unit of activity j.

Eq. (3) assumes producers maximize profits under perfect competition in product and labor markets. As a result, in the short run, they will hire employees of skill q until the labor remuneration rate for that skill, LR_q, equals the value of the marginal product of that labor skill.

Eq. (4) states that the remuneration rate of capital, KR, is equal to the value of its marginal product. Capital is assumed to be mobile between sectors, and thus, capital returns are the same for all sectors.

Eq. (5) fixes the supply of labor by skill type and equalizes this supply with the demand for that labor skill. The remuneration rate of labor by skill type carries the burden of adjusting demand to supply in the labor market.

Eq. (6) fixes the supply of capital and equalizes this supply to the demand in all activity levels. Here too, the remuneration rate for capital across activities carries the burden of adjusting demand to supply of capital for all activities. This is the

Table 1. Notations.

Indices: c = commodity categories (1 = agricultural, 2 = industrial, 3 = commercial, 4 = services). h = household groups (1 = URH, 2 = RUH, 3 = RSH, 4 = RLH, and 5 = firms). j = activity sectors (agriculture, industry, commercial services, and other services). q = (1 = low skilled labor, 2 = high skilled labor). Furthermore, use is made of the subscripts g and r to denote government and the rest of the world, respectively.

Endogenous variables: price, quantity, and value variables of activities and commodities

DP_c	Domestic price of domestic output by commodity c, with particular reference to DPc (industrial) which serves as numeraire, equal to 1.0
EP_c	Export price in domestic currency by commodity c
MP_c	Import price in domestic currency by commodity c
SP_c	Composite supply price by commodity c
XP_c	Producer price by commodity c
XP_j	Output price by activity j
DQ_c	Domestic output quantity sold domestically by commodity c
EQ_c	Exports quantity by commodity c
MQ_c	Imports quantity by commodity c
SQ_c	Composite supply quantity by commodity c
XQ_c	Domestic output quantity by commodity c
XQ_j	Gross output quantity by activity j
Xj	Gross output of activity j
V_j	Value added of activity j (value)

Endogenous variables: Others

C_{hc}	Consumption by household h of commodity c
C_c	Total consumption by commodity c
FCF	Foreign capital flow expressed in domestic currency. FCF is converted into an exogenous variable in an alternative specification of model closure
GBD_g	Government budget deficit
I	Installed investment
ICH	Inventory change
I_c	Installed investment deliveries by commodity c
KD_j	Demand for capital in activity j
KR	Rental rate of capital
LD_{qj}	Demand for labor of type q in activity j
LR_q	Remuneration rate of labor factor q
Y_h	Disposable income of household h, applies also for firms
Z_h	Factor income and received transfers of household group h, applies also to firms
Z_g	Government revenue

Exogenous variables

ep_c	Export price in foreign currency by commodity c
mp_c	Import price in foreign currency by commodity c
FXR	Foreign exchange rate (domestic currency per unit of foreign currency). FXR is converted into an endogenous variable in an alternative specification of model closure

Table 1. (*Continued*)

C_{gc}	Government consumption expenditure on commodity c
I_g	Government expenditure on installed investment
LS_q	Supply of labor factor production factor q
KS	Supply of capital stock in the whole economy
T_{gh}	Government transfer payments to household group h, extended to include firms
T_{rh}	Transfer from rest of world r to household h, extended to include firms
T_{rg}	Transfer from rest of world r to government g
Coefficients	
α_{jo}	Calibration parameter in production function of activity j
α_{cj}	Intermediate delivered quantity of c as input per unit of activity j
α_{co}	Calibration parameter for output transformation (CET) function
α_c	Share parameter for output transformation (CET) function
$\alpha_{c'}$	Exponent for output transformation (CET) function $(-1 < \alpha_{c'} < \infty)$
α_{rj}	Non-competitive import share in the output of activity j
β_{qj}	Labor elasticity of production relating to labor type q in activity j
χ_{co}	Calibration parameter for composite supply (Armington) function
χ_c	Share parameter for composite supply (Armington) function
$\chi_{c'}$	Exponent for composite supply (Armington) function $(-1 < \chi_c' < \infty)$
ε_{co}	Calibration parameter for exports by commodity c
ε_c	Export price elasticity by commodity c
γ_{hc}	Consumption price elasticity of commodity c by household group h
$\gamma_{hc\#}$	Consumption budget share of commodity c in the consumption of household group h
γ_{hco}	Calibration parameter in consumption functions
$\iota_o, \iota_k, \iota_g$	Private investment function coefficients, whereby ι_o is calibrated, ι_k is elasticity of investment with respect to rental rate of capital, and ι_g is with respect to public investment
ι_c	Distribution share of total investment on commodity c
μ_{co}	Calibration parameter for imports by commodity c
μ_c	Import price elasticity coefficient by commodity c
θ_{cj}, θ_{jc}	Converted units of commodity c per unit of activity j and otherwise
π_{jh}, π_{jg}	Profit distribution shares from activity j that go to household h (and firms) and to government g
$\rho_{h'h}$	Transfer payments (net) from household h' to h, as proportion of the income of the paying group h'
σ_h	Savings proportion in the disposable income of household group h
τ_{cg}	Sales tax rate by commodity c collected by government g
$\tau_{cg,\text{imp}}$	Import tariff rate by commodity c collected by government g
$\tau_{cg,\text{exp}}$	Export tax rate by commodity c collected by government g
τ_{hg}	Direct tax rate on income of household group h collected by government g
ω_{qjh}	Wages distribution shares from activity j for labor of skill type q received by household group h
υ_c	Inventory change in commodity c as proportion of the aggregate inventory change

case of the mobile situation for installed capital, which allows capital to shift from one activity to another in pursuit of higher rental differentials.

Box 1. Factor market: Production functions, factor use, and factor remuneration.

$X_j = XP_j\{1/(1 - \Sigma_c\alpha_{cj} - \mu_j\}[\alpha_{jo}\Pi LD_{qj}^{\beta qj} \cdot KD_j^{(1-\Sigma q\beta qj)}]$	j (1)
$V_j = \{1 - (\Sigma_j\alpha_{cj}SP_c/XP_j) - \alpha_{rj}\}X_j$	j (2)
$LR_q = \beta_{qj}V_j/LD_{qj}$	$q \cdot j$ (3)
$KR = (1 - \Sigma_q\beta_{qj})V_j/KD_j$	(4)
$\Sigma_j LD_{qj} = LS_q q$	(5)
$\Sigma_j KD_j = KS_j j$	(6)

The second block of equations, Box 2, relates to the income and spending of households and the government. In eq. (7), the total income of recipient household groups (and firms) is specified as consisting of factor remunerations distributed over household groups h via wage shares ω that are detailed by household group h, skill q, and sector j, and profit shares π detailed by household group and sector, thus ω_{hqj} and π_{hj}. The model can incorporate earnings details by sector of activity, which is an important element for policymaking. This is often missed in many CGE models due to the aggregative nature of the SAMs behind them which do not link household earnings to the sector where the income is earned. Next to factor incomes there can be income transfers paid to and received from other household groups which are assumed to be fixed proportions, $\rho_{h'h}$, of the income of the paying party. The equation incorporates the net results of these transfers. Furthermore, there are income transfers received from the government, T_{gh}, and net income transfers from the rest of the world, T_{rh}. The conversion of these foreign transfers from foreign currency to national currency via the foreign exchange rate, *FXR*, is explicitly incorporated in the equation.

In eq. (8), direct taxes are subtracted from the incomings of households to arrive at disposable income.

In eq. (9), consumers save a fixed proportion of their disposable income and spend the rest on consumption, i.e. $(1 - \sigma_h)Y_h$. This is their spending budget constraint. The consumption function assumes that the consumer maximizes a Cobb–Douglas utility function given the spending budget constraint. Accordingly, the distribution of the consumption expenditure on commodities is determined initially by the start budget shares γ_{hco} and adjusted subsequently to a price effect (via own and cross-price elasticities, γ_{hc}, in interaction with the composite prices of competing commodities, SP_c) and to an income effect (via the expenditure elasticity which is $(1-\Sigma_c\gamma_{hc})$, in interaction with the expenditure level). [The Cobb–Douglas utility function requires that the sum of the elasticities involved is equal to 1, hence the specification of the expenditure elasticity is $(1 - \Sigma_c \gamma_{hc})$. In the specific case where price elasticities equal zero and the expenditure elasticity equals 1.0, the distribution of spending on commodity c will be consistent with the initial budget shares, γ_{hco}.]

In eq. (10), total consumption expenditure for commodity c is the sum of private consumption by all households of commodity c and government consumption expenditure on commodity c, C_{gc}.

In eq. (11), installed investment[1] is broken down into public investment, taken exogenous, and private investment, which is specified as a behavioral function in terms of two main factors. One factor is the profit rate (private investment increases as the rental rate of capital increases via elasticity ι_k). The other factor is the complimentary character and crowding in the effect of public investment leading to more private investment via elasticity ι_g. In this equation, ι_o serves as the calibration coefficient.[2]

In eq. (12), installed investment deliveries classified by commodity c, that is, I_c, are a proportion ι_c of the total installed investment, I. Because there is only one commodity, denoted as industrial, which constitutes investment goods, we have $\iota_c = 1.0$ for the industrial commodity $c = 2$ and zero for all others.

In eq. (13), government revenue is defined to consist of factor income from the ownership of public enterprises, plus direct taxes from households (and firms), plus indirect taxes on domestic commodities, import duties, and export duties, plus net transfers relating to households (and firms), and net transfers from abroad converted to national currency.

In eq. (14), the left-hand side shows government expenditure consisting of current expenditure (consumption and transfers: $\Sigma_c C_{gc} + \Sigma_h T_{gh}$), plus fixed investment (I_g), while the right-hand side shows how they are financed, namely by government revenue, Z_g, and a budget deficit, GBD_g.

Box 2. Factor incomes, disposable incomes, private consumption, investment, and government.

$$Z_h = \Sigma_q \Sigma_j \omega_{qjh} LR_q \cdot LD_{qj} + \Sigma_j \pi_{jh} KR_j KD_j + \Sigma_{h'} \rho_{h'h} Z_{h'} + T_{gh} + FXR.T_{rh} \qquad h \quad (7)$$

$$Y_h = (1 - \tau_{hg}) Z_h \qquad h \quad (8)$$

$$C_{hc} = \gamma_{hco} \Pi_{hc} SP_c^{\gamma_{hc}} \{\gamma_{hc\#}(1 - \sigma_h) Y_h\}^{1-\Sigma c \gamma hc} \qquad h, c \quad (9)$$

$$C_c = \Sigma_h C_{hc} + C_{gc} \qquad c \quad (10)$$

(*Continued*)

(*Continued*)

$$I - I_g = \iota_0 KR^{\iota k} I_g^{\iota g} \quad (11)$$

$$I_c = i_c I \quad c \ (12)$$

$$Z_g = \Sigma_j \pi_{jg} KR_j \cdot KD_j + \Sigma_h \tau_{hg} Y_h + \Sigma_c \tau_{cg} DPc.DQc + \Sigma_c \tau_{cg,imp} FXR \cdot mp_c \cdot MQ_c + \Sigma_c \tau_{cg,exp} FXR \cdot ep_c \cdot EQ_c + FXR.T_{rg} \quad (13)$$

$$\Sigma_c C_{gc} + \Sigma_h T_{gh} + I_g = Z_g + GBD_g \quad (14)$$

The third block is in Box 3. The equations here relate to demand, supply, and prices in the product market. The price system of the model is elaborate, primarily as a result of the assumed quality differences between commodities of different origins and destinations (exports, imports, and domestic outputs used domestically). A distinction is made between the quantity and price level of the supply composite of commodities, SQ_c and SP_c, the quantity and price level of the domestic output of commodities that are sold domestically, DQ_c and DP_c, and the quantity and price level of the domestic output (that is sold domestically and is exported internationally), XQ_c and XP_c. Composite price variables SP_c are important, among others, in determining the distribution of consumption on commodity c (see eq. (9)) and clearing the product market (see eq. (27)). The domestic price variables DP_c are crucial in determining national contra foreign price competitiveness and the size of imports and exports, as will be incorporated in eqs. (17) and (21).

Composite supply (Armington function): Eqs. (15) and (16) specify the composite supply. In eq. (15), for each commodity, absorption (i.e. total domestic spending on the commodity) is the sum of spending on domestic output, including an upward adjustment for the sales tax and imports. All purchasers buying composite quantity SQ_c pay the composite price, SP_c. Prices of both domestically produced goods and imported goods are expressed in domestic currency, and they are both adjusted with their respective taxes. Eq. (16) deals with the imperfect substitutability between imports and domestic output. This is captured by a constant elasticity of substitution (CES) aggregation function in which the composite commodity that is supplied domestically is "produced" by domestic and imported commodities, and they enter this function as "inputs". This means demander preferences over imports and domestic output can be expressed as a CES function, along the lines proposed by Armington, the originator of the idea. The restriction on the value of χ_c', $(-1 < \chi_c' < \infty)$, assures that the corresponding isoquant is convex to the origin, in terms of production economics equivalent to a diminishing technical rate of substitution.

Import ratio and price: Eq. (17), which applies to imported commodities, specifies how the mix between the quantity of imports and the domestic output for commodity c is realized. It states that the domestic price/import price ratio determines the import/domestic demand ratio, subject to applicable elasticities. Eq. (18) gives a simple definition of the price of imported commodity c as the world market price converted to domestic currency and increased with the import tariff.

Domestic output (CET function): Turning now to domestic output details, eq. (19) defines the value of domestic output of commodity c, at producer prices, as the sum of the value of domestic output sold domestically and the export value expressed in domestic currency. The imperfect transformability between domestic output for exports and domestic sales is treated in eq. (20) via a constant elasticity of transformation (CET) function that captures the transformation. The CET function is identical to a CES function except for negative elasticities of substitution. The isoquant corresponding to the output transformation function will be concave to the origin given the restriction imposed on the value of $\alpha_{c'}(-1 < \alpha_{c''} < \infty)$. In economic terms, the difference between the Armington and CET functions is that the arguments in the former are inputs, and those in the latter are outputs. In case of commodities without exports, a_c equals 0, thus resulting in $XQ_c = DQ_c$.

Export ratio and price: Eqs. (21) and (22) for exports are like eqs. (15) and (16) for imports, above. The common formulation allows ratios of domestic and foreign prices and relating price elasticities to be influential in determining quantities of exports and imports by commodity. In eq. (21), determination of the mix for commodity c between the quantity of goods destined for exports and that for domestic use is specified. In eq. (22), the price of the exported commodity is defined as the world price times the foreign exchange rate and increased with the export tariff.

Output prices and quantities: Output prices and quantities are specified in eqs. (23), (24), and (25). In eq. (23), the domestic activity price is the domestic commodity price times a yield coefficient of commodity c per unit of activity j. In eq. (24), the quantity of the domestic output of the commodity c is derived from the corresponding activity product using the reversed yield coefficient of commodity c per unit of activity j. In eq. (25), the value is defined in terms of quantity and price.

Numeraire: The model uses eq. (26) as numeraire the price level of domestically produced industrial goods, $DP_{c(\text{industrial})}$, which is set at 1.0..0

Box 3. Commodities blocks: Product market balances and foreign payment balance.

Composite supply (Armington function)	
$SP_c \cdot SQ_c = (1 + \tau_{cg})DP_c \cdot DQ_c + (MP_c \cdot MQ_c)$	c (15)
$SQ_c = \chi_{co}\{\chi_c MQ_c^{-\chi c'} + (1 - \chi_c)DQ_c^{-\chi}c'\}^{-1/\chi c'}$	c (16)
Import ratio and price	
$MQ_c/DQ_c = \mu_{co}\{(DP_c/MP_c)^{\mu_c} \cdot (\chi_c/1 - \chi_c)\}^{1/1+\chi_c'}$	c (17)
$MP_c = (1 + \tau_{cg,imp}) \cdot FXR \cdot mp_c$	c (18)
Domestic output (CET function).	
$XP_c \cdot XQ_c = DP_c \cdot DQ_c + (EP_c \cdot EQ_c)$	c (19)
$XQ_c = \alpha_{co}\{\alpha_c EQ^{\alpha c'} + (1 - \alpha_c)DQ_c^{\alpha c'}\}^{1/\alpha c'}$	c (20)
Export ratio and price	
$EQ_c/DQ_c = \varepsilon_{co}\{(EP_c/DP_c)^{\varepsilon c} \cdot (1 - \alpha_c)/\alpha_c\}^{1/\alpha c - 1}$	c (21)
$EP_c = (1 - \tau_{cg,exp}) \cdot (FXR \cdot ep_c)$	c (22)
Output prices and quantities.	
$XP_j = \Sigma_c \theta_{cj} XP_c$	j (23)
$XQ_c = \Sigma_j \theta_{jc} XQ_j$	c (24)
$X_j = XP_j \cdot XQ_j$	j (25)
Numeraire	
$DP_{c(\text{industrial})} = 1.0$	(26)

The fourth block of equations, Box 4, displays national accounting balances. Eq. (27) is the composite commodity balances, which states that the total quantity of the commodity supplied equals demand, which is the intermediate demand in quantity terms, plus consumption demand plus investment demand, and inventory change, where applicable converted into quantity terms. The change in stocks is taken as a proportion υ_c of the total inventory change. The adjusters in the product market balances, which are c in number, are the composite prices SP_c for $c - 1$ and the aggregate inventory change IHC.

Eq. (28) is the savings–investment balance. The right-hand side shows total gross capital formation, which is installed investment and inventory change. These are financed by the left-hand sum of domestic savings and foreign savings.

Domestic savings are disposable income minus consumption expenditure for the private sector, and government savings are government revenues less current spending on consumption and transfers. The foreign savings destined to close the investment savings gap are net foreign capital flow expressed in national currency, FCF. The savings–investment balance can be generally described as the financial market balance in its most simplistic form. The adjuster in this market is foreign capital flow FCF, which goes together with assuming a regime of fixed foreign exchange rates, FXR. This setting will be maintained in several policy simulations for deductive reasons. We shall later on shift regimes and convert the foreign exchange rate, FXR, from its status as an exogenous variable into that of an endogenous variable. To maintain the determinacy of the model, and given the causal ordering of the CGE model, it is necessary that FCF is converted from the endogenous to the exogenous status.

At this point with its 28 sets of equations, the model is now complete. It contains 28 sets of endogenous variables that can be counted in the list of notations.

Box 4. National accounting balances

Composite commodity balances

$$SQ_c = \Sigma_j \alpha_{cj} XQ_j + C_c/SP_c + I_c/SP_c + \upsilon_c ICH/SP_c \qquad c \; (27)$$

Savings–investment balance

$$(\Sigma_h \sigma_h Y_h) + (Z_h - \Sigma_c C_{gc} - \Sigma_h T_{gh}) + FXR.FCF = I + ICH \qquad (28)$$

Foreign payments balance

$$\Sigma_c(FXR\ mp_c)QM_c + \Sigma_j \alpha_{rj} X_j = \Sigma_c(FXR\ ep_c)EQ_c + FXRT_{rg} + \Sigma_h T_{rh} + FXR \cdot FCF \qquad (A1)$$

There is an additional eq. (A1) that can be specified. Eq. (A1) is the foreign payments balance. The equation states that the total outgoing foreign payments, in lieu of competitive imports and intermediate imports, equal incoming payments in lieu of exports, transfers to the rest of the world, and foreign capital flow. Since there are accounting balances that are connected and form together a consistent system, this makes one of the accounting balances self-evident, i.e. the nth accounting balance. We take this to be the foreign payments balance, denoted as additional A1 and is not countable as a separate equation. This is congruent with Walras' law that states if $(n - 1)$ markets are cleared, the nth one is cleared as well. So, one of the accounting balances can be considered "redundant" and be left out. The generated results for the other accounting balances will reproduce eq. (A1) automatically and are consistent with this nth accounting balance. Although we choose to leave out the foreign payments balance, the same outcomes are obtained if instead of skipping the foreign payments balance the modeler would skip one of the c balances in the commodity product balances, in eq. (27), or the savings–investment balance, eq. (28).

Before examining the policy simulations, we discuss here one additional equation outside the model that can be handy in interpreting the results of the model or refining its parameters and robustness. Instead of the numeraire that we use, it is common to use a consumer price index, CPI, as a numeraire. This is constructed from the composite prices and the weights of commodities c. Even if CPI is not used as a numeraire and is not part of the CGE model applied here, consideration of CPI as a by variable tailed to the model is useful in summarizing information on changes in the general price level and real expenditure. CPI is defined in eq. (A2):

$$\mathrm{CPI} = \Sigma_c (SQ_c / \Sigma_c SQ_c) SP_c \tag{A2}$$

4. Application and Policy Simulations

Estimates of the parameters of the model are based on an SAM of Nepal, especially complied for the base year 1996, and other data sources. For details, see Acharya (2011). The analysis here can focus on selected policy simulations and further refinements of the model. Among the policy simulations that were run are the following four indicated by MLN, ELR, (MLN+ELR), and (MLN+ELR+EXR): under two different regimes regarding the dependence of FCF and FXR. The two alternative closures were discussed above as (FXR prefixed, FCF unknown) and (FCF prefixed, FXR unknown).

Under FXR prefixed and FCF unknown

1. MLN=Import liberalization by Nepal (simulated by reducing import tariff rates, τ_{cg}, by 10%).
2. ELR=Export liberalization by the rest of the world (simulated by raising export elasticities, ε_c, by 10%).
3. (MLN+ELR)= combination of the MLN and ELR simulations in one simulation.

Under FCF prefixed and FXR unknown

1. (MLN+ELR+EXR)= combination of MLN and ELR simulations in one simulation but under endogenous foreign exchange rate, FXR, in contrast to the other simulations under fixed FXR. The prefixed value of FCF is set at that obtained from the previous simulation of (MLN+ELR), plus 10%, to allow for more flexibility and analysis of the results.

We shall review the results of the four simulations. Compared to the benchmark data, the immediate effect of the policy simulation denoted by MLN is to reduce import and composite prices, SP_c, except for the agricultural commodity.[3] The strong decline in $SP_{(industrial)}$ induces industrial output and since this is heavily agro-based, agricultural output is enhanced as well. With limits on the factors of production, the expansion in these two sectors is counteracted by contraction in the services sectors, but the overall effect on *GDP* is positive, at plus 0.58%: Table 2. Factor reallocations among sectors follow the pattern consistent with growth by sectors. The expanding sectors absorb more factors, whereas the contracting sectors lose them. With constant factor supplies, all factor remuneration rates increase, with the rate of profit rising faster than that of wages.

As *GDP* gains, incomes and consumption of households gain as well. The distribution of the increased incomes is a different story. Factor income increases by 3.1% in industries but by only 1.4% in agriculture, where most of the population earn their income. The rural owning households, ROH, benefit most with an income shift upward of 0.7%. The rural middle households, RMH, and rural landless households, RLH, benefit less, with their income rising by 0.65% and 0.63%, respectively. On a per capita basis, the gain is minimal. Urban households, URH, gain the least, 0.52%, as they mostly draw their income from services which performed least. The contribution of the import liberalization policy to resolving income redistribution disparities and poverty is not compelling, given the above results. Furthermore, the government budget deficit soars, deficit increases by 22%, due to the reduction in customs duties that comprise almost one-third of the government revenue. This would require future reductions in government expenditure, with detrimental effects for the lowest income groups who rely heavily on public allocations for health, education, and other social provisions. The reduction in investment of 3% is also not a favorable sign for future economic growth.

The second policy simulation is denoted by FLR. Internationally, there is a consensus that the implementation of an import liberalization policy by the developing country should somehow be rewarded by the rest of the world by them taking measures that would stimulate exports of the liberalizing developing country. The ELR simulates the effects of such favoring measures (postulated to raise export elasticities by 10%). The immediate effect is a rise in agricultural exports and output, and because this elevated demand is not sufficiently met by supply, the composite price of agricultural commodity rises. Industrial exports and output jump also but supply is flexible, so the composite price is stable. The service sectors undergo price rises and output reductions, as factors of production shift to agriculture and industry. In similarity with the previous policy simulation, the reshuffling of labor skills and capital toward agriculture and industry results in a positive change in the GDP of about half a percent, 0.45%, Table 2. Factor remuneration increases, all households increase their incomes with the richer agriculturalists gaining the most, and the poorest landless agricultural group achieving the average gain. Urban dwellers who associate more with the retarding service sectors gain the least. The residual effects of the above developments are a reduction in total investment, I, by 2.5%, and an increase in government budget deficit, GBD, by 16%, which together act to maintain the level of foreign savings, FCF, at about its base value. The above results indicate that MLN scores more on growth while ELR scores more on the income equality dimension, though the differential magnitudes involved appear to be rather small.

The third policy simulation is (MLN + ELR), also in Table 2, third column, shows results that are closer to MLN than ELR, which suggests that the import mechanisms in the model are stronger than the export mechanisms in determining outcomes. There is no advantage in combining the two policies. Given the implied doubling of policy efforts that go with the combined policy simulation, the results do not bring anything close to double benefits, suggesting that it is more desirable to pursue separate lines of external liberalization, one at a time.

The fourth policy simulation is (MLN + ELR *under flexible FXR and given FCF*). A striking result of the simulation is the appreciation of the foreign exchange rate by about 3.1%, making exports in domestic currency cheaper. Prices of the imports go down as well because of import liberalization. These declines lead to the overall decline of the composite prices, SP_c, in a range varying between −1.6% and −2.6%; *CPI* is −1.9%, Table 2, fourth column. Accordingly, rates of factor remuneration fall down with a greater loss for lower than upper skills, −1.27% and −1.16%. The value added goes down too showing a negative effect on GDP, −1.39%. (Although agriculture and industry grow somewhat, the larger fall in the service sectors overrules.) Household incomes decline, especially that of the poorest group. Results for other variables that are important for future prospects show also a negative picture: Investments are down by 1.9%, and the government budget deficit is rising by 22%. As such, the four policy simulations cannot be recommended. A rerun of this policy simulation with a restricted value for the foreign capital inflow, FCF, at a much lower level than is customary for Nepal can reverse the negative predictions of the policy simulation. To get along with a lower level of FCF, it is necessary to restructure government budget revenues and spending so as to shore up government savings and reduce the need for FCF.[4]

In a CGE model, changes in relative prices of commodities force shifts in the allocation of production factors among activities. In all the four policy simulations, the average shift in factor use in all sectors varies narrowly between 1.62% and 1.84%. But there are significant differences at the factor and sector level. Industry and commercial services carry the largest shifts in factor use, with factors moving to industry from commercial services. Taking the example of the import liberalization policy, not shown in the table, the shift off commercial services in capital use is −2.69%, and the shift into industry is +2.64%. Shifts in the use of labor skills are close to this range.

Table 2. Selected results from four policy simulations in the static model: Percentage change of simulation results over base values 1996.

	Closure C: fixed foreign exchange rate FXR, endogenous foreign capital flow FCF			Closure D: flexible FXR, exogenous FCF
	Import liberalization by Nepal (MLN)	Export liberalization by rest of world (ELR)	(MLN) + (ELR)	(MLN) + (ELR)
Composite price SP_c				
Agricultural	0.40	0.30	0.39	−1.60
Industrial	−1.40	−1.30	−1.38	−2.10
Commercial services	−0.40	−0.10	−0.39	−2.20
Social services	−0.40	0.10	−0.40	−2.60
Sector output, XQ_j				
Agriculture	0.80	0.90	0.90	1.10
Industry	2.60	2.90	2.61	2.20
Commercial services	−2.80	−2.90	−2.80	−2.90
Social services	−0.80	−0.80	−0.80	−0.80
Shifts in pay rates				
Low skill	0.63	0.49	0.62	−1.27
High skill	0.85	0.71	0.84	−1.16
Rental rate of capital	0.48	0.48	0.48	−1.45
Average shifts in factor use in all sectors				
Low skill	1.67	1.83	1.67	1.67
High skill	1.62	1.82	1.62	1.75
Capital	1.68	1.84	1.69	1.68
GDP	0.58	0.45	0.58	−1.39
Income URH	0.52	0.40	0.52	−1.54
Income ROH	0.70	0.58	0.69	−1.21
Income RMH	0.65	0.52	0.65	−1.25
Income RLH, poorest	0.63	0.53	0.63	−1.26
Installed investment I	−3.00	−2.50	−2.90	−1.90
Budget deficit GBD	22.0	16.6	21.0	22.7
Foreign capital flow FCF	0.86	0.13	0.87	10.96(a)
CPI	−0.20	−0.10	−0.19	−1.86

Note: (a) Value of FCF is fixed exogenously to allow foreign exchange rate, FXR, to become endogenous. This policy simulation predicts a rise in the FXR of 3.1% compared to the base year.

The direction and strength of the shifts of factors between activities are central in determining the resulting configuration of growth and income distribution among household groups; this is obvious since these groups form the owner–work link between factors and activities. For a pro-poor growth strategy to succeed, it would require long-term restructuring of linkages between factors, activities, and households, in ways that converge toward pro-poor growth performances.

5. The Dynamic Model with a Restructured Economy

5.1. *General*

The results of the liberalization policies simulated above do not show a pro-poor growth despite the predicted expansion of economic activities. This is the turning point for closer cooperation between the policy modeler and the policy maker in analyzing the structure of the economy, pinpointing elements in the structure that need to adjust so as to generate a pro-poor growth that accompanies the implementation of liberalization reforms, redesigning the policy modeling activity accordingly, simulating the liberalization policies under the redesigned regime, assessing the policy implications, and testing for the plausibility of the outcomes. Our analysis of contrasting results indicates that the required elements in a restructuring strategy may take more years to implement before realizing the balanced benefits of liberalization reforms. Among the elements are (a) improvement of efficiency parameters and (b) redirection of labor endowments of poorer households toward their greater exploitation in high-growth expanding sectors that benefit from liberalization reforms and redirection of complementary investment to these sectors.

The intention is to incorporate these elements in the CGE model in several steps. First, it is necessary to update and restructure the social accounting matrix for 2006, so as to incorporate such structural changes. We have considered 10 years as a transformation period for this restructuring, 1996–2006. Second, it is also necessary to develop a dynamic CGE model that can link solutions for 1996 with those for 2006. Third, once the dynamic model is calibrated and verified, the same policy simulations of liberalization reforms can be applied and analyzed in relation to the same policy simulation with the non-restructured economy. Fourth, qualitative lessons can be drawn from the policy experiments that can be made operational at the real policymaking level.

5.2. *A restructured SAM for 2006*

Next to the SAM for 1996, a hypothetical but plausible SAM for 2006 is developed that is used for calibrating the CGE model for 2006. This is done in several rounds:

(i) Various data for 2006 are compiled to set up an SAM for 2006. Since the annual rate of inflation in the period 1996–2006 has been around 5%, all current year values for the year SAM 2006 have been deflated by this rate cumulatively over the 10 years.

(ii) To enhance efficiency in production activities, factor payment shares as a proportion of the total output are increased from 0.60 to 0.64 reflecting higher efficiency in a restructured economy. Intermediate deliveries as a proportion of the total output decline accordingly.

(iii) To maximize the gain for poorer households, they should enjoy a high participation in the reshuffling of labor endowments toward the high growth performing activities under liberalization reforms. When this occurs, the activity/factor/household income links would move in their favor. Furthermore, the upgrading of human capital from low to high skill will also benefit the poor. In the factor market, the wage shares in the value added are increased at the cost of profit share. These adjustments are represented by a 3% jump in the low-skilled wage share and 1.5% jump in the high-skilled earning share, which are compensated by a 4.5% decline in the profit share.

(iv) The above shifts in wages and profits are carried forward to the incomes of household groups with slight upscaling of the wage proportions earned by poorer groups. The decline in the profit share is carried forward to all household groups except the landless group who earn little or no profit.

(v) The shifts in wages and profit shares are carried backward to the activity accounts of agriculture, industry, and commercial services. The public service sector, being labor intensive, keeps to its factor distribution patterns as in 1996.

(vi) For the other accounts in the 2006 SAM, the distribution proportions are assumed to follow the same pattern as the 1996 SAM. To achieve full consistency between row totals, column totals, and the adjustments that were incorporated in (i)–(v), the RAS method was applied to the constructed 2006 SAM, ending up in what can be termed a policy SAM for 2006, that can be calibrated as CGE model for 2006.

5.3. *Extensions to a dynamic model*

The extension of the static to the dynamic model involves adding six sets of equations, along similar lines as was set in Chapter 10. The extensions aim at making endogenous the otherwise exogenously assumed supply of the labor and capital factors of production. Sustainable economic growth requires increments in the supply of factors. In correspondence with the added equations, there are six newly introduced endogenous variables, as listed in the following notations, Table 3. We shall specify each of the equations and summarize them together in Box 5.

Eq. (29) makes endogenous the supply of labor and its distribution on skill types. The labor force would grow annually by λ'. In Nepal, this amounts to 2.6%, which is increased in the policy simulations by an additional 10% to give 2.86%, as a reflection of enhanced work incentives that would lead to greater employment and ultimately benefit the populous poorer groups.

$$LS_{1,t} + LS_{2,t} = (LS_{1,t-1} + LS_{2,t-1})(1 + \lambda') \tag{29}$$

Table 3. Newly introduced endogenous variables and coefficients.

IAS	Investment accumulated over the 10-year period 1996–2006.
IGR	Investment growth rate
KS_j	Total capital stock (this was exogenous in the static model)
RHL_{t+n}	Ratio of high-skilled to low-skilled labor in a future prospective year $t+n$.
SL_1	Supply of low-skilled labor ($q=1$) (this was exogenous in the static model)
SL_2	Supply of high-skilled labor ($q=2$) (this was exogenous in the static model)
δ	Depreciation rate of capital goods
η_q	Educational cost incurred and earnings forgone in acquiring skill
λ'	Growth rate of the total labor force
λ_o	Calibration coefficient in the equation of the skill ratio
λ	Elasticity of skill upgrading in response to wage differentials
φ	Distributed lag adjustment coefficient for realizing long-term change in the skill ratio

In eq. (30), the future skills ratio of high to low skills, RHL_{t+n}, is considered to grow over time influenced by what is generally acknowledged as social demand (or sometimes called non-economically motivated behavior) and economically motivated behavior. Given the close association between the two factors, especially with regard to occupational education, it is functional to focus on economically motivated behavior, which can give a reasonable approximation of the effects of the combined behavior. The workers' choice between offering himself (or herself) to highskilled versus low-skilled employment depends on the relative benefit–cost ratios associated with the two skill types. Benefits are the remuneration of labor, LR_2 and LR_1, respectively. Costs are indicated by η_2 and η_1, respectively, and they include the education costs incurred in acquiring skill q and foregone earnings during the formal acquisition of the higher skill.[5] The incurred costs of η_2 and η_1 are interesting policy parameters, as they can be varied and their long-term effects on the structure of the labor force can be evaluated. However, in the application to Nepal, the estimates of η_1 and η_2 are kept constant at Rs. 1032 and Rs. 280 in 1996 prices.

Once earners make their choice as to what skill level they will pursue, it takes several years, say (n) years, before the effects of the choices are realized in a changed structure of the labor supplies. The (n) years may vary from about 4–10 years depending on the educational system and the classification range of high and low skills. The equation for the ratio of higher to lower labor skills, RHL_{t+n}, starts with the benchmark for the ratio at $(LS_2/LS_1)_o$, allows for some growth due to social demand expressed by λ_{sd}, and specifies its dynamics as a response to relative returns to both skills, with λ as the elasticity of skill upgrading due to differentials in skill returns: $\text{RHL}_{t+n} = (1+\lambda_{sd})(LS_2/LS_1)_0\{(LR_{2,t}/\eta_2)/(LR_{1,t}/\eta_1)\}^{\lambda}$.

For estimation purposes, the equation can be edited as in eq. (30):

$$\text{RHL}_{t+n} = \lambda_o\{(LR_{2,t}/\eta_2)/(LR_{1,t}/\eta_1)\}^{\lambda} \tag{30}$$

In this equation, the calibration coefficient λ_o can have a value equal to or higher than the benchmark for the skill ratio. There is the problem that the period (n) cannot be specified *a priori* since behind it are many lags and overlapping variables of the educational and demographic systems that do not permit a short cut. The value of (n) can only be specified along empiricist lines. It is clear also that when the period (n) is longer, RHL_{t+n} will tend to be higher and thus leading to a higher value of the skill upgrading elasticity. In principle, the equation can be regressed for various fixations for the (n) years, and the best fitting regression for λ_o and λ can be selected, in this way determining how long the number of years (n) should be. This may require data that may not be available. An alternative approach is to postulate that the elasticity λ assumes the value of unity and iterate from limited data the gestation period (n) that corresponds with the postulate of $\lambda = 1$. [The application for Nepal gave (n) = 10 years.]

Finally, eq. (31) states that the change in the skill ratio for the current year t, from last year $t-1$, is assumed to follow a distributed lag pattern in terms of its value in the future year of $t+n$ and in the past *year* $t-1$. This is done via adjustment coefficient, φ, as in eq. (31). For Nepal, the two periods relate to year t, 2006, and the benchmark year o, 1996. The two time periods are t and $t-10$. The proportion φ becomes $t-(t-10)/(t+n)-(t-10)$, giving a value of $10/(n+10)$. With $n = 10$ years, the value of φ gets fixed at 0.5.

$$(LS_2/LS_1)_t - (LS_{2,}/LS_1)_{t-1} = \varphi\left[\text{RHLS}_{t+n} - (LS_{2,}/LS_1)_{t-1}\right. \tag{31}$$

Turning to the dynamics of capital, there is the distinction between mobile and immobile situations. The CGE model of Nepal abides by the mobile situation where capital use can be shifted between activities. In this case, the extension is straightforward and requires only turning the total capital supply KS into an unknown and specifying how it develops annually. However, because this CGE model will not solve separately for each year between 1996 and 2006, but goes straight to solving the dynamic model for year $t = 2006$, that is, ten years later than the base year of 1996 (denoted by o), it is necessary to take investment accumulation summed over the 10-year period. This can be calculated as the sum of a geometric progression with the common factor derived from the annual growth of investment between t and o. The annual growth rate of investment, IGR, is imputed from eq. (32):

$$I_t = I_o(1 + \text{IGR})^t \tag{32}$$

The investment accumulation sum, IAS, after taking account of depreciations assumed at $\delta = 0.05$, is in eq. (31). The sum starts with I_o and ends with I_{t-1}, given the consideration that there is some time lag between investment spending and utilization of the newly installed capital.

$$\text{IAS}_t = I_0(1-\delta)^t + \sum_{n=0}^{n=t-1} I_o\,(1-\delta)^{t-n}(1+\text{IGR})^n \tag{33}$$

Eq. (34) specifies capital supply in year t. Nominal investment is converted into volume terms.

$$KS_t = KS_o(1-\delta)^t + \text{LAS}_t/XP_{j',t} \tag{34}$$

Box 5. Newly introduced equations.

$$LS_{1,t} + LS_{2,t} = LS_{1,t-1} + LS_{2,t-1}(1+\lambda') \tag{29}$$

$$\text{RHL}_{t+n} = \lambda_o\{(RL_{2,t}/\eta_2)/\left(RL_{1,t}/\eta_1\right\}^{\lambda} \tag{30}$$

$$(LS_2/LS_1)_t = (1-\varphi)(LS_2,/LS_1)_{o+}\varphi\text{RHL}_{t+n} \tag{31}$$

$$I_t = I_o(1+\text{IGR})^t \tag{32}$$

$$\text{IAS}_t = I_0(1-\delta)^t + \sum_{n=0}^{n=t-1} I_o(1-\delta)^{t-n}(1+\text{IGR})^n \tag{33}$$

$$KS_t = KS_o(1-\delta)^t + \text{LAS}_t/XP_{j',t} \tag{34}$$

5.4. *Simulation results of the dynamic model*

We make use of GAMS in calibrating the CGE to the updated and restructured SAM for 2006. Before proceeding with running the four policy simulations and examining their results, it is worthwhile to review the progress of the main variables between 1996 and 2006. The *GDP* is found to grow annually at 5.3%, distributed in the sectors as follows: agriculture 5.1%, industry 5.8%, and commercial and public services 5%, and 6.3%. The imputed annual growth rate for high-skill labor (3.4%) exceeds that of low-skilled labor (2.8%). The low-skilled to high-skilled wage ratio was 0.53 in 1996 and is projected to rise to 0.63 in 2006. The annual growth rate of investment is 6.4%. Changes in factor and activity composition of *GDP* have significant effects on income distribution among household groups. The restructuring scenario allows the rural landless group to gain in relative terms more than others.

The ways the policy simulations work in the static and dynamic models are the same; the differences in results lay in the changed values of parameters and in the expansion of factor supplies that is now made endogenous. Here, we shall

Table 4. Selected results from four policy simulations in the dynamic model: Percentage change of simulation results over base values 2006.

	Import liberalization by Nepal (MLN)	Export liberalization by ROW (ELR)	(MLN) + (ELR) under fixed foreign exchange rate	(MLN) + (ELR) under endogenous foreign exchange rate
Composite price SPc				
Agricultural	0.10	0.00	0.10	−2.30
Industrial	0.00	0.00	0.00	0.00
Commercial services	0.30	0.30	0.30	−1.50
Social services	−0.20	−0.30	−0.20	−2.70
Sector output, XQj				
Agriculture	1.53	0.02	−0.02	−0.03
Industry	3.47	0.21	−0.21	−0.91
Commercial services	−0.98	−0.18	0.19	−0.38
Social services	0.35	−0.17	0.17	0.05
Shifts in pay rates				
Low skill	−0.90	−1.04	−0.90	−3.58
High skill	0.69	0.55	0.69	−2.11
Rental rate of capital	1.36	1.27	1.36	−0.79
Average shifts in factor use in all sectors				
Low skill	2.43	2.42	2.42	2.33
High skill	1.66	1.78	1.67	1.56
Capital	1.58	1.73	1.59	1.46
GDP	1.64	1.50	1.63	−1.16
Income URH	1.19	1.02	1.19	−1.66
Income RRH	1.50	1.35	1.50	−1.23
Income RMH	1.87	1.76	1.87	−0.84
Income RLH, poorest	2.19	2.12	2.18	−0.58
Installed Investment I	−0.52	−0.02	−0.51	−0.26
Budget deficit GBD	19.88	12.35	19.86	23.12
Foreign capital flow FCF	2.39	1.80	2.38	12.63
CPI	−0.39	−0.29	−0.38	−2.64

Note: (a) Value of FCF is fixed exogenously to allow foreign exchange rate, FXR, to become endogenous.

limit our review of simulation results to pinpointing the differences between the static and dynamic versions, as shown in Tables 2 and 4. Taking first import liberalization by Nepal (MLN), it is observed that agriculture and industry grow more and commercial services contracts less in the dynamic as compared to the static model. The public service sector grows now by 0.35% compared to the contraction then by 0.8%. The aggregate result is that the rise in the GDP would be 1.64% in the dynamic compared to 0.58% in the static model. Imports overgrow exports, requiring an increase in foreign capital inflow of 2.4% in the dynamic, compared to a smaller rise of 0.9% in the static model. A favorable development is that due to the overall expansion in economic activities, government revenue rises at a higher rate with further decline in budget deficit by 20% in the dynamic, compared to a worsening of 22% in the static model.

Equally significant is that the results show larger magnitudes of shifts in the use of factors of production across sectors in the dynamic (ranging between 2.4% and 1.5%) compared to the static model (the range was between 1.8% and 1.6%). The greater shifts in factor use are accompanied by significant progressive income redistributions. In the static simulations, the rural richer households, ROH, gained more than rural landless households, RLH. This is reversed in the dynamic simulations. The MLN policy simulation raises the income of RLH, the poorest group, by 2.2% against an average national rise of 1.6%. Furthermore, the benefits of the next poor household group, RMH, are higher than the national average.

Results from four simulations confirm that the best results in terms of growth with redistribution are obtained in the first policy (import liberalization policy, MLN), and if the country would like to capture the benefits from the second policy (the complimentary export liberalization policy, ELR), then a sequencing of these policies may bring more favorable results than combining both at the same time. The third policy (the combined MLN + ELR) is not an attractive option in both the dynamic and static models. The fourth policy simulation of a flexible foreign exchange rate, if not accompanied by restricted foreign savings and upscaled domestic savings, has negative effects.

6. Concluding Remarks

The differences in simulation results obtained between a restructured dynamic CGE model and a neoclassical static CGE model indicate that there are promising possibilities, even for a lowest-income developing country, i.e. Nepal, for combining higher and pro-poor growth together with trade liberalization and market reforms. The whole thrust of this potential rests on the design of the restructured future economy.

In the dynamic Nepal CGE model, efficiency gains in activities are postulated via more efficient use of intermediate deliveries, both domestic and imported. The design for restructuring the distribution pattern of endowments goes through greater access of landless rural households to knowledge and skill training pertaining to agricultural and agro-based industrial activities, as these were found to be the sunshine activities in the case of Nepal. Complementary to this is the need for more incentives directed toward small-scale capital owners to invest in agriculture and agro-based industries.

When import liberalization and market reforms are simulated in the restructured dynamic CGE model, a particularly higher and pro-poor growth is obtained.

Furthermore, the following differences in other results are obtained. Budget deficit narrows down in the restructured economy. This contraction in the fiscal deficit has become possible by the higher growth of the economic activities and subsequent rise in tax revenues from higher institutional incomes and a broader tax base in the commodity market.

Endnotes

1. Installed investment is fixed investment. However, the word "fixed" may bring misunderstandings as we use the same word in the sense of fixing an exogenous value of the variable. To avoid such overlapping, we shall refer to fixed investment as installed investment or simply investment.
2. In principle, estimation of a private investment function should be econometrically tested. This is not feasible given the available data for Nepal. Under the circumstances, a Cobb–Douglas-type equation for investment demand offered a plausible solution with a profit effect and a crowding in public investment effect. Various studies suggest elasticity values for the public investment effect ranging between 0.8 and 0.4. We assume initially equal values for both elasticities $\imath_g = \imath_k = 0.5$. For more details, see Acharya (2011).
3. This is partly due to the strong growth of industry and strong input–output linkages that push the composite price of agricultural commodities upward.
4. For review of adaptation of the model to these considerations, application, and results, see Acharya (2011).
5. Taking ε'_q for the unit cost of educating labor of skill type q, ε''_q for the part of educational costs charged to the user, and ε'''_2 for foregone earnings during n years of educational upgrade from low to high skill, the total cost for skill type 2 can be abridged into $\varepsilon_2 = \varepsilon'_2 + \varepsilon''_2 + \varepsilon'''_2$. Similarly, the total cost for skill type 1 is $\varepsilon_1 = \varepsilon'_1 + \varepsilon''_1$. The equation makes use of the aggregated costs ε_2 and ε_1.

Chapter 12

Sustained Development of Agricultural Resources in a CGE Policy Model: Sudan

1. Introduction

Land degradation, deforestation, and desertification can seriously reduce the productivity of land and jeopardize economic growth. The conflict between environmental sustainability and economic growth is obvious in poorer developing countries. In general, four adverse interdependencies are commonly acknowledged. First, the inaccessibility of poor farmers to modern technical knowledge and information leads to the misuse of natural resources. Second, farm-gate prices in most developing countries are far below their world market levels. This discourages farmers' incentives for soil conservation and encourages soil depletion. Third, lack of well-defined private property rights over natural resources leads to overexploitation and degradation of these resources. Fourth, pressured by their poverty, poor people adopt short-term survival strategies and overuse land resources, thus giving environmental protection a low priority. The four interdependencies are supported by a large number of references which are summed up in Abdelgalil (2000).

There are few policy models in the literature that explore the links between economic growth and environmental conservation in the context of land use. Those focusing on agriculture include incentives for upland farmers in Indonesia for investing in soil conservation as an alternative to existing methods of cultivation that lead to considerable soil erosion, Barbier (1990). Others examined the deforesting behavior of smallholder agriculturists in rural Nepal as off-farm labor market conditions change in the context of an open access regime, Bluffstone (1995). There is also the computable general equilibrium (CGE) model for Costa Rica in which the effects of economy-wide government policies are traced to the development of agriculture and forestry, Persson and Munasinghe (1995). Some models have assumed a narrower scope in studying the environmental effects of stabilization and structural adjustment programs for Thailand: Reed (1992) and for Malawi: Cromwell and Winpenny (1993). The key conclusion drawn from a review of this literature is that the policy modeling of trade-offs between growth and conservation in the development context emphasizes the need for joint appraisals of economic incentives, property rights, population and poverty pressures, and modern farming knowledge. However, available models do not go beyond focussing on this one aspect to the exclusion of others.

This chapter focuses on the CGE modeling of the trade-off between economic growth and resource degradation as far as agricultural land use is concerned, defining agricultural activities in the broader sense to include croplands, forestry, and livestock. We take Sudan as a case study, a country very rich and diverse in land potential but equally so with ecological risks.[1] The model incorporates the joint appraisal of economic incentives, property rights, poverty pressure, and the role of modern farming knowledge in determining sustainable growth in subsectors of agriculture, forestry, and livestock, in short, the AFL sectors. The model links these AFL sectors with the non-agriculture sector in an economy-wide model that gives also due emphasis to relative prices in influencing the allocation of resources and shares other common features with CGE models.

This chapter is organized as follows. Section 2 specifies the model. Section 3 treats calibration and reflects on baseline results under alternative closures. Section 4 uses the model to appraise and combine alternative policies that reduce the trade-offs between growth and conservation. Section 5 concludes.

2. The Model

2.1. *Major features*

In introducing the model, the main features of the AFL sectors in Sudan are summed in the following. Agriculture in Sudan is commonly classified as irrigated, mechanized, and subsistence, which will be denoted by $j = 1, 2, 3$, respectively. Cultivated quantity of land for these sectors, measured in feddan, is denoted by NQ_j.[2] The product mix is different for the three sectors but not exclusively. The product of each sector is assumed to be a constant composite of all crops produced in that sector. Furthermore, the three sectors have different land tenure regimes and different sets of farming knowledge, marketing channels, and production technologies.

The irrigated land, NQ_1, producing wheat, cotton, sorghum, and groundnuts, is composed of government-owned schemes run by tenants. Tenancy renewal is automatic and the right of heirs to inherit the tenancy is recognized. There is a limited freehold. The price that producers in irrigated agriculture receive is set by the government marketing boards at a lower rate than the international market price at which the produce is exported. While this practice can have the advantage of stabilizing off-farm produce prices, it can form a disincentive to produce more in times of rising international market prices, cf. Faki *et al.* (1995).

The mechanized land, NQ_2, using mechanical traction power, produces sorghum, sunflower, sesame, and millet as the main crops and markets them freely. Land is composed of privately owned large-scale schemes mostly on leasehold basis from the state for periods between 15 and 25 years. Renewal of lease is not automatic, and farmers rate the tenancy system as insecure, cf. Ahmed and Sanders (1998).

The subsistence land, NQ_3, uses traditional methods of cultivation to produce millet, sorghum, sesame, and groundnuts as main crops, with a limited production of rain-fed cotton. All produce is freely marketed. Land is composed of small-scale family farms. Land tenure is based on customary rights and is more secure relative to that based on leasehold. Land productivity in subsistence cultivation is obstructed by land use patterns that are dominated by the need to survive. Poor subsistent farmers, in their daily struggle for survival, may often find themselves compelled by poverty to adopt cultivation practices that are harmful to the long-term sustainability of productivity.

Data on productivity, i.e. crop yield per unit of land, show that the irrigated is the highest followed by mechanized and subsistence.[3] As regards income, farmers in irrigated agriculture are a middle-income group and in mechanized agriculture are a high-income group, while subsistence farmers have the lowest income. A crucial input that determines the yield is the farming knowledge of farmers. This stands for education, training, information, and experience with modern technical packages for crops Due to extension services provided by the government, farmers in irrigated land NQ_1 have better access to education, training, and information than farmers in mechanized land, NQ_2, while the least access is in subsistence land, NQ_3.

The above features of Sudanese agriculture are manifested in the model by focussing on different factors that determine patterns of land use, productivity, and degradation in the different sectors. For example, the model emphasizes the role of prices that farmers receive for their cash crops in irrigated agriculture; the importance of land tenure security in mechanized agriculture, and the dominance of basic needs considerations in the exploitation of subsistence agriculture. Furthermore, the model elaborates on the dependence of productivity on the amount of farming knowledge farmers have, which happens to vary between the three sectors. These features suggest that the three sectors require developing different policies that address varying needs and motivations underlying three different settings.

Next, the forestry sector faces deforestation problems, which jeopardize sustainable exploitation. The driving forces behind deforestation are lack of well-defined property rights and poverty. For the most part, forestry land, NQ_4, is open access and, so, poor people cut trees and sell them as a source of income. Conversion of forestry land to agriculture is another major factor causing deforestation.

Finally, the livestock sector faces problems of overstocking of grazing land, NQ_5, the situation where animal population is in excess of grazing land carrying capacity, thus leading to land degradation. There are three main factors that determine grazing land carrying capacity. These are the size of the grazing land, its vegetation yield, and the number of grazing animals. The degradation of grazing land negatively affects both the natural growth rate of the livestock and its quality.

Land shifts between the above-stated uses are not in all directions. Extension of NQ_1 is a government decision. Documented shifts occurred mostly from forestry and livestock toward mechanized and subsistence agriculture. The relative prices for land in alternative uses are the dominant mechanism behind the shifts. After undergoing some restructuring investment costs, the transformed land is deployed to produce the average yield of its new destination. The specification of the model follows this factual stylization.

The AFL sectors and the rest of the economy, ROE, are linked via input–output relations, delivery of labor by AFL to ROE, and delivery of capital from ROE to itself and to the AFL sectors.

One important feature of the model is that practically all agricultural and forestry products of Sudan are exportable. World markets determine prices of these crops. Producers and exporters in a small player like Sudan look at these world prices as given. There can be a domestic price lower than the world price, as in the case of the irrigated sector due to government price controls, but the given world price at the macro level cannot be circumvented. There is, therefore, a reason to model domestic prices of agriculture and forestry sectors in terms of exogenous world prices. We make use of small letters $\mathrm{p}_{j,0}$ for the price of the product of sector j in the base year 0 and capital letters XP_j for the relative price index of the products of sector j to that of the irrigated sector 1, the latter being taken as a numeraire. As just mentioned, price indexes XP_j for the three agricultural subsectors, forestry and livestock products, $j = 1, 2, 3, 4, 5$, are equal to the exogenously given relative prices at the world level. In contrast, the domestic price level of the rest of the economy, $j = 6$, is endogenously determined as it includes both tradable and non-tradable. This price level is determined along the lines of computable general equilibrium (CGE) models. With respect to clearance in the financial market (savings–investment balance), the model follows the closure where the foreign exchange rate FXR is given and foreign capital flow, *FCF*, is unknown.

2.2. *Specification of the model*

The equations of the model will be described in four blocks, making use of the notations in Table 1. Two blocks deal with the AFL sectors, and the third block connects the AFL sectors with the rest of the economy, ROE. The fourth block treats national accounting balances and some additional policy equations.

Table 1. Notations.

Endogenous variables	
ASP_j	Attained degree of maximum sustainable productivity in activity j, $j = 1, \ldots, 5$
BTS_4	Biomass tree stock expressed as biomass per land unit, i.e. feddan
C_j	Total consumption delivered by sector j, $j = 1, \ldots, 6$
E_j	Exports less imports provided by sector j, $j = 1, \ldots, 6$
FCF	Foreign capital flow expressed in foreign currency
GSA	Government savings from all agriculture
I	Total value of installed investment
I_{psi}	Private demand for installed investment
I_{agr}	Total investment in the aggregated all agriculture sector
KD_6	Capital use in non-agriculture
LD_6	Labor use in non-agriculture
LVS_5	Average number of livestock unit per feddan
NP_j	Land price per unit of land in activity j, $j = 1, \ldots, 5$
NQ_j	Land quantity in cultivation by activity j. Endogenous variables apply to $j = 2, 3, 4, 5$
VGT_5	Vegetation measured in grass available in metric tons per feddan
V_j	Gross value added of sector j, $j = 1, \ldots, 6$
XP_6	Price index of products of the non-agriculture sector; relative to the price of irrigated agricultural products $j = 1$ (this latter is taken as numeraire)
X_j	Gross output by activity j, $j = 1, \ldots, 6$
YLD_j	Yield in volume per unit of land by activity j, defined as volume of applicable crop produce per feddan for $j = 1, 2, 3$ and as volume of biomass wood cutting per feddan in case of $j = 4$.
DCS_j	Degradation cost of agricultural activity j
GRN	Green GDP is GDP less the cost of natural resource degradation
TRD	Trade-off between growth and depletion of natural resources
Exogenous variables	
ep_6	Foreign export price of the non-agriculture sector denoted by $j = 6$
ANS_5	Artificial insemination in case of livestock breeding, assumed $= 0$
BTP_4	Biomass tree planting expressed as biomass per land unit, assumed $= 0$
FKN	Farming knowledge
FXR	Foreign exchange rate
I_g	Government expenditure on installed investment
ICH	Inventory change
LTS	Land tenure security

(Continued)

Table 1. (*Continued*)

MNC	Market incentives
NQ_1, NQ	Land quantity falling under irrigated croplands $j = 1$, and total land available for cultivation
$P_{j,o}XP_j$	XP_j is world price index of agricultural produce $j(1, 2, 3, 4, 5)$ relative to that of irrigated croplands $j(1)$, which is taken as numeraire. $P_{j,o}$ is price per unit of produce j in base year
ΔRFL	Exogenous variations in rainfall
T_{gj}	Transfers from government to households associated with agricultural activity j
ΔWLS	Controllable extensions of water wells
YBN_j	Total income for the population group associated with agricultural activity j that is required to meet basic needs satisfaction
Coefficients	
$a_{jj'}$	Coefficient of intermediate deliveries from sector j to sector j', $\quad j = 1, 2, 3, 4, 5$
a_{rj}	Non-competitive imports share in the output of sector j
$\beta_{4,\text{norm}}$	Sustainability norm of biomass trees in cubic meters per feddan of forestry land
β_4	Annual natural growth rate of biomass forestry under optimal conditions
β_4'	Elasticity of growth of biomass forestry in relation to attained sustainable productivity
χ_j	Calibration in function outlining attainment of sustainable productivity in activity j, $j = 1, 2, 3$
δ	Discount rate
ε_{6o}	Exports of non-agriculture as a proportion of the non-agriculture output for the benchmark year
ε_6	Export price elasticity of non-agriculture
ϕ_j	Elasticity of attaining greater sustainable productivity in activity j with respect to attaining greater farming knowledge FKN in activity j, applicable to $j = 1, 2, 3$
$\gamma_{jo}, \gamma_j, \gamma_j'$	Calibration coefficient, consumption expenditure share on sector j in the GDP, and elasticity of consumption of j with respect to relative price of j. Income elasticity is $1 - \Sigma_j \gamma_j'$
η_j	Incurred costs in the conversion of land from one use to another
ι_j	Share of investment by sector of origin j in total investment
φ_j	Cost of educating and training a farmer in activity j to acquire farming knowledge, $j = 1, 2, 3$
κ_j	Incremental capital–output ratio by activity j, $\quad j = 1, \ldots, 5$
λ_2	Elasticity of attaining greater sustainable productivity in activity j with respect to attaining greater security of land tenure in activity j, especially applicable to activity 2
ν_3	Elasticity of attaining greater sustainable productivity with respect to attaining greater satisfaction of basic needs, especially applicable to activity 3

(*Continued*)

Table 1. (*Continued*)

μ_j	Elasticity of the relative allocation of land quantities in alternative activities to their relative prices, taking as base the quantity and price of mechanized land
π_j	Growth rate of agricultural yield per feddan in j based on autonomous technical change
$\theta_{5,\text{norm}}$	Norm of vegetation per livestock unit that fosters sustainable development
$\theta_5, \theta_5', \theta_5'$	Elasticities of improved vegetation to higher rainfall, to enhanced wells, and to greater attained sustainable productivity, respectively.
ρ_j	Rental share for the land factor in the value added of activity j. $j = 1, \ldots, 5$
σ_j	Subsidy towards enhanced agricultural exports above the maximum limit as determined by potential productive capacity
τ_1	Elasticity of attaining greater sustainable productivity in relation to attaining greater market incentives, MNC, in terms of price tax reduction. Elasticity is especially applicable to activity $j = 1$.
τ_{jg}	Rate of indirect tax. In the case of agriculture this is an export levy by the state on activity j. $j = 1, \ldots, 5$, as proportion of the export price. For non-agriculture, τ_{6g} is indirect taxes as proportion of the gross output of non-agriculture, representing government revenue from the non-agriculture sector
υ_j	Proportion of sector j in total inventory change, $j = 1, \ldots, 6$. Whereby $\upsilon_6 = 1$, all others $= 0$
ϖ_5	Annual natural growth rate of livestock under optimal conditions
ϖ'_5	Elasticity of growth of livestock in relation to attained sustainable productivity in vegetation
ψ_{31}, ψ_{32},	Supplementary wages that subsistence farmers ($j = 3$) earn from work they deliver in irrigated and mechanized agriculture, expressed as proportions in the output of irrigated and mechanized agriculture
ζ_j	Reclamation cost as a proportion of foregone yield $j = 1, \ldots, 5$
Coefficients applicable solely to the non-agriculture sector	
α_{60}	Calibration in the Cobb–Douglas production function of the non-agriculture sector 6
β_6	Labor elasticity of production in the non-agriculture sector. Capital elasticity is $1 - \beta_6$
δ_6	Depreciation rate of capital in the non-agriculture sector 6
$\varepsilon_{6,o}$	Calibration in the (net) export function of the non-agriculture sector 6
ε_6	Elasticity of (net) exports with respect to output of the non-agriculture sector 6. Price elasticity is $1 - \varepsilon_6$
λ_6	Growth rate of the labor force in the non-agriculture sector 6

Notes: Index j refers to the sectors; for AFL sectors, $j = 1, 2, 3, 4, 5$ and for the non-agricultural sector, $j = 6$. Furthermore, g is used to identify variables and coefficients relating to the government.

The first block, referring to attained sustainable productivity and yield, constitutes equation sets 1–5. The first equation can be formulated generally for the AFL sectors. It postulates that an average piece of land has a sustainable productivity that can be standardized in an index ASP_j, which ranges from zero to unity, with unity representing the highest sustainable productivity possible. The sustainable productivity index reached in any actual case is determined by the nature and degree of land exploitation, which, in turn, is influenced by four conditions that include farming knowledge FKN_j, market incentives MNC_j, land tenure security LTS_j, and satisfaction of basic income needs for the poor, YBN_j.

Primary inputs of capital, labor, and intermediate inputs of fertilizers, water, seeds, etc., which correspond with an attained specific level of sustainable productivity, ASP_j, are assumed to be forthcoming and do not form a bottleneck, as will be apparent from later specifications for investment and intermediate goods deliveries. This allows us to deal more at length with the four influential factors behind attained sustainable productivity. Under the most optimal conditions for the four influential factors, the attainable sustainable productivity of a piece of land will be at its maximum level of 100%. The actually attained degree of sustainable productivity, which is always short of the maximum 100%, can be generally formulated as a production function in terms of the attained levels of the four factors, as follows:

$$ASP_j = f_j,(FKN_j,MNC_j,LTS_j,YBN_j,) \qquad j = 1, 2, 3, 4 \qquad (1)$$

Devising policies to enhance the attainment of the four factors would automatically enhance the attained sustainable productivity and lead to more realized production and income. It is proposed to specify the dependence of ASP_j on the four factors in the form of a Cobb–Douglas function. The degree of influence of each of the four factors depends on the specific agricultural sector.

The specification of eq. (1) for the AFL sectors, i.e. (1.1)–(1.5), is summarized in Box 1. A detailed description follows. Farming knowledge is the first factor. Take FKN_j to represent the proportion of farmers who have adequate farming knowledge and experience. This variable is policy controllable. The effect of attaining greater farming knowledge on raising ASP_j is captured by elasticity φ_j. Farming knowledge is highest in the irrigated sector, less in mechanized, and least in subsistence. The declining significance of the knowledge effect is reflected in the following values: $\phi_1 < \phi_2 < \phi_3$.

Market incentive, MNC_j, is the second factor. The model defines $p_{jo}XP_j$ as equilibrium prices of agricultural activity j, where p_{jo} is the unit price of activity j in the base year and XP_j is the index of relative prices expressed in terms of the price level of the irrigated product, which is taken as numeraire. All agricultural prices are exogenously given. The model assumes a competitive world, in which equilibrium prices are equal to the world prices. The market incentives of farmers are highest when farmers can obtain the equilibrium prices for their products, i.e.

$p_{jo}XP_j$. But farmers do not receive the world market price for their products since government marketing boards, which are the main purchasers of the products, withhold a price tax, to be denoted by τ_{jg}, so what they receive is $(1-\tau_{jg})p_{jo}XP_j$. It is argued that as the producer's farm-gate price approaches the expected equilibrium price, and thus the lower the price tax, τ_{jg}, the more the farmers have money and incentive to undertake soil conservation and improvement measures. The effect of greater market incentives on sustainable productivity with regard to $(1-\tau_{jg})$ is captured by the elasticity τ_i. This factor is especially relevant for irrigated agriculture so that $\tau_1 > 0$ while $\tau_2 = \tau_3 = 0$.

Land tenure security, LTS_j, is the third factor. LTS_j is defined as the ratio of the actual lease period to the relatively secure one, which is generally viewed to be 40 years. In the absence of land tenure security, farmers adopt short-term cultivation practices and neglect fallow periods, crop rotation, soil conservation, and improvements. All of these exhaust and degrade the land. A greater LTS_j leads to a greater ASP_h, and this effect is captured by elasticity λ_j. The LTS factor is especially relevant in mechanized agriculture where the actual lease term is between 15 and 25 years; hence, we focus on $\lambda_2 > 0$, while $\lambda_1 = \lambda_3 = 0$.

Satisfaction of basic needs is the fourth factor. If poor farmers earn enough to satisfy their basic needs, then they are motivated to exploit the land in more productive ways. The gap between what they earn (their value added from the land they cultivate, V_3, plus supplementary wages they receive for work they deliver in irrigated and mechanized agriculture, expressed as $\psi_{31}X_1$ and $\psi_{32}X_2$) and the income they need to fulfill their basic needs (denoted by YBN_j and which is externally normed) is crucial for enhancing productive efforts. It is proposed to simulate the positive effect of a narrowing of the income gap on the attained sustainable productivity via elasticity ν_i. This factor is particularly valid for poor farmers, who are primarily in the subsistence sector[4] so that $\nu_3 > 0$, while for other sectors, $\nu_j = 0$.

The above-stylized facts for irrigated, mechanized, and subsistence agriculture result in the specifications of ASP_j for the three sectors as in eqs. (1.1), (1.2), and (1.3). As stated earlier,the equations assume Cobb–Douglas specifications so that $\phi_1 + \tau_1 = 1, \phi_2 + \lambda_2 = 1$, and $\phi_3 + \nu_3 = 1$.

Specification of eq. (1.4) for biomass forestry ($j = 4$) requires elaboration. The attained sustainable productivity index, ASP_4, is expressed as the proportion of last year's actual stock of biomass trees in cubic meters per feddan of forestry land, $BTS_{4,t-1}$, to the technical norm $\beta_{4,\text{norm}}$ for sustainable development. As ASP_4 reaches the value of 1, forestry recovers back to its optimal level of sustainable productivity, for example, $ASP_4 = BTS_4/\beta_{4,\text{norm}}$. Specification of eq. (1.5) for the livestock sector is similar to that of forestry. The attained sustainable productivity index for livestock ASP_5 is the ratio of the first term representing last year's actual vegetation per livestock unit, measured in grass available in metric tons per feddan $VGT_{5,t-1}$ and divided by the average number of livestock unit per feddan, $LVS_{5,t-1}$, to the second term representing a normed vegetation per livestock unit for sustained development, $\theta_{5,\text{norm}}$, which is technically given by livestock experts. Attaining a value of $ASP_5 = 1$ is an ideal and optimal state.

Specifications of BTS_4, VGT_5, and LVS_5 are done in separate equations. BTS_4, which is the actual biomass trees in any one year, is specified in eq. (2) as the level of the previous year plus a natural growth based on an autonomous growth rate β_4, as well as its responsive accommodation to progress made in the sustainable productivity index $ASP_4/ASP_{4,0}$ via elasticity β_4', plus voluntary biomass tree planting per feddan, BTP_4, and less tree wood cutting per feddan, which is equivalent to the produce yield volume of the forestry activity, YLD_4. The absence of conservation knowledge and a private property rights system in forestry has often resulted in $BTP_4 = 0$, while wood cutting, YLD_4, that represents the output of the sector, has become a prosperous activity but with possibly negative environmental consequences. The three variables of BTS_4, BTP_4, and YLD_4, are expressed in biomass trees per unit of land, i.e. per feddan.

Vegetation state, VGT_5, is specified in eq. (3). Its annual improvement is influenced by exogenous variations in rainfall ΔRFL and by the controllable extension of water wells, ΔWLS, via appropriate elasticities θ_5 and θ_5'. The vegetation level is, as a whole, dependent on the change in the attained sustainable productivity index $(ASP_5/ASP_{5,0})$ via elasticity θ_5''. The constant economies of scale inherent in the Cobb–Douglas function require that $\theta_5 + \theta_5' + \theta_5'' = 1$.

The current livestock per feddan, LVS_5, is determined in eq. (4) by the previous livestock per feddan plus an autonomous net growth rate, ϖ_5, as well as its responsive accommodation to progress made in the sustainable productivity index $ASP_5/ASP_{5,0}$ via elasticity ϖ_5', plus artificial insemination, ANS_5, that remained at zero in the past, less average livestock slaughter per feddan, YLD_5, that represents the output of the livestock sector in physical terms.

Attention can be turned now to equation set 5 which determines the annual physical yield or volume of the produce per unit of land of activity j, YLD_j. Eq. (5) is detailed for each of the three agricultural activities as follows. Current yield is the product of the yield of the previous year and an annual growth rate, π_j, that follows improvements in production technologies that are partially exogenous but that are also dependent on the attained sustainable productivity. In this equation, the attained sustainable productivity index, ASP_j, is the accommodating variable that can be controlled policy-wise to influence the growth of the yield. Furthermore, the realization of any produce requires current and fixed inputs, such as intermediate deliveries and investment. The two inputs will be incorporated in related equations for agriculture that assume Leontief and Harrod–Domar technologies, respectively.

The actual yields in physical terms per feddan in the cases of forestry (i.e. wood cutting) and livestock (livestock slaughtered) are determined by a combination of technical, market, behavioral, and policy considerations, giving eqs. (5.4) and (5.5). The technical consideration lies in the fact that the yield per feddan in physical terms, whether it is wood cutting or livestock slaughter, Yd, in any current year needs to be standardized in terms of its equivalent quality in relation to the base year. This is done by adjusting the physical yield to the variation in the sustainable productivity index $ASP_j/ASP_{j,0}$. The market considerations lie in converting the adjusted physical yield into revenue terms. This is done by multiplying the adjusted physical yields by the produce price for the base year $p_{j,0}$, the world relative price index specific to the products of the respective activity XP_j, and their respective cultivated land quantities NQ_j. For a small country like Sudan, the world relative prices of AFL commodities are exogenously given, relative to the irrigated sector that serves as numeraire. The behavioral consideration lies in the urge of forestry and grazing households to engage respectively in wood cutting and livestock slaughter and sell these products up to the point at which they can earn a desirable income level that more or less satisfies the basic needs of their growing population. This level is fixed exogenously at YBN_j, as was proposed for the agricultural population. It can also be expressed in a simplified form as the previously attained income of the social group plus an exogenously stipulated annual addition. We shall keep to the general formulation of YBN_j, without further specification.

Finally, policy considerations enter if the government would allocate transfers and/or provisions in kind, denoted by T_{gj}, to the populations associated with forestry and livestock activities such that their gaps between required income and earned incomes are reduced. Poor people, in desperation to secure basic life needs, may be forced to destroy the environment. Therefore, if the government can help them through a transfer payment to partially close their poverty gap, then this may preserve the environment.[5]

Box 1. Attained sustainable productivity and yield in agriculture, forestry, and livestock activities.

Farming activities

$$ASP_1 = \chi_1(FKN_{1,t-1})^{\phi 1}(1 - \tau_{1g})^{\tau 1} \tag{1.1}$$

$$ASP_2 = \chi_2(FKN_{2,t-1})^{\phi 2}(LTS_{2,t-1})^{\lambda 2} \tag{1.2}$$

$$ASP_3 = \chi_3(FKN_{3,t-1})^{\phi 3}\{(V_3 + \psi_{31}X_1 + \psi_{32}X_2 + T_{g3})/YBN_3\}^{\nu 3} \tag{1.3}$$

Forestry and livestock

$$ASP_4 = BTS_{4,t-1}/\beta_{4,\text{norm}} \tag{1.4}$$

$$ASP_5 = (VGT_{5,t-1}/LVS_{5,t-1})/\theta_{5,\text{norm}} \tag{1.5}$$

$$BTS_4 = BTS_{4,t-1}(1 + \beta_4)(ASP_4/ASP_{4,0})^{\beta' 4} + BTP_4 - YLD_4;\quad BTP_4 = 0 \tag{2}$$

$$VGT_5 = VGT_{5,t-1}(\Delta RFL_5)^{\theta 5}(\Delta WLS_5)^{\theta' 5}(ASP_5/ASP_{5,0})^{\theta'' 5} \quad (3)$$

$$LVS_5 = LVS_{5,t-1}(1+\varpi_5)(ASP_5/ASP_{5,0})^{\varpi' 5} + ANS_5 - YLD_5 \; ANS_5 = 0 \quad (4)$$

Yield in the farming activities

$$YLD_j = YLD_{j,t-1}(1+\pi_j)ASP_j \qquad j = 1, 2, 3 \qquad (5.1, 5.2, 5.3)$$

Forestry and livestock

$$[p_{j,0}XP_j.YLD_j(ASP_j/ASP_{j,0})]NQ_j + T_{gj} = YBN_j \qquad j = 4, 5 \qquad (5.4, 5.5)$$

The second block, in Box 2, referring to eqs. (6)–(9), is to be written for all five land use activities. Eq. (6) gives the value per feddan for activity j, NP_j, as the rental share of the land factor in the yield per feddan, ρ_j, valued at world prices $p_{j0}XP_j$ and discounted with a constant discount rate δ.

Eq. (7) is a set of four equations. They specify the mechanism behind the distribution of types of land other than the predetermined irrigated land. The allocation is fully governed by market forces. Changes in land allocation between type j and mechanized agriculture (sector 2) from a base year are formulated as a function of relative changes in last year's land value as compared to the base year. Hence, μ_j is the land-to-value elasticity of substitution between sector $j = 2$ (mechanized land) and sectors $j = 3, 4, 5$. Practically speaking, land conversions proceeded in the past from forestry to subsistence and mechanized agriculture, but mostly to the latter, making it logical to take land values of mechanized agriculture as the numeraire for the purpose of clearance of the land market. To account for incurred costs η_j in the conversion of land i from one use to another and for the changing states of sustainable productivity ASP_j of the concerned land j, the term $\eta_j ASP_j$ is deducted from the value of the concerned land j as per the last year and the base year. Furthermore, equation set 7 contains the accounting identity stating the fixed sum of land for all sectors, *NQ*.

Eq. (8) gives the value of agricultural output, X_j, of activity j as the price of the product in the base year $p_{j,o}$ weighted by the relative price index for the current year XP_j, the numeraire being the price of the produce of irrigated agriculture. The price expression is then multiplied by both the actual yield per feddan YLD_j and the quantity of land under cultivation in that sector NQ_j.

Eq. (9) specifies the investment goods required by destination activity and adds these to give total investment in the aggregated agriculture sector, I_{agr}. The equation relates investment requirements in each AFL activity to production growth of the activity via sector incremental capital–output ratios, denoted by κ_j. Now that the output expansions of the land resource sectors are known from eqs. (1) to (6), the necessary investments that are complementary for these expansions are specified and summed in eq. (9).

Box 2. Other equations on agriculture, forestry, and livestock activities.

Value per unit of land

$$NP_j = (\rho_j p_{j0}.XP_j.YLD_j)/\delta \qquad j = 1, \ldots, 5 \qquad (6)$$

Distribution of land on agricultural activities

$$NQ_{j'}/NQ_j = (NQ_{j',o}/NQ_{j,o})[(NP_{j',t-1} - \eta_{j'}ASP_{j',t-1})$$
$$(NPj, o)/(NP_{j',o} - \eta_{j'}ASP_{j',0})(NPj, t-1)]^{\mu j} \quad j =, 3, 4, 5 \qquad (7.3, 7.4, 7.5)$$

$$NQ = NQ_1 + NQ_2 + NQ_3 + NQ_4 + NQ_5 \qquad (7)$$

Value of gross output by agricultural activity

$$X_j = p_{j,o}.XP_j.YLD_j NQ_j \qquad h = 1, \ldots, 5 \qquad (8)$$

Investment requirements of all agriculture

$$(I_{\text{agr,t}} + I_{\text{agr,t-1}})/2 = \Sigma_j \kappa_j (X_j - X_{j,t-1}) \qquad (9)$$

The third block of equations, in Box 3, consists of equations that specify the non-agriculture sector, denoted by $j = 6$, and connects it to the agriculture sectors $j = 1, \ldots, 5$ within an interindustry framework. Eqs. (10), (11), and (12) present a simplified modeling of the output of the non-agriculture sector. In eq. (10), output quantity follows a Cobb–Douglas production function, with labor and capital as factors of production. Eq. (11) specifies the growth of labor supply. Eq. (12) specifies the growth of capital formation. The annual non-agriculture investment added to the capital stock of non-agriculture is total investment less investment destined for agriculture.

Eq. (13) is written for agriculture and non-agriculture. Value added is obtained by deducting three items from the output: domestic intermediate input deliveries, imported intermediate deliveries, and indirect taxes. Domestic intermediate deliveries are quantity-based input–output coefficients, $\alpha_{j'j}$, that are adjusted to relative price indices of receiving and delivering sectors $XP_{j'}/XP_j$. Shares of non-competitive imports are α_{rj}, and rates of indirect taxes are τ_{jg}.

Eq. (14) specifies demand for consumption goods, C_j. These are based on Cobb–Douglas-like consumption demand functions in terms of the gross domestic product $\Sigma_j V_j$ and relative price indexes XP_j.

Eq. (15) specifies a behavioral function for private investment I_{psi}. One determining factor is the profit rate. Because this is not generated by the model, the price index of non-agriculture is used as a proxy. A higher price raises cost and can discourage investment, but the higher price can also be an incentive for greater investment. In Sudan, the larger part of the investment is imported and is thus not negatively affected by the domestic price. The net result is a positive price effect that can be represented by elasticity ι_p. The other factor is the crowding in the effect of public investment leading to more private investment via elasticity ι_g. With given values of the two elasticities, ι_o is obtained as the calibration coefficient.[6]

Eq. (16) defines installed investment,[7] I, as the sum of private investment I_{psi} and government investment I_g.

Eq. (17) specifies foreign trade at the sector level. As stated earlier, it is assumed that the agricultural sectors are able to export their products as long as the prices offered are equal to the international prices of these products. We assume thus that net exports E_j for sectors $j = 1, \ldots, 5$ are endogenous. The export–import balance for the non-agriculture sector, $j = 6$, is formulated such that the quantity of net exports of the sector is dependent on the output quantity of the sector (the first term), and the relative price of the sector to the given world price, and the export price elasticity ε_6 (the second term).

Eq. (18) specifies the positions of government revenue and spending. Government, by imposing price levies on irrigated agriculture, appropriates the difference between the world price for the irrigated product and that which it offers to farmers. The revenue that the government appropriates in this way is used to finance the following: (a) several spending items relating to agriculture, i.e. cost of policies relating to transfers to poor populations in subsistence cultivation and forestry $\sum_j T_{gj}$ and cost of policies for education and training of farmers, $\sum_j \varphi_j \Delta FKN_j$, and there is a subsidy to farmers if exportable agricultural surplus exceeds an upper limit $\sum_j \sigma_j(E_j - E_{j,\max})$.[8] (b) Government agricultural savings, *GSA*, is used for financing government consumption and investment in the whole economy. In Sudan, the incidence of total government revenue has been for many years roughly evenly split between agriculture and non-agriculture. The contribution of non-agriculture to government revenue and spending is specified as the indirect tax on output, $\tau_{6g} X_6$, on the right-hand side.

Box 3. Equations relating to non-agriculture and the whole economy.

Output of the non-agriculture sector

$$X_6/XP_6 = \{1/(1 - \Sigma_j \alpha_{j'6} - \alpha_{r6} - \tau_{6g})\} \left[\alpha_{6o} LD_6^{\beta 6} KD_6^{(1-\beta 6)}\right] \quad (10)$$

$$LD_{6,t} = LD_{6,t-1}(1 + \lambda_6) \quad (11)$$

$$KD_{6,t} = (1 - \delta_6) KD_{6,t-1} + (I - I_A) \quad (12)$$

Whole economy: value added, consumption, investment, foreign trade, and government

$$V_j = (1 - \Sigma_j \alpha_{j'j} XP_{j'}/XP_j) X_j - \alpha_{rj} X_j - \tau_{jg} X_j \qquad j = 1, \ldots, 6 \quad (13)$$

$$C_j = \gamma_{jo}(XP_j)^{\gamma' j} (\gamma_j \Sigma_j V_j)^{1 - \Sigma_j \gamma' j} \qquad j = 1, \ldots, 6 \quad (14)$$

$$I_{\text{psi}} = \iota_o (XP_{\text{non-agriculture}})^{\iota p} (I_g)^{\iota g} \quad (15)$$

$$I = I_{\text{psi}} + I_g \quad (16)$$

$$E_6/XP_6 = (\varepsilon_{6,o} X_6/XP_6)(XP_6/ep_6)^{\varepsilon 6} \quad (17)$$

$$\Sigma_j(\tau_{jg}.p_j XP_j \cdot YLD_j \cdot NQ_j) - \Sigma_j T_{gj} - \Sigma_j \phi_j \Delta FKN$$
$$- \Sigma_j \sigma_j (E_j - E_{j,\max}) + GSA = \tau_{6g} X_6 \quad (18)$$

The fourth block, in Box 4, displays the three national accounting balances and a few additional equations that are of interest for policy making and resource management. In eq. (19), the sector product balances by delivering sector state that total supply equals total demand of goods by the delivering sector j. The supply is the output of the sector. The demand comprises intermediate deliveries adjusted to the price indices of the receiving and delivering sector, consumption, investment, and net exports. The installed investment is specified by delivering sector. Since only the non-agriculture sector delivers capital goods, we have $\iota_6 = 1$, and $\iota_j = 0$ for the other sectors.

The equalization of supply and demand in the product markets runs differently for the agricultural sectors and for non-agriculture. The supply of agricultural sectors, X_j for $j = 1, 2, 3, 4, 5$ is already determined from the agricultural blocks in Boxes 1 and 2. The supply of non-agriculture goods, X_6, is solved from eqs. (10), (11), (12) in Box 3. On the demand side, the intermediate deliveries, consumption, and investment, along with net exports of non-agriculture, are all solved for and can be substituted in eq. (19). The result of the above discussion is that the six j balances are left with only the following adjuster variables to be determined: net exports of the five agricultural activities E_j for $j = 1$–5 and the price level of non-agriculture, XP_6, which is expressed in terms of the numeraire (i.e. the given prices of the irrigated activity products).

Looking for adjusters in the agricultural product balances, these can be only net exports E_j, which were specified earlier as endogenous. Because they are offered and traded at given exogenous international prices and since the size of the country's exports in the total world imports is marginal, it is very realistic to take E_j for the AFL sectors as endogenous. This makes net exports the natural adjusters in the AFL market balances.

In case of the product balance of non-agriculture, the natural adjuster is its output price XP_6. Inventory change, *IHC*, is incorporated in eq. (19) but has a subordinate role. It is insignificant in agriculture and mostly at the zero level so that all inventory change occurs in non-agriculture making $\upsilon_6 = 1$. The aggregate level of *IHC* is fixed at its level for the benchmark year, implying that its relative significance diminishes as the solutions of the model show economic growth for the coming years.

Eq. (20), the savings–investment balance, states the equality between the supply of financial funding (private savings, government savings, and foreign savings) and demand, consisting of investment and inventory changes. Since the foreign exchange rate *FXR* is fixed, the adjuster in this financial market balance is foreign savings, i.e. foreign capital flow *FCF*, expressed in foreign currency.

The model, with its 20 sets of equations, is mathematically complete at this point. When the accounting balances of sector product balances and savings–investment balances are substituted in each other, they automatically give the foreign payments balance of eq. (A1). This states the equality of foreign trade (exports less imports, or net exports $\Sigma_j E_j$ plus non-competitive imports $\Sigma_j \alpha_{rj} X_j$) to foreign capital inflow, FXR. *FCF*.[9] This equation is placed outside the model as it is an implied equation, generally highlighted by Walras's rule. The model of 20 sets of equations counts in total 54 single equations. The model counts an equal number of 54 endogenous variables. There are 28 endogenous variables that relate directly to the five AFL sectors (ASP_j, YLD_j, NP_j, X_j, four NQ_j variables relating to sectors 2,3,4,5, and four variables of BTS_4, VGT_5, LVS_5, and required investment of all agriculture I_{agr}). Furthermore, there are the remaining 26 endogenous variables that are directly or indirectly related to the whole economy consisting of 3 sets of variables in $j = 6$ sectors (they include V_j, C_j, and E_j) and 8 individual variables of output and labor and capital use in non-agriculture, X_6, LD_6 and KD_6, government savings, *GSA*, private installed investment, I_{psi}, total installed investment I, and the two adjuster variables of the output price of non-agriculture XP_6, and foreign capital flow *FCF*.

Counted otherwise, the model consists of 20 sets of endogenous variables derivable from 20 equation sets. It is important to underline that the formulation of the model is in two parts: (a) AFL sectors, consisting of eqs. (1)–(9), with its 9 sets of endogenous variables, and (b) the rest of the economy with the remaining

11 equation sets, eqs. (10)–(20), which contains 11 sets of endogenous variables. This divisional structure contributes substantially to the modeling of a simplified structure. Equations (1)–(9) is an autonomous system and is solved without access to the equations or variables of the rest of the economy part. But the solution for the rest of the economy part requires the prior solutions for the AFL sectors.

Box 4. National accounting balances and additional equations.

Product market balances

$$X_j = \Sigma_j(\alpha_{jj'}XP_j/XP_{j'})X_{j'} + C_j + \iota_j I + \upsilon_j ICH + E_j \quad j = 1, \ldots, 6 \quad (19)$$

Financial market balance (savings investment balance)

$$\Sigma_j(V_j - C_j) + GSA + FXR \cdot FCF = I + ICH \quad (20)$$

Foreign payments balance

$$\Sigma_j E_j + \Sigma_j \alpha_{rj} X_j = FXR \cdot FCF \quad (A1)$$

Effects of land degradation

$$DCS_i = \zeta_i(p_i XP_i \rho_i YLD_i)(1 - ASP_i)NQ_i \quad i = 1, \ldots, 5 \quad (A2)$$

Green GDP

$$GRN = \Sigma_j V_j - \Sigma_i DCS_i \quad (A3)$$

Trade-off economic growth and land degradation

$$TRD = \Delta\Sigma_j V_j / \Delta\Sigma_I DCS_i \quad (A4)$$

There are three additional equations meant to emphasize some policy considerations and can be seen as a linked tail to the model. Eq. (A2) underscores the effects of environmental degradation by estimating the degradation cost DCS_j to be incurred so as to reclaim foregone sustainable productivity, this being defined in relation to the desirable value of $ASP_j = 1$. Reclamation cost per feddan has been generally estimated for the average piece of land of average sustainable productivity at about 10% of the foregone yield per feddan as a result of resource degradation, i.e. $\zeta_h = 0.1$. Foregone yield per feddan is the lost rental product of the land factor $\rho_j YLD_j$ valued at the world price of the produced commodity $p_j XP_j$; the degree of loss being dependent on degradation level $(1 - ASP_j)$. If ASP_j is at its ideal level of 1, then the reclamation cost becomes zero. The degradation loss per feddan is then multiplied by NQ_j to give total degradation loss.[10]

The indicator of land degradation costs, $\Sigma_j DCS_j$, is useful in highlighting the environmental loss of economic growth since it gives the welfare loss due to natural resources' misuse and can tell how simulated agricultural policies will reduce the cost of environmental degradation. A supplementary indicator in eq. (A3) is *GRN*, for the green *GDP*, obtained by deducting degradation cost from *GDP*. Alternatively, eq. (A4) computes the ratio of the change in GDP to the ratio of change in $\Sigma_j DCS_j$, which gives a relative measure of the trade-off between growth and depletion, denoted by *TRD*, or broadly interpreted it would give the created income per added unit of degradation. Results from the absolute measure, i.e. GRN, and the relative measure, i.e. the trade-off ratio, do not necessarily point in the same direction.

The performance of degradation indicator DCS_j is decomposable into three elements: changes in yield per feddan YLD_j, changes in sustainable productivity ASP_j, and changes in the quantity of land exploited, NQ_j, although it is clear from the model that all three components are interrelated. Higher ASP_j enhances YLD_j and results in shifting land from more to less costly degrading sectors.

3. Estimation and Baseline Forecasts

The base year of the model is 1990. A Social Accounting Matrix (SAM) of Sudan for 1990, constructed in the context of the model, provided the required data for most variables and coefficient estimates.

The crop mix plays an important part in this study. Crop data were aggregated following the product mix per sector to give main variables by sectors. This applies to the crucial variables of land cultivated, land productivity, agricultural production, land values, and the sectoral time series of price indices.[11] Additional available data for other main variables allowed a calibration for 1990–1995, which was used to estimate missing values of some parameters. Various studies undertaken by the Ministry of Agriculture in Sudan allowed the estimation of elasticities relating to the sustainable productivity indices. Once the calibration was done, the entire model was solved annually for 10 years over the period 1991–2000. In these solutions, the exogenous variables were set to grow at their past growth of 1980–1990.[12] Our database and projections, which relate to the period 1990–2000, were conditioned by the time in which the study was implemented. An update of the database to 2010 is now feasible. Such a recommendable update can be helpful in giving further support to our findings.

The model is solved to reproduce the observed values in the year 1990 and solutions for the subsequent 10 years. Within the product markets, we make use of two price closure scenarios for the AFL sectors: the situation under unchanging relative prices (U), and the situation under exogenously changing relative prices, that is, varying relative prices (V), as projected from world market tendencies. It is likely that the actual relative prices in the future may be somewhere between the two scenarios. Though, because the numerical differences in relative prices between the two scenarios happen to be minor, the impact is minimal.[13] Even though the outcomes are not significantly different, comparing the growth and environmental results under unchanging and changing relative prices can give insight into the relevant aspects of world market price tendencies, as to whether these tendencies would favor growth or the environment. Results are shown in Table 2 for the closure with unchanging relative prices (U) in the 5th column and for changing/varying relative prices (V) in the 6th column.[14]

We consider first the (U) closure. In the irrigated sector, since neither sustainable productivity, ASP_1, nor irrigated land, NQ_1, undergoes changes, other variables of the irrigated sector are shown to grow annually at 4.9%, being fully dependent on the same projected growth of the yield, YLD_1. Results show that the mechanized and subsistence sectors will increase their land at the cost of forestry and livestock due to the relatively higher value of land in agriculture, but that relatively more land will shift to subsistence than mechanized. This is because as the income of subsistence farmers grows (indicated by $Y_{3,\text{poor}}$ in the table), their cultivation practices improve slightly and their sustainable productivity, ASP_3, is raised, while the mechanized sector undergoes no change in ASP_2, thus allowing the subsistence yield, YLD_3, to grow faster than the mechanized, ASP_2, making possible a greater appreciation of the value of land for subsistence, NP_3, than mechanized, NP_2. Growth of production and income will thus be higher in subsistence than mechanized, but growth in degradation costs is about the same, indicating less degradation per unit of growth in subsistence compared with mechanized. Taking all of agriculture together, total agricultural output, $\Sigma_{i=1}^{3} X_i$, and total agricultural value added, $\Sigma_{i=1}^{3} V_i$, grow annually by 6.0%, while agricultural degradation loss, $\Sigma_{i=1}^{3} D_i$, grows slightly faster at 6.3%.

Regarding the forestry sector, continued wood cutting under the pressure of meeting basic needs compels sustainable productivity ASP_4 to fall annually by 2.9%, leading to a greater fall in stock of trees biomass BTS_4 by 3.3%. There is a similar fall in land value, NP_4, triggering the shift of forestry land to agriculture that was already noted above. Forestry production and income grow annually at 5.1%, while degradation costs grow annually at a high level of 8.3%. Regarding livestock sector, both livestock, LVS_5, and vegetation yield, VGT_5, fall, leading to a deterioration in sustainable productivity, ASP_5, land value, NP_5, hardly changes, but some grazing land, NQ_5, nevertheless shifts to agriculture. Production and income grow annually at 1.1%, with degradation costs growing at 4.6%.

In the non-agriculture sector, output, X_6, and income, Y_6, grow annually by about 5.1% and the price index, XP_6, by 2.3%. For the economy as a whole, investment I and GDP grow annually by 5.2%.

We consider now the model solutions with changing/varying relative prices, the (V) closure. This can be argued to be the more complete closure since it captures substitution effects due to both internal and external stimuli and thus gives a more comprehensive treatment of land reallocation between the sectors. This closure incorporates future changes in relative prices in reallocating land. The observed post-benchmark trends of world prices for 1990–2000 appear to favor forestry and livestock relative to mechanized and subsistence. This period is characterized by relative world prices that are environment friendly. The result for Sudan is a moderation in the shift of land away from forestry and livestock to mechanized and subsistence when compared with the solutions under unchanging prices (U). The outcome is a lesser degradation, but, also, a lower growth. The improved environment is demonstrated to occur at the cost of less economic growth.

In agriculture, the irrigated sector remains unaffected. Performance of the mechanized improves and that of subsistence worsens, reflecting the slight positive bias of world prices to mechanized over subsistence. The reduced performance in subsistence reduces incomes and drives down sustainable productivity, land yield, and land value, making it less attractive for subsistence to attract more land. Results for other variables are about the same for both closures.

Although degradation increases at a higher rate than income, deducting degradation costs from the GDP gives positive and increasing values of what was termed "green GDP". This is demonstrated in Table 3. For the whole economy, GDP and degradation costs grow at slightly lower rates in the changing compared to the unchanging price regime. The reduction in GDP growth is 0.042% p.a. (i.e. 5.181–5.139), while the reduction in degradation growth is 0.001% p.a. (i.e. 6.284–6.283). As was stated above, the results show that the world pattern of changing relative prices at the turn of the century can be considered environmentally friendly, this being at the cost of a reduction in *GDP* growth. In relative terms, the loss in economic growth can be assessed to be more significant in magnitude than the gain in environment, if equal weights are assigned to a percentage change in growth and environment.

Several conclusions can be drawn. First, the model predicts land shifts from forestry and livestock uses to mechanized and subsistence because of land values under cultivation rising at a greater rate, caused by relatively higher sustainable productivities, APS_i, and, to a lesser extent, land yields, YLD_i, in agriculture.

Second, production and income would increase but so will degradation costs as land transfers from forestry and livestock to mechanized and subsistence agriculture, the latter being more resources depleting sectors. The average degradation cost per unit of land in mechanized and subsistence agriculture, the sectors to which land is reallocated, exceeds that of the forestry and livestock sectors, the sectors from which land is shifted. In the base year, the average degradation cost per unit of land was Ls 112.6 for mechanized, Ls 13.1 for subsistence, Ls 2.1 for forestry, and Ls 2.2 for livestock. In spite of the association of higher growth with higher degradation costs, there is a net increase in the green *GDP* when degradation costs are deducted from income, as shown in Table 3. This tendency is substantiated by

Table 2. Annual growth rates of variables in base run projections, under unchanging and changing relative prices, 1990–2000(% p.a.).

Symbol	Description	Measurement	Base year 1990	Unchanging Relative prices (U)	Changing Relative Prices (V)
ASP_1	Sustainable productivity	Index	0.700	0.000	0.000
YLD_1	Yield	Metric Ton	0.625	4.900	4.900
NP_1	Land value	LS	56241	4.900	4.900
NQ_1	Cultivated land	M. Feddan	5.0	0.000	0.000
V_1	GDP irrigated	M.LS	23647	4.900	4.900
DCS_1	Degradation costs	M.LS	843	4.900	4.900
Mechanized Agriculture					
ASP_2	Sustainable productivity	Index	0.463	0.000	0.000
YLD_2	Yield	Metric Ton	0.220	4.900	4.900
NP_2	Land Value	LS	20971	4.900	4.199
NQ_2	Cultivated land	M. Feddan	7.0	1.875	1.887
V_2	GDP mechanized	M. LS	11781	6.867	6.880
DCS_2	Degradation costs	M. LS	788	6.867	6.880
Subsistence Agriculture					
ASP_3	Sustainable productivity	Index	0.393	0.788	0.757
YLD_3	Yield	Metric Ton	0.095	5.727	5.694
NP_3	Land value	LS	2156	5.727	4.887
NQ_3	Cultivated land	M. Feddan	9.0	2.549	2.446
V_3	GDP subsistence	M. LS	5408	8.422	8.280
$Y_{3,\text{poor}}(a)$	Income poor	M. LS	13690	6.624	6.560
DCS_3	Degradation costs	M. LS	117	7.834	7.717
Forestry					
ASP_4	Sustainable productivity	Index	0.580	−2.912	−2.913
BTS_4	Stock/Feddan	Cubic meters	37.1	−3.320	−3.321
YLD_4	Output/Feddan	Cubic meters	0.104	5.271	5.271
NP_4	Land value	LS	1765	−3.320	−3.782
NQ_4	Woodland	M. Feddan	152	−0.169	−0.163
V_4	GDP forestry	M. LS	13104	5.093	5.099
DCS_4	Degradation costs	M. LS	314	8.322	8.329
Livestock					
ASP_5	Sustainable Productivity	Index	0.82	−0.890	−0.891
LVS_5	Stock/Feddan	LS	0.293	−1.258	−1.257
VGT_5	Vegetation/Feddan	Metric Ton	1.067	−0.713	−0.713
YLD_5	Output/Feddan	Livestock	0.033	1.237	1.232
NP_5	Land Value	LS	2056	0.046	0.046
NQ_5	Grazing land	M. Feddan	77	−0.176	−0.171
V_5	GDP livestock	M. LS	7762	1.060	1.059
DCS_5	Degradation costs	M. LS	169	4.615	4.611
Non-agriculture and whole economy					
E_6	Net exports	M. LS	−10831	8.187	8.200
XP_6	Price index	Index	1.0	2.345	7.161
X_6	Output	M. LS	196508	5.131	5.077
Y_6	GDP non-agriculture	M. LS	130955	5.131	5.077
I	Investment	M. LS	22631	5.116	5.003
$\Sigma_i V_i$	GDP all sectors	M. LS	192660	5.181	5.139
$\Sigma_i DCS_i$	Degradation costs all	M. LS	2234	6.284	6.283

Note: (a) As was defined in eq. (1.3), the income of subsistence farmers is $Y_{3,\text{poor}} = V_3 + \psi_{31} X_1 + \psi_{32} X_2 + T_{g3}$. M. = Million, LS = Sudanese Pound.

Table 3. Green *GDP* and degradation loss by sector of activity under unchanging (U) and changing varying relative prices (V), 1990–2000. Values are measured in million Sudanese pounds (LS).

	Green *GDP*			Degradation costs/*GDP*		
Sector	1990 Base value	2000 Unchanging prices %Δ p.a. (U)	2000 Changing prices % Δ p.a. (V).	1990 Base	2000 Unchanging prices % Δ p.a. (U)	2000 Changing prices % Δ p.a. (V)
Irrigated	22804.3	4.900	4.900	0.036	0.000	0.000
Mechanized	10993.4	6.867	6.880	0.067	0.000	0.000
Subsistence	5291.1	8.435	8.292	0.022	−0.542	−0.520
Forestry	12789.1	5.001	5.007	0.024	3.072	3.073
Livestock	7592.5	0.966	0.965	0.022	3.518	3.515
Economy	190426.0	5.167	5.125	0.012	1.049	1.088

empirical evidence from Sudan and other developing countries at a similar stage of economic development.

Third, the model shows slightly lower growth in sector output coupled with lower degradation costs under changing versus unchanging relative prices. Past trends in relative prices at the world level thus favor sustainable productivity in land use at the cost of more economic growth in Sudan. However, the net effect, if this can be represented by the green *GDP*, i.e. *GRN*, or by *TRD*, is less favorable under the changing than under the unchanging relative price.

4. Policy Simulations: Benefits and Costs

The economy-wide model with changing relative prices is used to appraise the following policies:

(i) educating and training of farmers in the three agricultural sectors (human capital),
(ii) reducing government tax on the irrigated sector (price incentives),
(iii) defining property rights in mechanized and forestry sectors (property rights security),
(iv) making transfers to the poor population in subsistence and forestry sectors (basic needs).

Each policy has costs and benefits. The policy of human capital involves costs of educating and training farmers. The price incentives policy is a tax reduction that diminishes government savings. The policy of basic needs involves transfers to the poor population that reduce government savings. The costs of these three policies are taken up in eq. (18). Implementing the policy of secure property rights would involve some cost, but this is relatively insignificant and is ignored. In all policies, the size of the effort has been put at a comparable level so as to make an unbiased comparative appraisal of policies. The percentage changes between the policy run results and the base run values for the year 2000 are presented in Table 4.

Simulation I: Human capital: The policy focuses on eqs. (1.1)–(1.3). The proportions of educated and trained farmers in each of the irrigated, mechanized, and subsistence sectors are adjusted upward by 30%. The impact is that the sustainable productivity indices rise in all agricultural sectors but mostly in subsistence where performance is above base forecasts by 22.1%. Subsistence farmers, now earning higher incomes, enhance their sustainable productivity further. Yield and value of land in various sectors increase unevenly, leading to land reallocation from mechanized, forestry, and livestock sectors to subsistence. Agricultural *GDP* grows significantly while degradation loss in agriculture falls. The costs of this policy are a fall in government savings by 20.1% as a result of the costs of training farmers and subsidies on exports that have exceeded prescribed limits. These costs are lower than those involved in alternative policies.

Greater exports of agricultural goods are compensated by greater imports of non-agricultural goods in a model of balance of payments equilibrium and constant foreign exchange rates. This reduces the growth of the non-agricultural *GDP* by 1%, as seen in Table 4. Forestry *GDP*, which is dependent on intermediate deliveries from non-agriculture, falls by 0.4%. Attained sustainable productivity, ASP_4, is unaffected while degradation costs DCG_4 fall. In contrast, livestock *GDP* rises by 0.4% due to enhanced final consumption demand for livestock products resulting from an elevated growth in overall *GDP*. The decline of livestock per feddan relieves the pressure on grazing land, and, as a result, the sustainable productivity index, APS_5, improves while degradation costs, DCS_5, fall. In summary, the policy of investing in human capital achieves a greater economic growth on the base forecast of 1.4% and a mitigation of degradation of 3.5%. The policy contributes significantly to the reduction of the trade-off between growth and environment.

Simulation II: Price incentives: This policy intervention focuses on the irrigated sector in eq. (1.1). The government tax rate on the price of irrigated products is reduced from 0.30 to 0.21, i.e. by 30%. Attained sustainable productivity rises by 10.2%. As a result, yield and land value rise by the same rate. Degradation cost falls by 16%. As subsistence farmers get additional earnings from working in the irrigated sector, their income, $Y_{3,\text{poor}}$, increases by 6.8%. This causes the attained sustainable productivity in subsistence agriculture to rise by 4.1%, as do yield and land value, leading to a reallocation of land from mechanized to subsistence agriculture. The policy results in a net decline in degradation loss. The costs of this policy consist of a decline in government revenue by 25.5% due to forgone tax income, and the cost of subsidizing agricultural exports that have exceeded their upper limit.

The GDP of the non-agricultural sector is negatively affected along the same lines as in the previous policy simulation and would fall by 1.4%. This causes a further fall in the output of forestry accompanied by a reduction in degradation loss. The livestock output is also diminished due to less slaughter and slow economic growth. These effects result in overstocking, a fall in the grazing land sustainable productivity index, and a rise in degradation loss. The overall impact of this policy is that the GDP of the whole economy grows by 0.3% while total degradation cost falls by 6%. The previous policy of human capital thus performs better than the policy of price incentives.

Simulation III: Property rights: The policy intervention here focuses on eqs. (1.2) and (1.4). The measure of land tenure security in the mechanized sector, denoted by LTS_2, is increased from 0.50 to 0.65, i.e. a 30% upward adjustment in lease term. The impact is that the sustainable productivity index in the mechanized sector increases by 20.2%, as do yield and value of land. Consequently, land moves from subsistence, forestry, and livestock activities to mechanized agriculture, where the value of land is rising faster relative to other land-using sectors. With the movement of land, degradation loss increases in mechanized agriculture since it is the sector with the highest degradation cost per unit of *GDP*. In subsistence agriculture, the productivity index increases by 2.9%, as do yield and value of land. At the same time, subsistence poor farmers' income, $Y_{3,\text{poor}}$, is boosted by growth in mechanized agriculture. Degradation loss decreases in subsistence agriculture as a result of land moving out of the sector to mechanized agriculture. Government revenue falls by 19.8% since it incurs the cost of subsidizing agricultural exports that have exceeded their upper limit. The balance of payments adjustments leads to a negative growth in non-agriculture of −2.1%.

We have introduced a similar property rights effect in forestry, not reported in the model specification. This allowed the stock of tree biomass per feddan to increase and, as a result, the sustainable productivity index rose while degradation loss declined. In the livestock sector, due to a higher consumption of meat caused by higher *GDP* growth, the sustainable productivity index rises, causing vegetation yield to rise and degradation loss to fall. *GDP* of the whole economy rises by 1.3%, but degradation costs rise by 4.8%. This is explained by the movement of land to mechanized agriculture, which has the highest degradation cost per unit of *GDP* among the land-using sectors. This policy has a more positive impact on achieving economic growth than that of price incentives, but it has higher degradation costs. The trade-off is intensified.

Simulation IV: Basic needs: This policy intervention focuses on eqs. (1.3) and (2) for the subsistence and forestry sectors, respectively. Income of the poor population in these two sectors is adjusted upward by 30% through a direct government transfer, T_g. The impact on subsistence agriculture is that the attained sustainable productivity, yield, and price f land rise by 15.6%. Land is moved from mechanized

Table 4. Percentage change of variables between policy runs and base run in year 2000.

Symbol	Description	Measurement	Baseline value	Human Δ value (%)	Price Δ value (%)	Property Δ value (%)	Basic Needs Δ value (%)
Irrigated Agriculture							
ASP_1	Sust. productivity	Index	0.700	5.4	10.2	0.0	0.0
YLD_1	Yield	Metric Ton	1.009	5.4	10.2	0.0	0.0
NP_1	Land value	LS	90742	5.4	10.2	0.0	0.0
NQ_1	Cultivated land	M. Feddan	5.0	0.0	0.0	0.0	0.0
V_1	GDP irrigated	M. LS	38155	5.4	10.2	0.0	0.0
DCS_1	Degradation costs	M. LS	1361	−7.9	−16.0	0.0	0.0
Mechanized Agriculture							
ASP_2	Sust. productivity	Index	0.463	8.2	0.0	20.2	0.0
YLD_2	Yield	Metric Ton	0.355	8.2	0.0	20.2	0.0
NP_2	Land Value	LS	31642	8.2	0.0	20.2	0.0
NQ_2	Cultivated land	M. Feddan	8.4	−4.1	−2.2	14.9	−8.3
V_2	GDP mechanized	M. LS	22917	3.7	−2.2	38.1	−8.3
DCS_2	Degradation costs	M. LS	1533	−3.6	−2.2	14.1	−8.3
Subsistence Agriculture							
ASP_3	Sust. productivity	Index	0.424	22.1	4.1	2.9	15.6
YLD_3	Yield	Metric Ton	0.165	22.1	4.1	2.9	15.6
NP_3	Land Value	LS	3475	22.1	4.1	2.9	15.6
NQ_3	Cultivated land	M. Feddan	11.5	8.0	1.8	−1.6	6.8
V_3	GDP mechanized	M. LS	11983	31.9	6.0	1.2	23.4
$Y_{3,poor}$	Income poor	M. LS	25844	17.5	6.8	4.9	25.8
DCS_3	Degradation costs	M. LS	248	10.4	2.8	−0.9	9.2
Forestry							
ASP_4	Sust. productivity	Ratio	0.432	0.0	0.0	0.2	1.0
BTS_4	Stock/Feddan	Cubic meters	26.5	0.0	0.0	0.3	1.2
YLD_4	Output/Feddan	Cubic meters	0.173	−0.2	−0.6	−0.4	−10.0
NP_4	Land value	LS	1201	0.0	0.0	0.3	1.2
NQ_4	Woodland	M. feddan	149.8	−0.3	0.0	−0.5	0.0
V_4	GDP forestry	M. LS	21548	−0.4	−0.6	−0.9	−10.0
DCS_4	Degradation costs	M. LS	701	−0.5	−0.6	−1.1	−10.6
Livestock							
ASP_5	Sust. Productivity	Ratio	0.749	0.8	−0.2	1.0	0.5
LVS_5	Stock/Feddan	LS	0.258	−0.3	0.0	−0.4	−0.1
VGT_5	Vegetation/Feddan	Metric Ton	0.993	0.7	−0.1	0.8	0.4
YLD_5	Output/Feddan	LS	0.038	0.7	−0.2	0.6	0.4
NP_5	Land Value	LS	2047	0.0	0.0	1.0	0.0
NQ_5	Grazing land	M. Feddans	75.7	−0.3	0.0	−0.5	0.0
V_5	GDP livestock	M. LS	8625	0.4	−0.2	1.0	0.3
DCS_5	Degradation costs	M. LS	266	−1.8	0.3	−2.4	−1.2
Non-agriculture and whole economy							
E_6	Net exports	M. LS	−23820	32.4	26.0	47.1	1.3
P_6	Price index	Index	2.0	−2.4	−0.2	−2.2	−16.3
X_6	Output	M. LS	322451	−1.0	−1.4	−2.1	1.0
Y_6	GDP non-agriculture	M. LS	214766	−1.0	−1.4	−2.1	1.0
I	Investment	M. LS	36876	0.1	0.0	0.1	0.4
$\Sigma_i Y_i$	GDP all sectors	M. LS	317993	1.421	0.287	1.314	0.280
$\Sigma_i DCS_i$	Degradation costs all	M. LS	4109	−3.507	−6.024	4.858	−4.444
Gov	Gov. revenue	M. LS	17023	−20.1	−25.5	−19.8	−43.7

to subsistence agriculture. Degradation costs fall in mechanized agriculture where land is moving out but increase in the subsistence sector where land is moving in. Government revenue falls by 43.7% as a result of making transfers to poor farmers. In a similar way, with an income transfer, forestry workers are less inclined to cut trees, so the tree stock biomass per feddan increases, attained sustainable productivity increases, and degradation costs decline. The sectoral income from cutting wood trees falls by the amount of the government transfer, i.e. 10%. *GDP* increases by 0.3%, while total degradation loss falls by 4.4%. The policy of making direct government transfers to the poor population in the subsistence and forestry sectors brings about more economic growth with less degradation. Population dependent on the livestock sector is also better off.[15] However, the transfer costs involved are the highest compared to other policies.

The relative performance of the four policies in relation to the base run forecasts is demonstrated graphically in Figures 1 and 2. In Figure 1, the dotted line is 45°. Policies that lie most below this line and are most stretched to the right contribute more to economic growth and to a reduction in degradation loss and, therefore, mitigate the trade-off between growth and environment. Policies that lie above the line thus perform least in resolving the trade-off. All the simulated policies, except that of property rights security, contribute to economic growth as well as reduce degradation loss when measured from the baseline. When the relative effectiveness of policy is evaluated in terms of this trade-off, the most effective policies across the 1990s are those of strengthening human capital and price incentives, with human capital "better" in *GDP* and price incentives "better" on environment. These are followed by the policy of basic needs. The policy of property rights, which lies closest to, and for a part above, the 45° line, tends to intensify the trade-off by promoting economic growth at the cost of more degradation loss.

In Figures 2a and 2b, the policy numbering (i.e. I, II, III, and IV) is the same as that shown in the legend at the bottom of Figure 1. Figure 2a shows the degradation loss due to policy intervention measured from the baseline for the year 2000. As shown, the policies of human capital (I), price incentives (II), and basic needs (IV) reduce degradation costs compared to the baseline of the year 2000. The policy of property rights security III increases degradation costs. Figure 2b shows the effect of policy intervention on *GDP* and green *GDP* (i.e. *GDP* after deduction of degradation loss) as measured from the baseline for the year 2000. The policy of human capital, i.e. (I), produces the highest green *GDP*. Price incentives (II) and basic needs (IV) show positive but moderate changes in green *GDP*. The real surprise here is in the policy of property rights security (III) which shows a strong positive performance in green *GDP*, reversing the impressions obtained from Figure 1. When deterioration of the environment is monetized and is allowed to be traded against the gains, then this policy climbs to second place in terms of green *GDP*.

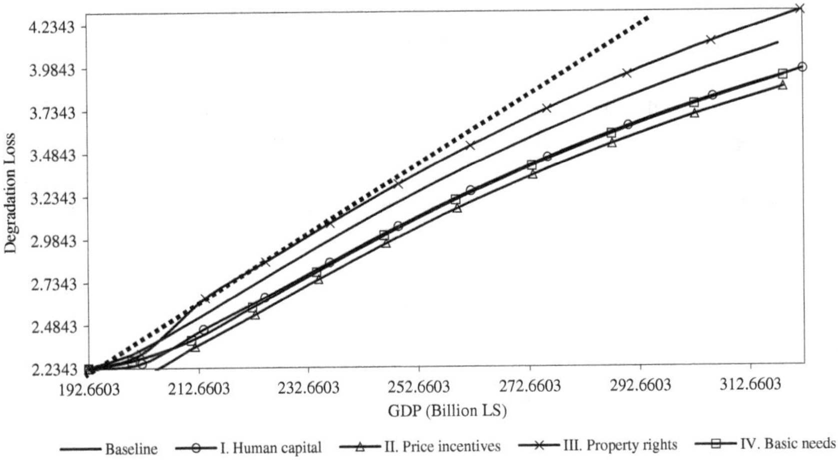

Figure 1. Trade-off between economic growth and degradation loss, 1990–2000, in billion LS.

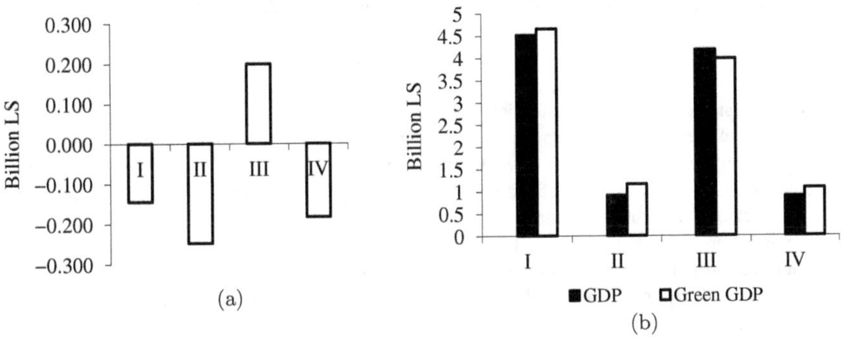

Figure 2. (a) Degradation loss: Difference between Policy and Baseline, 2000. (b) GDP and Green GDP: Difference between Policy and Baseline, 2000.

5. Concluding Remarks

Basically, traditional uses of land, i.e. subsistence cultivation, forestry, and grazing activities, have lower degradation costs per unit of output relative to the modern land uses, i.e. irrigated and mechanized. Economic development involves a shift of land from the first to the second. Therefore, reallocation of land from the traditional uses to the modern uses leads to more production, but at the same time, it involves more loss in terms of resource depletion. Fortunately, there are policies that can mitigate this trade-off between economic growth and resource degradation. The policy of investment in human capital and training programs appears to be the most effective in combating the trade-off and resolving the conflict between growth and environment. This policy is followed by price incentives and income transfers to maintain basic needs. The policy for promoting greater security in property rights favors growth at the cost of environment but scores high in terms of green *GDP*.

The specification that takes the economy-wide model and incorporates the effects of changing relative prices based on world market price trends represents a workable assessment of the trade-off between growth and environment. The observed trends in relative prices at the world level at the turn of the century (1990–2000) seem to favor environment but the effect is very marginal. The cost to economic growth of the environment-friendly relative prices is relatively greater, however. The net effect is a lower green *GDP* in Sudan. Given the present distribution of land use in the country, the results suggest that there is no need to worry about reaching a critical ecological balance between growth and environment any time soon.

Endnotes

1. Sudan is a typical country in which the 4 resource degrading factors apply, see Abdelgalil (2000). For example, the low level of farmers' education and training leads to overexploitation of arable land. Next, price controls imposed by the government on irrigated agriculture have discouraged farmers from adoption of long-term sustainable cultivation practices. Land tenure insecurity has pushed farmers in mechanized agriculture to "mine" arable land in pursuit of short-run gains. Finally, poverty in subsistence agriculture has compelled farmers to exploit arable land unsustainably. Furthermore, open access to woodland is a major cause behind the excessive clearance of forestland, and lack of well-defined property rights over grazing land has left no incentives for livestock owners to invest in improving the prevailing conditions in grazing land.
2. Irrigated land NQ_1 represents about 24% of the total cultivated area in Sudan; it is generally fixed, and its expansion requires significant public investments in irrigation works. Mechanized NQ_2 and subsistence NQ_3 are rain fed, and they form 33% and 43%, respectively. Rain-fed land can shift between subsistence and mechanized cultivation, very much governed by market forces, depending on the relative value of land in both alternatives. The rest of rain-fed land is used by forestry NQ_4 and livestock NQ_5. In 1990, NQ_4 was twice NQ_5. One feddan equals about 0.42 hectare or 1.038 acre.
3. This applies to cases of one and the same crop that is being produced in all three sectors, as well as when the aggregate productivity value per feddan is compared for the three sectors.
4. Unable to satisfy basic needs and having a limited time horizon, subsistence farmers often overexploit the land during their lifetime, cf. Barbier (2000). It has been regularly observed that the negligence of the fallow period, crop rotation, and soil conservation and improvement measures in subsistence rain-fed agriculture reflects both the poverty and the lack of necessary farming knowledge in this sector, cf. Kevane (1997). Subsistence farmers, being the poorest, are driven by this factor to cultivate the land more frequently and, hence, the fallow period becomes shorter and shorter or ignored completely. Ignoring crop rotation reflects the limited options they have when it comes to the issue of crop diversification. They mainly cultivate food crops (sorghum and millet) on which they depend for their survival, and it happens that these food crops are more soil erosive than others, cf. Coxhead and Jayasuriya (1994). The lack of crop rotation leads to soil nutrient depletion and soil erosion and consequently declining yield.

5. There can be rare but desirable situations from the environmental viewpoint where T_{gi} can function as a tax imposed by the government on households, i.e. $T_{gi} < 0$. If such a tax is levied on households, then wood cutting and livestock slaughter will have to increase so as to maintain their living standard as before the tax.
6. Ideally, a private investment function should be econometrically regressed from the country's data. The Sudanese data do not allow this. Instead, we followed here a Cobb–Douglas-type equation for investment demand and plugged an appropriate value for the crowding in public investment elasticity based on Taylor (1991), p. 166, and Ibrahim (1995), p. 54, at $\imath_g = 0.82$, so that the price effect elasticity can be set at $\imath_p = 1 - 0.82 = 0.18$.
7. Installed investment is fixed investment. However, the word "fixed" may bring misunderstandings as we use the same word in the sense of fixing an exogenous value of the variable. To avoid such overlapping, we shall refer to fixed investment as installed investment or simply investment.
8. We incorporate an upper limit to the permissible level of AFL exports, beyond which a government role is implied as a subsidiser of additional exports where certain costs have to be incurred to provide the additional supply.
9. FCF is assumed to grow at 5% per annum.
10. The cost of reclaiming a degraded feddan of arable land of an average quality is found to be about 10% of its foregone yield, cf. Gigengack *et al.* (1990). Note that arable land degradation can be seen as a process that ranges from mild degradation to extreme desertification.
11. Relative prices between the AFL sectors have moved very closely with those of the relative indices based on world market prices so that working with the latter is justified. The strong inflationary tendencies in Sudan were neutral in effect as far as these relative prices are concerned. The price elevation is about nine times for each of the AFL sectors. Taking the irrigated price index as numeraire, the relative price indices for all AFL sectors are calculated accordingly and set to grow exogenously based on the past growth path of relative world market prices. Note that, in contrast, the price index for the rest of the economy sector is endogenously solved. For more details, see Abdelgalil (2000).
12. The level of desired basic needs income, *YBN*, for the poor population engaged in subsistence agriculture, about 26% of the population, is calculated as being in the range of 13% of the gross domestic product, and is assumed to grow annually at 5%, same as that of GDP in the past. Government transfers to the poor population in subsistence and forestry sectors, T_{gj}, for the purpose of meeting basic needs is set to zero in the year 1990 but is simulated at positive levels in the policy runs. Agricultural labor force is assumed to grow by annual growth rate of 2.7%, as it did in previous decade.
13. The relative price indices are projected to move within a narrow range. For instance, while the numeraire price index of irrigated grows at 0.048% per annum, that of mechanized grows at 0.041%, giving a declining relative price index of mechanized at $XP_2 = 1.041/1.048 = 0.9933$. The magnitudes of the other indices are $XP_3 = 0.9924$, $XP_4 = 0.9952$, and $XP_5 = 0.9943$. These projections show XP_4 and XP_5 standing for forestry and livestock prices to experience slightly more favourable price trends than those of agricultural produce XP_2 and XP_3.
14. More results are discussed in Abdelgalil and Cohen (2001).
15. Livestock output per feddan increases because both non-agricultural output and the *GDP* work in the same direction to increase final consumption and intermediate demand for livestock products. This improves sustainable productivity, as vegetation yield rises while degradation costs declines.

Chapter 13

Development Analysis and Policy Modeling with Minimal Data: Suriname

1. Introduction

To start with, the following paragraphs provide a brief introduction to Suriname. The current population of Suriname is roughly 600,000 as of 31 December 2022, based on Worldometer elaboration of the latest United Nations data. The total land area is 156,000 km^2. This gives a population density of 4 per km^2, which is practically speaking the lowest in the world (with the exception of Western Sahara, Mongolia, Iceland, and Greenland). Half of the population lives in urban Paramaribo.

Suriname became a plantation colony under the Netherlands in 1667, with population drawn from Africa and Asia as slaved workers and contract laborers. The country became one of the most ethnically diversified in the world. Suriname gained independence in 1975. It had a difficult start with intermittent military and civilian regimes before it stabilized to civilian rule from 1991 onward, though political governance continued to be tense.

Suriname economy is highly dependent on its supply of mineral resources, mainly oil, gold, and bauxite, as their export and their prices. Less than 1% of Suriname's land is arable, and about half of this is cultivated, mostly rice. More than 90% of Suriname is tropical rainforest, and great timber resources exist but are not yet fully exploited. There is little industry. Tourism is picking but suffered immensely during the COVID epidemic.

The well-being of the country is strongly influenced by the political governance and by the primary economic dependence on commodity exports. The GDP per capita, which amounted to 2200 USD in 1980, reached its peak at 9470 USD in 2014; GDP per capita fell and was halved back to 4836 USD in 2020, in part due to the COVID epidemic. Economic recovery stabilized in 2021 and is expected to proceed slowly from 2022 onward. While many developing countries have been able to move their economies from the primary commodity-based type to a diversified-based type with sustainable economic growth, this has been less forthcoming in Suriname, in statistical terms. The backlog is noticeable in various spheres of the economy's development.

In Suriname, as in any other developing country, the cabinet and ministries require the support of a National Planning Department (NPD) to fulfill monitoring, research, and advisory functions relating to development progress, policies, and planning. Because of the situation in which Suriname finds itself, the urge to have a strengthened and viable NPD is essential and real. This chapter treats a number of extensions and refinements that were introduced and institutionalized in the monitoring, research, and planning activities of the National Planning Department of Suriname. The technical assistance aimed at transferring knowledge, use, and training in economy-wide modeling of development policies. The technical assistance to NPD Suriname dated from 2019 and was jointly sponsored and supported by the International Labor Office and Erasmus University Rotterdam. The participation of the Suriname General Bureau of Statistics (ABS) and the Institute for Graduate Studies and Research (IGSR) of the University of Suriname was significant. Although the advisory activities formally terminated in early 2022, online external support is available on an informal basis. See endnote for acknowledgements.

In the context of development planning, distinction is often made between three types of economic models and their associated statistical systems. These are (1) macro econometric model, (2) input–output table with related interindustry modeling and analysis, for short IOT, and (3) social accounting matrix, for short SAM, with related SAM-based economy-wide models that deal with broader socio-economic development problems and that can be elaborated further along computable general equilibrium models. Figuratively, the three modeling types and their associative statistical systems constitute a triangle toolbox, with macro on top and IOT and SAM on the two sides. Next to these, there are all other specific purpose models and analytical tools, which are not of immediate concern here.

In 2019, the NPD was practically speaking starting from square one in building its capacity regarding the above tools. It relied in the past on an annually-based calculative scheme for doing economic projections (SURYA model). Given the nature of the calculative scheme, it cannot be described as a macro econometric model or used as such in monitoring and the policy analysis of the economy. To fulfill its tasks, the NPD needed to acquire capabilities and proficiency with regard to the input–output table and related modeling (IOT), and the social accounting matrix and related modeling (SAM). The IOT is the most suitable tool for monitoring, analyzing, and formulating policies in the area of interindustry economics and structural development. The SAM is a broader framework that addresses socio-economic development issues with special reference to human resources and the workforce.

This chapter falls into four sections. Section 2 takes up construction and applied use of the IOT. Section 3 is on the construction and applied use of the SAM.

Section 4 discusses the use of the obtained analytical results and policymaking. Section 5 is on updates of the IOT and SAM to the newly revised data series. Section 6 is on formulating and applying Suriname SAM-based economywide model (SSEM), which is capable of treating economic growth next to socio-economic development objectives pertaining to employment, distribution, and poverty. The period 2022–2225 for which projections were done with SSEM corresponds with the recently issued Suriname Development Plan 2022–2025. Section 7 includes concluding remarks.

Some portions of what is contained in this chapter were treated in some previous chapters. To allow this chapter to be self-contained in terms of methods, we choose to repeat some basic introductory remarks on the methods. These remarks can be skipped by advanced readers.

2. Input–Output Table: Construction and Analysis

2.1. *Construction and estimation of the input–output tables Suriname*

An input–output table consists of four sections as shown in Table 1: (a) An inner transactions part of domestically produced and imported interindustry intermediate inputs by sector, supplemented downward by (b) primary factor inputs employed in the production process, that is, the GDP. The right-hand side of the table gives (c) expenditure on domestically produced and imported final demand goods such as consumption, investment, and exports, specified by sector, and (d) their summing totals which constitute the GDP from the expenditure side. As such, the required data for constructing the IOT are four sets of data shown in different colors, which should fit with each other to assure a consistent IOT.

Construction of an authentic IO table for Suriname based totally on national data is an enormous undertaking. It requires in-depth establishment surveys of major industrial enterprises and knowledge on the production technology and the commodity mix of major inputs and outputs, assuring consistency for major commodities (and industries) between the supply of goods (also called make) with their use (i.e. demand or absorption). Suppose that the balancing of supply and demand is reasonably and appropriately done, then there are various kinds of adjustments and choices pending which boil to four issues: (a) How to harmonize the different transactions in the table, some of which are expressed in basic prices, and others in market prices? (b) Which layout to choose for the IOT table? Possibilities are commodity x commodity, commodity by industry, or industry by industry. (c) Configuration of domestically produced intermediate goods and final products versus foreign-made intermediate goods (complimentary imports) and foreign-made final goods (competitive imports). Should the domestic production be separated from the foreign imports from the beginning and throughout, or

Table 1. Layout of the input–output table.

	Intermediate deliveries $A_{jj'}$				Final demand				Total Output
Sector j	$j = 1$	$j = 2, 3, \ldots$	$j = J$	Sum	C_j	G_j	I_j	E_j	X_j
$j = 1$	A_{11}	....	A_{1J}	ΣA_{1j}	C_1	G_1	I_1	E_1	X_1
.	.	....	.	.	.	.	.	.	.
.	.	....	.	.	.	.	.	.	.
$j = J$	A_{J1}	....	A_{JJ}	ΣA_{Jj}	C_J	G_J	I_J	E_J	X_J
Sum	ΣA_{j1}	....	ΣA_{Jj}	$\Sigma A_{jj'}$	ΣC_j	ΣG_j	ΣI_j	ΣE_j	ΣX_j
Imports	M_1	....	M_J	ΣM_j	M_c	M_g	M_i	M_e	M
GDP bp	$Y_{1\,(bp)}$	....	$Y_{J\,(bp)}$	$\Sigma Y_{j\,(bp)}$					$Y_{(bp)}$
Indt tx-sb	T_1	....	T_J	ΣT_j					T
GDP mp	$Y_{1\,(mp)}$	....	$Y_{J\,(mp)}$	$\Sigma Y_{j\,(mp)}$					$Y_{(mp)}$
Total Input	X_1	....	X_J	ΣX_j	C	G	I	E	

Notations: j = sector or industry, $j = 1, \ldots, J$.
Intermediate deliveries: $A_{jj'}$ = intermediate deliveries of sector j to j'.
Final demand: C = private consumption. G = Government consumption. I = Gross investment, E = Exports.
M = Imports, consisting of intermediate goods by sector, M_j, and final goods M_c, M_g, M_i, E_i.
Primary inputs: Y_j (bp) = GDP by sector j at basic prices. T_j = Indirect taxes less subsidies by sector j.
Y_j (mp) = GDP by sector at market prices.
X_j = Total production of sector j, (total output = total input).

should they be amalgamated together to give the national, and in later steps obtain the domestic parts by deducting the (foreign) imports from the national aggregates? Finally, (d) updating requires renewed data on GDP (and output) by industry and GDP by final demand components. The renewed final demands by sector can then be subtracted from the corresponding renewed outputs by sector to give the updated total intermediate inputs by sector. As these renewed updates do not fit with the old structures, the IOT inner matrix needs to be subjected to several rounds of iteration before IOT consistency is reached.

If and when the Suriname General Bureau of Statistics (ABS) decides to produce an authentic IO table for Suriname, it may take a few years to get the job done. Under such circumstances, to obtain an IOT for the country, input–output statisticians would construct the inner transaction part of interindustry deliveries based on contemporary technologies as found in several advanced representative countries and transplant this inner submatrix to fit with the country's primary factor inputs on the production side (down left) and the country's final demand on the expenditure side (up right and down right).

The transplantation venture is facilitated by the presence of a proxy IOT, known as Eora IOT, which has been commonly used in many countries and has proven to be reliable, effective, and adjustable. The Eora project (source: www.worldmrio.com), is backed by the World Bank, and its data bank is used by the World Bank among others. The Eora project produced proxy IOT for many countries and over more years. These IOTs are accessible for use. The following brief account on the Eora tables serves as background information. Eora starts with a 26-industry proxy IO table combining diverse industries and products from the Australian, US, UK, and Japanese economies and then scale it to match the available data that for that country, such as GDP, imports bundle, exports bundle, and the like.

There are four main issues which any IOT has to consider in the process of construction. How do the Eora tables treat these issues? (a) Eora allocates the trade and transport margins to their corresponding sectors, thus satisfying price harmonization. (b) Eora chooses an industry-by-industry layout of the input–output table. Commodity-to-industry transactions are converted to industry-by-industry transactions. (c) Eora separates domestically produced intermediate goods and final demand products from those that are foreign-made, that is, imports. This is interesting because it simplifies the accounting framework and allows for more flexibility in treating the imports components but at the same time requires some research effort in splitting the data of the aggregate final demand (consumption and investment) by-product into their domestic and imported parts. The separation between domestically produced and foreign-made (imports) is essential when the focus is on conducting IO economic analysis and formulating development policies. The aggregation in totals without separation in domestic and foreign is followed when data are scarcer and when the focus of the modeling analysis is less on economic strategies and more on broader socio-economic development issues. We shall shift to the aggregate approach in the context of the SAM. (d) As regards calibration and updating, the Eora applies various iteration methods to bring about consistency between the row totals and column totals of the adjusted input–output table to individual countries. We shall use the RAS method to realize these consistencies.

The preceding paragraph may give the impression that the Eora input–output tables for Suriname are readily available for use. This is very far from the real situation. The industries are classified differently in Eora and in Suriname's ABS. Interindustry transactions, factor payments on the production side, and final demand on the expenditure side are valued, aggregated, and reconciled differently, and there is no readily available documentation on how the production side is reconciled with the expenditure side in neither the Eora sources nor the Suriname ABS sources. Besides, the Eora figures are in USD and these need to be converted into SRD. The simple transposition of ABS data regarding GDP by sector, next to consumption, investment, exports, and imports in the Eora, would result in non-plausible negative figures for many entries and exaggerations for others. And yet the two data frameworks have a common origin and resemble two faces of the same coin. The adaptation of the Eora source to the ABS source is partly a matter of following an algorithm which is applied in the attached Excel file and partly an application of deductive reasoning and empirical investigation that entail several trials before reaching reconciliations. This is already apparent with regard to the selected benchmark year discussed in the following.

Table 2. Suriname: Input–output table 2015, in million SRD.

ISIC	1 agrcltr	2 fsry	3 mnng	4.1 fd prc	4.2 txtl mnf	4.3 wd prc	4.4 ptr chm	4.5 mtl prd	4.6 elc mry	4.7 trn eqp	4.8 otr mnf	5 EGW	6 cnstrctn	7 trade
1.Agriculture	1123	0	0	192	3	33	2	0	0	0	1	0	22	5
2.Fishery	2	164	0	232	0	0	0	1	0	0	9	0	0	16
3.Mining	6	3	852	2	0	2	129	58	1	2	35	135	110	2
4.1.Food prcsng	2	0	0	2	0	0	0	0	0	0	0	0	0	1
4.2.Txtile mnfctrng	1	2	0	1	19	2	2	1	4	3	3	0	8	9
4.3.Wood prcsng	5	0	0	16	1	40	8	6	8	3	8	1	77	31
4.4.Ptr, chemicals	32	4	4	17	11	17	127	23	55	32	17	5	263	27
4.5.Metal prdctn	0	0	0	1	0	0	1	8	4	2	0	0	9	0
4.6.Electric mchnry	1	0	1	1	0	1	2	8	59	33	1	1	29	8
4.7.Transport eqp	0	1	1	0	0	0	1	1	12	68	1	0	19	22
4.8.Other mnf	0	0	0	0	0	1	1	3	1	3	1	0	11	3
5.Elctricity,wtr,gas	23	1	11	23	6	27	73	112	47	12	5	161	39	87
6.Construction	14	1	21	9	2	12	34	44	36	7	3	64	1	90
7.Trade	29	4	3	38	10	27	53	63	133	52	15	5	423	129
8.Hotels, rstrnts	2	0	1	8	2	9	13	23	21	6	3	17	60	82
9.Transport,cmntn	21	3	7	23	4	20	39	50	73	21	15	26	258	410
10. Financial srvcs	8	0	2	5	2	4	14	9	30	9	2	4	64	92
11.Cmmrcl srvcs	9	0	2	6	2	4	15	10	32	10	2	4	70	101
12.Public admnstrn	1	0	0	0	0	0	1	1	1	0	0	0	1	2
13.Education	1	0	0	0	0	0	1	0	1	0	0	0	3	4
14.Health	1	0	0	1	0	1	1	1	2	1	0	1	8	12
15.Socal prsnl srv	0	0	0	0	0	0	0	0	0	0	0	0	1	1
Dmstc Intrm dlvrs	1281	185	905	577	63	200	517	422	522	264	123	425	1477	1136
imports	61	39	15	188	78	145	326	171	445	269	175	77	214	351
gross factor income	966	554	505	201	50	151	322	196	460	173	67	539	1496	2993
indrct txs less sbsds	104	59	54	22	5	16	35	21	49	19	7	58	161	321
GDP market prices	1069	613	559	222	55	168	356	217	510	192	74	597	1657	3315
Total input	2412	838	1479	987	195	512	1199	811	1478	724	372	1099	3348	4802

(Continued)

Table 2. (*Continued*)

ISIC	8 htl & rst	9 Tr & cm	10 fnc sev	11 cmr srv	12 pbl ad	13 edctn	14 hlth	15 slpr sr	intrmdt dlvrs	hshld cns	gvrn cns	invest ment	exports	final dmnd	Total Output
1.Agriculture	34	1	1	1	2	2	2	0	1425	174	46	16	751	987	2412
2.Fishery	116	0	1	1	1	3	3	3	552	95	0	1	178	275	838
3.Mining	2	48	0	0	15	1	1	1	1406	6	0	15	36	57	1479
4.1.Food prcsng	6	0	0	0	1	0	0	0	12	174	0	0	801	975	987
4.2.Txtile mnfctrng	2	3	0	0	4	2	2	2	69	49	0	0	78	126	195
4.3.Wood prcsng	11	27	4	4	25	5	6	5	290	26	0	0	197	223	512
4.4.Ptr, chemicals	14	115	3	3	51	23	24	8	875	141	0	0	187	328	1199
4.5.Metal prdctn	0	1	0	0	0	0	0	0	28	4	0	0	779	783	811
4.6.Electric mchnry	1	7	1	1	10	2	2	1	170	94	0	1048	167	1309	1478
4.7.Transport eqp	0	11	1	1	31	0	0	1	171	93	0	397	64	554	724
4.8.Other mnf	1	2	0	0	1	1	1	0	32	62	0	97	182	340	372
5.Elctricity,wtr,gas	79	66	6	6	61	22	24	8	899	141	21	0	41	203	1099
6.Construction	44	156	50	45	260	46	49	15	1002	3	15	2210	125	2353	3348
7.Trade	73	70	6	5	37	20	21	7	1223	1416	84	987	1099	3586	4802
8.Hotels, rstrnts	98	106	24	22	96	31	33	12	670	205	0	0	648	853	1519
9.Transport,cmntn	77	275	17	16	127	33	35	36	1587	334	40	236	1266	1875	3450
10. Financial srvcs	21	84	1	1	31	17	18	10	428	381	0	305	28	714	1138
11.Cmmrcl srvcs	23	92	1	1	34	19	20	11	470	308	0	237	22	567	1033
12.Public admnstrn	2	5	1	1	1	2	2	37	59	19	1153	551	214	1938	1997
13.Education	4	8	1	1	8	0	0	2	34	374	616	0	0	990	1024
14.Health	11	24	4	3	22	0	0	4	99	423	561	0	0	984	1082
15.Socal prsnl srv	0	1	0	0	0	0	0	0	5	314	82	0	0	396	401
Dmstc Intrm dlvrs	622	1101	123	112	816	228	241	164	11506	4836	2617	6100	6865	20418	31941
imports	130	344	191	173	312	119	126	89	4078	2652	101	1788		4540	8618
gross factor income	693	1811	745	676	785	611	646	134	14772						
indrct txs less sbsds	74	194	80	73	84	66	69	14	1585						
GDP market prices	767	2005	824	748	869	677	715	148	16357						
Total input	1519	3450	1138	1033	1997	1024	1082	401	31941	7488	2718	7888	6865	24959	

The evaluation of published data allowed for one-digit industry classification along ISIC Rev 3 (15 sectors). This was extended to include 2-digit manufacturing subsectors (bringing the whole to 22 sectors). The year 2015 was selected as a benchmark year, supplemented by 2014 as a checkup year. The construction of the table for the two consecutive years allowed for greater insight and for fruitful testing of table regularities over 2 years. It is important to underline that what the IOT and its economic analysis should capture is the underlying economic structure of the Suriname economy for the coming couple of years, and this is not necessarily coupled to one or the other specific year. Appendix I gives a stepwise description of the estimation procedure. The resulting IOT of Suriname for 2015 is Table 2.

2.2. *Input–output multipliers*

W. Leontief, the founder of IOT, outlined a production function with proportional technology, whereby the intermediate inputs of the giving industries j to the receiving industry j' are assumed to be a fraction of the total inputs of the receiving industry j'. The fractions of intermediate deliveries are expressed by the input–output coefficients $\alpha_{jj'}$. These coefficients are collected together in what is called the A matrix, input–output coefficients, or Leontief coefficients. The fractions of all intermediate inputs received together with payments for primary inputs for the receiving industry add to 1.0. See Table 3 showing the 22 × 22 matrix, which is the A matrix.

The basic equation in IOT can be written now in matrix algebra as $x = Ax + f$, where x is the vector (column) of sector production and f is the vector (column) of final demand specified by the supplying sector. By shifting terms, this equation becomes $x(I' - A) = f$, where I' is an identity matrix. Next, $x = 1/(I' - A)f$ or as in eq. (1).

$$x = (I' - A)^{-1} f = M_j f \tag{1}$$

The inverse $(I' - A)^{-1}$ is calculated using Excel. Inverse results are named Leontief multipliers and are denoted further on by M_j. Multiplication of the inverse results by final demand f gives x. Table 4 gives the production multipliers M_j. Example: Production multiplier of agriculture is 2.068.

On the whole, the IO model multipliers for Suriname show that in spite of an average production multiplier over all sectors of 1.62, the country is able to plow back no more than an average of 0.72 in GDP multipliers; the major part of the production multiplier is leakage into the intermediate deliveries multiplier of 0.90 (split into domestic intermediates 0.62 and imported intermediates 0.28). This implies that a final demand injection of 1.00 million SRD is able to generate a GDP of only 0.72 million SRD.

Table 3. The A matrix for 22 sectors and primary inputs, 2015.

	1	2	3	4.1	4.2	4.3	4.4	4.5	4.6	4.7	4.8	5	6	7	8	9	10	11	12	13	14	15
ISIC	agricul	fishery	mining	food prc	txtile mnf	wood prc	ptr chm	mtl prd	elc mry	trn eqp	otr mnf	EGW	cnstrctn	trade	htl & rst	tr & cm	fnc sev	cmr srv	pbl adm	education	health	scl prs srv
1	0.466	0.001	0.000	0.194	0.015	0.064	0.002	0.001	0.000	0.000	0.001	0.000	0.007	0.001	0.023	0.000	0.001	0.001	0.001	0.001	0.001	0.000
2	0.001	0.196	0.000	0.235	0.001	0.000	0.000	0.001	0.000	0.000	0.025	0.000	0.000	0.003	0.076	0.000	0.001	0.001	0.000	0.003	0.003	0.006
3	0.003	0.003	0.576	0.002	0.001	0.003	0.108	0.072	0.001	0.002	0.094	0.123	0.033	0.000	0.001	0.014	0.000	0.000	0.007	0.001	0.001	0.003
4.1	0.001	0.000	0.000	0.002	0.000	0.000	0.000	0.000	0.000	0.000	0.000	0.000	0.000	0.000	0.004	0.000	0.000	0.000	0.000	0.000	0.000	0.000
4.2	0.001	0.003	0.000	0.001	0.095	0.003	0.002	0.002	0.003	0.004	0.007	0.000	0.002	0.002	0.001	0.001	0.000	0.000	0.002	0.002	0.002	0.004
4.3	0.002	0.001	0.000	0.016	0.007	0.078	0.007	0.007	0.006	0.004	0.022	0.000	0.023	0.006	0.008	0.008	0.003	0.003	0.013	0.005	0.005	0.012
4.4	0.013	0.005	0.003	0.018	0.055	0.033	0.106	0.029	0.037	0.044	0.046	0.004	0.079	0.006	0.009	0.033	0.003	0.003	0.025	0.022	0.022	0.021
4.5	0.000	0.000	0.000	0.001	0.000	0.000	0.000	0.010	0.003	0.003	0.001	0.000	0.003	0.000	0.000	0.000	0.000	0.000	0.000	0.000	0.000	0.000
4.6	0.000	0.000	0.000	0.001	0.001	0.002	0.002	0.009	0.040	0.046	0.004	0.000	0.009	0.002	0.001	0.002	0.001	0.001	0.005	0.002	0.002	0.002
4.7	0.000	0.001	0.000	0.000	0.000	0.000	0.001	0.001	0.008	0.094	0.004	0.000	0.006	0.004	0.000	0.003	0.001	0.001	0.015	0.000	0.000	0.003
4.8	0.000	0.000	0.000	0.000	0.001	0.001	0.000	0.004	0.001	0.005	0.002	0.000	0.003	0.001	0.001	0.001	0.000	0.000	0.001	0.001	0.001	0.001
5	0.009	0.001	0.008	0.024	0.029	0.052	0.061	0.138	0.032	0.016	0.013	0.147	0.012	0.018	0.052	0.019	0.005	0.005	0.031	0.022	0.022	0.021
6	0.006	0.001	0.014	0.009	0.013	0.023	0.028	0.054	0.025	0.010	0.009	0.058	0.000	0.019	0.029	0.045	0.044	0.044	0.130	0.045	0.045	0.036
7	0.012	0.005	0.002	0.039	0.050	0.054	0.044	0.078	0.090	0.071	0.039	0.004	0.126	0.027	0.048	0.020	0.005	0.005	0.018	0.019	0.019	0.018
8	0.001	0.000	0.000	0.008	0.009	0.018	0.011	0.029	0.014	0.008	0.009	0.015	0.018	0.017	0.065	0.031	0.021	0.021	0.048	0.030	0.030	0.031
9	0.009	0.003	0.005	0.023	0.022	0.039	0.032	0.062	0.050	0.029	0.041	0.024	0.077	0.085	0.051	0.080	0.015	0.015	0.064	0.032	0.032	0.091
10	0.003	0.000	0.001	0.005	0.011	0.008	0.011	0.011	0.020	0.013	0.005	0.004	0.019	0.019	0.014	0.024	0.001	0.001	0.015	0.017	0.017	0.026
11	0.004	0.000	0.002	0.006	0.012	0.009	0.013	0.012	0.022	0.014	0.005	0.004	0.021	0.021	0.015	0.027	0.001	0.001	0.017	0.018	0.018	0.028
12	0.000	0.000	0.000	0.000	0.000	0.001	0.001	0.001	0.000	0.000	0.001	0.000	0.000	0.001	0.002	0.002	0.001	0.001	0.000	0.002	0.002	0.091
13	0.000	0.000	0.000	0.000	0.000	0.000	0.000	0.001	0.000	0.000	0.000	0.000	0.001	0.001	0.003	0.002	0.001	0.001	0.004	0.000	0.000	0.004
14	0.001	0.001	0.000	0.001	0.001	0.001	0.001	0.001	0.001	0.001	0.001	0.001	0.002	0.002	0.007	0.007	0.003	0.003	0.011	0.000	0.000	0.011
15	0.000	0.000	0.000	0.000	0.000	0.000	0.000	0.000	0.000	0.000	0.000	0.000	0.000	0.000	0.000	0.000	0.000	0.000	0.000	0.000	0.000	0.000
int inp	0.531	0.221	0.612	0.584	0.321	0.390	0.431	0.521	0.354	0.364	0.330	0.387	0.441	0.237	0.410	0.319	0.108	0.108	0.409	0.223	0.223	0.410
imported	0.025	0.047	0.010	0.191	0.397	0.283	0.272	0.211	0.301	0.371	0.471	0.070	0.064	0.073	0.085	0.100	0.168	0.168	0.156	0.117	0.117	0.221
GDP fc	0.400	0.661	0.342	0.203	0.254	0.295	0.268	0.242	0.312	0.239	0.179	0.491	0.447	0.623	0.456	0.525	0.654	0.654	0.393	0.597	0.597	0.333
Ind txls	0.043	0.071	0.037	0.022	0.027	0.032	0.029	0.026	0.033	0.026	0.019	0.053	0.048	0.067	0.049	0.056	0.070	0.070	0.042	0.064	0.064	0.036
GDP mp	0.443	0.732	0.378	0.225	0.282	0.327	0.297	0.268	0.345	0.265	0.199	0.543	0.495	0.690	0.505	0.581	0.724	0.724	0.435	0.661	0.661	0.369
Tl input	1.000	1.000	1.000	1.000	1.000	1.000	1.000	1.000	1.000	1.000	1.000	1.000	1.000	1.000	1.000	1.000	1.000	1.000	1.000	1.000	1.000	1.000

Table 4. Leontief multiplier matrix $(I' - A)^{-1}$, that is, Mj. Suriname 22 sectors, 2015.

	1	2	3	4.1	4.2	4.3	4.4	4.5	4.6	4.7	4.8	5	6	7	8	9	10	11	12	13	14	15
ISIC	agric	fishery	mining	food prc	txtile	wood prc	ptr chm	mtl prd	elc mry	trn eqp	otr mnf	EGW	cnstrct	trade	htl & rst	tr & cm	fnc sev	cmr srv	pbl adm	educat	health	sl pr srv
1	1.873	0.002	0.001	0.368	0.033	0.132	0.007	0.006	0.004	0.003	0.008	0.003	0.018	0.005	0.049	0.005	0.004	0.004	0.010	0.007	0.007	0.007
2	0.003	1.243	0.001	0.295	0.003	0.004	0.003	0.006	0.003	0.003	0.033	0.003	0.004	0.007	0.104	0.004	0.003	0.003	0.007	0.008	0.008	0.013
3	0.030	0.013	2.373	0.032	0.040	0.051	0.319	0.246	0.037	0.037	0.250	0.355	0.119	0.020	0.037	0.064	0.012	0.012	0.061	0.027	0.027	0.041
4.1	0.001	0.000	0.000	1.003	0.000	0.000	0.000	0.000	0.000	0.000	0.000	0.000	0.000	0.000	0.004	0.000	0.000	0.000	0.001	0.000	0.000	0.001
4.2	0.001	0.004	0.000	0.003	1.106	0.005	0.003	0.003	0.004	0.006	0.008	0.001	0.004	0.003	0.002	0.002	0.000	0.000	0.003	0.002	0.002	0.005
4.3	0.005	0.001	0.002	0.021	0.010	1.087	0.011	0.012	0.010	0.008	0.026	0.004	0.029	0.010	0.012	0.012	0.006	0.006	0.020	0.009	0.009	0.019
4.4	0.031	0.008	0.012	0.032	0.074	0.051	1.128	0.048	0.053	0.063	0.059	0.016	0.099	0.015	0.022	0.049	0.009	0.009	0.049	0.033	0.033	0.040
4.5	0.000	0.000	0.000	0.001	0.000	0.000	0.001	1.010	0.003	0.004	0.001	0.000	0.003	0.000	0.000	0.000	0.000	0.000	0.001	0.000	0.000	0.000
4.6	0.001	0.000	0.002	0.001	0.002	0.003	0.003	0.011	1.043	0.054	0.005	0.002	0.011	0.003	0.002	0.003	0.002	0.002	0.008	0.003	0.003	0.004
4.7	0.001	0.001	0.001	0.001	0.001	0.001	0.002	0.003	0.011	1.105	0.005	0.001	0.008	0.006	0.001	0.005	0.001	0.001	0.019	0.001	0.001	0.006
4.8	0.000	0.001	0.000	0.001	0.002	0.002	0.001	0.004	0.001	0.006	1.002	0.001	0.004	0.001	0.001	0.001	0.001	0.001	0.001	0.001	0.001	0.001
5	0.026	0.003	0.023	0.040	0.048	0.078	0.089	0.179	0.051	0.034	0.028	1.181	0.033	0.029	0.074	0.035	0.011	0.011	0.052	0.034	0.034	0.041
6	0.017	0.002	0.037	0.020	0.025	0.040	0.048	0.080	0.040	0.024	0.022	0.079	1.019	0.030	0.045	0.060	0.048	0.048	0.147	0.055	0.055	0.065
7	0.028	0.008	0.011	0.054	0.067	0.073	0.062	0.102	0.110	0.096	0.052	0.019	0.145	1.038	0.065	0.038	0.015	0.015	0.050	0.033	0.033	0.039
8	0.005	0.001	0.003	0.013	0.016	0.028	0.020	0.043	0.025	0.017	0.016	0.024	0.030	0.025	1.077	0.042	0.025	0.025	0.062	0.038	0.038	0.047
9	0.025	0.006	0.018	0.041	0.041	0.064	0.056	0.097	0.077	0.055	0.059	0.044	0.109	0.104	0.075	1.103	0.025	0.025	0.096	0.049	0.049	0.122
10	0.009	0.001	0.005	0.010	0.016	0.014	0.018	0.020	0.027	0.020	0.010	0.008	0.028	0.024	0.020	0.030	1.003	0.003	0.024	0.021	0.021	0.034
11	0.010	0.001	0.006	0.011	0.018	0.016	0.020	0.022	0.030	0.022	0.011	0.009	0.030	0.026	0.022	0.033	0.004	1.004	0.027	0.023	0.023	0.038
12	0.001	0.000	0.000	0.001	0.001	0.001	0.001	0.001	0.001	0.001	0.001	0.000	0.001	0.001	0.002	0.002	0.001	0.001	1.001	0.002	0.002	0.092
13	0.001	0.000	0.000	0.001	0.001	0.001	0.001	0.001	0.001	0.001	0.001	0.001	0.001	0.001	0.003	0.003	0.001	0.001	0.005	1.000	0.000	0.005
14	0.002	0.001	0.000	0.002	0.002	0.003	0.002	0.003	0.003	0.002	0.002	0.002	0.004	0.004	0.009	0.009	0.004	0.004	0.013	0.001	1.001	0.014
15	0.000	0.000	0.000	0.000	0.000	0.000	0.000	0.000	0.000	0.000	0.000	0.000	0.000	0.000	0.000	0.000	0.000	0.000	0.000	0.000	0.000	1.000
Multiplier	2.068	1.296	2.496	1.949	1.505	1.654	1.796	1.897	1.534	1.559	1.600	1.752	1.700	1.352	1.628	1.502	1.176	1.176	1.656	1.347	1.347	1.634

Table 5. Income multipliers and other multipliers.

	1	2	3	4.1	4.2	4.3	4.4	4.5	4.6	4.7	4.8	5	6	7	8	9	10	11	12	13	14	15	
	agriculture	fishery	mining	food prc	txtile mnf	wood prc	ptr chm	mtl prd	elc mry	trn eqp	otr mnf	EGW	cnstrctn	trade	htl & rst	tr & cm	fnc sev	cmr srv	pbl adm	education	health	scl prs srv	average
tl int inp	1.10	0.29	1.53	1.14	0.48	0.65	0.77	0.99	0.54	0.57	0.53	0.68	0.75	0.32	0.67	0.48	0.13	0.13	0.68	0.30	0.30	0.67	0.62
imported	0.05	0.06	0.02	0.37	0.60	0.47	0.49	0.40	0.46	0.58	0.75	0.12	0.11	0.10	0.14	0.15	0.20	0.20	0.26	0.16	0.16	0.36	0.28
GDP basic prices	0.83	0.86	0.85	0.40	0.38	0.49	0.48	0.46	0.48	0.37	0.29	0.86	0.76	0.84	0.74	0.79	0.77	0.77	0.65	0.80	0.80	0.54	0.65
Indirect tax-sbs	0.09	0.09	0.09	0.04	0.04	0.05	0.05	0.05	0.05	0.04	0.03	0.09	0.08	0.09	0.08	0.08	0.08	0.08	0.07	0.09	0.09	0.06	0.07
GDP mrkt prcs	0.92	0.95	0.94	0.44	0.42	0.54	0.53	0.51	0.53	0.41	0.32	0.95	0.84	0.93	0.82	0.87	0.85	0.85	0.72	0.89	0.89	0.60	0.72

Table 6. Multiplier effects of sector injections on income components.

	1	2	3	4.1	4.2	4.3	4.4	4.5	4.6	4.7	4.8	5	6	7	8	9	10	11	12	13	14	15	
	agriculture	fishery	mining	food prc	txtile mnf	wood prc	ptr chm	mtl prd	elc mry	trn eqp	otr mnf	EGW	cnstrctn	trade	htl & rst	tr & cm	fnc sev	cmr srv	pbl adm	education	health	scl prs srv	total
distributional proportions of GDP bp sector																							
compensa	0.13	0.32	0.17	0.34	0.51	0.49	0.37	0.55	0.52	0.47	0.50	0.22	0.62	0.55	0.55	0.47	0.26	0.26	0.26	0.59	0.60	0.60	0.60
Net opera	0.61	0.49	0.55	0.44	0.29	0.31	0.38	0.24	0.25	0.29	0.28	0.47	0.18	0.25	0.23	0.29	0.47	0.47	0.47	0.14	0.20	0.20	0.20
Net mixed	0.11	0.07	0.13	0.12	0.11	0.11	0.11	0.11	0.11	0.12	0.12	0.12	0.13	0.14	0.14	0.13	0.13	0.13	0.13	0.17	0.13	0.13	0.13
Net facto	0.85	0.88	0.84	0.90	0.91	0.91	0.86	0.89	0.88	0.88	0.90	0.80	0.92	0.93	0.92	0.89	0.85	0.85	0.85	0.90	0.93	0.93	0.93
cns fxd cp	0.15	0.12	0.16	0.10	0.09	0.09	0.14	0.11	0.12	0.12	0.10	0.20	0.08	0.07	0.08	0.11	0.15	0.15	0.15	0.10	0.07	0.07	0.07
gross fact	1.00	1.00	1.00	1.00	1.00	1.00	1.00	1.00	1.00	1.00	1.00	1.00	1.00	1	1	1	1	1	1	1	1	1	1
Multiplier effects of sector injections on income components																							
compensa	0.11	0.28	0.14	0.13	0.20	0.24	0.18	0.25	0.25	0.18	0.14	0.19	0.47	0.46	0.41	0.37	0.20	0.20	0.17	0.47	0.48	0.33	0.26
Net opera	0.51	0.42	0.47	0.17	0.11	0.15	0.18	0.11	0.12	0.11	0.08	0.40	0.13	0.21	0.17	0.23	0.36	0.36	0.31	0.11	0.16	0.11	0.23
Net mixed	0.09	0.06	0.11	0.05	0.04	0.05	0.05	0.05	0.05	0.04	0.03	0.10	0.10	0.12	0.11	0.10	0.10	0.10	0.08	0.14	0.11	0.07	0.08
Net facto	0.71	0.76	0.72	0.36	0.35	0.44	0.42	0.41	0.42	0.33	0.26	0.69	0.70	0.79	0.68	0.70	0.66	0.66	0.56	0.72	0.75	0.51	0.57
cns fxd cp	0.12	0.10	0.13	0.04	0.03	0.05	0.07	0.05	0.06	0.04	0.03	0.17	0.06	0.06	0.06	0.09	0.11	0.11	0.10	0.08	0.06	0.04	0.08
gross fact	0.83	0.86	0.85	0.40	0.38	0.49	0.48	0.46	0.48	0.37	0.29	0.86	0.76	0.84	0.74	0.79	0.77	0.77	0.65	0.80	0.80	0.54	0.65

Next to sectoral production multipliers, one can investigate sectoral income multipliers as done in Table 5, i.e. Multiplier of investigated variable z_j = (production multiplier M_j, from Table 4) * (alpha coefficient of the investigated variable in production α_{zj}, from Table 3).

The GDP income multipliers can be further split into its components of employment compensation, net operational surplus, and mixed returns on labor and capital. Multiplication of the distributional shares of the components by the GDP multiplier gives multiplier effects of the components. Table 6 gives the GDP distributional shares of the three components in the first part and the corresponding multiplier effects in the second part.

An important observation on the multiplier results is that although the production multiplier of mining (2.5) is higher than agriculture (2.1) and almost twice as much as fishery (1.3), the income generated is almost the same for the three sectors (0.85, 0.83, 0.86). And strikingly, the workforce in the fishery sector is better off with a wages multiplier of 0.28 compared to 0.14 in mining and 0.11 in agriculture. An attractive sector for development policy with emphasis on enhancing remunerative employment is the fishery sector.

2.3. *Overview of IO multiplier analysis*

This overview can be found in the extended literature on IOT and related economic modeling. The application for Suriname can be summarized in 12 points.

1. *IO Multiplier analysis (production, income, and other variables):* Examples of these were given above. These can be pursued further but would require additional data. How much of a primary factor of production, such as labor or capital, is needed for the production of a given final demand? If labor/production coefficients are available, then the employment effect of a change in final demand for sector j can be calculated. The total employment generated includes the direct employment effect in sector j plus indirect employment effects in other sectors j'. It is important to note that well-measured employment production elasticities are very low, labor inputs are not homogeneous, and labor participation is finite. Catching such relationships with IO analysis is insufficient. A SAM-based economy-wide modeling is more suited for tracing employment effects.

2. *Economy projections:* This is a variation in the impact analysis. If the final demand components are projected from some macro econometric model, these can be fed into the IO economy model to give projections of GDP at the sector level, as well as other projections relating to factor use and payments.

3. *Impact analysis:* What would production, value-added, and intermediate flows be if the final demand is changed? For any vector of final demands, f, one can

calculate the vector of industry production, j, making use of the production multipliers. Such an impact analysis was performed, and it showed that if extra final demand impulses are directed to infrastructure-related sectors (a total of 10.3% from basis 2015), the GDP growth would jump in 2020 to 9.8% from basis 2015. The sectors construction, transport, and related manufacturing sectors of machinery and transport equipment would increase their GDP shares in the total GDP by between 1% and 2%.

4. *Key sectors (backward and forward linkages):* The term key sectors is technically defined in IO analysis as $[\{(M_j/(\Sigma M_j)/J\}+\{(M_{j'}/(\Sigma M_{j'}/J)\}]/2$. where J is the number of sectors. In this formula, the first term refers to backward linkages and the second term to forward linkages. For backward linkages, a key sector should show that its own production multiplier over the rows, that is, the inputs side, M_j, is higher than the average of such multipliers over all sectors. For forward linkages, a key sector should show its production multiplier over the columns, that is, the outputs side, $M_{j'}$, is higher than the average of such multipliers over all sectors. A combined average score of above one is an indication of the presence of strong linkages for the sector concerned. Stimulation of key sectors pushes overall production to higher levels. The results are summarized in the first part of Table 7. In Suriname, the sizes of forward linkages (second term) are greater than backward linkages (first term). Agriculture, mining, petro chemicals, EGW, construction, trade, and transport sectors can be called key sectors as they show the highest combined scores on backward and forward linkages together. The sectors with the least linkages are those of public services which make little use of intermediate goods in the input–output context.

5. *Gainer loser index for sectors, GLI:* The index is defined for sector j by taking its multiplier j in terms of multipliers of all sectors after deducting the unit injection for sector j and for all sectors, whereby J stands for the number of sectors. The injected sector is denoted by $j^{\#}$:

$$GLI_{jj^{\#}} = \left[(M_{,jj\#} - 1)/(\Sigma_j M_{,jj\#} - 1^{*}J)\right] / \left[\text{Output}_{j,o}/\Sigma_j \text{Output}_{j,o}\right]$$

The first term gives the share of the added production effect of injecting sector j in all the added productions of all sectors. This term is divided by the actual production share of sector j in all sectors, in the IOT benchmark year. Sectors with $GLI_{jj\#} > 1$ are gainers, the so-called sunrise sectors. A sector with $GLI_{jj\#} < 1$ indicates a decreasing in the share economy. Because we simulate an equal injection of one unit in all sectors, the *GLI* index of sector j can be denoted by $GLI^{\#}_{j\ J}$. The results are summarized in the second part of Table 7. The gainers have favorable multiplier effects allowing them to pick higher shares of the multiplier effects than their actual shares in the economy. This indicates that these sectors are likely to increase their shares in the economy. They are growth sectors that are likely to grow at rates above the average growth rate of the economy. The data for 2014 and 2015 show that this prediction was realized.

Table 7. Results of key sector analysis, gainers losers analysis, and growth decomposition analysis.

		Key sector linkages analysis			Gainer loser analysis			Multiplier growth analysis		
		Back ward	For ward	Key sector	nomi- nator	denomi- nator	GL Index	M'14	M'15	M'15/M'14
1	Agriculture	1.28	1.58	1.43	0.08	0.08	1.04	2.07	2.08	0.99
2	Fishery	0.80	1.09	0.94	0.02	0.03	0.83	1.30	1.25	1.03
3	Mining	1.54	2.60	2.07	0.11	0.05	2.37	2.50	2.32	1.07
4.1	Food prcsng	1.20	0.63	0.91	0.07	0.03	2.25	1.95	1.98	0.99
4.2	Textile mnf	0.93	0.72	0.82	0.04	0.01	6.06	1.51	1.54	0.98
4.3	Wood prcsng	1.02	0.82	0.92	0.05	0.02	2.99	1.65	1.70	0.97
4.4	Ptr chm	1.11	1.19	1.15	0.06	0.04	1.56	1.80	1.88	0.96
4.5	Metal prdcts	1.17	0.63	0.90	0.07	0.03	2.60	1.90	1.96	0.97
4.6	Elctrc mchnry	0.95	0.72	0.83	0.04	0.05	0.85	1.53	1.59	0.97
4.7	Trnsprt eqp	0.96	0.73	0.85	0.04	0.02	1.81	1.56	1.64	0.95
4.8	Other mnf	0.99	0.64	0.81	0.04	0.01	3.77	1.60	1.63	0.98
5	ElctctyGsWtr	1.08	1.32	1.20	0.06	0.03	1.60	1.75	1.77	0.99
6	Construction	1.05	1.24	1.14	0.05	0.10	0.49	1.70	1.72	0.99
7	Trade	0.83	1.33	1.08	0.03	0.15	0.17	1.35	1.35	1.00
8	Hotels & rst	1.01	1.00	1.00	0.05	0.05	0.97	1.63	1.63	1.00
9	Trnsprt & cm	0.93	1.44	1.19	0.04	0.11	0.34	1.50	1.50	1.00
10	Fncl sev	0.73	0.84	0.79	0.01	0.04	0.36	1.18	1.19	0.99
11	Cmrl srv	0.73	0.87	0.80	0.01	0.03	0.40	1.18	1.19	0.99
12	Pblc adm	1.02	0.69	0.86	0.05	0.06	0.77	1.66	1.68	0.99
13	Education	0.83	0.64	0.73	0.03	0.03	0.80	1.35	1.37	0.99
14	Health	0.83	0.67	0.75	0.03	0.03	0.75	1.35	1.37	0.99
15	Scl prs srv	1.01	0.62	0.81	0.05	0.01	3.70	1.63	1.54	1.06
	Average							1.62	1.63	0.99

Table 7 explanations: Key sectors in column 3 is based on equal weights for backward and forward linkages

$[\{(M_j/(\Sigma M_j)/J\} + \{(M_{j'}/(\Sigma M_{j'}/J)\}]/2$

Table 7 explanations: Gainer loser index, GL index, in column 6 is defined as

$GLI^{\#}_{jJ} = [(M_{s,jj'} - 1)/(\Sigma_j M_{s,jj'} - 1 * J)]/[\text{Output}_{j,o}/\Sigma_j \text{Output}_{j,o}]$

6. *Growth decomposition analysis* focuses on the change δ in actual production X, or GDP, between two years, say 2015 and 2014, indicated by o, making use of the following formula:

$$\delta X = (M_o + \delta M)(f_o + \delta f) - M_o f_o = M_o \delta f + \delta M f_o + \delta M \delta f$$

Growth decomposition analysis is partially demonstrated in Table 7, which shows how much of the change in GDP between the two years is due to a deterioration in the production multipliers and how much is due to a deterioration in the final demand. Results are in the third part of Table 7. The comparison between the IOT multiplier for 2014 and 2015 shows a decrease from 1.630 to 1.619, a deterioration of $0.0109/1.6302 = 0.67\%$. This can be described as a deterioration of the production circular flow system of Suriname in 2015 by 0.67%. The actual fall in the GDP between the two years amounted to 3.4%. The difference is fully accounted for by the downfall in the final demand expenditure which accounted for the recession. The growth decomposition analysis shows that deterioration in the input–output production circular mechanisms formed a small proportion of the recession. This can be calculated as $0.67\%/3.4\% = 20\%$. The implication is that the fall in the final demand expenditure is dominant and determinant at 80%. This is a simple and quick decomposition of economic growth between 2014 and 2015 into its component parts, which adds insight into how the Suriname economy is operating.

7. *Extraction analysis* investigates the structural importance of a particular sector in the economy by hypothetically removing it from the IOT, rerunning the inverse, and contrasting the newly obtained multipliers without the particular sector to the multipliers with the particular sector.

8. *Insertion analysis is practically the opposite of extraction analysis:* The structural significance of a particular economic activity within mining, such as gold or oil, can be simulated in the IOT by inserting additional rows and columns for these sectors based on own country studies (or on borrowed IO data), redoing the inverse and evaluating the new set of multipliers to the standard set of multipliers without the inserted sectors. If the data of the inserted sectors and the ensuing multiplier analysis give reliable results, there is reason to include the inserted sectors as regular sectors. An insertion analysis is often simpler and achieves the same objective of sector simulation and evaluation.

9. *Sensitivity analysis* can be applied to a wide range of $\alpha_{jj'}$ coefficients. Change a specific cell or blocks of cells, redo the inverse, and observe how the multipliers are changed.

10. *Structural change analysis* would compare the changing tendencies in production multipliers over a series of several years. This is feasible if more IOT is available. Examples of analysis for 2015 and 2014 are shown in Table 7. The results show a slight decrease in average multipliers in 2015. The ranking of sectors remains the same with mining leading and followed by agriculture, food processing, metal, petroleum, EGW (electricity, gas, water), and construction, all of these with production multipliers above 1.7.

11. *Ghoshian multipliers:* While Leontief focuses on the relation between inputs and total production and thus moves downward along the columns to compute $a_{jj'}/X_{j'}$ and uses these alpha coefficients $\alpha_{jj'}$ in generating the Leontief multipliers M_j. Ghosh shifts the attention to the relation between outputs and total production and thus moves sideways to the right along the rows to compute $a_{jj'}/X_j$

and use the modified alpha coefficients $(\alpha_{jj'})_m$ in generating Ghoshian multipliers. Although there is controversy on the theoretical foundations of Ghoshian multipliers, their application can highlight hidden properties of forward linkages, production networks, and supply chains.

12. *Induced multiplier analysis:* The IO multipliers consider direct and indirect effects. But once these effects take place, the factors of production would employ their incomes in spending on FD which would create a first round of induced growth resulting in new rounds of IO multipliers to be followed by new rounds of induced growth, and so on. The IO table and IO model are not able to capture this element of the circular flow of the economy, which is very much the Keynesian element. There are applications which supplement the Leontief multiplier by adding to it the Keynesian element, resulting in the so-called induced multipliers. These are higher. The more systematic way of integrating the Loentief and Keynes multipliers is the social accounting matrix, which incorporates direct, indirect as well as induced effects. The IOT analytical framework can be described as partial when compared to the SAM which is describable as general.

3. Social Accounting Matrix: Construction and Analysis

3.1. *The SAM accounts*

The Social Accounting Matrix (SAM) is the comprehensive transformation of transactions between actors that take place in the circular flow of the economy into a statistical matrix of the accounts of these actors. In correspondence with circular flow, SAM contains the following seven account categories: (1) Industries j (also called sectors or activities) consist of payment received and paid for in and out deliveries among industries. This comes from the input–output table. (2) Factors of production earnings and payment for various workforce types, denoted by f, and capital returns. (3) Household population groups income and spending, denoted by h, are classifiable in alternative ways depending on the selected focus and available data. (4) Incorporated business firms, b. (5) Government, g. (6) Non-current account, n, which consists of savings and investment transactions aggregated over all institutions. (7) Rest of the world account, w, relates to exports, imports, foreign investment, and transfers.

Industries j are already discussed under input–output table, whereby the manufacturing sector is aggregated as one sector. There are simply no data available at the workforce level to apply subdivisions of the manufacturing sector.

Factors f are distinguished in seven factor compensations. Factor payments fall into employee compensation classified into four aggregated occupational groups following the ISCO, the category of small self-employed, the category of business employers, and finally the purely net operating surplus which go as capital returns to corporate business:

$f1$. Professionals + Managers + Technicians and Associate Professionals
$f2$. Administrative + Clerical Support Workers + Services and Sales Workers
$f3$. Skilled Agricultural, Forestry, and Fishery Workers + Craft and Related Trades Workers
$f4$. Elementary Occupations +Plant and Machine Operators and Assemblers
$f5$. Self-employed tiny enterprises with remuneration more aligned with wages than profits
$f6$. Employer and proprietor of larger firms with remuneration more aligned to profits than wages.
$f7$. Capital returns, i.e. corporate net operating surplus.

As to household population groups, h, an appraisal of what is desirable and what is feasible in the SAM context suggests that the total population of the country can best be classified into eight household population groups, six of which are directly mapped to earners of workforce categories distinguished above. The characteristic occupation-status of the six household earners f determines the identity of the household population group. The adult dependents (aged 15–65) and child dependents (aged <15) attached to a specific earner occupational group belong to that specific group. The other two population groups do not earn labor remuneration and are dependent on transfers: they are the unemployed and the seniors aged 65 years and above.

The relationship between the total population by age groups and status, their distribution on the active workforce factor types and non-actives, and their subsequent transformation in household population groups can be gathered from the following table. Dependent non-actives and children are added to household earners to obtain household population groups. Population >65 forms the seniors hpg. The distinction between earners, adult dependents, and child dependents, when combined with adult equivalence scales, gives the size of the household population groups in adult equivalents (in the last column). This is a very useful information for measuring consumption functions and tracing poverty incidence, as will be shown later on.

The SAM connects the seven accounts to each other in ways which correspond with the circular flow of the economy. Industries use intermediate inputs and primary inputs (factors of production such as various employed and remunerated labor types and capital returns) to produce final goods for consumption, investment, and foreign trade. Industries pay earnings to the factors of production. In turn, these factors bring their earnings to household groups to which they belong. Next, household population groups spend their incomes on consumption of final goods, and the rest they save. The savings are used for investment. In addition to households, there are corporates, governments, and the world; and the capital accumulation account. Corporates get the capital returns, do some payments, and save the rest. The government collects indirect taxes from and gives subsidies to industries, collects taxes from and makes transfers to households and taxes corporates, and engages in transfers with the world. The world account takes care of exports and imports sourced by industries, transfers sourced by the institutions of h, o, and g, and closes the gaps between total exports and total imports on the one hand and total savings and total investment through foreign capital flow on the other hand. The latter feeds the capital accumulation account.

3.2. *Estimation of the SAM*

1. Industries: The IOT manufacturing branches are aggregated to obtain one manufacturing sector. The interindustry deliveries part of the IOT are inserted in the SAM tabulation, in the upper left corner of Table 12. Furthermore, other cells in the primary inputs part of the IOT, such as factor payments by sector, indirect taxes less subsidies by sector, and capital maintenance by sector, and in the final demand part of the IOT, such as consumption, investment, exports, and imports per sector, are to be entered in their respective cells in the SAM tabulation.

2. Factors: Employee remuneration is to be split into the four occupational types, $f = 1, 2, 3, 4$. The summary equation is $R_{jf} = M_{jf}{}^{*}W^{*}P_{f}{}^{*}P_{f}$, where R_{jf} is the employee remuneration per sector j and occupation f, M_{jf} is the employment by sector and occupation, W is the average wage rate, P_j is the earnings productivity differential by sector, and P_f is the earnings differential by occupation. Mixed remuneration is to be split into two more workforce types: f_5 for self-employed and f_6 for employer proprietors.

Employment M_{jf} is obtained by extending household survey numbers from Paramaribo and Wanica to the whole of Suriname. Average wage W is obtained by dividing total employee compensation (from IOT) by total employees $(\Sigma \cdot M_{jf})$. W amounts to 45457 SRD, which is very close to the average labor cost in large enterprises as published by ABS.

Earnings productivity differentials by occupation, P_f, are derived from salary scales in the public sectors of public administration, health, and education, indicating a salary index range of 7 for professionals/managers, 5 for administrative/clerical, 3 for skilled workers, and 1 for elementary jobs.

Earnings productivity differentials by sector P_j are obtained as the difference between actual employee compensation by sector from IOT and the simulated values of $M_{jf}{}^{*}W^{*}P_{f}$.

Table 8. The eight household population groups: Gross income per adult equivalent.

Household groups	1	2	3	4	5	6	7	8	total	unit
gross income	2579	2931	1567	576	522	1228	139	277	9820	SRD mln
Adult equivalent	60759	88441	56769	61157	38180	5914	22190	30100	363510	AEU
gr inc per equiv	42447	33146	27600	9420	13663	207698	6269	9209	27014	SRD

The values of earning productivity differentials per sector, P_j, are found to amount to the following: agriculture $= 1.07$, etc. With all the above, R_{jf} become known and are inserted in the SAM.

The self-employed group is highly differentiated in terms of earnings as it includes well-remunerated own-account professionals but mostly self-employed and unpaid family workers. It was reasoned there that most self-employed workers fall in the occupational groups f_3 and f_4, supporting the selection of an average remuneration per worker based on f_3 and f_4. This average remuneration multiplied by the number of self-employed workers gives the total earnings of the self-employed group. Deducting this from the IOT total sum for mixed compensation gives the total earnings of employers group.

3. *Household groups:* We first handle the population and then proceed to receive in-payments and to spend out-payments each treat. The *population* of an earning household group consists of the number of earners in the group, plus dependent adults and dependent children, which are obtained from demographic data. The dependency rates are 0.84 and 0.74, respectively. For the unemployed group, the dependency rates are adjusted downward since many of the unemployed have no dependents. The seniors group is counted as it is, without dependents.

To obtain the sizes of the household groups in adult equivalent units, denoted by AEU, we apply scale in Sobhie (2017) and OECD (2008) which value adult dependents at 0.5, child dependents at 0.3, and seniors at 0.7. The formula is AEU $=$ earner $+$ adult dependents $*$ 0.5$+$ child dependents $*$ 0.3.

Next, we treat the *received in-payments*. Earned income by factors 1–6 goes directly to the hpg with which each factor is linked. The unemployed hpg (group 7) and the seniors hpg (group 8) do not receive earnings. They receive various transfers which were estimated based on their respective numbers, maintenance allowance rates, pension payments, and public allowance for elders (AOV). The results are in Table 8.

Next, we treat the *spent out-payments*. Disposable income of hpg is defined as gross income less direct taxes and public levies paid to the government. To bring more realism and simplicity to the SAM, we postulate the distinction between higher-income and lowest-income household groups (hg). The higher-income hg are groups 1, 2, 3, and 6. The least income hg are groups 4, 5, 7, and 8, that is, the employee household group with elementary occupations, self-employed tiny undertakings hg, the unemployed hg, and the seniors hg. We make the validated assumption that while the higher income groups pay, the least income groups are excused from such tax and levy payments. The sum of taxes and levies (457 SRD mln) is paid by groups 1, 2, 3, and 6 based on the proportional distribution of their gross incomes. The outcomes are inserted in the SAM.

The SAM requires breaking up disposable income in consumption and savings for each of the eight hpg separately. Household survey data (HBO) do not display disposable income, consumption, and savings. They focus on consumption expenditure patterns and demographic attributes of household types. We apply some devices to get around the lack of data and introduce differentiation in consumption and saving behavior between the eight household groups.

Formulate the consumption function $C/AEU = \alpha + \beta(Y/AEU)$, where C is the consumption expenditure, Y is the disposable income, and AEU is the adult equivalence unit; α and β are unknowns to be estimated. Apply this equation for the aggregated group of high income and the same for the low income, giving thus two equations. Assume tentatively that the low-income groups consume all their disposable income, later to be modified. Deducting this tentative (low-income) consumption from total consumption gives the tentative (high-income) consumption. With values available for the above variables, the two equations are solved to determine the two coefficients, that is, $\alpha = 3226.7$ and $\beta = 0.6784$. The consumption function can be restated as

$$C = \alpha AEU + \beta Y = 3226.7\ AEU + 0.6784\ Y$$

meaning that for every adult equivalent unit *AEU*, the amount of 3226.7 SRD is a basic consumption, and the rest of the consumption varies with income Y, at a consumption share of 0.68. The equation can now be used to project the consumption of each of the eight household groups. The results are consistent and confirm an increasing consumption ratio with lower income. They go further and show, as can be expected, negative savings for the least income groups with presumably the highest poverty incidence. The resulting values for consumption expenditure for each household group on the right-hand side of Table 9 are inserted in the consumption expenditure row by the household group in the SAM.

All the above is brought together in Table 9. The table calculates the negative savings ratio for employee workers with elementary jobs (*h4*), self-employed and family workers (*h5*), the unemployed (*h7*), and the seniors (*h8*). Negative savings are the other face of the poverty coin. Parts of these groups fall under the poverty line. The elementary jobs household group has an income short of their expenditure by about 2%. Depending on the skewness of the earnings within this group, the

Table 9. Estimation of consumption function and consumption projection by household group.

C/E = a + b (Y/E)
28299= a + b 37043
9985 = a + b that is a= 9985 - b 9985 =(1-b) 9985
substitute
28299= (1-b) 9985 + b 37043
28299=9985 + b (37043-9985)
18314 = b 27058
b = 0.676842
a= (1-b) 9985= 3226.7
Recall C/E = a + b (Y/E)
multiply by E gives enhanced consumption function
in terms of adult equivalent units and disposable income
C = a E + b Y
C= 3226.7 E + 0.67684 Y

Household group	Projections C	S	C/Y	S/Y
1.prf	1846	592	0.76	0.24
2.adm	2160	610	0.78	0.22
3.crftmn	1185	295	0.80	0.20
4.elmntry	587	-11	1.02	-0.02
5.slfmpl	476	45	0.91	0.09
6.emplyr	805	356	0.69	0.31
7.Unmplyd	166	-27	1.19	-0.19
8.Seniors	285	-8	1.03	-0.03
High Incm	5996	1853	0.76	0.24
Low Incm	1514	0	1.00	0.00
Total	7512	1854	0.80	0.20

dissaving shortage can be higher and be concentrated in a larger poverty struck portion within the group, of say 20%. Within the self-employed household group, there can be a similar poverty stuck portion of 20%. As earners in these two household groups constitute about 30% of all earners, working poverty would amount roughly to 6%, which is close to ILO's estimate of 5% working poverty for Suriname.

Next in the spent out-payments is the allocation of consumption expenditure to sectors. There are no direct data available that give each separate household group the consumption pattern by commodity/sector. In such a situation, there is no other alternative than making use of the national pattern of allocation of consumption by sector, which is also apparent in the IOT.

4. Corporate business: The incomings in this account are capital returns (net operating surplus) amounting to 4250 SRD mln and interest payments on the national government debt amounting to 140 SRD mln. Corporate business firms include creditor financial institutions that supply the government with loans to cover its budget deficits. There is a net negative transfer of capital returns to the world account amounting to 84 SRD mln. When this is deducted, the domestic revenue of the corporate account amounts to 4306 SRD mln. This is disposed of partly in corporate taxes 1359 and the remainder of 2947 as corporate savings that enter later on into total investment. The actual corporate tax rate amounts to 32% and the savings rate at 68% of their domestic revenue.

5. Government account: The government statistics on revenue and expenditures are from the Central Bank of Suriname and the ABS, and their distribution was assigned to the previously mentioned various accounts where applicable.

6. Institutions non-current account: The SAM's non-current account is an aggregation of non-current transactions of households, corporate, and government. The row of this account stands for receipts from industries (maintenance for capital depreciation (total 1468), from the institutions of households, corporate, and government (their savings amounting to respectively 1853, 2947, and −147), and net foreign capital flow from the world (net 1760). The total of the incomings row amounts to 7882 SRD mln. The column stands for the total outlay of the non-current account which is 7882 SRD mln in 2015. This is also the value of total investment in 2015. By definition, total savings equal total investment.

7. World account: Entries in the world account are simplified in the SAM by inserting net values of transactions with the world in the column and keeping the row empty with total incomings of zero. The first category of entries in the world column relates to exports and imports of goods and services by sector, which is taken from the IOT, showing a negative net trade balance of −1753 SRD mln. The second category of entries relates to net foreign transfers to institutions. For households, the transfer is a positive sum of 219 SRD mln. For corporate business firms, the net transfer is a negative sum of −84 SRD mln, representing capital returns that are transferred to foreign share-owning businesses. For the government, the net transfer is negative at −141 SRD mln, standing for interest payments and paybacks on the national debt that is financed by foreign institutions. The third category is the net foreign capital inflow which brings both the non-current account and the foreign payments account into equilibrium. The figures for net foreign capital inflow are readily available from ABS but are also derived as residuals from the SAM through the non-current account and the world account. Getting the same results through different channels is the most important test for the external and internal consistency of the SAM. The results are strikingly satisfying. Net foreign capital inflow via the non-current account amounted to 1762 SRD mln, and via the world account it is 1759 SRD mln; the difference is due to rounding errors. Net foreign capital inflow in the SAM corresponds with ABS statistics.

A brief summing of the steps employed in constructing and estimating the SAM is found in Appendix II. The final outcome of the estimation is the SAM as in Table 10.

Table 10. Social Accounting Matrix (Suriname, 2015: Million SRD).

	ACTIVITIES, INDUSTRIES, SECTORS J															intrmt	FACTORS f		
	$j1$	$j2$	$j3$	$j4$	$j5$	$j6$	$j7$	$j8$	$j9$	$j10$	$j11$	$j12$	$j13$	$j14$	$j15$	dlvrs	$f1$	$f2$	$f3$
$j1$. Agrcltr	1159	1	0	302	0	24	6	41	1	2	2	2	2	2	0	1561			
$j2$. Fishery	2	321	0	219	0	0	13	96	0	1	1	0	2	3	4	679			
$j3$. Mining	7	9	834	322	160	134	3	2	63	1	1	19	1	1	3	1577			
$j4$.Mnfctrng	46	24	6	921	7	498	125	46	213	15	14	153	41	44	38	2181			
$j5$. El wr gs	25	2	10	402	182	45	108	102	83	10	9	76	27	29	18	1126			
$j6$. Cstrctn	14	2	17	171	63	1	97	49	169	66	60	281	49	52	27	1113			
$j7$. Trade	25	10	2	419	4	382	125	73	68	7	6	35	18	20	12	1200			
$j8$. Htl Rstrnt	2	0	0	109	18	66	96	119	124	34	31	112	36	38	25	806			
$j9$.Trsprt cmn	23	8	6	334	29	299	508	99	340	26	24	156	40	42	78	2001			
$j10$.Fncl srv	16	1	4	183	8	133	206	49	187	2	2	69	37	39	40	972			
$j11$.Cmcl srv	17	1	4	187	8	137	211	50	191	2	2	70	38	40	41	995			
$j12$.Pblc adm	1	0	0	3	0	1	2	2	4	1	1	0	1	1	51	68			
$j13$.Edctn	0	0	0	2	0	2	3	3	7	1	1	6	0	0	2	29			
$j14$. Health	1	1	0	7	1	7	11	11	23	4	4	21	0	0	7	99			
$j15$.Otr srv	0	0	0	2	0	1	2	1	1	0	0	0	0	0	0	10			
ttl intrt inpts	1338	382	883	3583	481	1729	1517	743	1475	172	156	1002	294	311	346	14412			
$f1$. prfsnls	14	20	29	201	47	124	278	97	373	64	60	365	465	367	18	2522			
$f2$. admnstrv	13	18	23	197	37	81	1150	260	284	122	99	324	45	165	49	2866			
$f3$.ag mn wrk	87	121	11	307	26	665	163	7	59	4	9	26	2	7	37	1532			
$f4$. elmntry jb	15	20	22	54	7	52	41	14	135	2	6	31	7	9	10	424			
empl cmpnsn	128	179	85	759	117	922	1633	379	851	192	174	745	519	549	114	7344			
$f5$.slf emplyd	31	12	19	55	19	57	123	30	69	28	25	0	18	19	4	510			
$f6$.emplyr prp	73	29	45	130	44	134	290	70	163	66	60	0	43	45	9	1201			
mixed returns	104	41	64	185	63	190	413	100	232	94	85	0	61	65	13	1711			
$f7$. Nt opr srp	593	269	276	502	252	264	745	159	522	350	317	0	0	0	0	4250			
Nt fctr inc (bp)	825	489	426	1446	432	1376	2790	637	1604	636	577	745	581	613	127	13304			
$h1$. prfsnls																	2522		
$h2$. admnstrv																		2866	
$h3$.ag mn wrk																			1532
$h4$. elmntry jb																			
$h5$.slf emplyd																			
$h6$. emplyr prp																			
$h7$.unemployd																			
$h8$. seniors																			
Ttl hshld grps																	2522	2866	1532
Crprt firms																			
Ind txs - sbs	104	59	54	174	58	161	321	74	194	80	73	84	66	69	14	1585			
Non crrnt acnt	141	64	80	174	107	120	203	56	206	109	99	39	31	32	7	1468			
Rest Wrld																			
Total Input	2407	995	1443	5376	1078	3386	4832	1511	3480	997	904	1871	971	1026	494	30769	2522	2866	1532

Table 10. (*Continued*)

	FACTORS *f*	N O S			NFI			HOUSEHOLD GROUPS						Ttl hld	CRPR	GVRN	NON	RST of WRLD		Pymt	TTL
	*f*4	*f*5	*f*6	*f*7	bp	*h*1	*h*2	*h*3	*h*4	*h*5	*h*6	*h*7	*h*8	grps	FRMS	MNT	CRNT	EXPRT	IMPRT	blns	OTPT
*j*1. Agrcltr						61	72	39	19	16	27	5	9	249		48	20	751	207	544	2407
*j*2. Fishery						41	48	26	13	11	18	4	6	166		0	1	178	11	167	995
*j*3. Mining						6	7	4	2	2	3	1	1	25		0	19	36	199	−162	1443
*j*4.Mnfctrng						251	294	161	80	65	109	23	39	1021		0	1994	2505	2334	171	5376
*j*5. El wr gs						53	62	34	17	14	23	5	8	216		22	0	41	329	−288	1078
*j*6. Cstrctn						1	1	1	0	0	0	0	0	4		15	2852	125	729	−604	3386
*j*7. Trade						549	643	353	175	142	240	49	85	2235		87	1277	1049	1021	29	4832
*j*8. Htl Rstrnt						77	90	49	24	20	34	7	12	313		0	0	648	260	388	1511
*j*9.Trsprt cmn						124	145	80	39	32	54	11	19	505		41	305	1266	649	617	3480
*j*10.Fncl srv						143	168	92	46	37	63	13	22	583		0	394	28	986	−958	997
*j*11.Cmcl srv						116	135	74	37	30	50	10	18	470		0	307	22	896	−874	904
*j*12.Pblc adm						7	8	5	2	2	3	1	1	29		1198	713	214	352	−138	1871
*j*13.Edctn						147	171	94	47	38	64	13	23	596		640	0	0	294	−294	971
*j*14. Health						161	188	103	51	41	70	14	25	654		582	0	0	311	−311	1026
*j*15.Otr srv						108	127	70	34	28	47	10	17	441		85	0	0	41	−41	494
ttl intrt inpts						1846	2160	1185	587	476	805	166	285	7510		2718	7882	6865	8618	−1753	30769
*f*1. prfsnls																					2522
*f*2. admnstrv																					2866
*f*3.ag mn wrk																					1532
*f*4. elmntry jb																					424
empl cmpnsn																					7344
*f*5.slf emplyd																					948
*f*6.emplyr prp																					762
mixed returns																					1711
*f*7. Nt opr srp																					4250
Nt fctr inc (bp)																					13305
*h*1. prfsnls					2522										Dividend					57	2579
*h*2. admnstrv					2866										payments					65	2931
*h*3.ag mn wrk					1532										marginal					35	1567
*h*4. elmntry jb	424				424										tentative	142				10	576
*h*5.slf emplyd		510			510										zero					12	522
*h*6. emplyr prp			1201		1201															27	1228
*h*7.unemployd						inter hshld ppltn grp transfers fixed at zero										136				3	139
*h*8. seniors																271				6	277
Ttl hshld grps	424	510	1201		9055										0	549				219	9820
Crprt firms				4250												140				−84	4306
Ind txs − sbs					9055	142	161	86	0	0	68	0	0	457	1359					−141	3260
Non crrnt acnt						592	610	295	−11	45	356	−27	−8	1853	2947	−147				ca 1760	7882
Rest Wrld																					0
Total Input	424	510	1201	4250	13305	2579	2931	1567	576	522	1228	139	277	9820	4306	3260	7882			0	69342

3.3. *SAM uses: Descriptive analysis and multiplier analysis*

3.3.1. *Descriptive analysis*

SAM Suriname is the description of the social economy of the country in a compact matrix of 34 rows × 34 columns, plus additional rows and columns for subtotals. The matrix presents a multi-dimensional picture of the country that goes far beyond singular tables of one or the other aspect and hence allows for a wider comprehension and deeper insight into otherwise hidden features of the social economy. This section displays some examples of descriptive analysis.

The activities account was thoroughly treated in the IOT and can be skipped, except for noting that in 2015 the sum total of interindustry delivery inputs amounted to 14412 SRD mln, while the whole circular flow of the economy as indicated by the grand total of all seven accounts of the SAM amounted to 69342 SRD mln. The volume of the SAM transaction flows is about five times as much as IOT.

Factors: The degree of earnings productivity differentiation by sector as measured by highest/lowest values for P_j amounts to 9.57, where the highest is hotels and restaurants at 2.08 and the lowest is general services at 0.21. The earnings differential among occupation types expressed as highest to lowest is $1.7/.24 = 7.08$. This suggests that the economic surroundings in which the earner works are more influential than his/her own skill attributes in the determination of relative incomes. When the employer–employee status is considered, the earnings differentiation by status jumps to $4.65/.24 = 19.38$. The above suggests that remuneration differentials in the workforce at large are most influenced first by employment status, second by sector, and only third by occupation.

Household groups: In spite of the limited data available, the SAM presents verifiable adult equivalent units for the eight household groups, as well as measurements of consumption function implying consumption rates of 69% and savings rates of 31% for the richest and varying upward and downward to reach consumption rates of 119% and negative savings rates of −19% for the lowest-income receiving group of the unemployed. For all households, the average consumption rate is 80% and the savings rate is 20%.

Corporate business: The following four indicators are interesting: (1) Out of the total capital returns which corporate business receives, 4250 SRD mln, the sum of 48 SRD mln is repatriated as dividends to foreign-owning investors. The repatriation share is 11.3%. (2) Domestic financial institutions, which are included in the corporate account, provide about half of the government borrowings, and the other half is provided by foreign financial institutions. These ratios are reflected by the interest payments which government pays to the domestic financing corporate business and foreign financiers, 140 and 141 SRD mln, respectively. (3) The actual corporate tax rate that is collected by the government is found to amount to 18.4%. The legal company tax rate is 36%. The ratio of actual to nominal company tax rate amounts to 51%. (4) The SAM shows the savings rate of corporate business to amount to 68%. This implies that to meet its investment goals, corporate business supplements its savings on a yearly basis by another 28% of funding resources, presumably mostly from abroad.

3.3.2. *Derivation of SAM multipliers*

Methodologically, the SAM can be converted into a static model in very much the same way as this applied to IOT, with the difference that the SAM is a more comprehensive representation of the economy. Specific columns (and their respective rows) which are considered to be exogenous are placed in a separate exogenous vector on the right side, denoted by vector e. These are the accounts of the government, the world, and the non-current account. There are 31 endogenous variables placed on the left side, denoted by vector υ. The cells attached to these endogenous variables are converted in a coefficient matrix using the same IOT assumption of proportions expressed in terms of column totals. Denote this coefficient matrix by A. The system can be described now generally by eq. (1). Inversion of the matrix $(I' - A)^{-1}$ and solving give eq. (2), where *Ms* stands for the SAM matrix of multipliers. To distinguish the IOT multipliers from the SAM multipliers, we have denoted them by M and *Ms*, respectively:

$$\upsilon - A\upsilon = e \tag{1}$$

$$\upsilon = I' - A^{-1}e = Ms\,e \tag{2}$$

The SAM multipliers matrix, *Ms*, is a matrix of 31 rows by 31 columns. The multiplier analysis focuses on impacts initiated by three types of exogenous interventions denoted by $j^{\#}$. The exogenous interventions are sectoral injections, factor shifts, and household group income transfers. (1) Exogenous injections per production sector, the injected sector denoted by $j^{\#}$. Such injections are put into motion via spending by the government, investors, and the world, i.e., exports and imports. The question is as follows: How does a unit of these sectoral injections impact the 31 endogenous variables (consisting of sectoral productions $X_{jj}{}^{\#}$, factor earnings $Y_{fj}{}^{\#}$, and household incomes $Y_{hj}{}^{\#}$)? (2) There can be exogenous shifts in rewards and use per producing factor, expressed as $f^{\#}$, which are technologically induced but can also be influenced by government policy and global developments. The question is as follows: How does a unit of these factor changes impacts the 31 endogenous variables (consisting of sectoral productions $X_{jf}{}^{\#}$, factor earnings $Y_{ff}{}^{\#}$, and household incomes $Y_{hf}{}^{\#}$)? (3) There can be exogenous income transfers to a specific household group *h#* put into action via the government and the world. The question is as follows: How do these transfers impact the 31 endogenous variables (consisting of sectoral productions $X_{jh}{}^{\#}$, factor earnings $Y_{fh}{}^{\#}$, and household incomes $Y_{hh}{}^{\#}$)?

The 31 × 31 SAM matrix of multipliers is best analyzed when it is split into three submatrices corresponding to the above three questions:
(1) multipliers of sector injections: $Ms\ X_{jj}{}^{\#}$, $Ms\ Y_{fj}{}^{\#}$, $Ms\ Y_{hj}{}^{\#}$.
(2) multipliers of factor earnings shifts: $Ms\ X_{jf}{}^{\#}$, $Ms\ Y_{ff}{}^{\#}$, $Ms\ Y_{hf}{}^{\#}$.
(3) multipliers of household income transfers: $MsX_{jh}{}^{\#}$, $Ms\ Y_{fh}{}^{\#}$, $Ms\ Y_{hh}{}^{\#}$.
This chapter will further examine (1) in more detail and (2) and (3) in less detail.

3.3.3. *SAM multipliers of sector injections:* $MsX_{jj}{}^{\#}$, $Ms\ Y_{fj}{}^{\#}$, $Ms\ Y_{hj}{}^{\#}$

General analysis: Table 11 is the first portion relating to multipliers of sector injections: $Ms\ X_{jj}{}^{\#}$, $Ms\ Y_{fj}{}^{\#}$, and $Ms\ Y_{hj}{}^{\#}$. This shows effects on sectoral production and GDP, factor account, and household account, respectively.

Table 11. SAM multipliers of sector injections: $Ms\ X^{\#}_{jj}$, $Ms\ Y^{\#}_{fj}$, and $Ms\ Y^{\#}_{hj}$.

IMPACTED	MULTIPLIER EFFECTS OF A UNIT INJECTION IN SECTOR DEMAND														
	j1	j2	j3	j4	j5	j6	j7	j8	j9	j10	j11	j12	j13	j14	j15
Sector j															
1. Agriculture	1.97	0.05	0.04	0.19	0.05	0.11	0.08	0.13	0.08	0.06	0.06	0.10	0.10	0.10	0.10
2. Fishery	0.02	1.51	0.02	0.11	0.03	0.06	0.05	0.15	0.05	0.03	0.04	0.06	0.06	0.07	0.07
3. Mining	0.06	0.09	2.42	0.29	0.48	0.21	0.10	0.12	0.15	0.07	0.07	0.17	0.12	0.12	0.16
4. Manufacturing	0.12	0.15	0.10	1.37	0.13	0.36	0.21	0.22	0.25	0.14	0.14	0.34	0.28	0.28	0.32
5. Elct, Gs, Water	0.06	0.05	0.06	0.18	1.25	0.11	0.11	0.17	0.11	0.07	0.07	0.16	0.13	0.13	0.15
6. Construction	0.04	0.04	0.06	0.10	0.11	1.08	0.09	0.10	0.12	0.10	0.10	0.23	0.13	0.13	0.16
7. Trade	0.14	0.18	0.13	0.31	0.16	0.39	1.28	0.30	0.27	0.18	0.18	0.34	0.35	0.35	0.33
8. Hotels & rs	0.03	0.04	0.03	0.09	0.06	0.10	0.10	1.16	0.11	0.08	0.08	0.16	0.13	0.13	0.15
9. Trnsp & cm	0.09	0.10	0.08	0.22	0.13	0.26	0.26	0.22	1.25	0.13	0.13	0.28	0.23	0.23	0.36
10. Fnncl services	0.06	0.07	0.06	0.13	0.07	0.15	0.15	0.14	0.16	1.07	0.07	0.17	0.17	0.17	0.21
11. Cmrcl services	0.06	0.06	0.05	0.13	0.07	0.15	0.14	0.13	0.15	0.06	1.07	0.16	0.15	0.16	0.20
12. Public admstrn	0.00	0.01	0.00	0.01	0.00	0.01	0.01	0.01	0.01	0.01	0.01	1.01	0.01	0.01	0.11
13. Education	0.03	0.04	0.03	0.05	0.03	0.06	0.06	0.06	0.05	0.04	0.04	0.07	1.07	0.07	0.07
14. Health	0.03	0.04	0.03	0.06	0.04	0.07	0.07	0.07	0.07	0.05	0.05	0.09	0.08	1.08	0.09
15. Other services	0.03	0.03	0.02	0.03	0.02	0.04	0.04	0.04	0.04	0.03	0.03	0.05	0.05	0.05	1.04
All sectors	2.75	2.46	3.14	3.28	2.64	3.17	2.74	3.01	2.85	2.12	2.13	3.39	3.06	3.07	3.54
Factor f															
f1	0.07	0.11	0.11	0.18	0.14	0.20	0.20	0.21	0.25	0.15	0.16	0.38	0.65	0.53	0.25
f2	0.09	0.12	0.11	0.22	0.15	0.23	0.41	0.36	0.26	0.23	0.22	0.39	0.25	0.37	0.35
f3	0.10	0.21	0.05	0.15	0.08	0.27	0.10	0.08	0.09	0.05	0.06	0.12	0.08	0.09	0.17
f4	0.02	0.04	0.05	0.04	0.03	0.04	0.03	0.04	0.06	0.02	0.02	0.05	0.03	0.03	0.06
f5	0.04	0.04	0.05	0.05	0.05	0.06	0.06	0.06	0.05	0.05	0.05	0.04	0.06	0.06	0.05
f6	0.09	0.09	0.11	0.12	0.11	0.13	0.14	0.13	0.13	0.12	0.12	0.10	0.14	0.14	0.13
f7	0.61	0.56	0.58	0.49	0.52	0.44	0.45	0.46	0.47	0.53	0.53	0.39	0.34	0.35	0.42
All factors	1.03	1.17	1.05	1.25	1.07	1.38	1.39	1.34	1.31	1.15	1.15	1.48	1.55	1.56	1.42
Household h															
h1	0.07	0.11	0.11	0.18	0.14	0.20	0.20	0.21	0.25	0.15	0.16	0.38	0.65	0.53	0.25
h2	0.09	0.12	0.11	0.22	0.15	0.23	0.41	0.36	0.26	0.23	0.22	0.39	0.25	0.37	0.35
h3	0.10	0.21	0.05	0.15	0.08	0.27	0.10	0.08	0.09	0.05	0.06	0.12	0.08	0.09	0.17
h4	0.02	0.04	0.05	0.04	0.03	0.04	0.03	0.04	0.06	0.02	0.02	0.05	0.03	0.03	0.06
h5	0.04	0.04	0.05	0.05	0.05	0.06	0.06	0.06	0.05	0.05	0.05	0.04	0.06	0.06	0.05
h6	0.09	0.09	0.11	0.12	0.11	0.13	0.14	0.13	0.13	0.12	0.12	0.10	0.14	0.14	0.13
h7	0.00	0.00	0.00	0.00	0.00	0.00	0.00	0.00	0.00	0.00	0.00	0.00	0.00	0.00	0.00
h8	0.00	0.00	0.00	0.00	0.00	0.00	0.00	0.00	0.00	0.00	0.00	0.00	0.00	0.00	0.00
All hhlds	0.42	0.61	0.47	0.76	0.55	0.94	0.94	0.89	0.84	0.62	0.62	1.09	1.21	1.21	1.00
Corprate Firms	0.61	0.56	0.58	0.49	0.52	0.44	0.45	0.46	0.47	0.53	0.53	0.39	0.34	0.35	0.42

Table 12. SAM Suriname: Key sector analysis and aggregate gainer loser analysis.

	Key sector analysis					Aggregate Gainer loser analysis GL Index				
sector j	SAM Key sectors			IOT Key sector	SAM / IOT %	SAM GLI			IOT GLI	position in SAM vs IOT
	Back-ward linkage	Forward linkage	Key sector			Nomi-nator	Denomi-nator	SAM GLI		
1. Agriculture	0.95	1.11	1.03	1.07	96%	0.061	0.078	0.78	1.04	lower
2. Fishery	0.80	0.81	0.83	0.82	101%	0.051	0.032	1.58	0.83	higher
3. Mining	1.09	1.60	1.34	1.47	91%	0.075	0.047	1.60	2.37	lower
4. Mnfctrng	1.10	1.53	1.34	0.94	142%	0.080	0.175	0.46	2.74	lower
5. Elct wtr gs	0.91	0.97	0.94	0.96	99%	0.058	0.035	1.65	1.60	same
6. Construction	1.10	0.89	1.00	0.94	105%	0.076	0.110	0.69	0.49	higher
7. Trade	0.95	1.70	1.32	1.51	88%	0.061	0.157	0.39	0.17	higher
8. Hotels & rs	1.04	0.86	0.95	0.90	105%	0.071	0.049	1.44	0.97	higher
9. Trnsp & cm	0.99	1.37	1.18	1.28	92%	0.065	0.113	0.58	0.34	higher
10. Fncl srv	0.73	0.98	0.86	0.92	93%	0.039	0.032	1.21	0.36	higher
11. Cmrc srv	0.74	0.94	0.84	0.89	94%	0.040	0.029	1.35	0.40	higher
12. Pblc adm	1.18	0.42	0.80	0.61	131%	0.084	0.061	1.38	0.77	higher
13. Education	1.06	0.61	0.83	0.72	116%	0.072	0.032	2.29	0.80	higher
14. Health	1.06	0.66	0.86	0.76	113%	0.073	0.033	2.18	0.75	higher
15. Otr srv	1.23	0.53	0.86	0.71	125%	0.089	0.016	5.55	3.70	higher

Size of production multipliers: $MsX_{jj}{}^{\#}$ is the SAM multiplier showing how much sector production increases due to a unit injection in sector demand. A unit injection in agriculture results in a production multiplier of 2.75, of which 1.97 occurs in agriculture itself and 0.78 in the other sectors. The highest production multipliers >3.1 are scored by the sectors of mining, manufacturing, construction, public administration, and other services. The SAM average production multiplier for all sectors is 2.89.

A comparison of production multipliers between SAM and IOT shows that the average in SAM at 2.89 is higher than the average in IOT at 2.0039. This is because the SAM contains more circular flows of the economy while IOT is limited to interindustry transactions. Sectors which involve more economy-wide transactions would score higher multipliers in SAM versus IOT and this is apparent in the higher scores for the services sectors in the SAM as compared to IOT. These sectors are manufacturing, trade, public administration, education, health, and other services.

Key sectors analysis: Table 12 displays in the first and second rows the scores for backward and forward linkages, respectively. The third row gives key sectors when the two linkages are assigned equal weights.

$$\text{Key sector score} = (MsX_j/(\Sigma MsX_j)/J) + (MsX_j'/((\Sigma MsX_j')/J)\}/2,$$

where J stands for the number of sectors.

The results show that in the SAM mining, manufacturing, trade, and transport have the highest key sector scores. These were about the same as obtained in the IOT analysis, displayed in the fourth row. However, the scores are raised in the SAM above the IOT levels, reflecting the greater transaction flows in the SAM compared to the IOT. In relative terms, the scores of manufacturing and the services sectors are elevated in the SAM compared to the IOT (by + 42% to + 13%), as these sectors are more extensively engaged in the circular flow of the economy, while mining is diminished by −9%.

Gainers losers analysis: The formula for identifying gaining and losing sectors divides a sector's relative share in the sum of multipliers over all sectors after deducting all injections, by the sector's relative share in the actual total production of all sectors, that is, $[X_{j,o}/\Sigma j X_{j,o}]$. The result is gainer loser index $GLI^{\#}_{jJ}$. A gaining sector has a higher nominator than a denominator. A losing sector has the opposite. The formula can be repeated as follows:

$$GLI^{\#}_{jJ} = \left[(MsX_{jj}{}^{\#} - 1)/(\Sigma j(MsX_{jj}{}^{\#} - 1)\right] \Big/ \left[X_{j,o}/\Sigma j X_{j,o}\right] \tag{3}$$

where j and $j^{\#}$ denote receiving and injecting sectors, The first term gives the share of the added production effect of sector j in all the added productions of all sectors. This term is divided by the actual production share of sector j in all sectors, in the IOT benchmark year. Sectors with $GLI^{\#}_{jJ} > 1$ are gainers.

The gainer sectors with the GLI score significantly above 1.0 such as mining, EGW (electricity, gas, water), and the various public services sectors have favorable multiplier effects allowing them to pick higher shares of the multiplier effects than their actual shares in the economy. This indicates that these sectors are likely to increase their shares in the economy. They are growth sectors which are likely to grow with rates above the average growth in the near future. Between 2014 and 2015, the figures show this was realized. A qualifying note is that very tiny sectors starting from a very low share (which is typical for the public services sectors) tend to show a more favorable bias. Large share sectors cannot grow larger. SAM indicates five sectors as making losses in their shares; these are agriculture, manufacturing, construction, trade, and transport.

IOT has shown different gainers: mining, manufacturing, and services, and eleven sectors that are losers. The greater circular flow in the SAM allows more sectors to maintain and increase their shares in the economy. The limited circular flow of the IOT gives a distorted picture of structural change.

SAM multipliers can be analyzed in other ways as was reviewed in the IOT analysis. These are stated here for the sake of completeness: *insertion analysis*, *extraction analysis*, *growth decomposition analysis*, and *structural change analysis*. These are feasible if there are SAMs for two or more years.

So much for the SAM results on production multipliers as per Table 11. Table 11 displays as well the impact of injections in the sectors on other variables such as factor earnings and household incomes. The results on factor earnings are useful in computing employment multipliers that policy makers often ask for, while results on household incomes give insight into the built-in distribution mechanisms that are hidden in the economy and are not observable by policy makers.

To estimate the employment multiplier from an injection of 19 mln SRD in sector j, several alternatives are possible. The simplest formula is as follows:

created jobs = (total earnings multiplier of sector j) $*$
(10 mln SRD/average wage all sectors in mln SRD).

An example of injection in agriculture gives employment jobs $= 0.32 * 10/0.0455 = 71.2$ employment jobs. The simple formula is incomplete since the average wage can be defined by sector, by occupation, or by both combined.

An elaborate calculation would work with differentiated wage rates by sector and occupation and not one average wage for the whole economy, which is done in several steps. (a) Go to Table 13 and take the multiplier of factor payments for professionals from a 10 mln SRD injection in agriculture (that is, $0.0737 * 10$ ml SRD). (b) What is the average earnings of a professional employed in agriculture? The total payment of concern is obtainable from the SAM (Table 13 second block on the left-hand side gives total remuneration by occupation and sector) giving 14.46 mln SRD for professionals in agriculture. Division of this sum by the number of employed professionals in agriculture at 166.5 gives an average remuneration of.086850 mln SRD. (c) Dividing the multiplier value of 0.737 mln SRD by average earnings for a professional in agriculture of 0.08685 gives the number of created jobs in this category at 8.5. When the above is applied to the other occupations in agriculture, the results show +8.5 professionals +14 administrative +27 skilled workers +18 elementary jobs +16 self-employed. Summary: The total employment effect of 10 mln SRD injection in agriculture is the additional employment of 83.4 jobs.

Table 13 gives the direct and indirect employment multipliers of injections of 10 mln SRD in the 15 sectors, following the simple and elaborate formulas.

Table 13. Employment creation due to injection of 10 mln SRD in sector j: Simple and elaborate calculations.

	agr	fry	mng	mnf	egw	cns	trd	htl	trn	fnl	cml	adm	hlh	edc	srv
simple formula	71	116	80	141	97	177	176	165	157	111	111	217	235	236	192
ranked	15	10	14	9	13	5	6	7	8	11	12	3	2	1	4
elaborate formula	83	139	352	81	125	105	142	127	86	108	299	454	292	216	1009
ranked	15	8	3	14	10	12	7	8	13	11	4	2	5	5	1

Table 14. Income distribution impact of sector injections.

Recipients	agr	fry	mng	mnf	egw	cns	trd	htl	trn	fnl	cml	adm	edu	hlth	srv	average
All hsh grp	0.42	0.61	0.47	0.76	0.55	0.94	0.94	0.89	0.84	0.62	0.62	1.09	1.21	1.21	1.00	0.81
crp frms	0.61	0.56	0.58	0.49	0.52	0.44	0.45	0.46	0.47	0.53	0.53	0.39	0.34	0.35	0.42	0.48
Total	1.00	1.00	1.00	1.00	1.00	1.00	1.00	1.00	1.00	1.00	1.00	1.00	1.00	1.00	1.00	1.00
High incm	0.36	0.53	0.38	0.67	0.48	0.84	0.85	0.79	0.73	0.55	0.55	1.00	1.11	1.12	0.89	0.72
Low incm	0.06	0.08	0.09	0.09	0.07	0.10	0.09	0.09	0.12	0.07	0.07	0.09	0.09	0.09	0.11	0.09
low/high	0.17	0.15	0.24	0.13	0.16	0.12	0.11	0.12	0.16	0.12	0.13	0.09	0.08	0.08	0.12	0.13

Notation: Higher income hg applies to household groups h = 1,2,3,6.
Lower income hg applies to household groups h = 4,5,7,8.

The size of employment creation is much bigger when differentiated earnings are considered because most of the differentiated earnings are significantly below the average earnings. The ranking of sectors by their employment creation effect changes as well with the low earnings sectors like mining and services climbing up in their employment creation. These results open a discussion regarding which earnings norm should be considered in calculating employment multipliers. Employment multipliers that emphasize quantities of employment jobs created without due consideration to the remunerative level (which should be as close as possible to the average remuneration) are of little relevance.

The impact of sectoral injections on household incomes reflects on the multiplier pattern of income redistribution. Table 14 separates the multiplier impacts for lower income from the higher income households groups and divides in the fifth row the multiplier results for low income by higher income. Results show that injections in mining result in a ratio of low to high income of 0.24. This is the ratio with relatively most benefits to low-income households. Injections in the sectors of agriculture, forestry, manufacturing, energy, construction, trade, hotels, transport, financial, commercial, and general services distribute income between the poor and the rich in the ratio range of 0.16–0.11. A not too surprising but significant result is that economic growth in the public domain-related sectors such as public administration, education, and health appear to be the least progressive in their income distribution impact with a ratio of poor to rich of 0.09–0.08, reflecting a higher income composition of earners in these sectors, as well as indirectly a consumption expenditure pattern that may benefit low-income earners less than high-income earners.

3.3.4. *SAM multipliers of factor earnings shifts:* $Ms\,J^{\#}$, $Ms\,Y^{\#}_{ff}$, $Ms\,H^{\#}_{y}$

To complete the picture, Table 15 gives the impact of a unit of factor earnings shifts on each of the endogenous variables in the SAM relating to sectoral production, factor earnings, and household incomes. Shifts in factor earnings can be due to changes in levels of earnings or the number of earners.

Table 15. SAM multipliers of factor earnings shifts: $Ms\ J^{\#}$, $Ms\ Y^{\#}_{ff}$, $Ms\ H^{\#}_{y}$.

IMPACTED		MULTIPLIER EFFECTS OF A UNIT SHIFT IN FACTOR EARNINGS					
		f1	f2	f3	f4	f5	f6
production	j1	0.114	0.118	0.120	0.161	0.147	0.105
of	j2	0.068	0.070	0.072	0.097	0.088	0.063
sectors	j3	0.107	0.110	0.113	0.152	0.139	0.098
	j4	0.268	0.276	0.283	0.381	0.343	0.245
	j5	0.108	0.111	0.114	0.154	0.139	0.099
	j6	0.074	0.076	0.079	0.105	0.094	0.068
	j7	0.410	0.422	0.434	0.584	0.524	0.376
	j8	0.103	0.106	0.109	0.146	0.132	0.095
	j9	0.205	0.211	0.217	0.291	0.262	0.188
	j10	0.152	0.157	0.161	0.217	0.194	0.140
	j11	0.136	0.140	0.143	0.193	0.173	0.124
	j12	0.013	0.013	0.014	0.018	0.017	0.012
	j13	0.096	0.098	0.101	0.136	0.122	0.087
	j14	0.109	0.112	0.115	0.155	0.138	0.100
	j15	0.070	0.072	0.074	0.098	0.089	0.064
total production		2.032	2.093	2.149	2.889	2.601	1.862
earnings	f1	1.182	0.188	0.193	0.259	0.233	0.167
of	f2	0.216	1.222	0.228	0.306	0.275	0.197
factors	f3	0.072	0.074	1.076	0.102	0.092	0.066
	f4	0.025	0.026	0.027	1.036	0.032	0.023
	f5	0.039	0.040	0.041	0.055	1.049	0.035
	f6	0.091	0.094	0.096	0.129	0.116	1.083
	f7	0.329	0.339	0.348	0.468	0.421	0.301
total earnings		1.953	1.981	2.008	2.355	2.219	1.873
incomes	h1	1.182	0.188	0.193	0.259	0.233	0.167
of	h2	0.216	1.222	0.228	0.306	0.275	0.197
hshld	h3	0.072	0.074	1.076	0.102	0.092	0.066
p g	h4	0.025	0.026	0.027	1.036	0.032	0.023
	h5	0.039	0.040	0.041	0.055	1.049	0.035
	h6	0.091	0.094	0.096	0.129	0.116	1.083
	h7	0.000	0.000	0.000	0.000	0.000	0.000
	h8	0.000	0.000	0.000	0.000	0.000	0.000
total incomes		1.624	1.643	1.660	1.888	1.798	1.572
corporate firms		0.329	0.339	0.348	0.468	0.421	0.301

3.3.5. SAM multipliers of households income transfers: $Ms\ J^{\#}_{ha}$, $Ms\ Y^{\#}_{fh}$, $Ms\ Y^{\#}_{eh}$

To complete the picture fully, Table 16 gives the impact of a unit of income transfer to a household group on each of the endogenous variables in the SAM relating to sectoral production, factor earnings, and household incomes. Income transfers are affected by the government but can also originate from the rest of the world.

Table 16. SAM multipliers of household income transfers: $Ms\ J^{\#}_{ha}$, $Ms\ Y^{\#}_{fh}$, $Ms\ Y^{\#}_{eh}$.

IMPACTED		MULTIPLIER EFFECTS OF A UNIT TRANSFER TO THE HOUSEHOLD GROUPS							
		h1	h2	h3	h4	h5	h6	h7	h8
production	$j1$	0.114	0.118	0.120	0.161	0.147	0.105	0.184	0.161
of	$j2$	0.068	0.070	0.072	0.097	0.088	0.063	0.118	0.097
sectors	$j3$	0.107	0.110	0.113	0.152	0.139	0.098	0.187	0.154
	$j4$	0.268	0.276	0.283	0.381	0.343	0.245	0.451	0.387
	$j5$	0.108	0.111	0.114	0.154	0.139	0.099	0.182	0.155
	$j6$	0.074	0.076	0.079	0.105	0.094	0.068	0.124	0.106
	$j7$	0.410	0.422	0.434	0.584	0.524	0.376	0.682	0.591
	$j8$	0.103	0.106	0.109	0.146	0.132	0.095	0.173	0.149
	$j9$	0.205	0.211	0.217	0.291	0.262	0.188	0.342	0.295
	$j10$	0.152	0.157	0.161	0.217	0.194	0.140	0.254	0.218
	$j11$	0.136	0.140	0.143	0.193	0.173	0.124	0.223	0.196
	$j12$	0.013	0.013	0.014	0.018	0.017	0.012	0.024	0.018
	$j13$	0.096	0.098	0.101	0.136	0.122	0.087	0.158	0.139
	$j14$	0.109	0.112	0.115	0.155	0.138	0.100	0.178	0.157
	$j15$	0.070	0.072	0.074	0.098	0.089	0.064	0.118	0.101
total production		2.032	2.093	2.149	2.889	2.601	1.862	3.398	2.925
earnings	$f1$	0.182	0.188	0.193	0.259	0.233	0.167	0.303	0.263
of	$f2$	0.216	0.222	0.228	0.306	0.275	0.197	0.359	0.311
factors	$f3$	0.072	0.074	0.076	0.102	0.092	0.066	0.120	0.103
	$f4$	0.025	0.026	0.027	0.036	0.032	0.023	0.042	0.036
	$f5$	0.039	0.040	0.041	0.055	0.049	0.035	0.064	0.055
	$f6$	0.091	0.094	0.096	0.129	0.116	0.083	0.152	0.131
	$f7$	0.329	0.339	0.348	0.468	0.421	0.301	0.549	0.472
total earnings		0.953	0.981	1.008	1.355	1.219	0.873	1.590	1.372
incomes	$h1$	1.182	0.188	0.193	0.259	0.233	0.167	0.303	0.263
of	$h2$	0.216	1.222	0.228	0.306	0.275	0.197	0.359	0.311
household	$h3$	0.072	0.074	1.076	0.102	0.092	0.066	0.120	0.103
groups	$h4$	0.025	0.026	0.027	1.036	0.032	0.023	0.042	0.036
	$h5$	0.039	0.040	0.041	0.055	1.049	0.035	0.064	0.055
	$h6$	0.091	0.094	0.096	0.129	0.116	1.083	0.152	0.131
	$h7$	0.000	0.000	0.000	0.000	0.000	0.000	1.000	0.000
	$h8$	0.000	0.000	0.000	0.000	0.000	0.000	0.000	1.000
Total incomes		1.624	1.643	1.660	1.888	1.798	1.572	2.040	1.900
corporate firms		0.329	0.339	0.348	0.468	0.421	0.301	0.549	0.472

4. Update of IOT and SAM to Revised Sector Classification

In 2021, Suriname ABS stopped publishing its International Standard Industrial Classification ISIC Rev 3 (which represents the conventional economy) and replaced it with ISIC Rev4 (which emphasizes the rise of the information economy) as recommended by the UN Statistics Division. One main difference between Rev 3 and Rev 4 of special relevance here is in the introduction of two new sectors, such as professional, scientific, and technical activities and administrative and business support activities, next to dropping fishery as a separate sector and including it in the broader agriculture sector. Rev 4 is also characterized by an increase in overall detail, new concepts of information, and new application rules.

Adherence to Rev 4 required that the IOT and SAM be revised and updated to the new classification. Because there are no data on the input and output profiles of the new sectors, their intermediate delivery profiles were assumed to correspond with the sectors of communication and education, with adjustments based on supplementary data provided by ABS. This can be rightly described as a superficial accommodation until more data become available in the future. In some sense, Suriname's stage of economic development fits more with holding to Rev 3 than joining the caravan and adopting Rev 4. The deletion of the fishery as a separate sector ignores the significance of this sector for the socio-economic development of the country, while the newly introduced information servicing sectors are as yet of little significance in IOT and SAM analysis.

ABS rebased series of ISIC Rev 4 includes next to the reclassification and extension of sectors from 15 to 17, a revision in application rules: SNA consolidation in the old data series was based on production method, while in de rebased series consolidation is done along expenditure method, leading to a higher estimate of GDP + 7%. The shift increases further in 2016–2019, reaching 14% in 2019. The shifts in 2015 are unevenly distributed in the sectors; see the following table, with some pushed up (agriculture + 24%, mining + 41%, manufacturing + 21%) and others lowered (education and health reduced by −11% and −28%). These changes make the IOT update more substantive. By implication, the IO multipliers of the revised IOT of 17 sectors are somewhat higher than in the old IOT of 15 sectors, not because of the increase in the number of sectors from Rev 3 to Rev 4 but because of the re-estimates of a higher GDP. Production multipliers of the new IOT (average 1.88) are slightly higher than those of the old IOT (average 1.85), which is consistent with the revised higher output in the rebased series. The ranking pattern of production multipliers by sector is practically the same in old and new IOT. But on the whole, the patterns of IOT and SAM multiplier results reported in the preceding sections are practically the same as those obtained for the revised IOT and SAM.

5. Suriname SAM-Based Economy-wide Model (SSEM)

The economy of Suriname had its most difficult years between 2015 and 2020, partly due to commodity price volatility and internal political instability and mostly from the closure of the economy during the COVID epidemic in 2020. As was mentioned in the introduction, the GDP per capita in USD was halved in a period of five years. Next to interim recovery policy measures in the crisis years of 2020 and 2021, the government initiated work on the four-year development plan 2022–2026 with the objective of managing sustainable growth and balanced development. As usual, the National Planning Department of Suriname was assigned the task of coordinating and writing down the development plan, which culminated in the reference publication NPD Suriname (2021).

With the revised IOT and SAM available, the next move was to formulate and apply for Suriname an SAM-based economy-wide model (SSEM) that could be of some support as feedback for the development plan 2022–2026. Some of the results obtained from SSEM came in time and were incorporated in the five-year plan.

The SSEM model, and that holds for all economic models, cannot possibly reproduce the uncertain growth in a primary commodities-producing economy. Instead, there were four considerations that guided the formulation and application of the SSEM model. (a) In terms of content, there are the urges to assure sustainable economic growth and satisfy the income and consumption needs of the whole population, which are best done if an SAM-based economywide perspective is followed. (b) Projection and balancing of government revenue with expenditure (current and investment) is a primary task in formulating development plans; this is done by expanding the government-related equations in the model. (c) Focus on and orientation toward a development planning model that can be solved in stages (macro, IOT, and SAM) and that can be well comprehended and operated by the SPB staff, rather than a black box prediction model. (d) The limited data available in Suriname required taking the year 2015 as the base year of SSEM, for which the SAM is available, and supplemented with 10–20 time series data on growth, consumption, wages, employment, etc., for estimation of several behavioral equations.

The SSEM model counts 64 equational sets, broken down into an interindustry IOT block of 12 equations that is self-sufficient and is solvable on its own, and a SAM-based block of 52 equations that include variables relating to demographic counting, factor remuneration, household budgets, corporate business, extended government revenues and expenditures, and the world account. While it is formally and practically not feasible to display here the equations of the model, some estimation details and projection results can be highlighted.

A comparison of model solutions with observed values for 2015–2019 is done for aggregated variables such as gross domestic product (GDP) and its breakdown in consumption, investment, and the foreign trade balance of exports less imports and for the gross factor income (GFI) and its disaggregation into gross value added at factor cost per sector. Model solution and observed values for the aggregates are practically the same. Discrepancies appear regarding GFI by sector.

The year 2020, characterized by the COVID crisis, is exceptional and is practically beyond modeling. Nevertheless, the model was able to reproduce the observed decline in the GDP between 2019 and 2020 by 13%, and the observed positive foreign trade balance, as well as very low discrepancies in the major goods-producing sectors of agriculture, mining manufacturing, construction, and the distributive sectors of trade and transport. Although the model predicted major declines for the sector of hotels and restaurants, the observed decline was 25% higher, a similar tendency applied to the sector of financial and related services. The opposite occurs with SSEM solutions predicting declines for the government-related sectors. The observed values for the government sectors were higher, which is explainable by autonomous allocations in a crisis year that cannot be captured by a general model.

With the above satisfactory performance, the model was considered equipped for effective projection and planning. Solutions for macro variables are in Table 17. The model has been useful in providing the Development Plan 2022–2026 with baseline projections of the GDP at growth rates moving along the lines below 1.5% in 2022 and increasing further to a sustainable growth rate of 4% in 2026. These estimates are consistent with the public revenue and public spending expectations for the plan years as reported in the latest provided official document entitled MTFF.

The statement that the decade starting with 2015 was a lost decade in terms of economic well-being is unavoidable. It will take five to six coming years to return back in 2025 or 2026 to the same levels of consumption, investment, and GDP that were already present in 2015.

The gross value-added shares per sector at the start and the end of the development plan show some significant changes, Table 18. The share of public administration falls from a high of 11–8%, which is consistent with the intended policy to restrain public spending that has overgrown in past years. This sector depends heavily on the consumption expenditure of government (ministerial personnel salaries

Table 17. Macro projections of the SSEM model, SRD mln., in constant prices of 2015.

	2015	2020	2021	2022	2023	2024	2025	2026
CNSp consumption private	8693	7184	7250	7508	7813	8179	8621	9148
CNSg consumption government	2571	2016	2277	2076	1935	1863	1988	2067
INV investment	7888	4529	4724	5057	5441	5888	6415	7037
FCF frgn cptl flw (EXP-MP)	−1637	1901	1208	1049	814	490	−61	−611
GDP	17515	15630	15458	15690	16004	16420	16962	17640
GDP_t/GDP_{t-1}		0.87	0.989	1.015	1.02	1.026	1.033	1.04
GDP growth rate %		−13.00%	−1.10%	1.50%	2.00%	2.60%	3.30%	4.00%

Table 18. Sector shares in the gross value added: 2021 and 2026, constant prices of 2015.

	GFI. Gross value added			
	SRD mln		Share in total	
	2021	2026	2021	2026
1. Agriculture	935	1228	7%	8%
2. Mining	562	778	4%	5%
3. Manufacturing	2130	2347	15%	14%
4. Electricity, gas	281	350	2%	2%
5. Water	19	20	0%	0%
6. Construction	1112	1338	8%	8%
7. Trade	2116	2398	15%	15%
8. Transport	545	609	4%	4%
9. Hotels & restaurants	483	438	3%	3%
10. Information, communication	1466	1394	10%	9%
11. Financial services	926	1257	6%	8%
12. Commercial services	984	1109	7%	7%
13. Prfl tchn business services	178	121	1%	1%
14. Public administration	1566	1354	11%	8%
15. Education	306	563	2%	3%
16. Health	451	622	3%	4%
17. Other services	192	343	1%	2%
Total GFI	14253	16269	100%	100%

and public purchases of goods and services), and this is implied to diminish from 13.2% of the GDP in 2021 to 11.7% in 2026. Other sectors with a falling share of 1% are manufacturing and the newly introduced sector of information in the national accounts, which is disappointing in view of the generally held positive prospects. In contrast, agriculture, mining, finance, education, health, and public services will be able to increase their share by 1%. It is also interesting to note that after the devastating falls in 2020 and 2021, the sector of Hotels and restaurants is able to hold to its share in the gross value added of 3% in 2021 throughout 2026.

Some interpretations of estimates and obtained results from the SAM-related equations and variables are summarized below in eight boxes. Estimates are for the past years (PY) 2015–2021 and results are for the development plan period (DP) 2022–2026.

(1) Wage rate and labor productivity

The indexes of the real wage rate and real labor productivity have kept close track of each other in the past and continue to do so in spite of the interruption of the COVID year 2020 when labor productivity diminished significantly (by 12 index points) but the wage rate remained sticky with a fall of .04 in 2020, supplemented by another fall in 2021 of 0.07 index points. For the development plan years, both indexes move in the same direction and at about the same pace.

Box 1. Wage rate and labor productivity.

			INDEX		
	wage rate	labour productivity		WGR	LPY
2015	0.0533	0.0930	2015	1.0000	1.0004
2016	0.0529	0.0903	2016	0.9942	0.9715
2017	0.0566	0.0888	2017	1.0627	0.9548
2018	0.0567	0.0939	2018	1.0651	1.0094
2019	0.0567	0.0931	2019	1.0651	1.0007
2020	0.0543	0.0818	2020	1.0192	0.8798
2021	0.0507	0.0814	2021	0.9516	0.8747
2022	0.0521	0.0827	2022	0.9775	0.8887
2023	0.0542	0.0851	2023	1.0173	0.9149
2024	0.0564	0.0876	2024	1.0591	0.9421
2025	0.0592	0.0909	2025	1.1109	0.9774
2026	0.0625	0.0949	2026	1.1729	1.0207

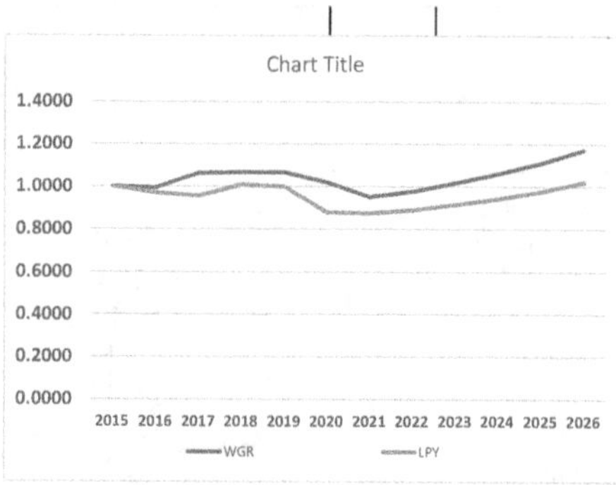

(2) Unemployment

The Suriname economy appears to be flexible in confronting the unemployment problem. Expectations of large downfalls in employment and high rates of unemployment in crises years are not realized, partly because of a downward trend of participation in the active labor force by newcomers and a reserved attitude of employer business firms and government toward preserving employment levels at their current levels as much as possible. This allows the unemployment rate to fluctuate within the small range of 7–9%. In the DP years, the unemployment rate, UMR, is predicted to be around 8% and diminishing somewhat over the years,

Box 2. Unemployment.

	Unemployment ratio
2015	0.0722
2016	0.0971
2017	0.0750
2018	0.0922
2019	0.0782
2020	0.0811
2021	0.0812
2022	0.0809
2023	0.0803
2024	0.0796
2015	0.0787
2026	0.0777

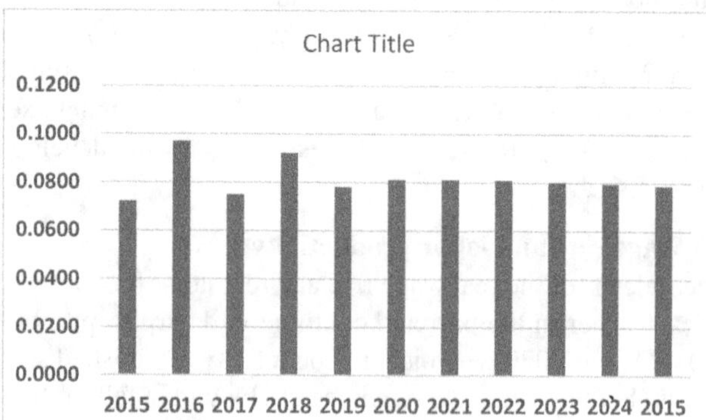

(3) Employment compensation/NFI and operating surplus/NFI

The long-term trend shows a rising share of employment compensation and a falling share of operating surplus (that is, gross profits) in Net Factor Income, NFI. In the recession year 2016 and in the COVID year 2020, this is reversed but immediately shifts back to the general trend. The trend implies rising incomes for the middle classes and falling incomes for employers.

Box 3. Employment compensation/NFI and Operating surplus/NFI.

	FRTq(1..6)/FRTn /NFI	
2015	0.6612	0.3388
2016	0.6676	0.3324
2017	0.6760	0.3240
2018	0.6833	0.3167
2019	0.6977	0.3023
2020	0.6990	0.3010
2021	0.7063	0.2937
2022	0.7145	0.2855
2023	0.7227	0.2773
2024	0.7309	0.2691
2015	0.7391	0.2609
2026	0.7477	0.2523

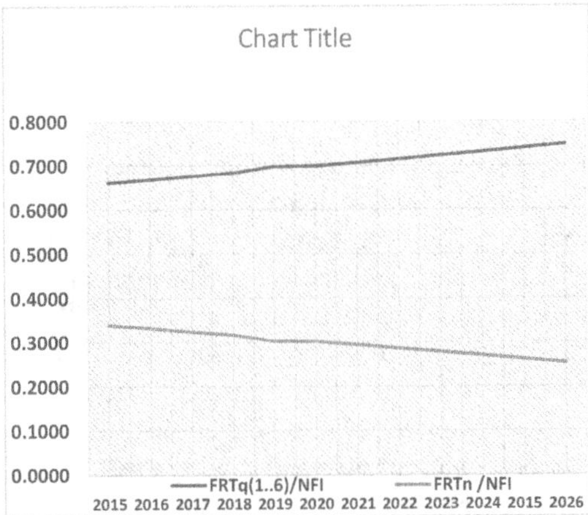

(4) Dissavings rates and well-being distribution

In 2021, all household groups taken together are estimated to save about 20% of their disposable income. In OP 2026, the general well-being allows all households to save 22%, which is an important well-being measure of over-satisfying basic and higher consumption needs. But included in all households are some low-income groups which are under-satisfying regarding consumption needs. These are the four household groups characterized by employees with elementary jobs, self-employed and family workers in informal jobs, the unemployed, and parts of the old age household group (65+). The chart shows that while the four groups are dissaving in 2021, the earning ones are happily above the zero line in DP 2026; the old age households are stuck with a negative savings rate of 6% and the unemployed group with a higher negative savings of 12%. The implication is that satisfaction of basic consumption needs for all would ultimately require some voluntary/conventionally motivated transfer from the employed to the unemployed and from the better-off aged households to the less-off aged households. As the following sections show, the government budget is overwhelmed with spending demands, making it necessary to look for voluntary/conventionally motivated interhousehold income maintenance transfers.

Box 4. Dissavings rates.

Dissavings rate as indicator of wellbeing distribution

	2021	2026
all Hholds	0.1969	0.2172
h=4 elmntry jobs	−0.0467	0.0104
h=6 Self employd	−0.0296	0.0166
h=8 Unemployed	−0.1101	−0.1221
h=9 Old age	−0.0534	−0.0567

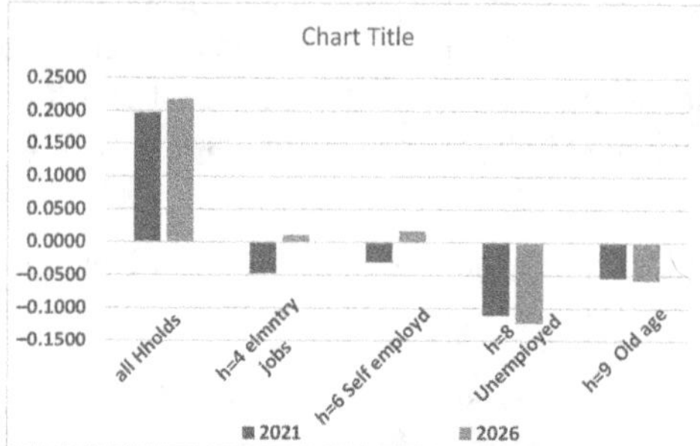

(5) The government sector: Budget deficit and the national debt

The DP inherits a budget deficit, BGD, amounting to about 12% of the GDP in 2021; both variables are deflated and represent real values. The DP targets for government revenue and spending as displayed in DP/MTFF (dated July 2021), and as was appropriately deflated in terms of 2015 prices (which applies to the whole SSEM model) to give real values, would result in reduced BGD/GDP over the DP years, ending at 8.0%. This is a reduction of 4%, which is equivalent to a one-third reduction in the budget deficit share. The model shows that this substantial reduction is accomplishable and is within reach.

In spite of this striking accomplishment, the national debt ratio, NDR, that is the accumulated national debt NDT divided by the GDP, is hardly affected and remains at the high level of about 78% for most years of the DP. The jump in NDR in the period 2020–2021 from a level of around 44–61%, which is partially due to the substantial devaluation of the foreign exchange rate, FXR, is not easy to turn back. Given the magnitudes involved, further reductions in current and capital government expenditure have no impact as the following charts show. The prospective escapes from the NDR dilemma are debt cancelation and a revalued FXR.

Box 5. Budget deficit and national debt.

	BGT / GDP	NDT / GDP
2015	0.07380	0.4069
2016	0.07194	0.4069
2017	0.07763	0.4022
2018	0.06500	0.4458
2019	0.13828	0.4387
2020	0.08988	0.6863
2021	0.11809	0.6125
2022	0.11156	0.7575
2023	0.08474	0.7944
2024	0.07400	0.7797
2015	0.08016	0.7856
2026	0.08028	0.7863

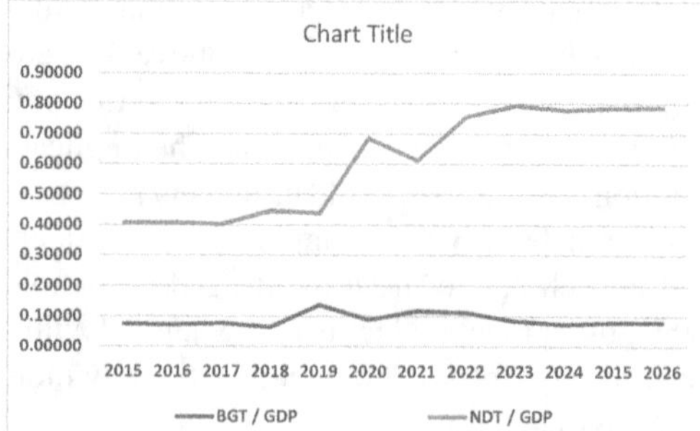

(6) Government current expenditure

The depicts real reductions in all government expenditure items. The model reproduces this picture as the following chart shows. One exception is the shortfall in AOW funding. The model comes out with higher values for the AOW funding, at 255 mln SRD, against a target figure of 115 mln SRD in the DP (MTFF). The model assumed the old age allowances to remain at the same rate as in 2000–2021. Transfers for unemployed households, denoted by TUN, remain moderate as unemployment remains moderate. The same applies to other household transfers that fall under transfers on behalf of children support (TKB) and Transfers on behalf of Needy and Poverty (TNP). Subsidies to non-profit and semi-Governmental Institutions (SGI) fall appreciably.

Box 6. Government current expenditure.

	CNSg	AOW deficit	UNM sprt	AKB sprt	NPY sprt	SBS sbsds
2015	2571	168	139	45	92	849
2016	2019	185	188	35	71	733
2017	1828	193	146	31	63	540
2018	1830	195	182	31	64	427
2019	2517	203	155	46	95	585
2020	2016	229	160	36	74	470
2021	2277	238	159	41	83	530
2022	2076	244	158	37	76	484
2023	1935	247	156	34	71	451
2024	1863	251	154	33	68	434
2015	1988	254	151	35	73	463
2026	2067	255	148	37	75	481

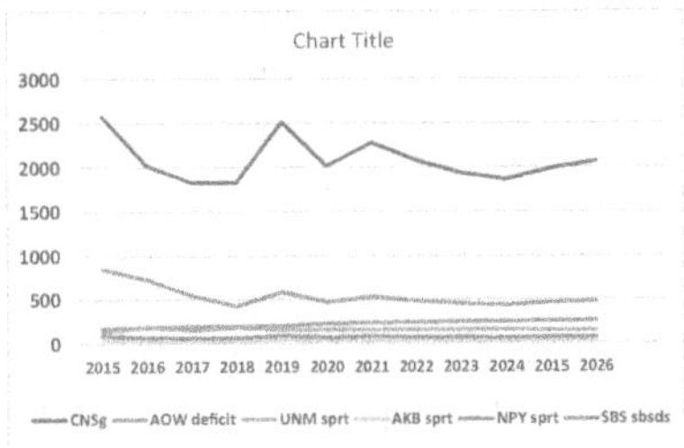

(7) Government investment INVg retreating and private investment INVp shooting

The past relationship between INVg and INVp in Suriname shows a high degree of complementarity. One tends to compensate for the other while maintaining a stable share in total investment of 12% for INVg and 88% for INVp. From 2021 onward, the model predicts a relative reduction of the contribution of government investment to total investment toward 9%, with private investment reaching 91% of total investment.

Box 7. Shares of public and private investment.

			shares in total INV	
	INVp	INVg	INVp	INVg
2015	7454	434	0.9450	0.0550
2016	5355	472	0.9189	0.0811
2017	4753	729	0.8670	0.1330
2018	5831	707	0.8918	0.1082
2019	6113	1193	0.8368	0.1632
2020	7454	332	0.9574	0.0426
2021	4358	366	0.9224	0.0776
2022	4509	549	0.8915	0.1085
2023	4953	487	0.9104	0.0896
2024	5401	487	0.9172	0.0828
2015	5905	510	0.9205	0.0795
2026	6507	530	0.9247	0.0753
			0.9086	0.0914

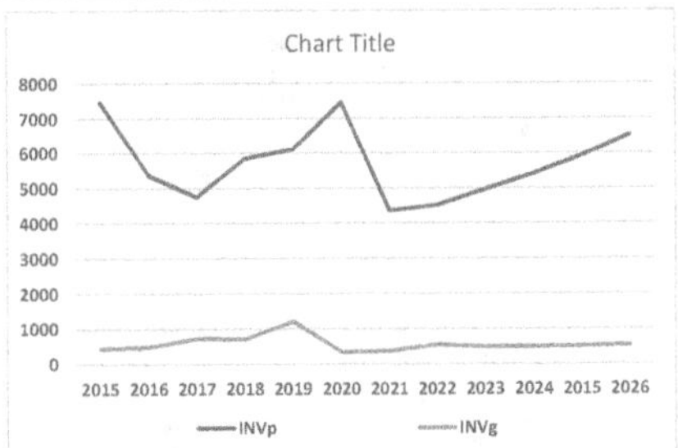

(8) The streamlining of the investment–savings balance with the foreign trade balance

Often, the domestic payment balances of the economy are discussed in isolation from the foreign payments balances, which is not correct. Policymaking needs to streamline both ends. The model produces the following chart showing one line savings (that is GDP less private and government consumption) and the other line investment. It is rare that the two would equal each other. There is always a savings–investment imbalance, a gap, and it is the foreign trade balance that is supposed to close this gap. This is the third line in the chart. If savings are below investment, there is a funding shortage, and it is the foreign capital inflow (that is, imports exceed exports) which fills this shortage. Where savings > investment, there is a foreign capital flow FCF out (that is, exports exceed imports).

The predicted savings and investment levels of the model for the DP years result in savings > investment for 2021–2025, meaning a positive foreign trade balance (exports less imports) and implying an FCF outflow. This trend is diminishing over the DP years and turns the other way round in 2025 and 2026, giving the contrasting picture of investments exceeding savings and hence imports exceeding exports and thus implying an FCF inflow of 61 mln SRD in 2025 and 611 mln SRD in 2026. These cyclical movements in the funding of national economic growth are due in principle equally to both the domestic conduct of savings and investment, and the foreign trade balance of exports and imports.

The SSEM makes handy use of the savings–investment balance in projecting a simplified outcome for the foreign trade balance without entering into detailed projections of exports and imports. The interindustry IOT block takes care of distributing the foreign trade balances of exports less imports at the sectoral level based on sectoral capacities and their growth, with due consideration to the requirement that the sum of sectoral exports less imports add up to the total foreign capital flow, FCF.

Box 8. Foreign and domestic financing of investment.

	FCF	Savings	Investment
2015	-1637	6249	7888
2016	-1015	5325	5827
2017	285	5765	5482
2018	663	7199	6538
2019	-1131	6135	7306
2020	1901	6430	4529
2021	1208	5931	4724
2022	1049	6047	5057
2023	814	6269	5441
2024	490	6378	5888
2025	-61	6354	6415
2026	-611	6426	7037

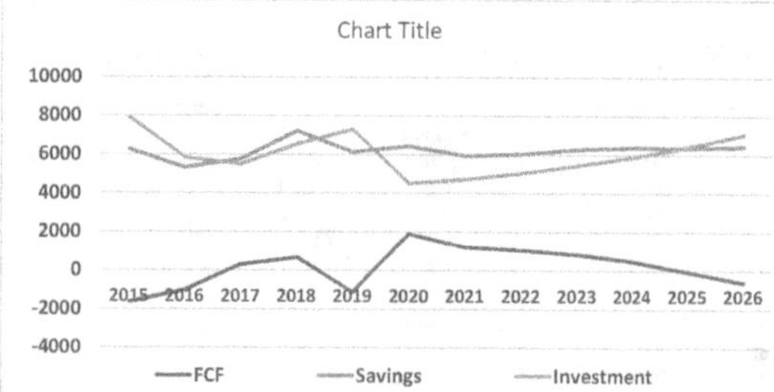

6. Concluding Remarks: Discussion on Analytical Results versus Policy Uses

This chapter presented various analytical results on IOT multipliers and SAM multipliers that rank key sectors in terms of their backward and forward linkages and classifies sectors into gainers and losers regarding their share in the total production. Multiplier impacts were extended to factor shares, treat income distribution, employment creation, poverty incidence, etc. In the discussion of analytical results, one important question raised by the SPB staff was the following: Which of the so many multiplier analytical results on sector performance is relevant for policy-making? If the country wants to grow quickly, which sector should the state select and promote for further investment?

This is a clear question, but it is a complicated issue to address. In the first place, any analytical result obtained on key sectors or gaining sectors is a partial result. The IOT multipliers are partial when compared to SAM, and the SAM is partial when compared to a dynamic multi-year model like the SSEM. Second, the multiplier impacts are valid for marginal injections only of a few percentage points. Any big injections would violate the given input–output structure and would require readjustments of inputs and outputs and production capacities elsewhere in the whole economy. Third, in a mixed market state economy, it is private investors who select their investible sectors, while the state facilitates such private investments by extending physical, human, information, and communication infrastructures. Fourth, regarding private investors, while the IOT and the more comprehensive SAM provide analytical results that can guide private investors in choosing their investible sectors, much depends on the individual orientation of the private investor. If the business investor in question happens to be positioned in the forward linkages plane, he/she will find key sector results emphasizing forward linkages highly interesting; another business investor may be more interested in key sectors emphasizing forward linkages. A conglomerate business investor may be interested in both linkages. A business investor oriented toward long-term high growth in turnover would find multiplier results on gainers and losers more interesting. Analytical and policy research generate multiplier results that can be used by the business investors but it is their decision to invest where they think it is most profitable, and expectedly they are wise and experienced and sufficiently informed to take the right investment decisions. The influence of the state is limited in this respect. Fifth, regarding state investments in infrastructures, neither the IOT nor the SAM has the necessary details to address the infrastructural investment choices. Though indirectly, the impact of infrastructural packages can be fruitfully evaluated via IOT and SAM as was done in a previous section. Sixth, all the above multiplier effects relate to the growth objective. Once the distribution (and employment) objective is considered, the problem of choosing sectors gets complicated. Of the many sectors, the sector of fishery in Suriname was found to combine high growth with positive redistribution prospects. Recommendation for state infrastructural spending in fishery activities is obvious. The results are mixed for the other sectors of economic activities, which implies that for redistribution policies, other areas of policy intervention than economic activities are more relevant, such as income transfers, provisions of public goods, enhancing human endowments, and extending land ownership.

Finally, here is a concluding remark as regards the SSEM model. This is the first time that the SPS has raised an economy-wide model that can trace and analyze past changes and gauge and plan future developments. While the breakup of the model into a macro part, an IO part, and an SAM-related part facilitates comprehension of SSEM and its partial operation by SPB staff, the prospects of the full operation of the model by the SPB staff are limited in the absence of a qualified econometrics graduate with experience in economy-wide models. While external assistance is available in the handling of SSEM, the institutionalization and maintenance of such modeling ventures require the presence of a nationally equipped professional team. It is hoped that the development planning results with minimal data that is characteristic of this chapter have laid down basic steps in the institutionalization of modeling activities in Suriname.

Appendix I. Stepwise Construction and Updating of the Input–Output Table Suriname

The Excel file of relevance is named SIC.IOT.2015(22 sectors).09.12.19. It is possible to request the Excel file from Suriname planning bureau at info_@planningofficesuriname.com.
Sheet 0 contains three parts: (1) The layout of IOT/S, (2) the sectors of IOT/S, and (3) ABS/Suriname data available for incorporation in the IOT/S.

(1) The layout of the IOT Suriname is characterized by the distinction between domestically produced and foreign-made (imports) intermediate goods and final goods. This is the announced standard IOT layout of Eora tables, but there may be exceptions. This IOT layout is most suited in the context of the economic analysis of input–output models. Aggregation of domestic and foreign to get national is more suited for SAM where the focus shifts to the broader economy-wide development issue. We shall adjust to the national layout when we construct the SAM.
(2) IOT/S sectors are ISIC Rev 3 plus the subsectors of manufacturing. In total, these are 22 sectors. The sheet contains the key for converting the Eora sectors into the 22 sectors.
(3) ABS/Suriname production data by sector j are to be tabulated in three rows:
GDP basic prices + Indirect taxes less subsidies = GDP market prices
Expenditure data for Household consumption, Government consumption, Investment, Exports, Imports
National accounts consistency requires Σ (GDP mp) j = Hhdcns+Gvrcns+Inv+Exp-Imp
Reconciliation is to be done via adjusting Hhdcns and Inv proportionately. Hopefully, the adjustment is small. At the end of the updating of IOT, there will be a second very marginal reconciliation.

Sheet 1. This is the Eora data file.

Sheet 2. Simplify foreign trade

Step 1. Sums exports of Suriname to all countries in one column of exports.

Step 2. Sum Suriname imports of intermediate goods and imports of final goods from all countries (separately).

Sheet 3. Simplify, adapt layout, and check national accounts consistency

Step 1. Divide values by 1000000.

Step 2. Adapt to the layout of IOT Suriname.

Step 3. Check national accounts consistency. Checked. OK.

Sheet 4. Contains several parts towards converting Eora into Suriname IOT

Part A is for reorganizing the sectors along the ISIC Rev 3 plus subsectors manufacturing.

Step 1. Rearrange the columns of the Final demand.

Step 2. Apply aggregation of Eora sectors where applicable.

Step 3. Split Eora combined sectors to cope with ISIC Rev 3 separated sectors where applicable. For the separation, use the distribution proportions of GDP for Suriname as given in Sheet 0.3.

Step 4. Remove redundant columns and rows after the completion of the sector reorganization.

Part B is meant to simplify the table by hiding/saving some portions of the table for use later on.

Step 5. This relates to the specification of gross factor income, that is GDP basic prices. Enclose this part within the border.

Step 6. Hold also separately the GDP bp distribution proportions of all manufacturing on subsectors manufacturing. To be used in sheet 0.3.

Part C is for conversion from USD to SRD.

Step 7. Do not use "official exchange rate". Use the underlying implicit exchange rate which equalizes GDP bp in Eora with GDP bp Suriname. This amounts to 3.65 in 2015.

Part D is for studying the Eora data and finding inconsistencies with Suriname ABS statistics, due to different ways of recording inputs and outputs.

Step 8. An adjustment for the mining sector is necessary. Apply correction.

Step 9. An adjustment for indirect taxes differences is unnecessary.

Part E gives the basic parameters to use in estimating IOT Suriname. This is the most crucial part of the updating.

Step 10. Calculate the technology relationship for each sector from the following domestic int deliveries j/gross factor income at basic prices j. These technology ratios are to be applied to the Suriname GDP bp per sector to determine the Suriname intermediate goods per sector. This will be done in the following sheet.

Step 11. Apply distribution proportions to determine the breakup of Suriname imports into intermediate and final demand components.

Sheet 5. Constructs the production and expenditure sides of the IOT Suriname

Step 1. Suriname production statistics. Recall three rows of Suriname: GDP bp, indirect tax less subsidy, and GDP at market prices from sheet 0.1.

Step 2. Prepare the production part of IOT Suriname. Bring here the last sheet 4.8.

Step 3. Bring here basic parameter sectoral domestic int deliveries/gross factor income at basic prices (E ttl int inp/Epri inp)j.

Step 4. Insert rows of Suriname primary inputs, GDP bp, Ind tax, and GDP mp. See Part 1.

Step 5. Multiply the Eora technical coefficient by sector of (Eora total intermediate input j/Eora primary input j) by Suriname's primary input by sector j to give Suriname's total intermediate input by sector j.

Step 6. Find adjuster per sector j for new intermediate Suriname/old intermediate Eora.

Step 7. Apply this adjuster to the individual cells of intermediary deliveries per sector column to give Suriname interindustry deliveries. Sum for checking.

Step 8. Calculate the row of Suriname imports deliveries. The total is 4077.86 (see bottom previous sheet). Adjust imported deliveries to the ratio of Suriname/Eora intermediate imports. Apply adjuster to imported deliveries. Sum to check.

Step 9. Sum domestic intermediate, imported intermediate, and primary inputs to give the total inputs.

Step 10. Sum across columns to give total intermediate deliveries outward per row. Step 11. Final demand. Step 12. Bring here Suriname values for FD components, Sheet 0.3, and split in domestic and foreign-produced using basic parameters from the bottom previous sheet 4. Step 13. Compute the distribution proportions of FD on sector j in Eora 2015 in a separate place.

Step 14. Compare and evaluate Eora 2015 versus Suriname 2014 expenditure pattern as constructed in the Excel document "Copy of egdp 2014-2016-propHBO2". The latter shows more validity despite the judgmental estimates it includes. Besides, this 2014 expenditure pattern has worked well for IOT Suriname 2014. Choose provisionally for Suriname 2014 in the absence of better estimates. Apply the FD expenditure pattern as was developed for 2014–2016 to give the total FD by sector.

Step 15. Transpose the sector input to become sector outputs and deduct from it total FD to give the tentative column of intermediary deliveries

Step 16. Study results and apply adjustments based on available knowledge and basic analysis to avoid negative intermediate deliveries. Note that the discrepancies are small and concentrated in a few sectors. When industry is aggregated as one sector, the negative signs are limited to two sectors only that deliver services.

Step 17. Indicate negative cells by yellow. To be compensated by cells to be decreased (red) and compensating cells to be increased (green). Trade sector is best suited for such compensating adjustments.

Step 18. Integrate end results of parts B and C in the IOT Suriname ready for iteration.

Insert the outcoming intermediate deliveries in the table. Table is ready for applying iteration.

Sheet 6. Application of RAS Method. Step 1. Apply the RAS method to the inner matrix of intermediate deliveries and repeat for several rounds starting from left to right and following with starting from above to below.

Step 2. Stop when the differences in the column total become negligible. It took 10 rounds of Ras method iterations to reach the final IOT for 2015 and 12 rounds to reach the final IOT for 2014.

Step 3. Add the differences to household consumption. If not feasible, then elsewhere.

Step 4. Carry the consequences through the columns of the Final demand and check for certainty the national accounts identity.

Sheet 7. Moving from the Input–output table to the input–output economy modeling analysis

Step 1. Bring here the IOT table.

Step 2. Compute the cells a jj' giving matrix.

Step 3. Compute the matrix $(I' - A)$

Step 4. Invert matrix $(I' - A)$ to give IO Multipliers.

Appendix II. Stepwise Estimation of the Social Accounting Matrix for Suriname

This summary is more intelligible when it is read and applied in concert with the Excel file: SIC.SAM.SURINAME.1.4.20. It is possible to request the Excel file from Suriname planning bureau at info_@planningofficesuriname.com.

The construction of the SAM is usually done in two parts: In the first part, the published estimates of the national accounts are sufficient to construct an aggregate matrix of incomings and outgoings for the accounts. In the second part, the accounts undergo further specification, and their connections are elaborated. In the situation at hand, some work has already been done regarding the first part, and there is already a well-operating IOT of 22 sectors for 2015. Proceed with further specifications along the following summary of stepwise procedures.

(1) *Industries:* There is available a well-operating IOT of 22 sectors for 2015. This needs to be compressed to 15 sectors along ISIC Rev 3. The first step is to aggregate the manufacturing branches to obtain one manufacturing sector, resulting in ISIC Rev 3.

(2) Other cells in the IOT such as indirect taxes less subsidies by sector, capital maintenance by sector, exports by sector, and imports by sector are to be entered in their respective cells in the SAM.

(3) *Factors:* There are employment numbers and payment transactions. The filling of the factors account requires several multiplications. The employment numbers by sector and by occupational types X the rates of differentiated earnings by sector and by occupation X the average earnings per employee.

(4) Capital returns, that is, net operating surplus, are allocated to corporate firms.

(5) *Household population groups (hpg):* There are demographic numbers and payment transactions (in and out). The filling of the in-payment transactions is a straightforward cross allocation of six factor earnings to the six earning hpg, $h = 1, .., 6$.

(6) *In-payments of $h7$:* The income sources of the unemployed hpg, $h7$, consist of unemployment allowances by government and there can be interhousehold transfers.

(7) *In-payments of $h7$:* The income sources of the seniors hpg, h8, consist of old-age benefits by government and pension incomings from previous savings.

(8) Tentative estimates for incomes of $h7$ and $h8$ are scaled to fit with government transfer allowances to these and other hps's.

(9) *Other in-payments received by hpg:* Hpg's receive or remit transfer payments with the world. Distribute such foreign transfer payments on hpg in proportion to their domestic income.

(10) *Out-payments of hpg:* Government statistics contain data on taxes and duties received from the hpg's. Distribute these on earning hpg in proportion to their domestic incomes.

(11) *Out-payments of hpg:* Next is relating consumption expenditure to the disposable incomes of the eight hpg. The remainder of disposable income goes into savings. This is a complex operation which is made simple and is fully verified and actualized by using handy statistical and econometric devices given the limited data available. See Excel sheets for the estimates of the consumption and savings ratios for each hpg.
(12) *Out-payments of hpg:* Information on the sectoral pattern of consumption by each hpg is lagging. In lack of such information, it is recommendable to use one uniform sectoral consumption pattern for all hpg, which is the one available from the IOT. There is a pending research paper that aims at obtaining such distribution proportions from survey data of the ABS/HB0 using indirect means of estimation. If such outcomes are meaningful and significant, they can be incorporated into the SAM.
(13) *Corporate firms:* Insert estimates relating to corporate firms: paid out dividends, taxes, and foreign transfers. The remainder is corporate savings.
(14) *Government:* Insert estimates relating to government spending, revenues, and domestic and foreign transfers. The remainder is government savings.
(15) *Complete the pending entries of the World Account:* The trade transactions are already inserted, and what needs still to be incorporated are transfer payments. These need to be done in concert with the corresponding transfers from the other accounts.
(16) *Check on consistency of the non-current account:* Foreign capital flow equivalent with the current payment balance and investment–savings balance.

Acknowledgements

I like to acknowledge my deep thanks for the hospitality and cooperation provided by the director and staff of the NPD Suriname, D. Lachman, L. Menke-Tangali, S. Wallerlei, and T. Elstak, staff at the General Bureau of Statistics Suriname, especially G. Koornaar, D. Sjahkit, S. Bisshop, and S. Presierie-Nijon, and to D. Rei and M. La Marca from the ILO. The same thanks and appreciation go to R. Woodly-Sobhi and S. Debipersad of the University of Suriname.

Chapter 14

Oil-Rich Labor Shortage Economies with Focus on Growth Only: Comparative Performance of UAE and GCC

1. Introduction

The six countries of the Gulf Cooperation Council (GCC), consisting of Bahrain, Kuwait, Oman, Qatar, Saudi Arabia, and the United Arab Emirates (i.e. UAE), are unique in the southern sphere. They are oil rich and are sparsely populated, allowing them to be among the richest in the world in terms of GDP per national citizen (nationals only and not total population per capita) and affording them to satisfy practically all material needs of their nationals.

From the perspective of country nationals, and this is what matters in this context, the country nationals are assured of high levels of well-being. This situation makes the twin goals of growth with redistribution (which would apply to normal countries and which is a main theme in this book) least relevant. The development goal in the GCC context is accordingly simplified to growth only.

Growth only seems easy to comprehend, but the devil is in the details. The growth-only objective falls into four connected and overlapping prerequisite dimensions which need to be satisfied in the context of UAE/GCC. There are trade-offs and complementarities between the four dimensions that require appraisal and resolution by the custodian decision makers. The four dimensions can be defined as in the following.

First dimension: Rapid economic growth requires increasingly mobilizing factors of production to produce (supply) and consume (demand). In GCC, the labor factor is amply available from migrant workers, and the other factors of production are financed by oil revenues. Production (supply) is thus secured. And the production (supply) creates its own consumption (demand). This is Say's law of the market. The circular flow is shifted upward every year and is kept in balance. The shift in the circular flow is largely determined by the oil revenues and the net inflow of migrant workers (NIMW). The question is what is the optimal or satisficing level of the NIMW? Economically speaking, in theory, the optimal NIMW is reached when the marginal national total costs of an additional NIMW (plus complimentary migrants servicing him) exceed the total marginal national benefits of this additional migrant worker (plus complimentary migrants servicing him), as perceived by the national citizens. Emphasis here is on total costs and benefits (monetary and non-monetary), as perceived by national citizens (solely Emirati).

Second dimension: Sustainable economic growth requires going beyond oil revenues and the regular economy, and entering into the knowledge economy, smart cities, the Fourth Industrial Revolution (4th IR), hi-tech startups, cooperation with international networks at full speed, etc. The policy questions raised are as follows: How much of the oil revenues should be devoted to the regular economy versus the knowledge economy and how to invest effectively in the knowledge economy? The general answer is to use part of the oil revenues to finance what is perceived as an optimal level of NIMW and use the leftover finance for the knowledge economy, or alternatively, investing less in the regular economy and stopping short of some optimal NIMW by $-x$ amount and enhancing the finance in the knowledge economy by $+x$ amount. Any specific answer entails implications for the NIMW and the economic activities in which they engage, and for the pace of the knowledge economy.

Third dimension: Influential economic growth is achieved by being big in terms of the economy (both the regular and the knowledge branches) being big in terms of the residential population. In the GCC context, Saudi Arabia is the biggest with the other five GCC generally seen as hanging around, which makes them partially dependent. Under the circumstances, each of the other five GCC tries to make their economies as influential and independent as possible. There is country competition within GCC to gain relative influence. This relative influence is measured by the dominance index based on GDP and population. The index shows UAE gaining influence at the cost of other GCC, mainly due to the surge in the residential population which is in turn caused by NIMW.

Fourth dimension: An economy that is significantly dependent on MW with nationals holding a marginal portion of the workforce can encounter more risks and uncertainties than a normal country with a majority of own nationals who are permanent settlers and manage to keep the economy in their own hands. Even though the risks of MW leaving the host country in masses or controlling the host country massively seem remote, they are feasible and are part of resolving the simple but complex growth-only objective. This dimension comes to what can be named securely nativized economic growth, also dubbed as Emiratization in UAE and Qatarization in Qatar. The issue is how to combine more *nativization* with secured stability in the NIMW, which is essential for economic growth. The issue is more actual in UAE and Qatar which are more dependent on MW than the other GCC countries with larger portions of the national population. Possible solutions to this issue lie in the extra promotion of the knowledge economy which requires less skilled labor but this is a partial answer since the knowledge economy requires hi-tech labor which is foreign as well and a complementary rise in the regular economy which requires more MW. Promising solutions can be also found in advancing shared national/foreign ownership of enterprises with national veto rights in management decisions where needed. Equally promising for assuring a stable NIMW are strategies toward a greater diversification of MW by country of origin.

Although the above four dimensions can be verbally described, it is practically impossible to quantify them as the variables of migrant workers and their economic activities weigh strongly in direct and indirect ways on the interactions between the four dimensions. Besides, national governing bodies do not appraise optimal or satisfactory points in designing development strategies. As trusted custodians of nationals and national interests, governors tend to apply development strategies which are perceived to be beneficial and welcomed by the over majority of the national citizens. What is feasible in terms of quantification is a comparative analysis of performance indicators relating to the four dimensions in the six countries. Such a comparative analysis would reflect on and gives insight into the underlying tacitly pursued development strategies in the oil-rich labor shortage economies of GCC.

The following sections will attempt to quantify each of the four dimensions in turn, with more focus on development performance and strategies in the UAE. Section 2 is on achieving rapid economic growth in the regular economy. Section 3 shifts development performance and strategy toward achieving sustained economic growth via entering into the knowledge economy. Section 4 considers respect to achieving influential economic growth. Section 5 discusses development performance and strategy regarding the secured nativization of economic growth. Section 6 contains concluding remarks.

2. Rapid Economic Growth in the Regular Economy

Achievement of rapid economic growth in the oil-rich labor shortage economy requires increasingly mobilizing migrant workers. With other factors of production amply financed by oil revenues, production (supply) is thus secured, and this creates its own consumption (demand). The circular flow is shifted upward every year as more oil revenues allow for more migrants to be put to work. The shift in the circular flow is largely determined by the net inflow of migrant workers (NIMW). The question is as follows: What is the optimal or satisfactory level of the NIMW in a particular year? In theory, the optimal NIMW is reached when the marginal national total costs of an additional NIMW (plus complimentary migrants that service his shelter, feeding, shopping, living services, etc.) exceed the total marginal national benefits of this additional migrant worker (AMW) and his complimentary servicing migrants, as perceived by the national citizens. The emphasis here is on total costs and benefits (monetary and non-monetary), as perceived by national citizens (solely Emirati in the UAE).

What to include in total benefits and total costs is controversial and lacks quantification. The monetary benefit from AMW is additional GDP, and there are no income taxes on MW that contribute to state revenue. Regarding costs, for every additional MW, there is additional infrastructure needed in terms of roads, transport and city facilities, and security which are funded by the government, and these are real national costs. Housing, health, and education services are paid for by the AMW and cannot be considered as national costs, but their regulation to meet acceptable standards is a national cost.

The non-monetary benefits are secured growth, higher well-being, satisfaction, and esteem from achieving developmental success. Obviously, the non-monetary benefits are non-quantifiable. The non-monetary costs can be high as these could include inevitable overcrowding and downgrading of AMW since each newly admitted AMW of an upper qualification and upper income requires and spends on the services of some complimentary AMWs of a lower qualification and lower income. Such developments lead to the emergence of a dualistic economy that has different origins than the conventional dual economy in developing countries as described by Lewis, Todaro, etc. The dualistic feature in the oil-rich labor shortage country expands rapidly when the country opens for entertaining wealthy expatriates as semi-permanent residents in luxury environments. Most of the wealthy expatriates are not AMW in the usual sense, but their residential environment requires significant inflows of AMWs in low-paid servicing activities. In turn, these low-paid AMWs would spend on and require for their living maintenance yet more complimentary AMWs of lower pays and lower skills. Often, for minimal payments and fees, AMWs succeed in in-migrating accompanied dependents with equal or lower skills. One and the other implies a further intensification of dualistic tendencies. At some point, explicitly distinguishable and highly distanced ways of living of guests can be perceived as negatively affecting the quality of life of the host. There are non-monetary trade-offs involved here that can hardly be investigated. But the trade-offs are real and often lead to the hosts enacting restraints on some aspects of the foreign inflow of human resources.

Given the above-discussed limitations on quantification, what is the sense of formulating the problem as the search for the optimal or satisfactory level of the NIMW in a particular year? One general answer is that statement of the problem in a logical setup helps in understanding the problem. A practical answer is the following. Governors in the GCC context, confronted with alternative paths, often make a judgment based on the general opinion and consensus of their national population whom they represent or protect. They observe and examine the attitude of their people, conform to such attitudes, and decide accordingly. Assuming that the situation in a particular year is an equilibrium situation where the attained value of NIMW reflects the consensus of the national population on the satisficing number of NIMW that the nation can live with, then that number can be interpreted as an approximation of the optimal number of NIMW absorption as being tacitly perceived by Emiratis nationals and governors. The case when the level of NIMW reaches a peak and is followed by a turnaround downward can be interpreted as an expression of reduced preference by Emiratis for more MW. The preferential interpretation does not contradict the contention that the downturn can be economically explained (that it may be caused by a reduction in economic activity or a rise in labor productivity). Both the preferential and the economic interpretations are valid. For example, from 2010 to 2015, the net inflow of migrant workers in UAE was 270 thousand. In the period between 2015 and 2020, NIMW went down to 200 thousand. The downturn is a reduction in the optimal number perceived as nationally permissible, which is the preferential interpretation. Equally valid is the economic explanation that the diminished NIMW was due more to a rise in average labor productivity (partly due to labor-saving impacts of the knowledge economy) rather than a reduction in economic activity. The further reduction in MW during the COVID epidemic of 2021 is explainable in terms of reduced economic activity and reduced need for MW, but the reduction can also be perceived as Emirati's preference for less MW during the COVID epidemic.

A closely related indicator to watch is the labor productivity index (LBI) expressed as GDP in USD per worker, indexed at 100 for 1990, Figure 1. Labor productivity attained its highest level with values of above 170 in 1980 and 1981. Since then, the index declined gradually to reach 53 in 2009. The index moved up in a range of around 70 in the years 2010–2020, reflecting the diminished NIMW in these years. The frequent oscillations in the index are due to abrupt movements in the oil revenues.

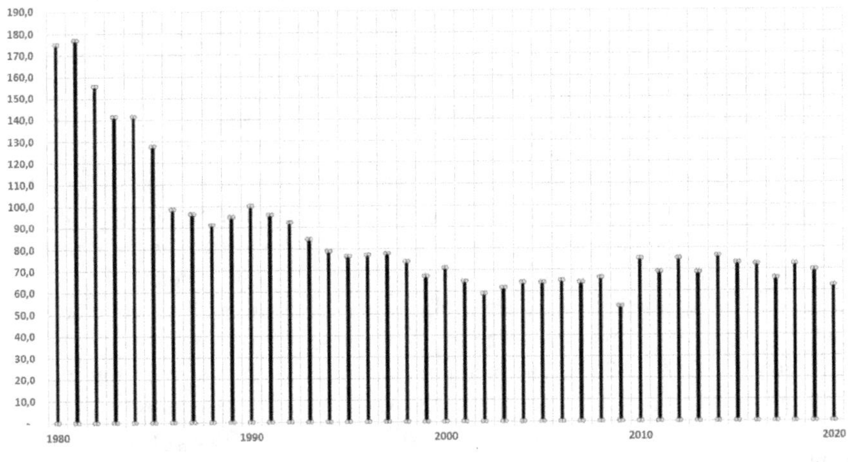

Figure 1. UAE Labor productivity index 1980–2020 (GDP in USD dollars per worker, indexed 1990 at 100).

Sources: 1980–2008 are from www.ilo.org/kilm. For later years, the GDP data are from the World Bank, and the employment data are from UAE Employed Persons, 2008–2016 CEIC Data, and 2016–2020 UAE annual reports 2016–2021, converted to index form.

Table 1. Industrial Operating Establishments (IPO) in GCC Countries in 1998–2000.

	Bahrain	Kuwait	Oman	Qatar	S. Arabia	UAE	Total
Total number IPO	327	725	751	382	3,004	2,054	7,243
Population mln	0.71	1.93	2.34	0.65	21.5	3.28	30.41
Number of IPO per capita	461	376	321	588	140	626	238

Source: Gulf Organization for Industrial Consulting: "Industrial Data Bank" GOIC: http://www.goic.org.qa/.

While generally speaking a declining LPI is considered a weak performance, this is not the case for the economy of UAE which can count on cheap MW. With having economic growth (expansion of the GDP) as the primary objective, it is worthwhile to employ additional MW as long as the employment of an additional MW adds more value added than what the MW costs, even though this can result in a decreasing LPI. In the context of UAE and GCC, higher economic growth goes with decreasing labor productivity. At some points, the NIMW stabilizes or diminishes or the GDP is lifted, allowing the LPI to shift upward. The extent that the LPI in the other GCC countries is not falling as much as in UAE suggests that the other GCC countries are missing opportunities for expanding their GDP when compared with UAE.

Notwithstanding the diminishing trend in labor productivity in UAE, the achievement pace in industrial development in the UAE is ahead of the GCC. Some indicators and explanations demonstrate the situation in the forthcoming tables. While in 1998–2000 the number of industrial establishments in Saudi Arabia exceeded UAE, the number of industrial establishments per capita in UAE is almost five times as much as in Saudi Arabia and is about 2.6 times as much as the whole GCC, Table 1.

The LPI is an average for all sectors of production taken together. The average covers highly capital-intensive sectors with rising LP as well as highly labor-intensive sectors with high economic growth driven by MW labor inputs. The UAE economy shows greater degrees of segmentation in terms of economic activities with higher and lower productivities than the GCC, rendering a more dualistic structure in UAE as compared to GCC. Table 2 shows a relatively greater occurrence of small firms in the manufacturing sector in UAE as compared to GCC. About 44% of manufacturing fall in the category of small firms in UAE; the figure for GCC is 39%. The medium and large together account for 56% in UAE and 61% in GCC. To the extent that small firms are associated with lower productivity and the informal sector, this will show itself up in a greater duality in UAE as compared to GCC.

Table 3 presents data on the number of firms in manufacturing, their capital investment and their employed labor. In manufacturing, it is generally the case that the higher the capital/labor intensity, the greater the productivity of the activity. The results for manufacturing show that the intensity amounts to 56,306 US dollars of

Table 2. Manufacturing: Distribution of the number of firms by size, 1998–2000.

Country	Small	Medium & large	Total	% Small in total	% Medium & large in total
UAE	806	1040	1846	43.7%	56.3%
GCC	2766	4322	7088	39.0%	61.0%

Source: Shiha (2000), p. 22. Base of size distribution is the number of workers in the firm.

Table 3. Manufacturing: Number of firms, capital invested, labor employed, and capital/labor intensity, 1998–2000.

Country	Number of firms	%	Capital invested mil US$	%	Number of labor employed	%	Capital/labor in US$
UAE	1846	26.0	8362	10.3	148509	26.6	56306
GCC	7088	100	81367	100	559352	100	145467

Source: Shiha (2000), p. 21.

capital per worker in UAE, as compared to 145,467 in GCC, reflecting the greater share of tiny and small enterprises in UAE referred to earlier as a cause of the low productivity.

3. Sustained Economic Growth via the Knowledge Economy

The knowledge economy (KE), standing for internet, communication, information, digitalization, and all that goes under the Fourth Industrial Revolution, is transforming the whole fabric of economic and societal relationships. KE is perceived as an unstoppable progress. The issues are which countries take the lead in managing the institutional setup so as to make the transition as comfortable and effective as possible for as many people involved as possible. UAE was among the earliest countries to take the lead in declaring the transformation to a KE as a development objective so as to assure sustained and heightened economic growth. Preceding the turn of the century the UAE reinvested strategically and enacted governance regulations in favor of the KE.

The notion of KE has been systematized by the World Bank along the lines of Figure 2, operationalized with various indicator measurements, and applied in ranking individual countries. The WB modeling framework known as the Knowledge Assessment Methodology produced the Knowledge Economy Index (KEI). The KEI considers four components or pillars: (a) the economic incentive and institutional regime, meant to provide incentives for the efficient use of existing and new knowledge and the flourishing of entrepreneurship, (b) education and human resources assures creating, sharing, and using knowledge effectively and extensively, (c) research and development, and (d) information communication

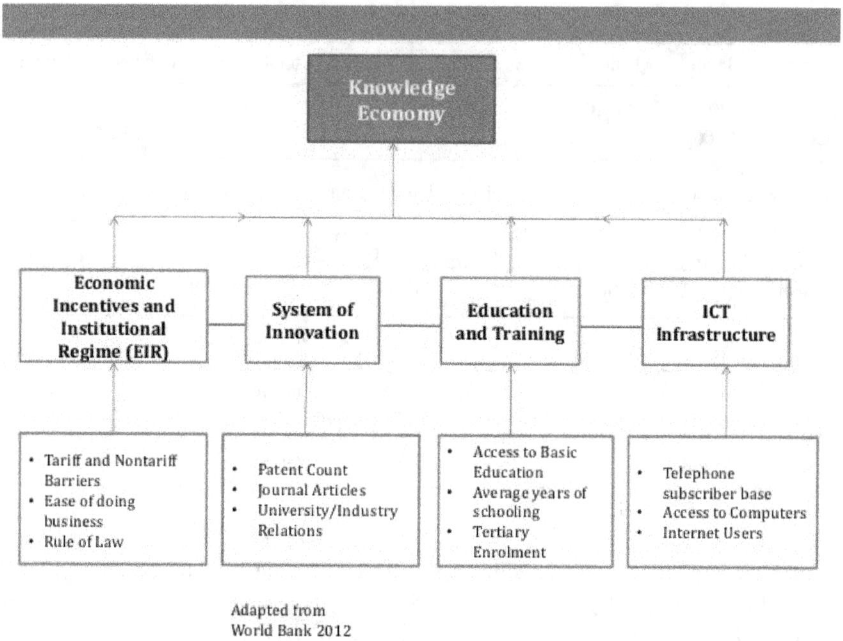

Figure 2. World Bank indicators on knowledge economy.

technology, ICT. The Knowledge Economy Index works with three indicators for each of the four pillars, thus totaling 12 knowledge indicators, as shown in the following: (a) Economic and institutional regime: extent of tariff and non-tariff barriers, regulatory quality, and rule of law. (b) Education and skill: adult literacy rate, gross secondary enrollment rate, and gross tertiary enrollment rate. (c) Research and development: royalty payments and receipts, US$ per person, technical journal articles per million people, and patents granted to nationals by the US Patent and Trademark Office per million people. (d) Information structure: telephones per 1,000 people, computers per 1,000 people, and Internet users per 1,000 people. The average score per pillar is summed over the four pillars and is again averaged equally. Data are updated by year as they become available.

The scores in Table 4 refer to 2015 and show the highest four ranking countries in descending order, a few other countries, and the GCC countries. Denmark is first with a score of 9.58, followed by Sweden, Finland, and the Netherlands. Other countries shown are Canada, the USA, Japan, and Hong Kong China with ranks of 6, 9, 19, and 26, respectively. The GCC countries are led by UAE, followed by Qatar, Bahrain, Kuwait, Oman, and Saudi Arabia with ranks of 42, 45, 50, 51, 62, and 65, respectively.

Table 4. Knowledge economy index (KEI). Scores of selected countries for 2015.

Country	KE Index	Economy	Innovation	Education	ICT	2015 Rank
Denmark	9.58	9.66	9.57	9.8	9.28	1
Sweden	9.52	9.18	9.79	9.4	9.69	2
Finland	9.37	9.47	9.66	9.78	8.56	3
Netherlands	9.32	9.18	9.48	9.26	9.36	4
Canada	9.21	9.42	9.43	9.26	8.74	6
USA	9.08	9.16	9.45	8.77	8.93	9
Japan	8.56	7.71	9.15	8.71	8.66	19
China (Hong Kong)	8.2	9.6	8.64	5.3	9.26	26
UAE	6.66	6.95	6.74	4.78	8.18	42
Qatar	6.15	5.99	5.77	5.29	7.56	45
Bahrain	6.02	6.84	4.2	5.82	7.22	50
Kuwait	6.01	7.01	5.05	4.87	7.13	51
Oman	5.37	7.32	4.95	4.3	4.9	62
Saudi Arabia	5.15	5.39	4.04	4.87	6.29	65

Source: World Bank.

In the GCC, the awareness of and preparation for the intrusion of the knowledge economy can be traced back two to three decades ago. All six countries, especially UAE and Qatar, took various measures in the past 30 years to bolster hi-tech industrial development. The investment in KE has culminated in striking achievements in advanced applications in research and development, digitalization, and information and communication technologies. UAE's World Expo 2022 and the moon landing 2022 are two highlights.

This section will attempt to assess the scores of the six countries along similar lines as those of the World Bank, making use of available indicator data which supplement the WB-selected indicators. The studied indicators go a step further than the WB KEI by distinguishing between input indicators and output indicators of KE. By dividing the composite score of the output indicators by the composite score of the input indicators, we obtain an output–input ratio for each country which reflects on the effectivity of the knowledge policies pursued in each country.

Use is made of a set of four indicators that give an idea of the magnitude and shape of inputs aligned with the knowledge economy. Table 5 gives expenditure on higher education per capita in UAE and GCC. The figures show that UAE devotes about half as much resources compared to GCC, i.e. 63 US$ per capita in UAE compared to 102 US$ in GCC. Other indicators are R&D expenditure per capita, R&D full-time equivalent researchers per 100,000 persons, and R&D support personnel per 100,000 persons. Here too, the input values in UAE are lower than in GCC. The indexes for these indicators are calculated with the GCC values as the denominator and set at 100. The average of the indexes shows UAE investing less resources in the knowledge economy at 64 points compared to 100 points for GCC.

Table 5. Various input indicators relating to the knowledge economy: UAE and GCC, around 2000.

	Higher education expenditure mln USD per capita	R&D expenditure mil USD per capita	R&D FTE researchers per 100,000 persons	R&D support personnel per 100,000 persons	Average index
UAE	63.0	4.64	4.5	8.6	
GCC	102.0	11.52	6.1	11.0	
UAE Index	63	40	74	78	64
GCC Index	100	100	100	100	100

Source: Adapted from ESCWA–UNESCO, Research and Development System in the Arab States: Development of Science and Technology Indicators, 1998 (E/ESCWA/TECH/1998/Rev. 1).

The next set of indicators deals with outcomes associated with the above inputs effort. Table 6 shows the extent of published papers in science and technology disciplines and those that were jointly co-authored with foreign institutions. Two productivity indicators can be calculated. The number of papers per full-time equivalent researcher shows UAE performing about the same as GCC in 1995, with about 1.3 publications per FTE researcher, compared to 1.7 for GCC. Notwithstanding, the international exposure of the research effort in UAE is greater than in GCC, with twice as much international exposure. The table shows the percentage of joint publications for UAE at 40% and for GCC at 21%. Table 6 presents also electronically released data on patents originating from the GCC countries and registered in the United States during the period 1990–1999. The comparatively small number of 170 patents generated, probably by foreign institutions operating in the Gulf countries, indicates the initially low level of innovative activity taking place in the region compared with other developing countries with a longer experience in technological development, such as Korea, Chile, and others, with ranges between 356 and 1343 patents during the same period. Calculating the number of patents per billion dollars of invested capital gives a productivity index for UAE of 1.8 patents, which is not far from that for the GCC of 2.1 patents. In interpreting patent figures, it is important to keep in mind that innovative firms may prefer not to file for patent rights for their innovations, such a decision being part of its competitive strategy. There is no information on this aspect in UAE and GCC. The table provides an overview of technology transfer activities undertaken in areas that relate to information and communication technologies (ICT) during 1992 and 1998. The highest value of contracts in information technologies is achieved by UAE, followed by Saudi Arabia and Kuwait. The highest value of contracts in telecommunication technologies is achieved by Saudi Arabia followed by UAE and Kuwait. On average, the figures of contract values per capita show UAE to be three times as much as the GCC, that is, 694 US$ for UAE compared to 229 US$ for GCC. The table provides also data on advanced methods of information and communication technology, i.e. the numbers of personal computers per 1,000 persons and internet

Table 6. Various outcome indicators relating to the knowledge economy: UAE and GCC, around 2000.

	Productivity: Published papers per FTE researcher	Exposure: Share of joint papers %	Patents/ capital investment billion USD	ICT contracts mil USD per capita	Personal computers per 1,000 persons	Internet users per 1,000 persons	Average index
UAE	1.28	40.1	1.79	694	62	301	
GCC	1.70	20.9	2.09	229	46	190	
UAE Index	75	192	86	303	135	158	158
GCC Index	100	100	100	100	100	100	100

Sources: Columns 1 and 2 from ESCWA (1999) Science and Technology Policies and Strategies for the Twenty-First Century, p. 13. Column 3 from United States Patent and Trademark Office, website: www.uspto.gov. Column 4 from Middle East Economic Digest: MEED 1992–1998. Columns 5 and 6 from www.econstats.com/wdi.wdiv_610htm.

users per 1,000 people. Both indicators show UAE as leading in GCC. The indexes for the six indicators are calculated with the GCC values as the denominator and set at 100. The average of the indexes shows UAE getting more outcomes relating to the knowledge economy, with 158 points for UAE compared to 100 points for GCC.

The averaged results for outcome and inputs indicators for the new economy show that in spite of the relatively lower inputs invested by UAE compared to GCC, there are on average higher outcomes in UAE than in GCC, as can be gathered from a division of average outcomes by average inputs, giving a benefit–cost ratio of $158/64 = 2.46$ for UAE, as compared a benefit–cost ratio of $100/100 = 1.0$ to GCC. The results suggest that the UAE has a greater ability to attract, lure, and exploit the potential of the knowledge economy supplied by expatriate experts and enterprises compared to other GCC. This is explainable by the generally acknowledged higher levels of hospitality access available for expatriate experts and investors in the UAE.

The knowledge economy and the regular economy interact in many ways. To sustain growth and development, it is necessary to shore up the share of the knowledge economy in the whole economy, which suggests that there is a zero-sum competition between the regular and the knowledge parts. This requires qualification as the knowledge economy enters in and introduces into the regular economy technologies that are knowledge-intensive, and labor-saving (less MW). In return, the regular economy entertains the world's highest quality levels of hospitality for the knowledge expatriates which allows the UAE to achieve the noted great ability and success in attracting and exploiting the potential of the expatriate-based knowledge economy. As such, the two branches of the economy complement each other in a win-win cooperation.

4. Influentially Powered Economic Growth

The third dimension of the growth-only development objective is the urge to gain influence. Influential economic growth is achieved not only by being big in terms of the GDP but also by being big in terms of the residential population, which relies on MW. The arguments for representing a country's economic influence in a group of countries by its relative sizes in the GDP and population in the referred group were explored in chapter 3. In the GCC context, Saudi Arabia is the biggest country in terms of both GDP and population. Each member of the GCC strives to make its economy as influential as possible. The country competition within GCC to gain influence is actual and is one of the dimensions of the development objective of growth only. It is proposed to measure this dimension by the dominance index based on GDP and population (The dominance index was previously encountered in Chapter 3).

The dominance index of country c, DIc, has two arguments: the relative share of the population of the member country in the GCC (that is *PPLc*) and the relative share of value added (that is *GDPc*):

$$DI_c = (\omega_1 PPLc + \omega_2 GDPc) \tag{1}$$

In this equation, there are two share parameters that represent influence. The dominance index proposes that the greater the shares of agents and transformed value added of a country, the greater the country's economic influential power. In this equation, ω_1 and ω_2 are equal weights applying to the two shares.

Table 7. Dominance index in the GCC, 1980–2020.

Year	UAE	Bahrain	Kuwait	Oman	Qatar	Saudi Arabia	All GCC
Country share in total population of GCC							
1980	0.073	0.026	0.108	0.074	0.020	0.700	1.000
1990	0.085	0.023	0.075	0.081	0.020	0.717	1.000
2000	0.108	0.023	0.063	0.077	0.021	0.707	1.000
2010	0.182	0.026	0.063	0.062	0.037	0.631	1.000
2020	0.162	0.026	0.076	0.079	0.048	0.609	1.000
Country share in total GDP of GCC							
1980	0.168	0.012	0.121	0.021	0.038	0.640	1.000
1990	0.256	0.022	0.071	0.056	0.033	0.562	1.000
2000	0.279	0.025	0.091	0.051	0.050	0.504	1.000
2010	0.246	0.021	0.097	0.053	0.099	0.484	1.000
2020	0.243	0.022	0.078	0.047	0.100	0.510	1.000
Dominance index *DIc*							
1980	0.120	0.019	0.114	0.047	0.029	0.670	1.000
1990	0.170	0.022	0.073	0.068	0.026	0.639	1.000
2000	0.193	0.024	0.077	0.064	0.036	0.605	1.000
2010	0.214	0.024	0.080	0.057	0.068	0.558	1.000
2020	0.203	0.024	0.077	0.063	0.074	0.560	1.000

Table 7 gives the results of the Dominance Index for the GCC countries. UAE is shown to gain influence at the cost of other GCC throughout 40 years, mainly due to the greater surge in resident population which is in turn caused by higher NIMW in UAE than GCC, next to higher GDP growth which is again due in part to higher NIMW in UAE than in GCC. The dominance index of UAE shows a slight decline of 0.01 in 2020 compared to 2010, which is due to the relative decline in the population share, as the UAE seems to be reaching a stabilizing population level in 2020 of around 10 million, with a diminishing NIMW in recent years as mentioned earlier. The Dominance Index of UAE at 20% compared to Saudi Arabia at 56% in 2020 does not consider the impact of a more advanced knowledge economy in UAE than in Saudi Arabia. A plausible speculation is that when the premium of the knowledge economy is considered, the economic influential power of the UAE can be approximated at half that of Saudi Arabia in the GCC.

5. Securely Nativized Economic Growth

The fourth dimension to be reviewed relates to national security. An economy that is significantly dependent on MW with nationals holding a marginal portion of the workforce can encounter more risks and uncertainties than a normal country with a majority of own nationals who are permanent settlers and manage to keep the economy in their own hands. Even though the risks of MW leaving the host country in masses or controlling the host country massively seem remote, they are feasible and are part of resolving the simple but complex growth-only objective. To minimize the security risks of an economy-wide open to MW, the countries aim at assuring securely nativized economic growth, also dubbed as Emiratization in UAE and Qatarization in Qatar. The issue is how to combine more nativization with secured stability in the NIMW, which is essential for economic growth. The issue is more actual in UAE and Qatar which are more dependent on MW than the other GCC countries with larger portions of the national population. Table 8 shows that practically speaking the GCC countries have the highest shares of migrant population in the world, which place them uniqely apart in resolving risks of dependence on foreigners.

Possible solutions lie in the extra promotion of the knowledge economy which requires less skilled labor but this is a partial answer since the knowledge economy requires hi-tech labor which is foreign as well and a complementary rise in the regular economy which requires more MW. Promising solutions can be also found in advancing shared national/foreign ownership of enterprises, with national veto rights where needed in management. Equally promising for assuring a stable NIMW are strategies toward greater diversification of MW by country of origin

Table 8. Countries with highest share of immigrants in the total population > 30%, year 2020.

Country	Immigrants	% of population
United Arab Emirates	8716332	88.1
Qatar	2226192	77.3
Kuwait	3110159	72.8
Bahrain	936094	55.0
Luxembourg	298062	47.6
Oman	2372836	46.5
Singapore	2523648	43.1
Saudi Arabia	13454842	38.7
Jordan	3457691	33.9
Australia	7685860	30.1

Source: Immigration by Country 2023 (worldpopulationreview.com).

and sectoral employment. There is a scarcity of knowledge and research on how these solutions are addressed in the GCC countries.

6. Concluding Remarks

Oil-rich labor shortage economies such as the GCC countries are guided by the economic growth-only objective. The income distribution goal can be considered as not applicable. While this simplifies socio-economic development issues, achievement of economic growth becomes significantly dependent on migrant workers. This raises complex issues regarding the optimal net inflow of migrant workers over the years, especially in the context of the introduction of the knowledge economy which saves on migrant labor but which also favors the luxury of being serviced by cheap migrant labor. Individual GCC countries are also under conflicting pressures to increase national power via enlarging the migrant labor force and the total resident population and to minimize security risks of dependence on foreign resident citizens. The comparative analysis in this chapter shows the UAE to be forerunner among the GCC countries in tackling development policies of oil-rich labor shortage economies.

Part V

Human Resource Development and Policies

Chapter 15

Analytics of Labor Force Information Systems

1. Introduction

Policymaking regarding labor market issues critically rests on the availability of well-organized data and analysis. Labor market information systems (LMIS) provide an essential basis for organizing labor data for useful monitoring, assessments, analysis, and policies. LMIS is a database or system that collects, stores, manages, and disseminates data and information about the labor market. The information typically includes data on employment, unemployment, wages, skill requirements, job vacancies, and other indicators that help describe the demand and supply of labor in a particular geographic area or industry. The purpose of an LMIS is to provide accurate, relevant, and up-to-date information on the labor market to inform policy decisions, support workforce development and job placement programs, and inform job seekers, employers, and other stakeholders about local labor market conditions. See Mangozho (2003), Swinwood (2013), and Schmillen (2019).

In many developing economies, the setting up of functioning of LMIS is hampered by various constraints, such as incomplete overview of the available labor data sets and how they relate to each other, little clarity on the differentiated analytical uses of labor data, indecision as to what to which data to include and exclude in LMIS, and how to combine these data in developing indicators of the labor market that can be relevant for policymaking. Furthermore, although labor market matching institutions collect matching data and report on market tendencies, they are lightly engaged in the analysis of these data.

Information feeding the LMIS is usually obtainable from two main sources: (1) periodical labor force survey and (2) labor market matching statistics collected and tabulated by the public employment service and private matching agencies. Other secondary sources are employment and earnings data as found in annual establishment surveys, and training statistics published by vocational, technical, and educational institutions, and there can be non-tabulated information supplied by key informants who are acquainted with employment counseling, career development, training services, etc.

The two main data types mentioned above are vital for obtaining a clearer description of the imbalances in the labor market and the processes behind them. To the extent that the analysis of this information is subject to formal methods, the methods actually employed take usually the form of an assessment of trends of indicators often displayed in statistical tables and graphical presentations.

The object of this chapter is to raise the use of the labor market information from the labor force surveys and from labor market matching statistics toward higher levels of understanding in data organization, monitoring assessments, analytical studies, and policymaking. This chapter falls into two sections: First, we use the labor force survey to construct a comprehensive labor force matrix. Second, we employ labor market matching statistics to monitor developments, highlight changes, and analyze them in terms of explanatory variables using simplified regression analysis. The case studies recalled here refer to applications to Pakistan in the 1980s. Although the numbers in the statistics displayed are of little relevance for the actualities of today, they should be perceived as examples in demonstrating the analytics methods involved in the upgrading of the labor market information system for use in analysis and policies. Accordingly, the focus of this chapter is on analytics methods with applicability in more countries and over time.

2. Labor Force Matrix: Example from Pakistan

This section reports on technical assistance in support of establishing a multi-sided LMIS under the auspices of the Ministry of Labor Affairs, Pakistan. In Pakistan, as in most developing countries, there is the labor force survey which is conducted by the statistics division annually or over periods of a few years. The survey contains scores of labor force data relating to un/employment by sector, age, sex, occupation, education, etc., but these data are loosely related to each other. Analysis and policy preparation in the area of human resource development can be significantly enhanced if these data are brought together and related to each other in the framework of some labor force information system. Loose sets of labor force data, no matter how well tabulated and documented, get the status of an information system when these sets are related to each other in a labor force matrix (LFM) that reveals a consistent, comprehensive, and summarized picture of the whole. The LFM is usable for quick and effective assessments.

The idea and the feasibility of a labor force information system have been a subject of discussion at the UN statistical division and the ILO, among others. An ambitious standpoint sees the information system as one in which data modules can be properly linked to allow the user to establish his/her own linkages. This permits the user to zoom into a topic and allows the user direct and indirect access to increasingly more detailed data modules. Our objective is more pragmatic and is limited to the direct use of the available data. We use statistics from the labor force surveys to sketch an LFM in which relevant categories of human resources and their attributes are displayed; we show ways in which this LFM is made useful in the context of analytical studies and policy preparation.

A student or an official acquainted with an economy like Pakistan may know that about 30% of the labor force work in urban areas, that 15% work in manufacturing, that 30% are employees, that 70% are illiterate or below primary school level, and perhaps that 25% are production workers. What neither the student nor his teacher would know is the combined number or percentage of illiterate production workers functioning as employees in manufacturing in urban areas. Similarly, for various purposes, one may desire to know how many persons work in various types of cross-combinations in terms of location, age, sex, activity, occupation, education, and status, but this information is not readily available. However, bits of information can be gathered and organized in a labor force matrix, LFM.

Table 1 is an LEM of 70 rows by 63 columns, giving in total 4410 cells. The LFM falls in an urban part and a rural part. We utilize the rows for classifications of location (two categories of urban and rural), status (five categories), and education by achieved level, while the columns are reserved for sectors of activity and occupational classification. One can read that the group referred to above (illiterate production workers functioning as employees in manufacturing in urban areas) falls in row 8 and column 21. This group counts 481,732 persons out of a total labor force of 26.1 million persons or 18% of the total labor force. In the same way, the absolute or relative size of other groups in the labor force can be directly calculated.

How is the LFM constructed? The published data of the labor force survey are usually described via simple cross-tabulations by sector/occupation, sector/status, occupation/education, and the like. Under certain assumptions, an appropriate LFM can be constructed from the published cross-tabulations. The procedure we follow makes use of joint probabilities of cross-tabulations. Take the available cross-tabulations to consist of the following: *IS*, *IQ*, *QS*, and *QK*, where I = sector, S = status, Q = occupation, and K = education. A combined use of these cross-tabulations would necessarily require starting with the three cross-tabulations involving I, S, and Q, while *QK*, which brings in K for the first time, is to be entered at a later stage. For *IS*, *IQ*, and *QS*, determine which cross-tabulation is the most independent, i.e. least dependent, on the basis of the lowest χ^2. Such a test shows *IS* and *IQ* to have the highest χ^2, while *QS* shows the lowest χ^2. As a result, an initial tableau can be worked out from *IS* and *IQ*, assuming *QS* to be initially irrelevant. The joint probabilities of the elements of Q and S in I can be determined, for instance, by $(Q_1/I_1) * (S_1/I_1)$, which gives the probability of Q_1 S_1 in I_1, Q_2S_2 in I_2, etc. The initial tableau can be constructed on the basis of these probabilities and the given values of I. The given subtotals from QS can be inserted now. Finally, the matrix of IS by Q can be extended to K in the columns by splitting up relevant cells using the information on *QK*. The result is a labor

Table 1. The labor force matrix of Pakistan 1982/3, urban.

A. Status and Education by Activity and Occupation Urban 1982

		AGRICULTURE							MINING							MANUFACTURING						
		PROF	ADMI	CLER	SALE	SERV	AGRI	PROD	PROF	ADMI	CLER	SALE	SERV	AGRI	PROD	PROF	ADMI	CLER	SALE	SERV	AGRI	PROD
EMPR	BPRI	7	0	2	20	61	16621	85	25	338	0	0	156	0	123	18	446	19	16	169	0	
	PRIM	5	0	2	8	14	2449	23	18	169	0	0	37	0	34	12	223	13	6	40	0	
	MSEC	8	0	3	7	9	1563	17	26	253	0	0	22	0	25	18	335	22	6	24	0	
	MSEC	30	0	20	7	8	1042	15	103	8B6	0	0	20	0	21	72	1171	170	6	22	0	
	INTE	17	0	11	2	2	521	2	58	464	0	0	5	0	3	40	611	94	2	5	0	
	DEGR	32	0	7	1	1	417	2	107	949	0	0	3	0	2	75	1255	56	1	3	0	
	POST	30	0	1	1	0	261	0	101	802	0	0	0	0	0	70	1060	7	0	0	0	
EMPE	BPRI	43	0	47	71	302	63791	865	90	94	0	0	471	0	771	6115	1198	2384	333	4962	0	
	PRIM	31	0	33	28	71	9399	238	64	47	0	0	111	0	212	4332	599	1658	129	1172	0	
	MSEC	45	0	55	26	42	5999	175	94	70	0	0	66	0	156	6370	899	2798	123	690	0	
	MSEC	177	0	422	26	39	3999	150	368	246	0	0	61	0	134	24970	3146	21452	124	642	0	
	INTE	99	0	232	7	10	2000	24	207	129	0	0	15	0	22	14014	1648	11814	34	161	0	
	DEGR	184	0	138	4	5	1600	16	384	263	0	0	8	0	14	25989	3370	7047	IB	80	0	
	POST	174	0	16	2	0	1000	2	361	222	0	0	0	0	2	24460	2846	829	10	0	0	
SELF	BPRI	52	0	4	182	340	127573	1834	0	0	0	0	0	0	0	227	589	69	265	1729	0	
	PRIM	37	0	3	71	80	18796	505	0	0	0	0	0	0	0	161	295	48	103	408	0	
	MSEC	54	0	5	67	47	11997	372	0	0	0	0	0	0	0	236	442	81	98	241	0	
	HSEC	212	0	39	68	44	7996	319	0	0	0	0	0	0	0	925	1546	620	98	224	0	
	INTE	119	0	22	19	11	3999	51	0	0	0	0	0	0	0	519	810	341	27	56	0	
	DEGR	221	0	13	10	6	3199	34	0	0	0	0	0	0	0	963	1657	204	14	28	0	
	POST	208	0	2	5	0	2000	5	0	0	0	0	0	0	0	907	1399	24	8	0	0	
FAMW	BPRI	22	0	3	128	481	101070	1382	0	0	0	0	0	0	0	47	436	26	93	1217	0	
	PRIM	15	0	2	50	114	14891	380	0	0	0	0	0	0	0	33	218	18	36	2	0	
	MSEC	23	0	4	47	67	9505	280	0	0	0	0	0	0	0	49	327	30	34	87	0	
	HSEC	89	0	30	48	62	6337	240	0	0	0	0	0	0	0	192	1145	234	35	169	0	
	INTE	50	0	16	13	16	3168	39	0	0	0	0	0	0	0	108	600	129	9	157	0	
	DEGR	92	0	10	7	8	2535	26	0	0	0	0	0	0	0	200	1225	77	5	39	0	
	POST	87	0	1	4	0	1584	4	0	0	0	0	0	0	0	188	1036	9	3	20 0	0	
UNF.M	BPRI	12	0	11	32	93	21986	334	9	8	0	0	50	0	104	55	98	176	48	482	0	
	PRIM	9	0	8	12	22	3239	92	6	4	0	0	12	0	29	39	49	123	19	114	0	
	MSEC	13	0	13	12	13	2068	68	9	6	0	0	7	0	21	37	74	207	18	67	0	
	HSEC	50	0	98	12	12	1378	58	36	22	0	0	7	0	18	223	258	1588	18	62	0	
	INTE	28	0	54	3	3	689	9	20	12	0	0	2	0	3	125	135	875	5	16	0	
	DEGR	52	0	32	2	2	551	6	38	24	0	0	1	0	2	232	276	522	3	8	0	
	POST	49	0	4	1	0	345	1	35	20	0	0	0	0	0	218	233	61	1	0	0	

		ELECTRICITY							CONSTRUCTION							TRADE						
		PROF	ADMI	CLER	SALE	SERV	AGRI	PROD	PROF	ADMI	CLER	SALE	SERV	AGR	PROD	PROF	ADMI	CLER	SALE	SERV	AGRI	PROD
EMPR	BPRI	0	0	0	0	0	0	0	26	1333	4	0	264	0	4705	2	179	6	20996	2484	25	1068
	PRIM	0	0	0	0	0	0	0	18	666	3	0	62	0	1294	1	90	4	8153	587	4	294
	MSEC	0	0	0	0	0	0	0	27	999	5	0	37	0	945	2	134	8	7732	346	2	216
	HSEC	0	0	0	0	0	0	0	106	3498	38	0	34	0	817	7	471	58	7797	321	2	185
	INTE	0	0	0	0	0	0	0	60	1832	21	0	9	0	131	4	247	32	2135	80	1	30
	DEGR	0	0	0	0	0	0	0	111	3748	12	0	4	0	88	7	504	19	1132	40	1	20
	POST	0	0	0	0	0	0	0	104	3165	1	0	0	0	13	7	426	2	615	0	0	3
EMPE	BPRI	660	171	1900	270	5737	1079	23491	490	1940	288	0	1481	0	154056	11	91	154	84563	13736	108	12186
	PRIM	467	86	1322	105	1355	159	6461	347	970	201	0	986	0	42374	8	46	107	32835	3245	16	3352
	MSEC	687	128	2230	99	798	101	4762	510	1455	339	0	582	0	31232	11	68	181	31141	1911	10	2470
	HSEC	2695	449	17098	100	743	68	4080	2000	5093	2595	0	541	0	26758	45	239	1386	31402	1778	7	2117
	INTE	1512	238	9416	27	186	34	656	1122	2668	1429	0	135	0	4299	25	125	763	8600	445	3	340
	DEGR	2805	481	5617	15	93	27	441	2082	5457	853	0	68	0	2895	47	256	455	4560	222	3	229
	POST	2640	407	661	8	0	17	67	1959	4608	100	0	0	0	539	44	216	54	2476	0	2	35
SELF	BPRI	21	7	5	19	176	59	1353	108	570	5	0	870	0	60335	25	281	28	420860	29985	416	50063
	PRIM	15	4	3	7	42	9	372	77	285	3	0	206	0	16596	18	140	19	153416	7084	61	13770
	MSEC	22	6	6	7	24	6	274	113	427	6	0	121	0	12232	27	210	33	154985	4173	39	10149
	HSEC	88	19	43	7	23	4	235	443	1496	45	0	113	0	10480	104	736	251	156282	3862	26	8695
	INTE	49	10	24	2	6	2	38	248	783	25	0	28	0	1684	58	386	138	42799	970	13	1397
	DEGR	91	21	14	1	3	1	25	461	1603	15	0	14	0	1134	108	789	82	22697	485	10	941
	POST	86	17	2	1	0	1	4	434	1353	2	0	0	0	172	102	666	10	12321	• 0	7	143
FAMW	BPRI	0	0	0	0	0	0	0	2	42	0	0	61	0	2237	4	164	8	116729	16650	129	14611
	PRIM	0	0	0	0	0	0	0	2	21	0	0	14	0	515	3	62	6	15325	3934	19	4074
	MSEC	0	0	0	0	0	0	0	2	31	0	0	8	0	454	4	123	10	42986	2317	12	3003
	HSEC	0	0	0	0	0	0	0	9	109	2	0	8	0	389	17	430	75	43346	2155	8	2573
	INTF	0	0	0	0	0	0	0	5	57	1	0	2	0	62	9	225	41	11871	539	4	413
	DEGR	0	0	0	0	0	0	0	10	117	1	0	1	0	42	18	461	25	6295	269	3	278
	POST	0	0	0	0	0	0	0	9	99	0	0	0	0	6	17	389	3	3417	0	2	42
UNEM	BPRI	21	5	49	13	196	41	1011	28	104	14	0	265	0	21343	3	23	35	37472	4115	36	1605
	PRIM	15	2	34	5	46	6	278	20	52	10	0	63	0	3395	2	11	24	14550	972	5	1267
	MSEC	21	4	58	5	27	4	205	30	78	16	0	37	0	2502	3	17	41	13799	573	3	934
	HSEC	84	13	444	5	25	3	176	116	272	126	0	34	0	2144	12	60	317	13915	533	2	800
	INTE	47	7	245	1	6	1	28	65	143	69	0	9	0	344	7	32	174	3811	133	1	128
	DEGR	86	14	146	1	3	1	19	121	292	41	0	4	0	232	13	65	104	2021	67	1	87
	POST	82	12	17	0	0	1	3	114	246	5	0	0	0	35	12	55	12	1097	0	1	13

		TRANSPORT							FINANCE							SERVICES						
		PROF	ADMI	CLER	SALE	SERV	AGRI	PROD	PROF	ADMI	CLER	SALE	SERV	AGRI	PROD	PROF	ADMI	CLER	SALE	SERV	AGRI	PROD
EMPR	BPRI	2	98	16	0	130	8	1238	30	1109	33	144	223	0	15	113	168	19	7	1361	57	664
	PRIM	6	49	11	0	31	1	341	21	555	23	56	53	0	4	80	84	13	3	321	8	183
	MSEC	9	74	18	0	18	1	251	31	832	39	53	31	0	3	118	126	22	3	189	5	135
	HSEC	36	258	141	0	17	1	215	123	2911	298	53	29	0	3	462	442	169	3	176	4	115
	INTE	20	135	78	0	4	0	35	69	1525	164	15	7	0	0	259	232	93	1	44	2	19
	DEGR	38	277	46	0	2	0	23	128	3119	98	8	4	0	0	481	474	55	0	22	1	12
	POST	36	234	5	0	0	0	4	120	2634	12	4	0	0	0	45	400	7	0	0	1	2
EMPE	BPRI	721	616	4575	0	8843	416	173797	934	2665	3731	2751	5847	0	798	3	1792	9322	638	157852	5081	158611
	PRIM	510	308	3183	0	2089	61	47804	662	1333	2595	1068	1381	0	219	15545	896	6485	247	37245	749	43627
	MSEC	751	462	5371	0	1231	39	35234	973	1999	4379	1013	814	0	162	11011	1344	10943	234	21939	478	32156
	HSEC	2942	1616	41178	0	1145	26	30187	3814	5996	33576	1022	757	0	139	16192	4704	83899	236	20408	319	27549
	INTE	1651	846	22678	0	286	13	4850	2141	3664	18491	280	189	0	22	63474	2464	46205	65	5102	159	4426
	DEGR	3062	1731	13527	0	143	10	3266	3970	7495	11030	148	95	0	15	35623	5040	27561	34	2551	127	2981
	POST	2882	1462	1591	0	0	7	495	3736	6329	1298	81	0	0	2	66065	4256	3242	19	0	80	452
SELF	BPRI	188	213	93	0	2167	180	80168	119	451	37	753	702	0	180	62179	511	156	293	31880	1823	80364
	PRIM	133	106	65	0	512	27	22051	85	226	26	292	166	0	50	3344	256	109	114	7532	269	16603
	MSEC	196	160	109	0	302	17	16253	124	339	44	277	98	0	37	2369	384	184	108	4436	171	12238
	HSEC	767	559	837	0	281	11	13924	487	1185	334	280	91	0	31	3484	1342	1407	109	4127	114	10485
	INTE	431	293	161	0	70	6	2237	273	621	184	77	23	0	5	13657	703	775	30	1032	57	1684
	DEGR	798	599	275	0	35	5	1507	507	1270	110	41	11	0	3	7664	1438	262	16	516	46	1134
	POST	751	506	32	0	0	3	228	477	1072	13	22	0	0	1	14214 13378	1215	54	9	0	29	172
FAMW	BPRI	16	64	14	0	623	29	12268	13	173	7	137	256	0	35	472	257	40	70	15243	488	15378
	PRIM	11	32	10	0	147	4	3375	9	87	5	53	61	0	10	334	129	28	27	3601	72	4230
	MSEC	17	48	17	0	87	3	2487	13	130	9	50	36	0	7	494	193	47	26	2121	46	3118
	HSEC	65	169	129	0	81	2	2131	53	455	65	51	33	0	6	1925	675	360	26	1973	31	2671
	INTE	37	88	71	0	20	1	342	30	239	36	14	8	0	1	1081	351	198	7	493	15	429
	DEGR	68	181	42	0	10	1	231	55	488	21	7	4	0	1	2004	723	118	4	247	12	289
	POST	64	153	5	0	0	0	35	52	412	3	4	0	0	0	1886	611	14	2	0	8	44
UNEM	BPRI	45	36	240	0	608	32	15066	86	225	285	409	587	0	101	1065	113	530	70	11777	427	14945
	PRIM	32	18	167	0	144	5	4145	61	113	198	159	139	0	28	754	56	369	27	2782	63	4111
	MSEC	47	27	281	0	85	3	3055	90	169	335	150	82	0	20	1109	85	623	26	1639	40	3030
	HSEC	185	94	2156	0	79	2	2597	351	591	2567	152	76	0	18	4347	296	4774	26	1525	27	2596
	INTE	104	49	1187	0	20	1	420	197	310	1414	42	19	0	3	2440	155	2629	7	381	13	417
	DEGR	193	100	708	0	10	1	283	365	634	843	22	10	0	2	4524	317	1568	4	191	11	281
	POST	181	85	83	0	0	1	43	344	535	99	12	0	0	0	4258	268	185	2	0	7	43

(*Continued*)

Table 1. The labor force matrix of Pakistan 1982/3, rural.

B. Status and Education by Activity and Occupation Rural 1982

		AGRICULTURE							MINING							MANUFACTURING						
		PROF	ADMI	CLER	SALE	SERV	AGRI	PROD	PROF	ADMI	CLER	SALE	SERV	AGRI	PROD	PROF	ADMI	CLER	SALE	SERV	AGRI	PROD
EMPR	BPRI	42	0	38	0	0	261724	672	0	0	0	0	0	0	0	19	321	43	0	396	18	13673
	PRIM	16	0	40	0	0	28943	149	0	0	0	0	0	0	0	7	193	45	0	91	2	3021
	MSEC	35	0	38	0	0	16136	82	0	0	0	0	0	0	0	16	193	43	0	80	1	1664
	HSFC	112	0	162	0	0	8269	35	0	0	0	0	0	0	0	51	193	182	0	25	J	720
	INTE	39	0	52	0	0	1034	53	0	0	0	0	0	0	0	18	128	59	0	2	0	1086
	DEGR	28	0	24	0	0	328	2	0	0	0	0	0	0	0	13	321	27	0	2	0	35
	POST	26	0	7	0	0	429	2	0	0	0	0	0	0	0	12	0	8	0	0	0	35
EMPE	BPRI	115	0	206	0	0	1117187	4071	0	717	251	0	0	0	1629	219	422	986	0	6825	330	350302
	PRIM	44	0	219	0	0	123546	900	0	430	267	0	0	0	1686	84	253	1048	0	1575	36	77408
	MSEC	95	0	206	0	0	68875	495	0	430	251	0	0	0	928	181	253	986	0	1386	20	42635
	MSEC	306	0	883	0	0	35299	214	0	430	1075	0	0	0	402	586	253	4222	0	438	10	18445
	INTE	106	0	283	0	0	4412	323	0	287	345	0	0	0	606	202	169	1356	0	29	1	27819
	DEGR	77	0	129	0	0	1399	11	0	717	157	0	0	0	20	147	422	616	0	29	0	907
	POST	73	0	39	0	0	1830	11	0	0	47	0	0	0	20	139	0	185	0	0	1	907
SELF	BPRI	188	0	24	0	0	4307999	16423	0	67	1	0	0	0	1032	148	485	47	0	9662	525	583396
	PRIM	72	0	25	0	0	476407	3629	0	40	1	0	0	0	228	57	291	50	0	2230	58	128916
	MSEC	155	0	24	0	0	265593	1999	0	40	1	0	0	0	126	123	291	47	0	1961	32	71005
	HSEC	502	0	102	0	0	136116	865	0	40	4	0	0	0	54	397	291	200	0	619	17	30718
	INTE	173	0	33	0	0	17015	1304	0	27	1	0	0	0	82	137	194	64	0	41	2	46329
	DEGR	126	0	15	0	0	5395	43	0	67	1	0	0	0	3	100	485	29	0	41	1	1511
	POST	119	0	4	0	0	7055	43	0	0	0	0	0	0	3	94	0	9	0	0	1	1511
PAMW	BPRI	55	0	0	0	0	4679354	17310	0	0	0	0	0	0	1003	14	0	0	0	4826	179	193565
	PRIM	21	0	0	0	0	517474	3825	0	0	0	0	0	0	222	5	0	0	0	1114	20	42773
	MSEC	46	0	0	0	0	288487	2107	0	0	0	0	0	0	122	11	0	0	0	980	11	23559
	HSEC	148	0	0	0	0	147850	911	0	0	0	0	0	0	53	37	0	0	0	309	6	10192
	INTE	51	0	0	0	0	18481	1375	0	0	0	0	0	0	80	13	0	0	0	2b	1	15372
	DEGR	37	0	0	0	0	5860	45	0	0	0	0	0	0	3	9	0	0	0	21	0	501
	POST	35	0	0	0	0	7663	45	0	0	0	0	0	0	8	9	0	0	0	0	0	501
UNEM	BPRI	24	0	63	0	0	348134	1257	0	0	0	0	0	0	0	16	0	107	0	811	36	38299
	PRIM	9	0	67	0	0	38499	278	0	0	0	0	0	0	0	6	0	113	0	187	4	8463
	MSEC	20	0	63	0	0	21463	153	0	0	0	0	0	0	0	13	0	107	0	165	2	4661
	HSEC	63	0	270	0	0	11000	66	0	0	0	0	0	0	0	43	0	457	0	52	1	2017
	INTE	22	0	87	0	0	1375	100	0	0	0	0	0	0	0	15	0	147	0	3	0	3041
	DEGR	16	0	39	0	0	436	3	0	0	0	0	0	0	0	11	0	67	0	3	0	99
	POST	15	0	12	0	0	570	3	0	0	0	0	0	0	0	10	0	20	0	0	0	99

		ELECTRICITY							CONSTRUCTION							TRADE						
		PROF	ADMI	CLER	SALE	SERV	AGRI	PROD	PROF	ADMI	CLER	SALE	SERV	AGRI	PROD	PROF	ADMI	CLER	SALE	SERV	AGRI	PROD
EMPR	BPRI	10	0	59	10	219	15	452	0	285	0	0	13	0	3338	0	162	7	16458	2239	413	830
	PRIM	4	0	63	3	51	2	100	0	171	0	0	3	0	738	0	97	7	5377	517	46	183
	MSEC	8	0	59	2	44	1	55	0	171	0	0	3	0	406	0	97	7	3652	455	25	101
	HSEC	27	0	252	1	14	0	24	0	171	0	0	1	0	176	0	97	28	1751	114	13	44
	INTE	9	0	81	0	1	0	36	0	114	0	0	0	0	265	0	65	9	600	10	2	66
	DEGR	7	0	37	0	1	0	1	0	285	0	0	0	0	9	0	162	4	150	10	1	2
	POST	7	0	11	0	0	0	1	0	0	0	0	0	0	9	0	0	1	0	0	1	2
EMPE	BPRI	566	0	6370	289	17634	1276	54180	0	1738	0	0	963	0	399425	0	38	26	17356	6780	132	3742
	PRIM	218	0	6768	94	4069	141	11972	0	1043	0	0	222	0	88263	0	23	28	5671	1586	15	827
	MSEC	468	0	6370	64	3580	79	6594	0	1043	0	0	196	0	48614	0	23	26	3851	1377	8	455
	HSEC	1513	0	27271	31	1130	40	2853	0	1043	0	0	62	0	21031	0	23	113	1846	435	4	197
	INTE	523	0	8758	11	75	5	4303	0	695	0	0	4	0	31720	0	15	36	633	29	1	297
	DEGR	381	0	3981	3	75	2	140	0	1738	0	0	4	0	1034	0	38	17	158	29	0	10
	POST	359	0	1194	0	0	2	140	0	0	0	0	0	0	1034	0	0	5	0	0	0	10
SELF	BPRI	3	0	2	11	187	15	675	0	273	0	0	187	0	91077	0	251	7	519323	55762	1222	36176
	PRIM	I	0	2	4	43	2	149	0	164	0	0	43	0	20126	0	151	8	169688	12868	135	7994
	MSEC	2	0	2	2	38	1	82	0	164	0	0	38	0	11085	0	151	7	115230	11319	75	4403
	HSEC	8	0	10	1	12	0	36	0	164	0	0	12	0	4796	0	151	31	55247	3575	39	1905
	INTE	3	0	3	0	1	0	54	0	109	0	0	1	0	7233	0	100	10	18942	238	5	2873
	DEGR	2	0	1	0	1	0	2	0	273	0	0	1	0	236	0	251	5	4735	238	2	94
	POST	2	0	0	0	0	0	2	0	0	0	0	0	0	236	0	0	1	0	0	2	94
FAMW	BPRI	1	0	0	10	273	15	655	0	0	0	0	47	0	15209	0	0	0	107033	18531	278	7986
	PRIM	0	0	0	3	63	2	145	0	0	0	0	11	0	3361	0	0	0	34973	4276	31	1765
	MSEC	1	0	0	2	55	1	80	0	0	0	0	10	0	1851	0	0	0	23749	3762	17	972
	HSEC	2	0	0	1	17	0	35	0	0	0	0	3	0	801	0	0	0	11386	1188	9	420
	INTE	1	0	0	0	1	0	52	0	0	0	0	0	0	1208	0	0	0	3904	79	1	634
	DEGR	0	0	0	0	1	0	2	0	0	0	0	0	0	39	0	0	0	976	79	0	21
	POST	0	0	0	0	0	0	2	0	0	0	0	0	0	39	0	0	0	0	0	0	21
UNEM	BPRI	4	0	72	10	220	15	623	0	0	0	0	62	0	23653	0	0	11	22340	3142	57	1594
	PRIM	2	0	77	3	51	2	138	0	0	0	0	14	0	5227	0	0	12	7299	725	6	352
	MSEC	4	0	72	2	45	1	76	0	0	0	0	13	0	2879	0	0	11	4957	638	4	194
	HSEC	12	0	310	1	14	0	88	0	0	0	0	4	0	1245	0	0	48	2377	201	2	84
	INTE	4	0	100	0	1	0	49	0	0	0	0	0	0	1878	0	0	15	815	13	0	127
	DEGR	3	0	45	0	1	0	2	0	0	0	0	0	0	61	0	0	7	204	13	0	4
	POST	3	0	14	0	0	0	2	0	0	0	0	0	0	61	0	0	2	0	0	0	4

		TRANSPORT							FINANCE							SERVICES						
		PROF	ADMI	CLER	SALE	SERV	AGRI	PROD	PROF	ADMI	CLER	SALE	SERV	AGRI	PROD	PROF	ADMI	CLER	SALE	SERV	AGRI	PROD
EMPR	BPRI	4	1340	828	0	94	7	1516	105	1190	57	0	327	0	0	0	51	135	0	2688	87	1147
	PRIM	2	804	880	0	22	1	335	40	714	60	0	76	0	0	0	30	143	0	620	10	254
	MSEC	3	804	828	0	19	0	185	87	714	57	0	66	0	0	0	30	135	0	546	5	140
	HSEC	11	804	3544	0	6	0	80	280	714	243	0	21	0	0	0	30	576	0	172	3	60
	INTE	4	536	1138	0	0	0	120	97	476	78	0	1	0	0	0	20	185	0	11	0	91
	DEGR	3	1340	517	0	0	0	4	70	1190	36	0	1	0	0	0	51	84	0	11	0	3
	POST	3	0	155	0	0	0	4	66	0	11	0	0	0	0	0	0	25	0	0	0	3
EMPE	BPRI	218	841	9231	0	7767	656	186940	1310	1683	1415	0	6063	0	0	0	277	12891	0	191663	6474	121702
	PRIM	84	505	9808	0	1792	73	41309	504	1010	1503	0	1399	0	0	0	166	13697	0	44230	718	26893
	MSEC	180	505	9231	0	1577	40	22752	1083	1010	1415	0	1231	0	0	0	166	12891	0	38906	399	14812
	HSEC	583	505	39520	0	498	21	9843	3501	1010	6058	0	389	0	0	0	166	55191	0	12286	205	6408
	INTE	201	336	12692	0	33	3	14846	1209	673	1946	0	26	0	0	0	111	17726	0	819	26	9665
	DEGR	147	841	5769	0	33	1	484	882	1683	884	0	26	0	0	0	277	8057	0	819	8	315
	POST	139	0	1731	0	0	1	484	831	0	265	0	0	0	0	0	0	2417	0	0	11	315
SELF	BPRI	46	302	137	0	3436	326	97279	87	189	7	0	837	0	0	0	101	195	0	86625	3290	64709
	PRIM	18	181	145	0	793	36	21496	33	113	7	0	193	0	0	0	61	208	0	19990	364	14299
	MSEC	38	181	137	0	697	20	11840	72	113	7	0	170	0	0	0	61	195	0	17584	203	7876
	HSEC	124	181	586	0	220	10	5122	231	113	28	0	54	0	0	0	61	836	0	5553	104	3407
	INTE	43	121	188	0	15	1	7725	80	75	9	0	4	0	0	0	41	269	0	370	13	5139
	DEGR	31	302	86	0	15	0	252	58	189	4	0	4	0	0	0	101	122	0	370	4	168
	POST	28	0	26	0	0	1	252	55	0	1	0	0	0	0	0	0	37	0	0	5	168
FAMW	BPRI	3	0	0	0	1140	74	21431	0	0	0	0	0	0	0	0	0	0	0	42908	1116	21290
	PRIM	1	0	0	0	263	8	4736	0	0	0	0	0	0	0	0	0	0	0	9902	123	4704
	MSEC	2	0	0	0	231	5	2608	0	0	0	0	0	0	0	0	0	0	0	8710	69	2591
	HSEC	8	0	0	0	73	2	1128	0	0	0	0	0	0	0	0	0	0	0	2751	35	1121
	INTE	3	0	0	0	5	0	1702	0	0	0	0	0	0	0	0	0	0	0	183	4	1691
	DEGR	2	0	0	0	5	0	55	0	0	0	0	0	0	0	0	0	0	0	183	1	55
	POST	2	0	0	0	0	0	55	0	0	0	0	0	0	0	0	0	0	0	0	2	55
UNEM	BPRI	7	0	434	0	401	314	8876	44	0	70	0	329	0	0	0	0	712	0	11635	365	6798
	PRIM	3	0	461	0	93	35	1962	17	0	74	0	76	0	0	0	0	757	0	2685	40	1502
	MSEC	6	0	434	0	81	19	1081	36	0	70	0	67	0	0	0	0	712	0	2362	23	827
	HSEC	19	0	1856	0	26	10	467	117	0	300	0	21	0	0	0	0	3049	0	746	12	358
	INTE	6	0	596	0	2	1	705	40	0	96	0	1	0	0	0	0	979	0	50	1	540
	DEGR	5	0	271	0	2	0	23	30	0	44	0	1	0	0	0	0	445	0	50	0	18
	POST	4	0	81	0	0	1	23	28	0	13	0	0	0	0	0	0	134	0	0	1	18

force matrix in the dimensions *IS* in the rows by *QK* in the columns. In view of the lack of verification, the resulting matrix of *IS* by *QK* should be seen as a tentative approximation of the real figures. Of course, a labor force matrix can be directly programmed from the original questionnaire of the labor force survey, making it feasible to check on the reliability of the procedure used here.

How is the LFM designed? The size of a labor force matrix is determined by the available data and the chosen disaggregation. In this particular case, the rows count 70 lines which represent two locational disaggregation (rural and urban), three status types, and five educational types. The columns count 63 which is the result of including 9 sectors and 7 occupations.

It is up to the designer to make a choice on what to include in the columns and the rows. Our particular design here has been motivated by the consideration that employment by sector and occupation are determined primarily by demand factors, while the labor force by location, status, and education is largely a matter of supply factors. Registering demanders in the columns and suppliers in the rows is in equivalence with input–output accounting in which the row items are deliverers to the column items. This particular arrangement of rows and columns can be shown to increase the flexibility of the LFM for purposes of forecasting and policymaking where a specific shape of demand for labor is given and a solution of the supply pattern is sought or otherwise. It is noted that the chosen design regarding what should come in the rows and columns does not affect the results.

A final note is on the treatment of the unemployed. While their education, occupation, and status (wage earners) are known, the eventual sector of activity in which they may be employed in the future or which they have left is unknown. Because such data on their future/past sector of activity are unknown, the choice was either to exclude the unemployed from the matrix (which devaluates the matrix) or to assure that the activity distribution of the unemployed can be approximated by the activity distribution of wage employment, which enriches the matrix by the inclusion of the unemployed though in an approximative way.

Hence, the presentation of their numbers is in italics. Inclusion of the unemployed allows the matrix to be named a labor force matrix and not only an employment matrix.

In which ways can the LFM be presented? Table 1 is the matrix in its full form. But the matrix is flexible and can be aggregated to whatever classifications are thought desirable.

Furthermore, the LFM can be expressed in percentages which add up to 100.0% as in Table 2, which throws light on structural relations. To save space, Table 2 shows only the grouped sectors of trade, transport, finance, and services and the total of all sectors.

What are the uses of the LFM? From a welfare economics viewpoint, there is support for the contention that the proportion which a particular labor group has in the whole labor force can be a guideline for the degree of attention which may be devoted by policy makers and public authorities at large to that particular labor

Table 2. Abridged LFM of Pakistan 1982/3, in persons and in proportions.

Grouped sectors of	Trade/Transp/Finance/Serv (in persons)					Trade/Transp/Finance/Services (in proportions)				
	prfn	adm/cl	slr/srv	prdwrk	Total	prfn	adm/cl	slr/srv	prdwrk	Total
WAGE	**594857**	**694105**	**933233**	**1077321**	**7913626**	**0.0228**	**0.0265**	**0.0357**	**0.0412**	**0.3027**
Blw prmry	58565	54746	550814	677718	4384834	0.0022	0.0021	0.0211	0.0259	0.1677
Primary	28145	45257	148584	167325	955991	0.0011	0.0017	0.0057	0.0064	0.0366
Mid scndry	52156	53939	118335	110084	701471	0.0020	0.0021	0.0045	0.0042	0.0268
High scndry	181034	286964	82692	77747	967709	0.0069	0.0110	0.0032	0.0030	0.0370
Intermediat	77824	133784	19415	35017	420741	0.0030	0.0051	0.0007	0.0013	0.0161
Degree	101529	92637	10198	7516	301020	0.0039	0.0035	0.0004	0.0003	0.0115
Post-gradua	95604	26778	3195	1914	181860	0.0037	0.0010	0.0001	0.0001	0.0070
NON-WAGE	**138761**	**38767**	**2778081**	**776958**	**17212560**	**0.0053**	**0.0015**	**0.1063**	**0.0297**	**0.6584**
Blw prmry	13472	3686	1471943	491509	12643528	0.0005	0.0001	0.0563	0.0188	0.4836
Primary	6535	2200	485210	120306	1990117	0.0002	0.0001	0.0186	0.0046	0.0761
Mid scndry	12038	2892	393454	78259	1282745	0.0005	0.0001	0.0150	0.0030	0.0491
High scndry	41909	10996	292764	54010	844623	0.0016	0.0004	0.0112	0.0021	0.0323
Intermediat	18159	5626	81693	26392	266639	0.0007	0.0002	0.0031	0.0010	0.0102
Degree	24025	8144	37242	5113	111646	0.0009	0.0003	0.0014	0.0002	0.0043
Post-gradua	22623	5223	15775	1369	73262	0.0009	0.0002	0.0006	0.0001	0.0028
LYD	***31518***	***38181***	***175671***	***86192***	***1017661***	**0.0012**	**0.0015**	**0.0067**	**0.0033**	**0.0389**
TOTAL	**765136**	**771053**	**3886985**	**1940471**	**26143847**	**0.0293**	**0.0295**	**0.1487**	**0.0742**	**1.0000**

group. In a simple application of this guideline, go to Table 1, cells 50 by 6 and 57 by 6, say groups A and B. These two cells have the largest number of persons, over 4 million each, and should get in equivalence with their shares, around 15% each of the policy research and planning effort in the nation. Groups *A* and *B* also happen to be the most deprived in terms of welfare. Actually, the attention which such groups receive is likely to be very minor and much below 15%. In contrast, much more attention goes to minor groups, which are usually better off, say *C*.

As a second guideline, we may add that only in the presence of positive group linkages whereby the benefit which accrues to group *C* may trickle down to groups *A* and *B* through expenditure by *C* or taxation of *C* followed by differentiated public spending will it be justifiable to increase the development effort in *C* at the cost of *A* and *B* in spite of a smaller share of *C* than *A* or *B* in the labor force. In directing the development effort, the use of proportional structure in the LFM, in combination with information on group linkages as provided by the Social Accounting Matrix, SAM, that was discussed in previous chapters, would open the possibility of achieving higher social welfare.

The LFM can be a helpful guide to relevant policy research in a related aspect. A particular group can not only be located in the LFM but its multi-dimensional characteristics can also be made more apparent. The matrix indicates the kind of characteristics which decision makers have to cope with in their encounters with particular groups. The type of problems faced by a specific group may even be anticipated based on the apparent characteristics.

The matrix can also function as a reference framework for labor market monitoring and matching in the short term as well as a sampling framework for labor force surveys or for the study of selected target groups.

Although the LFM gives a static picture, the availability of LFMs for more countries and more years would allow detecting and analyzing structural patterns in the labor force.

Another interesting use of the LFM is in the following. The Sixth Five-Year Manpower Plan of Pakistan was estimated on tentative assumptions regarding future government policy as of early 1983. The Sixth Plan considered a domestic labor force (excluding net migration) of 27.5 million in mid-1983 which grows to 30.8 million in mid-1988. With a terminal unemployment figure of 1.0 million, a target employment of about 29.8 million was obtained. The model we utilized for breaking up the employment figures by destination is similar to those in the following two chapters. The outcomes of the manpower plan can be rearranged in the form of a target LFM for 1988, which gives plan projections of employment by sector, status, occupation, and education next to projected unemployment by status, occupation, and education. The observed LFM of the initial year of the plan (i.e. 1982/3, Table 1) can then be compared with the LFM for the end of the plan (1988). Such comparisons were made and showed approximately the same patterns for 1982/3 and for planned 1988.

The human resource development perspective pays attention not only to the labor force but also to the population at large, that is, including the dependent population. The LFM is extendable to consider the dependent population as well or, more generally, the non-active population. The result is a population matrix. To do this, an additional dimension to the LFM can be added which divides the labor force between heads of household, HH, and other members of the household. The HH is the main link between a labor force and the number of inactives in a population group matrix.

There are other conceivable elaborations which are capable of converting the LFM from a static to a dynamic matrix, allowing basic questions relating to labor mobility to be treated in the dynamic context, as was developed in demographic accounting by Stone (1971).

3. Labor Market Matching Data for Assessment and Analysis: Examples from Pakistan

An important source of LMIS is the labor market matching statistics collected by public and private employment agencies. These are recurrent and are usually reported on a quarterly basis. These labor force matching statistics allow assessments of the short-term trends in job vacancies, job seekers, unemployment, and sometimes if collected, data on job remuneration rates as well.

Employment exchanges are unique in their double roles of promoting employment through matching and other related activities and of collecting and processing labor market information. As is well known, the main activity of employment exchanges in most countries is the matching of registration of job seekers against notifications of vacancies with the objective of achieving maximum placements in the concerned district. The secondary activities include conduct of establishment enquiries, training surveys, *ad hoc* employment surveys, registration essential personnel, reviews of exchange areas, vocational guidance, and employment counseling. In the process, matching statistics at the district level are constantly being created, and these can form an important source of labor market information.

Although the various types of labor information which employment exchanges in most developing countries collect are tabulated and published at provincial and/or federal levels, they are only seldom analyzed. The deficiencies of the collected data are often held as reasons for not carrying out additional analysis of the data.[1] We believe that demonstrating some uses of what is available is a more constructive attitude. It is also by working with what is available that one can demonstrate the more significant deficiencies in statistics and hope to give convincing arguments for improving the database.

The objective of this and the following section is to demonstrate some useful analysis of matching data, in the context of employment exchanges in Pakistan.[2] In particular, matching statistics can be useful in two respects: first, in assessing labor market trends and, second, in monitoring the matching performances at the district level. These two uses can be named external analysis and internal analysis, respectively. First, even though they are partial, the matching statistics can give an external description of certain trends in the labor market, and in a more elaborate analysis, they can be modeled and simulated so as to predict the future outlook regarding demand and supply. Second, as far as matching statistics reflect the internal functioning of the individual employment exchanges, these statistics can be utilized to assess the performance of the employment service and give guidelines toward increasing their internal efficiency.

What employment exchanges do by way of recording the job seekers, notified vacancies, and placements of job seekers against vacancies boils actually down to matching the demand and supply of manpower in the short run and at the local level. This yields aggregate and specific information on shortages and surpluses. This information could help in making the assessment of certain segments of the labor market and perhaps estimate their tendencies in the medium run as well as provide guidelines for training programs and recruitment possibilities.

The matching activities of employment exchanges cannot cover the many dimensions of the labor market or, for that matter, can any agency, how elaborate it is, be able to give comprehensive information on the complex and dynamic labor market. So which segments of the labor market do matching activities highlight? And how well do they represent them?

Matching activities usually take place in urban areas and can be assumed to be predominantly oriented toward the organized sector. In assessing the extent of labor market coverage by the matching activities, one has to compare the placements with employment creation in the urban-organized segment since this is the main segment they serve. It can be estimated on the basis of the Economic Surveys that in the period 1973–1981 urban employment in Pakistan increased annually by about 140,000 persons. On the basis of the Labor Force Surveys, it can be further estimated that about half, i.e. 70,000 persons, found new jobs in the organized sector. An examination of the placement figures of employment exchanges in Table 3 shows these to average about 55,000 persons in the same period. Dividing one by the other gives a coverage of about 80%.

This brings us to the question of how far is the 80% sample a reasonable representation of what happens in organized labor. It is important to realize that the coverage is distorted by the limited number and spread of employment exchanges and by the facts that registration of job seekers covers those with and without jobs, while notified vacancies can be the result of new jobs as well as turnover, and the notified do not coincide with actual vacancies since notification is not compulsory. As a result, the readily available data on matching activities do not allow an assessment of the representativeness of the organized segment. We shall give them the benefit of the doubt and assume them to be reasonably representative. The real picture may not be too far from that given by the 80% sample, considering that the sample contains several overlapping and that some overlapping may neutralize each other.

Table 3 presents national data for registrations, notifications, and placements, while Figure 1 shows these trends from 1973 to 1982. Registration of job seekers averaged about 260,000 with the highest level in 1975 at 300,000 and the lowest only 2 years later in 1977 at 197,000. This trend is understandable in the light of (1) higher incentives to go overseas as migrant workers to oil-producing Arab countries than to seek a domestic job and (2) the realization that there is little gain from registering when urban industrial activity, notifications, and placements are

Table 3. Pakistan: Registration of job seekers, vacancies, and placements at employment exchanges, *n*. thousands, migrant workers leaving the country, in thousands of persons, and index of industrial production.

	1973	1974	1975	1976	1977	1978	1979	1980	1981	1982	Average
Job seekers	287	284	300	260	197	240	232	249	247	271	257
Vacancies	60	60	70	63	51	54	54	58	66	66	60
Placements	50	52	62	57	48	49	51	54	62	64	55
Migrant workers	14	23	27	40	145	135	125	135	165	145	
Index industrial production	100	99	98	97	112	120	134	148	169	185	

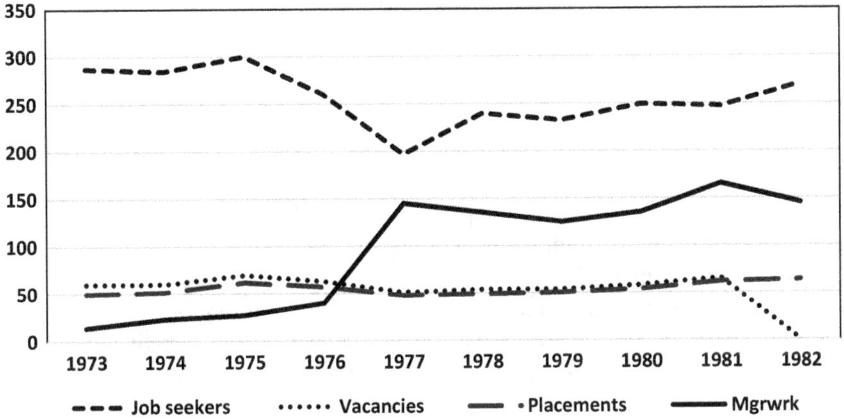

Figure 1. Pakistan. Trends of matching statistics.

sluggish and prospects for getting a local job are less prosperous. Figure 1, which plots the number of migrant workers and the index of industrial activity, against indicators of job-seeking registrations, notifications, and placement, shows such associations.

The trends shown above are not independent of the domestic economic activity and the international setting. A basic model can be formulated and quantified to highlight these interdependencies and, in turn, serve as an analytic tool for assessing the future outlook. The basic model presented in the following will aim at explaining the three aggregate variables of the matching process: *JBS* is the registration of job seekers during a year, *VCN* is the notification of vacancies during a year, and *PLM* is the placements during a year.

Eq. (1) is on explaining registrations. As stated above, registration can be seen to be a negative function of migrant workers (the higher the overseas opportunities for migrant workers, the less incentive to register as a job seeker, β_1 negative) and a positive function of the level of domestic industrial activity (the more the volume of production, the more the incentive to register as a job seeker, γ_1 positive).

$$JBS = \alpha_1 + \beta_1 MIG + \gamma_1 VIP \tag{1}$$

where *MIG* is the number of migrant workers and *VIP* is the index of volume of industrial production.

Registered vacancies, in eq. (2), can be expected to be positively dependent on the volume of industrial production, γ_2 positive. Notifications are also likely to be influenced by migrant workers in different ways. Shortages create vacancies. But to the extent that (a part of) the migrant workers engage in creating new jobs, their departure may cancel such vacancies and their return may stimulate new vacancies.

The combined overall effect can render β_2 to be either negative or positive.

$$VCN = \alpha_2 + \beta_2 MIG + \gamma_3 VIP \tag{2}$$

Placements, in eq. (3), are in turn positively dependent on the number of vacancies, in a situation where the employment exchanges are able to devote their resources fully toward placing job seekers, β_3 positive. However, the tasks of registering and placing job seekers compete with each other in terms of staff time and available resources at the employment exchanges. More of the first is at the cost of the second. Since employment exchanges are obliged by law to register job seekers when they apply, the placement activity may suffer from too high levels of registration activities. The negative dependence is reflected in γ_3 negative. It will be shown to be a statistically valid and significant effect.

$$PLM = \alpha_3 + \beta_3 - \gamma_3 JBS \tag{3}$$

This basic equation was estimated from the observations in Table 3 to give the results of Table 4.

The regression coefficients have the expected signs. The standard errors within parentheses are very low by usual norms. The degree of explanation as reflected by the adjusted R^2 is 0.86 for registrations in eq. (1), and 0.92 for placements in eq. (3), which are high and assuring. The explanation of notifications with an adjusted $R^2 = 0.46$ proves to be more difficult. This is likely to be the result of working with aggregate data. A disaggregation of notifications into those forthcoming from the private and public sectors and an explanation of each separately can improve results significantly.

The regression results for registrations of job seekers would imply that there is yearly a more or less constant flow of job seekers amounting to 206 thousands ($\alpha_1 = 206.2$) and that changes above or below this level are induced by industrial activity and migrant workers. The volume index of industrial production (1976 = 100) amounted in 1982 to 184. An 8% growth in industrial production—equivalent to 15 additional points would increase registered job seekers by 14,000 (that is, 15 × 0.9265), while a net reduction of 20,000 migrant workers would

Table 4. Ordinary least square estimates of the basic model.

Explained	Intercept	*MIG*	*VIP*	*VCN*	*JBR*	R^2
JBR	206.2	−0.7190		+0.9265		0.86
		(0.0971)	(0.1939)			
VCN	43.8	−0.1127		+0.2119		0.46
		(0.0373)	(0.0745)			
PLM	3.4			+1.2894	−0.1025	0.92
				(0.1466)	(0.0288)	

increase registration of job seekers by another 16,000 (that is, 20 × 0.7190). This is about what has happened during 1983, the first year after the observation period when registrations increased by about 30,000 to another record level of 301,000. This trend toward further increases has materialized in later years in view of both industrial prospects and returning migrants.

As regards registration of vacancies, the model predicts a departure from the average level of 60,000 to higher levels in view of returning migrants and the maintained pace of industrial growth. This is also borne out by preliminary figures for 1983 when notifications exceeded 70,000 for the first time.

As regards placements, the model predicts greater lags behind notifications than was customary in the past, especially if under pressure of more registrations in the future less resources would be made available for the placement function.

Finally, and as a result of the above, the gap between registrations, on the one hand, and notifications and placements on the other hand, which amounted to an average ratio of 4.5 to 1.0 in the observation period has a built-in tendency to increase, which was realized in later years.

This ratio is high by the standards of other countries. But, what significance should be given to this ratio? The very high registration must include, besides serious candidates, a vast number of job seekers who are either (1) badly informed about the limited possibilities of getting a job in the organized sector, or (2) overrate their ability in terms of meeting the requirements of the organized sector, or (3) register as a matter of routine, the motivation being job-hunting rather than job-seeking.

Closely related to the height of the ratio is the negative effect of registration on placement in eq. (3). This is alarming. Too many persons register, and much staff time goes into the registration activity with little staff time left for persuading the placement activity. The spread of more information on available but limited vacancies, the observance of trade tests, verification of certificates, and above all, more scrutiny and selectivity in registering job seekers who are presently enjoying jobs which match their qualifications could reduce the load of registration and free resources for more effective activities in the employment service. This aspect will be treated in more detail in the following section.

In concluding this part, it is important to note that the number of observations used in estimating the model is only ten but these will be significantly higher if provincial and quarterly data are used. This will allow testing more sophisticated relations that were done here.

The external analysis of the labor market can now move from aggregate variables to disaggregation by occupations and educational levels. Use is made of published data for job seekers and vacancies by occupational level. As examples, Table 5 gives the percentage distribution of job seekers by major occupations and educational level. Table 6 gives the percentage distribution of achieved placements by occupation and education. While Table 5 describes the supply pattern of job

Table 5. Registration of job seekers: Distribution by occupation and education.

Registration of Job seekers		1973	1974	1975	1976	1977	1978	1979	1980	1981	1982	Average
Percentage distribution of job seekers by occupation (%)												
0,1	Professional	11.8	12.9	16.7	12.4	12.5	10	9.7	10.7	10.4	11.3	11.8
2	Administrative	0.3	0.2	0.2	0.2	0.2	0.2	0.2	0.3	0.2	0.3	0.2
3	Clerical	31.8	29.5	28.2	30.4	28	30.2	30.2	30.3	30.6	32.1	30.1
4	Sales workers	0.1	0.4	0.1	0.2	0.1	0.1	0.2	0.2	0.2	0.3	0.2
5	Service workers	24.2	26.7	27.6	28.6	29.6	32.1	32.1	32.9	34.4	33.1	30.1
6	Agriculture wrkrs	1.5	1.9	2.9	3.4	3.7	4	3.7	3.6	3.6	3.7	3.2
7,8,9	Production wrkrs	29.2	28.6	24.2	24.9	26	23.4	23.8	22.9	20.3	19.3	24.3
Percentage distribution of job seekers by education (%)												
1	Illiterate	27.2	26.6	24.3	24.3	26.2	23.4	24.5	25.9	24.3	23.7	25.0
2	Below matric	28.9	31.4	30	31.6	33.1	30.3	31.6	30.8	32.4	28.6	30.9
3	Some matric	28.5	26.5	26.6	26.7	24.5	27.6	28.8	29	28.6	33.3	28.0
4	Matric crtfct	8.9	11.1	13.1	11.3	11.2	12.8	10.5	8.7	8.7	8.1	10.4
5	Matric diploma	1.5	1	1.8	1.8	1.1	1.6	1	1.4	1.5	1.6	1.4
6	Polytechnic dplm	0.7	0.6	0.6	0.8	0.8	0.8	0.9	0.7	0.7	1	0.8
7	Graduate	3.7	2.5	3	3.3	2.8	3.2	2.5	3.1	3.3	3	3.0
9	Post graduate	0.6	0.4	0.4	0.4	0.3	0.7	0.2	0.3	0.4	9.7	1.3

seekers, Table 6 describes the demand pattern of the wage economy, as it refers to matched placements, i.e. filled vacancies that are put forward by business firms. Table 7 divides the cells in Table 6 by their corresponding cells in Table 5 to give measures of the comparative advantage of the employment exchanges in their employment matching operations.

As can be seen, the supply pattern of job seekers hardly corresponds with that of the labor force in the LFS. There are relatively many more job seekers among clerical and service workers than in the LFS and relatively many less job seekers among sales and production workers than in the LFS.

Instead, the occupational pattern of job seekers is rather a reflection of vacancies; compare also the trends in Table 5, showing, with a few exceptions which we discuss in the following, consistent movements in the occupational patterns between job seekers and vacancies. This is an indication that the supply of the labor force does not determine significantly the supply of job seekers and that the organized labor market in Pakistan, as far as it can be described by matching statistics, is characterized by an awareness of job seekers as regards unfilled vacancies. Job seekers register in the expectation of securing a placement and their expectations seem to correspond in broad lines with the realization of the placements. In both the aggregate analysis — eq. (1), Table 4 — as in the disaggregate analysis — Tables 5 and 6 — the evidence is that the labor supply of

Table 6. Placements: Percentage distribution by occupation and education.

Placements		1973	1974	1975	1976	1977	1978	1979	1980	1981	1982	Average
Percentage distribution of placements by occupation (%)												
0,1	Professional	19.1	14.8	15.8	13.4	9.8	12.7	12.2	12.4	15.2	15.5	14.1
2	Administrative	0.2	0.2	0.2	0.3	0.3	0.3	0.2	0.2	0.3	0.2	0.2
3	Clerical	12.3	13.4	12.8	14.2	13.1	16.5	15.4	15.7	14.3	16.7	14.4
4	Sales workers	1.1	1.3	0.8	0.6	0.6	0.9	0.9	0.9	0.8	0.9	0.9
5	Service workers	28.3	34	37.4	37.5	34.5	31.4	33.2	34.1	38.8	37.2	34.6
6	Agriculture wrkrs	3.5	3.3	2.9	3.8	4.6	5.4	5.8	4.6	5.8	6.3	4.6
7,8,9	Production wrkrs	34.9	33	28.9	30.5	37	32.8	32.2	32.2	25	23.3	31.0
Percentage distribution of placements by education (%)												
1	Illiterate	31	32.3	28	28.2	31.9	29.1	29.9	34.4	29.9	27.6	30.2
2	Below matric	29.6	35	37	35.1	37.3	33.7	37.2	29.7	30.3	29.1	33.4
3	Some matric	19.7	19	16.2	18.1	16.9	16.7	20	22.1	24.5	26.8	20.0
4	Matric crtfct	13.9	10.8	14.5	13.4	10.3	12	8.7	9.9	9.6	11.8	11.5
5	Matric diploma	2.4	1.1	2.1	2.3	1.4	1.6	1.5	1.6	1.7	1.6	1.7
6	Polytechnic dplm	0.4	0.4	0.5	0.7	0.7	1.2	0.8	0.5	0.7	0.6	0.7
7	Graduate	2.4	1.3	1.4	2.2	1.1	2.5	1.9	1.6	2.9	2.3	2.0
9	Post-graduate	0.3	0.1	0.2	0.2	0.1	0.7	0	0.2	0.2	0.3	0.2

job seekers is generally elastic to the demand for labor as represented by notified vacancies.

The above-mentioned high correspondence between job seekers and vacancies does not exclude certain autonomous preferences among job seekers. For instance, it is noted in Table 5 that there is a very stable and stubborn persistence among job seekers to register for clerical occupations reflecting a preference for white-collar public sector jobs (30% share) in spite of low expectations of finding vacancies (15% share). This bias in registration is a waste and can have detrimental effects on the performance of other activities of the employment exchanges, as will be treated in the following section.

Among vacancies — but also among job seekers — a rising trend is noted in Table 6 for service workers and a falling trend for production workers. For a country at an early stage of developing its industrial base, one would like to see the opposite. The obtained picture is the result of the bias toward more representation of the public as against the private sector in notifications of vacancies. The public sector is known to make relatively more use of service workers while the private sector makes relatively more use of production workers. The shares of public and private sectors in notified vacancies (and approximately in placements) are 66% and 34%, respectively, over 1973–1982. Actual urban employment is more evenly distributed in the two sectors. This weak element of representation in the vacancy data can be ratified by applying more appropriate weights for the public and private sectors.

Tables 5 and 6 give the educational patterns of job seekers and vacancies. Generally speaking, there is more accessibility to register among the better than the less educated, in spite of relatively lower expectations for filling a vacancy. Taking illiterates and below matric together, these form 55% of job seekers while the demand for them had a share of 66%. The better educated — remaining categories — have a share of 45% in the total supply and only 34% in the total demand. The gap becomes greater at the higher levels of graduate and post-graduate.

Among vacancies, there is a trend for decreasing shares of illiterate and below matric levels and a rising trend for matric level. The other educational levels tend to fluctuate in the demand portfolio.

Finally, it is striking to note some similarities between the short-term trends of matching statistics and the medium-term manpower projections for the Fifth Plan and Sixth Plan.[3] The relative positions of supply (job seekers) and demand (vacancies) for (a) production workers in contrast to (b) non-production workers show equivalent signs of shortages in (a) and surpluses in (b), in both the short-term trends of the matching statistics and in the medium-term trends of the manpower plans. Also with regard to education, it seems that there is a tighter labor market at the lower than at the upper end, both in matching statistics and in the medium-term manpower plans.

Matching statistics can be rearranged to assess the performance of the employment service as a whole or of particular employment exchanges. For this purpose, various indicators of internal efficiency can be constructed. At an aggregate level, an indicator of matching efficiency is obtained by dividing placements % by job seekers %. Table 7 shows very low values of the indicator at 21% for 1973–1982. Only about one in five job seekers is placed. In terms of efficiency, there is a redundancy of registrations. If the probability of one good match would require registering two candidates, then there must have been three costly and unnecessary registrations to the detriment of other activities in employment exchanges such as the placement itself and also other non-matching activities. But, of course, registration can be an objective by itself. In such situations, policy makers may have to weigh the opportunity cost of additional registrations. For example, an autonomous increase of 50,000 in registrations would be at the cost of reductions in placements by 5000 (assuming eq. (3) in Table 4 is valid, the relevant regression coefficient is 0.1025). As a result, the new placement/registration average ratio will be reduced from 21% to become 16% only: $PLM/REG = (54 - 5)/(256 + 50) = 0.16$.

Should, under the circumstances, the extensive registration be reduced one day and be limited to where the comparative advantages of matching activities are, then the operations data of the employment exchanges in Tables 5, 6 and 7 suggest that the relative advantages of employment exchanges as far as matching and placement are concerned lie in the following rank of comparative advantage

Table 7. Indicators of matching efficiency: Placements/job seeking by occupation and education.

Placements/Job seekers		1973	1974	1975	1976	1977	1978	1979	1980	1981	1982	Average
By occupation												
0, 1	Professional	1.62	1.15	0.95	1.08	0.78	1.27	1.26	1.16	1.46	1.37	1.19
2	Administrative	0.67	1.00	1.00	1.50	1.50	1.50	1.00	0.67	1.50	0.67	1.04
3	Clerical	0.39	0.45	0.45	0.47	0.47	0.55	0.51	0.52	0.47	0.52	0.48
4	Sales workers	11.00	3.25	8.00	3.00	6.00	9.00	4.50	4.50	4.00	3.00	4.63
5	Service workers	1.17	1.27	1.36	1.31	1.17	0.98	1.03	1.04	1.13	1.12	1.15
6	Agriculture wrkrs	2.33	1.74	1.00	1.12	1.24	1.35	1.57	1.28	1.61	1.70	1.44
7, 8, 9	Production wrkrs	1.20	1.15	1.19	1.22	1.42	1.40	1.35	1.41	1.23	1.21	1.28
By education												
1	Illiterate	1.14	1.21	1.15	1.16	1.22	1.24	1.22	1.33	1.23	1.16	1.21
2	Below matric	1.02	1.11	1.23	1.11	1.13	1.11	1.18	0.96	0.94	1.02	1.08
3	Some matric	0.69	0.72	0.61	0.68	0.69	0.61	0.69	0.76	0.86	0.80	0.71
4	Matric crtfct	1.56	0.97	1.11	1.19	0.92	0.94	0.83	1.14	1.10	1.46	1.10
5	Matric diploma	1.60	1.10	1.17	1.28	1.27	1.00	1.50	1.14	1.13	1.00	1.21
6	Polytechnic dplm	0.57	0.67	0.8	0.88	0.88	1.50	0.89	0.71	1.00	0.60	0.86
7	Graduate	0.65	0.52	0.47	0.67	0.39	0.78	0.76	0.52	0.88	0.77	0.64
9	Post-graduate	0.50	0.25	0.50	0.50	0.33	1.00	0.00	0.67	0.50	0.03	0.17

from high to low: sales, agricultural, production workers, service workers, professional, administrative, and the least is in the clerical occupations. In view of previous observations on the inelastic market response of this group, limits on registration of such occupations could have beneficial operational effects in the placements task of other occupations.

A similar ranking can be done by educational levels giving a more efficient rating of above unity for metric diploma, metric certificate, below matric, and the illiterate level, and a less efficient rating of below unity for the other levels, the rate for graduates being 0.7 and for post-graduates 0.4. Here too, for the matching of demand for and supply of graduates and post-graduates, other agents than employment exchanges may have a comparative advantage. It is important to note also that the classification of educational levels pursued and registered by the employment exchanges is different than the classification used by the Central Bureau of Statistics and the Ministry of Education. Overlapping classifications in the collection of data stand in the way of using common data in different contexts.

4. Concluding Remarks

The periodical survey of the labor force can be used to construct a labor force matrix that allows one to read the number of persons (and their percentage in the whole) who belong to a specific combination of location, status, sector, occupation, and education and is therefore superior to two-dimensional cross-tabulations. An LFM is a flexible tool, extendable to dynamic analysis and social system modeling. It can serve as a guide in the allocation of research and planning efforts for competing groups of the population and a sampling framework. Under plausible assumptions, such matrices have been constructed from published data of the labor force surveys of Pakistan of 1978/1979 and 1982/1983 and projected to 1988. Out of many interesting experimentations with the LFM, we chose to simulate the Sixth Plan by means of a model which generates demand and supply targets and a planned LFM for 1988. A comparison between the two matrices supported the contention that the plan does not foresee any major changes in the structure of the labor force.

Matching statistics can be subjected to a fruitful analysis with the twofold purpose of highlighting current movements in the labor market (in particular, the organized segment) and directing attention to issues of internal efficiency in matching activities. This chapter produced a tentative model explaining supply, demand, and employment as proxied by registrations, notifications, and placements, respectively, as well as various indicators showing occupational and educational gaps between demand and supply, a generally elastic response of job seekers to vacancies, a rigid response in some groups, a trade-off between registration and placements, and insights on the comparative advantages of employment exchanges in matching activities. Some suggestions were also made toward improving the presentation and analysis of matching statistics.

Endnotes

1. For a comprehensive account of deficiencies in the data collected by employment exchanges, see S. Hoda (1982) and K. Shah (1981).
2. Matching statistics of registrations, notifications, and placements are produced monthly, quarterly, and yearly for the 36 employment exchanges distributed on the four provinces of Pakistan, albeit with delay. These are aggregated for the provincial and national levels and are published in the Pakistan Manpower Review of the Ministry of Labor and Manpower. This used to be done without comment until 1990. Since then, the matching statistics are being supported by analytical reports along lines similar to this chapter.
3. Pakistan Manpower Division (1981, 1984).

Chapter 16

National and Regional Manpower Modeling and Projections for Development Plan: Indonesia

1. Introduction

Manpower planning and forecasting for a whole country involves analyzing current and future workforce needs and developing strategies to meet those needs. The following approaches are often used for conducting manpower projections for development plans: (1) The econometric approach employs historical data and predictive analytics techniques to forecast future workforce needs, which are then supplemented by demographic analysis of population growth, aging, and migration patterns to forecast future workforce supply and the modeling of the educational system and its graduates so as to specify the supply further on by qualification. (2) The industry-specific approach involves focusing on the specific needs of individual industries and developing workforce plans accordingly. (3) The partial skills focused approaches identify the skills and competencies that will be in high demand in the future and develop strategies to provide a workforce with those skills. (4) The consultative approach involves partnering with stakeholders such as employers, educational institutions, and government agencies to develop comprehensive workforce plans.

A recent review of manpower planning and forecasting practices in developing countries is found in Mabele (2018). The econometric approach appears to be the most common, which is about the same situation as was decades ago. This chapter presents manpower planning applications that align with the econometric approach. Recent literature on manpower planning and forecasting in advanced countries highlights the importance of considering the impacts of technology and automation on the workforce, as well as the need to develop flexible and adaptive workforce plans that can respond to rapidly changing labor market conditions and that copy and adopt best practices in workforce planning at more micro levels. We leave this literature for what it is as it does not elaborate on the application in the context of developing countries.

This chapter employs a simulative model that confronts projections of the demand for manpower types by sectors, occupation, education, and status with projections of the supply of manpower classified in the same categories. The model analyzes alternative ways to resolve the imbalances between demand and supply. The model and its results served as a primary input among others in the preparation of the development plan of Indonesia (1986–1990) in the areas of manpower and education. The model gives for the period 1980–1990 projections of human resources in the labor force and the educational system at the national level and their distributions at the regional level.

In general terms, demand *DM* and supply *SP* of manpower with attribute *k* can be formulated generally as follows:

$$DM_k = f(\text{Sectoral product, various labor input coefficients}) \quad \text{(i)}$$

$$SP_k = f(\text{Available manpower of type k+ inflows from educational system}) \quad \text{(ii)}$$

Manpower planning is the balancing of the future values of DM_k and SP_k. There are four types of approaches toward the balancing of demand with supply of manpower:

1. The first type treats demand exogenously and supply endogenously. The manpower balance is maintained by utilizing instruments from the supply side, i.e. expansion of formal education.
2. The second type treats supply exogenously and demand endogenously. The manpower balance is maintained by utilizing instruments from the demand side.
3. The third type treats both the demand for and the supply of manpower endogenously. Instruments to maintain a manpower balance can be sought on both demand and supply sides.
4. The fourth type is the simulative approach which is more pragmatic and is most in use. It makes first independent projections of demand and supply and, second, confronts the projections with each other. Expansion or reduction of components of demand or supply is then scheduled to eliminate shortages and surpluses. We make use of the simulative approach, which gave the Indonesian policy makers a flexible framework for combining manpower policies and taking measures to resolve the imbalances between supply and demand.

Regarding the regionalization of the national forecasts, there are two conceivable ways for doing a consistent and realistic assessment of manpower demand and supply at both the regional and national levels:

(1) conducting forecasts of demand and supply for each region separately and adding over all regions to give the national forecast.
(2) making first a national forecast and conducting second tentative regional forecasts which are then adjusted in such a way that the sum of the adjusted regional forecasts is equal to the national forecast.

In coordination with the ministerial authorities, the second option was chosen. Most analysts choose this option too in view of the lack of sufficient and reliable data for forecasting immediately at the regional level, the desirability of maintaining a flexible framework of national assessment which permits a quick application, and the desirability of employing a method which checks upon the correctness and consistency of both national and regional databases and parameters. Section 2 of this chapter gives the formulations of the supply and demand models at the national level. Section 3 treats the regional disaggregation. Sections 4 and 5 report on the applications. Section 6 concludes.

2. The National Simulation Model

The supply part: The national model consists of a supply part and a demand part. The supply part aims at giving projections of the available labor force disaggregated by educational level k. Indonesia distinguishes between nine educational levels k. These are as follows:

1 = No school, 2 = Some primary (Some SD), 3 = Primary (SD), 4 = Secondary General (SMP/G), 5 = Secondary Vocational (SMP/V), 6 = High General (SMA/G), 7 = High Vocational (SMA/V), 8 = Academy diploma, 9 = University degree.

The supply part contains equations which model the educational system throughout the entry of pupils to schools, enrolment, transition through classes and levels, ending in graduation, and participation in the labor force. The general reader can skip the following box which describes the equations. The specifications are more relevant for the technical modelers of the educational system and projections of the labor force.

The supply part: The first equation gives the total supply of the labor force on the basis of a projected growth rate.

$$SP_t = SP_{t-1}(1 + \lambda) \tag{1}$$

Eq. (2) permits the calculation of enrolment, *NR*, in school level k in each class c as a result of promotions from the previous class, repetitions in the current class, and new entrants *NE* where applicable.

$$NR_{kct} = (1 - \xi_{kc-1} - \rho_{kc-1})\sigma_{k-1}NR_{c-1,t-1} + \rho_{kc}\sigma_{kc}NR_{kct-1} + NE \quad \text{for } k = 2,..,9 \quad (2)$$

where ξ_{kc} is the rate of leaving school k at the end of class c, ρ_{kc} is the rate of repetition applicable to school k and class c, and σ is the rate of survival.

In eq. (3), the newly enrolled students *NE* are determined on the basis of a rate of admission to an upper level k from graduating school leavers of the last class $c'1$ of a lower level k', denoted by $\xi_{kk'}$. The equation applies to all levels except the primary level since new admissions here are taken directly from available projections by the Ministry of Education.

$$NE_{kct} = \zeta_{kk'}\zeta_{k'c}NR_{kct-1} \quad \text{for } k = 2,..,9 \quad (3)$$

In eq. (4), the current supply of the labor force distinguished by educational level is identical with the surviving previous stock after attritions due to migration, retirements, and deaths, plus those school leavers from school level k who join the labor force. This equation applies to the labor force for each educational level except the labor category which did not undertake formal education, $k = 2,..,9$

$$SP_{kt} = \sigma_k SP_{kt-1} + \Sigma_{kc}\varphi_{k'kc}\tau_{kc}(\zeta_{kc}NR_{kct} - NE_{kct}) \quad \text{for } k = 2,..,9 \quad (4)$$

where τ is the rate of participation in the labor force and φ is the rate which converts students by school type and class to labor force by educational level.

As for the supply of the labor category which did not follow formal education, and which is generally named as No School, index $k = 1$, this is found in a residual way in eq. (4.1) as the difference between the total supply and the various supplies by other educational levels, $k = 2,..,9$.

$$SP_{kt} = SP_t - \Sigma_k SP_{kt} \text{(where sum of } k \text{ refers to } k = 2,..,9)) \quad \text{for } k = 1 \quad (4.1)$$

Finally, eq. (5) gives a conversion of supply by educational levels into a supply by occupational levels making use of a coefficient matrix which cross-tabulates occupations in the rows and education in the columns. Here, λ_{qk} stand for coefficients which distribute the labor force over educational levels into a labor force by occupational groups. The occupational groups q are the broad categories of the International Standard Classification of Occupations: 1 = Professional, 2 = Administrative, 3 = Clerical, 4 = Sales workers, 5 = Service workers, 6 = Farmworkers, 7 = Production operators, 8 = Others.

$$SP_{qt} = SP_{qt-1} + \Sigma_k \lambda_{qk}(SP_{kt} - SP_{kt-1}) \quad \text{for } q = 1,..,8 \quad (5)$$

The demand part: The demand part aims at projecting manpower requirements by occupational types q. Economic growth is assumed to be given in the form of the most likely growth by sectoral activity for each specified year. This simplification reduces the demand model to fourteen equations: four for determining employment by status/sector, five for determining employment by status/occupations, and five for determining employment by status/education. An important distinction which holds throughout the demand model is with regard to the two status categories of wage and non-wage employment, indicated by index w and n, respectively. The w index covers modern establishments and the n index covers the non-wage segment consisting mainly of self-employed and family workers, which is typical for small household establishments. Following previous notations, we use j for sectors, q for occupations, and k for education. The demand part projects the number of workers demanded specified by the above-mentioned indexes. The general reader can skip the box describing the following equations.

The demand part: To start with, take the demand for manpower by status. DM_{wjt} and DM_{njt} stand for wage and non-wage employment by sector for year t. These are determined by among others: P_{jt} standing for the growth rate of the value added by sector by year, ε_{wjt} and ε_{njt} standing for the employment-output elasticities for wage and non-wage employment by sector and year, and ϕ_6 and ϕ_7 representing calibration factors required to adjust forecasts to ex-post observed trends.

Eq. (6) relates to wage employment.

$$DM_{wjt} = DM_{wjt-1}(1 + \phi_6 \varepsilon_{wjt} P_{jt}) \tag{6}$$

Eq. (7) relates to tentative solutions of non-wage employment by sector by year, hence the notation #.

$$DM_{wjt\#} = DM_{wjt-1}(1 + \phi_7 \varepsilon_{wjt} P_{jt}) \tag{7}$$

The tentative solutions for non-wage employment $DM_{njt\#}$ are rescaled to obtain definitive solutions of $DM_{njt\#}$ via eq. (7.1) which postulates the residual character of non-wage employment. Non-wage employment DM_{njt} is affected by the unemployment rate, μ, total supply, SP, and wage employment, DM_{wjt}. A positive difference between the definitive and tentative solutions can be interpreted as a surge in underemployment while a negative difference is a reduction in the underemployment of the self-employed and family workers. The rescaling effect appearing in { } in eq. (7.1) can be called "adjustment coefficient", whereby values of { } > 1 indicate a surge in underemployment and { } < 1 a reduction. The adjustment coefficient will be subjected to further comments in the analysis of results.

$$DM_{njt} = \{[1 - \mu)SP - \Sigma_j DM_{wjt} / \Sigma_j DM_{njt\#}]\} DM_{njt\#} \tag{7.1}$$

Eq. (8) gives the total wage and non-wage employment by sector.

$$DM_{jt} = DM_{wjt} + DM_{njt} \tag{8}$$

Forecasts of the demand for manpower by status and occupation are determined in eqs. (9)–(13):

$$DM_{wqjt} = \phi_9 \lambda_{wqj} DM_{wjt} \tag{9}$$

$$DM_{nqjt} = \phi_{10} \lambda_{nqj} DM_{njt} \tag{10}$$

$$DM_{wqt} = \Sigma_j DM_{wqjt} \tag{11}$$

$$DM_{nqt} = \Sigma_j DM_{nqjt} \tag{12}$$

$$DM_{qt} = DM_{wqt} + DM_{nqt} \tag{13}$$

where λ_{wqj} and λ_{nqj} stand for coefficients of matrices which distribute manpower by sector j to manpower by occupation q, for wage and non-wage employment status w and n, respectively, and ϕ_9 and ϕ_{10} are calibration factors necessary to calibrate forecasted imbalances to the generally observed trends of imbalances by occupations during the *ex post* observation period.

Forecasts of demand for manpower by status and education are determined in eqs. (14)–(18):

$$DM_{wkqt} = \phi_{14} \lambda_{wkq} DM_{wqt} \tag{14}$$

$$DM_{nkqt} = \phi_{15} \lambda_{nkq} DM_{nqt} \tag{15}$$

$$DM_{wkt} = \Sigma_q DM_{wkqt} \tag{16}$$

$$DM_{nkt} = \Sigma_q DM_{nkqt} \tag{17}$$

$$DM_{kt} = DM_{wkt} + DM_{nkt} \tag{18}$$

where λ_{wkq} and λ_{nkq} stand for coefficients of matrices which distribute manpower by occupation q to manpower by education k, for wage and non-wage employment types, w and n, respectively, and ϕ_{14} and ϕ_{15} are calibration factors necessary to calibrate forecasted imbalances to the generally observed trends in imbalances by educational level during the ex-post observation period.

3. Regionalisation

In a vast country like Indonesia with a population of 147 million in 1980 and 180 million in the nineties (and 275 million in 2022), the regional implications of the national projections are essential for policymaking. It is normal and common sense that the planning authorities required and wanted to see and examine how the manpower projections work out at the regional level. To meet the requirement, the national model of 18 equations was applied separately to each region. The regional administration of Indonesia distinguishes between nine regions, $r = 1, .., 9$:

1 = Jakarta, 2 = West Java, 3 = Central Java, 4 = Yogyakarta, 5 = East Java, 6 = Sumatera, 7 = Kalimantan, 8 = Sulawesi, 9 = Other Islands.

The regional applications gave for each region tentative projections for each set of variables. The model of 18 equational sets was estimated and applied to each of the nine regions. The sum of the regional tentative projections for a particular variable is seldom equal to the nationally projected value for the particular variable, and it can be lower or higher for a particular variable by say an x proportion. To assure consistency of projections at the national and regional levels, the tentative regional projection is adjusted by the x proportion to give the definite regional projection. The adjustments are applied to each variable.

The following example gives the adjustment for the variable of labor supply SP, eq. (1). For each region r, there is eq. (1r) which projects the tentative supply of the labor force in the region, expressed by $SP_{rt\#}$, whereby SP is the labor supply, r is the region, t is the year, and # stands for the tentative value. The projection is based on a given regional growth rate, λ_r. This supply is tentative, hence the attachment #.

$$SP_{rt\#} = SP_{r\,t-1}(1 + \lambda_r) \tag{1r}$$

To obtain the definitive supply in the region, we use eq. (1r.d), which multiplies the tentative value by an *x proportion* that is defined as $SP_{t,national}/\Sigma SP_{rt\#})$

$$SP_{rt} = (SP_{t,national}/\Sigma SP_{rt\#})SP_{rt\#} \tag{1r.d}$$

Each regional variable in the model is adjusted similarly to assure consistency between projections for the nation and the regional totals.

4. Application of the National Model

This section reports on the application of the national model to Indonesia for the period 1980–1990, implemented halfway through this period with data available from 1971 and up to 1984/1985. The supply results are treated first, followed by the demand results.

According to the 1980 population census, out of a population of 147 million people, 52 million were counted as economically active or as belonging to the labor force. This implies a crude labor force participation rate of 35.1%.

In the period 1971–1980, the growth rate of the labor force, at 2.6% per annum, substantially exceeded the population growth rate of 2.3%. The difference can largely be accounted for by the rapid increase in the working-age population, which increased by 2.9% per year in the period 1971–1980 mainly on account of the population boom in the 1950s and higher survival rates in the relevant age groups. This effect was to some extent offset by a small decline in labor force participation rates in the same period.

The same factors seem to persist in 1981–1990 leading to higher annual growth rates of the labor force, compared to population, 2.7–2.0%, respectively, giving for 1990 labor at 69 million and population at 184 million. This implies an increase in the crude labor force participation rate.

Now that the supply of the labor force is known from eq. (1), the details of this supply by level of education require solving eqs. (2)–(4). In these equations, transition rates for students from one level to another are calculated from educational statistics supplied by the Ministry of Education. The school leaving rate is about 3% for SD, 2.7% for SMP, 2.2% for SMA, and estimated at 10% for higher education. A school leaving rate of 3% for SD seems to be very small if compared with such rates in other developing countries.

New entrants to each educational level are estimated at initial percentages based on 1980/1981 and 1981/1982 and are allowed to increase until they reach planned targets as provided by the Ministry of Education. A check on the financial feasibility of the planned target by applying total enrolment by school level to rough estimates of cost for each school type, summing and relating the whole to the GDP, showed the results to be comparable with past developments and the educational burden in other countries.

Future labor supply by education is estimated as the stock of the previous year minus attrition due to death and retirement plus new graduates participating in the labor force. The model worked with an estimate of the attrition rate at 2%; the attrition rates are assumed equal for all education levels. To estimate participation rates in the labor force for graduates from each educational level, the study used the 1980 census on employment figures. These ranged from 53.8% for some schools to 91.1% for higher education graduates[ii]. The labor force belonging to the category "no school" is obtained as a residual after deducting labor with education from the total labor force, as displayed in eq. (4.1).

The labor force by occupational classifications, eq. (5), is obtained via the use of labor coefficients which convert educational levels into occupations, appropriately simulated to reflect the past changes in upgrading. The occupational groups q are the broad categories of the International Standard Classification of Occupations.

Tables 1 and 2 give forecasts of the labor supply by educational levels k and occupational groups q, respectively. This is the outcome of eqs. (1)–(5). The workforce is shown to increase between 1980 and 1990 by 16.6 million, meaning an annual increase of about 1.5 million. A workforce growing annually by 1.5 million, together with just the official rate of unemployment of 4% means that Indonesia in the eighties should experience a minimum of 3.5 million job seekers per year.

Table 1. Forecast of labor supply by educational levels, Indonesia, 1980–1990.

	In thousands		In percent		
Education	1980	1990	1980	1990	Annual growth rate
No School	15462	18965	29.1	27.5	2.1
Some SD	19664	23752	37.1	34.4	1.8
SD	11433	15740	21.9	22.8	3.4
SMP General	2103	3384	4.0	4.9	5.5
SMP Vocational	601	615	1.2	0.9	2.3
SMA General	1296	2907	2.5	4.2	4.9
SMA Vocational	1722	2976	3.3	4.3	6.6
Academy diploma	226	284	0.5	0.4	2.3
University degree	199	403	0.4	0.6	9.3
Total	52421	69026	100.0	100.0	2.8

Table 2. Forecast of labor supply by occupational grouping, Indonesia, 1980–1990.

	In thousands		In percent		
Education	1980	1990	1980	1990	Annual growth rate
1. Professional	1647	2878	3.1	4.2	6.8
2. Administrative	57	108	0.1	0.2	8.1
3. Clerical	1925	3460	3.8	5.6	7.2
4. Sales	6806	9098	13.0	13.2	3.0
5. Services	2363	2907	4.5	4.2	2.1
6. Farm	34633	44318	66.1	64.2	2.5
7. Production	4930	6172	9.4	8.9	2.3
8. Others	60	85	0.1	0.1	3.8
Total	52421	69026	100.0	100.0	2.8

During the ten-year period of 1981–1990, the structure of the workforce would still be characterized by low educational achievement with about 85% having elementary or no education. The huge development effort that has been launched by the Indonesian government in education has upgraded the educational structure of the workforce in several ways, except for the SMP Vocational and Diploma categories which show a small decline. Other educational categories demonstrate increases, some of which are substantial. For example, the university category achieved the highest growth rate with an annual increase of 9.3%, while the SMA Vocational is the second highest with a growth rate of 6.6%.

As regards the supply of the labor force by occupational category, Table 2 shows the continued dominance of agriculture in the Indonesian economy where about two-thirds of the workforce pursue farm-related occupations. This trend is gradually maintained between 1980 and 1990 as the share of workforce with farm-related occupations has gone only slightly lower from 66.1% in 1980 to 64.2% in 1990. Nevertheless, the results show an upgrading of the occupational structure as the supply proportions of professional, managerial, administrative, and clerical workforce are forecasted to become larger, indicating an acceleration in job qualifications, which was also realized *ex post*. The upward movement in the occupational structure is reflected in the faster rates of annual growth for these categories of between 7% and 8% as compared to 2.8% for the whole. This tendency is observed to continue for years after 1990, though at a slower pace.

We turn now to labor demand projections based on the prospects and targets for economic development during the second half of the 1980s, which were laid down in Repelita IV. The major goals of economic development in this Five-Year Plan were agricultural development in order to attain self-sufficiency in food and to provide raw materials for industrial processing, and the development of heavy and light machinery industry to generate growth potential for the longer run. In addition, a number of social objectives were made explicit such as the development of lagging regions and meeting basic needs for the poor. Other priorities included improvement in the transport and communication infrastructure, as well as the promotion of non-oil/LNG exports and import substitution.

Repelita IV paths of sectoral growth rates are presented in Table 3. These show the highest growth rate to occur in the manufacturing sector. This sector is expected to make an important contribution to accelerating non-oil/LNG exports. For comparison, World Bank projections published in 1984/1985 of components of GDP are presented, too. These projections turn out to be at variance with the plan projections. The third column gives estimates from other sources. As it appeared later, the realization of the growth objectives was strongly dependent on the external environment, especially the international oil market. Less favorable developments regarding the price of oil, combined with enhanced exports, have affected the realized sectoral outcomes appreciably in the last column.

Table 3. Indonesia annual growth rates of GDP by sector in constant prices, 1985–1990.

Sector	Repelita IV	World Bank	BIES	Realization
Agriculture	3.0	3.7	4.2	3.4
Mining	2.5	3.1	2.4	2.8
Manufacturing	9.5	8.2	9.5	10.2
Construction	5.0	6.0	6.2	6.6
Transport	5.2	5.5	6.2	6.5
Other	5.0	5.5	6.2	7.5
Total GDP	5.0	5.0	6.2	6.2

Sources: Column 1: supplied by Bappenas in Repelita IV; column 2: supplied by World Bank country mission, 1984/85; column 3: *BIES. Bulletin of Indonesian Economic Studies* Vol. 26, No. 1, p. 5 and Vol. 27, No. 1, p. 10.

Eqs. (6) and (7) make use of employment output elasticities by employment status (wage versus non-wage employment) and sector. Here too, alternative simulations were done. However, the basic run adjusts the elasticities obtained from the past trends of 1970–1980 to the performance of the model in the observation period 1981–1984.

Before assessing future manpower demand, some thought should be given to the structure of employment. Table 4 shows the past trends of the distribution of employment by status for each sector. Non-wage employment has increased its significance at the cost of wage employment in manufacturing and services. Although the share of agriculture in non-wage employment declined from three-quarters in 1971 to two-thirds in 1990, nevertheless, the employment pattern within agriculture itself has shown the same trend of a more rapidly falling share of the wage status in favor of the non-wage status. This information is important in terms of its implications for educational and occupational requirements. Since the majority of the additional demand would go to non-wage, this would moderate the required increase in educational requirements in the future.

The elasticities for wage employment (indexed m) are expected and commonly found to be less than those for non-wage employment (indexed n). Modern technologies typical of wage employment are inclined to use more capital-intensive methods of production while traditional technologies typical of non-wage employment are more oriented toward labor-intensive processes of production. It is found that the wage employment in 1980 is 29.96% of total employment. It decreases to 24.70% in 1985 and decreases further to 24.20% in 1990. More people would have to rely on their livelihood on the small scale and very tiny household enterprises. This fact has important bearings on national policy. For example, the spectrum of investment and educational policy should be widened to cover the kinds of infrastructure and training needed by the small-scale and the so-called unorganized

Table 4. Distribution of employment by sector and status in percentage for 1971, 1980, and 1990.

	Wage			Non-wage		
Sector	1971	1980	1990	1971	1980	1990
1. Agriculture	46.95	32.71	20.19	74.59	66.79	62.09
2. Mining	0.50	1.19	2.92	0.03	0.56	0.39
3. Manufacturing	10.39	15.52	20.20	4.14	6.32	7.08
4. Electricity	0.23	0.37	0.65	0.0008	0.02	0.05
5. Construction	3.82	7.33	8.88	0.32	1.45	2.29
6. Trade	5.33	4.23	3.42	13.35	16.69	19.80
7. Transportation	4.62	5.26	5.20	0.90	1.82	1.55
8. Finance	0.58	1.81	4.27	0.01	0.06	0.14
9. Services	27.58	31.58	34.26	6.63	6.28	6.61
Total	100.00	100.00	100.00	100.00	100.00	100.00

branches of economic activity. The extent of the non-wage employment which increases from 70% in 1980 to 75% in 1990 is indicative of these needs.

Once wage and non-wage employment by sector are forecasted as shown in the last two columns of Table 4, these are subdivided further by occupations. The projected distribution is obtained by using the labor coefficients $\lambda\ wqj$ and $\lambda\ nqj$ in eqs. (8)–(13).

Since one of the main purposes of the reported study is to obtain information useful for education planning, the projected employment by occupation was broken up further into the level of education. This is done via $\lambda\ wkq$ and $\lambda\ nkq$ in eqs. (14)–(18).

The above-mentioned four coefficient sets were calculated separately for wage and non-wage employment from the Population Census of 1980 and were appropriately adjusted so as to calibrate the trend during the observation period of 1981–1984.

Supply–demand imbalances: Even if one treats the above projections of incremental demand for manpower as being indicators of orders of magnitude, it is legitimate to ask if supply can approximately match them. The rest of this section discusses the forecasted imbalance by educational levels and occupational categories.

The projected imbalances by education for 1990 are presented in Table 5. For 1990, the forecasts show three shortages. First, manpower with some SD shows a shortage of 690,000 (2.9%), indicating the continuing dominance and growth of the informal sector in the Indonesian economy and accentuating the duality of the country's economy. Second, the largest shortage in terms of relative percentages is at the SMP Vocational category, which is mainly due to previous government action in Repelita II to reduce secondary vocational schools to the advantage of a higher SMA level. The result is a big shortage for SMP vocational of 119,000 (19.4%)

Table 5. Supply–demand imbalances by educational level in thousands, 1990.

Education	Supply SP_k	Wage DM_{wk}	Non-wage DM_{nk}	Total DM_k	Imbalance $SP_k - DM_k$	Percentage[1] $(SP_k - DM_k)/SP_k$
No school	18965	5887	13017	18904	61	0.33
Some SD	23752	1472	22970	24442	−690	−2.91
SD	15740	3590	11681	15271	469	2.98
SMP Gen.	3384	1297	1757	3054	330	9.76
SMA Voc.	615	362	372	734	−119	−19.42
SMA Gen.	2907	1208	743	1951	956	32.89
SMA Voc.	2976	2008	617	2625	351	11.81
Academy	284	264	44	308	−24	−8.45
University	403	278	48	326	77	19.00
Total	69026	16366	51249	67615	1411	2.00

Table 6. Supply–demand imbalances by occupational categories in thousands, 1990.

Occupation	Supply *SP q*	Wage *DM wq*	Non-wage *DM nq*	Total *DM q*	Imbalance $SP\ q - DM\ q$	Percentage[1] $(SP\ q - DM\ q)/SP\ q$
Professional	2878	1871	399	2270	608	21.12
Administration	108	71	28	99	9	3.93
Clerical	3460	2554	237	2791	669	19.33
Sales	9098	561	10218	10779	−1681	−18.47
Service	2907	1538	1121	2659	248	8.56
Farm	44318	6717	35706	42423	1895	4.28
Production	6172	3005	3517	6522	−350	−5.67
Other	85	50	22	72	13	14.89
Total	69026	16367	51248	67615	1411	2.00

as demand for this manpower continued to grow while the supply decreased drastically. Third, the academy level small shortage of about 5,000 (2%) which was found in 1981 continued to grow and reached its peak of 26,000 (10.3%) in 1987. This shortage is to decrease after 1988 because the supply of academy graduates is to grow at a faster rate than the demand, ending in 1990 with 24,000 (8.5%).

The imbalance in occupational groupings is presented in Table 6. In 1980, there were small oversupplies in all occupational categories. Since 1981, an undersupply of about 1.68 million and 0.35 million applied for sales and production categories respectively due to the relatively faster growth of the demand. Both categories still lag behind in supply, causing shortages of about 18% and 6%, respectively.

The big push that the government gives to university education has created an oversupply of its graduates for all occupational categories. Policy-relevant questions come up from this observation such as should the government continue with its past effort to step up university education which would certainly accelerate the oversupply of university graduates or should it redirect its effort to meet the above-mentioned shortages of 1.68 million sales workers and 0.35 million production workers.

5. Regional Applications

There are two conceivable approaches toward regionalization: separate forecasts for each region and adding them to give the national forecast, or making first a national forecast and conducting second tentative regional forecasts which are then adjusted in such a way that the sum of the adjusted regional forecasts is equal to the national forecast.

The second option was followed in view of the lack of sufficient and reliable data for appropriate forecasting at the regional level, and the desirability of maintaining a flexible framework of national assessment and quick applications of national simulations. The projected regional values of a variable are adjusted downward or upward so that their sum corresponds to the projected national value. In this regard, most results show the adjustment factors to be very small, in the range of 0–3%, which indicates very high degrees of consistency between national and regional forecasts. The exceptions are with regard to the supply of manpower by educational levels SMA general and university where the discrepancies between national and regional forecasts reach in 1990 a range of 10% and 14%, respectively. In particular, the national forecasts exceed the regional forecasts in SMA by 10%, while the regional forecasts exceed the national forecasts in the case of university supply by 14%. In assessing the forecasts for 1990, these two margins of possible error should be kept in mind.

Another feature of the procedure followed is to assure consistency between disaggregated forecasts and aggregate forecasts for each type of classification in the same region. This is done at the occupational levels by letting the demand and supply of the category of farm workers be calculated as a residual. Similarly, for the educational levels, we let the demand and supply of the category of persons without formal education — no school — be calculated as a residual. The procedure renders realistic results which can be normally expected.

The detailed supply and demand results by status, sector, education, and occupation for the nine regions are very extensive for reporting here. Instead, summary outcomes on surpluses and shortages are reported in the following. The regional assessment shows the regions of Jakarta and Central Java to be especially surplus regions while Kalimantan and Sulawesi are shortage regions, Table 7.

The regional assessment goes further in specifying the forecast shortages and surpluses by occupation and education. Table 8 gives the pattern of imbalances for the nation and for Jakarta in 1990.

The results show a relatively tight market for professional, administrative, and clerical jobs in Jakarta as compared to the national average, and a relatively more

Table 7. Forecasted surpluses (+) and shortages (−) by region for 1980, 1985, and 1990, in percentage.

Region	1980	1985	1990
Nation	1.65	2.00	2.00
Jakarta	1.71	11.96	19.37
West Java	−0.79	2.05	5.18
Central Java	13.13	13.71	14.47
Yogyakarta	−1.90	−4.35	−6.08
East Java	−1.40	−3.23	−4.98
Sumatera	−2.07	2.71	7.41
Kalimantan	6.23	−7.60	−24.72
Sulawesi	−4.03	−12.95	−26.72
Other islands	−1.85	−1.19	0.08

Table 8. Forecasted surpluses (+) and shortages (−) by occupation and education, 1990, in percentage.

Occupation	Nation	Jakarta	Education	Nation	Jakarta
Professional	21.12	4.75	No School	0.33	74.82
Administrative	3.93	−4.68	Some SD	−2.91	−11.57
Clerical	19.33	−1.85	SD	2.98	−14.42
Sales	−18.47	27.32	SMP Gen	9.76	−5.16
Service	8.56	18.87	SMP Voc	−19.42	−10.85
Farm	4.22	32.44	SMA Gen	32.89	10.86
Production	−5.67	17.54	SMA Voc	11.81	2.91
Other	14.89	17.65	Academy	−8.45	−10.26
			University	19.00	2.67
Total	2.00	19.37	Total	2.00	19.37

abundant supply for the lower occupational groups (sales, service, farm, and production workers) in Jakarta as compared to the national average. The results for Jakarta are striking in that they give a different pattern than that of most other regions. These tendencies reflect a twofold concentration in the Jakarta region of modern activities requiring high occupations and of supplies of labor with lower occupations. Removal of these imbalances implies action on all three fronts of demand, supply, and migration. The occupational imbalances work themselves through in educational imbalances, the second part of Table 8, which shows an excess supply of no school labor and relative shortages of labor by almost all other educational levels in Jakarta as compared to the national average. In particular, the applications predict a relatively tight market for university graduates in Jakarta as compared to the national average (2.6% surplus and 19.0% surplus, respectively).

6. Concluding Remarks

The national assessment in this chapter made use of a projections model of the supply of demand for labor status, sector, occupation, and education. Among its main features was the differentiated treatment of wage employment and self-employment. The model was calibrated and appropriately adjusted to the period 1980–1984 before it was used in an *ex ante* way to forecast 1985–1990.

The demand submodel assumed growth of the economy by separate activities lower than planned, variable employment-output elasticities, and constant open unemployment at the level of the earlier eighties. The supply submodel gave the outflow from the educational system into the labor force and the conversion of the latter into occupational groups. This allowed obtaining labor force imbalances in terms of both educational and occupational categories.

Wage employment which formed 28% in 1971 and increased to 32% in 1980 was predicted to fall back to 24% in 1990. In 1980, wage employment amounted to 15.8 million and was estimated to reach in 1990 only 16.4 million. Alternative simulations of absorption and growth gave about the same results: a small wage employment sector (about one-quarter) as compared to a dominating self-employment sector (about three-quarters). These forecasts have been realized.

The structure of wage employment is seen to change appreciably toward more higher education and technical occupations. Changes in the structure of self-employment regarding education and occupation are less. A positive trend is that the degree of absorption into self-employment which held in the past may not diminish in the near future so that the existing levels of underemployment will not be increased. However, the absolute gap in labor productivity between the two segments will increase by implication.

Regional forecasts were obtained in several steps. First, a national forecast was done, then separate forecasts were done for each region, and finally these last were added and adjusted upward or downward to assume consistency with the national forecasts. The size of the adjustments was found to be generally small with a few exceptions. Forecasts of the labor imbalances for the nine regions showed that the solution of the regional imbalances with regard to occupations and education can be relieved to a certain extent by induced migration, especially from such surplus regions as Jakarta and Central Java to shortage regions like Kalimantan and Sulawesi. The regionalized model provided further insight into the educational and occupational types of migrants which could be stimulated to transmigrate.

The displayed model for the balancing of demand and supply of the workforce and its links to the supplying educational system and links to the employing sectors of production is a compact model consisting of 18 equational sets. The data needed for estimating coefficients entered in the model are readily available for most countries. The regional decomposition of the results is highly relevant for the regional balancing of demand and supply. Besides the application of the model to Indonesia, similar applications were done for manpower planning in Pakistan and Kenya in simplified forms. The model can be readily implemented in other developing countries, not only in the context of manpower planning but also for analytical purposes and policymaking. The applications and the obtained results demonstrate the usefulness of pursuing a balancing approach to the modeling of demand for and supply of human resources.

Chapter 17

Labor Market Imbalances and Adjustments: Korea, Pakistan, and Colombia

1. Introduction

The origin of this chapter goes back to advisory work on labor markets and manpower planning in the 1980s and 1990s in Colombia, Korea, Pakistan, Kenya, and other countries.[1] The manpower forecasts at the time were open-ended in the sense that they made independent forecasts of demand and supplies of skills and gave little consideration to labor market interactions and adjustments that took place between *ex ante* expectations of skill demanders, i.e. employing firms; and *ex ante* expectations of skill suppliers. It is these interactions and adjustments by demanders and suppliers of skills that lead to the *ex post* observed states (realizations of employment and unemployment).

The closest theoretical and empirical works that relate to the adjustment processes between demand and supply are the labor market search studies which focus more on the search by the job seekers rather than job providers, that is the employing firms. Theoretical models of labor market search are typically built upon classical models of job search and unemployment, incorporating additional variables and mechanisms to explain the behavior of job seekers and employers in the labor market. Empirical studies often use data from surveys, administrative records, or field experiments to test predictions from these models and to identify key determinants of job search behavior. The economics of labor market search is very well covered in Rogerson and Shimer (2010). Confronted with mismatches of demand and supply between some five or more occupational types and some five or more educational types it is simply impossible to operationalize and apply partial theories of labor market search and adjustment to the mismatch problem at hand.

There is an absence of an analytical framework that could separate *ex ante* from the *ex post* states of the labor market and lay out the adjustment processes between demand and supply for large numbers of categories of occupation and education. Our approach to the labor market search and the clearance of labor market shortages and surpluses focuses on the combined outcome of all partial search and balancing considerations that result in employment decisions. Our interest lies in the ultimate direction of labor market adjustments. This chapter aims at developing and applying an analytical framework that resolves labor market imbalances.

The supplementation of forecasting models of labor demand and supply by subsequent modeling of adjustment processes and the clearance of labor markets presented themselves as challenges that require resolution, testing, and applied use. The challenges are relevant from the viewpoints of both academic inquiry and policymaking concerns. The objective of this chapter is to extend manpower forecasting methods toward incorporating iterative labor market adjustments that can be approximated by RAS iterations and investigate in retrospect the results and implications in the context of three countries mentioned above: Colombia, Korea, and Pakistan.

This chapter is organized as follows. In the first part of this chapter, we lay out the past background: Section 2 presents *ex ante* forecasts of demand and supply of labor skills by sector of activity[2]; while Section 3 extends the forecasts of demand and supply to occupational qualifications and educational levels. Many details which are specific to the individual countries for which the manpower forecasts were developed are avoided on purpose in this presentation so as to keep to a minimum the number of generally applicable equations to all three countries[3] and to assure that the same classifications of occupations and education are followed consistently. Section 4 departs from forecasts of imbalance and enters into the simulation of the labor adjustment process that results ultimately in resolving forecasted *ex ante* imbalances and clearance of the labor market. The approach followed is to specify additional equations that describe the adjustment processes between demanders and suppliers of occupations and educations and generation of the *ex post* values of employment and unemployment along the lines of iterations applied to the RAS method. Section 5 applies and validates the approach and examines the results for the three countries. Section 6 concludes.

2. Aggregate Labor Demand and Supply at the Sector Level

A main feature of modeling the labor market in the development context is the disaggregation of the economy into modern and non-modern sectors. In the modern sectors employers and employees work under relatively fixed labor contracts and working conditions, enterprises have access to credit and modern equipment, the firms are usually registered and regular statistics are collected on them. Labor can be assumed to work commercially at productive norms, which are technically prescribed. Underemployment can therefore be excluded. In the non-modern sector, the primary mode of employment is that of the self-employed and family workers, where non-commercial motives are present and underemployment feasible. Although clear-cut criteria for dividing the economy into modern and non-modern sectors are usually lacking, a useful rule of thumb is to take the non-modern sector as consisting of household production units with a majority of self-employed and family workers. This adds to considering most agriculture as the non-modern sector and most non-agriculture as the modern sector.

Rules that clear quantities in the labor market differ for the two sectors. In the modern sectors, employment is determined by the demand for employing enterprises, in the non-modern sectors employment is determined by the supply of the active population. In the non-modern sector, the supply of labor (total labor force less open unemployment less modern employment) manages to find work in self-employment, as paid and unpaid apprentices or as family workers, so that supply = employment. It is also well established that the (technical) demand for labor is below the (residual) supply of labor in this sector: supply > technical demand. As a result, some hidden underemployment is inevitable; this is measurable by employment less technical demand.

As regards open unemployment, policy makers tend to work under the assumption of a fixed unemployment rate that they conceive of as a policy target for the short and medium terms.

The aggregate model incorporates the above statements in eqs. (1) and (2). Eq. (1) determines employment in the modern sectors, LD_j, making use of yearly labor input rates per unit of the gross value added of modern sector j, λ_j, and planned or projected yearly gross domestic product by modern sector j, V_j. Eq. (2) determines employment in the lump-summed non-modern sector j', denoted by $LD_{j'}$, as a residual: obtained by deducting the above-mentioned sum of labor requirements in the modern sectors, $\Sigma_j LD_j$, and the given unemployment rate, *LU*, from the exogenously given supply of the labor force, *LS*:

$$LD_j = \lambda_1 V_j \qquad j \quad (1)$$

$$LD_{j'} = (1 - LU)\text{LS} - \Sigma_j LD_j \qquad (2)$$

where LD_j and $LD_{j'}$ are employment in the modern and non-modern sectors, respectively.

To facilitate comparisons across countries, relevant data for Colombia, Korea, and Pakistan were reclassified and aggregated. For practical purposes and because

Table 1. Annual growth rates of GDP, employment, and labor productivity in modern and non-modern sectors and the labor force for the periods 1970–1980 and 1980–1990.

	Colombia		Korea		Pakistan	
	1970–1980	1980–1990	1970–1980	1980–1990	1970–1980	1980–1990
Modern sectors						
Value added, $\Sigma_j V_j$	7.0	6.7	8.5	14.0	5.7	7.7
Employment $\Sigma_j LD_j$	4.8	5.5	4.9	5.7	1.9	3.4
Labor productivity	2.2	1.2	3.6	8.3	3.8	4.3
Non-modern sector						
$GDP - \Sigma_j V_j$	4.1	4.0	4.6	7.6	2.6	4.9
Employment $LD_{j'}$	3.7	−1.0	2.6	2.0	2.1	2.5
Labor productivity	0.4	5.0	2.0	5.6	0.5	2.4
underemployment (b)	1.8	−3.0	1.6	2.6	3.2	1.9
labor supply LS	4.5	3.0	3.8	2.7	3.0	3.0
Unemplymnt rt LU (a)	14.0	7.0	4.0	4.0	2.0	2.0

Notes: (a) Unemployment rate at end of period: 1980 and 1990 in percentage. (b) Added underemployment in the non-modern sector is realized employment in the non-modern sector less demand for labor based on labor input rates that apply for the modern sectors.

of lack of directly comparable disaggregated data the application takes the agricultural sector as a close approximation of the non-modern sector. The non-agricultural sectors constitute the modern sectors. Table 1 summarizes the growth rates obtained for the above variables for the three countries for two ten-year forecast periods ending 1980 and 1990.

3. Demand and Supply by Occupation and Education: Forecast Model

The forecast model of demand and supply for labor focuses on the *modern sectors.* The forecast model contains six equations and makes use of two indexes: Index q is for the occupational qualification, distinguishing the following categories, basically along the International Standard Classification of Occupations lines:

1 = professional/technical, 2 = administrative and clerical, 3 = sales personnel, 4 = farm workers, 5 = production workers, and 6 = service workers. Index e is for the educational classifications; following UNESCO practice, four levels are distinguished: 1 = higher, 2 = secondary, 3 = primary, and 4 = none.

Eqs. (3) and (4) are demand equations. Eq. (3) converts employment demand by sector j, LD_j into employment demand by occupation q, LD_q, via labor input coefficients λ_{qj}

$$LD_q = \Sigma_j \lambda_{qj}\, LD_j \tag{3}$$

Eq. (4) converts these occupational demands into educational demands. In doing this use is made of distributive coefficients obtainable from cross-tabulations by occupation and education, denoted by $\lambda_{eq,o}$. These are available with frequencies of several years as part of labor or population surveys. Since the coefficients of such a matrix are subject to changes and adjustments over time, as will be discussed later, the forecast is no more than an indication of the "hypothetical" demand by educational level. Because educational demand is "hypothetical" the variable is denoted by LD_e^{Θ}. Thus, eq. (4) assumes that the most recent matrix of e by q reflects in an initial way the conversion rates which business would use, *ceteris paribus*, to convert their occupational employment into a hypothetical demand by educational levels.

$$LD_e^{\Theta} = \Sigma_q \lambda_{eq,o}\, LD_q \tag{4}$$

where LD_e^{Θ} is the "hypothetical" demand for labor by educational level e and $\lambda_{eq,o}$ is the proportion of labor by educational level e in occupational qualification q, for the most recent period o.

Eqs. (5) and (6) are supply equations. Eq. (5) permits calculation of current enrollment in year course c, denoted by NT_c, (in many countries, c amounts to 18 annual courses distributed evenly on primary, secondary, and higher education levels, with each level consisting of 6 annual courses). Current enrollment in year t in course c is the result of (a) transitions from year $t-1$ in the forms of promotions, repetitions, leavers, and deaths from own and other courses and (b) new entrants in the educational system, denoted by NE_c. These usually take place in the first-year course in primary education and are dependent, among other things, on government enrollment policies and available finances. They are exogenously given:

$$NT_{c,t} = \Sigma_{c'} \delta_{cc'} (1 - \gamma_{c'} - \rho_{c'}) \sigma_{c'} NT_{c',t-1} + NE_{c,t} \qquad c \quad (5)$$

where NT_c is the enrollment in course c, NE_c is the new entrants in course c, $\delta_{cc'}$ is the rates distributing promoted pupil from course c to course $c,'$ always $c > c'$, γ_c is the rate of graduating and leaving the educational system at the end of course c, ρ_c is the rate of repetition applicable to course c, and σ_c is the rate of demographic survival (i.e. 1– rate of mortality) applicable to course c.

In eq. (6), labor supply distinguished by educational level e is a function of its lagged variable and the inflow of school leavers from the educational system that participates in the labor force. The inflow of school leavers is certified from course c and assigned as having attained educational level e via attainment coefficients α_{ce}:

$$LS_{e,t} = \sigma_e LS_{e,t-1} + \sigma_c \alpha_{ce} \pi_c \gamma_c NE_{c,t-1} \qquad e = 1, 2, 3 \quad (6)$$

where LS_e is the labor supply by educational level, π_c is the rate of participation of school leavers of course c in the labor force, and α_{ce} is the rates converting course c into educational level e.

In eq. (7), labor supply with no education, indexed as $e = 4$, is obtainable as the difference between the just obtained labor supply by the other educational levels and the exogenous total labor supply.

$$LS = \Sigma_e LS_e \tag{7}$$

In eq. (8), as in eq. (4), a transposed matrix of q by e for a recent period o can be assumed to reflect, initially, the pattern of conversion which, *ceteris paribus*, guide the labor force by educational levels to reassemble into a "hypothetical" supply by occupational groups, hence the use of LS_q^{Θ} to denote such a hypothetical supply.

$$LS_q^{\Theta} = \Sigma_e \lambda_{qe,o} LS_e \tag{8}$$

where $LS_q^{\Theta}1$ is the hypothetical supply of labor by occupational qualification q and $\lambda_{qe,o}$ is the proportion of labor by occupation q in labor with education attainment e, for the most recent period.

The outcomes of eqs. (4) and (8) are independent forecasts of demand and supply by occupation and education. Table 2 shows the occupational imbalances forecasted, and Table 3 shows the educational imbalances forecasted. Both tables are found a few pages further on. Traditional manpower forecasts and planning tended to present these two tables as end results, leaving it for authorities and their advisors to pursue various kinds of policy strategies in closing the occupational and educational gaps. However, the forecasted imbalances obtained from the above equations cannot claim to be more than an "initial round" of forecasts in the absence of a privately functioning labor market. How these first round forecasts would turn out in "consecutive rounds" of interactions and adjustment within the privately functioning labor market and what are the consequences are the subject matter of the rest of this chapter.

4. Labor Market Adjustments Modeled as RAS Iterations

A major bias of planning exercises in manpower and education is the assignment of a predominant role for policy makers in the balancing of supply and demand by occupation and education. The real situation is that the labor market has its own mechanism of adjustment which holds irrespective of whether the government intervenes or not. When there is potential for large discrepancies between demand and supply of manpower types it is inevitable that both demanders and suppliers of these manpower types adjust their positions and move toward a balanced situation; this may involve adjustment in other types as well, given the presence of substitutability between the types. In this section, we incorporate the simulation of these interactions.

One simple and validated way of incorporating a balancing mechanism via the labor market would be to allow the coefficient matrix of the occupational/educational mix $\lambda_{eq,o}$ (and $\lambda_{qe,o}$) to become endogenous fully (or partly) in such a way that a realistic balance is reached between demand for and supply of occupations and demand for and supply of education.

In fact, there are long- and short-run labor market adjustments which shape this occupational/educational distribution, cf. Zymelman (1969). Regarding the long run, adjustments toward more capital and skill-intensive production processes are an inherent part of economic development and imply regular rises in the skill level of most occupations. Furthermore, younger members of the labor force have more formal education than older members because of the general tendency to increase years of compulsory education. As a result, there is a built-in upward trend to shift the median years of formal education in occupations. Regarding the short run, in times of labor shortage, employers accept workers with less formal education. But in the context of a labor surplus in a given occupation, employers are more strict in their recruitment criteria and demand more years of educational attainment and higher certificates. Thus, an occupational shortage tends to induce a downgrading of educational requirements for entering the concerned occupation, while a surplus tends to induce an upgrading. Seen from the point of view of the workforce, a shortage of labor at a particular educational level often induces the respective graduate to join the labor force instead of taking up further education. A surplus of labor at a particular educational level tends to induce the respective school leaver to postpone entry into the labor force and instead continue further education.

In theory, the differential between a *desired* wage in a desired job with a particular sector/occupation/educational specification and the *actual* wage in a directly available job with another sector/occupation/education specification plays a dominating role in the decision of the individual to take up an offered job or postpone a decision. The modeling of the behavioral framework within which such decisions are taken is hardly possible in view of the multiplicity of options and the absence of cross-tabulated data on wages by sector/occupation/education. Given these limitations, simulation of labor market adjustment in a probabilistic manner, albeit mechanistic, makes more sense. This is outlined in eqs. (9)–(13). The following chapter will explore some aspects of the difference between desired and actual wages, and their consequences for the operation of the labor market.

Eq. (9) states that in the final analysis, the resolution of the occupation/educational imbalance can be described as a trial and error search by the suppliers of occupations q and demanders of education e, resulting in certain upgrading and downgrading. Both parties, starting from a (past) initial occupation/educational mix, as represented by $\lambda_{eq,o}$, would try to adjust the mix so as to exhaust their excesses and satisfy their shortages as implied by the hypothetical forecasts of demand and supply. The newly installed mix is an equilibrium mix and can be indicated by $\lambda_{eq,r}$. This new mix assures the clearance of the labor market subject to the overall open unemployment constraint.

This trial and error adjustment process can be simulated by applying the RAS method. The RAS method is due to Stone (1961), which he applied to update an input–output table for a given year to a future year. The RAS method was tested extensively by Bacharach (1970) and extended to applications in related areas by Hewings (1969), and Oosterveen *et al.* (1986), among others. Although the RAS method was designed to update input–output tables, it can be considered as a general estimation aid for the unknown interior of matrix tables with an initial probability matrix as a point of departure and with prescribed column and row totals. Every column of the initial matrix is multiplied by a specific factor chosen such that the column total becomes equal to the prescribed total; the same is done for the rows. However, while normalizing rows to their prescribed totals, the column totals are disturbed again. Thus, a new normalization of columns will be necessary and of rows, of columns again, and so on.

Application of the RAS method proceeded as follows. We want to predict an adjusted or a new occupational/education matrix $\lambda_{eq,r}$ in 1980 based on the initial matrix $\lambda_{eq,o}$ that belonged to 1970; the prescribed row totals are the predicted supply by education LS_e, while the column totals are the predicted demand by occupation LD_q plus a given provisional allowance for unemployment among q based on recent figures or eventually fixed as policy targets; so that the grand total of the predicted supply by education and the grand total of the predicted supply by occupation are made equal, to allow for the application of the RAS method. The definite unemployment rates by q and e will be among the outcomes of the RAS application.

$$\lambda_{eq,r} = \text{function of } [\lambda_{eq,o}, LS_e, (LD_q + \text{unemployment } q)] \tag{9}$$

The RAS method in the present context can be explained in terms of a search for the appropriate row multiplicators RM_e and column multiplicators CM_q, as in eq. (10); so as to satisfy equalization of forecasts of supply by e and of demand by q (plus *provisional* figures of unemployment by q), as in eq. (11).

$$\lambda_{eq,r} = RM_e\ \lambda_{eq,o}\ CM_q \tag{10}$$

$$LS_e = \lambda_{eq,r}\ [LD_q + \text{unemployment } q] \tag{11}$$

In the process of realizing adjustment in the labor market, it is feasible that the assumed magnitudes in the demand and supply models be revised by employers and workers as part of the adjustment process. For instance, in the case of shortages employers may revise their plans and cut down the predetermined production levels or the predetermined unemployment level may undergo adjustment downward. However, if the predetermined values for production and unemployment were correctly forecasted, their revision is, by definition, excluded.

The ability of the model to produce realistic results is the ultimate test of its viability. Fortunately, the predicted occupational/educational matrix for Colombia, Korea, and Pakistan for 1980 corresponded very closely to the observed one for 1980, which encouraged us to proceed further with the analysis. Once found, the adapted $\lambda_{eq,r}$ are utilized to convert demand LD_q into new equilibrium values of realized employment LD_e as in eq. (12). Application of a transposed matrix λ_{qer} to forecasts of LS_e gives equilibrium values of the realized labor force, LS_q, as in eq. (13).

$$LD_e = \Sigma_q \lambda_{eq,r} LD_q \tag{12}$$

$$LS_q = \Sigma_e \lambda_{qe,r} LS_e \tag{13}$$

These solutions assure the following approximate balances: $LD_q \sim LS_q$ and $LD_e \sim LS_e$. Relative discrepancies can be expected to be in the neighborhood of the general unemployment rate, as will be seen from the applications in Tables 4 and 5. These results are discussed in the following sections.

Note that the model can go straight to simulating labor market adjustment, instead of implementing the two stages of (first) solving for the forecasted imbalances (via eqs. (4) and (8)) and (second) applying the RAS to simulate market clearance (via eqs. (9)–(13)). Going straight is to skip eqs. (4) and (8). We follow here the phasing of the model in two stages, which is helpful in emphasizing an *expected ex ante state of imbalances* based on diverging expectations of demanders and suppliers of the labor force, as distinguished from the *observed ex post equilibrium state.* The differences provide important information on the size and pattern of the necessary labor market adjustments, which policy makers can use in designing development strategies.

Before reviewing the results of the application, it is worth noting that use of the RAS method in manpower forecasting is not new, but the form in which the method is applied here is new and economically meaningful. Evans and Lindley (1973) used the RAS method in what amounts to generating new values of the education occupation cells after modifying the values of some specific cells. Their concern was to obtain statistical consistency. Our approach is different. We use the RAS method to simulate the interaction in the labor market between demanders of occupations and suppliers of education so as to clear the market.

5. Applications

The model is calibrated and solved to give forecasts of demand–supply imbalances for the two periods of 1980 and 1990. Required values for exogenous variables such as V_j are either plan targets or semi-official projections. *LS*, *NE*, and unemployment estimates are either semi-official or own projections, depending on the country. Required estimates of the labor input coefficients λ_{qj} are mostly projections based on in-depth analysis of various labor force surveys, conducted in the individual countries. Estimates of coefficients in eqs. (5) and (6), were collected from ministerial sources and applied for or around 1980. They were kept at their values of around 1980, for obtaining solutions for 1980 and 1990. Finally, as was stated earlier, the matrices giving λ_{eq} (and λ_{qe}) are from the most recent cross-tabulation of occupation by education in the 1970s. These matrices were used in eqs. (4) and (8) to generate demand forecasts by education e and supply forecasts by occupation q, respectively.

The same matrix of education by occupation is employed in eq. (9) but in a different context and for a different use. As eq. (9) explains, the matrix is fed with manpower forecasts of (educational) row totals and (occupational) column totals for 1980 and iterated in a number of runs to give RAS solutions for 1980. The results can be considered to represent the end state in 1980 of the labor market adjustment processes that took place in the period ending in 1980 so as to clear the labor market imbalances within given unemployment margins.

The obtained RAS-ed matrix for 1980 was fed in turn with forecasted row and column totals for 1990 and subjected to several iteration rounds to give RAS solutions for 1990. In similarity with the above, the RAS-ed matrix for 1990 was considered to represent the labor market adjustment processes that took place in the period ending in 1990 so as to clear the labor market imbalances within given unemployment margins.

Simulation of the labor market adjustment (LMA) in this manner, along the lines of eq. (9), needs to be validated. The simulation can be validated by comparing the RAS-ed λ_{eq} cells for 1980 with the observed data of λ_{eq} for 1980, where available. Such a validation was feasible for all three countries. as their statistical sources provided the matrix for both 1970 and 1980. The RAS-ed matrix of 1970 with the row and column totals for the 1980 year showed general correspondences with the observed matrix for 1980. There were other indications that the results for 1980 and 1990 are also generally valid. For instance, the RAS-ed adjustments were found to be concentrated in similar cell clusters in all the three countries. The pattern of adjustment is highly consistent among the countries and over time. The size of the adjustment in the cell clusters with the highest changes rarely exceeded 15% over 10 years. Altogether, the simulated results indicate the use of the RAS to simulate adjustment of the labor market is operational and meaningful.

Table 2 displays forecasts of demand–supply imbalance by occupation, and shows how these imbalances are cleared in the process of LMA, which is approximated by the RAS model. With little exception, the imbalances forecasts across countries show growth in supply to surpass growth in demand for the groups of professional/technical, administrative/clerical, and sales personnel. In contrast, the primarily manual groups including farm, production, and service workers experience a somewhat higher or equal growth in demand than in supply.

Table 2. Occupations: Forecasts of periodical growth rates per annum of demand and supply, imbalance rates, and unemployment rates after labor market adjustment for 1980 and 1990.

	Colombia				Korea				Pakistan			
	Annual growth				Annual growth				Annual growth			
	LD_q	LS_q^{Θ}	Imbal-ance	Un-employ-ment	LD_q	LS_q^{Θ}	Imbal-ance	Un-employ-ment	LD_q	LS_q^{Θ}	Imbal-ance	Un-employ-ment
1970–1980												
Prof/technical	7.9	9.6	25	12	3.8	6.5	26	5	4.4	6.0	−14	4
Adm/clerical	6.0	6.2	16	13	5.8	9.3	24	5	6.3	4.7	−14	5
Sales personnel	6.0	1.1	14	13	2.0	5.1	10	4	2.3	2.2	1	2
Farm workers	1.3	1.6	14	14	2.0	0.7	−10	3	2.3	2.6	4	1
Production workers	2.2	2.0	11	14	5.4	6.0	9	4	5.2	5.2	3	1
Service	8.4	8.7	13	14	2.4	2.8	8	4	6.1	6.2	3	1
1980–1990												
Prof/technical	5.6	8.3	42	6	4.6	7.0	41	5	3.0	4.5	17	5
Adm/clerical	5.6	5.8	17	6	5.2	6.5	34	5	3.3	5.0	20	5
Sales personnel	5.0	5.8	17	6	4.5	4.0	6	4	3.9	4.1	5	2
Farm workers	−0.8	−2.5	−10	8	−2.0	−2.7	−26	3	2.5	2.2	−2	1
Production workers	5.1	4.0	1	7	6.6	5.8	1	4	3.4	3.4	1	2
Service	5.6	3.6	−6	7	4.6	3.9	0	4	3.2	3.2	1	2

Note: Imbalance rates = $(LS_q^{\Theta} - LD_q)/LS_q^{\Theta}$. Unemployment rates = $(LS_q - LD_q)/LS_q$.

Defining the surplus occupational imbalance rate as $(LS_q^{\Theta} - LD_q)LS_q^{\Theta}$, third column, Table 2, the results show that the surplus imbalance rates are highest for professionals, with the exception of Pakistan.[4] The surplus imbalance can be interpreted as a "preference" of the labor force for non-manual jobs as opposed to a "preference" of the employing economy for manual jobs. The occupational imbalances are forecasted to be generally higher for 1990 than for 1980. Application of the RAS model, eqs. (9)–(13), ends up in adjusting the positions of demanders and suppliers to each other. As job preferences and searches by the employing business and the labor force iterate to each other in the adjustment processes, they converge toward definite unemployment rates that are lower than the imbalance rates and also vary within a narrower range than the imbalance rates. The unemployment rates are defined as $(LS_q - LD_q)LS_q$, fourth column in Table 2.

Table 3 presents corresponding forecasts of demand–supply imbalances by education and their subsequent clearance via the LMA-RAS model. The forecasts indicate higher growth rates in demand for and supply of manpower with more advanced educational levels as compared to those with less education. Furthermore, educational imbalance rates $(LS_e^{\Theta} - LD_e)/LS^{\Theta}$, generally show surpluses for manpower with higher and secondary education (again, with the exception of

Table 3. Education: Forecasts of periodical growth rates per annum of demand and supply, imbalance rates, and unemployment rates after labor market adjustment for 1980 and 1990.

	Colombia				Republic of Korea				Pakistan			
	Annual growth				Annual growth				Annual growth			
	LDe	LS_e^{Θ}	Imbal-ance	Un-employ-ment	LDe	LS_e^{Θ}	Imbal-ance	Un-employ-ment	LDe	LS_e^{Θ}	Imbal-ance	Un-employ-ment
1970–1980												
1. Higher	4.2	8.1	38	12	5.3	8.5	29	5	7.7	4.8	−34	5
2. Secondary	4.0	5.0	20	12	5.7	9.3	27	5	5.4	3.4	−21	6
3. Primary	4.1	2.9	2	15	1.5	0.3	−8	3	5.0	5.0	−1	3
4. None	0.6	3.0	31	14	3.4	0.4	−36	2	1.8	2.3	5	1
1980–1990												
1. Higher	5.4	12.3	68	8	4.9	9.1	52	5	3.1	4.6	19	6
2. Secondary	5.3	5.5	22	8	4.5	4.2	24	4	3.2	5.4	24	7
3. Primary	3.7	2.3	−12	6	2.4	0.4	−31	3	3.2	5.0	18	3
4. None	2.4	−2.0	−11	5	−0.2	−1.2	−52	2	2.9	2.3	−5	1

Note: Imbalance rates $= (LS_e^{\Theta} - LD_e)/LS_e^{\Theta}$ Unemployment rates $= (LS_e - LD_e)/LS_e$.

Pakistan in 1980). The imbalance rates for higher and secondary education are generally higher in the 1990s than in the 1980s, which is evidence of a heightened gap between the economy and education. Application of the RAS method shows outcomes for unemployment rates by education, $(LS_e - LD_e)/LS_e$ at lower levels, and diverge less than the *ex ante* imbalance rates. Higher unemployment rates are still predicted for manpower with advanced as compared to lower educational levels.

Comparative results in the two tables support the following. In economies that develop slowly, demand for and supply of labor tends to keep track of each other. Imbalance rates are close to unemployment rates and there is a diminished role for labor market adjustments. In contrast, a more rapidly developing economy, i.e. Korea is characterized by major structural changes which are manifested, among others, in vigorous adaptations of labor demand and supply to each other, with regard to both occupations and education. The more rapid the growth of the economy, the greater the gap between (i) forecasted imbalance rates and (ii) realized unemployment rates and the more intensive labor market adjustments. These tendencies are apparent in the results, showing the more rapidly growing Korea to have greater imbalances and greater LMA than Colombia or Pakistan.

Further analysis of the LMA results can be done making use of Theil's coefficient of inequality which provides a systematic measure of the *intensity* of LMA. Theil's coefficient would relate (i) and (ii): the higher the value of the coefficient, the more intensive the LMA. Table. 4 gives Theil's coefficient by occupational LMA and educational LMA, across countries and periods. There

Table 4. Intensity of forecasted labor market adjustment as measured by Theil's coefficient.

	Colombia		Republic of Korea		Pakistan	
	1980	1990	1980	1990	1980	1990
1. Occupational LMA	0.4	2.4	2.9	5.0	2.0	2.4
2. Educational LMA	1.3	4.5	6.0	10.4	3.9	2.7
3. Educational LMA/occupational LMA	3.3	1.9	2.1	2.1	2.0	1.1

are two types of conclusions. First, more rapidly changing economies show higher intensities of LMA. Across countries, the Republic of Korea has the highest growth rates of value added and labor productivity. Korea also has the highest values of Theil's coefficient. Over the years, the 1980s, which have higher growth and productivity, are predicted to have greater labor market adjustments than the 1970s. In general, the quicker the pace of economic development, the greater the educational requirements of specific occupations and the less job-oriented the educational system. Second, the value of Theil's coefficient is lower for manpower by occupational groups than by educational levels, which indicates a less intensive LMA among occupations than among education. The reason is that imbalances in different occupations are often shifted to a particular education while imbalances in a particular education are often distributed over many occupations. For example, occupation $q = 4$ (farm workers) which is highly concentrated in education $e = 4$ (no education), as against the same level of education $e = 4$ (no education), which is spread over more occupations $q = 1, \ldots, 6$.

In retrospect, as more standard certification for specific jobs takes place over the years, specific occupations and a specific education can be expected to associate more exclusively with each other. As a result, the intensity of LMA among occupations and education would tend to converge with development. This is also borne out by Theil's coefficient which shows on average a value for educational LMA which is 2.7 times the occupational LMA in 1980, as compared to the lower value of 1.7 times in 1990.

Analysis of the pattern of adjustment is facilitated by examining the row multiplicators and column multiplicators, *RM* and *CM*, implied in the conversion[5] of λ_o; into λ_r. Row multiplicators give the factors by which $\lambda_{\varepsilon q,o}$ should be appropriately multiplied to give $\lambda_{\varepsilon q,r}$. *RM* represents adjustments which the employer undertakes to restructure the educational composition of his occupational requirements to meet long-term technological trends and future restrictions on the labor market. Table 5 gives a summary of results for row and column multiplicators.

For 1970–1980, last two columns, the average *RM* for higher education is 1.28, meaning that employers upgrade their requirements for higher education by 28% in

Table 5. Row multiplicators, *RM*, and column multiplicators, *CM*, for 1970–1980 and 1980–1990.

	Colombia		Korea		Pakistan		Average	
	1970–1980	1980–1990	1970–1980	1980–1990	1970–1980	1980–1990	1970–1980	1980–1990
RM								
I. Higher	1.60	2.60	1.72	1.79	0.53	1.47	1.28	1.95
2. Secondary	1.16	1.24	1.39	1.01	0.62	1.48	1.05	1.24
3. Primary	0.85	0.88	0.83	0.81	0.94	1.22	0.87	0.97
4. None	1.23	0.57	0.63	0.83	1.07	0.91	0.98	0.77
CM								
I. Prof/technical	0.96	0.64	0.68	0.70	1.42	0.83	1.02	0.72
2. Adm/clrcl	0.95	0.84	0.74	0.79	1.47	0.82	1.05	0.82
3. Sales prsnl	0.95	0.84	0.96	1.02	1.02	0.97	0.98	0.94
4. Farm workers	1.02	1.29	1.22	1.16	0.95	1.06	1.06	1.17
5. Prdctn wrkrs	1.21	1.09	1.02	1.10	1.00	1.04	1.08	1.08
6. Service wrkrs	1.76	1.51	0.99	1.07	1.03	1.08	1.26	1.22

less than one decade. The upgrading is less for required manpower with secondary education, i.e. an upgrading of 5% during the period ($RM_2 = 1.05$). This upgrading happens at the cost of reduced requirements for primary education, less 13%, and no education, less 2% ($RM_3 = 0.87$ and $RM_4 = 0.98$). The average row multiplicators are generally higher for 1980–1990 than for 1970–1980, except for manpower with no education for whom requirements are forecasted to be squeezed appreciably. In the figures, *RM* for 1980–1990 should be 1.95, 1.24, 0.97, and 0.77 for the four educational levels, respectively. On an annual basis, an upgrading is predicted for employment of manpower with higher education by 6.9%, an upgrading of secondary education by 2.2%, a slight downgrading of primary education by –0.3%, and an appreciable downgrading of no education by −2.6%. These shifts are associated with an average annual growth rate of GDP in the non-agricultural sectors of 9.5% in the 1980s. Predicted elasticities of the educational LMA with respect to GDP in the 1980s suggest the following values for the four educational levels, respectively: 0.7, 0.2, −0.03, and −0.3. At an average annual growth rate of labor productivity in the non-agricultural sector of 4.6%, predicted elasticities of the educational LMA with respect to labor productivity are at about twice the above values.

Regarding column multiplicators, their lower values imply that the occupational LMA is milder than the educational LMA. Nevertheless, the prediction is that for the 1980s the labor force may be forced, or ready, to solicit less for non-manual jobs, as apparent from CM_1, for the professional/technical group = 0.72. LMA for administrative/clerical and for sales personnel shows similar but less pronounced trends, $CM_2 = 0.82$ and $C_3 = 0.94$. Opposite behavior is expected from the labor force with regard to the primarily manual occupations. More of the labor force is to be channeled into the occupational groups of farm, production, and service workers, with CM> 1.0. The policy implications of the above trends for general education and vocational training are obvious.

More specifically, as an aid for policymaking at the individual country level, one may examine the predicted adjustments to be brought about in the individual elements for $\lambda_{eq,r}$ (and $\lambda_{qe,r}$). Table 6 lists the largest adjustments in $\lambda_{qe,r}$ for Colombia, Korea, and Pakistan for 1980–1990. Each change in the educational row e is neutralized by compensating changes in the nearest educational row and within the same occupational column q. The table predicts systematic shifts in the educational/occupational mix which three countries at different levels of development are likely to undergo in the 1980s. The detailed results on which the table is based constitute essential information for effective planning of the development and utilization of human resources.

As stated earlier, governments have instruments they can use in controlling the parameters of demand and supply. But once the future occupational demand and the future educational supply positions are set, anticipated changes in λ_{eq} would occur because of the free play of market forces. In principle, government policy has very little control over these market forces. This is generally valid even though the anticipated changes may take place more smoothly if the government encourages the dissemination of information on the future demand and supply conditions and encourages or discourages upward and downward wage revisions by occupation and education, as the case may be. The more significant use of the model lies in the fact that knowledge by policy makers of the nature of anticipated changes in λ_{eq} is essential for effective use of the instruments which policy makers can use in setting the right demand and supply positions in the future. Effective planning of manpower demand and supply requires knowledge of how labor markets adjust to the overlapping between supply and demand.

In this chapter, we dealt exclusively with LMA in terms of quantities of labor any allocation of quantities implies a certain set of prices. The shift from matrix

Table 6. Predicted major adjustments in the educational/occupational mix for 1980–1990 (Colombia (C), Korea (K), and Pakistan (P)).

	Occupation					
Education	1. Prof/technical	2. Admin/clerical	3. Sales	4. Farm w.	5. Production w.	6. Service w.
1. Higher	C+, K+	C+, K+	C+, K+			
2. Secondary	P+	P+		K+		
3. Primary					C+, K−	K−
4. None			P−	C−, P−	P−	C−, P−

$\lambda_{eq,o}$ to $\lambda_{qe,o}$ implies changes in remuneration patterns by occupation and education. Given rigidities in wage changes for certain occupations/education, the simulation of the adjustment process should observe such restrictions. The model by itself treats only labor adjustment and cannot predict the adjustment in earnings which accompanies labor reallocation. To do that requires the estimation of earning functions by occupation and education. In the following chapter, an exploratory attempt is made to connect earnings imbalances with quantity imbalances in labor market adjustments.

6. Concluding Remarks

An open-ended forecast of demand for and supply of manpower by sector, occupation, and education offers a more flexible tool in the planning of manpower and education than other approaches, ie manpower requirements. Besides simulating balancing policies by the government, the open-ended framework can be extended to simulate adjustments in the labor market (LMA). Resolution of occupational and educational imbalance can be described as a trial and error search by the demanders and suppliers of educational skills and occupational titles. The RAS method is shown to be a helpful tool in simulating this adjustment process. In general, analysis is more realistic and useful in a framework that considers interactions in the labor market. Theil's coefficient of inequality is helpful in measuring the intensity of LMA, while row and column multiplicators derived from the application of the RAS method are effective means of reflecting on the pattern of LMA.

The imbalances in terms of labor quantities have their counterpart in converging expectations on earnings. This will be demonstrated in the following chapter by formulating and applying earnings expectations based on two contrasting expectations as viewed by suppliers and by employers. One is based on human capital theory which tends to overestimate educational returns and underestimate occupational returns. The other is job competition theory which predicts more returns for occupations and less for education. The results of the cost–benefit analysis based on return expectations are discussed in the following chapter. It will be seen that the results from returns analysis are consistent with the forecasted scarcities and surpluses in 1970–1980, and their reversal in 1980–1990.

Endnotes

1. Related assignments in various countries resulted in several reports that prepared the way for a concerted effort toward resolving the problem of forecasted imbalances and the shaping of labor market adjustments. The reports are listed as follows: (a) Cohen, S.I. and. Sarmiento, A. (1982): Sistema de Planeacion de Recursos Humanos, Sena Press, Bogota. (b) A Study of the Occupational and Educational Manpower Requirements and Supply of the Fifth Plan, Manpower Division, Government

of Pakistan, Islamabad. 1981. (c) Projection of Human Resource Development in the Framework of the Fifth Kenyan Development Plan 1984–1988, report for the European Commission, Brussels, and Government of Kenya, Nairobi, 1983. (d) Structural Changes in the Indonesian Employment Situation, commissioned report by the World Bank Seventh Education Project and Government of Indonesia, Washington and Jakarta, 1988. This chapter makes use of the applied work for Colombia and Pakistan and supplements the results with similar applications for Korea.

2. The number of sectors distinguished varies in the applications between 9 and 32 depending on the country.
3. The mode takes the variables of the GDP per sector to be exogenously given by policy makers and official plans, for all four countries. But when first applied in Pakistan and Korea, these variables were embedded also within an economy-wide model which includes more aspects of the circular flow.
4. Pakistan in 1980 shows low or some negative imbalances for professional but also for manual occupations, which is due to labor migration to the Gulf countries.
5. The adjusted $\lambda_{eq,r}$ is related to the initial $\lambda_{eq,o}$, via RM_e, in the following way: $\lambda_{eq,r} = RM_e.\lambda_{eq,o}/\Sigma_e RM_e.\lambda_{eq,o}$.

Chapter 18

Earnings Imbalances: Human Capital versus Job Competition

1. Introduction

Cost–benefit analysis (CBA) of education is a method of evaluating the economic value of investments in education. It involves comparing the benefits that are expected to accrue from additional years of education and the costs involved. The benefits of education can include higher earnings for individuals, increased productivity for businesses and society, improved health and well-being, and reduced crime and poverty. The costs of education include direct expenses such as tuition and fees, as well as indirect costs like lost earnings from time spent in school. CBA of education is a complex process that requires a comprehensive understanding of the various costs and benefits involved and may also require the use of advanced statistical and economic methods to make valid comparisons and projections, as can be gathered from updated works in Psacharopoulos and Patrinos (2018). Other works relevant to CBA of education are Hanushek and Welch (2006) and Burgess (2016).

The new element that we bring in this chapter is that the earnings expectations of additional years of education by graduating students leaving the educational system can be valued, differently from employers who place the school graduates in occupational jobs. The employers' valuation is guided by the job productivities rather than the educational qualifications.

We dealt in the previous chapter exclusively with labor market adjustments in terms of quantities of labor, and we did not touch earnings. An allocation of a set of quantities implies a certain set of prices. The explained demand–supply gaps in quantities in the previous chapter infer the presence of expectation gaps with regard to the remuneration patterns by occupations and education. The model in the previous chapter focused on labor adjustment and it was not meant to analyze the adjustment in earnings which accompanies labor reallocation. To do that requires the estimation of earning functions by occupation and education. In this chapter, we explore the use of cost–benefit analysis (CBA) in replicating and connecting earnings imbalances with quantity imbalances in labor market adjustments.

In correspondence with the imbalances in demand and supply, there is logic in assuming that there can be also an imbalance in earnings expectations. There are two contrasting models of earnings expectations; that tend to associate with supply and demand imbalances in labor quantities. The first earnings expectations model is supply oriented and is based on human capital theory which reflects the earnings expectations of school leavers. The second earnings expectations model shifts attention from the educational impact and the supply side to occupational impact and the demand side. Job competition theory emphasizes occupational demand in the determination of earnings.

The first earnings expectations model represents conventional methods for estimating returns to education rely on *human capital theory*, i.e. Becker (1973), equate earnings to the marginal productivity of the worker, and explain the latter in terms of the education attained by the worker.

The second and alternative earnings expectations model, based on *Job competition theory*, is equally legitimate in many contexts. It deflects the impact of education on earnings and assigns instead a primary role for occupational demand in determining wages. Job competition theory, as was first formulated by Thurow (1969) and recalled in Cohen (1994), asserts that it is the marginal productivity of the job, or the occupation, that determines the wage rate to which a worker will be matched. Wages are paid on the basis of the characteristics of a job or an occupation. Occupations differ in their intensities of using capital, handling information, and practicing leadership. More demanding occupations are paid higher wages. Productivity is an attribute of occupation. In the job competition model, workers are matched to occupations by specific worker characteristics and job requirements.

While in the human capital model education has a direct link with productivity and wage, in the job competition model the role of education in influencing wages is indirect and secondary, namely via occupational upgrading. More education gives access to better occupations with higher pay. Investment by students in schooling and their expected wages are linked to each other in the job competition model by the expectations of an occupational upgrading, and hence, a higher occupational wage. Employers undergo significant transaction costs in matching the right selection of persons to jobs. Educational certificates can serve as a screening device in the selection process and can save transaction costs. Entrants to the labor force, aware of employers' behavior, expand on and use higher educational certificates as a signaling device. This often results in an inflation of certificates of higher education.

2. Cost–Benefit Analysis Based on Contrasting Expectations

In human capital theory, the basis for calculating the rate of return to investment in educational level *e* is estimated directly from earning functions or indirectly by employing age-earnings profiles by educational levels to estimate future benefits and finding the discount rate that equates costs to benefits. Under simplified assumptions that all earnings can be explained by education, a constant stream of benefits, foregone earnings incurred in the first year, and no schooling costs, the rate of return is obtained as a benefit–cost ratio, eq. (1).

$$(LR_e \ - LR_{e-1})/(LR_{e-1,o}.n_e) = RHC_e \tag{1}$$

where RHC_e is the rate of return to educational level *e* following human capital theory, LR_e is the annual average earnings of workers with completed educational level k, $LR_{e-1,o}$ is the initial average earnings of workers who forego educational level k, or simply starting wage, and n_e is the foregone years of earning during education e, or simply the duration of education e.

In job competition theory, the impact of additional education on enhanced earnings is found by considering that more education gives access to an upgraded occupational mix with higher labor productivities and earnings. Returns to education in this case are captured by the internal rate of return in eq. (2). The left-hand terms give the discounted net benefits over the working years. The right-hand terms give discounted foregone earnings during the educational course. The equation allows for variable occupational wages over time and for changing compositions over time of the occupational-educational matrix of which λ_{qe} are elements. Changing compositions over time in the present context is equivalent to occupational mobility. In job competition theory, wages are coupled to occupations in a manner that reflects the relative productivities of different occupations. More productive occupations are remunerated with higher wages. Wage formation is assumed to be more dependent on the specifics of the job and less on the personal characteristics of the particular job holder.

$$\begin{aligned} &\Sigma_{t=1,\ldots,w}[\Sigma_q(\lambda_{qe}\, LR_q - \lambda_{qe-1}\, LR_q)(1+RJC_e)^{-t}] \\ &\quad = \Sigma_{t=1,\ldots,n}[(\lambda_{qe-1}LR_{q,o})(1+RJC_e)^{-t}] \end{aligned} \tag{2}$$

where RJC_e is the rate of return to educational level *e* following the job competition theory, LR_q = annual average earnings of occupation q, $LR_{q,o}$ is the initial average earnings of occupation q or simply starting wage, λ_{qe} is the proportion of the labor force with education k in occupation q, n_e is the duration of education e, and w is the working years after completing education k.

As was stated earlier, in many countries there are cross-tabulations of occupational and educational distributions $q \times e$ that can be used in combination with earnings data to apply the above rates of returns. In the long run, there are persistent substitution tendencies toward more capital and skill-intensive production processes. These tendencies are part of economic development and imply a regular rise in the skill level of most occupations. In the shorter run, and in times of labor shortages, employers will accept people with less formal education. In times of labor surplus, employers become stricter in their recruitment criteria and may demand higher certificates. The longer-run tendencies are more relevant to our purpose.

3. Application and Results

We apply both approaches to Indonesia and Pakistan under simplified assumptions to give the rates of return to education under both models. We let RHC_k and RJC_k, represent the rates of return under the human capital model and the job competition model, respectively, with k denoting the educational level, i.e. primary, secondary, and higher levels, see Appendix 2 for a formal discussion. The rate of return, RHC_k, is calculated from earning functions for the different educational levels. In contrast, the rate of return, RJC_k, is based on wage functions by occupations and cross-matrices that convert occupational to educational mixes. Remuneration, educational, and occupational data from Indonesia and Pakistan are used for calculating the rates of return. The data are from the Labor Force Surveys and Household Income and Expenditure Surveys of Indonesia and Pakistan. These are supplemented by data on schooling costs from ministerial sources.

Figure 1 and Table 1 show the rates of return based on the two approaches considering three educational levels: primary, secondary, and higher and making use of the distinction between seven major occupational categories.

The empirical literature is full of calculations of *RHC* for many countries, but there is none following *RJC*. Psacharopoulus (1980) has shown that the general pattern of *RHC* found among most developing countries is that of higher returns to primary than secondary or higher education. While our *RHC* results for Indonesia

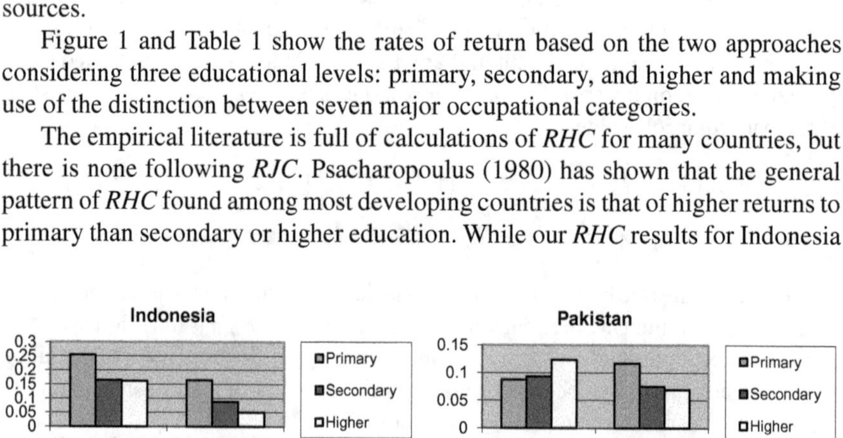

Figure 1. Shifts in educational returns under human capital and job competition.

Table 1. Results of different frameworks for estimation of rates of return to education.

Indonesia				Pakistan			
	Primary	Secondary	Higher		Primary	Secondary	Higher
RHC_k	0.254	0.164	0.162	RHC_k	0.087	0.093	0.123
RJC_k	0.164	0.087	0.050	RJC_k	0.117	0.075	0.069

Source: Cohen (1994).

confirm this pattern, our *RHC* results for Pakistan show a reverse of the ranking pattern of returns, with a lower returns for primary education; being one of the few exceptions in the developing countries. The results obtained here for Pakistan are consistent with and fall within the range of previously estimated rates for Pakistan (Khan and Irfan, 1985). The shown reverse pattern for Pakistan is likely to reflect an income earnings distribution that rewards less education cheaply and more education by steep overpayments.

Six comments are made on the obtained results. First, RJC_k are generally lower than RHC_k. The average returns on all educational levels following RJC_k are about 50% lower in Indonesia and about 15% lower in Pakistan. Results are also consistent with the expectation that the reduction in returns is greater for higher educational levels and is moderate for lower educational levels. The human capital model emphasizes the remuneration premium of additional education. The job competition model eliminates the premium and assigns all earnings to the job irrespective of the education of the employee. Consequently, the job competition approach tends to downgrade the returns to education across the board, particularly for higher educational levels. As a result, there is a tendency that $RHC_k > RJC_k$ for all k.

Second, as reductions in the returns are more pronounced the higher the educational level, the job competition model gives substantive support to the hypothesis of decreasing returns to increased education. The model also suggests that greater returns to education would occur for the type of education that leads to greater upward occupational mobility, especially toward the higher paid jobs. Primary education, being a crucial threshold for occupational mobility, scores greater returns in comparison to secondary or higher education. The general tendency in the human capital model for greater rates of return for primary education is further accentuated in the job competition model.

Third, there are greater increases in returns for Indonesia than for Pakistan, as one moves from the human capital model to the job competition model. The differences between the two countries are likely due to the presence of exaggerated premiums to education following *RHC* in Pakistan than *RHC* in Indonesia and that there is lower variation in earnings between occupational categories in Pakistan following *RJC* as compared to Indonesia following *RJC*. It is as if Pakistan is more inclined to follow *RHC* and overemphasize educational returns to higher education, while the results for Indonesian reflect the operation of the *RJC* more vividly.

Fourth, which of the two expectations models is more applicable in a particular country is a question that cannot be addressed with our estimates. It is likely that both expectations models are valid for different types of behaving agents. In its simplest form, the *RHC* model considers educational achievement as the one and only screening device for obtaining a job with higher earnings. While there is ample evidence on the use of education as a signaling device for remuneration by both employment seekers and employing firms. Many occupational/sector mixes (simply jobs) have predetermined remuneration levels for these jobs based on the productivity expectations of the job.

Fifthly, in how far do the earnings imbalance between *RHC* and *RJC* of this chapter correspond and fit with the supply–demand quantity imbalances found earlier under LMA in the previous chapter? RHC_e, showing highest values for higher and secondary education fits with the LMA forecast for 1970–1980 showing the highest shortage imbalances for higher and secondary education. RJC_e results are a reversal of rates of return favoring primary education over upper levels. This is consistent with a corresponding reversal of forecasted imbalances for 1980–1990 which show a shortage imbalance for primary education and surpluses for upper education. It is encouraging to note that the results obtained from the quantity side and those from the earnings side reinforce and are consistent with each other. Furthermore, the combined results forecast that for 1980–1990 a reversal in relative returns to the advantage of less-educated labor and to the disadvantage of the more educated will be in conformity with the changing scarcities as predicted by the manpower forecasts.

Finally, the demonstrated divergence in expectation results between the HC and the JC models can be related to the generally observed institutional bias in many countries that tends to exaggerate labor returns to certified education, and sometimes to an over-investment in university education. It is likely that the behavior of school entrants and leavers, and their influential parents, is more guided by the supply-oriented human capital theory than the demand-oriented job competition theory. The misinformed beliefs may lead to lower benefits and higher costs and a misallocation of resources, and can thus stand in the way of achieving the development goals of higher economic growth and more equitable distribution.

4. Concluding Remarks

Applications of human capital theory to earning expectations tend to overrate educational returns, which may lead to a bias toward more investment in higher education at the cost of intermediate education, and in general at the cost of vocational education. In both cases marginal labor productivities are not equal to earnings, investment incentives are distorted, and positive externalities are not utilized; hence, losses are incurred in terms of securing higher growth and equity. These findings would recommend giving equal attention to appraisals and evaluations based on occupational returns and job competition theory.

Chapter 19

Normed Planning of Human Resource Development: Ethiopia

1. Introduction

The first economic planning model of human resource development (HRD) that was formulated and applied dates back to the early 1960s and is due to the joint work of Hector Correa and Jan Tinbergen (1962).[1] Since then, practically speaking, many kinds of manpower planning models and cost–benefit analyses of educational paths have been applied in the third world, often with assistance from UN international organizations. More recently, UNDP showed interest in the modeling of HRD and provided support in sponsoring HRD policymaking devices that aim at integrating approaches based on economic planning models with those based on international comparative assessments. We call the integrated approach "normed planning model." This chapter is based on a recently carried advisory assignment on behalf of UNDP to the Ministry of Education (MOE), Ethiopia.

Outlining a roadmap for human resource development (HRD) for the coming 20–30 years for a developing country cannot rely on methods of manpower forecasts or educational returns and market signaling which are valid for the short and medium terms. Given the pace of technological change and the rapidly changing sectoral configuration in the economy and global competition, these methods may not even be valid for the medium term. The policy modeling of a 20-year roadmap can better be drawn by making judgmental use of the past experience of selected countries that are known to have performed better in HRD, and whose realized structure of the education sector can be projected backward so as to apply to the developing country in question. The country is Ethiopia. If the predicted paths of the select group of countries are followed along with associated institutions and policies; it is most likely that similar successful performances would occur in Ethiopia.

Drawing from the experience, policies, and allocative practices of selected better-performing countries in HRD, a normed planning model is developed with regressed parameters from the data sets of the selected best-performing countries, and the model is then applied to Ethiopia with the object of laying out a roadmap for HRD for the next two to three decades. In particular, for the developing country in question: what should be the targeted education mix at large in terms of enrolments, teachers, etc. at the various educational level? What are the shortfall gaps between the targeted education mix and the existing education mix? Which crucial features within the education system account for the shortfall gaps? What are the implications for the public and private financing of the educational plan? Which other factors outside the education system are considered to be critical for realizing the targeted education mix needs to be identified, monitored, and integrated? The model is called normed planning model because all parameters are derived as norms from pooled international data reflecting worldwide best performances in HRD, these norms are then applied to the developing country to give their "normed" profiles of HRD, which are usually upgrades of their "observed" profiles. The gaps constitute the areas for policy actions.

The application is organized as follows. Section 2 considers a select group of countries whose development pattern will be used to outline the Ethiopia roadmap. In Sections 3 and 4, a model is formulated and applied for planning basic parameters of the educational system such as enrolments, teachers, recurrent and capital costs, and the breakup of finance into government and private resources. The model is estimated from data of the select group, applied to Ethiopia, and alternative transitional paths simulated. Section 5 comments on qualitative features in HRD that made achievements in the select countries feasible, and which are prerequisites for the realization of the modeling results. The section examines also how prepared are the various regions in Ethiopia toward adopting the roadmap and how to bridge the lags. Ultimately, any transformations along the lines of the roadmap have to take place in the regions and regional conditions are known to vary significantly. Section 6 treats matching aspects between the demand and supply of human resources in the medium term. Section 7 emphasizes that there are non-HRD aspects that have been critical for the socio-economic development of the select countries; and if the roadmap is to be followed, its success requires that links with the non-HRD aspects need to be specified, measured, and realized. The section reflects on forecasts of related economy-wide imbalances in Ethiopia. Finally, Section 8 concludes.

2. The Targeted Select Group of Countries

UNDP's Human Development Index, HDI, ranked Ethiopia in 2005 as number 169 out of 177 countries.[2] In 1990, Ethiopia was ranked as number 111 out of 130 countries, implying that the country was relatively better off in the past. Lifting human resource development, HRD, in Ethiopia to levels comparable with middle-level countries is a long-term undertaking and may require a couple of decades or more of concentrated and consistent long-range perspective investment under governmental direction. This comes to drawing an HRD-education sector roadmap for 20–30 years that coincides with the development pattern and paths of a selected group of countries.

Several criteria were formulated and used in the selection of the targeted countries. The criteria aim at selecting the best-performing countries in HRD and economic development at large. The countries should (a) belong to the medium-level development group, (b) have a ranked Human Development Index higher than the ranked index of GDP per capita in $ppp, (c) have achieved a high economic growth in the last decade and is expected to continue, and (d) have a population size comparable to Ethiopia or bigger.

These criteria have assured an optimal selection of top performers. The selection resulted in eight countries. These are China, Vietnam, Indonesia, the Philippines, India, Egypt, Brazil, and Russia. On the request of MOE authorities, two more Asian countries lying much further ahead are added to the select group; these are Korea and Japan, resulting in 10 countries. The 10 countries show big jumps in their ranked HDI over the last decade. It is not surprising that six of the ten countries come from broader East Asia, which is the world region with the highest socio-economic performance.[3] The modeling approach is to use data from the eight countries over the period 1990–2005 in estimating a long-range conditional forecasting model that can then be applied to Ethiopia toward the year 2030. Since this database is incomplete for some countries/years the forecasts may not fully reflect the experiences for the missing countries/years.

Once selected, a compact databank was then set up for the selected 10 countries for the period 1990–2005, which was then used to estimate the equations of the model.

3. Long-Range Targeting Model for HRD

The model aims to display the destination structures of the educational system over the long term. The elements in these structures cover the mix between primary, secondary, and higher education, as regards quantity (i.e. relative enrolments), quality (i.e. relative teacher–student ratios), and balanced costs, as well as the financing of these levels by government and private sources.

The basic assumption made is that HRD structural variables follow paths that are interdependent with the socio-economic development phase, as represented by GDP *per capita* in dollars of purchasing power parity, $ppp. The HRD variables are specified as dependent on the GDP *per capita*. The model contains seven reaction equations with regression coefficients to be estimated from the select countries'

Table 1. Notations.

Index e denotes educational level, where $e = 1$ for primary, $e = 2$ for secondary, and $e = 3$ for tertiary.	
Endogenous variables and (structural ratios)	
ENR_e	Number of enrolled students by level e
TCH_e	Number of teachers by level e
REE_e	Recurrent expenditure cost of education by level e
GTS	Government total spending on all sectors
GTE	Government total expenditure on education
GRE	Government recurrent expenditure on education
GRE_e	Government recurrent expenditure on education by level e
GRO	Government recurrent expenditure on education in overhead and other activities
NRE_e	Non-government recurrent expenditure on education by level e
TGN	Total government and non-government expenditure on capital and recurrent costs of education
GER_e	Gross enrolment ratio by level e
STR_e	Student/teacher ratio by level e
RCS_e	Recurrent cost per student by level e expressed relative to resource base, i.e. recurrent cost per student/GDP per capita, both are measured in national currency
KRC	Ratio of capital cost/recurrent cost
TVS	Share of TVET (technical and vocational education training) enrolment in total secondary enrolment
NSA	Share of natural sciences students in total tertiary enrolment
Exogenous variables	
$GDPpc$	Gross domestic product per capita in \$ ppp, in constant prices of year 2000
GDP	Ethiopia's Gross domestic product in Birr millions, in constant prices of 2000
POP	Ethiopia's total population
$SAGe$	Ehiopia's share of the age group e, corresponding with level e, in the total population

databank. The model contains also seven definitional equations that hold the educational system together and allows formulating a consistent and comprehensive development plan for the educational sector as a whole, and its balanced financing. Together, the model consists of 14 sets of equations in 14 sets of endogenous variables that have to be solved, assuring thus a determinate model.

Some of the endogenous variables, that are explained in regressions, are structural ratios such as the gross enrolment ratios by educational level, denoted by GER_e. Other structural variables are student–teacher ratio, STR_e, and recurrent cost per student, RCS_e.

The equations in Box 1 can be briefly described, making use of the notations in Table 1. All the reaction equations are specified below in a general linear form, but when estimated the best-fitting form of the equation was selected which need not be the linear form. Table A1 in the appendix gives the selected best fits. The model is very simple and is solved by consecutive substitutions. Take first eqs. (1)–(6). Regressions of reaction eqs. (1), (3), and (5) allows predicting for

Ethiopia from these three equations the prospective Gross enrolment ratios, GER_e, the student–teacher ratios, STR_e and the Recurrent cost per student, RCS_e, respectively. Next, inserting these outcomes in eqs. (2), (4), and (6) results in number of enrolments, ENR_e, number of teachers, TCH_e, and the recurrent expenditure costs of education by level, REE_e. Reaction eq. (7) specifies the dependence of the capital cost/recurrent cost ratio, *KRC*, on *GDP pc*. This is formulated for all educational levels taken together.

Turning to the equations for governmental financing of education, there are here two reaction equations of (8) and (9), which determine consecutively the size of the overall government budget for spending on all sectors, *GTS*, and that part of which that goes to education, *GTE*.[4]

In eq. (10), capital costs of education are deducted from total spending on education to give government recurrent expenditure on all education, *GRE*. Equation (11) is a regression equation which estimates the distribution of this *GRE* on the three educational levels to give, GRE_e. Eq. (12) is a definitoional equation. *GRE* does not add up to the sum of GRE_e because there is the spending on overheads and other activities in education, *GRO*, which has to be accounted for. This is obtained as a residual. This variable occurs only in this equation and does not impact other variables in the model, but it is an item which is highly informative for the work of budget planners in balancing the various components of educational expenditure.

To find the non-government recurrent expenditure on education by level, NRE_e, deduct the government recurrent spending by level from the total recurrent expenditure per level, as in eq. (13).

Furthermore, the model sums in eq. (14) all educational expenditure to give total government and non-government expenditure on education including all recurrent and capital costs, to give total government and non-government spending on education, *TGN*.

Box 1. Model specification.

Educational structure of enrolments, teachers, and cost

$$GER_e = \alpha_{1e} + \beta_{1e}\, GDP\,pc \qquad e = 1,2,3 \qquad (1)$$

$$ENR_e = GER_e \cdot SAG_e \cdot POP \qquad e = 1,2,3 \qquad (2)$$

$$STR_e = \alpha_{3e} + \beta_{3e}\, GDP\,pc \qquad e = 1.2.3 \qquad (3)$$

$$TCH_e = [1/STR_e]\, ENR_e \qquad e = 1,2,3 \qquad (4)$$

$$RCS_e = \alpha_{5e} + \beta_{5e}\, GDP\,pc \qquad e = 1,2,3 \qquad (5)$$

$$REE_e = RCS_e \cdot ENR_e \qquad e = 1,2,3 \qquad (6)$$

$$KRC = \alpha_{7e} + \beta_{7e}\, GDP\,pc \qquad (7)$$

(*Continued*)

(*Continued*)

Public and private financing of education		
$GTS/GDP = \alpha_8 + \beta_8 GDPpc$		(8)
$GTE/GTS = \alpha_9 + \beta_9 GDPpc$		(9)
$GRE = [1/1 + KRC]GTE$		(10)
$GRE_e/GRE = \alpha_{11e} + \beta_{11e} GDPpc$	$e = 1, 2, 3$	(11)
$GRO = GRE - GRE_1 - GRE_2 - GRE_3$		(12)
$NRE_e = REE_e - GRE_e$	$e = 1, 2, 3$	(13)
$TGN = GTE + (1 + KRC)\ \Sigma_e\ NRE_e$		(14)

Simple as it is, besides comprehensively projecting the various components of a plan for education, the model provides checks on important key relations such as the distribution structures of enrolments, teachers, and spending, and the comparative gross enrolment ratios and student–teacher ratios in the three levels. The model allows also evaluating the cost per teacher per level and its relation to the *GDP per capita*. For policy appraisal purposes, the total expenditure on education can be calculated as a proportion of the GDP, i.e. *TGN/GDP*.

As the roadmap model contains some basic structural relationships *within* each level of education and *between* the various levels of the education sector, the roadmap results have the additional advantage of providing systematic and comprehensive sets of monitoring indicators to check the pace of achievement and lag for specific items of HRD at specific future periods.

4. Roadmap Results and Transition Paths to Destinations

4.1. *Estimation, results, and apparent gaps*

For estimation of the regression equations, a compact databank was set up that brings together data for the above variables for the 10 countries in the period 1990–2005. The databank relies heavily on the World Bank Development Indicators Databank, next to additional material from UNESCO, UN Population Division, and UNDP Human Development Reports. The number of observations covered from the 10 countries varied per estimated relational equation depending on data availability and validity. The shapes of the relational equations fitted included linear, logarithmic, powered, and polynomial, as shown in the appendix. An indication of the extent to which the observations of the ten countries fit together in case of a specific estimated relational equation is provided by calculation of R^2 for that

Table 2. HRD positions: Gaps between required levels for 2005 and Ethiopia actual in 2005.

	Actual	Required levels	Gap
GER = Gross enrolment ratio			
Primary	0.86	0.85	0.01
Secondary	0.19	0.45	−0.57
Tertiary	0.031	0.06	−0.48
STR = Student/teacher ratio			
Primary	62	30	1.08
Secondary	49	36	0.36
Tertiary	36	27	0.33
RCS = recurrent cost per student/GDPpc			
Primary	0.154	0.107	0.44
Secondary	0.484	0.268	0.81
Tertiary	4.987	3.4	0.47
KRC = Capital/recurrent cost ratio	0.33	0.25	0.32
GTS/GDP, Share gov spending all services	0.31	0.31	0.00
GTE/GTS, Share gov total exp on education	0.18	0.148	0.22
GRE_e/GRE Share gov re-current exp			
Primary	0.59	0.34	0.74
Secondary	0.18	0.28	−0.37
Tertiary	0.16	0.19	−0.15

equation. The average R^2 for all the estimated relational equations based on data from the ten countries is $R^2 = 0.73$. The figure of 0.73 is reasonable by conventional standards, given the diversity of the ten countries in definitions and data coverage. It is also important to note that the model has the advantage of including several checks and balances via definitional equations that correct for off-line regression estimates that may creep in.

The first use of the estimated model is to fill in the GDP per capita of Ethiopia for 2005 in the equations and solve for the predicted HRD positions of Ethiopia for 2005. These can be checked with the actual positions of the country in 2005. This is done in Table 2. The gaps tell a lot about the current imbalances assessed in the framework of the select countries. Take, for instance, primary gross enrolment rate in primary education, its actual value is higher than the expected, which is not surprising given the very high priority that Ethiopia assigns to this target variable. But apart from this advantage, Ethiopia shows a lag in all other target variables including student–teacher ratios and recurrent cost per student in all three levels, next to significant gaps in gross enrolment roles in secondary and tertiary education reaching 57% and 48%, respectively. Although the actual total and expected total government financing of education are close to each other, the distribution of government spending differs and reflects Ethiopia's greater preference for primary at the cost of secondary and tertiary. The roadmap assessment suggests that the government has overspent in primary and underspent in secondary and tertiary HRD.

4.2. *Roadmap results of the whole model*

All equations of the model are then solved as a whole system to give solutions for the years 2015 and 2030. To do this, exogenous variables of Ethiopia are required for these future years. These are the population growth projections for Ethiopia as published by UN and the population and its breakup by eligible enrolment age groups, as in Table 3. For source, see endnote.[5]

These are consistent with the estimates of the Ten-Year Development Plan up to 2015.

Table 3. Projected population by age groups and total.

		Share of age groups, SAG_e, %			Population in millions		
Educational level	Age-group	2005	2015	2030	2005	2015	2030
Primary	7–14	0.1996	0.2025	0.1934	14.75	19.13	24.27
Secondary	15–18	0.0915	0.0910	0.0950	6.76	8.60	11.93
Tertiary	19–22	0.076	0.0760	0.0794	5.65	7.18	9.97
Rest	(<6 + >22)	0.6324	0.6306	0.6322	46.74	59.59	79.34
Total population	POP	1	1	1	73.9	94.5	125.5

The other exogenous variable for future years is the GDP per capita in \$ppp, in constant prices of 2000. This amounted to \$965 in 2005.[6] We take for 2005–2015 an annual growth of the GDP per capita at 5% (7.5% GDP growth less 2.5% population growth), this gives a total growth over 10 years of 163%. Starting from the value of \$965 in 2005, the projection is \$1573 for 2015. For the next 15 years 2015–2030, the annual growth of GDP per capita can rise by a half percent every 5 years in view of the greater momentum with economic development, and reductions in population growth that are feasible in view of their correspondence with UN population projections. An annual growth of GDP per capita of 5.5% in 2015–2020 would result in \$2056 in 2020, followed by an annual growth 6.0% in 2020–2025 resulting in \$ 2751 in 2025, and finally, an annual growth of 6.5% in 2025–2030 giving \$ 3770 for 2030.

The equivalent of the GDP per capita in 2005 in Birr amounted to 1144 Birr, both assumed to grow at the same rates and at constant prices of 2000.[7] Multiplying by population gives the GDP in national currency. The above data are found in Table 4.

Applying these exogenous data to the model gives roadmap requirements (or projections) as in Tables 5 and 6. The model generates the structure of the educational system for 2030, based on projections of variables relating to number of

Table 4. Projected GDP and GDP per capita.

	2005	2015	2030
GDPpc in $ppp thousands in constant prices	0.965	1.573	3.770
GDPpc Birr thousands in constant prices	1.144	1.865	4.470
Total population million	73.9	94.5	125.5
GDP Birr million, constant prices	84553	137826	330326

enrolments, teachers, and recurrent and capital expenditure for the three levels and the division of these into government and non-government sources. Together, these variables form the ingredients of a comprehensive plan for the education sector. Table 5 gives the details of the roadmap projections, and Table 6 gives a summing structure of the educational sector as depicted by the roadmap. We shall focus on Table 6.

The roadmap expects the growth of enrolments in primary education to be lower than that of secondary and tertiary so as to fulfill expected targets of gross enrolment ratios at percentages 100:71:18, for the three levels respectively in 2030. The enrolment structure consistent with these targets is a distribution of students along the following percentages 70:25:05 for 2030, as shown in rows 1 and 2 of Table 6.

Student/teacher ratios are required to converge in the three levels by 2030 towards 21:27:19 students per teacher in the three educational levels, respectively, thus resulting in a distribution of teachers similar to that of enrolments, at 74:20:6 for primary, secondary, and tertiary levels in 2030, as shown in rows 3 and 4 of Table 6.

While the recurrent cost per student/GDP per capita is supposed to remain stable for primary education, the roadmap path expects the relative cost to increase for secondary and decrease for tertiary but, nevertheless, keeping significant distances from each other, as shown in row 5 of Table 6. When taking unit cost and the other costing aspects mentioned above the recurrent expenditure structure is expected to be more or less equally divided in one-third for each level by 2030, precisely in the percentages of 35:33:35, as shown in row 6 of Table 6.

The roadmap shows that for 2030, the government would have to allocate its educational expenditure among the three levels in the percentages 36:30:15, with the remainder in others and overhead. In contrast, non-government sources are supposed to fund primary and secondary education in equal proportions of 30% and 31% and devote more to tertiary education, 39%; these figures are shown in rows 7 and 8 of Table 6. This pattern is generally the case in the world at large, as user charges and returns to tertiary education are tied to the private beneficiaries.

The structure of financing education shifts over time toward relatively less from government and more from non-government resources. The ratio moves from 71%

Table 5. Future development paths of enrolments, teachers, and expenditure by educational level. All Birr values are in constant prices of 2000.

Actual	Plan		Roadmap			Gap	
2005	2015	Variable	2005	2015	2030	2005	2015
		Primary educational level					
0.86	1.109	Gross enrolment ratio	0.85	0.89	> 1.0	0.01	−0.25
12.66	21.22	Enrolments, millions	12.538	17.031	24.272	0.01	−0.25
62	47	Student/teacher ratio	30	27	21	1.08	−0.74
203.0	451534	Teachers, thousands	417.9	630.8	1155.8	−0.51	0.28
0.154		Recurrent cost pr student/GDP pc	0.107	0.110	0.120	0.44	1.00
176	200	Recurrent cost per student in Birr	122.4	205.2	536.4	0.44	0.03
2228	4245	Primary recurrent exp in Bm	1535	3494	13019	0.45	−0.21
		Secondary educational level					
0.19	0.4213	Gross enrolment ratio, %.	0.45	0.54	0.71	−0.57	0.22
1.314	3.623	Enrolments millions	3.042	4.644	8.465	−0.57	0.22
49	40	Student/teacher ratio.	36	32	27	0.36	−0.25
26.93	90574	Teachers, thousands	84.5	145.1	313.5	−0.68	0.38
0.484		Recurrent cost pr student/GDP pc.	0.268	0.281	0.326	0.81	1.00
554	557	Recurrent cost per student in Birr	306.6	524.1	1457.2	0.81	−0.06
728	2019	Secondary recurrent exp in Bm	933	2434	12335	−0.22	0.17
		Tertiary educational level					
0.031	0.0551	Gross enrolment ratio, %	0.06	0.08	0.18	−0.48	0.31
0.1739	0.396	Enrolments millions	0.337	0.575	1.794	−0.48	0.31
36	28	Student/teacher ratio	27	25	19	0.33	−0.12
4.85	14133	Teachers, thousands	12.5	23.0	94.4	−0.61	0.39
4.987		Recurrent cost per student/GDP pc.	3.4	2.7	1.5	0.47	1.00
5705	7863	Recurrent cost per student in Birr	3890	5036	6705	0.47	−0.56
992	3111	Tertiary recurrent expenditure in Bm	1311	2893	12026	−0.24	−0.08
		All levels					
3948	9375	Total recurrent expenditure	3779	8821	37380	0.04	−0.06
0.33	0.316	Capital/recurrent cost ratio	0.25	0.22	0.145	0.32	−0.44
5250	12337	Total recurrent and capital exp	4723	10762	42800	0.11	−0.15
		Public and private financing					
0.31	0.31	National budget/GDP	0.31	0.31	0.28	0.00	0.00
0.18	0.15	Share gov exp edu in national budget	0.148	0.138	0.12	0.22	−0.09
0.59	0.53	Share gov rec exp on primary edu	0.34	0.34	0.36	0.74	−0.56
0.18	0.164	Share gov rec exp on secondary edu.	0.28	0.28	0.3	−0.37	0.41
0.16	0.251	Share gov rec exp on tertiary edu	0.19	0.18	0.16	−0.15	−0.39
0.07	0.055	Share gov rec exp others, overhead	0.19	0.2	0.18	−0.62	0.73
		Other indicators					
0.0558	0.0465	Gov total exp on education/GDP	0.0459	0.0428	0.0336	−0.22	−0.09
0.0104	0.0261	Non-gov total exp on ed/GDP	0.0187	0.0268	0.0487	0.44	0.03
0.0662	0.0726	Total gov, non-gov exp on ed/GDP	0.0646	0.0696	0.0823	0.03	0.04

(*Continued*)

Table 5. (*Continued*)

Actual	Plan		Roadmap			Gap	
2005	2015	Variable	2005	2015	2030	2005	2015
0.84	0.64	Share education finance by gov	0.71	0.61	0.41	0.19	0.04
0.16	0.36	Share of ed finance by non-gov	0.29	0.39	0.59	−0.46	0.07
(a)		Average of summed shaded gaps				−0.28	−0.12
(a)		Average of absolute shaded gaps				0.38	0.23

Notes: Gap 2005 = (actual-roadmap)/roadmap, Gap 2015 = (plan-roadmap)/roadmap, Actual and Plan figures are from Education Statistics Annual Abstract 2006, and MOE 10 Years Education Sector Plan 2006/07–2015/16, respectively. (a) The average absolute gap removes the negative signs before averaging. The average summed gap does not. Both are indicative of the required adjustments to bring the educational system to its preconceived balanced pattern. Bm = Birr millions.

Table 6. Roadmap structures of HRD in terms of educational levels of primary: secondary: tertiary. (prm: scn: trt, respectively).

	2005	2015	2030
	prm: scn: trt	prm: scn: trt	prm: scn: trt
1. Enrolment ratios	85: 45: 06	89: 54: 08	100: 71: 18
2. Enrolments numbers, % distribution	79: 19: 02	77: 21: 03	70: 25: 05
3. Students/teacher ratios	30: 36: 27	27: 32: 25	21: 27: 19
4. Teacher numbers, % distribution	81: 16: 02	79: 18: 03	74: 20: 06
5. Recurrent cost student/GDP pc	.11: .27: 2.30	.11: .28: 2.00	.12: .33: 1.30
6. Recurrent costs, % distribution	41: 25: 35	40: 28: 33	35: 33: 34
7. Government expenditure % distribution	34: 28: 19	34: 28: 18	36: 30: 16
8. Non-gvr expenditure, % distribution	38: 05: 57	36: 18: 46	30: 31: 39
9. Share gvr in total educational exp	71	61	41
10. Share non-gvr in total edc exp	29	39	59

Note: Row 7. Government expenditure on overheads and others form the remaining share.

government to 29% non-government in 2005 to 61% to 39% in 2015 and to a change in major roles toward 41% to 59% in 2030, rows 9 and 10 of Table 6.

What can be stated about the height and pattern of the gaps shown in Table 5? Taking 2005 as a benchmark, the gaps between the actual and expected are significant, as can be gathered from focusing on the ten variables of enrolments, teachers, and recurrent expenditure for the three levels and total expenditure on education/GDP. The average of the summed gaps for these ten variables is 28%, while the average of the absolute gaps is 38%, see bottom of Table 5. The striking thing about the 2005 gaps is that while the total expenditure on education as a proportion of the GDP is about 6.5% for both the actual and expected and is thus well balanced; nevertheless, significant gaps arise in the subdivisions of the educational system, due to various factors that will be examined in the following.

The gaps are due to differences in the development profiles of Ethiopia and the composite of the select countries. Apart from this obvious statement, the gaps are significantly large and are explainable in terms of non-controllable factors and controllable factors, which are discussed in the following.

The initial situation of Ethiopia in terms of a relatively large school-age population and a low GDP is given and cannot be controlled. Ethiopia is at the top of its demographic transition when population growth is at its highest rate. With a school-going population comprising almost 40% of the population the targeted enrolment rates would require massive spending on education that cannot be maintained with the low GDP resources available. The absolute levels of population and GDP are at opposite ends, causing thus significant gaps in enrolments, teachers, and expenditures. To demonstrate the influence of the demographic factor results can be reported from a simulation applied to the model. The simulation fixed the population for 2005 at a reduced level of 10%, 66.5 instead of 73.9 million. At the expected gross enrolment ratios, required enrolments at all three levels were diminished, and accordingly for required teachers and finances. The average summed gap fell from −0.28 to −0.22, a reduction of 6 points, or 27%.

Regarding controllable factors causing the gaps, these lie in (first) pursued educational policies aiming at universal enrolment in primary education, and (second) the generally very costly unit costs at all levels in relative terms.

First, more resources have gone to raising enrolment in primary education so as to meet the millennium goal of universal coverage by 2015; this has gone beyond the required paths as depicted by the select countries. As a result, much less than expected resources have gone to secondary and tertiary education. The results are enrolment imbalances in all three levels. The greater focus on enrolment numbers coincided with a lower than expected quality of education, as represented by higher than expected student/teacher ratios which apply for all three levels. In primary education, the actual str is double the expected str. In secondary and tertiary education the gap is half as much.

Second, unit recurrent costs in all three levels in relation to the GDP per capita are much higher than expected following the select countries. This is also true if other countries than those selected were taken as the reference point. Unit costs (i.e. teacher salary) relative to GDP per capita in Ethiopia are remarkably high. Because the non-teacher costs vary between 6% and 15% of the recurrent costs, and because of the very low number of teachers per student that varies between 1:60 to 1:35, depending on the level of education, the fault lies in the relatively very high salary scales of teachers compared to GDP per capita. As an example, the average annual salary for a primary school teacher in the reported period was 8191 Birr for the country as a whole, against a GDP per capita of 1380 Birr. This gives a ratio of about six times as much. In the select countries, the ratios vary around four times. In relative terms, there is thus a 50% more pay for primary teachers than the expected norm. For secondary and tertiary teachers, the pay beyond the expected norm runs at levels reaching 100%.[8] The high cost is also due to a high non-academic staff/teachers ratio, especially in tertiary education.[9]

Ten years later, in 2015, the ESDP IV plans a more balanced educational system that is closer to the expected paths of the selected countries. If the plan for 2015 is realized, Table 5 shows that the average summed gaps would fall significantly from the high level of −0.28 to −0.12. In terms of the average absolute gap, the improvement is from 0.38 to 0.23, which is reduction in gaps of 40%. The causes behind the gaps in 2015 are similar to those in 2005. The large population combined with a low GDP is a mainly non-controllable cause. A simulation of a 10% lesser population for 2015 diminishes the average summed gap to only −0.03, down from a value of −0.12. The effect in 2015 is bigger than in 2005 due to the larger school-going population in 2015, which is reduced accordingly. Among the controllable policies, the continued overinvestment in the primary level as planned for 2015 causes gaps in all three levels. On the other hand, if the plan figures for reductions in recurrent unit costs, implying lower teacher salaries, would materialize in 2015, then a major cause of the gaps would be eliminated. [Table 6 shows some reduction in the recurrent unit costs between 2005 and 2015, and a tendency to approach the roadmap pattern.]

One point on the realization prospects of ESDP IV and the related gap, that needs emphasis, is the following. Tha data show that the planned total expenditure from government and non-government sources as a percentage of the GDP is 7.3% in 2015. This is 0.6% higher than 2005 and 0.3% higher than the roadmap pattern for 2015. While government provisions can be assumed to happen, realization of the non-government provisions would require increased efforts to mobilize domestic sources, i.e. parents and graduates paying user charges, and local communities and business circles paying back for external benefits from a more skilled labor force, as well as foreign assistance.

4.3. *The transition phase: Flexible routes to roadmap destinations*

The gaps between the observed situation in 2005 and the trajectory are supposed to be bridged during a transition phase and the duration of this phase is flexible, as long as the course of development links with the trajectory. Of course, the costs are less, and the benefits are more the shorter the transition period. Obviously, the indicated gaps are too big to be resolved in 10 or 15 years. [This is not only because of the size of the gaps but also because any decision to adjust the current policies may not take place before 2010 or 2015 given the already drawn-up plans and their

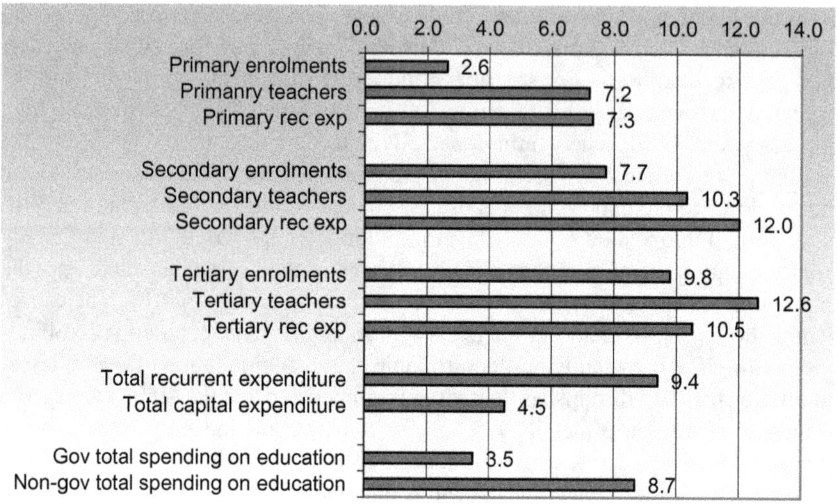

Figure 1. Anticipated annual growth rates of main variables of the education system 2005–2030 according to the roadmap, percentages.

implementation.] The obvious way out is to take the whole period 2005–2030 as one of a gradual transition toward the roadmap destinations, which is the surest way of reaching the destination in time. The annual growth rate over the 25 years for each element of the roadmap is a helpful guide in applying the required adjustment. These growth rates are displayed in Figure 1 for the main variables.

Table A2 in the appendix gives a larger coverage of the transition details, and the growth paths of all variables in the model along the years 2015, 2020, 2025, and their destination in 2030. The transition paths shown in the appendix table are flexible and what cannot be bridged for some variables in one period can be done in more periods. This applies especially to shaded variables with annual growth rates of 10% and above, i.e. enrolments and teachers in secondary and tertiary education, and non-government expenditure on all three levels. Especially in this area, incentives need to be instituted to mobilize greater efforts from the private sector in financing HRD.

This approach is the most flexible one and has the additional advantage of avoiding the simulation and appraisal of alternative strategies to bridge this or that gap. Such alternative strategies often reflect arbitrary choices, advisor preferences, and untested schedules, which are not convincing to policy makers. Furthermore, Table A2 in the appendix specifies the target values of structural indicators that relate the various parts of the education sector to each other, for various periods until 2030. These structural indicators and their targets are especially suited to monitor the pace of implementation toward the roadmap destinations.

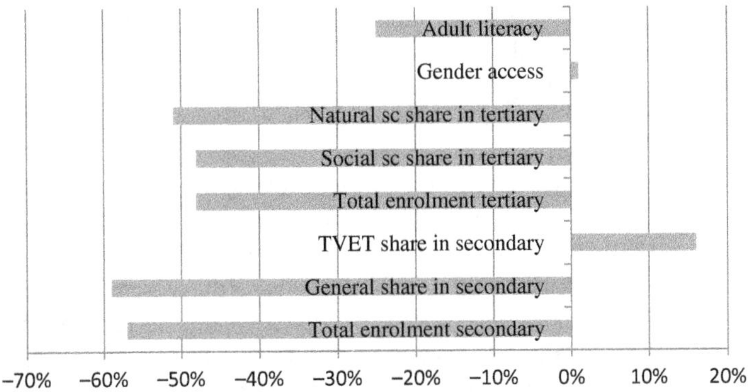

Figure 2. Roadmap gaps for subdivisions within secondary and tertiary education, gender access and adult literacy, benchmark 2005.

4.4. *More roadmap specifications: Technical, non-technical, gender, and literacy*

The model contains additional equations that specify the HRD profile in more detail. For example, one equation gives the share of technical enrolments in total secondary enrolment. The equation is formulated as in the other regressed equations: the share is made dependent on the GDP per capita, and the data employed to estimate the equation is that of the select countries. Applying the estimates of the equation to the Ethiopian GDP per capita gives the anticipated roadmap share of technical secondary enrolments for Ethiopia. From this share, and the anticipated roadmap target for total secondary enrolments, the latter is then disaggregated into its two components: general and technical. A similar equation has been estimated to split tertiary education into its two components of enrolment in natural sciences and in social sciences. The gaps between the actual distribution and the roadmap distribution are depicted in Figure 2. The gaps indicate that Ethiopia has a positive balance in technical secondary education of + 16% and a negative balance in general secondary education of −59%. The gap for total secondary education is −57%. The situation for tertiary education shows about the same negative balance for natural and social sciences.

To assess the anticipated gap in gender performance the actual versus predicted performance for the *girls to boy's ratio* in primary and secondary enrolments, a regression was run to explain this ratio GBR in terms of the GDP per capita. The data for the select group shows that an equal gender ratio of one was realized at a GDP per capita of $4000 ppp. Observations falling below this point belonged to Egypt, India, Indonesia, Vietnam, and some early years in China.[10] For Ethiopia, the required GBR is 77% in 2005, which is exactly equal to the 77% reached in 2005. This is clearly shown in Figure 2. Eliminating the remaining gender gap as the GDP per capita of Ethiopia approaches the $4000 level in 2030 is thus a target within very easy reach.

The positive performance regarding gender stands in contrast with an excessive negative gap regarding adult literacy. An equation outlining the adult literacy ratio, ALR, as a long-term function of the GDP per capita was tested. Application of the regressed equation[11] to Ethiopia gave results implying that would require that Ethiopia should have an ALR of 57% in 2005, 61% in 2010, and increasing to 65% and to 88% in 2015 and 2030, respectively. The situation is that the actual adult literacy ratio for 2005 is only 36% against the required 57%, Figure 2. This is a gap 21%. Although the size of the literacy gap is moderate when compared to others, the required finance for its elimination surpasses all other gaps calculated so far. The gap is financially too huge to be closed by conventional literacy campaigns. The situation suggests a need to employ non-conventional policy approaches toward greater participation and integration of the least literate population.

5. Additional Refinements

The quantitatively targeted structure of the educational system as was displayed above in the roadmap cannot be considered in isolation from the qualitative educational features that circumvent the educational system. These features are also broadly defined as the educational institutions along which the educational system is activated and runs. Accordingly, the policy model was supplemented with a separately implemented comparative descriptive review of qualitative HRD features of the educational system in the 10 select countries that have been pivotal for their higher performance. As these qualitative considerations fall outside the focus of the book they are left out. Notwithstanding, it is important to acknowledge that one cannot take over and transplant the quantitative results from a normed planning model that is estimated from the database of select countries, and hope that this performance can be realized elsewhere, without giving due consideration to the qualitative foundations in which the quantitative results were formed.

While the roadmap sketches and focuses on the national contours of HRD, actual implementation is for the greatest part always at the regional level. How prepared are the various regions in Ethiopia toward adopting the roadmap? Which regions are furthest from the roadmap, and would thus require more attention and resources in the coming years? Since the policy modeler is also a policy advisor, he/she should attempt to answer these questions which are central to policymaking.

Use is made of regional data on gross enrolment ratios, *GER*, and on student–teacher ratios, *STR*, in both the primary and secondary levels of education, for specifying and quantifying a Regional Index of Educational Development. The two indicators and the Index are shown in Table 7, they are sufficiently broad

Table 7. Regional indicators (2006/2007) and regional index of educational development (a).

	Gross enrolment Ratio, *GER*		Student–teacher Ratio, *STR*				Share government enrolment in total	
Region	Primary	Secondary	Primary	Secondary	Regional index of educational development	Regional rank	Primary	Secondary
Tigray	104.8	28.2	42	43	0.58	6	96%	97%
Afar	22.2	4.6	31	27	0.52	7	76%	77%
Amhara	93.1	22.05	58	53	0.46	8	95%	99%
Oromiya	91.4	21.15	64	50	0.45	9	98%	96%
Somali	38.6	3.65	137	92	0.19	11	96%	100%
Benishangul-Gumuz	127.9	26.55	47	36	0.62	5	99%	100%
Snnpr	97.8	18	68	53	0.44	10	96%	98%
Gambella	181.4	28.8	35	31	0.78	3	97%	100%
Harari	116.8	51.6	30	31	0.81	2	91%	96%
Addis Abeba	146.6	63.9	28	31	0.92	1	46%	76%
Dire dawa	80	40.05	33	36	0.67	4	78%	84%
Total	91.7	21.4	59	48	0.47(b)		95%	96%

Source: ESDP 2008 Annual Review Meeting. (a) Index is obtained by converting (Str) to its inverse so as to work with increasing values as a development measure. Indicators of columns 1–4 are to be indexed in terms of the highest regional value and averaged over the four columns. (b) Simple average of the column gives 0.59.

to cover the quantity and quality aspects of education. Of course, the education sector contains many other aspects relating to graduation, dropouts, efficiency, cost, returns, and differing stakeholder interests; that cannot be dealt with at the regional level often because of limited data. Fortunately, performances regarding *GER* and *STR*, tend to correlate with most of the other aspects, so that the Index can give reasonable answers to the posed questions.

When applied to Ethiopia the results show Addis Abeba to be at the top with an index value of about 0.9, followed by Harari and Gambella with index values of around 0.8. Next, there are Dire Dawa and Benishangul-Gumus at around 0.65, Tigray and Afar at around 0.55, Amhara, Oromia, and Snnpr at the lower end of 0.45, and Somali at only 0.19. The HRD status of the last four mentioned regions, namely Amhara, Oromiya, Snnpr, and Somali, is at about half or less than that achieved in Addis Abeba, suggesting that major efforts are needed in these regions to bring them on par with the rest. Strengthened effort applies also to Tigray and Afar but to a lesser extent.

Table 7 supplements regional performances with regional data on the share of government enrolment in total enrolment at the primary and secondary levels. This gives an idea of the self-help efforts and dependence on government versus non-government resources in the various regions. The high performances in Addis

Abeba and Dire Dawa are made possible by a greater role of the non-government sector, as compared to other regions. It is also worth noting that the higher development ranks of Harari, Gambella, and Benishangul-Gumuz correspond with the highest shares of government enrolments. On the other hand, afar ranks seventh out of eleven regions in spite of a relatively lower involvement of the government sector. As far as the optimal mixture of government and non-government resources in education as depicted by the roadmap is concerned, it can be observed that Addis Abeba, Dire Dawa, and Afar are closest to the roadmap features.

6. Matching of the Labor Market in the Short and Medium Terms

While the roadmap is focused on reaching a balanced structure of HRD in the long term in conformity with selected criteria, it is not meant to answer questions on detailed supply and demand of the labor market in the short and medium terms. Such questions as how to tackle the problems of temporary and enduring unemployment,[12] how many technicians for the various trades should be trained, or how many engineers, physicians, managers, accountants, and the like should exit from tertiary education, in a couple of years or so to meet market requirements are very important, but they are supposed to be resolved at more detailed policy levels than the roadmap level, though within its boundaries.

In a mature economy, the matching of demand and supply of HRD is resolved and decided upon by the stakeholders in the labor market. Stakeholders generate and use signals of labor market information, LMI, to help them in deciding where to enroll in education and training and where to apply for appropriate jobs that match their qualifications. In a developing country, as very typical of Ethiopia, the labor market is embodied in barriers that prevent its fluid functioning. The barriers are fourfold; the labor market is highly segmented, labor market information is lagging, absorption of LMI by agents is minimal, and even if the above conditions are fulfilled, conditions for elastic mobility of agents between the segments are usually unfavorable. Moreover, established mobility barriers between regions substantiate the segmentation tendencies further. On the other hand, the labor market matching tasks of the government in Ethiopia are facilitated by the fact that currently major shares of the employment of secondary and tertiary graduates are in government activities, while at the same time, public education is the dominant supplier. With both ends in the same hands matching exercises by the government are relatively simple for now. But, as the share of the private sector increases in both the employment and supply of education and training, government's ability in matching labor market gets more complex, and reliance on an LMI system becomes indispensable. In this regard, a few comments can be added on the state of the LMI system in Ethiopia.

The labor force surveys, LFS, are the major source of LM information. The detailed elaboration of HRD programs by manpower type requires much more data than those contained in LFS. Such programing is supposed to be done by making use of (a) training needs assessments, (b) manpower forecasts, (c) analysis of educational returns, and (d) labor market signaling, within the broad destination structures that are depicted in the road map. Regarding (a) and (b), ministerial departments engaged in the employment and provision of training are well equipped to make training needs assessments at a meaningful and usable detailed level. But little or nothing has been done in skilled manpower forecasts in Ethiopia; though such forecasts face many weaknesses that limit their effective use in HRD programming. Regarding (c), there are calculations of educational returns to the three educational levels in Ethiopia. An elaborate review is found in World Bank (2005). There are various studies that show the returns to primary education are lower than to secondary or higher, i.e. 10.6 against 15.9 and 15.1, respectively, which is in variance with many developing countries. However, the results of the roadmap model which suggest an overinvestment in primary education at the cost of secondary and tertiary education tend to justify the empirical findings on low comparative returns to primary education in Ethiopia. Notwithstanding, calculations of educational returns can hide serious misunderstandings since the activity segment in which they were calculated conditions the educational returns, and there can be multiple segments. Besides, when positive externalities such as contribution to awareness and innovation are considered the returns to primary education would turn higher. But that will also apply to the other levels if the analysis is extended. Moreover, the level of aggregation in calculations of educational returns is very aggregate and is not helpful for any detailed HRD programming for specific skills. Finally, regarding (d), labor market signaling in the forms of gauging the number of vacancies and rates of remuneration by skills is more useful for making decisions on education and training than manpower forecasts or educational returns. The Federal Civil Service (FCS) appears to have updated market information on vacant positions and remuneration rates for many skilled occupations, which information is used flexibly by the FCS for scaling new recruits and upgrading the salary scales of skilled personnel in public sector.[13]

7. The Roadmap as Part of a Sustained Development Trajectory: Anticipated Economy-Wide Imbalances

HRD in general, including the education sector in particular, do not work in isolation from the rest of the economy, polity, and society. We pinpoint four crucial conditions in overall development that the select countries have fulfilled and which can serve as guidelines for a balanced path of socio-economic development for Ethiopia. These are (I) quick demographic transition, (II) speeded industrial transformation, (III) greater outward orientation, and (IV) restraints in income inequalities.

(I) Quick demographic transition: The UN sources project an annual population growth of Ethiopia to fall to 2.06 in 2015, and to 1.72 by 2030. These projections have been used in the model so far. How do these trends match with the experience of the select countries? We tested a logarithmic function that gave significant results in which average annual population growth for 5-year periods: 1975–1980, and so on up to 2005–2010, for the select countries is made dependent on GDP per capita for initial years of 5-year periods, i.e. 1975, and so on until 2005, see Figure A1 in the appendix.

$$(\text{Annual growth of population}) = m2.236e^{-0.0946\ \text{Periodical GDPpc}} \quad R^2 = 0.78 \quad (15)$$

Application of the estimated equation to Ethiopia predicts an annual population growth in 2025–2030 of about 1.6%. The UN projected path for Ethiopia is 1.72%, which is fractionally higher than the select path. The difference is 1.72% −1.6% = 0.12, which is about 7% more. It can be argued that some slight additional effort to restrain population growth may be required to bring population growth in Ethiopia in line with that in the select countries.

(II) Speeded industrial transformation: All select countries have passed, or are passing, through a swift industrialization process in which the shares of the labor force and of the value-added move from agriculture to the non-agriculture sectors. The share of the labor force is the best indication of the concentration and interaction of agents, and the more agents in industrial activities the greater is the industrialization process. And the share of the value added that is generated in industrial activities is an expression of the extent of industrial transactions taking place and the pace of industrialization. These two indicators are transformed into an industrialization index by summing the two shares and regressing the outcome against the GDP per capita. for the select countries between 1980 and 2005. This gave the following well-performing estimated equation; see Figure A2 in the appendix.

$$\text{Industrialisation Index} = 14.644\ Ln\ GDPpc + 51.821 \quad R^2 = 0.9 \quad (16)$$

The select countries already reached values of the index ranging between 97 and 72 in 2005. Applied to Ethiopia the equation would recommend that Ethiopia should have an index value of 52, while the actual value is only 36 in 2005. The gap is about 30%, which is in line with other gaps reviewed so far for 2005. The required value for 2030 is 72. The transition path from the actual 2005 to the required value for 2030 over a period of 25 years implies an annual change in the index of 3.6%. This adjustment growth rate is lower than the adjustments required in mainstream educational variables, suggesting that it may be easier to cope with broader conditions of development sustainability than with education.

(III) Greater global orientation: In all select countries, and in the world at large, economies become more outward-oriented with more economic development over time. Capturing this process in an analytically operational way is not easy. The indicators of foreign direct investment FDI as % of GDP and foreign merchandise trade FMT as % of GDP are often used to indicate the degree of outward orientation of the economy. The regressing of the FDI/GDP indicator for the select countries did not deliver reportable results. The results for FMT/GDP were better but not fully satisfactory, see Figure A3 in the appendix. A tested equation gave the following rather weak results.

$$(FMT/GDP)\% = 23.65 + 2.3684\ GDPpc \qquad R^2 = 0.69 \quad (17)$$

The required value following the tested estimates should be 26% in 2005 and rise to 33% in 2030. Ethiopia is ahead of the norm path regarding outward orientation, having an actual *FMT/GDP* in 2005 of 44%. This can be seen as a positive sign. But it can be also judged as an imbalance that feeds and maintains other imbalances such as the backlog regarding income disparities discussed in the following. Given the weak estimates, more refined analysis may be needed to validate the above assertions.

(IV) Restraints in income disparities: It is generally established that reductions in regional disparities and strengthened processes of national integration and political stability are essential for sustainable development. This is manifested in the select countries and the world at large. Taking the select countries as the norm, an equation was tested that regresses an equality indicator to GDP per capita. The equality indicator is the income share of the richest 20% of the population divided by the income share of the poorest 20% of the population. A value of 1 is total equality, and a higher value indicates inequality degrees. The fitted equation is a sort of Kuznet curve. As generally acknowledged, it takes the shape of an S-curve: there is a tendency for inequality to increase during take-off, followed by more equality in the middle range, and more inequality in the highest range; see Figure A4 in the appendix.

$$\text{Equality index} = 0.008\ \text{GDP}pc^3 - 0.327\ \text{GDP}pc^2 + 3.3891\ \text{GDP}pc - 0.6896 \qquad R^2 = 0.61\ (18)$$

The expected value of the equality index for Ethiopia in 2005 is 2.2, while the actual value for 2000 was 4.3, almost double.[14] The roadmap approach suggests that there are established grounds for reducing current inequalities should the profile of the select countries be consistently followed.

Following the anticipated path of the select countries the implications for Ethiopia, drawn in Figure 3, indicate a combination of backlogs in the demographic transition, industrialization pace, and income equality, with a better than the expected outward orientation of the economy. Though tentative, the results suggest that some adjustments may be required on all four fronts and especially

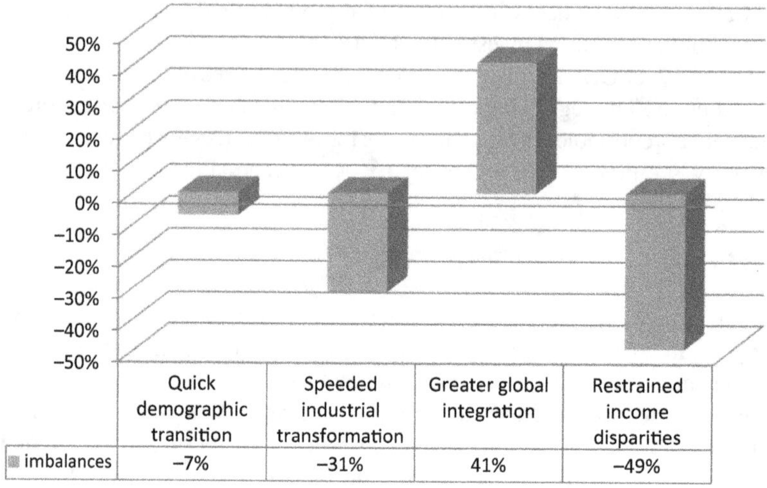

Figure 3. HRD Roadmap and anticipated imbalances elsewhere.

industrial transformation and reduction of income disparities to resolve possible contradictions between them, and to lead the socio-economy along the norm path.

8. Summary and Conclusions

Lifting human resource development, HRD, in Ethiopia to appreciable levels comparable with middle-level countries would take more than a couple of decades. A roadmap model toward that end can only be specified, and estimated by making judgmental use of the experience of selected countries that are known to have performed better in HRD, and whose realized structure of the education sector can be projected backward so as to apply to Ethiopia. Several selection criteria emphasizing the highest HRD performance produced in 10 select countries. A model was subsequently formulated for planning basic parameters of the educational system such as enrolments, teachers, recurrent and capital costs, and the breakup of finance into government and private resources. This was done for the primary, secondary and tertiary levels, with some detail about general and technical education. When applied to Ethiopia, the results show for benchmark year 2005 that while the total expenditure on education as a proportion of the GDP is about 6.5% for both the actual and expected, and is thus well balanced; nevertheless, significant shortfalls in the subdivisions of the educational system occur; reaching an average gap of 28% from the roadmap norms. Ethiopia's high population growth explains the gaps for a part, but also the pursued policy for universal primary education and the very costly unit costs at all levels in relative terms (read a too high salary per teacher in relation to GDP per capita) are major causes of the gaps. These obstacles cause imbalances elsewhere in the education system resulting in shortfalls toward reaching the enrolment norms in secondary and tertiary levels, as well as the required teachers.

The official plan for 2015 was simulated. If realized, the average summed gaps would fall significantly from the high level of 28% in 2005 to 12% in 2015. A simulation of a 10% less population for 2015 diminishes the average summed gap to only 3%. This is not feasible, however. A policy shift of focus to secondary and higher education and a relative reduction in the current cost per pupil are essential to get Ethiopia's HRD in line with the roadmap.

Other features of the roadmap model that can be highlighted are the ability of the model to stylize the optimal distribution of educational expenditure government and non-government sources, for the whole sector as well as to the three levels separately, and the proposed flexibility for closing the gaps by taking the whole period 2005–2030 as one of a gradual and flexible transition toward the roadmap destinations. Since ultimately any transformations along the lines of the roadmap must take place in the regions and regional conditions are known to vary significantly, it was necessary to formulate and apply an Index of Regional Index of Educational Development to identify which regions are closest to the roadmap profile, and which are most distanced, and would thus require a greater effort to align them with the roadmap profile.

Finally, the educational sector is part of a whole socio-politico-economic system. There are qualitative and non-educational economic aspects that have been critical for the socio-economic development of the select group. Following the norm path of the select countries, Ethiopia is shown to have a combination of backlogs in the demographic transition, industrialization pace, and income equality, with a better-than-expected outward orientation of the economy. Adjustments are required on most of these fronts to bring the country's development in line with the profile of the select countries.

Appendix

Table A1. Estimated equations and detailed assessment of estimated variables.

Eq.	Dependent variable	Estimated equation
(1)	*Gross enrolment ratio*	$GER_e = \alpha_{1,e} + \beta_{1,e}\ GDPpc$
	Primary	$GER_1 = 77.5 + .0075\ GDPpc$
	Secondary	$GER_2 = 44.4 + 19.47\ Ln\ GDPpc$
	Tertiary	$GER_3 = 0.9 + 4.57\ GDPpc$
(3)	*Student/teacher ratio*	$STR_e = \alpha_{3,e} + \beta_{3,e}\ GDPpc$
	Primary	$STR_1 = 29.7 - 6.16\ Ln\ GDPpc$
	Secondary	$STR_2 = 34.6 - 5.99\ Ln\ GDPpc$
	Tertiary	$STR_3 = 27.3 - 6.10\ Ln\ GDPpc$
(5)	*Recurrent cost per student/GDPpc*	$RCS_e = \alpha_{5,e} + \beta_{5,e}\ GDPpc$
	Primary	$RCS_1 = 0.1029 + 0.0045\ GDPpc$
	Secondary	$RCS_2 = .2481 + .0208\ GDPpc$
	Tertiary	$RCS_3 = 3.7005\ GDPpc^{-0.7394}$
(7)	*Capital/recurrent cost ratio*	$KRC = -0.0122 + 0.0509\ GDPpc - 0.0024\ GDPpc^2$
(8)	*Share gov exp in GDP*	$GTS/GDP = \alpha_8 + \beta_8\ GDPpc$
(9)	*Share gov edc exp*	$GTE/GTS = 15.15 - 1.2863\ GDPpc + 0.1326\ GDPpc^2 - .0035\ GDPpc^3$
(11)	*Share gov recurrent expenditure on education*	$GRE_e/GRE = \alpha_{11,e} + \beta_{11,e}\ GDPpc$
	Share primary education	$GRE_1/GRE = 0.3306 + 0.0087\ GDPpc$
	Share secondary education	$GRE_2/GRE = 0.2689 + 0.0088\ GDPpc$
	Share tertiary education	$GRE_3/GRE = 0.1967 + 0.0101\ GDPpc$

Table A2. Roadmap transition paths. See abbreviations in footnote.

Actual		Roadmap transition path			Destination	An.gr. %
2005	Variable	2015	2020	2025	2030	2005–30
	Primary education					
0.86	*Gross enrolment ratio*	0.91	0.94	0.97	1	0.61
12.66	Enrolments millions	17.448	19.642	21.933	24.272	2.64
62	*Student/teacher ratio*	40.34	32.45	26.10	21	-4.26
203.0	Teachers, thousands	432.5	605.2	840.2	1155.8	7.21
0.154	*Rcrnt cost ps / GDP pc*	0.14	0.132	0.126	0.120	-0.99
176	Rcrnt cost ps B	259.7	322.9	411.2	536.4	4.56
2228	Rcrnt exp Bm	4531	6343	9019	13019	7.32
	Secondary education					
0.19	*Gross enrolment ratio*	0.33	0.423	0.548	0.71	5.32
1.314	Enrolments millions	2.807	4.089	5.910	8.465	7.74
49	*Student/teacher ratio*	38.51	34.21	30.39	27	-2.34
269.3	Teachers, thousands	72.9	119.5	194.5	313.5	10.32
0.484	*Rcrnt cost psB / GDPpcB*	0.41	0.38	0.35	0.326	-1.55
554	Rcrnt cost ps B, cnst pr	772.0	933.2	1155.0	1457.2	3.95
728	Rcrnt exp Bm	2167	3816	6826	12335	12.00
	Tertiary education					
0.031	*Gross enrolment ratio*	0.06	0.09	0.13	0.18	7.30
0.1739	Enrolments millions	0.450	0.719	1.141	1.794	9.79
36	*Student/teacher ratio*	27.82	24.5	21.6	19	-2.51
.0048	Teachers, thousands	16161	29350	52876	.094	12.61
4.987	*Rcrnt cost psB/ GDP pcB*	3.08	2.4	1.9	1.5	-4.70
5705	Rcrnt cost psB, cns prc	5747	5904	6210	6705	0.63
992	Rcrnt exp Bm	2584	4245	7085	12026	10.50
	All educational levels					
3948	Rcr exp edc Bm	9282	14404	22929	37380	9.41
‘1302	Cpt exp edc Bm	2206	2905	3924	5420	4.16
5250	Rcr + capital exp edc Bm	11488	17309	26853	42800	8.75
0.33	*Ratio cpt /rcr exp edc*	0.24	0.202	0.171	0.145	-3.23
	Government spending					
4718	Gvr exp edc Bm, *of which*	8016	10485	13931	18841	3.48
3539	Gvr rcr exp edc Bm	6477	8725	11895	16455	4.11
2089	Gvr rcr exp prm edc Bm	3138	3829	4728	5924	2.08
625	Gvr rcr exp scd edc Bm	1412	2114	3202	4937	6.34
571	Gvr rcr exp trt edc Bm	1042	1401	1908	2633	4.08
253	Gvr other exp edc Bm	885	1381	2058	2962	8.03
0.59	*Share gvr rcr exp prm edc*	0.48	0.439	0.397	0.36	-1.96
0.18	*Share gvr rcr exp scd edc*	0.22	0.242	0.269	0.30	2.13
0.16	*Share gvr rcr exp trt edc*	0.16	0.161	0.160	0.16	-0.03
0.07	*Share gvr other exp edc*	0.14	0.16	0.17	0.18	3.76
26211	Gvr total exp Bm	52436	74417	107295	157010	5.17
0.18	*Share gvr exp edc/gvr exp*	0.15	0.141	0.130	0.120	-1.62
	Non-government spending					
881	Ngv exp edc Bm, *of which*	3784	8484	15332	27334	15.69
138	Ngv rcr exp prm edc Bm	1393	2515	4291	7090	18.44
103	Ngv rcr exp scd edc Bm	755	1702	3623	7394	19.82
421	Ngv rcr exp trt edc Bm	1542	2844	5177	9389	13.72
662	Ngv rcr exp all ed Bm	3690	7060	13091	23872	16.38
219	Ngv other exp edc Bm	94	1424	2241	3462	
	Related spending indicators					
5599	Gvr+Ngv exp edc Bm	12859	18969	29263	46175	8.67
.84	*Share gvr financing edc*	0.68	0.55	0.48	0.41	.84
.16	*Share ngv financing edc*	0.32	0.45	0.52	0.59	.16
0.31	*Ratio gvr total exp /GDP*	0.30	0.291	0.286	0.28	-0.41
0.0558	*Ratio gvr exp edc/GDP*	0.0455	0.0411	0.0371	0.0336	
0.0104	*Ratio ngv exp edc/GDP*	0.0215	0.0332	0.0408	0.0487	
0.0662	*(gvr+ ngv exp edc)/GDP*	0.0670	0.0743	0.0779	0.0823	

Abbreviations: Cost per student = cost ps. GDP per capita= GDP pc. Currency Birr=B. Birr million=Bm. Constant prices=cns prc. Recurrent=rcr. Capital=cpt. Expenditure=exp. Government=gvr. Non-government=ngv. Primary=prm. Secondary=scd. Tertiary=trt. Education=edc.

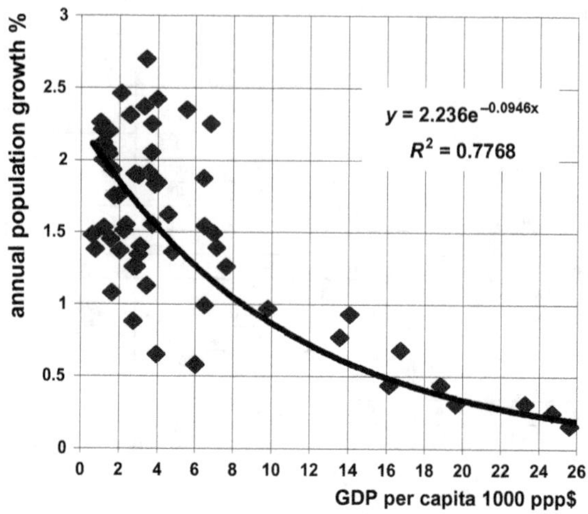

Figure A1. Equation (15). Y = Periodical Annual Population Growth,%.

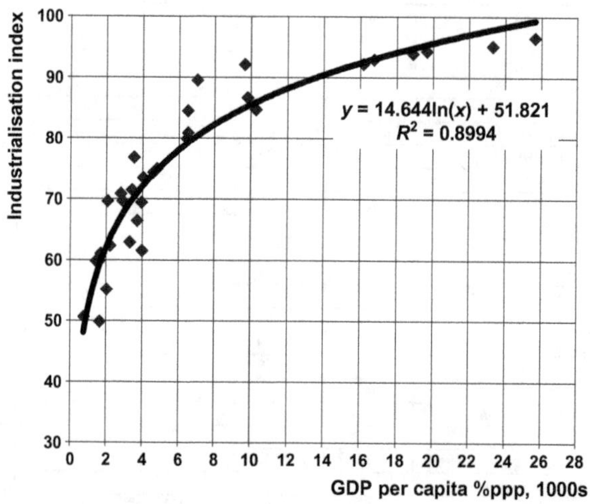

Figure A2. Equation (16). Y = Industrialization Index.

Notes: Average annual population growth for 5-year periods 1975–1980 and so on up to 2005–2010 is from UN http://www.un.org/esa/population/publications. These are regressed against GDPpc for the initial years of 5-year periods, i.e. 1975, and so on until 2005. Russia is excluded, having had a different demographic transition much earlier in the 20th century.

The industrialization index is the average share of the population in non-agriculture and the share of GDP in non-agriculture.

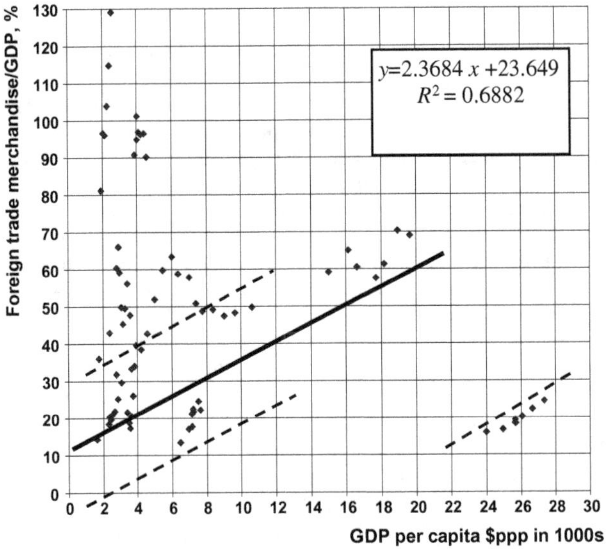

Figure A3. Equation (17). Y = Foreign merchandise trade FMT/GDP, %.

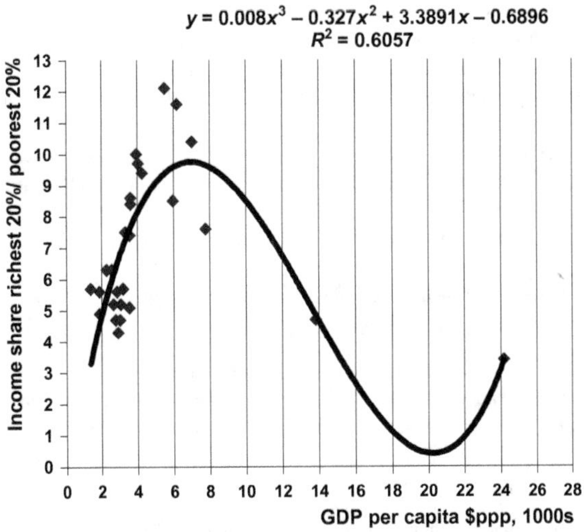

Figure A4. Equation (18). Y = Income shares of richest 20%/poorest 20%.

Notes: *FMT/GDP* as % is for years in 1991–2005. Outliers outside the range indicated by dashed lines are left out. For the income disparity indicator, Brazil is left out as an outlier, having about the highest income inequality in the world.

Endnotes

1. Correa, H. and Tinbergen, J. (1962). Later published, with other contributions on human resource development, as Tinbergen, J. (1965).
2. HDI is an equally weighted index of indicators of health (life expectancy) and education (adult literacy rate and combined primary and secondary enrolment ratios).
3. It is understandable that the selection resulted in the absence of sub-Saharan African countries in view of the subperformance of the region. Even though South Africa has a relatively advanced educational state, the progress in the HDI is significantly behind that of the index of GDP per capita, −22 points in 2004; the HDI ranking has deteriorated, and GDP growth is moderate.
4. This is consistent with conventional decision-making that is based on first knowing the size of the government spending budget on all sectors, *GTS*, and second, there is the decision as to that part of the budget that will be expended on the education sector, *GTE*.
5. The percentage distribution of age groups 7–14 and 15–18 for 2005 and 2015 is derived from the Ten-Year Education Sector Plan 2006/2007–2015/2016, backed by the simulation model of enrolments and other educational variables at the MOE planning department. As no data are classified for the age group 19–22, this is taken as 4/5th of age group 20–24, for which data are available. For 2030, and due to the projected diminished growth rate of the population, the share of the 7–14 age group is projected to decrease between 2015 and 2030 by about 4.5%. The shares of the age groups 15–18 and 19–22 are assumed to increase by the same margin of 4.5%. Population projections to 2015 are as in the plan. For later years, we apply UN/Ethiopia projected average annual growth for consecutive periods of 5 years. The annual growth rates behind the projections are 3.2, 2.6, 2.3, 2.08, 1.92, and 1.72 for the periods 2000–2005, 2005–2010, 2010–2015, 2015–2020, 2020–2025, and 2025–2030, respectively.
6. Note that $965 is the GDP per capita in $ppp in 2005, in constant prices of 2000. This is different that the GDP per capita in US dollars in 2005 in the current prices of 2005. While not relevant for the analysis here, this later figure amounted to $ 150 only. The difference between the two figures lie in expressing the GDP per capita in $ppp and in constant prices dating back to 5 years earlier.
7. The deflation index to convert 2005 Birr back to 2000 is 0.8585, from WB/Development Indicators database.
8. The problem is acknowledged by authorities as reflected in documented policies that aim to bring the ratio of teacher salary to GDP per capita across all education toward four times from its current levels of six to eight times.
9. The ratio of non-academic to academic staff in Ethiopia is 2:1; this is 3:1 in African countries, ESDP III, p. 20.
10. The regression gave the following weak results for the equation.

    $$GBR = 0.074\ GDPpc + 0.7012; \quad Gbps = 1.0\ for\ GDPpc > 4; \qquad R^2 = 0.63$$

11. The magnitude of the backlog can be measured from eq. (16), which relates the adult literacy rate, ALR, to GDPpc. The tendencies show a 100% adult literacy at GDPpc at $ppp of 8000 and above. For the observation period 1991–2005, Korea, Japan, and Russia had 100% throughout and are thus left out.

    $$ALR = 21.615\ Ln\ GDPpc + 54.746 \qquad R^2 = 0.69$$

12. The LFS of 2001 shows the unemployment rate for first time entrants in the labor force to jump from 1.6% for entrants with no schooling to 6.9% for primary graduates, 30.6% for secondary graduates, and 9.1% for tertiary graduates, reflecting interactions between search time and job opportunities. For workers of all ages, the unemployment rates take a more balanced profile at 3.7%, 5.7%, 19.9%, and 7.1% for the four educational levels, respectively. In 2001, the unemployment rate for all ages was 5.2%. In 2005, this was 5.0%, with about the same educational distribution.

13. For example, shortages in ICT skills have been compensated by salary adjustments upward for ICT graduates by up to 20% above non-ICT graduates with equivalent years of education. The variations in the salary scales are rich sources of information that can be fruitfully used in programing education and training activities and in resolving LM mismatches by stimulating graduates to pursue the more demanded jobs/training types.
14. The height of income disparity can be also gathered from the 6 to 10 times discrepancy between average teacher salaries and the GDP per capita, discussed earlier in the roadmap projections.

Chapter 20

A Survey Analysis of Generational Mobility: Pakistan

1. Introduction

Socio-economic development causes important changes in the socio-economic position of people within one generation and between generations. While studies of upward and downward mobility of human resources and the factors which are involved in these processes are available for advanced countries, there is generally an information gap and an absence of analytical frameworks regarding changes in socio-economic profiles and mobility trends in developing countries.

This chapter reports on a partial attempt to fill this lacuna, making use of conventional analytical methods applied to survey data as can be found in Ellis *et al.* (2018), among others. A specially designed questionnaire has been applied with the purpose of describing the changing socio-economic positions in the modern segment of Pakistan over different generations and their association with their endowments of social, human, and physical capital and other socio-economic characteristics. The assessment of the nature of mobility trends would make it possible to identify the processes through which different socio-economic groups attempt to improve their positions in a changing society.

The chapter is organized as follows. Section 2 describes the data set of the field inquiry undertaken in 1986. Section 3 gives the socio-economic profiles for two generations of "sons" and "fathers". Sections 4 and 5 outline a framework which takes into account two forms of mobility and reflect on the empirical findings. Section 6 comments on additional results. Section 7 concludes.

2. Data Sets and Descriptive Profile

The purpose of the study is not to assess the magnitudes of socio-economic mobility in Pakistan, a complex society with a highly diversified population of about

96 million in 1986 (and counting 230 million in 2022). Instead, the interest lies more in studying the nature and shape of the transformation processes among those who have a high potential of being transformed. Especially in a country like Pakistan, which is experiencing a gradual transition from a traditional agrarian society to a modern industrialized and service-oriented society, it is inviting to select those pockets of the labor force where mobility and social change are expected to have gained momentum. These pockets are found among elder males in urban areas and wage and salary earners in the modern segment.

As such, the sample does not claim to represent Pakistan but rather its modern segments. In selecting the sample of respondents, we focused therefore on male individuals working in the wage sector, engaged in non-agricultural activities of the economy, and residing in 10 major industrialized city districts of Pakistan.

The *a priori* known distribution over the working status of the male urban working force in the ten city districts was used as an approximation for the distribution of the 1200 respondents in the sample. The benchmark data show that 55% of the male working population in urban areas is occupied in the wage sector, leaving 45% for the non-wage sector; see pages 40–41. The actually selected sample deviates slightly from the above proportions: 61% of the respondents fall in the wage sector and 39% in the non-wage sector. Their difference is too small to require weighting.

The survey was further directed at respondents who were older than 40 years of age, and they were interviewed at the places of their work. The reason for going for this age group was to make sure that the respondents could report on substantial changes during their careers and to allow for the possibility of having children of a mature age. As a consequence, the average age of the target group of the study is higher than applicable for urban males in Pakistan. This will be reflected in differences in characteristics regarding income, occupation, etc. between the target group of the study and the urban male population as a whole.

The study of long-term changes in major socio-economic profiles and of mobility trends among urban males over at least two, and preferably three generations, would require developing a questionnaire which links the personal characteristics, achievements, etc. of the urban male respondent of the present generation, to those of (a) the respondents' brothers who evidently belong to the same generation, (b) the respondent's father who belongs to a past generation, and (c) the respondents' children belonging to a forthcoming generation. The questionnaire, which was solely filled in by the respondent, included corresponding sections on the respondent, his brothers, his father, and his children.

In addition, to study the impact of marriage networks on the respondent's achievement, the questionnaire incorporated questions on the characteristics of the wife and the father-in-law. Besides, the questionnaire included questions of an attitudinal nature as well as questions on the respondent's desirable level of income, size of family, etc.

Table 1 gives the sample composition of the respondents and relatives by place and regions of birth and residence, working status, and occupational category. Sons (all respondents and their brothers taken together) originate for 39% from India, while their fathers originate for 53% from India. The rural–urban origin is in the ratio of 1 to 4 for sons and 1 to 3 for their fathers. It is also shown that sons and fathers have strikingly different patterns of status and occupation, representing important shifts toward a modernizing society. In particular, while the sons of the present generation consist relatively more of employers and employees in professional and managerial occupations, the elder generation of the fathers had relatively more self-employment and agricultural occupations.

It is interesting to observe that in comparing the fathers with sons, it appears that in several respects there is a progression in the position of sons by about 40%. A generational progress of 40% can be noted in Table 1 for the share of self-employment (38.8% versus 59.3%) and in Table 2 for the number of educational years (9 for fathers and 13 for responding sons), monthly income (Rs. 4400 versus Rs. 6200), and value of the house owned (about Rs. 227,000 versus Rs. 327,000). However, possession of agricultural land becomes a lower priority among sons than fathers, and the average size of land owned is reduced to 4.2 acres from 9.2 acres. As can be expected, there is a reduction in the family size among responding sons as compared to fathers (number of children 4.6 as compared to 5.8).

Furthermore, only 26.3% of responding sons have performed Umra/Haj as compared to 43.7% among their fathers. Finally, the occurrence of high-positioned relatives has significantly increased in the present generation. Counting the difference in average age between son and father, the period in which the above changes have taken place is 24 years.

Similar tendencies exist if respondents are compared to their brothers indicating that the sample of respondents succeeds in securing more representation from the more mobile segments of the population. For instance, the average age of respondents is somewhat higher than that of the average son (49 compared to 46 years, columns 1 and 3 in Table 2). The average education is slightly higher (13 compared to 12 years of education). The average income of respondents from the main job is higher: Rs. 6199 as compared to Rs. 5814 for the average son. The same applies to income and wealth by other specifications. Older in age, with likely relatively more inherited properties, more years of education, and more modern occupations, the respondents are on average better off than their brothers. This edge associates with networks of positioned relatives which are more advantageous to respondents than to their brothers, cf. row 14 and 15. Respondents appear to be

Table 1. Sample composition of respondents and related persons.

Profile characteristic	Respondents %	Sons (a)%	Fathers (b)%
Province/Region of Present Residence			
Baluchistan	4.3	2.7	2.5
N.W.F.P.	12.5	11.7	13.6
Punjab	49.9	48.1	48.7
Sind	33.4	30.5	25.8
India	na	1.4	8.1
Other Countries	na	5.6	1.3
Number of Valid Cases	1199	3714	1192
Province/Region of Birth			
Baluchistan	2.9	2.9	2.1
N.W.F.P.	13.7	12.8	13.6
Punjab	32.8	36.3	25.1
Sind	6.3	7.7	4.9
India	42.9	38.9	53.1
Other Countries	1.4	1.4	1.3
Number of Valid Cases	1198	3713	1195
Place of Birth			
Rural	19.3	19.8	24.3
Urban	80.7	80.2	75.7
Number of Valid Cases	1199	3720	1190
Working Status			
Employer	16.3	9.4	6.3
Employee (Government)	27.8	27.1	24.7
Employee (Private)	17.2	19.0	8.8
Self-employed	38.8	42.0	59.3
Unpaid Family Worker	na	1.2	0.1
Unemployed	na	1.4	0.8
Number of Valid Cases	1192	3696	1183
Occupational category			
Professional Technical	11.2	9.6	4.0
Professional Non-technical	9.3	8.3	6.7
Managerial	29.3	17.5	6.8
Clerical	10.0	12.8	15.8
Sales	14.3	21.4	22.7
Services	2.8	2.2	2.5
Agricultural	0.3	4.7	18.6
Production Workers	22.8	21.4	20.4
Army	0	1.5	2.5
Number of Valid Cases	1196	3696	1169

Note: na = not appliable. (a) Includes respondents and their brothers. (b) The questionnaire distinguishes between fathers who are alive and deceased. The profile data on fathers represent the latest state reached by the father of which the respondent has knowledge. If the father is deceased, then it is the state prior to his death which is reported.

Table 2. Profile of respondents and profiles of sons and fathers.

Characteristics	Respondents		Sons		Fathers	
	Mean	SD	Mean	SD	Mean	SD
Age	49	8	46	10	73	9
Education attained (years)	13	5	12	5	9	7
Income from main job (Rs.)	6199	7504	5814	8222	4402	8476
Income from other sources (Rs)	567	2745	325	2690	296	1597
Income from family transfers (Rs.)	338	3292	216	2282	211	802
Value of house owned (000 Rs.)	327	766	294	1146	227	452
Land owned (acres)	4.2	26.4	3.7	28.4	9.2	30.1
Value of land owned (000 Rs.)	122	777	119	877	310	1102
Plot owned (yards)	58	446	40	324	10	116
Value of plot owned (000 Rs.)	29	292	16	183	15	222
Worked abroad (%)	13.50	na	13.60	na	3.10	na
No. of years worked abroad	0.48	1.91	0.81	3.07	0.52	4.10
Performed umra/haj (%)	26.30	na	20.60	na	43.70	na
No. of high-positioned relatives	0.81	1.26	0.67	1.15	0.57	1.13
Percentage having high-positioned relatives	43.60	na	36.80	na	20.80	na
No. of children	4.63	2.35	3.91	2.54	5.83	2.41

Note: na = not applicable.

more religious than their brothers, cf. row 13, and internationally less mobile, cf. row 12.

3. Changing Patterns of Correlations between Generations

The changing pattern over time of the interrelationships between socio-economic characteristics can be studied by comparing matrices of Pearson correlation coefficients among the characteristics for the past and the present generation. Correlation matrices for "fathers" and for "all sons" — combining respondents and brothers together — are presented in the upper and lower blocks of Table 3, respectively. Six characteristics are considered, namely value of wealth, total factor income, age, years of education, years worked abroad and the number of relatives in high positions as an indicator of the network.

One can observe positive correlations between education, network, and income. These characteristics, which relate in different ways to performance in the labor market, correlate significantly at acceptable levels in the case of the sons. Also, regarding the level of wealth, the above characteristics (except education) show significant correlations in the case of the sons. However, these correlations are less pronounced among the generation of the fathers. It is interesting to note also that the increased availability of educational institutes in Pakistan over time has led to

Table 3. Pearson's correlation coefficients for characteristics of living fathers and their sons.

Characteristics	Wealth	Income	Age	Education	Worked Abroad	Network
Fathers						
1. Wealth	1.000	0.192	0.120	0.060	−0.019	0.054
2. Income		1.000	0.062	0.064	0.216	0.059
3. Age			1.000	−0.143	0.046	−0.096
4. Education				1.000	0.008	0.157
5. Worked Abroad					1.000	−0.027
6. Network						1.000
Sons						
1. Wealth	1.000	0.349	0.168	0.087	0.095	0.246
2. Income		1.000	0.043	0.123	0.274	0.174
3. Age			1.000	−0.023	0.004	0.089
4. Education				1.000	0.064	0.170
5. Worked Abroad					1.000	0.101
6. Network						1.000

a positive correction in the correlation between age and education in the case of sons, whereas they are negatively associated in the case of the fathers.

The higher correlations of profile characteristics obtained for the sons are in contrast to the weaker correlation for the fathers. This may be the result of the formation of more coherent profile patterns in the process of socio-economic development. Personal characteristics seem to be more associated with each other now than some 24 years ago. Of course, the reported data on fathers is bound to be less reliable than for sons and this may explain partly why the correlations for fathers are less than for sons.

4. Intergenerational Mobility

In the analysis of mobility, a distinction can be made between (a) intergenerational mobility and (b) intragenerational mobility. In the case of intergenerational mobility, the focus of analysis is on mobility between the past and the present generations, while in the case of intragenerational mobility, it is the mobility of persons within one and the same generation that constitutes the object of study.

Furthermore, mobility is determined by two mechanisms: (i) the transmission of tastes, preferences, and socio-economic positions within the family — the internal environment, and (ii) the influence of the socio-economic development — the external environment. These two mechanisms are, to a large extent, interconnected. $INTER_{ij}$ defines intergenerational mobility in terms of the family unit. Defining mobility in terms of all sons and all fathers, irrespective of the family to which sons and fathers belong, is a less attractive alternative which may hide other efforts.

$$INTER_{ij} = C_{ij}/C_{kj} \qquad (1)$$

where C stands for a characteristic of mobility, i for the son from the present generation, and k for the father from the past generation, all belonging to the same family j.

The ratio measures the mobility of an individual (son) of the present generation compared with that of his father. Upward (positive) mobility is observed when the values of the indicators are above 1 and downward (negative) mobility is indicated when the values of the indicators are below 1.

$INTER_{ij}$ can be estimated for alternative characteristics of an individual, important among which could be income and wealth, or ranks of occupation, working status, and favored places of residence of a person. But not all of the latter characteristics can be easily expressed in acceptable standardized units and made comparable with some degree of accuracy. Income and wealth are perhaps the only two characteristics, in the present context, which can easily be made comparable across individuals over time and space. Therefore, the analysis will be limited to these two characteristics.

Experience has shown that the respondent is not reluctant to provide information on the accumulated wealth in terms of land, houses, and plots (residential and commercial). This information has been used to construct total wealth. The income of an individual was estimated by totaling the income from his main job as well as from other jobs and from properties.

The analysis of intergenerational mobility is done in four parts. First, the results are presented relating to the magnitude and incidence of mobility as regards wealth and income criteria separately. Second, we study the relationship of mobility indicators with socio-economic characteristics. This exercise, while complementing some of the earlier analyses, should bring sharply into focus those variables which have played a key role in intergenerational mobility in the target group. Third, the incidence of upward mobility by places of birth and residence, working status, and occupations is considered. Fourth, transition probabilities are estimated and applied to generate future generational patterns.

Table 4 presents magnitudes of the mean *INTER* across families as well as estimates of the occurrence of income and wealth mobility. As regards the averages, the estimates show that the individual sons have about 4 times as much income as their fathers, which is partly due to a different rate of accumulation of real wealth but is also partly due to inflationary effects. In the case of wealth, sons hold about 84 times as much wealth as their fathers. Wealth redistribution over generations is far more skewed than income distribution.

As regards the incidence of intergenerational mobility, Table 5 indicates that, using the wealth criterion, 31% of the sons have done better than their fathers. It has also been found, but not shown here, that in 56% of the cases, wealth ratios were

Table 4. Magnitudes of intergenerational mobility indicators of wealth and income and of the incidence of upward mobility.

	$INTER_{ij}$ wealth	$INTER_{ij}$ income
Mean	83.72	4.15
Standard deviation	281.10	7.16
Number of incidences of upward mobility/total sample	1010/3258	601/1003
Percentage upward mobility	31	60

Table 5. Coefficients of correlation between intergenerational mobility indicators of wealth and income and characteristics of fathers who are alive and those of their sons.

	INTER wealth		*INTER* income	
Characteristics	Father	Sons	Father	Sons
1. Income	0.092	0.092	0.100	0.100
2. Age	0.095	0.200	0.128	0.102
3. Education	0.100	0.038	0.108	0.003
4. Years worked abroad	−0.035	0.045	−0.058	0.177
5. Social network	0.037	0.109	0.007	−0.038

equal to zero. Therefore, the number of low cases of wealth mobility can be partly explained by the fact that there was a large percentage of sons who did not have any wealth at all. However, using the income criterion, the incidence of upward mobility reaches 60%.

These results should be interpreted in the light of the fact that in the present generation, not many people accumulate wealth in the same forms as the past generation did. Furthermore, since age was observed to be one of the most important factors associated with wealth, it can be expected that sons of a lesser age than their fathers have still many years to go in the future to accumulate wealth.

Table 5 presents coefficients of correlation between mobility indicators for wealth and income and different characteristics of fathers and sons. In almost every situation, the ages of fathers and sons appear to be very closely associated with intergenerational mobility. The ages of these two types were also observed to be closely associated with their absolute income and wealth. In the present context, these results may imply that as the population ages in Pakistan, the income and wealth mobility of the present generation may also go up.

It is also evident that the fathers' characteristics in terms of education exert an influence on the income and wealth mobility of sons in a significant and coherent pattern. In addition, it should be mentioned that sons' network also exerts a significant positive influence on wealth mobility. One could also note that the number of years worked abroad correlates positively with their income mobility.

Next, the incidences of wealth and income mobility are disaggregated by two selected characteristics of fathers and sons: status and occupation. Whether one takes the wealth or income, in both cases, one observes that there is a transition from *traditional* activities to the *modern* ones in Pakistan. For example in Table 6 in the case of working status one finds that there were 566 sons whose fathers were self-employed but there are only 393 sons who had that working status. This fact reflects the tendency of sons to become either an employer or an employee in the private and public sectors rather than becoming self-employed. In the case of occupational patterns, there is a tendency among sons to adopt technical and managerial lines and leave agricultural and clerical jobs.

Table 6. Incidence of intergenerational upward wealth mobility INTER defined for wealth and for income, by working status and occupations of fathers who are alive and their sons.

	$INTER_{ij}$ wealth		$INTER_{ij}$ income	
	Fathers	Sons	Fathers	Sons
Working status				
1. Employer	22	39	35	54
	(67)	(77)	(46)	(95)
2. Government employee	32	22	81	56
	(262)	(265)	(179)	(179)
3. Private employee	31	31	67	69
	(83)	(240)	(124)	(153)
4. Self-employed	29	37	50	58
	(566)	(393)	(310)	(214)
Occupational categories				
1. Professional technical	30	32	56	67
	(53)	(112)	(79)	(72)
2. Professional non-technical	22	22	43	63
	(72)	(98)	(46)	(68)
3. Managerial	44	38	42	66
	(77)	(162)	(45)	(104)
4. Clerical	33	18	78	52
	(176)	(110)	(132)	(77)
5. Sales	38	34	54	45
	(175)	(202)	(91)	(103)
6. Services	6	31	83	54
	(16)	(60)	(89)	(67)
7. Agricultural	17	2	47	35
	(222)	(44)	(130)	(61)
8. Production workers	39	39	63	79
	(201)	(217)	(95)	(118)
9. Army	23	12	91	70
	(26)	(16)	(113)	(80)

Notes: Figures in brackets are total number of cases having both downward and upward mobility in a particular category. These figures may not add up to the "total" as some of the cases (unpaid family workers/unemployed) have been ignored being too few.

Reflecting on wealth mobility by status, it is noted that sons whose fathers are employers have the lowest incidence of mobility as compared to other working statuses. This was somewhat expected as the employer father had on average more wealth than the non-employer fathers. On the other hand, one observes the highest incidence of mobility for sons who themselves are employers. An interesting case is that of sons whose fathers are government employees *vis-à-vis* those sons who themselves have the same status. The former category has had greater mobility (33%) compared to 22% of the latter. This decline is the result of the transition of 41% of sons with fathers in the self-employed status (in particular farmers) to the government employee status. Fathers in the self-employed farmer category had relatively more wealth than fathers who were government employees. Hence, we observe less wealth mobility among the farmers' sons. On the other hand, fathers who are government employees are likely to have a strong social network to place their sons in good positions.

As regards wealth mobility by occupation it is highest when either fathers or sons were in managerial positions and lowest for sons in agriculture. The latter is understandable, but the former represents a somewhat complicated case. This could indicate that sons of fathers in managerial positions performed on average better than their fathers in terms of wealth. One may conclude from this that not only the fathers' position was transferred to sons but also some more and better opportunities were available to sons of managerial fathers. Moreover, it is interesting to note that both in the case of clerical and army occupations, the incidence of wealth mobility decreases from fathers to sons. In both cases, this pattern occurs for sons whose fathers were in agriculture and where the sons took jobs in the army or as clerks.

Except for the higher incidence of mobility, the results based on income mobility present more or less the same picture which was observed when the estimates are based on wealth mobility.

As to geographical characteristics, not shown here, it was found that the better-ranked fathers and sons seem to play a significant role in sons' wealth mobility. The results indicate that those sons whose fathers, or who themselves, originated from Punjab, Sind, and India stood greater chances of gaining wealth mobility. Furthermore, the better-ranked places of residence are associate positively with income mobility in the cases of sons suggesting that sons living at present in Punjab, Sind, and abroad have a relatively high chance of surpassing their fathers in incomes.

Finally, intergenerational mobility can be modeled as a Markov chain. From the survey data, a square matrix of transitional probabilities for status (and for occupations) can be defined such that P_{ik} is the probability that in any time period, an individual will transfer from state k into state i. Given an initial column vector X^0, the next period's column vector X^1 is obtainable as follows:

$$X^1 = PX^0 \tag{2}$$

Table 7. Matrix of transitional probabilities.

Fathers/Sons	1. Employer	2. Gvrn emplyd	3. Prvt emplyd	4. Self-emplyd	5. Unpaid fmlynwrk	6. Unemplyd	Total	Stable share after 7 runs
1. Emplyr	0.441	0.062	0.037	0.046	0.033	0.042	0.068	0.087
2. Gov. emplyd	0.279	0.411	0.309	0.193	0	0.292	0.260	0.295
3. Prvt. emplyd	0.191	0.307	0.395	0.184	0	0.375	0.081	0.278
4. Self-emplyd	0.074	0.204	0.247	0.539	0.667	0.208	0.564	0.319
5. Unpaid fw	0	0.004	0.012	0.034	0	0	0.003	0.015
6. Unemplyd	0.015	0.012	0	0.004	0	0.083	0.024	0.007

Table 7 gives the matrix of transitional probabilities for different categories of working status. For example, the probability that a son of an employer may become an employer is 0.441, while that for a son of a self-employed to become an employer is only 0.046.

Application of eq. (2) to the initial working status of fathers subsequently for n times results in a stable equilibrium distribution of individuals over the status categories in period n. Table 7 gives this equilibrium distribution which is reached after 7 periods/generations. The largest shift occurs from the self-employed to employees in the private sector; as a result, the self-employed end up with a share of 32% (was 56%), while private employees end with 28% (was 8%), suggesting a tendency toward equivalent shares of public employees, private employees, and non-wage employment.

The transition with regard to occupations, if eq. (2) is applied to the relevant data on occupations from the survey, shows a sharp increase of technical and managerial occupations from the initial 10% to an equilibrium share of 31% in three periods/generations. The implications of the above for technical training are obvious.

5. Intragenerational Mobility

The questionnaire does not include details on the state of job, income, wealth, etc. of the individual on entry in the labor market, or on leaving school, say at age 15, and his attained state at the time of the questionnaire, some 25 years later. This impedes developing an effective indicator for intragenerational mobility. $INTRA_{ij}$ in eq. (3) is the ratio of the performance of everyone i in the family j regarding income C_{ij} (or wealth) to the average performance of all individuals (sons) in a family, C_j. Although $INTRA_{ij}$ is a measure of dispersion, it can be a helpful indicator for assessing the incidence of intragenerational mobility so far that an indication of higher income dispersion within a family can represent a breakthrough for one or

Table 8. Magnitudes of intragenerational mobility indicators of wealth and income and of the incidence of upward mobility.

	$INTRA_{ij}$ wealth	$INTRA_{ij}$ income
Mean	1.00	1.00
Standard deviation	0.877	0.603
Number of incidences of upward mobility/total sample	1194/3618	1196/3987
Percentage upward mobility	33	30

more members of the family.

$$INTRA_{ij} = C_{ij}/C_j \tag{3}$$

By definition, the mean of $INTRA_{ij}$ is 1.0, individuals with values above 1.0 are cases of upward mobility, and values below 1.0 indicate downward mobility. The standard deviation of a characteristic within the same family is also relevant and may also be derived from the above.

Table 8 displays the results. The incidences of upward wealth mobility indicate that about the same incidence of upward wealth mobility (33%) is observed between sons (i.e. intragenerational) as was observed in the previous section between fathers and sons (i.e. intergenerational). However, the upward incidence of income mobility between sons (i.e. 30%) is lower than that between fathers and sons as was previously found.

After having standardized the income and wealth standard deviation within families, it is noted that around 30% and 33% of the families in the sample show higher inequalities in income and wealth among sons respectively than the overall sample inequalities in income and wealth. This analysis of intragenerational mobility can be further supplemented by other indicators as was done in the previous section.

6. Attitudinal Responses

Besides studying the actual characteristics of different actors the survey also tried to capture the preferences and attitudes of the respondents. Comparing desirable with actually attained levels throws light on achievement motivations and mobility prospects.

For example, most respondents do not desire to move to other areas as the preferred areas of residence coincide largely with the present places of residence. Only 3% of the respondents expressed their desire to go abroad, of which 1.2% to USA/Canada, 0.8% to the Middle East, 0.6% to Europe, and 0.5% to other countries.

Regarding working status, the relationship between desirable to actual is more favorable for becoming an employer and less favorable for becoming a private or government employee. There were 25.8% of respondents who wanted to become employers (actual 16%), private employees 11% (actual 17%), and public employees 23% (actual 28%). As regards preferences for occupations, significant differences in the same directions were observed between the actual and desired occupations.

Turning to the desired level of income (Rs. 9458) and comparing it with the total amount of income from all sources, it can be calculated that the desired amount is 33% higher. The desired level of wealth (value of house, land, and residential plot) was observed to be Rs. 1,398,000 which is almost 3 times higher than the actual average. The respondents generally desired more education for their male children (15 years as opposed to 13 years actual), but the desired level for their female children was not well reported. The desired number of children is close to the actual observed.

About 80% of the respondents indicated having frequent (at least twice a month) contact with their parents, which points out that close family relations appear to be maintained in the changing society. Finally, most of the respondents believed that they have done at least as good in life as their brothers. Only 12.1% thought that they have performed poorly.

7. Concluding Remarks

The target group for the study of generational mobility was on purpose composed of modern-type families. These are likely to have experienced significant gains in socio-economic mobility in the recent past. Given the purpose, we surveyed elder males in the wage sector, engaged in non-agricultural activities and residing in urban areas. It is essential that we reiterate this bias to set the background for the following concluding remarks.

Besides producing otherwise very scarce information on socio-economic mobility in the context of developing countries, the survey reported upon here allowed (a) an analysis of intergenerational mobility, in particular, explanations of the underlying factors behind wealth and income mobility and forecasts of the future composition of the modern labor force in terms of status, occupation, residence, etc. via applying Markov chains, (b) description of basic trends in intragenerational mobility, and (c) a challenging analysis of attitudinal traits and desirable achievements which can be compared with attained levels and thus throws more light on the mobility prospects of the respective respondents.

Part VI

World Governance and International Development Policies

Chapter 21

The Shifting Economic Power of Countries and Regions

1. Introduction

In discussions in economic and political forums at the world level, there have been an increasing interest in and lengthy discussions on the prospective major shifts in the economic and political powers of leading countries in the world and their implications for world governance. This discussion took for granted two premises: that the magnitude of the GDP is the correct indicator of a country's global power and its rank in world leadership and that for running world affairs it is sufficient to focus on and consult within the few top leading countries with the highest GDP. These two premises formed the basis for consulting, finding solutions, and shaping contemporary world governance. The latest development in world governance is the establishment of the G-20, which is a form of political leaders of the 20 leading economies in the world; whereby qualification for inclusion in the top 20 is based on a county's rank in terms of the country's size of the GDP, though this is not literally updated and followed.

The discussion and the forwarded solutions are flawed in two major respects: One, there is obsession with the size of the GDP as the measure of economic and political influence potential, with no attention to the population factor which is very relevant in understanding global power and in managing world governance. Two, there is the obsession with focusing on individual countries as the unit of analysis in global issues, whereas world regions are more relevant for a better understanding and policy making.

On the first count, the GDP criterion is a poor indication of the influence potential of a particular country in the context of an interactive world of voluminous populations. Interactive influence is not only the result of the relative size of economic transformations but also the result of the relative size of the transforming populations. There is a need to develop and apply a dominance index that represents the influence potential of GDP and population in relative terms more effectively.

On the second count, pronouncing and pushing forward individual countries with the highest GDP as individual leading countries may not command global authority or fair legitimacy because such identification of individual leading countries does not consider regional power or regional representation. The G-20 approach ignores all the past progress made by mankind in defining constitutional democracy and representational rights. The world cannot be seen as a loose collection of individual countries. Any individual country is allied to other countries and is as such a member of an interest group that has common interests. Responsive actions to global failure would require global governance that is representative of regional and country interests. The division of the world into eight regions, which coincides with the practiced consensus in international organizations, is our answer in this paper to the representation problem.

This chapter defines the problems of global power and world governance in terms of system-based world regions that compete and cooperate in the economic, political, and social spheres, and in terms of economic and demographic driving forces that determine the relative weights of competing regions. The outline of the chapter is as follows. Section 2 will present an analytical framework for measuring global dominance via a dominance index that combines population size and GDP size, and that can measure dominance at the country and regional levels. Section 4 applies the analytical framework to the world at large for the years 2000 and 2012. The dominance index will be applied at various levels showing country influence, interregional influence, and intraregional influence. Section 5 uses projections and forecasts for exploring future perspectives of global dominance in few coming decades. Section 5 ends with concluding remarks.

2. Measurement of Influence Potential by Country and Region

The study of global dominance is highly relevant, important, and strategic, and has been receiving increasingly more attention. The relative size of the GDP of a leading country has so far been serving as an indicator of global leadership and dominance. The US has become the leading country not only in terms of having the largest GDP but also in view of its systemic dominance in the commercial, monetary, and financial spheres worldwide. Dominance in these spheres tends to increase with a greater GDP. Moreover, global dominance in terms of political, military, and technological levels tends to associate with economic power as well. There is thus a tendency for the dominant economy to become the core of the global system, giving its national representatives more leverage in the determination of world governance and the management of world affairs. Dominating countries drive, carry, transport, and transplant their own economic system baggage to other countries elsewhere. Fourth, the future economic prospects of countries that are competing for global leadership are crucial for their dominance prospects, may have downgrading effects for the incumbent leaders, and can create serious challenges to the adaptation of world governance and management to the new situation.

Current approaches that single the relative size of the GDP of leading countries as an indication of global dominance have been argued above as incomplete and insufficient for two reasons:

1. The GDP criterion is a poor indication of the influence potential of a particular country in the context of an interactive world of voluminous populations. Interactive influence is the combined result of the relative size of economic transformations and the relative size of the transforming populations. There is a need to develop and apply a dominance index that reflects these realities.
2. Pronouncing and pushing forward individual countries with the highest GDP as individual leading countries may not command global authority or fair legitimacy because such an identification of individual leading countries does not consider regional power or regional representation.

In this section, an analytical framework is formulated that considers these two issues. First, the GDP is a biased indicator of dominance. Macroeconomics is more concerned with the size of the transformed value added, i.e. the GDP, than the number of agents who are engaged in the value-added transformation. In contrast, microeconomic theory focuses on the agents (that is the population at large) who activate the value-added transformations, consumption, investment, and interactions that eventually result in outcomes and influential patterns. In representing global dominance population matters at least as much as the GDP. The spectacular rise in the GDP of China and India, which has prepared them to become leading countries, is due for the largest part to the magnitude and growth of labor inputs, cf. Cohen (2015). Each of the two countries has population of around one billion or more. In a globalizing world with an increasingly free movement of people and communication, population numbers carry influential power and contribute to global dominance. The influence potential of a unit as a whole is a complex matter and cannot be fruitfully assessed without a systematization of concepts of influence potential. In the study of economic systems, in Cohen (2009 and 2015), a distinction is made between two types of influence potential: interactive influence, and regulative influence. In both types of influences, it is essential to jointly consider the GDP factor and the population factor.

Interactive influence emerges from interacting agents and the transactions they generate. Microeconomic foundations support formulating an interactive *dominance index* that expresses the interactive influence potential of an entity y among all the entities of the same kind y'. The dominance index is denoted by $DI(y/y')$.

An entity can be a firm, a town, a country, or a world region. In this paper, we shall apply this index to the contexts of countries and regions.

The index has two arguments as shown in eq. (1): the relative share of agents, A, in y among all y', that is $(A_y/\Sigma A_{y'})$; and the relative share of value added transformations, V, in y among all y', that is $V_y/\Sigma V_{y'}$. In this equation, ρ_1 and ρ_2 are equal weighting rates applying to these two shares, whereby $\rho_1 + \rho_2 = 1$, and $\rho_1 = \rho_2$. Other weighting rates can be used.

$$DI(y/y') = \rho_1(A_y/\Sigma A_{y'}) + \rho_2(V_y/\Sigma V_{y'}) \quad (1)$$

The value of *DI* for an entity y is a proportion, whereby $\Sigma DI(y/y') = 1$. An entity that scores a very high value of the index tends to dominate the other entities of the same kind. Once the index for an entity reaches a critical mass the influence potential of that entity can be expected to benefit from network externalities and to become practically the dominant player among all member entities of the same set. There are different views concerning the likely value of the critical mass for becoming the dominant player. A value of 3/4th is among the most quoted in the literature on a critical mass, cf. Simon (1993). There is thus justification for fixing the value of this threshold at 0.8, or thereabout.

Regulative influence is the other type of influence potential. This refers to a situation in which an entity, or country y, happens to stand higher in relation to the hierarchy of all countries y', allowing y to set behavioral rules typical of y that other countries y' should abide with. In this way, the behavioral type of$y$overrides y', allowing the further spread of behavioral norms of y at the cost of those of y'. It is not feasible to quantify measures of regulative influence along the lines of interactive influence due to mounting difficulties in standardizing diversified measures of regulation. It is likely that there is a positive association between the two notions of influence potential, in the sense that a country powerful in interactive influence would in the long run become generally powerful in regulative influence. This will add to the importance of the dominance index.

While interactive influence represents the results of *horizontal* contacts, regulative influence is a *vertical* relationship. There is ground for speculating that the nature of the horizontal channels makes their effect more endurable as they are generated via experiencing, learning, and adoption. The contribution of horizontal channels toward converging behavioral patterns across countries is likely to be more influential and more permanent than that of vertical channels. In the case of vertically accommodated behavioral attitudes, the regulative influence can terminate abruptly if the regulative mechanisms become too demanding due to technological loopholes, or the rationale for the binding restrictions disappears, or the balance of power between y and y' reverses.

The general form of the dominance index in eq. (1) can be adapted to give three specific forms of dominance: First, the dominance index of a country c in all countries, that is, the world total, w, denoted by $DI(c/w)$. Second, the dominance index of a region r in all regions or world total w, denoted by $DI(r/w)$. Third, the dominance index of a country c in its region r, denoted by $DI(c/r)$.

First, the general form of eq. (1) can be specified to give the dominance index of a country c in all countries, that is, the world total, denoted by w, as in eq. (2). Note that entity y in eq. (1) is specified as country c in eq. (2) and the sum of all entities y' is specified as the world, w. Eq. (2) combines two share parameters to give the influence potential of a particular country in an interactive world of all countries. The first is the share of the population in country c, with respect to all populations in all countries w. The second is the share of commodities transformed in country c, with respect to all transformed commodities in all countries; in other words, the total GDP of the world, w.

$$DI(c/w) = \rho_1(A_c/A_w) + \rho_2(V_c/V_w) \tag{2}$$

Eq. (2) states that the greater the combined shares of the population and the GDP of a particular country in the world totals, the greater the influence potential of that country relative to other countries.

While the dominance index of a country in the world context cannot pretend to cover all types of influences in the economic domain, not to mention influences in the non-economic domains that have bearings on the economic sphere, it gives a meaningful representation of the general valid and widely recognized facts that the larger the number of agents and the larger the size of the economic transformation in one subsystem the greater the influence will be of that subsystem in its interactions with other subsystems.

Second, the world cannot be seen as a loose collection of individual countries. Any individual country is allied to other countries in a regional formation and is as such a member of a regional interest group that has common interests. For instance, the US conducts its world affairs and is viewed by others, as part of the Western advanced economies. The remedy to the country bias is to study global dominance in an analytical framework that gives attention to interregional and intraregional next to country dominance. It is both logical and realistic that in constructing a representative and real global governance the starting point should be the influence potential of the world regions and not individual countries. Once that starting point is resolved, the next step is to descend to regional representation that is indeed at the country level.

Adapting eq. (1) toward the measurement of interregional dominance gives eq. (3) where entity y is specified as region r and all entities y' are specified as all regions, that is, the world w.

$$DI(r/w) = \rho_1(A_r/A_w) + \rho_2(V_r/V_w) \tag{3}$$

Third, adapting of eq. (1) toward the measurement of intraregional dominance gives eq. (4) where entity y is specified as country c and all entities y' are specified as all relating countries in the same region r.

$$DI(c/r) = \rho_1(A_c/A_r) + \rho_2(V_c/V_r) \tag{4}$$

How do the three dominance indexes relate to each other? How do eqs. (2), (3), and (4) combine? The dominance index of a country in the world, $DI(c/w)$ as in eq. (2), is decomposable into two parts: the *DI* of leading regions r at the world level w, giving thus $DI(r/w)$ as in eq. (3); and the *DI* for leading countries, c, at the regional level, r, giving thus $DI(c/r)$ as in eq. (4). The decomposition is laid down in eq. (5).

$$DI(c/w) = DI(r/w) \cdot DI(c/r) \tag{5}$$

While $DI(r/w)$ can be described to stand for interregional dominance, $DI(c/r)$ represents intraregional dominance.

Application of eqs. (3) and (4) would require a relevant and meaningful division of the world, w, into regions r and the classification of countries c along these regions. In Cohen (2014) the world economy is divided into eight regional groups based on their shared type of economic system, common features and regional vicinity. The classification is displayed in Chapter 2, Table 1 of this book. The classification distinguishes between two developed regions (the F-group consisting of firm centered western economies and the S-group consisting of state centered economies such as Russia and some former ex-Soviet Union countries), and six development regions specified as East Asia and Pacific (EAP), South Asia (SA), Central Asia and Caspian (CAC), Middle East and North Africa (MENA), Sub-Saharan Africa (SSA), and Latin America and Caribbean (LAC). The classification corresponds closely with those operational at the World Bank and United Nations. Comparative indicators on economic structures, conduct, and performances of the eight regions and their constituent countries are discussed at length in Chapter 2 and recalled in other chapters.

3. Applications for 2000 and 2012

This section will apply *DI* for leading countries at the world level, and will subsequently treat the decomposition of the *DI* into interregional dominance and intraregional dominance.

Leading countries at the world level. The relevant equation here is eq. (2). Application of this equation for the years 2000 and 2012 gives the Dominance Index for (c/w) as shown in Table 1. The obtained results can be described in four points. First, while in 2000 the *DI* of US preceded China by 7 percentage points, pp, (18.3-11.0,

Table 1. Population shares, GDP shares, and Dominance Index of leading countries at world level, %. World population = 100%, world GDP = 100%.

	Population share, %		GDP share, %		Dominance index, %	
	2000	2012	2000	2012	2000	2012
F group total	17.4	16.0	79.5	62.7	48.5	39.4
USA	4.9	4.7	31.8	22.7	18.3	13.7
Japan	2.2	1.9	14.6	8.3	8.4	5.1
Canada	0.5	0.5	2.2	2.5	1.4	1.5
Korea, R.	0.8	0.7	1.6	1.6	1.2	1.2
Australia	0.3	0.3	1.3	2.1	0.8	1.2
Germany	1.4	1.2	5.8	4.8	3.6	3.0
France	1.1	1.0	4.1	3.7	2.6	2.3
U. Kingdom	1.0	0.9	4.6	3.5	2.8	2.2
Italy	1.0	0.9	3.4	2.8	2.2	1.9
Spain	0.7	0.7	1.8	1.9	1.2	1.3
Poland	0.7	0.6	0.5	0.7	0.6	0.6
Netherlands	0.3	0.2	1.2	1.1	0.7	0.7
Others	2.6	2.3	6.6	7.0	4.6	4.7
S-group total	3.56	2.98	0.94	3.15	2.25	3.06
Russia	2.40	2.04	0.79	2.77	1.60	2.41
Ukraine	0.81	0.65	0.10	0.24	0.45	0.45
Others	0.3416	0.28	0.06	0.13	0.20	0.211
EAP total	25.7	28.3	5.8	14.7	15.8	21.5
China	17.9	19.1	4.2	11.7	11.0	15.4
Indonesia	2.9	3.5	0.5	1.2	1.7	2.3
Philippines	1.1	1.4	0.2	0.3	0.7	0.9
Thailand	0.9	0.9	0.4	0.5	0.6	0.7
Vietnam	1.1	1.2	0.1	0.2	0.6	0.7
Malaysia	0.3	0.4	0.3	0.4	0.3	0.4
Others	1.5	1.7	0.1	0.2	0.8	1.0
SA total	19.6	23.4	1.9	3.2	10.8	13.3
India	14.8	17.6	1.4	2.6	8.1	10.1
Pakistan	2.0	2.5	0.2	0.3	1.1	1.4
Bangladesh	1.9	2.2	0.1	0.2	1.0	1.2
Sri Lanka	0.3	0.3	0.0	0.1	0.2	0.2
Others	0.6	0.8	0.0	0.1	0.3	0.4
CAC total	2.73	3.19	1.25	2.36	1.99	2.78
Türkiye	0.90	1.05	0.81	1.09	0.85	1.07
Iran	0.94	1.08	0.31	0.76	0.62	0.92
Kazakhstan	0.21	0.24	0.06	0.28	0.13	0.26
Uzbekistan	0.35	0.42	0.04	0.07	0.20	0.25
Others	0.33	0.39	0.03	0.16	0.20	0.27

	Population share, %		GDP share, %		Dominance index, %	
	2000	2012	2000	2012	2000	2012
MENA total	4.02	4.52	2.65	4.09	3.34	4.31
S Arabia	0.33	0.40	0.57	0.98	0.45	0.69
UAE	0.05	0.13	0.32	0.53	0.18	0.33
Kuwait	0.03	0.05	0.11	0.25	0.07	0.15
Qatar	0.01	0.03	0.05	0.26	0.03	0.15
Oman	0.04	0.05	0.06	0.11	0.05	0.08
Bahrain	0.01	0.02	0.03	0.04	0.02	0.03
Egypt	0.94	1.15	0.30	0.36	0.62	0.76
Algeria	0.45	0.55	0.17	0.28	0.31	0.41
Iraq	0.34	0.46	0.19	0.30	0.26	0.38
Morocco	0.40	0.46	0.11	0.13	0.26	0.30
Israel	0.09	0.11	0.38	0.35	0.24	0.23
Syria	0.23	0.32	0.06	0.09	0.15	0.21
Others	0.63	0.80	0.29	0.40	0.46	0.60
SSA total	9.4	13.0	1.05	1.8	5.2	7.4
Nigeria	1.7	2.4	0.14	0.4122	0.9	1.4
Ethiopia	0.9	1.3	0.02	0.1	0.5	0.7
Sudan	0.4	0.5	0.04	0.1	0.2	0.3
Ghana	0.3	0.4	0.02	0.1	0.1	0.2
Others (a)	1.7	2.4	0.12	0.2	0.9	1.3
S Africa	0.6	0.7	0.40	0.5	0.5	0.7
Angola	0.2	0.3	0.03	0.2	0.1	0.2
Congo DR	0. 7	0.9	0.01	0.0	0.3	0.5
Kenya	0.4	0.6	0.04	0.1	0.2	0.3
Others (b)	2.4	3.3	0.23	0.3	1.3	1.8
LAC total	7.46	8.64	6.86	8.00	7.16	8.32
Mexico	1.47	1.72	2.10	1.62	1.79	1.67
Guatemala	0.16	0.21	0.06	0.07	0.11	0.14
Cuba	0.16	0.16	0.09	0.11	0.13	0.13
Dominican	0.12	0.15	0.07	0.08	0.10	0.11
Others (c)	0.58	0.67	0.46	0.42	0.52	0.55
Brazil	2.48	2.82	1.95	3.09	2.22	2.95
Argentina	0.52	0.58	0.86	0.65	0.69	0.62
Colombia	0.57	0.68	0.30	0.51	0.43	0.59
Venezuela	0.35	0.43	0.36	0.52	0.35	0.47
Peru	0.37	0.43	0.16	0.28	0.27	0.35
Chile	0.22	0.25	0.24	0.37	0.23	0.31
Others (d)	0.46	0.55	0.20	0.30	0.33	0.42

Notes: The *F*-group of countries was also named Western alliance in other chapters. It is one and the same group. The categories of Others in SSA are subdivided geographically into Others SSA(a) = upper belt, and Others SSA(b) = lower belt. Similarly, the categories of Others in LAC are subdivided into Others LAC(c) = Central America and Caribbean, and Others LAC(d) = South America.

column 3), this ranking reversed in 2012 with *DI* in China at 15.4 and US at 13.7, due to higher growth in China of both the population and GDP. The same applies for the relationship between Japan and India. While Japan was ahead of India in the *DI* in 2000, this reversed in 2012.

Second, the *DI* of all *F*-countries amounted to 48.5 pp in 2000, with 30.4 held by the non-European group (US, Japan, etc), and 18.1 in the EU group. In 2012, the *DI* of all F countries is diminished by 8 pp to become 39.3 pp with 23.1 held by the non-European group and 16.2 held by the EU group. These figures show that within the firm-centered countries, European countries have gained and non-European countries have lost in influence potential, over the last decade.

Third, a striking fact is the significantly low influence potential of Russia at the world level, which is only 2.4 pp. This is in the neighborhood of the *DI* for countries like France, the United Kingdom, Indonesia, and Brazil.

Fourth, for practically all countries in the years between 2000 and 2012, the relative change in the GDP was greater than the relative change in the population with the exception of the sub-Saharan African countries where population growth was greater than GDP growth. This means that while the change in a country's dominance is less accountable by demographic than economic growth, this is reversed in the case of the African countries where demographic growth was larger than economic growth.

Interregional dominance: The relevant equation for this application is eq. (3) which gives the *DI* of leading regions r at the world level, that is *DI* (r/w). Table 2 displays the results of *DI* for the two developed regions and the six development regions as fractions of the whole world. The sum of *DI* over the eight regions is 100%. The most remarkable development in the period 2000–2012 is the reduction in the value of *DI* in the developed regions. The firm-centered Western countries (*F*-countries, i.e., US, EU, and Japan) have lost significantly with a reduction in their dominance of 18.7%. The state-centered countries (*S*-countries, i.e. Russia) gained, mainly due to the recovery after years of recession following the collapse of the communist regime, which does not make it a real advance. The main gainers and advancers are the development regions. For example, *DI* for the advanced regions diminished from 50.7 in 2000 to 42.2 in 2012 (a reduction of 16%, column 7), and the development regions reversed their subordinate position of 2000 and acquired a majority in 2012 (as they moved from 49.3 to 57.6). The *DI* of the development regions of EAP, CAC, MENA, and SSA increased by between 36% and 41%, the increase in SA and LAC was lower at 24% and 16%. If Table 2 would be computed for the world situation half a century ago a totally different picture would come out, with *F*-countries (that is, the Western countries), *S*-countries (i.e. Soviet Union and allies), and the developing countries having more or less equal levels of *DI* at 33% each.

Table 2. World regions: Population shares, GDP shares, and Dominance Index, %.

	Population, %		GDP, %		Dominance Index		
	2000	2012	2000	2012	2000	2012	Change, %
Developed regions	21.0	19.0	80.5	65.9	50.7	42.4	−16.4
Developing regions	79.0	81.0	19.5	34.1	49.3	57.6	16.8
Developed regions							
F-countries	17.4	16.0	79.5	62.7	48.5	39.4	−18.7
S-countries	3.6	3.0	0.9	3.1	2.2	3.1	36.2
Developing regions							
EAP	25.7	28.3	5.8	14.7	15.8	21.5	36.0
SA	19.6	23.4	1.9	3.2	10.8	13.3	23.5
CAC	2.7	3.2	1.2	2.4	2.0	2.8	39.6
MENA	3.5	4.5	2.6	4.1	3.1	4.3	40.5
SSA	9.4	13.0	1.0	1.8	5.2	7.4	41.0
LAC	7.5	8.6	6.9	8.0	7.2	8.3	16.3
World total	100.00	100.00	100.00	100.00	100.0	100.0	
World total values	6102	7044	32873	72682			

Intraregional dominance: The Dominance Index is also computable for individual countries within each region, as in eq. (4). The sum of the relative shares of population and GDP, when applied to each country within a region, gives the degree of interactive influence of each country in the region. The higher the index of a leading country, the greater its influence in passing its behavioral features to other countries in the same region. Table 3 shows leading country configurations in the two developed and six development regions. In order not to enter into unnecessary details we limit the presentation to the two most leading countries in each region. Within the F-group, the population is about evenly divided between non-European and European countries. The share of the GDP that goes to non-Europeans is about 10% higher than the European, but this difference is shrinking. The result is a DI in 2012 that gives the non-European a greater influence at 56% against the European at 44%. As the last column shows, this difference shrank over the past 12 years by 2 percentage points (pp), suggesting that within the F-group, European countries have gained while non-European countries, i.e. US and Japan, have lost in influence potential, over the last decade.

Computation of the dominance index for the S-region shows Russia dominating with a DI of 75.7% in 2000, and increasing to 78.3% in 2012. This is very close to the situation where the threshold of 80% is likely to be passed, allowing an anchored dominance. Other countries in the region have very limited and declining influential powers.[1]

Table 3. Leading countries in world regions: Population shares, GDP shares, and Dominance Index, %.

	Share in total population		Share in total GDP		Dominance Index		
	2000	2012	2000	2012	2000	2012	Change, %
F-group							
Non-European	50.8	51.9	65.4	60.5	58.1	56.2	−3.3
United States	27.9	29.2	39.9	36.3	33.9	32.7	*−3.6*
Japan	12.6	11.9	18.4	13.3	15.5	12.6	*−18.6*
European	49.1	48.1	34.6	39.5	41.9	43.8	4.5
Germany	8.1	7.5	7.3	7.7	7.7	7.6	*−2.1*
France	6.0	6.1	5.1	5.8	5.6	6.0	*6.8*
S-group							
Russia	68	68	84	88	75.7	78.3	3.5
Ukraine	23	22	10	8	16.4	14.7	−10.2
EAP							
China	69.5	67.7	71.7	80.1	70.6	73.9	4.6
Indonesia	11.4	12.3	8.6	8.2	10.0	10.3	2.5
SA							
India	75.4	75.0	76.1	80.7	75.8	77.8	2.7
Pakistan	10.4	10.9	11.8	9.8	11.1	10.3	−7.1
CAC							
Türkiye	32.9	32.9	65.0	46.1	48.9	39.5	−19.3
Iran	34.3	34.0	24.7	32.3	29.5	33.1	12.3
MENA							
Egypt	26.9	25.5	11.5	8.8	19.2	17.2	−10.5
Saudi Arabia	8.2	8.8	21.7	23.9	15.0	16.4	9.5
SSA							
Nigeria	18.5	18.5	13.5	19.8	16.0	19.1	19.8
South Africa	6.6	5.7	38.6	28.9	22.6	17.3	−29.1
LAC							
Brazil	33.2	32.6	28.5	38.6	30.9	35.6	15.4
Mexico	19.8	19.9	30.6	20.2	25.2	20.0	−20.5

In the EAP region, in 2012, China constituted 80.1% of the total population and 73.9% of the total GDP, resulting in a *DI* of 74%; in 2000, the *DI* was 71%, a rise by 5 pp. Indonesia follows with a long distance at *DI* of 10%, that is, maintained at that level in 2012. The huge size and the positive change of *DI* in China mean that *DI* in most other EAP countries is not only tiny but is shrinking as well.

In the SA region, in 2012, India has about 75% of the total population and stands stable at this share. The ratio of (GDP of India)/(GDP of SA) is 80.7% and had a rising tendency. Taken together, *DI* for India in 2000 was at 76% in 2000 and rose to 78% in 2012. The next country is Pakistan with a *DI* index of 11%, and has been falling. Other countries show also a decreasing *DI*, last column.

In the Central Asia and Caspian region, CAC, Türkiye, and Iran are numbers one and two, with *DI* at 49% and 30% in 2000, but the gap closed down rapidly to give respectively 40% and 33% in 2012. The dominance profile in CAC can be described as that of a majority-based duo leadership, which allows the two leading countries to exercise major influence. The duo leadership can lead to rivalry between Türkiye and Iran in acquiring more economic and political influences in this and neighboring regions.

In MENA, the two leading countries are Egypt and Saudi Arabia; they mastered in 2012 less than one-third of the total population of the region and account for only about one-third of the total GDP. Their *DI*s are limited to 17% and 16%, respectively. The sum of this duo leadership does not go beyond 33%. The dominance profile of MENA is best described as a minority-based duo leadership. Various factors such as the sparsely populated vast space, transport barriers, unequal resource endowments, nationalist sentiments driven by foreign interventions, and public approvals of authoritarian governments, tended to undermine the otherwise highly unifying factors such as common language, religious, and cultural traits.

The sparsely spread distribution pattern of *DI* among the member countries in SSA is similar to that in MENA and is best described as a minority-based duo leadership. Together, the two leaders, which are Nigeria and South Africa, command a dominance of only 36%. Cultural, religious, political, and not least geophysical barriers stand in the way of greater interaction and integration between SSA countries and restrict the eventual enlargement of dominating influences of leading countries.

The LAC region, consisting of 41 countries, has a majority-based duo leadership similar to the case of the CAC region. The two leaders are Brazil with *DI* at 36% and Mexico at 20%. Together, these two leading countries command a *DI* of 56%.

Although leadership patterns in the country/region context differ between the regions, some common features are present, significant, and meaningful in understanding and managing world development. One feature is that the *DI* of US as the leading country in the F-region is at 33%, which compares very poorly with *DI* for leading countries in the S-region, in EAP and in SA, that is Russia at 78%, China at 74% and India at 78%, respectively. It is directly seen that the degree of influence which US can practice in the F-region is much more limited than what the other three countries can do in their respective regions. The influential power of Russia, China, and India in their regional groups is more than twice the influential power of US in the F-group (i.e. $74/33 = 2.2$). Although Russia dominates the S-region by 78%, it is a special case. The S-region itself has become quite tiny on the total world stage, with a modest *DI* at 3%.

A second feature is that one can speak of a majority-shared duo leadership in the regions of CAC and LAC (with leading countries Türkiye and Iran in CAC, and Brazil and Mexico in LAC). Country leadership in these two regions is highly contested. The leadership pattern is otherwise in the regions of MENA and SSA, which are characterized by minority-shared duo leadership. The combined *DI* of leading countries like Egypt and Saudi Arabia in MENA, and Nigeria and South Africa in SSA do not go beyond 33% and 36%. The dispersed *DI* in these two regions is a reflection of multi-faceted fragmentations. Various intraregional barriers stand in the way of regional integration.

4. Projections into the Future

The future distribution of potential influence among competing regions and leading countries, as expressed in the Dominance Index will change, and this can have significant impacts on world development and world governance. In this and the following section, we project the main tendencies in the distribution of *DI* among regions and countries in the near future and examine world governance in the light of these projections.

To compute the Dominance Index for leading countries in future years one needs projections of the population shares and the GDP shares of leading countries in the world's total population and GDP, respectively. United Nations Demographic Division is the source for population projections. The PWC Economics (2017) is the source of projections for the GDP. These two types of projections are employed to compute *DI* for leading countries for 2030 and 2050. Results in Table 4 show that sometime between 2000 and 2012, the *DI* of China surpassed US already, and by 2030 India is projected to be equal to, and thereafter surpass US. In 2030, China and India are numbers 1 and 2, followed by US, and after a distance, come Brazil, Indonesia, Japan, Nigeria, and Mexico. The *DI* of leading EU countries is in the range of 2.0% to 1.5%. The *DI* of Russia and Türkiye are also in this range. All other countries in the rest of the world, next to Saudi Arabia and South Africa, are projected to have the *DI* at levels lower than 1%. Countries in the rest of the world hold together a *DI* amounting to 34 pp, which is projected to be stable.

Just as important, and perhaps even more relevant, is the projection of *DI* by world regions; since the regional leadership dimension adds crucial influential significance to the country leadership dimension. The influence potential of the eight regions as indicated by calculations of *DI* (r/w) in the years 2012, 2030 and 2050 are projected in Table 5. The same sources as in Table 4 were used to make the projections.

The focus of the presented results is to view the changing world development and influence spheres from the angle of regional influences, hence their reproduction in Figure 1. While the displacement discussions have been preoccupied with the situation of individual countries, such as China and India versus US, EU, and Japan, we contend here that deliberations on global governance are better served when the focus is on world groups rather than on individual countries.

Table 4. Projected changes in the influence potential of leading countries, as measured by the Dominance Index, %. Total = 100.0%.

2012		2030		2050		2012		2030		2050	
China	15.4	China	18.6	China	18.3	Indonesia	2.3	France	1.9	Russia	2.1
US	13.7	India	11.6	India	14.2	UK	2.2	Nigeria	1.9	Germany	1.6
India	10.1	US	11.5	US	10.3	Mexico	1.7	Mexico	1.9	France	1.6
Japan	5.1	Japan	3.4	Brazil	3.3	Nigeria	1.4	UK	1.8	UK	1.5
Germany	3.0	Brazil	3.3	Indonesia	3.0	Türkiye	1.1	Türkiye	1.4	Türkiye	1.5
Brazil	3.0	Indonesia	2.7	Japan	2.3	S. Arabia	0.7	S. Arabia	0.8	S Arabia	1.0
Russia	2.4	Russia	2.3	Nigeria	2.2	S. Africa	0.6	S. Africa	0.6	S. Africa	0.8
France	2.3	Germany	2.2	Mexico	2.2	Others	35.0	Others	33.9	Others	34.1

Source: Computation of the Dominance Index requires projections of population and GDP. The Population projections are from United Nations Population Division: World Development Prospects, at https://population.un.org/wpp. GDP projections are from PWC (2017).

Table 5. Projected distribution of the Dominance Index by world region: 2012, 2030, 2050.

2012		2030		2050	
Western allied	39.4	Western allied	30.6	Western allied	25.6
EAP	21.5	EAP	25.0	EAP	24.8
SA	13.3	SA	15.0	SA	18.2
LAC	8.3	LAC	9.2	LAC	9.6
SSA	7.4	SSA	8.5	SSA	9.6
MENA	4.3	MENA	5.3	MENA	6.2
Russia allied	3.1	CAC	3.4	CAC	3.7
CAC	2.8	Russia allied	2.8	Russia allied	2.5
World total	100.0	World total	100.0	World total	100.0

Source: Population projections are from United Nations Population Division: World Development prospects, at https://population.un.org/wpp. GDP projections are from PWC (2017).

Figure 1 shows the F-group of countries to continue dominating in 2012, 2030, and 2050 as well. In 2050, the value of DI for the F-group is projected at 25.6 pp, which is slightly higher but practically equal to the DI of EAP at 24.8 pp. This is a projected future situation of shared leadership that has a trajectory of some 38 years before the shared leadership is to be realized. The lengthy horizon of the trajectory gives ample opportunities for the two leading regional groups to adapt to each other in redesigning global governance and responding collectively to the challenges of global failures.

Would intercourse between parties with equal influential powers lead to more confrontation or more understanding? It is generally true that when the contending parties have influential powers that are more or less equal, as suggested in Figure 1 for 2050, and perceive the situation as such, the parties will be more inclined to use reason and knowledge and adopt cooperative attitudes in managing collective

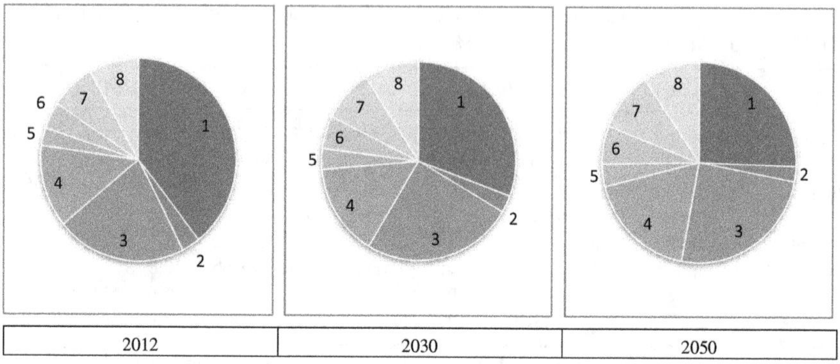

Figure 1. Projected distribution of the Dominance Index by world region: 2012, 2030, 2050.
Notes: Key: 1 = F-group, 2 = S-group, 3 = EAP, 4 = SA, 5 = CAC, 6 = MENA, 7 = SSA, 8 = LAC

actions and avoiding bilateral frictions. Under a skew distribution of influential powers, it is more likely that a non-collaborative attitude emerges. Figure 1 predicts a future world in 2050 with a more equal balance of influence than in 2012 and thus feeds the expectation that in the long run, the new country/systems competition will be more collaborative. Furthermore, the collaborative scenario is collectively superior to an isolationist, a protectionist, or a non-collaborative one. The collaborative scenario promotes borrowing, testing, and adaptation of successful institutions from one system to another but also experimenting with new designs and institutions of global governance.

It is worth mentioning that the South Asia region is projected at the third position with DI at 18 pp, and LAC at the fourth position with DI at 10 pp. The displacement at the regional level is thus less striking than the displacement at the country level. The figure reveals other interesting features of world development as well. The underdog position of SSA is reversed by 2050, allowing SSA to catch up with LAC with the same influence potential of 10 pp. MENA and CAC secure the sixth and seventh positions with DI at 6 pp and 4 pp, respectively. The S-group, which is practically Russia, reaches no more than 2.5 pp, which is equivalent to one-tenth of the influence potential of either EAP or F-group.

In what ways would the projected displacement of US, EU, and Japan by China and India affect the economic systems of the leading incumbent countries and the economic systems of the leading newcomer countries? And how could the projected displacement affect world development and world governance?

In discussing these questions, it is necessary first to sum up the crucial features of the socio-economic systems of US and EU as contrasted to those of China and India. As is well known, profit-maximizing firms, markets, and supportive institutions are the main driving agents in the US and EU; hence, our denotation of countries sharing this system by the F-group. In contrast, institutional behavior in China and India incorporates greater influences from kinship and household settings when compared to US and EU. There is also greater collaboration between the higher strata of the firm and state subsystems in China and India compared to US and EU; this closer collaboration between firm and state agents at the top is partly due to close kin relationships between leading agents in leading firms and state agencies. Furthermore, persuasion settings seeking consensus are much more active in coordinating and streamlining the social system in China and India than in US and EU; which is logical, given the demographic dynamics and the multi-polar differentiation of the social system in these two giant countries.

As the projections favoring the newcomers on the incumbents become a reality, the established institutions in US and EU are likely to come under pressure in such institutional areas as separation between business and government, free competition, transparent governance, merit goods, and social benefits of the welfare state. The fiscal budget may shift in favor of capital and firms at the cost of labor and consumers. The national economies are prone to apply more protectionism, cartelism, and state corporatism. The polity may also be affected by a weakening of decision-making in open parliaments and strengthened non-transparencies. The new country/system competition may work otherwise and motivate firms and states in F-countries to come closer, integrate, and reorganize with the object of raising the performance of their national economies; see Sinn (2002) and Lindbeck (2003) for elaborations on consequences of the new systems competition and protectionism. The reorganization in F-countries may borrow features of the leading newcomers. Firm-centered countries may let go and replace parts of the profit-maximizing institutions with coordination mechanisms that rely on community sharing, politicized rent, and persuasive settings. How far would this adaptation go? One view is that fundamental changes in F-countries cannot happen because given the embedded character of firm-oriented institutions; the cost of reorganization is higher than the benefit of breaking away from the embedded institutions and the historical path. The other view, based on interactive influence, allows for open-ended indeterminate courses, dependent on the degree of agent participation across the world regions and across competing regional systems, and if the returns in the competing regional systems are higher agents would either physically move to the better performing regional system or institutionally redirect their own system to incorporate elements from elsewhere. It very much depends on the relative shares of the dissatisfied versus loyalists.

The new country/system competition would have also consequences for leading newcomers. Given their growth premium in the future, there may be less incentive for the newcomer country/systems to incorporate, test, or adapt some of the institutions that proved successful in the context of the F-countries such as those of the competitive entrepreneurship, welfare state, medical insurance, and parliamentary democracy. This would imply a low degree of interaction between the economic systems that limits their evolution. But if the incumbent leading countries in the

F-group would take initiating steps in an adaptation process, this can engage leading newcomers in a mutual process of co-adaptations and co-integration, which would make global governance a lot easier.

Speculation on what will happen in the future, considering the huge uncertainties in world development and the multitudes of intervening factors, is not a worthwhile activity and loses relevance in terms of developing action rationales and policy intentions. What is more relevant in terms of policy is to bolster favorable conditions for all agents in all regional systems so as to allow agents to digest, compare and evaluate what is happening across the regional systems, and so as to allow agents to decide freely on entering, exiting, voicing, or reforming across the regional systems. Whatever outcome is realized at the end of the day regarding the prospects of a particular regional system is logical and defendable if the outcome is the result of fair starts, undistorted processes, comparative evaluations, and rational choices. These conditions are vital for the natural evolutions of the regional systems and for creating unbiased and fluid world governance that strives toward resolving global failures.

5. Concluding Remarks

Country dominance can be specified in different ways; some ways are more useful than others. We make use of a generalized notion of influence potential, which is expressed in terms of the relative shares of agent interaction and economic transformation, equally weighted, and giving thus the Dominance Index, *DI*. Displacement of incumbent leading countries by newcomers when measured along comparative *DI*s of competing countries, occurs at a quicker pace than when measured solely in terms of the GDP; this is due to the population effect in *DI* that favors developing over developed countries. Results of *DI* indicate that the displacement has already occurred, as the *DI* of China is higher than that of US in 2012, i.e. 15.4 pp and 13.7 pp, respectively.

The country dominance index at the world level, that is *DI* of country/world, is decomposable into *DI* of country/region (this reflects intraregional dominance), and *DI* of region/world (reflecting interregional dominance). The decomposition adds insights.

Regarding intraregional dominance, US has a low dominance of 33% in its region.; when compared to such countries as China, India, and Russia that score very high degree of dominance in their regions, i.e., *DI* around 75%. The results suggest that in relative terms, the influence potential of the US in global matters is hampered by its low intraregional dominance, while the other three countries command more influence in their respective regions.

Regarding interregional dominance, leadership displacement of the western industrialized region by the EAP region is projected to take place at a much slower rate than in the case of country displacement of US versus China. The displacement calculus in this paper predicts that the western industrialized region (which we also call the firm-centered region) and the EAP region will have equivalent *DI*s in 2050, at 25.6 pp, and at 24.8 pp, respectively. The interesting thing about this projected equal sharing of influence is that when the contending parties have influential powers that are more or less equal, as suggested in Figure 1, and perceive the situation as such, the parties will be more inclined to use reason and knowledge and adopt cooperative attitudes in managing collective actions and in avoiding bilateral frictions. Under skew distributions of influential powers, it is more likely that a non-collaborative attitude emerges. The obtained results feed expectations that in the long run, the new regional system competition will be more collaborative, a situation that promotes borrowing, testing, and adaptation of successful institutions from one regional system to another. With a time span of 38 years to go, the resetting of rules of global governance can be done gradually, and world responses to the mounting global failures can be made more effective and timely.

For democratic and effectively run world governance the interregional perspective should precede the intraregional and country perspectives. Global governance, in contrast to the more advanced organization of the national polity, is at an early stage of evolvement and is far from being in shape to tackle the list of mounting global failures. By way of demonstration, we applied the *DI* at the regional and country levels in composing a world top of presidential leaders, to be entrusted with coordinating global governance and resolving global failure. The result was the first chamber with a limited number of 16 leading countries, or G-16, which is more compact, representative, and effectively real than the G-20. It was postulated also that there is a rationale for supplementing the G-16 with a second chamber of eight regional ambassadors, call it R-8, which can represent the interests of *other* countries in the eight regions *other* than those of the leading country.

As world development evolves, partly determined by internal mechanisms, and partly by external events, the outcomes are not predictable. That is the reason for strengthening global governance based on principles of participatory democracy and interactive influence. The context of the world national polity is very different from that of the world polity. Remarkable advances have been achieved in the past centuries in circumventing and consolidating the institutional setup of the national polity. Some of these advances can be fruitfully used in programming the institutions of global governance, but the global governance of differentiated and interactive systems/regions/countries is unique and new, and it has to discover its own program and path.

Endnote

1. In this chapter, the Russian-led *S*-group includes Ukraine. In updating the classification, and in the light of recent political developments, it would seem justifiable to remove Ukraine from the Russian influence sphere. Because of the small size of Ukraine, exclusion of Ukraine would not significantly affect the obtained empirical results for this region.

Chapter 22

World Governance and the G-20: An Alternative Design

1. Introduction

The challenges of global governance with leading countries having different economic systems are diverse and complex. Some of the main issues include different views on economic policy. Leading countries with different economic political systems may have fundamentally different views on how to address economic challenges and promote economic growth, such as the role of government, the balance between free markets and government intervention, and the importance of social welfare programs. This can make it difficult for them to reach an agreement on economic policy initiatives that are effective and beneficial for all. Leading countries at different stages of economic development have different priorities, which can limit their ability to work together effectively. Leading countries may see themselves as rivals in the competition for power and influence in the global governance arena, which can limit their ability to cooperate and collaborate effectively. Political leaders of leading countries have different views on the benefits and drawbacks of globalization, which can limit their ability to reach an agreement on issues related to global governance and international trade. These challenges highlight the complexity of global governance and the need for effective solutions that address the different perspectives and needs of leading countries. Addressing these challenges will require a commitment to compromise, cooperation, and collaboration, as well as a deep understanding of the economic, political, and cultural differences that shape the views of leading countries on global governance issues.

The need for global governance can be presented otherwise. Technical and behavioral barriers that exist at the national level and that lead to economic failures at the national level are also present at the regional and world levels though in different and more complex forms. Market failures that apply at the micro level between interacting agents apply also internationally between interacting countries.

In general, coordination failures become more severe when the interaction involves competing countries that follow different economic systems. Global failures are likely to be more severe in the future because of the entry into the world scene of leading countries that have distinctly different economic systems (for instance, China, and India) from leading incumbents (US and EU) and because the new competition (country cum system) is likely to be perceived by newcomers and incumbents as a zero-sum game. It is crucial in such circumstances to have a design of world governance that can respond adequately to global failures.

The G-20 is a twenty-plus group of presidents and prime ministers of leading countries and unions in the world which meets annually to discuss and resolve rising issues in global governance. Research on global governance and the G-20 has become a mainstream topic of interest in recent years as demonstrated in the edited works of Kirton and Wilson (2017), and Collins and Kirton (2021). There are specific studies of what the G-20 did not do, did do, and can do in various areas of global reform such as Frieden (2016) on international finance. There are also studies with a broader scope such as Slaughter (2020) on global power and leadership legitimacy. Our chapter on the G-20 focuses on its representation character and not on resolving problems arising in specific areas. As such, this chapter is less close to the work of De Lombaerde and Kirton and is closer to the work of Hill and White.

The initiative of establishing and convening the G-20 is a response to the felt need for greater effective global actions toward combating global failures. The G-20 is one such design, but this is handicapped by its narrow scope (i.e. GDP), and undemocratic composition (selection of individual countries and not regional representation, next to being inconsistent and outdated). This chapter formulates and applies an index of influence potential that combines population and GDP, which is measurable at the region and country levels. This chapter employs these outcomes in drawing up a more fair representative participation by regions/countries in world governance and explores the effects of the changing distribution of influence potential on global development and economic systems.

The outline of this chapter is as follows. Section 2 sums up the examples of global failure and reviews current global governance for addressing these failures, and in particular the G-20. Section 3 discusses the shortcomings of the design of the G-20 and presents an analytical framework for dealing with the shortcomings. Sections 4 and 5 apply the framework. Section 6 discusses a few aspects of the interactive influence of leading regions and countries in the near future. Section 7 concludes.

2. Global Failures and World Governance

At the national level, microeconomics and welfare economics single out four categories of economic failures and search for remedies to combat them. The four economic failures in national economic systems relate to the presence of indivisibilities, uncertainties, externalities, and collective needs.

Examples of global failures in indivisibilities abandon. Some collective tasks at the international level are indivisible and can be only operated by one or a couple of the largest countries. These would include complex military operations, mega internet networks, mega space explorations, etc., and this gives monopoly power to the engaging lead country at the cost of the non-engaging countries. US is often the engaging country. Demands by leading newcomers for regulating these activities are likely to be challenged by the lead incumbent.

Examples of uncertainties and confidence failure in the world economy are encountered mostly in investment and finance. For instance, when giant enterprises from Brazil, Russia, China, and India, some of them state-sponsored, have solicited to buy and own US and EU enterprises; this is often seen in the incumbent countries as an unfair play that allows foreign countries to control western interests. In reaction firms and states in the incumbent countries have tended to take concerted action and protective measures to avoid foreign takeovers.[1] It is usually difficult to ascertain whether in such situations the national loss is a result of fair play or strategic trespassing. Whether protectionism is justified or not, counter-protection usually follows, which weakens the economic systems of both incumbents and newcomers. The current tension in hi-tech investment and trade between US and China undermines world welfare.

Examples of negative externalities at the world level are numerous. At the micro level, an externality problem arises in situations when each agent acts to raise one's own benefits without taking into account the negative effects of the act on other agents. Where there are significant interdependencies between agent actions private and social interests diverge. To reach more efficiency and satisfaction for all agents the externalities need to be internalized so that when both agents would interact again the externality effects would be incorporated into their mutual decisions. The credit crunch of 2007, followed by the financial meltdown of 2008 and the economic recession of 2008–2009 is one example. The regulated foreign finance in some leading newcomers (i.e. Russia and China) allowed their governments to accumulate large USD foreign exchange reserves. These USD reserves are mostly loaned back to the US economy allowing it to finance much more spending than economically permissible; some of this spending was backed by financially very risky warrants and regulatory loopholes. The credit crunch in the US that started with defaults in mortgage payments was sufficient to expose the financial risks of a world economy. The interdependent interactions between leading countries (with their economic systems having different rules of coordination and motivations) were basic ingredients of the externality failures behind the financial crises and the economic recession. Other externality problems next to risky finance, economic recessions, and trade protectionism, are global warming, cyber insecurity, war refugees, health hazards, whale protection, tax havens, and diverging fiscal and regulatory regimes.

Finally, the list of newly arising collective needs at the world level is increasing and includes space insecurity, violation of human rights, poverty reduction, fighting terrorism, exploiting ocean resources, controlling nuclear capabilities, and combating world epidemics. The collective actions required to satisfy these needs are perceived differently in countries with different economic systems and/or in different phases of economic development.

In short, global failures are imminent and require global governance that fixes indivisibilities, promotes confidence, internalizes externalities, and organizes collective actions to attend to newly arising collective needs at the global level At the international level, interactions between leading countries in the world economic system would be accompanied by global economy failures, similar to the economy failures encountered in the national economic system, as will be shown in the following by some examples. In the meantime, the current system of world governance is not sufficiently developed to deal with these global failures. Moreover, global failures are likely to be more severe in the future compared to today because of the entry into the world scene of leading countries that have distinctly different economic systems (that is, China and India) from the systems of the leading incumbents (that is, US and EU), and because application of the influence potentials of the leading newcomers and of the leading incumbents are likely to be perceived as a zero-sum game. What are the responses in terms of world governance to the challenges of global failures?

The current world governance system was shaped by the advent of WWII and has undergone a few additional changes since then. The United Nations Assembly consists of 193 member states. The UN security council, UNSC, consists of five permanent members with veto rights: China, France, Russian Federation, the United Kingdom, and the United States, and ten non-permanent members elected for 2-year terms by the General Assembly. These are currently Argentina, Australia, Chad, Chile, Jordan, Lithuania, Luxembourg, Nigeria, Korea, and Rwanda. This list of 5 plus 10 members of the Security Council looks obscure and uninformed when evaluated against the background of our findings on the Dominance Index in the world at large. Next to the UNSC, there are permanent international agencies on trade, finance, law, and major areas of social and economic activities, and intermittent conferences on newly rising global challenges.

The latest development in global governance was the establishment of the G-20, which is a forum of political leaders of the 20 leading economies in the world. The members of the G-20 are Argentina, Australia, Brazil, Canada, China, France, Germany, India, Indonesia, Italy, Japan, the Republic of Korea, Mexico, Russia, Saudi Arabia, South Africa, Türkiye, the United Kingdom, the United States, and the European Union. Spain is an honorary member. Together, they represent about two-thirds of the world's population, 85% of global gross domestic product, and over 75% of global trade. The president of G-20 rotates annually. Each year the G-20 president invites several guest countries to participate in G-20 events and contribute to the agenda. The work of G-20 members is supported by several international organizations that provide policy advice. The G-20 also regularly engages with the non-state sectors. The G-20 is an important addition to world governance, even though memberships are not fully consistent with the GDP figures.

There are four major shortcomings in the G-20 approach which are not solvable within the G-20 approach and to which this chapter will offer alternatives. The first shortcoming is that current country membership is inconsistent with factual data on the economic power of the member countries. The second shortcoming is that the economic power of nations is dramatically and rapidly changing, making it necessary to take a forward-looking prospective of the relative strength of leading powers. The third shortcoming is that focus on the GDP criterion does not reflect the real influence potential of countries when we perceive the world as an interactive process of voluminous agents. Population matters. The fourth problem is that a selection based on individual countries cannot command global authority or legitimacy because it does not consider regional power or regional representation, respectively. The solution to these problems is to incorporate the last three arguments in a broad analytical framework that can be consistently applied to select a more effective governance forum than the current G-20. The following section elaborates on the four problems and presents the broader analytical framework.

3. The G-20: Problems and Remedies

The first problem is that G-20 memberships are not fully consistent with the GDP figures. For instance, the Netherlands ranks number 18 in the world GDP, but it is not included. The latest estimates of the GDP show Nigeria to surpass South Africa, but South Africa is included, and Nigeria is excluded. The inclusion of Argentina is also problematic as its GDP does not fall in the top 20. Next to EU individual countries, the EU is also a member which involves double counting. Spain is added as a hosting country. The number is thus actually 22 and not 20. These can be perceived as minor problems relating to definition consistency and can be remedied over time, but there will be friction and lobbying complications when some de facto members (and their presidents) are dropped for the sake of greater consistency.

The second problem is that as the current top dominant countries, US and EU, are challenged by newcomers such as China and India whose political and economic systems are differently orientated than the leading incumbents, the current governance rules of the G-20 need to adapt to different orientations. Functionality requires that world governance should reflect not only the current but also the prospective influential power of the dominating country(ies)/systems; hence,

Table 1. Leadership replacement tendencies in the future.

GDP in terms of PPP (2011 US$bn)						GDP in terms of MER (2011 US$bn)					
2011		2030		2050		2011		2030		2050	
US	15,094	**China**	30,634	**China**	53,856	US	15,094	**China**	24,356	**China**	48,477
China	11,347	US	23,376	US	37,998	**China**	7,298	US	23,376	US	37,998
India	4,531	**India**	13,716	**India**	34,704	Japan	5,867	**India**	7,918	**India**	26,895
Japan	4,381	Japan	5,842	Brazil	8,825	FRG	3,571	Japan	6,817	Brazil	8,950
FRG	3,221	Russia	5,308	Japan	8,065	France	2,773	Brazil	4,883	Japan	8,065
Russia	3,031	Brazil	4,685	Russia	8,013	Brazil	2,477	FRG	4,374	Russia	7,115

Source: PWC Economics (2013) and PWC Economics (2017).

institutions of world governance should be forward-looking in terms of both representation and rules. The G-20, in both its composition and operation, is not sufficiently forward-looking and underestimates the pace and magnitude of the leadership replacement tendencies. This is demonstrated in Table 1, The displacement hypothesis,[2] stated that the upcoming large economies of China and India would have greater magnitudes of GDP than the US and Japan in the near future. Today, the projected displacement timeline of BRIC-2003 is best described as outdated when compared with the latest revisions. For instance, 10 years later, PWC (2013) adapted the same BRIC model to more updated and accumulated data, and improved methods of forecasting future foreign exchange rates. The PWC (2013) forecasts, summarized in the following, show the displacement to occur much earlier than was thought, in spite of the recently observed slowness in the tempo of leading developing countries. It is predicted that the GDP of China would overpass the GDP of US in 2017, in terms of purchasing power parity, and by 2027 in terms of market exchange rates. India would come close to US in 2050, and a long way ahead of the next batch of medium-sized countries. See Appendix table.

It is likely that the incumbent leading countries (for instance, US and EU) may oppose changing the rules of the game, surrendering influential power, or accommodating to the newcomers (China and India). The problem of world governance becomes more complex with the expected change of the guards in world leaders. Signs of increased tension in world governance are already showing off especially when important appointments in international agencies are due and when agendas for collective actions are prepared.

The third problem with the G-20 approach is that the GDP criterion is a poor indication of the influence potential of a particular country in the context of an interactive world of voluminous populations. Interactive influence is not only the result of the relative size of economic transformations but also the result of the relative size of the transforming populations. We elaborate in the following on proposed remedies.

In Chapters 2, 3, and 21, microeconomic foundations were set for formulating a *Dominance Index* (*DI*) to express the interactive influence of an entity y on other entities of the same kind y', denoted by DI_y. An entity can be a firm, a town, a country, or a world region. In this chapter, we shall adapt this index to the contexts of countries and regions, and in the following section, we shall apply it and demonstrate its empirical implications.

The index has two arguments as shown in eq. (1): the relative share of agents in y among all y', and the relative share of transformations in y among all y'.

$$DI_y = (\omega_1 A_y + \omega_2 C_y) \tag{1}$$

In this equation, there are two share parameters that reflect the influence potential of a particular country in an interactive world of all countries. A_y is the share of the population in country y, with respect to all populations in all countries y'. C_y is the share of commodities transformed in country y, with respect to all transformed commodities in all countries y', or in other words, the share of the GDP of country y in the world GDP. Eq. (1) proposes that the greater the shares of the population and GDP in a particular country, the greater the influence potential of that country relative to other countries. In this equation, ω_1 and ω_2 are equal weights applying to these two shares, whereby $\omega_1 + \omega_2 = 1$. The value of DI_y is a proportion, and $\Sigma DI_y = 1$. An entity which scores a very high value on the index tends to dominate the other entities. Once the index for an entity reaches a critical mass the influence potential of that entity can be expected to benefit from network externalities and to become practically the dominant player among all entities. There are different views concerning the likely value of the critical mass. A value of 3/4th is among the most quoted in the literature on a critical mass, cf. Simon (1993). There is thus justification for fixing the value of this threshold at 0.8, or thereabout.

Quantification of the Dominance Index (*DI*) for leading countries gives the projected results in Table 2, which is also found in the previous chapter. The leadership pattern in Table 2 is significantly different from that in Table 1. The *DI* places China and India way above the USA and the EU, and upgrades the positions of Brazil, Indonesia, Nigeria, and Mexico in the top ten worldwide.

A qualifying note is necessary. While the dominance index expresses the interactive influence of one entity on other interacting entities, the index does not cover regulative influence which is another type of influence potential. This refers to a situation in which an entity or country y happens to stand higher in relation to y' in the hierarchy of countries; allowing y to set behavioral rules typical of y that other countries y' should abide with. In this way, the behavioral type of$y$overrides y', allowing the further spread of behavioral norms of y at the cost of those of y'. The interactive influence represents the results of *horizontal* contact. Regulative

Table 2. Projected changes in the influence potential of leading countries, as measured by the Dominance Index, %. Total = 100.0%.

2012		2030		2050		2012		2030		2050	
China	15.4	China	18.6	China	18.3	Indonesia	2.3	France	1.9	Russia	2.1
US	13.7	India	11.6	India	14.2	UK	2.2	Nigeria	1.9	Germany	1.6
India	10.1	US	11.5	US	10.3	Mexico	1.7	Mexico	1.9	France	1.6
Japan	5.1	Japan	3.4	Brazil	3.3	Nigeria	1.4	UK	1.8	UK	1.5
Germany	3.0	Brazil	3.3	Indonesia	3.0	Türkiye	1.1	Türkiye	1.4	Türkiye	1.5
Brazil	3.0	Indonesia	2.7	Japan	2.3	S. Arabia	0.7	S. Arabia	0.8	S. Arabia	1.0
Russia	2.4	Russia	2.3	Nigeria	2.2	S. Africa	0.6	S. Africa	0.6	S. Africa	0.8
France	2.3	Germany	2.2	Mexico	2.2	Others world	35.0	Others	33.9	Others	34.11

Source: Computation of the Dominance Index requires projections of population and GDP. The Population projections are from United Nations Population Division: World Development Prospects, at https://population.un.org/wpp. GDP projections are from PWC (2017).

influence is a *vertical* relationship. It is not feasible to quantify measures of regulative influence along the lines of interactive influence due to mounting difficulties in standardizing diversified measures of regulation. It is likely that there is a positive association between the two notions of influence potential, in the sense that a country powerful in interactive influence would in the long run become generally powerful in regulative influence. This will add to the importance of the dominance index. There is also ground for speculating that the nature of the horizontal channels makes their effect more endurable as they are generated via experiencing, learning, and adoption. The contribution of horizontal channels toward converging behavioral patterns across countries is likely to be more influential and more permanent than that of vertical channels. In the case of vertically accommodated behavioral attitudes, the regulative influence can terminate abruptly if the regulative mechanisms become too demanding due to technological loopholes, or the rationale for the binding restrictions disappears, or the balance of power between y and y' reverses.

The fourth problem with the G-20 approach is that its loose selection of individual countries cannot command global authority or legitimacy because the selection does not consider regional power or regional representation. The G-20 approach ignores all the past progress made by mankind in defining constitutional democracy and representational rights. The world cannot be seen as a loose collection of individual countries. Ant individual country is allied to other countries and is as such a member of an interest group that has common interests. Ignoring this fact can result in over-accommodation for a specific group (for instance, the number of Western industrial countries at 11 forms together the majority in the G-20), at the cost of under-accommodation of vast regions in Africa and Asia. In Chapter 2, the world economy was divided into eight regional groups based on their shared type of economic system, common features, and regional vicinity. Some regional classifications like the one followed in this book should form the basis for composing a constitutionally acceptable platform of a representative world government. The regional classification followed throughout the book distinguishes between the

Table 3. Projections of regional distributions of population, GDP, and Dominance Index 2030, 2050.

	Population share, %			GDP share, %			Dominance Index, %		
	2012	2030	2050	2012	2030	2050	2012	2030	2050
Western allied	16.0	13.6	12.3	62.7	48.6	39.7	39.4	30.6	25.6
Russia allied	3.0	2.2	1.6	3.1	3.6	3.4	3.1	2.8	2.5
EAP	28.3	26.7	23.8	14.7	24.2	26.6	21.5	25.0	24.8
SA	23.4	22.6	22.5	3.2	7.9	14.5	13.3	15.0	18.2
CAC	3.2	3.3	3.2	2.4	3.7	4.3	2.8	3.4	3.7
MENA	4.5	6.1	7.2	4.1	4.8	5.4	4.3	5.3	6.2
SSA	13	13.2	14.5	1.8	3.9	5.0	7.4	8.5	9.6
LAC	8.6	8.3	8.0	8	10.4	11.5	8.3	9.2	9.6
World total	100.0	100.0	100.0	100.0	100.0	100.0	100.0	100.0	100.0
World values	7,044	8,214	9,322	72,682	125,914	231,871			

Source: Population projections are from United Nations Population Division: World Development prospects, at https://population.un.org/wpp. GDP projections are from PWC (2017).

F-group of countries consisting of firm-centered Western allied economies and the S-group consisting of state-centered economies such as Russia and some allied former ex-Soviet Union countries. Then there are six development regions specified as East Asia and Pacific (EAP), South Asia (SA), Central Asia and Caspian (CAC), Middle East and North Africa (MENA), Sub-Saharan Africa (SSA), and Latin America and Caribbean (LAC). Table 3, which was encountered in the previous chapter and displayed here in a different order, gives projections of population and GDP for the eight regions for the years 2030 and 2050. These projections allow computing expected paths of the Dominant Indexes at the regional and country level. The relative distribution of the DI among the eight regions would roughly result in a representation of 5 seats for the F countries, 1 seat for the S-countries, 2 seats for EAP, 2 seats for SA, 1 seat each for CAC and MENA, and 2 seats each for SSA and LAC, in total 16 seats.

4. An Alternative Composition of G-20

Responsive actions to global failure require global governance that is fairly representative of regional and country interests. A world polity, for example, G-20, that circles around individual countries with the highest GDP is ineffective in a world of 193 countries with 173 of them not participating. We worked our way by focusing on eight world regions that were shown to be internally converging, as is empirically validated in Cohen (2015). The structural and performance variation among member countries of these regions were shown to be decreasing as well, with the rare exception of the SSA region regarding some elements. The starting point in representative global governance should be the influence potential of the eight regions and not individual countries. Once that starting point is resolved, the next step is to descend to regional representation which is indeed at the country level.

It is instructive to demonstrate how the composition of a world top of presidential leaders (to be entrusted with coordinating global governance and resolving global failure) along our lines of thought would look like. Our list will be very different from the above-mentioned G-20, for several reasons. First, we employ influence potential based on population and GDP, which is more democratic and more real. Second, our starting point will be regional representation, followed by naming countries, which is more democratic, and more logic. Third, subject to explicitly set minimum and maximum rules, our outcome regarding representation is straightforward. This is not the case with G-20, which includes countries that do not qualify for the GDP criteria and excludes others which do qualify, pointing thus to manipulated selections.[3] Fourth, a forum of 20 top leaders is too big to be effective. Our list ends up with 16 members.

Box 1 applies a step-by-step approach to constructing our list. By elimination, it ends up in a list of G-16, as shown in Table 4. The list consists of US, Japan, Germany, France, United Kingdom (for *F*-group), Russia (for *S*-group), China, Indonesia (for EAP), India, Pakistan (for SA), Türkiye (for CAC), Saudi Arabia (for MENA), Nigeria, South Africa (for SSA), and Brazil, Mexico (for LAC). The G-16 allows also for shared/rotating memberships in the case of some regions, as indicated in the bottom line of Table 4. The leadership sharing remedy would reflect intraregional fairness and would apply in the CAC region for Türkiye and Iran, and in the MENA region for Saudi Arabia and Egypt.

It is noted that this list of G-16 leading countries accounts for about two-thirds of the full scale of the world DI, with the rest of the countries, about 180 controlling one-third of the world DI. There is a rationale for supplementing the G-16 with a chamber of regional ambassadors who can represent the interests of the countries in the region other than that of the leading country. We refer here to the EU in the F-group, the ASEAN in EAP, SARC in SA, OAU in SSA, the Arab League in MENA, etc. A chamber of eight regional ambassadors (say, the presidents of the above-mentioned organizations) can be installed to that effect, call it R-8, and it can convene on a regular basis in much the same way as the G-16, and cooperate together in fixing global governance and global failures. Such an arrangement is already accommodated in the G-20 with respect to the EU; and it proves essential for streamlining policies at the country, regional and world levels. The notion of two chambers, which is a conventional practice in national governance, is applicable and adaptable to world governance.

Finally, *DI* values in 2012 were used as a benchmark in the listing of the G-16 leading countries., and further adjusted to the expected changes in *DI* in the next few decades, as the list would require updating, which implies establishing a scheme of changing membership based on influential power.

Box 1. Applying DI in global governance: Region/country composition of world top.

The interesting thing about the number 20 is that when the full range of the dominance index of 100 pp is divided by 20, this gives the right to claim one position in G-20 for a bunch of 5 percentage points (pp) on the dominance index. Table 4 displays regional *DI*s in row 1 and by dividing by 5, the regionals are obtained in row 2.

A number of refinements can be applied to Table 4. The rounding off of the regional claims guarantees the *S*-region and CAC one position each even though their claim is 0.6 of a position each, but that means that world leadership positions are increased to 22. The rounding off of the claims is shown in row 3, Table 4.

The next refinement relates to applying maximum and minimum rules for regional inclusion in the world top. In filling the regional quota with leading countries, it is logical to keep to indivisibility principles, which means that a qualifying country can claim/send one position/president only irrespective of the height of its *DI* (this can be viewed as fixing a maximum) and that a minor country cannot obtain a position just because it belongs to a region with a high quota that is boosted by the membership of a superpower. For example, EAP has a high quota because of China and Indonesia. This should not give the Philippines, Thailand, or Vietnam the advantage of inclusion in the world top unless such a country manifests a high *DI* of its own. A similar situation applies to SA where India outflanks its neighbors. For inclusion, indivisibility requires thus fixing a minimum *DI* for country/region, of say 5%. Application of maximum and minimum rules gives row 4, Table 4.

The application so far reduces the membership positions of EAP and SA below their regional claims, by 3 seats. Inter regional fairness would require applying an equivalent reduction of membership positions of the *F*-group from its regional claim, from 8 to say 5. This results in a total membership of 16 seats, which is more operational than 20 seats, as shown in row 5, Table 4.

The G-16 countries roll out automatically from applying the above accommodations to the *DI* results for 2012. The outcome is displayed in row 6, Table 4.

There are instances in some regions where the included country has a *DI* that is marginally higher but practically equal to that of the next country in line. Türkiye is marginally higher than Iran in the CAC region. The same applies to Saudi Arabia and Egypt in MENA. Intra regional fairness may require shared or rotating membership in the G-16, as displayed in row 7, Table 4.

Table 4. Alternative design of G-14.

	F-group	*S*-group	EAP	SA	CAC	MENA	SSA	LAC	Outcome
1. *DI*	39.4	3.1	21.5	13.3	2.8	4.3	7.4	8.3	100
2. *DI/5*	7.9	0.6	4.3	2.7	0.6	0.9	1.5	1.7	20
3. Rounding	8.0	1.0	4.0	3.0	1.0	1.0	2.0	2.0	22
4. Max, min	8.0	1.0	2.0	2.0	1.0	1.0	2.0	2.0	19
5. Inter rgnl fairness	5.0	1.0	2.0	2.0	1.0	1.0	2.0	2.0	16
6. Leading Countries	US Japan Germany France UK	Russia	China Indonesia	India Pakistan	Turkiye	S Arabia	Nigeria S Africa	Brazil Mexico	16
7. Intra rgnl fairness					Turkiye/ Iran	S Arabia/ Egypt			

5. Overview

In a couple of decades, US and EU are likely to be displaced and surpassed by China and India as global leaders. Global governance is destined to go through a transition in which rules are reset so as to reflect the changing balance of influence between incumbents and newcomers.

The optimistic scenario is that as leading newcomers bring to the world scene their own systemic features, some of these new features are likely to be taken over by incumbent leading countries and integrated into their socio-economic systems. The newcomers in turn may take over systemic elements from the incumbents.

The pessimistic scenario would not see convergence taking place any time soon. Instead, global failures and conflicts are likely to accentuate when the world prospects are viewed by newcomer leaders and by incumbent leaders as a zero-sum game.

The definition of displacement is open for discussion. There is displacement defined in terms of the GDP in one country overtaking the GDP of another country. There is the more generalized notion of influence potential, which we express in terms of the relative shares of agent interaction and economic transformation, equally weighted, and giving thus the Dominance Index, *DI*. Displacement, when measured by *DI*, occurs at a quicker pace than when measured solely in terms of the GDP; this is due to the population effect in *DI* which favors developing over developed countries. Results of *DI* indicate that the displacement has already occurred, as the *DI* of China is higher than that of US in 2012, i.e. 15.4 pp and 13.7 pp, respectively.

Displacement calculus can be applied to individual countries as constituents of the world total, but can also be applied to the eight regions with which we worked throughout. For democratic and effectively run world governance the regional perspective would precede the country perspective. Regional displacement of the western industrialized region by the EAP region is projected to take place at a much slower rate than in the case of country displacement of US versus China. The displacement calculus in this chapter predicts that the western industrialized region (which we also call the firm-centered region) and the EAP region will have equivalent *DI*s in 2050, at 25.6 pp, and at 24.8 pp, respectively. The interesting thing about this projected equal sharing of influence is that when the contending parties have influential powers that are more or less equal, as suggested by the above mentioned equivalent DIs, and perceive the situation as such, the parties will be more inclined to use reason and knowledge and adopt cooperative attitudes in managing collective actions and in avoiding bilateral frictions. Under skew distributions of influential powers, it is more likely that a non-collaborative attitude emerges. The obtained results feed expectations that in the long run, the new regional system competition will be more collaborative, a situation that promotes borrowing, testing, and adaptation of successful institutions from one regional system to another. With a time span of 38 years to go, the resetting of rules of global governance can be done gradually, and world responses to the mounting global failures can be made more effective and timely.

Global governance, in contrast to the more advanced organization of the national polity, is at an early stage of evolvement and is far from being in shape to tackle the list of mounting global failures. A basic step in making global governance more effective is the application of principles of democracy with realism in matters of collective decisions. By way of demonstration, we applied the *DI* at the regional and country levels in composing a world top of presidential leaders, to be entrusted with coordinating global governance and resolving global failure. The result was the first chamber with a limited number of 16 leading countries, or G-16, which is different from the G-20. We postulated also that there is a rationale for supplementing the G-16 with a second chamber of eight regional chancellors, denoted by R-8, who can represent the interests of *other* countries in the eight regions *other* than those of the leading country.

As world development evolves, partly determined by internal mechanisms, and partly by external events, the outcomes are not predictable. That is the reason for strengthening global governance based on principles of participatory democracy and interactive influence. The context of the world national polity is very different from that of the world polity. Remarkable advances have been achieved in the past centuries in circumventing and consolidating the institutional setup of the national polity. Some of these advances can be fruitfully used in programming the institutions of global governance, but the global governance of differentiated and interactive systems/regions/countries is unique and new, and it has to discover its own program and path.

In appraising the G-20 versus the G-16, it is important to note that global functionality requires that world governance should be representative of the world regions and should reflect not only the current but also the prospective influential power of the dominating regions/countries and their socio-economic systems. Stated otherwise, institutions of world governance need to be forward-looking in terms of both representation and rules. The G-20, in both its composition and operation, when compared to the G-16, is not sufficiently forward-looking as it underestimates the pace and magnitude of the leadership replacement tendencies.

Endnotes

1. The call by Germany to veto takeovers of EU companies by Chinese and Russian state controlled companies is a case. French opposition to India's Mittal takeover of Arcelor is another, as well as the French policy of close collaboration between companies and the state to strengthen and consolidate French global industrial players. In the US, Chinese takeovers in the energy sector were prohibited as in the case of the unsuccessful bid by the Chinese oil company CNOOC for the California-based oil producer Uncoal. However, in less strategic sectors, no obstacles were laid down when parts of American IBM were sold to China's LP.
2. The displacement hypothesis was first launched by Wilson and Purushothaman (2003) and known as the BRIC report.
3. For instance, Nigeria is left out, and South Africa is included while the latest GDP figures show Nigeria ahead of South Africa. The place of Argentina is disputable, while the Netherlands had a GDP within the top 20. The group is in fact 20+1, as it includes a permanent position for Spain, which is an arbitrary accommodation.

References

Abdelgalil, E. (2000). Economic policies for sustainable resource development: Models applied for the Sudan. PhD thesis, Erasmus University, Faculty of Economic Sciences, Rotterdam.

Abdelgalil, E. and Cohen, S.I. (2001). Policy modelling of the trade-off between agricultural development and land degradation-the Sudan. *Journal of Policy Modeling*, November 2001, 847–874.

Acemoglu, D. and Robinson, J.A. (2010). The role of institutions in growth and development. *Review of Economics and Institutions*, 1(2), 1–33.

Acharya, S. (2011). *Pro-poor Growth and Liberalization in Developing Economies: The Case of Nepal*. London: Routledge.

Adelman, I. and Robinson, S. (1978). *Income Distribution Policy in Developing Countries: A Case Study of Korea*. Oxford, UK: Oxford University Press (for the World Bank).

Ahmed, M. and Sanders, J. (1998). Shifting from extensive to intensive agricultural systems: A case study in the Sudan. *Agricultural Systems*, 58(2): 253–268.

Alesina, A., Ditella, R. and Macculloch, R. (2001). *Inequality and Happiness: Are Europeans and Americans Different?* CEPR Discussion Paper 2877, July 2001.

Amendola, A., Easaw, J. and Savoia, A. (2013). Inequality in developing economies: The role of institutional development. *Public Choice*, 155: 43–60.

Anand, S. and Kanbur, S.M.R. (1993). Inequality and development: A critique. *Journal of Development Economics*, 41: 19–43.

Bacharach, M. (1970). *Biproportional Matrices and Input-Output Change*. Cambridge: Cambridge University Press.

Ballard, C., Fullerton, D., Shoven, J.B. and Whalley, J. (1985). *A General Equilibrium Model for Tax Policy Evaluation*. Chicago: University of Chicago Press.

Bandara, J.S. and Yu, W. (2003). Desirable is the south Asian free trade area? A quantitative economic assessment. *The World Economy*, 26(9): 1293–1323.

Banerjee, A. (1992). A simple model of herd behaviour. *Quarterly Journal of Economics*, 107: 797–818.

Banerjee, A.V. and Duflo, E. (2005). *Growth Theory through the Lens of Development Economics*. Massachusetts Institute of Technology (MIT). http://ssrn.com/abstract=651483.

Bardhan, P. (1974). Redistribution with Growth, some country experience. In Chenery, H. *et al.*, *Redistribution with Growth*. London: Oxford University Press.

Bardhan, P. (2005). Institutions and Development. University of California at Berkeley. Available at https://eml.berkeley.edu/~webfac/bardhan/papers/BardhanInstitutionsandDev.pdf.

Basu, S. and Stiglitz, J. (Eds.). (2016). *Inequality and Growth: Patterns and Poliicies*. Palgrave Macmillan.

Barbier, E. (1990). The farm-level economics of soil conservation: The uplands of Java. *Land Economics*, 66(2): 199–211.

Barbier, E. (2000). The economic linkages between rural poverty and land degradation: Some evidence from Africa. *Agriculture, Ecosystems and Environment*, 82: 355–370.

Baumol, W.J. (1967). The macro economies of unbalanced growth. *American Economic Review* 57: 415–426.

Becker, G.S. (1964). *Human Capital: A Theoretical and Empirical Analysis*, NBER.

Becker, G.S. (1973). *Human Capital: A Theoretical and Empirical Analysis, with Special Reference to Education*, 2nd edn. New York: Columbia University Press.

Bennet, M.K. (1948). International disparities in consumption levels. *American Economic Review*, XXXVII.

Berg, A., Ostry, J.D. and Yahshilikov, Y. (2018). Redistribution, inequality and growth in developing countries. *Journal of Economic Growth*, 23(3), 259–305.

Bikhchandani, S., Hirshleifer, D. and Welch, I. (1998). Learning from behaviour of others: Conformity, fads and informational cascades. *Journal of Economic Perspectives*, 12(3): 151–170.

Borcherding, T.E., Ferries, J.S. and Garazoni, A. (2002). *The Growth of Real Government, Handbook of Public Choice*. London: Edward Elgar.

Bosworth, B. and Collins, S.M. (1996). Economic growth in east Asia: Accumulation versus assimilation. *Brookings Papers and Proceedings*, 2: 135–191.

Brueckner, J.K. and Smirnov, O. (2004). *Workings of the Melting Pot: Social Networks and the Evolution of Social Attributes*. CESIFO Working Paper No. 1320, October 2003.

Burgess, S. (2016). Human capital and education: The state of the art in the economics of education. *SSRN Electronic Journal*, April 2016.

Caldwell, J.C. *et al.* (2006). *Demographic Transition Theory*. Dordrecht: Springer.

Chenery, H. *et al.* (Ed.). (1974). *Redistribution with Growth*. London: Oxford University Press.

Chitiga, M., Kandiero, T. and Mabugu, R. (2005). Computable general equilibrium micro-simulation analysis of the impact of trade policies on poverty. *Zimbabwe. Poverty and Economic Policy* (PEP) Research Network (www.pep-net.org), Working Paper No. 01, 2005.

Cockburn, J. (2001). *Trade Liberalisation and Poverty in Nepal: A Computable General Equilibrium Micro Simulation Analysis*. Working Paper, Centre for the Study of African Economics and Nuffield College (Oxford University) and CREFA.

Cohen, S.I. (1968). *The Level of Living Index in UK, Netherlands, Japan and Czechoslovakia, in 1920–1965*. Discussion Paper, UNRISD, Geneva.

Cohen, S.I. (1975). *Production, Manpower and Social Planning*. Rotterdam: Rotterdam University Press/Saxon House.

Cohen, S.I. (1977). *Development Models with Different Decision-Makers*. Polish Academy of Science and World Future Studies Federation "Future Research, Planning and Decision-making," Proceedings of a Conference Held in Jablonna.

Cohen, S.I. (1978). *Agrarian Structures and Agrarian Reform*. Leiden/Boston: Martinus NijhofT Social Sciences Division, Kluwer.

Cohen, S.I. (1981). Distribution of power and agrarian reform, an explanatory model applied to India and Chile. *Journal of Policy Modelling*, 3(1): 37–59.

Cohen, S.I. (1986). A comparative study of needs and their satisfaction. *Bulletin of the European Association of Development Institutes*, 1: 103–120.

Cohen, S.I. (1988). A social accounting matrix analysis for the Netherlands. *De Economist*, 136(2), 253–272.

Cohen, S.I. (1989). Multiplier analysis in social accounting and input-output frameworks; Evidence for several countries. In R. Miller, K.P. Polenske and A. Rose (Eds.) *Frontiers of Input-Output Analysis*. Oxford: Oxford University Press.

Cohen, S.I. (Ed.). (1993). *Patterns of Economic Restructuring for Eastern Europe*. Aldershot: Avebury-Ashgate Publishing.

Cohen, S.I. (1994). *Human Resource Development and Utilization*. Aldershot: Avebury.

Cohen, S.I. (2001). *Microeconomic Policy*. Routledge: London.

Cohen, S.I. (2002a). *Social Accounting and Economic Modelling for Developing Countries*. Aldershot: Ashgate.

Cohen, S.I. (2002b). *Social Accounting for Industrial and Transition Economies, Economy-Wide Models for Analysis and Policy*. Aldershot: Ashgate.

Cohen, S.I. (2009). *Economic Systems Analysis and Policies: Explaining Global Differences, Transitions, Development*. Palgrave MacMillan.

Cohen, S.I. (2013). *Economic Models for Policy Making: Principles and Designs Revisited*. London: Routledge.

Cohen, S.I. (2015). *World Development and Economic Systems: Theory and Applications*. Singapore, London: World Scientific Publishers.

Cohen, S.I. and Sarmiento, A. (1982). *Sistema de Planeacion de Recursos Humanos*. Bogota: Sena Press.

Collins, S. and Kirton, J. (Eds.). (2021). *The G20 and Global Governance*. London: Routledge.

Comite Interamericano de Dessarrollo Agricola, CIDA. (1966). *Tenencia de la Terra y Dessarrollo Socio-Economico del Sector Agricola*. Santiago de Chile: CIDA.

Correa, H. and Tinbergen, J. (1962). Quantitative adaptation of education to economic growth. *Kyklos* 18(4): 776–786.

Coxhead, I. and Jayasuriya, S. (1994). Technical change in agriculture and land degradation in developing countries: A general equilibrium analysis. *Land Economics*, 70(1): 20–37.

Crafts, N. (2001). Historical perspectives on development. In G.M. Meier and J.E. Stiglitz (Eds.) *Frontiers of Development Economics*. Oxford: Oxford University Press.

Cromwell, E. and Winpenny, J. (1993). Does economic reform harm the environment? A review of structural adjustment in Malawi. *Journal of International Development*, 5(6): 623–649.

Dasgupta, S., Laplante, B., Wang, H. and Wheeler, D. (2002). Confronting the environmental Kuznets Curve. *The Journal of Economic Perspectives*, 16(1): 147–168.

Dervis, K., Melo, de J. and Robinson, S. (1982). *General Equilibrium Models for Development Policy*. UK: Cambridge University Press.

Dixon, P.B. and Parmenter, B.R. (1996). Computable general equilibrium modeling for policy analysis and forecasting. In H.M. Amman, D.A. Kendrick and J. Rust (Eds.) *Handbook of Computational Economics*, vol. I (pp. 3–85). Amsterdam: North-Holland.

Dixon, P.B. and Rimmer, M. (2002). *Dynamic General Equilibrium Modelling for Forecasting and Policy: A Practical Guide and Documentation of MONASH*. North Holland.

Drewnowski, J. and Scott, W. (1967). *The Level of Living Index*. Discussion Paper, UNRISD, Geneva.

Eastwood, R. and Lipton, M. (2004). *The Rural-Urban Dimension of Inequality Change*. In Corina, Govanni (ed.) *Inequality, Growth and Poverty in an Era of Liberalization and Globalization*. Oxford: Oxford University Press.

Easterly, W. and Rebelo, S. (1993). Fiscal policy and economic growth: An empirical investigation. *Journal of Monetary Economics*, 32: 458–493.

Ellis, L., Hoskin, A.W. and Ratnasingam, M. (2018). *Handbook of Social Status Correlates*. Amsterdam: Elsevier.

Evans, G.J. and Lindley, R.M. (1973). The use of RAS and related models in manpower forecasting. *Economics of Planning*, 13(1–2).

Faki, H., Gumma, Y. and Ismail M. (1995). Potential of the Sudan irrigated sector in cereal grains production: Analysis of various policy options. *Agricultural Systems*, 48: 457–483.

Feindouno, S., Goujon, M. and Wagner, L. (2016). *Internal Violence Index: A Composite and Quantitative Measure of Internal Violence and Crime in Developing Countries*. Fondation pour les études et recherches sur le développement international, Paris. Working Paper No. 151, April 2016.

Frank, R. (1988). *Passions Within Reason*. New York: Norton.

Frieden, J. (2016). The governance of international finance. *Annual Review of Political Science*, 2016, 33–48.

Garth, F. (2006). Inequality and development across and within countries. *World Development*, 34(9): 1459–1481.

Gigengack, A.R., Jepma, C.J., MacRae, D. and Poldy, F. (1990). Global modelling of dryland degradation. In J.A. Dixon, D.E. James, P.B. Sherman (Eds.). *Dry Management: Economic Case Studies*. London: Earth Scan Publications Ltd.

Goodin, R.E. (1993). Moral atrophy in the welfare state. *Policy Sciences*, 26: 63–78.

Griffin, K. (1972). *The Green Revolution, an Economic Analysis*. Geneva: International Labour Office.

Grier, K.G. and Tullock, G. (1989). An empirical analysis of cross-national economic growth, 1951–1980. *Journal of Monetary Economics*, 24: 259–279.

Hanushek, E. and Welsch, F. (2006). *The Economics of Education*. Elsevier.

Hayek, F.A. (1960). *The Constitution of Liberty*. Chicago: University of Chicago Press.

Heritage Foundation. (2000). *Index of Economic Freedom*. New York: The Wall Street Journal and The Heritage Foundation.

Herrera, A. *et al.* (1974). *Latin American World Model*. Fundaci6n Bariloche, 8 volumes, International Institute of Applied Systems Analysis, Luxenburg.

Hewings, G.J.D. (1969). Regional input-output models using national data: The structure of the west midlands economy. *The Annals of Regional Science*, 3(1): 179–191.

Hoda, S.S. (1982). Labor market information programme of the employment organization in Pakistan. *Pakistan Manpower Review*, VIII.

Ianchovichina, E., Nicita, A. and Soloaga, I. (2001). *Trade Reform and Household Welfare: The Case of Mexico.* Working Paper No. 2386, the World Bank, DECRG-Trade; 2001.

Ibrahim, O.A. (1995). *Constraints of Development in Sudan: A Three-Gap Model Analysis.* M.A Thesis, Institute of Social Studies, the Hague.

Janvry, A. and Sadoulet, E. (2021). *Development Economics: Theory and Practice.* Routledge, New York.

Johansen, L. (1960). *A Multi-sectoral Study of Economic Growth.* Amsterdam: North-Holland.

Joshi, P.C. (1975). *Land Reforms in India.* Allied Publishers: New Delhi.

Kanbur, P. (2000). Chapter 13: Income distribution and development. In Atkinson, A.B. and Bourguignon, F. (Eds.) *Handbook of Income Distribution* (p. 791). North-Holland.

Kevane, M. (1997). Land tenure and rental in Western Sudan. *Land Use Policy* 1997, 14(4): 295–310.

Khan, S.R. and Irfan, M. (1985). Family background and other determinants of earnings and rates of return to education in Pakistan. *Annual Meeting of the Pakistan Society of Development Economics*, Islamabad.

Kidron, M. and Smith, D. (1983). *The War Atlas.* London: Heinemann.

Kirton, J. and Wilson, M. (Eds.). (2017). *The G20 and Global Economic Governance: Challenges and Opportunities.* London: Routledge.

Knight, J. (1992). *Institutions and Social Conflict.* New York: Cambridge University Press.

Knudsen, M.B., Pedersen, L.H., Petersen, T.W., Stephensen, P., and Trier, P. (1998). Danish rational economic agents model – DREAM, Version 1.2. *Statistics Denmark.*

Koopmans, T. and Montias, J.M. (1971). On the description and comparison of economic systems. In A. Eckstein (Ed.), *Comparison of Economic Systems*, pp. 27–28.

Krugman, P.R. (1981). Trade, accumulation and uneven development. *Journal of Development Economics*, 8: 149–161.

Kuznets, S. (1955). Economic growth and income inequality. *American Economic Review*, 4 March, 1–28.

Lewis, W.A. (1955). *The Theory of Economic Growth.* University Books.

Lewis, D.K. (1969). *Convention: A Philosophical Study.* Cambridge: Harvard University Press.

Lindbeck, A. (2003). *An Essay on Welfare State Dynamics.* CESifo Working Paper No. 976, July 2003.

Lipton, M. (1977). *Why Poor People Stay Poor: A Study of Urban Bias in World Development.* Temple-Smith: London.

Löfgren, H., El-Said, M. and Robinson S. (1999). *Trade Liberalization and Complementary Domestic Policies: A Rural–Urban General Equilibrium Analysis of Morocco.* Discussion Paper 41, International Food Policy Research Institute (IFPRI), Washington DC.

Lofgren, H., Harris, G. and Robinson, S. (2001). *A Standard Computable General Equilibrium (CGE) Model in GAMS.* Discussion Paper No. 75, Trade and Macroeconomic Division, International Food Policy Research Institute (IFPRI), Washington DC.

Lysy, F. and Taylor, L. (1977). *A Computable General Equilibrium Model for the Functional Income Distribution: Experiments for Brazil, 1959–1971*. Washington, D.C.: World Bank.

Mabele, W.S. (2018). Application of manpower requirement approach to educational planning in developing countries. *Journal of Educational Studies*, 2018, 8–15.

Mattes, R. and Moreno, A. (2017). *Social and Political Trust in Developing Countries*. Glasgow: University of Strathclyde. See https://www.researchgate.net/publication/330887004.

McKitrick, R.R. (1998). The econometric critique of computable general equilibrium modeling: The role of functional forms. *Economic Modelling*, 15: 543–573.

Mitra-Kahn, B. H. (2008). *Debunking the Myths of Computable General Equilibrium Models*. Schwab Center for Economic Policy Analysis. SCEPA Working Papers, no. 2008-1, Stockholm.

Mohan G., Brown, E., Milward, B. and Zack-Williams, A.B.(2000). *Structural Adjustment: Theory, Practice and Impacts*. London: Routledge.

Mangozho, N. (2003). Current practices in labour market information systems development for human resources development planning in developed, developing and transition economies. EMP/SKILLS Working Paper No. 13, ILO, Geneva.

Myrdal, G. (1968). *Asian Drama, an Inquiry into the Poverty of Nations*. New York: Twenty Century Fund.

Nkurunziza, J. and Bates, R.H. (2003). *Political Institutions and Economic Growth in Africa*. Harvard University and CSAE Oxford University, Working Paper Series, 2003/3.

North, D. (2003). *The Role of Institutions in Economic Development*. United Nations UNECE Discussion Papers Series No. 2003.2.

NPD Suriname (2021). *Development Plan Suriname 2022–2026*. English translation of Meerjaren Ontwikkelingsplan 2022–2026 van de Republiek Suriname. Draft August 2021. Suriname National Planning Bureau, Paramaribo.

OECD (2021). *Compendium of Productivity Indicators 2021*, at https://doi.org/10.1787/f25cdb25-en.

Okun, A. (1975). *Equality and Efficiency: The Big Tradeoff*. Washington D.C.: Brookings Institution.

Parsons, T. (1956). *Economy and Society: A Study in the Integration of Economic and Social Theory*. Routledge and Kegan Paul.

Persson, A. and Munasinghe, M. (1995). Natural resources management and economywide policies in Costa Rica: A computable general equilibrium (CGE) modelling approach. *The World Bank Economic Review*, 9(2): 259–285.

PIDE. (1985). *The Social Accounting Matrix of Pakistan 1978/9*. Islamabad: Pakistan Institute of Development Economics.

Piketty, T. (2017). *Capital in the Twenty First Century*. Harvard University Press.

PMD. (1981). *A Study of the Occupational and Educational Manpower Requirements and Supply of the Fifth Five Year Plan*. Islamabad: Pakistan Manpower Division.

PMD. (1983). *A Study of the Occupational and Educational Manpower Requirements and Supply of the Sixth Five Year Plan*. Islamabad: Pakistan Manpower Division.

Psacharopoulos, G. and Patrinos, H.A. (2018). *Returns to Investment in Education: A Decennial Review of the Global Literature*. Washington: World Bank Group.

PWC Economics. (2013). World in 2050, the BRICS and beyond. Price Waterhouse Coopers.

PWC Economics. (2017). The Long View How will the global economic order change by 2050? London: Price Waterhouse Coopers.

Pyatt, G. and Roe, A. (1977). *Social Accounting for Development Planning*. Cambridge: Cambridge University Press.

Ranis, G. (2003). *Is Dualism Worth Revisiting?* Yale University, Economic Growth Center, Discussion Paper No. 870, September 2003.

Ravallion, M. (2014). Income inequality in the developing world. *Science*, 344: 851. http://www.sciencemag.org/cgi/collection/economics.

Reed, D. (Ed.). (1992). *Structural Adjustment and the Environment*. Boulder: Westview Press.

Robinson, S., Yuñez-Naude, A., Hinojosa-Ojeda, Lewis, R.J. and Devarajan, S. (1999). From stylized to applied models: Building multisector CGE models for policy analysis. *North American Journal of Economics and Finance*, 10: 5–38.

Rogerson, R. and Shimer, R. (2010). Search in macroeconomic models of the labor market. NBER Working Paper Series 15901. Massachusetts.

Rosenstein-Rodan, P. N. (1943). Problems of industrialization of eastern and south eastern Europe. *Economic Journal*, 53: 202–212.

Sala-i-Martin, X. (2002). *The Disturbing Rise of Global Income Inequality*. NBER Working Paper 8904, http://www.nber.org/papers/w8904.

Scarf, H. (1969). An example of an algorithm for calculating general equilibrium prices. *American Economic Review, 59*(4): 669–677.

Scarf, H. and Shoven, J.B. (Eds.) (1984). *Applied General Equilibrium Analysis*. UK: Cambridge University Press.

Schelling, T.C. (1978). *Micro Motives and Macro Behaviour*. W.W. Norton and Company.

Schmillen, A.D. (2019). *Labor Market Information — An Introduction*. Washington: World Bank.

Schotter, A. (1981). *The Economic Theory of Social Institutions*. New York: Cambridge University Press.

Sen, A.K. (1982). *Choice, Welfare end Measurement*. Cambridge Mass: MIT Press.

Sened, I. (1997). *The Political Institution of Private Property*. Cambridge: Cambridge University Press.

Shah, K. (1981). Labour market information in Pakistan. *Pakistan Manpower Review*, VII.

Simon, H. A. (1952). A formal theory of interaction in social groups. *American Sociological Review*, 17, 202–211.

Simon, H.A. (1953). Causal Ordering and Identifiability. In W.C. Hood and T.C. Koopmans (Eds.) *Studies in Econometric Method*. Cowles Commission Monograph No. 15, New York.

Simon, H.A. (1993). Altruism and economics. *American Economic Association, Papers and Proceedings*, May 1993.

Sinn, H.W. (2002). *The New Systems Competition*. NBER Working Paper No. 8747, January 2002.

Slaughter, S. (2020). *The Power of the G20, the Politics of Legitimacy in Global Governance*. London: Routledge.

Smith, A. (1961). An Inquiry into the True Nature and Causes of the Wealth of Nations, dated 1776 edition b Cannon, 1961.

Stiglitz, J.E. (2016). Inequality and economic growth. https://doi.org/10.1111/1467-923X.12237.

Stone, J.R.N. (1947). On the interdependence of blocks of transactions. *Journal of the Royal Statistical Society* (Supplement) 9: 1–45.

Stone, J.R.N. (1971). Demographic Accounting and Model Building. OECS, Paris.

Stone, J.R.N. (1978). The disaggregation of the household sector in the national accounts. In Paper Presented at the *World Bank Conference on Social Accounting Methods in Development Planning*, Cambridge.

Swinwood, P. (2013). Labour Market Information Methods and Methodologies, CARICOM Education for Employment Program (C-EFE) 1, Georgetown, Guyana.

Szirmai, A. (2005). *The Dynamics of Socio-Economic Development*. Cambridge: Cambridge University Press.

Taylor, L. (1990). Structuralist CGE models. In L. Taylor (Ed.) *Socially Relevant Policy Analysis*. Cambridge, MA: MIT Press.

Taylor, L. (1991). *Income Distribution, Inflation and Growth: Lectures on Structuralist Macroeconomic Theory*. Cambridge: MIT Press.

Taylor, E. and Lybbert, T.J. (2020). *Essentials of Development Economics*. University of California Press.

Thirlwall, A.P. and Lopez, P.P. (2017). *Economics of Development: Theory and Evidence*. Macmillan, UK.

Thorbecke, E. (1990). *Adjustment, Growth and Income Distribution in Indonesia*. Paris: OECD Development Center.

Thurow, L. (1969). *Poverty and Discrimination*. Washington DC: Brookings Institution.

Tinbergen, J. (1965). *Econometric Models of Education*. Paris: OECD.

Tinbergen, J. (1970). Planning and economic forecasting. *Research Priorities in Quantitative Socio-Economic Development Planning*. International Institute of Quantitative Economics: Montreal.

Todaro, M.P. and Smith, S.C. (2020). *Economic Development*. Pearson, UK.

Transparency International. (2022). Corruption Perception Index. See https://www.transparency/org/en/.

United Nations. (1966). *Preliminary Report of Targets on Social Development*. ECOSOC.

United Nations. (1971). *Second United Nations Development Decade: A System of Overall Review and Appraisal of the Objectives and Policies of the International Development Strategy*. ECOSOC.

Williamson, O.E. (1985). *The Economic Institutions of Capitalism: Firms, Markets, Relational Contracting*. New York: The Free Press.

Wilson, D. and Purushothaman, R. (2003). *Dreaming with BRICS: The Path to 2050*. Goldman Sachs.

World Bank. (1997). *The State in a Changing World, World Development Report 1997*. Oxford: Oxford University Press.

World Bank. (2003). *Global Development Finance 2003: Striving for Stability in Development Finance*. Washington: World Bank.

World Bank. (2005). *Education in Ethiopia*. Washington: World Bank.

World Bank/EBRD. (1999–2003). *Business Environment and Enterprise Performance Survey* (Mid-1999 and later years). Washington: World Bank.

World Economic Forum. (2020). *The Global Social Mobility Report.* Produced by the World Economic Forum (WEF): Davos.

Yi-Chia Wang (2024). Optimal Resource Allocation on Physical and Human Capital: Theoretical Modelling and Empirical Case Study of the United States. *Theoretical Economics Letters* 14(1): 107–124.

Zymelman, M. (1969). Skill requirements for industrialization. *Industrialization and Productivity Bulletin*, No. 14, United Nations, New York.

Zysman, J. (1994). How institutions create historically rooted trajectories of growth. *Industrial and Corporate Change* 3(1): 243–283.

Subject Index

T

U

W

Author Index

F

G

H

I

J

K

L

M

N

O

P

R

S

About the Author

(Suleiman) Solomon I. Cohen is Professor Emeritus of Economics at Erasmus University Rotterdam, the Netherlands. His areas of specialization and publication include development economics and planning, economic and policy modeling, microeconomic policy, human resource development, social system analysis, and world economic development. In addition to being a tenured Professor, he was also the Founder/Director of the Foundation for Economic Research Rotterdam and acted as a regular advisor and team leader in the context of technical assistance and development policy sponsored by the World Bank, UN, and EU agencies. Born in 1942 in El Fayoum, Egypt, he obtained BSc from the University of Khartoum, Sudan, and MSc and PhD from The Netherlands School of Economics, where he joined as a student assistant and worked closely with Jan Tinbergen and the associated team of development economists.

www.ingramcontent.com/pod-product-compliance
Lightning Source LLC
LaVergne TN
LVHW011655200926
848484LV00004B/949
* 9 7 8 9 8 1 1 2 7 7 0 7 8 *